Genealogical Abstracts from

The Banner

1893
in Clanton
Chilton County, Alabama

Charlene Vinson

HERITAGE BOOKS
2008

HERITAGE BOOKS
AN IMPRINT OF HERITAGE BOOKS, INC.

Books, CDs, and more—Worldwide

For our listing of thousands of titles see our website at
www.HeritageBooks.com

Published 2008 by
HERITAGE BOOKS, INC.
Publishing Division
100 Railroad Ave. #104
Westminster, Maryland 21157

Copyright © 1999 Charlene Vinson

Other books by the author:

Genealogical Abstracts from The Autauga Citizen, *1853, in Prattville, Autauga County, Alabama*

Genealogical Abstracts from The Autauga Citizen, *1854, in Prattville, Autauga County, Alabama*

All rights reserved. No part of this book may be reproduced or transmitted in any form or by any means, electronic or mechanical, including photocopying, recording or by any information storage and retrieval system without written permission from the author, except for the inclusion of brief quotations in a review.

International Standard Book Number: 978-0-7884-1325-4

Contents

The Banner, Vol. 1, Clanton, Ala., Thursday, January 26, 1893, No. 11 1
The Banner, Vol. 1, Clanton, Ala., Thursday, February 2, 1893, No. 12 7
The Banner, Vol. 1, Clanton, Ala., Thursday, February 9, 1893, No. 13 17
The Banner, Vol. 1, Clanton, Ala., Thursday, March 2, 1893, No. 16 25
The Banner, Vol. 1, Clanton, Ala., Thursday, March 9, 1893, No. 18 35
The Banner, Vol. 1, Clanton, Ala., Thursday, March 30, 1893, No. 21 41
The Banner, Vol. 1, Clanton, Ala., Thursday, April 6, 1893, No. 22 47
The Banner, Vol. 1, Clanton, Ala., Thursday, April 13, 1893, No. 23 53
The Banner, Vol. 1, Clanton, Ala., Thursday, April 20, 1893, No. 24 59
The Banner, Vol. 1, Clanton, Ala., Thursday, April 27, 1893, No. 25 65
The Banner, Vol. 1, Clanton, Ala., Thursday, May 4, 1893, No. 26 69
The Banner, Vol. 1, Clanton, Ala., Thursday, May 18, 1893, No. 28 77
The Banner, Vol. 1, Clanton, Ala., Thursday, May 25, 1893, No. 29 83
The Banner, Vol. 1, Clanton, Ala., Thursday, June 1, 1893, No. 30 89
The Banner, Vol. 1, Clanton, Ala., Thursday, June 8, 1893, No. 31 95
The Banner, Vol. 1, Clanton, Ala., Thursday, June 15, 1893, No. 32 103
The Banner, Vol. 1, Clanton, Ala., Thursday, June 22, 1893, No. 33 107
The Banner, Vol. 1, Clanton, Ala., Thursday, June 29, 1893, No. 34 113
The Banner, Vol. 1, Clanton, Ala., Thursday, July 6, 1893, No. 35 121
The Banner, Vol. 1, Clanton, Ala., Thursday, July 13, 1893, No. 36 129
The Banner, Vol. 1, Clanton, Ala., Thursday, July 20, 1893, No. 37 139
The Banner, Vol. 1, Clanton, Ala., Thursday, July 27, 1893, No. 38 149
The Banner, Vol. 1, Clanton, Ala., Thursday, August 3, 1893, No. 39 157
The Banner, Vol. 1, Clanton, Ala., Thursday, August 10, 1893, No. 40 167
The Banner, Vol. 1, Clanton, Ala., Thursday, August 17, 1893, No. 41 175
The Banner, Vol. 1, Clanton, Ala., Thursday, August 24, 1893, No. 42 181
The Banner, Vol. 1, Clanton, Ala., Thursday, August 31, 1893, No. 43 191
The Banner, Vol. 1, Clanton, Ala., Thursday, September 7, 1893, No. 44 203
The Banner, Vol. 1, Clanton, Ala., Thursday, September 14, 1893, No. 45 211
The Banner, Vol. 1, Clanton, Ala., Thursday, September 21, 1893, No. 46 219
The Banner, Vol. 1, Clanton, Ala., Thursday, September 28, 1893, No. 47 225
The Banner, Vol. 1, Clanton, Ala., Thursday, October 5, 1893, No. 48 233
The Banner, Vol. 1, Clanton, Ala., Thursday, October 12, 1893, No. 49 241
The Banner, Vol. 1, Clanton, Ala., Thursday, October 19, 1893, No. 50 245
The Banner, Vol. 1, Clanton, Ala., Thursday, October 26, 1893, No. 51 249
The Banner, Vol. 1, Clanton, Ala., Thursday, November 2, 1893, No. 52 257
The Banner, Vol. II, Clanton, Ala., Thursday, November 9, 1893, No. 1 265
The Banner, Vol. II, Clanton, Ala., Thursday, November 16, 1893, No. 2 273
The Banner, Vol. II, Clanton, Ala., Thursday, November 23, 1893, No. 3 281
The Banner, Vol. II, Clanton, Ala., Thursday, November 30, 1893, No. 4 287
The Banner, Vol. II, Clanton, Ala., Thursday, December 7, 1893, No. 5 291
The Banner, Vol. II, Clanton, Ala., Saturday, December 16, 1893, No. 6 299
The Banner, Vol. II, Clanton, Ala., Saturday, December 23, 1893, No. 7 309
The Banner, Vol. II, Clanton, Ala., Saturday, December 30, 1893, No. 8 317
Index 325

Dedicated to
Elizabeth J. Collins
for her encouragement, support and friendship

Introduction

The following pages have been compiled from microfilmed copies of "The Banner" newspaper, edited by T. H. White. This book covers the year 1893. The paper was published in Clanton, Chilton County, Alabama. The information compiled not only covers the local news, but also the state, national and some worldwide news for this year. There are stories reporting births, deaths, marriages, elections, sickness and much more. Much care has been taken to correctly spell the names in these newspapers, but as you will find, the newspaper, at times, has used variations of the names, sometimes within the same story. I have tried to maintain this inconsistency, as I did not want to take it upon myself to decide which variation was correct. I have also indexed these variations. There are areas where you will see "...". I have used this to indicate that there was more of the story printed, but I did not see any genealogical value in these parts of the stories. If you want the complete story, you can check the microfilm. In other areas, you wil find "(?)" notations. These areas were not readable, because of torn pages on these newspapers. I tried to pull as much information on these stories as I could, as I didn't want to leave them out. They might have been my ancestors, too. The following issues were missing: February 16, 23, March 16, 23, May 11.

The Banner, Vol. 1, Clanton, Ala., Thursday, January 26, 1893, No. 11

A Horrible Death - Mrs. A.F. Woods wife of a prominent pioneer citizen of Hardin County, LA., has just died at Union of what is said to have been leprosy of the most malignant form. She was bedridden and utterly helpless for a number of years, her body finally becoming so shrunken, distorted and disfigured that she scarcely resembled a human being. A part of her face fingers, toes and portions of her lower limbs were eaten away by the ravages of the terrible disease.

Her Life Crushed Out - The body of Miss Eliza McDonald, a teacher in the State Female college at Greensboro, N.C., was found recently on the track of the Cape Fear and Yadkin Valley railroad, evidently crushed to death by being run over by a train. Miss McDonald was a highly estimable young lady, and had a large circle of friends.

Ex-President Hays Dead - Ex-President Rutherford B. Hays died at 10 o'clock Tuesday night...The first intelligence of this was received when Webb C. Hays came down and quietly announced that his father had just died...the encouragement given them by Dr. Hilbert, the family physician, led them to believe that the patient would soon recover...While Dr. Hilbert remained almost constantly by the patient's side, no alarming symptoms appeared until evening when he became rapidly worse...Rutherford Buchard Hays, eighteenth President of the United States, was born in Ohio nearly seventy-one years ago.

Duel To The Death - A crowded passenger coach on the outgoing Atlanta and Florida train from Atlanta was the scene of a sensational shooting affray...As the train reached a suburban station, McEachen started for Hewell. The latter, to avoid problem, stepped on the platform. McEachen followed and facing Hewell, called him the vilest of names, and drawing a knife started for him. Hewell warned him off, but it had no effect. Then Hewell drew a revolver and put a bullet in McEachen's brain, killing him instantly.

A Wreck on the A.G.S. - A tail end collision occurred on the Alabama Great Southern, 18 miles south of Chattanooga, about 4 o'clock Wednesday morning, between the pay train and freight No. 117, both southbound...Engineer Pat O'Brien had a leg broken.

A Mad Dog Runs Amuck - A mad dog in his brief career in the southern part of Springfield, Ohio, bit twenty people before he could be killed...The dog was a water spaniel, owned by Chas. Cutinan, a contractor.

It is Governor Turney - At noon Wednesday, the special committee of the legislature and officers of the Supreme Court went to the home of governor-elect Turney, at Winchester, Tenn., and swore in the new executive. Governor Turney was unable to leave his bed, and only the brief ceremony of the induction was performed.

John Cultice, the postmaster of Red Key, Ind., who has kept the place for ten years, is totally blind.

The Banner has been adopted as official organ of the Knights of Labor in this state, all official notices will henceforth be published therein. A.J. Henley, S.M.W.K. of L.

Messrs. A. G. Dake and O. M. Martin of Clanton; Mr. Ira Campbell of Jemison and L. B. Pounds of Maplesville are duly authorized to collect and receipt for subscriptions to The

Banner. T.H. White, Editor

Representative Cate, of Arkansas, wants coinage of silver dollars for his constituents satisfaction....

Justice Lamar died suddenly at Vineville, a suburb of Macon, Ga., on Monday the 23d instant.

President-elect Cleveland when asked recently by a reporter: "Do you oppose free coinage of silver?" answered "I have nothing to say on this question."

The committee on Privileges and Elections has declared Mr. Carter was not duly elected to the legislature from Pike County and have given the seat to Mr. Townsend, the Populist candidate.

The County Court, R.M. Honeycutt presiding, convenes on the first Monday of each month. The next term promises to be an unusually interesting one; quite a number of cases are set down for trial and Solicitor Nolan will be kept busy.

General Master Workman Powderly says, "I believe the railroad are public highways, and should be nationalized and the telegraph system should be owned and operated by the government."

Mr. Cleveland, with the arrogance characteristic of his party, intimated to the sovereign state of New York that the choice of Mr. Murphy for United States senator would be distasteful to him personally. In spite of this expression from a would-be dictator, Murphy was elected by the New York legislature.

Representative G. W. Ward, of Jefferson County, has introduced a bill in the House, providing for the payment of employees every two weeks by corporations and individuals in Jefferson County.....

Our Court Officers: Circuit Clerk Vandiver - Our highly efficient and genial Circuit Clerk, Mr. Joseph P. Vandiver, the subject of our sketch this week, was born in the city of Montgomery in November 1858. In November 1885, at the age of 17, he came into Chilton County, residing at Clear Creek, where he engaged in farming and merchandising, with considerable success, so that five years later, in 1880. he was enabled to take unto himself a wife, and was happily united to Miss Cornelia McMath, of Montevallo, who has been his aid and support in all the trials and triumphs of his life. At the early age of 18 he was appointed postmaster at Clear Creek, and one year later was elected Justice of the Peace, both of which positions he held with credit to himself and satisfaction to his fellow citizens until the time of his election to Circuit Clerk. In 1891 Mr. Vandiver removed to Jemison, where he lived until recently, when he purchased the handsome residence of Mr. Merritt, at Clanton, which property he is about to improve at a considerable outlay. Mr. Vandiver is not only a member of the Masonic fraternity, but is one of the most prominent officers in his lodge. He is the owner of the only quarry of roofing slate in this slate. Mr. Vandiver will unquestionably give as great satisfaction to his fellow-citizens in the responsible office he now occupies as he has hitherto done in his former official positions, and when the time arrives for him to retire will have earned for himself at the hands of his fellow citizens the verdict of "Well done, thou good and faithful servant."

State Assembly Knights of Labor in Alabama - The annual session of the State Assembly of the Knights of Labor of Alabama convened in Labor Hall, Selma on Tuesday, January 17, 1893 and was called to order by Master Workman A.J. Henley...Bro. J. W. Bell introduced a resolution, which was adopted, making it obligatory upon any local assembly, where the State Assembly may convene, to provide homes and take care of delegates while in attendance at such state meeting, but shall not be permitted to vote upon any question. Adopted. The officers elected for the ensuing year are: Master Workman-A.J. Henley, Worthy Foreman-W. S. Barefield, Rec. Sec. & Sec. Treas.-Ira Campbell, Executive Board: S. M. Franklin, H. Foshee, A. J. Leibert. Delegate to the G. A. - T. H. White....Ira Campbell, Sec. Treas.

Ad - Birmingham Business College and School of Shorthand and Typewriting, Birmingham, Ala.............Address all letters to Amos Ward, President

Ad - Low Prices Always Prevail At Simpson Brothers, The One Price Clothier....Birmingham, Ala.

Ad - Warner, Smiley & Co., Undertakers and Embalmers, Birmingham, Ala.

Ad - Seals Brothers Pianos and Organs...Birmingham, Ala.

Ad - L & N Railroad

Ad - Post Office, Clanton...B. H. Chestnut, Postmaster

Ad - Robert H. Knox, Attorney-At-Law, Clanton, Ala.

Town Items - One Car Acid Phosphate just received. W. L. Sampey
.
When you visit Birmingham, patronize the Metropolitan Hotel, next the depot, kept by the well known and popular firm Lesser & Co.
.
Will Kemp and Fonza Culp will open with a fine stock of goods at Mullins' old store.
.
Miss Emma Cox, who resides with John H. Collins, is suffering from a severe attack of pneumonia.
.
Mrs. Sara Collins' son is recovering from an attack of fever accompanied with pneumonia.

Energy Dottings - Our school, managed by Professor J. D. Adair, had three days vacation on account of the inclement weather...
.
Dr. R. O'Connell, of Pine Mills, Texas, spent the Christmas holidays here. His aged mother returned with him to make Texas her future home...
.
Will make special delivered prices in mixed car load lots of German milled oats, corn, bran, flour, etc. For further information address: Geo. A. Gowan, State Agent, Nashville Tenn.

Notice For Publication (Page Edge Torn) - Notice No. 13,419, Land Office at Montgomery, January 25, 1893, Notice is hereby given that the following - named settler has filed notice of her intention to make final proof in support of her claim and that said proof will be made before The Clerk of the Circuit Court at Clanton, Alabama, on march 18, 1893, viz.: Bethany S. Leopard, widow of John G. Leopard, Homestead entry No. 15,583, for the NW 1/4 of SW 1/4 of Section 12, Township 23, North of Range 13 E. She names the following witnesses to prove her continuous residence upon (land) cultivation of said land. viz.: J. J. Green, Mason Northcutt, Zacharaiah Avery and W.R. Lowery, all of Jemison, Ala. J. H. Bingham, Register.

Ad - New York College of Commerce, Birmingham, Alabama...M. M. Fields, Vice President; Leonard Lippman, President; F. W. Dryburgh, Sec'y and Treas.

Program of Chilton County Teacher's Institute - ...2. Address of Welcome, J. Alex Moore 3. Response, by Sup't J. W. Moore
Subjects For Discussion
1. Unwise Punishments. J.M. Scott, L. B. Pounds and E. E. Todd.
2. Model Recitation in Geography, conducted by G. L. Speer
3. An Ideal Teacher, Paper by Miss Lula Eddings, Discussions opened by L. C. Parnell
4. Language Work in Our Count Schools, David Moore and R. A. Roscoe...
6. Educational Addresses, by State Sup't J. G. Harris and others.
7. Recitation by Miss O. Garner...
Devotional Exercises
1. The Relationship of Teacher, Parent and Pupil, by E. G. Godsey...General Discussion
2. Class in Arithmetic, conducted by W. C. Robinson
3. How much work should be required of a pupil in a given time in any given branch of study? R.E.R. Hicks and H. L. Davis
Notice-Every teacher in the County is earnestly invited to attend the next institute. An effort will be made to have Hon. John G. Harris, State Sup't of Education, deliver an address on education. Let all come prepared to discuss every subject on the program. Collins Chapel is 2 miles east of Strasburg. Parties wishing to attend the Institute will correspond with J. Alex Moore, Jemison, Ala., who will furnish conveyance from the railroad at Strasburg to the Chapel.   G. L. Speer, F. G. Godsey, J. Alex Moore, Committee

Ad - Chickens And Eggs, Persons wishing to dispose of the above species of Farm Produce will find it to their interest to address or call on T. H. White, The Banner Office, Clanton

Notice to Subscribers To the People's Party Banner - All parties having subscribed to The Banner will please forward their Names and Addresses to the office of said paper, together with date of subscription and amount paid; the late fire having destroyed our subscription list. T. H. White, Editor

Ad - After The Grip...Hood's Sarsaparilla Cures...Mrs. Isiah Emerson, Manchester, N.H.

Ad - Cures Scrofula
Mrs. E. J. Rowell, Medford, Mass. says her mother has been cured of scrofula after the used of four bottles of S.S.S. after having much other treatment and being reduced to quite a low condition of health, as it was thought she could not live...
Cured my little boy of hereditary scrofula which appeared all over his face. For a year I had given up all hope of his recovery, when finally I was induced to use S.S.S. A few

bottles cured him and no symptoms of the disease remain. Mrs. T.L. Mathers, Mathersville, Miss.

Ad - Interested In Newspaper Work?...Don't Start a Paper without writing to A. E. Leishman...Birmingham, Ala.

Ad - Fruit Trees...E. Moody & Sons, Lockport, N. Y.

Working For His Former Slave: - "What a great of whirligig time is, to be sure," said C. A. Shneider, a native of Louisiana. "There is in New Orleans today a man working for a negro he once owned, but lost at a game of cards. Before the war, James M. Coleman was a well-to-do Mississippi planter. He owned thirty or forty slaves, had a fine plantation, and was what would be called a "high roller". He spent much of his time at Memphis and New Orleans and thought nothing of a blow out that could cost him a cool thousand. One day he was coming down the river and indulging his weakness for draw poker, he lost his roll. He had a bright mulatto boy with him, whose business it was to see that "massa" got safely to bed when he chanced to get an overdose of bourbon. He put the boy up against a thousand and lost. Dissipation and the war ruined him in health and fortune and two years ago he came to New Orleans in search of something to do that would provide his daily bread. The boy he had sold had become a contractor and employed several men and teams. He met his old "massa" and employed him to keep his accounts and that is what he is doing today - St. Louis Globe - Democrat

State of Ohio, City of Toledo} s.s.
Lucas County
Frank J. Cheney makes oath that he is the senior partner of the firm of F. J. Cheney & Co., doing business in the City of Toledo, County and State aforesaid, and that said firm will pay the sum of $100 for each and every case of catarrh that cannot be cured by the use of Hall's Catarrh Cure. Frank J. Cheney
Sworn before me and subscribed in my presence, this 6th day of December, A.D., 1886
{Seal} A. W. Gleason

Ad - "Three Thousand Tons of Shine"
Morse Bros., of Canton, Mass., made the largest sale of "The Rising Sun Stove Polish" during the year 1892 they ever made since they began its manufacture thirty years ago....

Ad - If afflicted with sore eyes use Dr. Isaac Thompson's Eye-water...

Ad (page torn) - "August Flower"
I used August Flower for lost vitality and general debility. A(fter) taking two bottles I gained 69 p(ounds). I have sold more of your Aug(ust) Flower since I have been in busin(ess) than any other medicine I ever kep(t). Mr. Peter Zinville says he was made a new man by the use of August Flower, recommended by me...George W. Dye, Sardis, Mason, Co., Ky.

Ad - A woman has very little desire to enjoy the pleasures of life and is entirely unfitted for the cares of housekeeping on any ordinary duties if afflicted with SICK HEADACHE DAY AFTER DAY and yet there are few diseases that yield more promptly to proper medical treatment...During a period of more than 60 YEARS there has been no instance reported where such cases have not been permanently and PROMPTLY CURED by the use of a single box of the genuine and justly celebrated Dr. C. McLane's Liver Pills...Fleming

Brothers Co., Pittsburgh, Pa.

Ad - Catarrh - sold by druggists or sent by mail 50 cents E. T. Haselltine, Warren, Pa.

Ad - Opium Morphine habit cured in 10 to 20 days. No pay till cured. Dr. J. Stephens, Lebanon, Ohio

Ad - To Young Men
Splendid Opportunity to learn a business that will give steady employment and a salary of $10000 a year...Address: Geo. H. Lawrence, 53 E 10th, N. Y. City

James G. Blaine - His Public Career From Manhood To Old Age.

James Gillespie Blaine was born on the 31st of January 1830, at West Brownsville, Penn., in a house built by his great grandfather before the War of the Revolution, which still stands. The Gillespies and Blaines were people of standing before the revolution, Colonel Blaine, who was Commissary General of the Northern Department of Washington's Army during the Revolution, when eleven years old, he went to live with (Unc)le Thomas Ewing, in Ohio, where his mother's father, Neal Gillespie, an accomplished scholar directed his studies. Later he attended Washington College, at Washington, Penn., graduating at the age of seventeen. After leaving college he taught school at Blue Lick Springs, Ky. It was as a professor in the military school there that he made the acquaintance of the lady - a school teacher from Maine - who afterwards became his wife. Later he went to Philadelphia, where he taught school and studied law. But after two years he abandoned law studies and went to Maine, and became proprietor and editor of Kennebec Journal. At the birth of the Republican Party, he was a delegate to the Philadelphia Convention in 1856, which nominated F. Fremont. After serving as Speaker of the Maine Legislature, he was sent to Congress and began his national career in 1862, with the outbreak of the war. During the Forty-first Forty-second and Forty-third Congresses he was Speaker of the House. Mr. Blaine's administration of the Speakership is commonly regarded as one of the most brilliant and most successful in the annals of the House. He had rare aptitude and equipment for the duties of presiding officer, and his complete mastery of Parliamentary law, his dexterity and physical endurance, his rapid dispatch of business, and his firm and impartial spirit were recognized on all sides. It was during his occupancy of the Speaker's chair in 1874 that he took the floor and succeeded in defeating the passage of the original "Force Bill". The political revulsion of 1874 placed the Democrats in control of the House, Mr. Blaine became the leader of the minority period. The session preceding the Presidential contest of 1876 was a period of stormy vehement contention. On the 21 of May a resolution was adopted in the House to investigate an alleged Union Pacific Railroad Company of certain bonds of the Little Rock and the Fort Smith Railroad Company. It soon became evident that the investigation was aimed at Mr. Blaine. An extended business correspondence on his part with Warren Fisher, of Boston, running through years and relating to various transactions, had fallen into the hands of a clerk named Mulligan, and it was alleged that the production of this correspondence would confirm the imputation against Mr. Blaine. When Mulligan was summoned to the fifth of June, 1874, he rose to a personal explanation, and after denying the power of the House to compel the production of his private papers, and his willingness to go to any extremities in defense of his rights, he declared that he proposed to reserve nothing. Holding up the letter he exclaimed, "Thank God, I am not ashamed to show them. There is the very original package. And with some sense of humiliation, with a mortification I do not attempt to conceal, with a sense of outrage which I think any man in my position would feel, I invite the confidence of 40,000,000 of my countrymen while I read these letters from my desk. The demonstration closed with a dramatic scene which Josiah Caldwell, one of the originators of the Little Rock and Fort Smith Railroad who had full knowledge of the whole transaction was traveling in Europe and both sides were seeking to communicate with him. After finishing the reading of the letter Mr. Blaine turned to the Chairman of the Committee and demanded to know whether he had received any dispatch from Mr. Caldwell. Receiving an evasive answer Mr. Blaine asserted as within his own knowledge, that the Chairman had received such a dispatch "completely and absolutely exonerating me from discharge and you have suppressed it." In 1875 Mr. Blaine was appointed to the Senate to fill the vacancy caused by the resignation of Senator Morrill, and the next winter was elected by the Legislature to the succeeding term. His career in the Senate was both brilliant and distinguished, as it had been in the House. He was called from the Senate to enter President Garfield's Cabinet as Secretary of State. It was while passing through the railroad depot leaning on Mr. Blaine's arm and pleasantly chatting with him about his coming holiday that Garfield received the assassin's fatal bullet. The death of Mr. Garfield led to Mr. Blaine's retirement from the Cabinet in December 1882. From that date until he entered Mr. Harrison's Cabinet as Secretary of State, he was in private life except during his campaign for the Presidency in 1884. During his retirement Mr. Blaine wrote his "Twenty Years in Congress", a work of his great historical value. It was in accordance with his original suggestion and due to his earnest efforts the provision was made in the McKinley bill for the reciprocity treaties which formed such prominent features of National policy. The Samoan difficulties, the complications arising out of the lynching of Italians at New Orleans, and the killing of American seaman at Valparaiso were also disposed of by Mr. Blaine was at the head of the State Department. The events preceding and attending the recent Minneapolis Convention are too recent almost to need recounting. Mr. Blaine was induced to permit his name to be used as a candidate and resigned his place in the Cabinet. Whether in public position or in private life, he always remained a central figure in National affairs.

BLAINE'S LIFE IN WASHINGTON.

For nearly 30 Mr. Blaine has been a resident of Washington. While he never gave up his homelife in Maine, where he had a town residence in Augusta and summer residence at Bar Harbor, yet he also had a home in Washington. It was only a few years after going there as a Member of Congress that he bought the residence at 821 Fifteenth street, where he lived so many years. This was about the year 1860, when he was elected Speaker of the House for the first time. The house he bought was one of a row which had just been built and was regarded at that time as one of the chief architectural features of the city. He made his home at 821 Fifteenth street for over ten years, and then having built the fine residence fronting on Dupont Circle, he sold the old house and took possession of the new one. The death of Garfield and Mr. Blaine's retirement from public life caused a change in his plans and he leased his Dupont Circle house to Mr. Leiter. He was absent from the city for several years, although he spent a portion of one or two winters there and occupied the house on Lafayette Square adjoining General Beale's residence, which is owned by the daughter of the late Representative Scott, of Pennsylvania, Mrs. Scott Townsend. About the beginning of his administration he purchased his late home, which is on the opposite side of Lafayette Square, and is considered notoriously unlucky, two tragedies having occurred within its portals. During Buchanan's administration it was occupied as a clubhouse. One day Philip Barton Key, the young and handsome District Attorney of the District of Columbia had just left the clubhouse when he was shot down by Congressman Sickles, of New York. Mr. Key was carried back to the clubhouse. An intrigue which Key had been carrying on with Sickle's wife was the cause of the encounter. Two years after this occurrence the home, which was for a time unoccupied, was taken by the then Secretary of State William H. Seward, and he moved into it with his family. On the night of April 14, 1865, while Mr. Seward lay sick in bed in one of the upper rooms, a big oak complexioned broad shouldered man rang the doorbell and told the servant who admitted him that he had a package of medicine which the Secretary's physician had ordered to be delivered to him personally. The servant refused to allow him to go upstairs and the Secretary's son, Frederick W. Seward, also opposed him; but the stranger, making a feint of departure, suddenly sprang at Frederick and felled him to the floor with a butt of a revolver, almost on the same instant slashing the servant with knife. He then darted forward and reached the sick chamber where Secretary Seward was sitting up in bed. The knife gleamed again and Mr. Seward, weak and helpless, was stabbed in the face and neck, but the bandages that swathed his neck saved him from a mortal wound. As the murderous intruder retreated he was again intercepted, this time by Major Augustus H. Seward and an attendant, but he shook them off, and running downstairs, leaped on his horse and rode off. He was captured a few days later, and being fully identified as Lewis Payne, one of the men implicated in President Lincoln's death, was tried, condemned and executed with his fellow-conspirators. So great was the alarm excited by the attempt on Mr. Seward's life that from 1865 to 1869 a soldier was kept on guard in front of the old mansion. The Secretary recovered, but his only daughter, who had witnessed Payne's assault, was so terribly shaken by the affair that she died not long afterward. Secretary of War Belknap was the next tenant of the house of misfortune, and for a time the sober old edifice became gay with the life of the Grant regime. Before a twelvemonth its evil genius had again asserted and Mrs. Belknap lay dead under its roof after a brief illness. Then, after the Belknaps vacated it again did duty as in the earlier days, as a boarding-house, but Washington had somehow got the impression that the place was uncanny and that its tenants were dogged by an evil fate. For a time the Commissary General's staff had possession, then when they had moved to the War Department's new building it was again tenantless. It was about this time that Mr. Blaine, shortly after his appointment as Secretary of State by President Harrison, astonished his friends by renting the ill-omened house for ten years at $3000 a year. He decorated and renovated it throughout, tearing down the walls of the room in which the attempt on Mr. Seward's life took place and by generous expenditures transformed the dingy old wide-roomed house into a magnificent modern residence. Yet all the changes failed to eradicate the characteristics attributed to the mansion by the superstitious Washingtonians. Becoming its tenant, Mr. Blaine has encountered the greatest reverses to his ambitions and experienced the keenest sorrows of his life.

MR. BLAINE'S PROPERTY

Although known as a man of comparatively large wealth, Mr. Blaine's life during his term as Secretary of State was far from being ostentatious. His home on Lafayette Square was well suited for entertainment, out, owing to the fact that what is called the "administration circle" has been almost constantly in mourning during the past four years, it has been used but little for that purpose. Mr. Blaine's fortune had its origin in tracts of land in Western Pennsylvania, which were left by his father, Ephraim L. Blaine who had himself inherited them from the elder James Gillespie Blaine. The most valuable of these properties was a tract of coal land near the Monongahela River. Mr. Blaine made most of his money out of these lands and out of the investment West Virginia. Mr. Blaine's last visit to the Capitol on a public occasion was when he attended with other members of the Cabinet, the Congressional funeral of Samuel J. Randall. Mr. Blaine had always a great respect and admiration for Mr. Randall, who had led the minority in the House when Mr. Blaine was the Speaker. His last appearance before a committee was when he protested to the Senate Finance Committee against the passage of the McKinley Tariff but in the form in which it had come from the House and brought forward his policy of reciprocity with the other republics of this continent. Mr. Blaine's last visit to the White House was when he attended the funeral services of Mrs. Harrison.

MR. BLAINE'S HOUSEHOLD

Of Mr. Blaine's six children, three-two sons and a daughter-were suddenly stricken down by death after reaching maturity. His eldest son, Walker Blaine, a young man of fine parts, who had given evidence of rare abilities and was apparently destined to a brilliant future, died two years ago. Emmons Blaine, his second son, a bright businessman, in manner and character closely resembling his father, also died suddenly in the heyday of youth and prosperity. A third and crushing bereavement was the death of the eldest daughter, Alice Blaine, who was married to Lieutenant Colonel John J. Coppinger. It followed closely on the death of her brother, Walker Blaine, whose funeral she was attending when seized by the fatal illness. Of the three surviving children, the son, James G. Blaine, made an unfortunate marriage, the results of which embittered the latter years of his father's life. One of the daughters, Miss Margaret Blaine, is married to Mr. Walter Damrosch, the famous New York musical director, and the other, Miss Harriet Blaine, is unmarried. Mrs. Blaine is still and active and brilliant and active lady. She has been a devoted wife to the great statesman, whom she married forty-one years ago when both were school teachers in a country district with but little to indicate the prominent place they were destined to fill in the highest circles of the Nation.

ITEMS OF INTEREST -...The Grand Duke of Baden has presented the order of "Zachringen" to Dr. W. J. Hoffman, of the Smithsonian Institution, Washington, in recognition of his distinguished contributors to ethnological science...

Ten more buffaloes consigned to Austin Corbin's game preserve on Croydon Mountain, have arrive at their destination. This increases the herd to thirty-three, making it, with one exception, the largest private herd in the United States.

William Black, the novelist, does his literary work in a room at the top of his house, above the noise of the street, and away from all unnecessary interruptions. Mr. Black's room, apart from a bookshelves and a desk, is almost bare of comforts.

TELEGRAPHIC NEWS ITEMS. - CONDENSED NOTES FROM ALL SECTIONS OF THE UNITED STATES AND EUROPE
...Jules B. Kampe, Cincinnati, manager of the Washington Life insurance company, fell short $1,075 and suicided to escape arrest.

Henry Sumner died suddenly in a cheap lodging house at Hartford, Conn., and it was afterward discovered that he was the possessor of $50,000 in cold cash.

...While digging a vault in his back yard, William Hall of Colorado Springs, Colo., struck a rich vein of silver ore, and now the whole population has begun to dig up their backyards.

Dr. McGlynn, a famous Catholic of New York is to visit his friend, Bishop John Moore, at St. Augustine, Florida, and deliver a course of lectures at the Cathedral there.

Mrs. Crum, the mother of the child who was recently run over and maimed by Cornelius Vanderbilt's carriage, brought suit for $365 damages. The millionaire paid it and additional $35 costs.

Ex-Gov. Ryerson of Lower California, says that the continued dry weather is becoming serious. Never before in forty years has there been a time where the cattle could not find food in the valley lands.

At St. Joseph Mo., Walter E. Brooks, the defaulting agent of the Sioux City & Northern, was located at the home of a friend Friday night. Detectives surrounded the house, but Brooks leaped from a third story window and made his escape....

The Iron Hall requisitions which Gov. Brown of Maryland, declined to honor, were issued under the administration of Gov. Chase, and it is thought by Indiana officials that the question can be taken up again if it is presented to Gov. Matthews in another form.

....The Supreme Court of Illinois has decided that women can vote in school elections. The decision was on the appeal of Martha E. Plummer, who last May defeated two male candidates by the aid of the votes of 293 women which the county court decided were illegal.

...A Sioux Falls, S.D., sensational proceedings have been begun by Madame Maud Alexandrina Lopez against Gen. Enrique Lopez of Buenos Ayres, Argentine Republic. Madame Lopez is one of the distinguished Lloyd family of London, England and was married to Gen. Lopez in London in June, 1882. She says that her husband is squandering her money.

Alexander Volz of St. Louis will doubtless escape the gallows because the statement of a wife cannot be taken in evidence. Mrs. Volz says she believes her husband murdered Jessie Simmons, because his relations with her were suspicious, and after the murder she washed some clothes for her husband that had blood on them, and he told her that if he was arrested for murder he wanted her to swear that the blood came there accidentally.

He Deserved Lynching. - One of the most horrible crimes ever committed at New Orleans occurred Tuesday evening and resulting in a woman's throat being cut from ear to ear, a man being murdered, and another being lynched. Mrs. Martha McMahon, an aged woman, kept a grocery store, and recently hired a negro ex-convict named Fischer. She sent him on an errand and complained at the trifling purchase he made for her. The negro without warning reached over to where a large meat knife was, and taking it up, rushed for the woman. He caught her by the hair and cut her throat. Her screams brought John Barrett, a fireman, to the scene. He caught the negro, but like a flash, the latter turned and stabbed him three times. killing him instantly. The negro was shortly afterwards captured and strung up by the infuriated citizens.

Justice Lamar's Death. - Justice Lucius Quintus Cincinnatus Lamar died at Macon, Ga., Monday evening at 8:50 o'clock. Death was sudden and the extreme, for, although he has been ailing for some time, Justice Lamar appeared to be gradually gaining in health. Bright's disease, with angina pectoris was the direct cause of Mr. Lamar's death, and as given by the physicians as being the chief complications in the case. The attack was very severe while it lasted, and the physician, Dr. A. H. Parker, who had been in attendance, arrived only a few minutes before death. Justice Lamar was born in Putnam county, Ga., September 17, 1825. President Cleveland appointed him secretary of the interior, and afterwards elevated him to a seat on the supreme bench.

The National Alliance - The annual convention of the National Farmers' Alliance opened at the Sherman House, at Chicago, Tuesday. The meeting was not largely attended, but twenty delegates being present. The only states represented were Illinois, Ohio and Iowa. W. H. Likins presided. In his address of welcome he stated that, although the organization had not increased in numbers, it was on a stronger footing than ever before.

The bill to incorporate Clanton has been introduced by Representative O.M. Mastin. We sincerely trust that that body will see fit to pass it.

Ben Terrell, Our Capitol National Lecturer, thus discourses upon the necessity for a new party: "I am a man independent in politics; vote with the people's party in the last election because it advocated measures I believe to be the interest of all people, and with the present light before me will do again. I believe a new party inevitable because the present party alignments are not in lines of interest. The South and West must and will join hands in a new party, but to build up and extend the Alliance until all who eligible to membership are in its ranks is the duty of all members of this order. Let our speakers, then talk Alliance not party; let our press-the Alliance press- go to work for the Alliance, and cease to be partisan; let every member go to work for Alliance and we can make it one of the greatest engines for good this country has ever known. I beg of you - each of you - to work to extend and build it up. The National Economists discoursing anent the situation, says; "There is no longer any doubt that the retiring administration is not working day and night to prepare a downy bed of ease for the incoming administration. It is now clear that they are determined Mr. Cleveland shall wrestle with the silver question and that the present administration is doing all it possibly can to prevent any silver legislation at this session of congress." Regarding the Hatch anti-option bill, the Economist says: "The Hatch anti-option bill still drags in the Senate, and Tuesday, the 31st Jan., is the day set for a vote. If it comes to a vote, the indications are that it will pass."

The County Alliance Meeting. - Tuesday, the morning of the 24th January, dawned fair and clear, and but for the scattered and fast melting patches of snow, the twittering of birds and the mildness of the atmosphere would have fain made the wayfarer believe that the reign, ever-welcome Spring had commenced. To add to the illusion from the fields came the well-known sound of "Gee" and "Whoa", showing that the patient husbandman had once more commenced his toil, sure in the promise that seed time and harvest shall not cease as long as earth endures. Through the courtesy of Sheriff Moore your editor enjoyed a delightful ride through the hills and dales of Chilton for a distance of twenty-six miles his Mecca being Valley Creek Alliance located four miles west of Plantersville. We stayed that night at the hospitable home of Brother J. W. Letcher, who with the aid of his kindly and charming wife entertained us in a manner we shall long remember. Early next morning we winded our way to the church house, where the Alliance holds, which in contradiction of its title we found located on the summit of a hill. Our worthy president, Bro. Moses Robinson, our no less worthy ex-president Judge Honeycutt, shortly arrived, and about 11 o'clock the Alliance was called to order in open session period. President Robinson made the opening address, in which he dwelt in an eloquent manner upon the advantages of the Alliance organization and its non-political character. He was followed by ex-President Honeycutt, who in a lucid and forcible manner explained the principles of our noble organization, and his devotion to its cause. "God forbid" he said, "that I should forget the hand that has conferred honor upon me; my life will ever be spent in behalf of the people." Amongst other remarks he said, most truly, "The exchange is the regulator of prices; it is the incalculable benefit. Even if its sales failed to clear its expenses, yet its existence regulated prices both in town and country." The eloquent brother closed by begging Alliancemen to hold on to the organization. Your editor being called upon responded by calling attention to the necessity of educating our people in Alliance principles, and appealed for the moral and financial assistance of the order for The Banner, the advocate of reform. The President then appointed Brothers Honeycutt and Bailey a committee on credentials and adjourned until 1 o'clock. At that hour the President called the Alliance to order; and remained in session until 5p.m., then adjourned to meet at 8 the following morning. During the afternoon session a resolution was adopted endorsing the Banner, which read as follows: "We resolve to assist and help the brother in publishing the Banner to give it our entire interest and support as long as it supports the principles of the F.A. & L. U. A resolution, inviting Mayor T. Key, of Montgomery to address the County Alliance at its next meeting was so adopted. Reform Alliance South secured the coveted honor of the next County Alliance, which will convene in April. We spent the night at Brother Sam Harris' hospitable home, together with Brothers Williams and Robinson. The Alliance met at 8:30 the following morning and adjourned at noon to met in April next. The Secretary's books were audited and found correct; a well-deserved compliment being paid Bro. W. H. Shaw for the neat and businesslike manner in which they were kept. The executive Board (Bros. E. W. Bailey, Wylie Foshee, and T. H. White) acted as auditing committee. A resolution of thanks to the brethren of Valley Creek for their very hardy and generous hospitality was unanimously adopted. Our honored State President failed to be present to the very great disappointment of the brethren. His absence was doubtless due to ill health, he having recently been afflicted with a stroke of paralysis.

OUR COUNTY OFFICERS, SHERIFF MOORE - The preservation of law and order being the first principle of all civilized communities it devolves upon the part of the people that they procure good and efficient officers for that purpose, and one of the most essential points in county government is the absolute necessity of having a man of undoubted integrity and courage to fill the onerous post of sheriff. In this respect Chilton county can congratulate itself upon the man who was elected to fill this position, and who has a short time since his election proven himself a vigilant, faithful and thoroughly efficient officer. P. M. Moore, or as he is more popularly known, Pink Moore. Sheriff of Chilton county, was born in the county of Bibb, May 6, 1846; he is of real old Chilton stock, his father, B. H. Moore having been born, in 1817, in Chilton county, which at that time formed part of the county of Bibb. While now in the very prime of manhood, Sheriff Moore has from his childhood up been inured to a life of toil, which has given him the sinewy athletic frame with which to cope with evil-doers. Whether following the plow or chasing lawbreakers our gallant sheriff goes about his work with a purpose so intent upon accomplishing his object that failure is to him an unknown quality. Pink early discovered that for a man to remain single was a mistake, and when he was twenty-one years of age he was more firmly convinced of this fact by the charms of Miss Martha A. Jones, of Bibb county, to whom he was married. January 4, 1867. Living a happy domestic life with his fair, accomplished wife, the Sheriff passed his days in peace and contentment, until the voice of the people called him to fill the sheriff's office, when he moved to Clanton, where the manifold virtues and attractions of his accomplished family at once made for them a host of friends. He has eight children, three whom are married. For fifteen years Sheriff Moore has been a member of the Baptist church, and for several years a strong supporter and member of the Alliance. He has already made himself a terror to violators of the law, and promises by his energetic course of action to make for himself a state reputation as a perfectly fearless and trustworthy official. It is such a man as this the people delighted to honor.

Knights of Labor - The meeting of the State Assembly at Selma last week signalizes the commencement of another era in the history of our noble Order in this state. The re-election of Bros. A. J. Henley and Ira Campbell as State Master Workman and Secretary Treasurer respectively, was a well-deserved tribute to the devotion they have shown for the best interest of the Order, and their unwearied perseverance of the face of many obstacles and discouragements... In our report of the proceedings " not " was inadvertently inserted in Bro. Bell' s resolution and thus altered the sense thereof. The resolution provides that " all members in good standing in the local where the State Assembly is held shall be admitted into the meeting, but shall not be permitted to vote upon any question "... Send all contributions to General Secretary John W. Hayes, 814 Broad Street, Philadelphia, Pa. General Master Workman T.V. Powderly has revived the degree of Philosopher's Stone, and will confer it upon those who perform signal service for the order...

TOWN ITEMS (page torn) - Mr. James Higginbotham is better; he is suffering from an attack of pneumonia, and not from typhoid as stated last week.

.
The residence of Mr. James D. Bivings narrowly escaped destruction by fire Saturday last. A fire screen and some rubbish having caught on fire in a disused fireplace resulted in the mantle board being badly damaged and a hole burnt in the floor. A quick alarm and prompt assistance prevented further damage.

Mr. Jeff Parnell of Dixie, and Miss Annie Carter of Billingsley, Autauga county, were married last Sunday at the home of the bride's mother at Billingsley. The Banner wishes them all happiness.

.
Mr. Samuel Yates, aged 72, died at Coopers last week, and was buried with Masonic honors last Sunday at Coopers. For 38 years he was a member of the Baptist Church, and for several years a member of the Masonic fraternity. He was followed by his resting place in God's acre by a large concourse of sorrowing friends.

.
B. M. Gentry, the genial tax collector paid us a list of subscribers.

.
Mr. Nolan Representative of Coosa County paid his son Solicitor Nolan a short visit this week.

.
Joseph Varden of Liberty Hill and Miss Mattie Maddox of Chandlers old mill were married Tuesday at Hobert Milford's house.

.
Rev. A. C. Wells returned from Sistrunk and Jordan's on Tuesday, he held a good meeting, forty mourners came up for prayer during its holding period.

.
There is to be preaching at the Congregation church on Sunday. Mr. Wells will be assisted by Rev. S.E. Bassett of Fort Valley, Ga.

.
Mr. C. D. Foshee of Mulberry was unfortunate enough to have three sheep killed by dogs this week.

.
Parson J. M. Dykes killed two pigs ___ months and 11 days old ___ 430 pounds.

Notice For Publication. - NOTICE No. 13, 419. Land Office At Montgomery, Jan.25, 1893
Notice is hereby given at the following named settler has filed notice of her intention to make final proof in support of her claim, and that said proof will be made before The Clerk of the Circuit Court at Clanton, Alabama, on March 18, 1893, viz.: Bethany S. Leopard, widow of John G. Leopard. Homestead entry No.15, 583, for the NW 1/4 of SW 1/4 of Section 12 Township 23, north of Range 13E. Site names the following witnesses to prove her continuous residence upon and cultivation of said land. Viz.: J. J. Green, Mason

Northcutt, Zacharaiah Avery and W. R. Lowery, all of Jemison, Ala. J. H. Bingham, Register

ALABAMA STATE ASSEMBLY - A synopsis of the work being done in the Senate and House
TWENTY-FOURTH DAY
Senate-President Compton called the Senate at 10:30 a. m. On calling the row 24 senators, a quorum, answered to their names. The following people introduced bills:
Mr. I. Inzer, Mr. Milner, Mr. McRae
For the relief of Mrs. Jefferson Davis To amend section two of an act entitled an act to incorporate the Montgomery, Hayneville Camden railroad. Approved Dec.11, 1893.
Also introducing bills were Mr. Pettus, Mr. McCall, Mr. Sayre, Mr. Forman, Mr. Joiner
TWENTY-FIFTH DAY
The following people introduced bills:
Mr. Inzer, Mr. Berry, Mr. McRae, Mr. Goodwin, Mr. Goodwyn, Mr. Amason, Mr. Shaw
TWENTY-SIXTH DAY
The following people introduced bills:
SENATE - A few unimportant bills were introduced and the calendar was cleared long before the hour for the special order business arrived.
HOUSE - The following people introduced bills:
Mr. Joiner, Mr. Biggers, Mr. Elam, Mr. Case
In the case of J. H. Wilson against J. A. Joiner, from Talladega county, contest was dismissed.
In the case of J. M. Wallace against Jas. E. NeSmith, from Lawrence county, the committee reported a resolution to the effect that Mr. NeSmith had been duly elected.
TWENTY-SEVENTH DAY
SENATE - President Compton called the Senate to order at 10:30 a. m.... Bills on the calendar were taken up and acted upon.
HOUSE - ... Mr. Ferguson's bill to require all legal advertising in counties where there are more than one newspaper, to let the contract to the lowest bidder, but a newspaper must be one year old before it can be a competent bidder.
TWENTY - EIGHTH DAY
SENATE - ... Mr. Inzer introduced a bill to do away with the convict lease system.
The bill for the relief of Mrs. V. Jefferson Davis was taken up. The bill was favored by Messrs. Block, Porter, Goodwyn, Milner, Davie, Smith, Lackey and , Downy, and Messrs. , McRae, Almon, Hundley, Whorton, Pearson, Samford, NeSmith, Cunningham and, Bogart spoke in opposition to it.
Mr. McRae moved to indefinitely postpone the bill, which was lost by a vote of 15 to 17. The bill was lost, yeas 15, nays 17.
Yeas - Messrs. Present, Block, Davie, Downy, Goodwyn, Harris, Kemp, Lackey, Milner, Porter, Reynolds, Smith, Steiner, Tumlin, Walker - 15.
Nays - Messrs. Almon, Austill, Berry, Bogart, Bradley, Cunningham, Darby, Hundley, Inzer, McRae, Minge, NeSmith, Pearson, Samford, Stansel, Whorton, and , Williamson - 17.
HOUSE - ... In the contest case of G. C. Townsend against J. M. Carter, contest for seat in the House from Pike county. Mr. Townsend, populist, was seated, and Mr. Carter was deprived of his seat.

Rare Signatures of Notables Sold - A sale of autograph letters and signatures of various notables was held at an auction room in New York City last week. George Washington' s letters Sold for less than half what they usually bring. One written by Washington to Richard Henry Lee went for $37. Another to Thomas Jefferson concerning his continuance in office, brought but $34. Signers of the declaration of independence fared hardly better. An autograph of Thomas Lynch, the rarest of all signers, went for $24, while the signatures of modern men of prominence in title and artistic line went for a few cents each.

A Royal Wedding - The marriage of Princess Marguerite Sophie and Duke Albrecht of Wurtemburg, was solemnized Tuesday at Vienna, in the church of the Hofrath. Cardinal Gruscha, archbishop of Vienna, officiated. The wedding was one of great brilliancy, being attended by Emperor Francis Joseph, several archdukes and archduchesses, the King and Queen of Wurtemburg, and other members of the royal family of Wurtemburg.

Dempsey Convicted - A telegraph from Pittsburgh, Pa., says: Hugh F. Dempsey, District Master Workman of D. A. No.3, K. of L., was found guilty and indicted Friday for causing poison to be administer to non-union men employed in the Homestead mill. The jury retired at 12p. m., and, after being out until 1:10, came in for further instructions from the court. The judge told the jury that if they found the defendant guilty at all, it must be on the first count charging Dempsey with assaulting W. E. Griffiths with intent to commit murder. Several questions of an unimportant nature, but which showed plainly that the jury intended to bring in a verdict of guilty, were asked and answered by the court. Ten minutes later they returned their verdict and were discharged from further service with the thanks of the court. Dempsey was in a measure prepared for the verdict and betrayed no signs of emotion. He left the court room and a crowd gathered about him and offered their sympathy. His attorneys said the verdict was a false one and he would move for a new trial.

Bishop Brooks Dead - Bishop Phillips Brooks of the Episcopal church, died at Boston, Monday morning, at 6:30, of pneumonia. He died of heart failure, brought on by a fit of coughing. He was taken ill Thursday night with a sore throat, but nothing serious showed until Sunday, Bishop Brooks was born in Boston, December 13, 1835. A few years ago he was made bishop. He was one of the those eminent devines in America

Beatty on Trial - Robert Beatty, who is charged with being an accomplice of Hugh Dempsey in the attempt to close down the Homestead steel works during the strike by administering poison to the non-union workmen, was on trial in the criminal court in Pittsburgh Tuesday morning. Beatty, it will be remembered, was arrested in Louisville and brought back on extradition papers after a hard battle.

The Banner, Vol. 1, Clanton, Ala., Thursday, February 9, 1893, No. 13

Three Girls and a Boy - At New Orleans, Mrs. Gus Blondo gave birth to quadruplets, three girls and a boy. One of the girls died, but the others appear to be healthy. The mother is doing well. This is the first case on record in New Orleans.

TELEGRAPHIC NEWS ITEMS - Condensed Notes From All Sections Of The United States And Europe

J. H. Clamp of Fairfield county, South Carolina, was waylaid and shot to death.

George C. Grover, Royal British Commissioner to the World's Fair, was found dead in bed at Chicago.

An old lady named Guthrie of Effingham, Ill., has held notes to the amount of $50, 000 until they are outlawed.

Major Morris advocates martial law on the Rio Grande border and talks interestingly of the trouble in capturing insurgents.

Deputy United States Marshall H. N. Faulkinbury was killed in Baxter county, Arkansas, by timber cutters whom he was trying to arrest

United States Senator Carey proposes to amend the House bill to admit New Mexico so as to admit also Utah, Arizona and Oklahoma.

There is no prospect of an adjustment of difficulties in the Kansas dual House. Senator Perkins will not personally contest Judge Martin's seat.

Andrew Carnegie has made a statement in reference to the affairs of the Carnegie Steel Company, in which he highly commends Chairman Frick's management.

Mr. A. G. Del Campello has been appointed royal vice-delegate from Spain to the World's Fair. He was formerly secretary of the Spanish legislation in this city.

While walking on the sidewalk directly the spouting of the Grand Opera House at Kokomo, Ind., Thomas C. Pearson, a young man, was struck on the head by a huge icicle and instantly killed.

Miss Sadie Conley, daughter of the St. Louis millionaire, William Conley, ran away from home and was married at Chicago to John Mooney, a jockey. The Chicago police were notified, but the pair managed to outwit them in some manner.

S. B. Dole, now president of the provisional government of Hawaii, is a one of late American missionaries to Hawaii, is a graduate of Williams College, and has been second associate justice of the Supreme Court of Hawaii. He is a scholarly man of acknowledged legal and judicial ability...

The Postmaster-General last March announced that he would present a gold medal to the railway postal clerk in each of the 11 divisions of the railway mail service who, under the rules prescribed by the general superintendent and approved by the second Postmaster-General, made during the calendar year, the best record in his division. The medal winners are as follows: W. A. Manchester, Boston & Albany, Harry P. Swift, Greensport & New York; H. T. Gregory, Washington & Charleston; W. L. M. Austin, Charlotte & Atlanta; J. C. Edgerson.

A special from Jackson, Mich., says a combination has just in day one effected whereby the Columbian Straw Paper Company, with headquarters at Chicago, secures control of 41 straw mills in the states of Ohio, Michigan, Indiana, Illinois, Wisconsin, Iowa, Missouri, Nebraska, and Dakota. The company is organized under the laws of New Jersey, with a capital stock of $40, 000, 000. The Central City Paper Company, of this city, has been purchased by the combined for about $40, 000. The principal officers of the trust are: P. D. Beard, Buffalo, N. Y., president; F. G. Trebien, Xenia, O., vice-president; E. Stein, Chicago, treasurer.

OUR COUNTY OFFICERS: COUNTY TREASURER SAMPEY - This week we have the pleasure of giving our readers a brief sketch of our courteous County Treasurer W. L. Sampey. The gentleman himself is so well known that it is almost superfluous to say that the respect and esteem in which he is held by his fellow citizens is well deserved by his considerate and kindly treatment of all who come in contact with him, and his courtesy is appreciated by everyone in the community. He was born at Ramer, Montgomery county, Ala., and devoting his youthful days to study acquired a sound education, finally graduating at Howard College, Marion, Ala., in June 1885. Having now to face the stern realities of life, Mr. Sampey selected Clanton as the best place to commence his campaign, and after leaving Howard College settled here and began merchandising. His business acumen and sound judgment, together with his urbane and courteous demeanor, soon placed him as one of our leading men, and today Mr. Sampey's reputation among Alabama merchants stands deservedly high. " One thing at a time and that done well. " being the motto Mr. Sampey has pinned his faith to, he, after firmly establishing himself in business, proceeded to establish himself for life, and having secured the affections of one of Tuskegee's most delightful daughters was united in the holy bonds of matrimony to Miss Lula Pinckard - thereby giving another evidence of his judgment. The young couple were warmly welcomed in Clanton society, and soon won an abiding place in the hearts of friends and neighbors, and it is not too much to say that their loss to society would be a most severe blow, but fortunately their is no prospect of any such untoward event. Mr. Sampey, in politics, is a consistent democrat - with broad views and a sense of what is right and just between man and man. His business being recognized his fellow-citizens he was, at their request, appointed by Governor Jones Treasurer for Chilton county in November last, in the place of Mr. J.M. Parish, who was elected to the position but failed to make the requisite bond. Judging from the way in which he conducts his own business interests there is no doubt but that the interests of Chilton county could not be entrusted to more capable hands.

Jemison Jingles - The all adage that " Death loves a shining mark, " was verified on the 2d inst. near Collins Chapel. Miss Ada Collins, aged 18 years, after a brief illness with pneumonia, crossed over the river. We condole with the grief stricken parents and friends. On 3d inst. Miss Emma Coe, aged 14, died, after a week's illness with hemorrhage of the lungs. She was an orphan, well cared for, however, and had a decent burial, thanks to the neighborhood. These two deaths at the same time were in separate families, but were very near by. Mr. Robert Martin was buried at the Chapel on January 29th, particulars not known.

Mr. J. P. Langston is suffering with a severe ailment of the throat, which almost prostrates him; it is to be hoped he will soon recover and resume his busy life as formerly.

Mr. Jake Woody, who recently married our esteemed friend Mrs. Allen, has opened up a new store at Jemison in close proximity to the dwelling house and Mrs. Woody's millinery establishment. To say that we wish this happy couple prosperity is the mildest way of expressing our sentiments.

Kincheon Ketchings - Jones and Brothers, the famous beaver hunters of this county, are contemplating going back to Autauga on another beaver hunt, as they met with such grand success before.

Mr. John Moore and wife of Autauga, were the guests of Mr. John Dennis last Saturday and Sunday.

FROM OUR FRIENDS - Maplesville, Ala., Feb.6, 1893
Editor Banner: - I see that there is a demand now for the people and advocates of political re-formation who to keep silent. " Let the people rest. " This comes from the bosses and their truckers, and to them it is important that the people be kept silent, as they are just now nearing a crisis in their diabolical schemes for the disfranchisement of the masses of the people. Heretofore they have beaten the people by their convention tricks, demagoguery, ballot stealing and fraudulent counts, and any and all mean, low, postillanimous methods that corrupt and depraved minds may become master of. For a while all thing moved serenely on, and they were fully satisfied and had no compunctions of conscience - but lo! All at once they pretend to awake to the dreadful enormity of these past crimes, they begin to see the awful precedents which they are setting the rising generation, and hypocritically pretend that by all means such a course most be arrested, some wise plan of their own must be instituted that will be safe, reliable and lawful. " That virtue and intelligence may rule! " and in order to do this a constitutional convention must be had that will result in the disfranchisement who of three fourths of our voters, and fully fortify themselves in power for all time to come. Yes, keep the people quiet, or divert their attention to other matters until this particular point is passed: wait until they secure on you the shackles of slavery by prestige of law, and force them deeper in the vale of poverty by increased burdens of taxation, and when all liberty is lost, all means of recovering the game, gone - then let the fool commoners of the masses kick as much as they please. But now, if you don't keep quiet until their little game is played, you are a disturber of the people, a pestilent fellow, a chronic grumbler, a demagogue, a fanatic, a fool, etc. Now, anyone who pretends he desires a new constitution in order to prevent future trouble in elections, and at the same time does not approve of righting the wrongs already perpetrated against the people, is both a knave and a fool. It is not the love of virtue and right that prompts these political henchman of plutocracy to advocate the changes they propose: if it were from this cause they would be prompted by the same principle to induct those whom the people have elected into the positions to which they have been chosen, or at least institute a fair means of investigation of the alleged frauds at the two past elections - but, you must let the people rest. Now, my countrymen, let us not hear their siren song for to keep quiet now is to allow this " infernal " constitutional scheme to work, is to bid a long farewell to all that we call liberty. It is to skulk like cowards, to shrink from duty; it is for our children and posterity to rise up and call us accursed cowards and scallions of plutocracy, to remain quiet at this time. So speak out, and say you are willing now to accept the Mississippi franchise law for Alabama. Yours, till the war is over, L. B. Pounds

TOWN ITEMS (Page Torn) - We are sorry to learn that Mrs. M.E. Stanley, the efficient secretary, of our local alliance, seriously cut her foot last week.

Mr. Robert Martin has lost his wife. She died January 30th, leaving an infant but nine days old. The deceased was a daughter of Mr. Mordecai Robinson, and leaves a large (?) of sorrowing friends to mourn (?) loss.

Rev. A.L. Foshee was happily married to Miss Rosa Mims, daughter of (?) Mims, on Thursday, Feb.2, (?) R.M. Honeycutt performed the ceremony. The Banner wishes the wedded pair long life and fe(?).

Probate Judge Honeycutt issued an order on Saturday for the admission of Mr. Wm. Norrels wife to the asylum at Tuscaloosa.

Mrs. Jim Dawson is visiting relatives at Robinson Springs and Montgomery.

(?)ewt Kicker left the classic pre(?) of Dukes mill last Sunday, and spent the they with friends in town.

Miss. Annie Smith paid a short visit to her brother, Mr. Tom Smith, at Mountain Creek.

Mr. O.A. Dukes is about to remove to Bainbridge, Ga., where he has an interest in a large saw mill.

GUANO NOTICE. I am now prepared to deliver guano and phosphates to my customers. Please come forward promptly and haul your fertilizers, as my warehouse is crowded.
W.L. SAMPEY

Mrs. J.M. Stanfield is visiting Miss (?)nna Gillespie at our capital city.

Mr. Ray made a trip to Montgomery on business last Tuesday.

Sheriff Moore is, we are sorry to say, on the sick list. Instead of his having the grip on someone else the grip is on him.

Rev. S.E. Bassett preached Sunday morning and evening to large congregations at the Congregational church. The reverend gentleman left on Monday for South Calera.

Mr. G.W. Gore has just completed and moved into his new residents, (?) miles north of Clanton.

Mr. K.R. Burnett has erected a substantial new dwelling house seven miles north of Clanton, and moved family into it this week.

Mr. F.W. Denty has moved his family from the Channel house to a house occupied by Mr. H. Boyd.

Mr. H.B. Roper and Miss Lula Young will marry on Sunday. The Banner presents its congratulations in advance on this happy occasion.

Mr. J.W. Sauls and Mrs. Sarah Mills all of Kincheon will marry on Sunday. The Banner wishes for them all happiness.

Plantersville Pickings - Mr. R.H. Gaines has been very sick, but is now improving. Mrs. David Martin is very sick, with not much chance of recovering.
.
Dr. Little, of Stanton, is erecting a good many houses for rent there.
.
Mr. Frank Harris and family paid a visit to Mrs. Harris' father and mother at Clanton last week. Mr. David Moore is getting better from his wound, and is visiting friends. Mr. A.R. Wigginton, of Birmingham, paid a visit to his brother here, returning home last Monday.
.
Mr. J.G. Gay has moved from Six-mile to his native home near Plantersville.

Ad - Mr. Wm. Wade of Lowell, INDIGESTION RELIEVED
Good Appetite and Good Health Restored by HOOD'S
Mr. Wm. Wade, the well known boot and shoe dealer at 17 Merrimack St., near the Postoffice, Lowell says: " When I find a *good thing* I feel like praising it, and I know from personal experience that Hood's Sarsaparilla is a fine medicine. I have for a good many years been seriously troubled with Distress in My Stomach and indigestion. I had medical advice, prescriptions and various medicines, but my trouble was not relieved. At last I thought I would try Hood's Sarsaparilla and I must say *the effect was surprising*. Soon after I began taking it I found great relief, and man Hood's Sarsaparilla Cures. Eat without having that terrible distress. I also rest well at night and am in good health, for all of which I thank Hood's Sarsaparilla. " Wm. Wade

ALABAMA STATE ASSEMBLY - A Synopsis of the Work Being Done in the Senate and House.
TWENTY-NINTH DAY
... The following people introduced bills:
Mr. Wiley, Mr. Austill, Mr. Porter, Mr. Hundley, Mr. Inzer, Mr. Stansel...
THIRTIETH DAY
...For the relief of Mrs. V. Jefferson Davis, Reconsidered and was Passed.
Yeas - Messrs. President, Block, Davie, Downy, Goodwyn, Harris, Kemp, Lackey, Milner, Porter, Reynolds, Smith, Steiner, Samford, Stansel, Tumlin, Walker - 17
Nays - Messrs. , Almon, Austill, Berry, Bogart, Cunningham, Darby, Hundley, Inzer, McRae, Minge, NeSmith, Pearson, Whorton and Williamson - 14...
HOUSE - Speaker Pettus called the house to order...
THIRTY-FIRST DAY
SENATE - President Compton calld the Senate to order..The whole day was spent discussing the election contest bill and, after adopting it, and a number of amendments, passed it. There was no other business of any importance transacted.
The following is the vote:
Yeas - Messrs. President, Almond, Berry, Bogart, Cunningham, Darby, Goodwyn, Hundley, Inzer, Milner, NeSmith, Pearson, Reynolds, Samford, Smith, Tumlin, Walker, Whorton, Wiley, and Williamson - 20
Nays - Messrs., Austill, Block, Davie, Downey, Harris, Kemp, Lackey, McRae, Minge, Porter, Stansel - 11...
HOUSE - Speaker Pettus called the house to order....
The following bills were called up, read a third time and disposed of:

For the relief of Mr. J. Sorel. Passed
To regulate the sale of winous, spirtuous, or milt liquors in the town of Opelika. It provides a license tax of $1,000 in the Opelika district. Mr. Jackson offered an amendment to make this license $500, but is was lost and the bill carried....
THIRTY-SECOND DAY
SENATE - President Compton called the Senate to order...
Resolutions of respect to the late Justice L.Q.C. Lamar and James G. Blaine were passed
HOUSE - ...Speaker Pettus residing...
In the pressure for time the House did not fail to express its feelings in the country's loss of three of her noblest citizens in the statesman James G. Blaine; the jurist L.Q.C. Lamar; and Chancellor John A. Foster, the latter of this State. Resolutions of condolence were passed.

RAILROAD NOTES - ...A. A. Allen succeeds J. J. Frey as general superintendent of the of the M., K. & T.,, with headquarters at Parsons, Jan....

Sullivan Sat Upon - John L. Sullivan and party registered at the Hotel Buehl, Akron, O., one day last week and the ruffian immediately proceeded to raise a disturbance. Colonel Wood, the proprietor of the hotel, informed John L. that he would not tolerate such conduct, even from an ex-champion, and stated emphatically to the burly fellow that unless he subsided the patrol wagon would be called for his exclusive benefit. Sullivan wished to discuss matters, but through his manager he finally quieted down.

ALL AROUND IN THE STATE - The News of a Week's Happenings Condensed for the Hasty Reader
.
Will Strickland of Lowndes county killed two hogs that weighed, respectively, 490 and 460 pounds.
.
The broom factory of Dr. T. A. Davis, of Anniston is filling a 12,000 ton order of pipe for Providence, R.I.
.
Judge W. C. Darden's gin house at Lafayette, with fifteen bales of cotton, were burned last week, caused by a young man trying to light a cigarette. Accidentally the cotton lighted and caught on fire. No insurance.
.
The Mobile Shingle Association held an annual meeting the other day and elected officers as follows: Paul A. Savage, president; C.W. Butt, vice-president and John R. Simpson, secretary and treasurer.
.
William Scroggins was hanged in the jail yard in Birmingham, Friday, for the murder of S. Shustig, a Jewish peddler, whom he killed near Warrior eight months ago. Scroggins was a young white man 20 years of age. He was uneducated. His home was in Baldwin county, Ala.
.
Jerry Underwood, the notorious burglar and thief, was taken before Judge Taylor at Huntsville, and in default of a bond of $1, 000 was committed to jail. He is also wanted, it is said, in Chattanooga for burglary, but he will dig coal in this state before engaging in that business for Tennessee.
.

Mr. Dan Dunkin, Greenville's noted truck farmer, stock raiser and horticulturist, killed eight shoats thirteen months old a week or two ago, and the lightest one weighed 250 to 275 pounds, as pretty a lot of hogs as any man need want to look at.

Mrs. Martha H. Bradford, one of Huntsville's oldest and most warmly esteemed ladies died last Wednesday afternoon in 84d year. She was a sister-in-law of Col. Ed Richardson of New Orleans, and in her early years made her home one of great hospitality in a noted social circle.

Six prisoners confined in the temporary jail at Selma made their escape by making an aperture in the 16-inch wall with a piece of wire from around the stove. Among the number was Bryant Gunter, charged with murder. The Dallas county jail was burned about three weeks ago, and the temporary jail was an old warehouse.

E.B. Miller has sold the William M. Douglass farm situated on Pulaski road about seven miles from Huntsville, to James Karney, an experienced farmer from Minnesota, for $3,000. The purchaser will return to Minnesota at once and return to the county by the 15th of next month, bringing with him three other families.

W.J. Hutto and H.M. Davis, farmers living about three miles from Abbeville, are rivals in hog raising. Each of these men has a hog which will weigh not less than 700 pounds net, and will very probably tip the beam at 750 or 860. They are endeavoring to surpass Mr. James Ward, who, two years ago, killed a hog that weighed 744. It is hard to tell which of these two hogs is the larger.

Issues Missing

The Banner, Vol. 1, Clanton, Ala., Thursday, March 2, 1893, No. 16

STATE ASSEMBLY - A Synopsis of the Work Being Done In the Senate and House.
FORTY-FOURTH DAY
SENATE - President Compton called the Senate to order..
HOUSE - ... Speaker Pettus presiding...
FORTY-FIFTH DAY
SENATE - President Compton called the Senate to order...
A resolution recommending Gen. Wheeler for Commissioner of Agriculture to President-elect Cleveland, was adopted...
HOUSE - ... Speaker Pettus in the chair...
FORTY-SIXTH DAY
SENATE - President Compton called the Senate to order...
The Governor made the following nominations to the Senate to compose the Board of Convict Managers, who were promptly confirmed:
S. H. Dent of the 3rd congressional district; S. W. John of the 9th congressional district; J. G. Bush of the 4th congressional district; to be members for the term of six years.
J. C. Clark of the 1st congressional district; S. C. M. Amason of the 6th congressional district; M. P. LeGrand, Sr. of the 2nd congressional district; to be managers for the term of four years.
G. R. Cather of the 7th congressional district; W. A. Handley of the 5th congressional district; and R. T. Simpson of the 8th congressional district; to be managers for the term of two years.
HOUSE - The House was called to order at 10:30 o'clock by Speaker Pettus.. The discussion was the most animated of the session, and the author of the bill by a scathing denunciation of Mr. Seymour of Sumter, brought the most distinctly personal element into debate that has been seen during the meeting of the General Assembly...
FIFTIETH DAY
SENATE - A message was received from the Governor transmitting the nomination of General J. T. Holtclaw for Railroad Commission to fill the unexpired term of General Levi W. Lawler, also the following Trustees of the University of Alabama:
M.L. Stansel, 6th district; John Little, 6th district; W.W. Haralson, 7th district for 6 years, from March 1st, 1893; W.T. Northington, 5th district, for 6 years from March 1st, 1893; J.E. Webb, 9th district, for 6 years from February 24th, 1893, all of which were promptly confirmed by the Senate.

Sent to the Pen for One Day - Judge Chrisman at Jackson, Miss., has passed a novel sentence upon a young white boy in Circuit Court, now in session at Raymond. The boy, Joseph Holiday, is about 17 years old, and was tried for arson. He pleaded guilty, but the lawyers and friends of the youth brought the facts before the court in such a light that the judge saw fit to sentence him to the penitentiary for only one day. Sheriff Harding brought him Saturday morning, and he was put in stripes, and has been working out his sentence all day. Three hundred citizens sent up a petition to the governor to pardon him, so he would not lose his citizenship, but under the new code the governor was powerless to grant pardon, the law requiring a petition to be printed for 30 days before pardon can be had. The boy will have to appeal to the legislature to restore his citizenship.

Big Batch of Bandits - Brigadier - General Frank Wheaton, commander of the military department at San Antonio, received a telegram Saturday from Capt. John G. Bourke, of the Third Calvary, stating that he had just returned to fourth day Fort Ringgold from detached service in the field, and that he bought in with him fifteen bandits, who were captured by troop in Starr county. In addition to the captured bandit prisoners he brought in four others, who surrendered peaceably. This is the biggest piece of work yet accomplished by the United States troops on the lower Rio Grande border, and Capt. Bourke is highly commended for the success of his scouting expedition by the military authorities.

May Resume if it Chooses - Some two weeks ago the Vicksburg Electric Street Railway company Michigan at, after a hearing by Judge Gilland, was granted permission to continue laying its track between Cherry Street crossing and the Washington Hotel, upon giving bond in the sum of $1,000. The bond was made Saturday evening and filed with the circuit clerk, but whether the road expects to resume construction at once is not known.

STATE NEWS - A Careful Summary of the Week's Doings Served in Briefest Form.
C.W. Guice has been elected city assessor of Eufaula.

Mrs. R.E. Booth has resigned as postmistress at Dothan.

The Methodist church at Alco was dedicated by Bishop Joyce Sunday.

Rev. J.W. Mitchell has been called as pastor of the Baptist church at Six Mile, Bibb county.

Mr. Waller is progressing very rapidly in putting down the water mains for the Greensboro water works.

James Harris, who lives near Choccolocco, is the father of the biggest boy to his age in the country. The youngster is only four years old and weighs 94 pounds.

Albertville, Marshall county, eighteen miles above Gadsden, furnishes a prodigy in Dollie Glanton, 6 years old, who reads chapter after chapter in the Bible and can play any piece of music given her. She has attended school only six months.

At a meeting of the stockholders of the basket factory at Fort Payne, the following officers were elected: M.D. Fuller, general manager; R.H. Hunt, C.D. Henly, M.W. Howard, Z, A.B. Green,Jr., M.D. Fuller and W.T. Folsom, board of directors.

The municipal election at Warrior resulted in the election of R.D. Jones, prohibitionist, mayor, over J.L. Brake, opposition, by thirty majority. The following is the list of aldermen elected: L.K. Moss, Dr. Thomas Cross, J.M. Bibb, John Mathews and D.F. South.

The governor has appointed the following as trustees of the Agriculture and Mechanical College at Auburn, Ala.: First District, J.C. Rich of Mobile; Second District, I.F. Culver of Union Springs, vice Kolb; Third, J.C. Armstrong of Lee, reappointed; Sixth district, William Smaw of Green county; Ninth District, R.H. Duggar; Seventh District, John A. Bilbro of Gadsden.

The Charles Henderson fire company, Troy, have elected the following officers: President, Charles Henderson; vice-president, W.R. White; secretary, E.R. Brannen; treasurer, C.F. White; foreman, L.E. Gillerstedt; assistant foremen W.B. Nail and J.L. Gilmore; engineer, P.H. Lafliteau; assistant engineer, Oscar Benton; Chief of the department, W.B. Talbot.

The stockholders of the Gadsden Land company met at the company's office in Gadsden last week and elected the following board of directors: A.H. Parker and L.B. Turner of Anniston, F.F. Weihl of Chattanooga, J.C. Street of Goodwater, L.W. Hammond of Cincinnati, R.A. Mitchell and W.R. Dorth of Gadsden. The officers for the ensuing year will be elected next week.

The Eufaula Board of Trade had a pleasant and enthusiastic meeting last night a the rooms of the Grocer's Exchange. An election of officers to serve for the ensuing year was held, which resulted as follows: E.B. Young, president,; Bert Scheuer, first president; R.Q. Edmondson,Sr., second vice-president; William Perry, secretary; George C. McCormick, William D. Jelks, Morris Beringer, John W. Tullis,Sr., J.M. Thweatt, Charles B. Goetchius, Levi W. Foy, directors.

G.A. Chastian, who works at the foundry of Noble Bros. & Company at Anniston, met with a most painful and serious accident last Friday morning. Just as the band was thrown on one of the " rattlers " and it placed to work, he reached over to oil the cogs. He was wearing a hand leather on his right wrist at the time, and it catching in the rapidly moving cogs, pulled his arm in, and before the machine could be stopped it was mashed into a shapeless mass. A surgeon was hastily sent for, who amputated the arm just above the elbow.

Abbeville is perhaps ahead of any other town in Alabama in raising big hogs. Henry M. Davis killed one last week that was about two and a half years old and weighed, net, 636 pounds. W.J. Martin also has a shote about two years old which will weigh somewhere from 600 to 700, and for which he has been offered a good bale of cotton. Robert Newman has one of these large hogs besides several others that will be killed here soon, and which will weigh nearly as heavy as those mentioned. From this showing it seems that the farmers would find economy in raising their meat and lard at home instead of paying 12 1-2 and 15 cents for it with 7 cents cotton.

Better Take Them In, Too - Among those who arrived on the Australian Monowai at San Francisco, were ex-American Consul A. Rick and Mrs. Rick, from Butaritari, Gilbert Islands. Mr. Rick said he received a letter for the State Department last November ordering him to close his office and return home, as the seizing of the islands by England made his further stay there unnecessary. Mr. Rick shut up shop November 26th and sailed for Sidney. He said the old king made a pathetic appeal to him to interest the American government in his behalf, as he claims his people prefer American to and English protectorate. He says American trade will soon be ruined, as the British traders are favored by their government and the feeling against Americans is strong. The natives prefer to deal with Americans, but they are given to understand that it will not be healthy for them to do this.

GENERAL NEWS - Current Events of General Interest Epitomized and Grouped.
Secretary Noble has authorized the payment of $125,000 "reserved claims" to the Chippewa Indians of Minnesota.

The Arizona legislature has passed a bill authorizing a reward of $5,000 for the body of Kid, the renegade Apache, dead or alive.

Dr. Blount, State quarantine inspector at Galveston, Tex., has received a telegram from Dr. Swearingen, Texas health officer, directing him to inspect all trans-Atlantic steamers for cholera.

.

Signor Grimaldi, Italian minister of finance, says that the monetary conference probably will not assemble next May, as European governments are convinced that nothing would come of it.

.

The United Ireland, Parnellite organ, expresses the opinion that the new home rule bill is inferior to the home rule bill of 1886, which Mr. Parnell did not regard as a complete settlement.

.

Premier Cuero has warned the editors of newspapers in Colombia that in the future they must not criticise public officers in their publications. Even the local police are not to be criticised by the newspapers.

.

One of the most notable banquets given in Chicago in many years was tendered Saturday night to Judge Henry W. Brodgett, who recently resigned from the Federal bench to become one of the counsel in the Behring Sea controversy.

.

Mr. J.J. Grinlinton, special commissioner from Ceylon to the Chicago exposition, who arrived in New York Thursday, has gone to Chicago, where he will be met by 50 native Singalese, who are now enroute to that city from San Francisco.

.

Dr. Kempster has gone to Dresden to attend the international cholera conference, as a representative of the United States. Dr. Kempster will later go to Egypt to investigate the business of rag exportation and methods of preventing the conveyance of disease germs in rags.

Since our last issue President Cleveland has announced the names of the remaining members of his cabinet, viz.: Hilary A. Herbert, of Alabama, Secretary of the Navy; Hoke Smith, of Georgia, Secretary of the Interior: J. Sterling Morton, of Nebraska, Secretary of Agriculture; and Richard H. Olney, of Massachusetts, Attorney-General.

We clip the following, with much pleasure, from the columns of the Alliance Herald - " Mastin, of Chilton, is one of the hard headed and resolute characters that one often meets whose frankness, candor and boldness render them attractive and win admiration. Mastin is exactly what he claims to be, and he does not care who knows it. He is also for the people of Chilton county, and he has never had any other thought or purpose, except to reflect their will by his action. He has made a good representative. "

To this fitting tribute we may add that in no single instance he has swerved from his allegiance to cause of reform, and his name is enrolled for all time to come with those of the gallant band who fought and battled so bravely for the rights and liberties of our citizens in the late legislature, as its records attest.

Below we give the vote recorded on the election bill in the House. Mr. Brewer, who voted nay, went to this same company on the ballot to seat Brown, of Conecuh, and voted for Jones, the sitting member, hence it appears that Mr. Brewer's cake will be dough. The bill, on the third reading, was passed by 50 votes against 45.

Yeas - Messrs. Pettus, Baker, Bartee, Biggers, Bolling, Brown, Calhoun, Cox, Clark, of Montgomery, DeLacey, Ferguson, Fontaine, Fletcher, Gewin, Gibbons, Goldsby, Hanson, Hardy, Holt, Joiner, Jones, of Clark, Jones of Conecuh, Kennedy, Knight, Lavretta, Lovelace, Lloyd, Morris, McCarron, McDonald, McQueen, Nisbet, O'Brien, Ott, Rather, Rice, Roach, Rogers, Sayre, Sowell, Smaw, Spier, Steele, Stockton, Turner, Ward, of Henry, West, Williams, of Calhoun, White, of Autauga, White, of Perry - Total 50.

Nays - Messrs. Amason, Barbour, Bellenger, Burks, Brewer, Case, Coleman, Clark, of Marion, Dawsey, Dent, Eiland, Ellis, Evans, Ewing, Finley, Ford, Forman, Fuller, Frazier, Gaines, Gilbert, Hill, Hollis, of Fayette, Hollis, of Lamar, Huffman, Jackson, Killebrew, Kyle, Langley, Lary, Mastin, Mills, Mixson, McCall, NeSmith, Nolen, Seymour, Shugart, Smith, Taylor, Townsend, Ward, of Jefferson, Williams, of Covington, Williamson, Whitten, Youngblood, - Total 46.

The four members not voting were Messrs. Dawson, Meador, Poole, and Ramsey,. Dawson was absent on sick leave, he not having been present since the recess, and Meador was absent by the vote of the House: they would have voted for the bill. Poole and Ramsey were either not in the house or declined voting.

OUR COUNTY OFFICERS. COMMISSIONER BAILEY - County commissioners as a rule, perform valuable services to the community by whom they are elected, without receiving any great amount of thanks or remuneration for the work they do. The commissioners get through a large quantity of work, and watch over the interests of their county without, in many instances, the public being made acquainted with the details of their labors. Our roads and bridges, with their constant need of repairs, are under their supervision, and it is owing to their vigilance that the expenditure of the county is kept within reasonable bounces. It is to them the unfortunate poor in their hour of need apply in vain. These are some of the many duties of our county commissioners, and happy are we in having such well-qualified gentlemen as compose our present board, a short sketch of one of the members we have much pleasure in appending hereto. Mr. E.W. Bailey was born in Bartow county, Georgia, October 31, 1859, his parents, Jason T. Bailey and L.A. Bailey having moved there from South Carolina. His education he partly received at the neighborhood schools, and completed at the Tennessee University at Knoxville, graduating in 1880. After moving to this state he married, December 16, 1888, Miss Della Ferry, of Dallas county, and immediately thereafter took up his residence in this county, locating in beat eight near Valley Creek church, where he owns and cultivates a well tilled farm. Brother Bailey has been a member of the Baptist church for the past fifteen years. He joined the Alliance in 1888, and has always been noted as a zealous and untiring worker in its ranks. He is a staunch member of the People's Party, and never loses an opportunity of forwarding the cause of reform. In the course of his life he has taught school, done newspaper work, and farmed, and in his various occupations he has always been remarked as a man of great application and determination of character. By his fellow-citizens he is highly esteemed for his many excellent qualities of heart and mind, and last August was elected as Commissioner for the Fourth District of this county. A man of sterling worth and strict integrity, Chilton county is proud to number him amongst its officials.

Chilton County Teachers' Institute - The Chilton County Teacher's Institute convened at Collins Chapel Friday Feb'y 17, 1893. The institute was called to order by Sup't J.W. Moore. Mr. F.G. Godsey led in prayer for the Divine blessing on the Institute and upon the labors of the teachers progress of education. Sup't Moore spoke to the teachers in regard to their duty in cooperating with his efforts in order to make the work interesting and profitable. There were twenty-one teachers present owing to flooding rains a number of teachers could not attend. J. Alex Moore was elected Sec'y for the ensuing year " Unwise Punishments ", discussion opened by Mr. W.I. Pruett, remarks made by Messrs. Godsey and Robinson.. " Language Work in our County Schools, " discussion by Messrs. Robinson, Godsey, Pruett and D. Mason. " Ideal Teacher. " paper by Miss Lula Eddings, this paper was carefully prepared and contained invaluable suggestions to teachers on individual improvement...

SATURDAY - Institute called to order by Sup't J. W. Moore. Devotional exercises conducted by Mr. S.J. Jennings. Supt. Moore announced the following committees Executive R.E. Hicks, G.L. Speer and J. Alex More. Resolutions, F.G. Godsey, D. Moore, S.J. Jennings, " How much work should be required of a pupil in a given time, " discussed by Messrs. Davis, Harwood and Jennings...

Kincheon Ketchings - Dear Brother Editor: - it has been some time since I sent you any news. The weather is fine, which delights our thrifty farmers Mr. Henry Culp's wife is quite sick; their little infant babe died on the 19th Feb., their many friends sympathize with them in their bereavement.

Charley Boles, son of Mr. George Boles, while shooting at a gourd with his bow and arrow was struck in the eye by the arrow bouncing back and will most likely lose the sight of that eye; little Charley will never be able to do any hard work

Mr. H.W. Friday paid his father, who is 87 years old, a visit at his home in south-west Chilton; he is quite lively in his old age.

Mr. Willie Gray paid our neighborhood a flying visit on his way home from Autauga.

MONEY TO LOAN - The undersigned is prepared to negotiate Loans upon Real Estate, in sums of $200 and upwards, upon reasonable terms, of 5 and 10 years time, in and through the MANHATTAN TWO AND THREE PER CENT. LOAN AND MORTGAGE COMPANY. Alex G. Dake, Agent.

OFFICE IN GRAND JURY ROOM AT COURT HOUSE, CLANTON, ALA.

TOWN ITEMS - On Sunday deputy Sheriff Will Hayes arrested Mr. Ed Willis charged with trading mortgaged property. Mr. Willis stood his trial on Wednesday before Judge Honeycutt and was fined five dollars and costs.

Mrs. G.I. Phillips will re-open her millinery establishment this week, with an entire new stock of Spring hats, flowers, trimmings, all of the latest fashion. She will be pleased to have all her friends from the country call and inspect her stock in her new quarters in the store formerly occupied by Mr. McRae.

Mr. G.P. Aldridge is having some improvements done on his premises.

The painting on Dr. Matthews house will soon be completed.

Mr. W.T. Aldridge spent Saturday and Sunday in Clanton, to the delight of his family circle.

Rev. A.A. Hutto, of Howard College, last Sunday in the Baptist church.

Rev. J.F. Smith, of Talladega held divine service at the Episcopal church on Tuesday evening. There will be a divine service (D. V.) held at this church on the Tuesday after the fourth Sunday in this month.

Tax collector B.M. Gentry, Mr. Ben Wells, ex-Sheriff Hayes and a host of other friends called at The Banner office this week and each brought a goodly list of subscribers to swell the list of Banner readers.

NOTICE - (Anyone) indebted to Alex G. Dake for guano and otherwise, whose notes, etc., were destroyed by fire, January 5, 1893, will save costs by calling and arranging the same at an early date, otherwise suit will be brought against them. ALEX G. DAKE. Clanton, Ala., Feb.14, 1893

Dr. Jackson the dental man is in town.

We regret that our genial depot agent Mr. Martin leaves to take the position of agent at Wetumpka.

Rev. A.C. Wells reports having held a good meeting in Autauga recently.

Rev. J.L. Busby, of South Calera, is expected to preach here next Sunday. He has been called to take charge of the Congregational church this year, the Rev. A.C. Wells having resigned on account of other churches. While we regret to lose Mr. Wells we heartily welcome Mr. Busby.

Mr. Ab Eiland of Strasburg, paid us a pleasant call this week.

Mr. E.O. Boyd, of Birmingham, visited town this week he has returned home with his wife, who has been visiting friends here for the past week.

A CARD OF THANKS - On the first Sunday in November my dwelling, smokehouse and kitchen were totally destroyed by fire between the hours of 10 and 1 a. m. I saved most of my furniture. My church and my neighbors came to my assistance most generously, and in two weeks time I had once more a good roof over my head, everyone without exception helped me. For this kindly help I desire to return my heartfelt thanks through the columns of the Banner. J.J. McDowell.

FROM THE STATE LECTURER - To the Alliance of Alabama. In answer to the many invitations extended to me urging that I attend meetings in April. I will say that I would be delighted to do so, but owing to the delay and neglect of many of the counties in making reports and remitting dues to the state secretary I am informed that there is little money in the state treasury to expenses. Hence where counties desire me to visit them, the president or secretary will please notify me that my expenses will be paid by the county. I am ready and anxious to do all in my power in the interest of our cause, and I am standing now where I have always stood, and shall ever stand, in the middle of the road. Fraternally, S.M. Adams
Randolph, Feb.10, 1893

KNIGHTS OF LABOR - The address of State Master Workman A.J. Henley, will be until further notice is given, 446 Lauderdale St., Memphis, Tenn.

Notice For Publication - NOTICE NO.13,494. LAND OFFICE AT MONTGOMERY, February 20, 1893, Notice is hereby given that the following named settler has filed notice of his intention to make final proof in support of his claim, and that said proof will be made before The Clerk of the Circuit Court of Clanton, Alabama, on April 15, 1893, viz.: William G. Davis, Homestead entry No.20595 for the S 1/2 of NW 1/4 of Section 18, Tp 22, north of Range 15 E. The names the following witnesses to prove his continuance residence and cultivation of said land, viz.: James Knox, John Dutton, William Headly, John Knox, all of Clanton, Ala. J.H. Bingham, Register

THE STATE OF ALABAMA, Chilton County - To the Hon. R.M. Honeycutt, Judge of the Probate Court of Chilton County, Alabama: We, the undersigned residing in Beat 1 Chilton County, Alabama, hereby certify that we are acquainted with James F. McKee and he is possessed of a good moral character and is an all respects a proper person to be licensed, we recommend that the said James F. McKee be granted license as a liquor dealer at James F. McKee's old stand on his place in beat No.1 in said County and State, for the year 1893.
FREEHOLDERS: S.L. Arledge, C.B. Arledge, E.H. Arledge, Eli McGuin, John Giles, S.L. Wagoner, W.P. Murreh, J.W. Williamson, Frank Willis, H.J. Wilson, J.J. Wilson, S.L. Ellison, Howard Glasscock, Henry Gentry, J.J. Marcus, W.L. Littlefield, R.M. Porter, C.R. Martin, J.W. Roberson, R.M. Aycock, R.N. Barett, W.A. Bennett, S.M. Brewer, T.P. Brewer, James Burnett, J.G. Barnett, C.S. Ellison, E.M. Bean, J.T. Cleckler, J.H. Collins, L.P. Carter, R.S. Callum, D.C. Cillum, J.M. Campbell, W.A. Callum, W.L. Collins, Elsza Headley, C.N. Headley, M.H. Jones, H.B. Jordan, G.W.A. Jones, J.W. Morton, S.W. Roberson, C.C. Ray, T.J. Roberson, J.M. Roper, R.I. Varden, J.N. Glasscock, C.J. Roberson, J.L. Marcus, W.R. Lowery, M. Robinson, W.T. Ellison, G.W. Bate, C.L. Davis
HOUSEHOLDERS: J.M. Benson, John A. Bean, J.S. Giles, J.M. Robinson, A.G.W. Lowery, W.E. Van Zant, Thomas, Ray, Lee Gewen, J.M. Gewen, Clemmon Giles
Sworn to, &c., this 11th February, 1893. S.L. ARLEDGE, N. P. & Ex-of. J. P.
Sworn to. &c., this 17th February, 1893. R.M. Honeycutt, Judge of Probate. At the request of a number of citizens in beat one, I have had the above petition with signatures thereto, published. R.M. Honeycutt

Ad - Hood's Cures
A Father's Gratitude, Impels Him to Tell How His Son Was Saved
White Swelling and Scrofula Cured. " I write this simply because I feel it is a duty to humanity, so that others affected as my son was may know how to be cured. When the was 7 years old a white swelling came on his right leg below his knee, drawing his leg up at right angles, and causing him intense suffering. He could not walk and I considered him a confirmed cripple. The swelling was lanced and discharged freely. At length we decided to take him to Cincinnati for a surgical operation. He was so week and poor we gave him Hood's Sarsaparilla to build of up his strength. To our great surprise, Hood's Sarsaparilla not only a strength but caused the sore, after discharging several pieces of bone, to entirely heal up. His leg straightened out, and he now runs everywhere, as lively as any boy. "J.L. McMurray, Notary Republic, Ravenswood, W. Va.

Ad - W.L. Douglas $3.00 SHOE...Address W. L. Douglas, Brockton, Mass.

CONGRESSIONAL - ... Mr. Quay offered a resolution, which gave notice of an amendment to an appropriation bill, making appropriations elected with the world's fair conditional on Sunday closing... Mr. Quay withdrew his objections to the world's fair items, being assured that the ground had been covered and they were passed... Mr. Faulkner gave notice that in consequence of the very serious illness of one of the late Senator Kenna's children, the memorial services were postponed from next Saturday until Monday... The amendment was offered by Mr. Sherman, and a point of order raised against it by Mr. Stewart...

Gave Her Her Choice - Sam Jones, in one of his recent sermons in New York City, told this story: " If people get married they're one ain't they? Now, how can one have a row? How can one get divorced? Most marriages nowadays ain't marriages at all - that's the trouble. If I like 'er I'll keep 'er, says he. If I like him I'll live with him, says she. An old friend of mine celebrated his wedding recently and he and his wife seemed such a happy couple that I asked him the secret of his happiness. He thought for a moment and then he said:' A good understanding to start with, that's all. The morning after we were married, I woke and looked at my wife. She was awake, and as we looked around the room there were two chairs and two piles of clothes on them. I said: Wife, get up an take your choice. But say, wife, whichever you take now you've got to stick to. All right, says she, and she got up and took the dress and left me the trousers, and she's worn the dress ever since.

34

The Banner, Vol. 1, Clanton, Ala., Thursday, March 9, 1893, No. 18

' 84 THE INAUGURATION ' 92 - For the Second Time Grover Cleveland is Inaugurated Chief Magistrate of our Great and Glorious Republic, YEA, A MIGHTY MULTITUDE, Fully Fifty Thousand, Braved the Whistling Winds to March in the Great Parade. The decorations for the Inaugural Ball Bewildering and Entrancing in Their Brilliant Elegance. Washington, March 4 - Grover Cleveland of New York, thrice nominated for President of the United states Michigan at and twice elected, was today successfully inducted into that high office for his second term with all appropriate ceremonies and the gathering of a mighty multitude...

THE RIDE TO THE CAPITAL

Shortly after 11 o'clock President elect Cleveland and Vice-President-elect Stevenson, accompanied by the Senate on arrangements, entered the executive mansion. They were received by President Harrison in the blue room... The inaugural which was under command of Gen. Martin G. McMahon, of New York, grand Marshall, was of two grand divisions, each division being in turn subdivided into divisions and brigades... Lieutenant Colonel E.C. Bainbridge commanded the artillery. Maj. R.W. Huntington, of the United States marine corps, commanded the marines, and Captain Bell of the Seventh Calvary commanded the squadron of light calvary... The first popular outburst came when Gov. Robert E. Pattison of Pennsylvania in front of the reviewing stand, followed by his staff and the National Guard of the State of Pennsylvania. The South Carolina contingent came next, headed by a man who has recently become famous throughout the Union as a defender of States' rights. It was Gov. Ben Tillman. The hearts of the old soldiers swelled with pride when the Fourth Division of the G. A. R. contingent passed the reviewing stand under the command of Department Commander S.E. Faunce. Men yelled themselves horse as Governor Flower and staff hove(?) sight, but the great enthusiasm of the hour was reserved for the "Tam(?) Society of New York. "

Major Thomas Key of Montgomery is of the opinion that the fruit was not injured by the late cold snap.

President Cleveland was duly inaugurated last Saturday as President of the United States of America. Chief Justice Fuller, of the Supreme Court, administered the oath of office. The Bible used on this occasion belonged to the President's mother, and was also used by him at his first inauguration. The weather was very unfavorable, being bitterly cold; notwithstanding, immense crowds gathered to witness the ceremony.

The Montgomery Journal, commenting on the utterance of the Birmingham News, regarding President Cleveland and his administration, that " the simple fact is the politicians are not in it " - says: " From the foundation of this government, politicians have shaped and added, perhaps, to its dignity. It will be a radical departure and a radical change for them to be ignored at the beginning of the republic's centennial Jubilee, and will be an experiment worth the watching. It will be an ideal administration and one that promises little for the two old parties, but a good deal for the new party - a party with Judge Gresham at its head, for instance. "...

OUR COUNTY OFFICERS. COMMISSIONER GLASSCOCK - Alexander Glasscock, the county officer we present you this week, was born in Bibb county, December 24, 1844, of South Carolinian parents - although his father and mother,

Benjamin and Margaret Glasscock, having been brought to this state when quite young children might almost be said to be Alabamians. At the age when most youths are best able to acquire and appreciate the advantages of an education, Brother Glasscock, in passing through the stormy and unsettled period preceding the late unpleasantness between the states, had but little for going to school. In the school of life he has well learned his part, and in the military necessities of strict discipline and unquestioning obedience he learned a lesson which has molded the remainder of his life. When 18 years old he enlisted in the service of his country, and was drafted into Company D, 29th Alabama, and faithfully served under the gallant Colonel Conley, of Dallas county. After the war, in the fall of 1865, he became a member of the Baptist Church, and in the following January was married to Miss Perdelia Hubbard, of this county, and happily together they have fought the battle of life. A military training had shown Brother Glasscock the advantages of organization and acting in concert with others. He became a hearty adherent of the Farmer's Alliance, and was one of the charter members of Macedonia Alliance, and right well has he at all times and seasons advanced the cause of the Alliance by all the means in his our. In addition to his farming he also follows the occupation of public ginner. For on a farm, raised on a farm, all his life (with the exception of the period of his military service) spent on a farm. Brother Glasscock is a man thoroughly well qualified to the benefits derived by the farming community from the Farmer's Alliance. He is a grand example of the Southern farmer, who under all the terrible trials and discomforts attending the reconstructive epoch nobly fought against and surmounted the difficulties which beset their path. In the last election he was elected Commissioner for Beats 2 and 3, and is making a capital officer.

Jemison Jingles - The heavy wind on the night of the 3rd blew down Tax Collector B.M. Gentry's buggy house, badly injuring his buggy; the wind also blew down a great quantity of fencing and timber on his and neighboring farms, it also blew the tops off several buildings in the neighborhood of Jemison.

Dixie Dots - Mr. D.A. Friday, of Dixie, has purchased a new home in Bibb Co. six miles south-west of Randolph, he expects to moved there next fall.

Mr. Jasper Wylie of this place is deserving of praise who, he settled in the wilderness three years ago without anything, now he has a comfortable home with plenty of the world's comforts. He is now 69 years old, he was at the log rolling last week and knocked out Corbett, Sullivan, Goddard, Hall, and all the balance in the last round, he wears the champion's belt among the log rollers.

Our esteemed friend, Brigham Young, has purchased Mr. Harris' steam mill near Plantersville, he is going to move it westward as far as Oakmulgee.

Messrs. George Little, J.M. Shepherd, and J.G. Ward of Waco, Texas are visiting the family of W.M. Price.

The Rev. S.M. Adams well preach at Fellowship church, the 3rd Sunday of this month, and I the people will turn out to hear him.

H.B. Gilden and F.H. Lunny will leave for Birmingham Thursday evening next, to celebrate the 17th, their national day.

TOWN ITEMS - We are glad to welcome Mr. W.W. Duncan, the new depot agent, to

Clanton. He comes from Verbena here, being promoted.

Mr. Tom Gullahorn has moved his family to Verbena.

Professor Carpenter contemplates returning to Clanton, and reopening his school.

Rev. A.C. Wells has decided not to move from Clanton, this will be welcome news to his many friends.

The Rev. J.L. Busby, who has been called to take charge of the Congregation church, did not arrive as expected last Sunday. The Rev. A.C. Wells officiated in his stead and deliver a very effective discourse to an attentive audience.

(Divine) service is held on the 2nd (?) Sundays in each month at (?) Methodist Episcopal Church South, at the hours of 11 a.m. and 7 p.m. Rev. B.B. Feagin, Pastor

Ex-treasurer J.M. Parrish called us this week, we are always glad to meet this old and faithful servant of the county.

Tax Assessor E.G. Rollins was in town Wednesday finishing up his second round.

Death visited the home of Brother Gundy Logan last Sunday night, taking his beloved daughter, Mrs. Jeannie Wilkerson. She leaves three orphan children together with their grandparents, to mourn her loss.

Bro. Wylie Foshee gave us a pleasant call on Thursday.

Ex-sheriff Lee Hayes dropped in the same day, busy and hustling as usual.

The L & N. pump engine was taken charge of by Mr. Forrest Potts, of Decatur, on the 1st.

Mr. H.C. Martin and family move to Wetumpka this week.

Senator Stewart of Nevada will make several speeches in favor of free silver, in Alabama this summer.

HELP YE ONE ANOTHER -
An Appeal For Aid For Destitute And Suffering People In Chambers County
At a meeting of citizens held in the court house at Lafayette on Monday, March 6, 1893, the undersigned were appointed a committee to make an appeal through the press to the citizens of Alabama in behalf of be unfortunate sufferers from the terrible cyclone that swept through the northern part of Chambers county on the evening of March 3... Send all contributions to J.D. Norman, of Lafayette, all of which will be used faithfully to the purposes intended. J.D. Norman, W.N. Brogan, S.M. Richards, Committee

Inauguration Of President Cleveland Continued - ... This division which was composed exclusively of Western political organizations from the States of Illinois, Iowa, Wisconsin, Indiana, Missouri, Kansas, Ohio, and other States, was under the command of Col. John P. Hopkins, of Chicago. The Sixth Division was under the command of Gen. Pierce Young, of Georgia, on whose staff were M.J. Barmon, Of Louisville, Ky.... Mr. Cleveland's competitor for the nomination last June ad his personality impressed on the multitude through the medium of David B. Hill Guard, of Richfield Springs. Hon. John M. Birch, minister to Japan, under the former Cleveland administration, led the 250 members of the Young Men's Club of Wheeling, W. Va. A chorus of yells heralded the Kentucky delegation, which was headed by an express cart bearing a life-size representation of the star-eyed goddess. The Bandana Club of the same State displayed between ranks pictures of Carlisle, Lindsey, Watterson, Grady, and other living and dead apostles of the Democratic faith.... Without going to the rooms reserved for them, the president and his wife started on a tour of the ball-room. The president led the way, on the arm of General Schofield, while Mrs. Cleveland followed under escort of Justice Gray, of the Supreme Court. Following them came Col. and Mrs. Daniel S. Lamont, Mr. and Mrs. William S. Bissell, with their daughter-in-law; Mr. Hoke Smith, Mr. and Mrs. J. Sterling Morton, Mr. and Mrs. E.C. Benedict, Miss Benedict and a number of others... The coming secretary of the navy, Mr. Herbert, there joined the party with Mrs. Herbert... Mr. and Mrs. Stevenson, with their son, daughter and their friends, accompanied them to Washington, then joined the president and Mrs. Cleveland in their rooms... Mr. Carlisle was one of those who remained and he and Mrs. Carlisle held several impromptu receptions in various parts of the hall.

Extra Session Of The Senate - The President has issued a proclamation convening the Senate in extra session on the 4th of March. The proclamation opens thus: Whereas, Public interest require that the Senate should be convened that 12 o'clock on the 4th day of March next to receive such communications as may be made by the executive: Now, therefore, I, Benjamin Harrison, President of the United States, do hereby proclaim and declare that an extraordinary occasion requires the Senate of the United States to convene at the capitol, in the city of Washington, on the 4th of March next, at 12 o'clock, of reach all persons who shall at that time be entitled to act as members of that body are hereby required to take notice... Benjamin Harrison.
By the President: William F. Wharton, Acting Secretary of State...

Aged 104 And Wants A Wife - A special from Little Rock, Ark., says: William Ware, colored, 104 years old, obtained a license to marry Lou Grant, a colored widow, 55 years old, in this county. The old man was tottering and hardly able to walk, but says he feels as young as when he was married 20 years ago.

NOTES AND COMMENTS - The discovery was made the other day that the only authentic of the coat-of-arms of the State of Pennsylvania had disappeared from the walls of Independence Hall. An investigation was made, and then it came out, although no one had noticed the omission, that the copy had been missing for several years from among the shields of the various States that may be seen hanging side by side. Capt. Hanson, a member of the Pennsylvania Board of World's Fair, who wanted to have a duplicate made for use at Chicago, can explain the disappearance only in this way, " In 1874 or thereabouts the Legislature appropriated $300 for the express purpose of correcting certain defects which were said to exist in the coat-of-arms used on official seals. To accomplish this work a committee, consisting of the Governor, Attorney-General, and Secretary of State was appointed and empowered to act. So far as I know or can discover this committee has never reported. It is possible that the Committee appointed by the Legislature removed it in 1875 to have copies made, and that it now lies hidden in some painter's shop or in some one's attic or cellar. "

Dr. Gatling is getting even more fastidious in the matter of guns than he used to be. He has harnessed to a new one an electric motor that gives a result of 2,000 shots a minute, according to his own claims.

Ad - Hood's Cures, Terrible Headaches, Distressed And Discouraged
Health all Broken, Thoroughly Built up by Hood's Sarsaparilla
" I am glad to have my experience with Hood's Sarsaparilla widely known, because the medicine has done me so much good, I think it will benefit others who are out of health. I was in a very distressing and discouraging condition. I had no appetite whatever; could not sleep well; suffered with excruciating headaches. I felt tired and languid. Had no ambition and seemed all broken down. After I had taken medicine prescribed by two of our best physicians, a kind neighbor advised me to try Hood's Sarsaparilla. I followed her advice, and the result is, I am perfectly well. I do not have the headaches now, sleep well, that tired feeling is vanished, and I am bright and ambitious. I can eat heartily at every meal, and have gained in weight from 95 to 105 pounds. I do not have any distress in my stomach and epileptic fits, to which I was formerly subject come never trouble me now. I cheerfully recommend Hood's Sarsaparilla and do not wish to be without it. " Miss Eva Covert, Bath, Stuben County, N. Y.

ISSUES MISSING

The Banner, Vol. 1, Clanton, Ala., Thursday, March 30, 1893, No. 21

A Letter From Dr. McCune on the Labor Movement - An important letter from Dr. McCune, editor of the official organ of the Farmer's alliance. was read at the meeting of the Central labor Union at New York recently...

AN ADDRESS - The following address to the Farmer's Alliance of West Virginia by S.A. Houston is of such merit that we take the liberty of reproducing it here and command its careful perusal by our many readers...

Washington Notes - The National Association of Democratic Clubs has issued a notice recommending a simultaneous celebration on April 13 next, of the birthday of Thomas Jefferson. At the caucus of the Democrats which nominated a ticket for senatorial officers, it was agreed that certain Republicans should not be disturbed. Among them are the venerable assistant doorkeeper, Charles B. Reed. Secretary Carlisle recently accorded an audience to a committee representing The American Institute of Architects... Ex-sheriff C.E. Dexter, of Three Rivers, Mich., has been appointed head usher at the White House, to fill the vacancy caused by the death of Capt. Densmore. The army has secured its flying machine. The military balloon which is to form part of the war department exhibit at Chicago, has been purchased by Gen. Greely, of the French balloon maker, La Chambra...

An Affecting Scene - A pleasant incident occurred at the White House a few days ago. Col. Oates of Alabama brought up Maj. I.F. Culver of Union Springs, who is an applicant for Marshall of the Middle District. While they were waiting to see the president, Senator Gordon of Georgia entered. When he and Mr. Culver saw each other, both men rush forward and embraced. Culver had been major in the Sixth Alabama when Gen. Gordon commanded the regiment, and the to men had not since the war (?)

THE COTTON CROP - Address of Senator George to Farmers In The South.
Senator George, of Mississippi, who since April last, has been engaged in an investigation of the causes of agricultural depression prevailing in the cotton states, has prepared an address to the cotton farmers of the United States. In view of the importance of the question and urgency in connection with the planting of next year's crop, so soon to be entered upon, Senator George has thought proper to give immediate publicity to the conclusion he has arrived ... Very respectfully, C.S. George

Presidential Appointments - Among the ones made by President Cleveland the past week we note the following: J.B. Eustis, minister to France; Theodore Runyon, minister to Germany; J.E. Eisley, minister to Denmark,; J.G. Jenkins, Judge of the Seventh Circuit; Wade Hamton, commissioner of railroad; (?).S. Seymour, commissioner of patents; S.W. Lamoreaux, general land commissioner; W.H. Sims, first assistant secretary of the interior; H.H. Lurton, Judge of the Sixth Circuit, and Max Judd for consul at Vienna.

Failed to Convict - Thomas W. Steele, son of Ex-Probate Judge Steele of Colbert county, was tried at Tuscumbia last week for the killing of John W. Goodwin. The jury failed to agree, six being for acquittal and six for conviction. The interest in this trial has been very intense, owing to the prominence of the parties. Public opinion of the verdict is like the jury - divided. Steele will apply for bail.

On Monday April 10th Dr. B.W. Groce, President of the State Alliance will deliver a speech at the Court House, Clanton. We hope that everyone will turn out to hear the worthy Doctor, he is an able and interesting speaker, we are satisfied at all who attend will be benefited.

General Edmund Kirby Smith died at his home in Sewanee, Tenn., on the 28th of March, in the 69th year of his age. He was the last of the confederate officers who held the rank of general. General Smith was graduated from West Point Military Academy in 1845, and served in the war with Mexico at the close of the late war he was in command of the trans-Mississippi Department. His wife and six of his family were with him. He died as he lived - bright, strong and confident in his Christian faith and hope. One of his very last connected utterances was a verse from the 23rd Psalm, " Though I walk through the Valley of the Shadow of Death, I will fear no evil for Thou art with me. "

With the Farmer's Alliance came knowledge... And they know perfectly well that hundreds and thousands of honest Democrats all over the land are holding the leaders on probation. " One more trial and man if you don't do something! " - That's the murmur all through the ranks - Tom Watson, in People's Party Paper.

It is reported that J. Pierpont Morgan, of the firm of Drexal & Morgan, New York bankers, has gone to England to negotiate $50,000,000 for the new administration.

Under the decisions of Judge Box as rendered in the case of Pitts vs. Geeper on Tuesday last the Kolb or Peoples ticket was elected in this county last August by about 1300 majority. - Peoples Advocate

In another column we publish a letter by Senator James Z. George, of Mississippi, addressed to cotton planters on the present state of the cotton trade. We believe a careful perusal of this letter by our readers will be instructive to them, and of much benefit if they heed the advice therein contained.

And now it is said that President Cleveland thanks some of the men who followed Capt. Kolb in August, but who voted for him in November should be recognized in the appointments...

Free - Until further notice a World's Fair souvenir coin goes free with every twenty Dollar Purchase. Alex Rice, Montgomery.

President Woolfold, of the Montgomery, Tuskaloosa and Memphis Railroad Company, on Monday last paid to the Tuskaloosa Coal, Iron and Land Company the purchase money for the Tuskaloosa Northern Railroad and the Tuskaloosa Belt Railway...

IMPORTANT TO LODGES AND INSURANCE SOCIETIES - The Ancient Order of United Workmen must pay the heirs of C.P. Smith the sum of $2,000 - so says the Supreme Court of Pennsylvania. C.P. Smith became a member of a Lodge of the United Workmen in May, 1883, in Cincinnati, Ohio, and removed in 1890 to Harrisburg, Pa. He then withdrew from his Lodge in Cincinnati, expecting to affiliate with a Lodge in Harrisburg. Upon being balloted he was rejected and could not, according to the rules of that order, again apply for admission until after the expiration of three months. Smith, however, died before the three months passed, leaving the assessments unpaid, which the Lodge in Harrisburg refused to accept from Smith on the grounds that he was not a member in good standing at the time. The Order of United Workmen then refused to pay the Dead Claim that of $2,000, upon the grounds that Smith at the time of his death was not a member in good standing in a Lodge of said organization and had not paid the two previous Death Claim assessments. The case was carried into the Courts and was hotly contested, with the result, however, in favor of the heirs of Smith, as stated above.

Collins Chapel - This beautiful Spring weather has revived the Sunday-school at this place under the superintendence of Mr. T.J. Collins.

There was singing last Sunday, and a number of visitors attended; the young men west of Strasburg think it is their duty to visit our community on the Sabbath. Mr. B.N. Martin cannot attend church services, he says he must stay home with the babies.

Mr. John Robinson, one of the oldest citizens of the county, died on the 24th inst.: for more than two years he had been a patient sufferer.

Mr. J.W. Collins has been confined to his room for several weeks; we are anxious to see Mr. Collins well and out among his many friends.

Reform South Alliance - At a late meeting the following resolution was passed: RESOLVED: That this Alliance No.1364, extends an invitation to Bethsalem Church and community to be with and partake of all the public deliberations with us at the County Alliance, and we further extend this invitation to all distant friends. Respectfully submitted. David Moore, Chairman

PROGRAM OF THIRD DISTRICT UNITY BAPTIST ASSOCIATION, To Be Held At Salem Church On The Big Island Road, April 28, 29, 30.
Introductory sermon by Rev. J.M. McCord, Alternate J.L. Long
Subjects to be debated.
1. What is the Duty of Deacons to their Church? - Opened by Moses Robinson and R.D. May.
2. The Duties of Church Members to their Church. - Opened by John Aldridge and Eliza Parish.
3. How can we best carry out the injunction of Solomon, where he says: " Raise up a child in the way you would have it to go, and when it is old it will not depart from it. " - Opened by Oliver Mullins and William Santor.
4. Is the Sabbath School a place where the Old should meet and impart knowledge to the Young? - Opened by P.C. Dennis and Will Strock.
5. Can there be any great good derived from a Sabbath School? - Opened by Rev. J.L. Long and N.J. Callaway. J.C. Alred, N.J. Callaway, Rev. W.A. Wood, Committee

DR. TALMAGE ON POLITICS - " There will be little difference between this administration and the last, "he said." I have paid some attention to the policies and the doctrines of the two great political parties, and I can see very little difference between them. Of course, they must have some ostensible difference in their platforms, and the tariff was selected for that purpose. The Republicans say they believe in a certain degree of tariff reform, and the democrats say they are in favor of free trade absolutely, and the results of it all is that when you get down to its fine expression you must look for any large differences with a microscope. The chief, and to my mind the only difference, is one of

100,000 office-holders between them. When the republican administration is in power the Republicans hold office, and when the democrats take office the democrats are appointed. Personally, I do not blame them for seeking office. "

TOWN ITEMS - Dick Taylor, col'd, was arrested by Sheriff Moore at Jemison on Monday charged with assault with a weapon.
.
Mr. Frank Moore is visiting his brother our efficient sheriff.
.
Mrs. Tom Smith, of Mountain Creek, is on a visit to Uncle Pat this week.
.
Deputy sheriff Will Hayes is down with the measles he is progressing as favorably as possible under the circumstances. His many friends will be glad to see him out again.
.
We offered our heartfelt condolences to Mr. Patrick Smith and family on the death of his beloved daughter, Mrs. John Parker, of consumption, which sad event happened on Tuesday, March 21st. The deceased lady was taken to her eternal rest while yet in the boom of womanhood, leaving a sorrowing husband and three little children. She died at her home in Coosa and was buried in Salem. " She is not dead, but sleepeth. "
.
A deputy sheriff from Birmingham came down to Kincheon on Thursday 23rd of March to arrest Willie Malachi a Negro, suspected of stealing a large quantity of jewelry in that city but the Negro made his escape.
.
Divine service was held that the Episcopalian church on Tuesday night Rev. J.F. Smith officiating.
.
Mr. J.E. Littleton living in the Jumbo settlement had eleven sheep killed this week by dogs Mr. Wm. Jones in the same settlement also lost some sheep from the same cause this week.
.
Mr. Tom Smith, of Mountain Creek, accompanied his mother, Mrs. Patrick Smith to Coosa, last week, on a visit to their sick sister and daughter, but to their great grief arrived too late.
.
 Ed. Henry, colored, was arrested Monday morning on a charge by O.R. Bell for assault with a stick on Mr. Bell's cook on Sunday. He gave bond.
.
Mrs. Minnie Sellers at Kilgore and Gentrys coaling died on Wednesday 22nd inst. and was buried at Cane Creek church on Thursday. She has been ailing ever since she had the measles about four years ago.
.
Messrs. John Garner and W.H. Phillips went to Birmingham on Monday.
.
Sheriff Moore and deputy sheriff Will Hayes paid a visit on Sunday to ex-sheriff Hayes.
.
Dr. Dawson has returned from Mobile where he has been attending a session of Medical College.
.
An excellent sample of homemade sugar was brought to us from the farm of Mr. E.H.

Smith. It was made by Mrs. Smith from ribbon cane: she made 150 pounds of sugar and 30 gallons of syrup from a half-acre of cane. Mr. Smith says he raised the cane without using any fertilizer, but the year previous he used fertilizer from the Alabama Fertilizer Co., and the half-acre of cane made 200 pounds of sugar and 70 gallons syrup.

Reform South Alliance No.1364 meets Saturday evening before the second and fourth Sunday in each month. J.S. Popwell, Pres; R.W. Scott, Sec; J.R. Vinson, Trustee

Ad - J.P. Givhan, Surgeon and Physician, Jemison, Ala.
Will attend cause at all hours day or night.

NOTICE - Dr. W.B. Groce, President of the State Alliance, will deliver a public address at the Court House, on Monday, April 10th, 1893.

Ad - Sufferers from Dyspepsia, Here's Something for You to Read, Distress in the Stomach CURED by HOOD'S. " When I began taking Hood's Sarsaparilla, I could eat nothing but very light food, without having terrible distress in my stomach. I had tried other medicines, which did me no good. Before I had taken 1 bottle of Hood's I saw that it was doing me good. I continued to grow vector while taking 5 bottles, this and now I can eat anything. I have had no distress or months, and I think there is no medicine for dyspepsia like Hood's Sarsaparilla. My appetite is excellent, and my health is very much better than for years. " Miss Jennie Cunningham, South Newcastle, Me.

The Banner, Vol. 1, Clanton, Ala., Thursday, April 6, 1893, No. 22

A RUFFIAN'S REWARD - We clip the following from the Virginia Sun: " Mr. Hoke Smith, editor of an Atlanta newspaper, has been appointed Secretary of the Interior by Mr. Cleveland. This is the Hoke Smith who, when Gen. Weaver was in Georgia, set on foot a ruffian bureau to mob him and drive him out of Georgia. Mr. Hoke Smith printed the most rascally, brutal, lying accounts about General Weaver and his treatment of the Southern people. Mr. Hoke Smith hired his ruffians to break up Gen. Weaver's meetings in Georgia, wherever they could. These ruffians, in the pay of Hoke Smith, followed Gen. Weaver and decided riots wherever it was possible, by throwing rotten eggs and other unlawful and disgraceful acts, thus defying free speech. Mr. Hoke Smith's agents followed Gen. Weaver to Virginia, when they were there informed that Gen. Weaver would be protected they desisted and returned to Georgia. Now Mr. Hoke Smith is rewarded for his ruffianism by an appointment in Mr. Cleveland's cabinet.

OPINION BOLDLY EXPRESSED - It takes a man of steady nerve and strong personality to rise above the man-worship which characterized visitors to the Inauguration, and speak as did Gov. R.B. Tillman of South Carolina. " I do not like to voice any sentiment that may be in the least suggestive of Democratic disaster. Our party is now in possession, for the first time in many years, of all the departments of the Government, and, of course, the country is looking to a Democratic administration, for relief and reform...

Tired Of Hiding Out - A Negro named Alonzo Street arrived in Union Springs, a few days since, and inquired for the city marshal. Finding the desired officer the Negro informed him that he belonged to a gang of counterfeiters at Oglethorpe, Ga., which was broken up two years since. It is remembered that a Negro by the name of Street escaped and has been pursued through Florida, Alabama, and Georgia. The actions of this man, however, in surrendering, is looked upon with suspicion; but he may be the right party. His object in giving up, he said, was because he was tired of fleeing from justice. A strange feature in the case is that two white men while pursuing this same Negro have lost their lives. One was assassinated by unknown parties in Florida. The other was killed at the depot in Montgomery.

Queer Place for a Still - Revenue officers from North Carolina have just reported the seizure of the oddest, illicit distillery ever captured in that State. It was in Moore county, and was operated by Lawrence Goins. The officers had received information of Goins' still and had made several searches for it to no purpose. Finally they found that was located in the middle of Tuckshoe Pond, in small trees which stand thickly. The only means of access was by boat. Goins had cut off the tops of small trees and on these built a shanty in which was the moonshine outfit. Deputy Collector Hall and a posse made the capture, having discovered a boat. The steel of sixty-five gallons capacity was in full blast. Goins was completely surprised. He admitted that he conducted the business some time, and said he thought his location entirely safe.

Because Dr. Mosely expressed a preference for Capt. Kolb the agonized have recommenced last years cry of Kolbism is Republicanism. What they term the union of the agonized with Bill Stevens and his cohorts we are at a loss to imagine.

On Monday next Dr. B.W. Groce the President of the State Alliance will deliver a public address at the Court House, everybody is invited to attend. We hope there will be a large turn out, we may be sure the Dr. will have something to tell us worthy of our time and attention.

The County Alliance will convene with the brethren of Reform South Alliance Wednesday April 26th. All who have the pleasure of attending this session will meet with a hearty reception, the brethren of Reform South are famed for their progressive and hospitable spirit. Amongst other good things in store, Major Thos. Key of the Southern Agriculturist has promised to be there and in all probability Bro. I.L. Brock, more widely known as "Warwick", our efficient State Secretary-Treasurer, will also be present and favor us with an address.

THE OUTLOOK FOR 1894 - Referring to the statement that Dr. Mosely, chairman of the state republican committee, had expressed a preference for Capt. Kolb for governor, a friend of Capt. Kolb said to a Journal reporter: " The statement, or intimidation, that Captain Kolb would affiliate with the republican party, or run other than as a straight Jeffersonian democratic in 1894, is untrue and is without any foundation...

The South Carolina newspapers have been wringing their hands and crying calamity ever since Governor Tillman was first elected...

In another column we publish the call of Chairman A.T. Goodwyn, of the State Executive Committee of the Jeffersonian Democracy, for a meeting of that body to be held in Birmingham, May 11th...

TERRIBLE MURDER AT PLANTERSVILLE - James Harris Shot and Instantly Killed By Alex Shelton
On Monday morning last, about nine o'clock, Mr. James Harris was shot in the head and instantly killed by Alex Shelton. Shelton had stolen some money from a colored woman in Chilton county, and was also charged with selling mortgaged property in Dallas county, near Plantersville. The warrants were handed to Deputy Sheriff J. Wiley Letcher to execute, and he, thinking that if Shelton saw him coming would run and get away, as he had made several ineffectual attempts previously to arrest the negro, procured the assistance of Mr. James Harris, who would better be able to approach Shelton, who would be unaware of the fact that Mr. Harris was deputized. Mr. Harris approached Shelton, who was working in the woods, his gun laying beside him. Accosting him, he told the negro to consider himself under arrest. Immediately the report of two pistol shots rung out, followed by the report of a gun. Mr. Letcher, who was waiting behind some shrubbery about seventy-five yards distant, ran forward, and seeing the negro fleeing, gun in hand, and Mr. Harris on the ground, face downward, he fired at the criminal with a gun loaded with small shot, failed to stop him. On reaching Mr. Harris he found him lifeless, shot in the under jaw, the charge having torn away part of the jaw and broken the neck. From the marks of powder burns in Mr. Harris' right arm and the flesh being torn off the fore-arm, it is evident that he made an effort to throw up Shelton's gun. Mr. Letcher immediately gave the alarm and sent a dispatch to Sheriff Moore to come with hounds. The Sheriff at once went to work and in as short time as possible procured dogs from Jemison and proceeded to the scene of the crime. A posse was organized and the search commenced, but it was Wednesday morning before any reliable information could be obtained. A negro had found Shelton in a fodderhouse, where he had been hidden, within a mile of the where the crime was committed. The negro said that Shelton had begged for money and food, and had left his

gun, he being wounded in the arm. The hounds were put on the trail, which was followed until late in the evening, when a heavy hail-storm destroyed the scent. Sheriff Moore returned home Friday morning, and informs us that a diligent search was being made by the citizens, and we hope before this reaches the eyes of our readers the murderer will in a power of justice. The Sheriff sent a dispatch to Mr. T.J. Driskell, asking if the criminal was caught yet, and for the particulars, and before noon received a reply that the search still continues, nothing definite known. The unfortunate victim of this awful crime was the son of the late Mr. Frank Harris, of Plantersville, and was an unmarried man, aged twenty-six, greatly liked and respected by all who knew him.

Our neighbor, the " View ", has changed hands, Editor Lawrence having sold out to Mr. F.B. Baldwin of Verbena. We welcome Mr. Baldwin's advent to journalism.

JEFFERSONIAN DEMOCRACY - Headquarters State Ex. Com., Montgomery, Ala., April 3, 1893
The State Executive Committee of the Jeffersonian Democracy of Alabama is hereby called to meet at Erswell Hall in the city of Birmingham, on Thursday, May 11, 1893... A.T. Goodwyn, Chairman State Ex. Com.

OUR COUNTY OFFICERS, COMMISSIONER PATE - As we were unable to obtain the necessary particulars at the time we were publishing " Our County Officers " we were compelled to leave the list incomplete, but now repair the omission, and have much pleasure in giving a short sketch of our worthy friend, Commissioner Samuel Pate. This gentleman first saw the light of day on August 18th, 1843, at his parents' home, in this county, two miles west from Strasburg, his father being Steven Pate, a North Carolinian, and his mother, Betsy Ann Pate, whose maiden name was Martin, a native of the Palmetto State, his mother died forty-five years ago, but his father still enjoys the declining years of an upright life. Brother Pate's youthful days were mainly passed in hard work, his schooling being limited to a period of rather less than two years. When not quite nineteen years old, while the struggle between the States was at its height, he joined Company C, 31st Alabama Regiment, serving under those gallant heroes, Kirby, Smith and, Beauregard, in the army of the Tennessee, and after nine months service was discharged on account of sickness. After recovering his health, and his country still needing his services in a military capacity, he volunteered into company D,6th Arknsas, in Boan and Loring's division, Johnson commander and was soon raised to the rank of sergeant and was afterwards promoted to adjutant. He served until the surrender at Greensboro, N. C., in April 1865, released him from military duty, when he returned home an went to farming with unabated vigor and a determination to make a home by the sweat of his brow. The homestead being ready and lacking the presence of the loved one who alone can make a homestead a home, he was married, December 27th, 1867, to Miss Carrie Collins, the fair daughter of Mr. John Long, of Shelby county, and seven children, four boys and three girls, have gladdened their hearts and enlivened their home. Brother Pate is a staunch Allianceman, having joined the third primary alliance organized in this county in March, 1887, and at the present time is a member of Collins Chapel Alliance. He is a member of the Baptist church, which denomination he entered in 1890, and is clerk of his church. In August, 1888, he was elected Justice of the Peace for Beat One, and dispensed justice with great impartiality, giving much satisfaction to his constituents, who mark their appreciation of his services by electing him County Commissioner for the same beat at the election last August. Commissioner Pate is a gentleman of sterling worth and ability, and is deservedly popular.

Clear Creek Clippings - Rev. Billie Woods will preach at Oak Grove school house, near Clear Creek, on Saturday night, April 8th.

Ad - Goetter, Weil & Co., Designers and Leaders of Fashion, Montgomery, Ala.

TOWN ITEMS - County Court convened on Monday Probate R.M. Honeycutt presiding, there were seven cases set for trial State vs. Ed. Henry plead guilty and was fined $10 and costs, State Vs. Dick Taylor, nol prossed by county Attorney Nolen on account of the youth of the offender his offense thrashing a boy he in turn has been soundly thrashed. The other cases will be carried to the Circuit Court.

Mr. J.B. Farley handed us in a fine specimen of the English pea vine last Saturday, it was fully eighteen inches in length.

We were glad to see Deputy sheriff Will Hayes out again after his attack of measles.

Martin Bates of Shelby was in town on Tuesday.

Judge Honeycutt made a trip to the Magic City this week.

Felix Dudley is convalescing after a spell of the measles.

(?)d and Miss Fanny Hicks (?)rried this week. Mr. (?) Duke's mill on Monday morning for Montgomery, and Miss Hicks left on Tuesday for the same city. They both then went on to (?)each Bloom, where they were married, and for the present will make that politically named village their home.

Mrs. Crew, of Goodwater, accompanied by her pretty little granddaughter, Miss Emma Bentley, are on a visit to the daughter of the (?) named lady, the charming wife of Square W.B. Nolen.

Professor Dill, of Birmingham will (?)r a lecture on the evening of the (?) for the benefit of the Baptist church. Subject " Lights and Shadows (?)me Life "

Rev. A.C. Wells has just (?) a visit to Sistrunk's and Jordan. He says that everywhere (?)rs are busy from sunrise to sun(?). He reports a good meeting last Sunday at Sistrunks. Next Sunday he will preach at Union church, Elmore county.

Rev. A.C. Wells will preach a funeral sermon on Mrs. Goldston wife of John Sidney Goldston at Tallahassee on the fifth Sunday in this month. The lady was well-known in this county, living here many years.

L.D. Beard of Washington, Ga. owns an Italian violin that is nearly 250 years old.

Ad - I Vote for Hood's, Forty Years in the Ministry
"Having taken Hood's Sarsaparilla five months I am satisfied it is an excellent remedy. I have had Rheumatism, afflicting my body, but especially my right arm from elbow to shoulder, so severe I feared I should lose the use of it. I felt better soon after I began with Hood's Sarsaparilla, and when I had taken 4 bottles the rheumatism entirely left me. I have been a minister of the M. E. Church 40 years and like many others of sedentary habits

to have suffered with Dyspepsia and Insomnia, but while taking Hood's Sarsaparilla I have had a good appetite, food digested well, I gained several pounds and sleep better. I vote for Hood's. Rev. W.R. Pepper, Richford, Vt.

Not Particular As To Weapons - One of men who figured conspicuously in the pioneer days of Nebraska was Col. Peter A. Sarpy, a distinguished Indian trader and member of the famous American Fur Company. An old settler tells the following story about this eccentric pioneer: Colonel Sarpy preferred the freedom of prairies to the society of civilized life and spent a great deal of his time in visiting Omaha wigwams near the old trading posts. He was regarded by the Omahas as their Nekagahha or big chief. In fact he married an Omaha woman, Nakoma, to whose intercessions he was more than once indebted for the preservation of his life when attacked by Indians. One night a crowd of frontiersmen were gathered in the store of Colonel Sarpy and the conversation turned upon the treatment of the Indians Sarpy portrayed in glowing colors the noble traits of the red man and the injustice heaped upon them by the whites. A tall, gaunt looking specimen over in the corner, who was busily engaged in whittling, listen with considerable interest. He suddenly looked up and interrupted the speaker. " This yere talk about the Indians as good and brave and intelligent may suit traders who have been swapping gewgaws for their valuable buffalo robes and stealing their annuities, but I have lived among them too. I want you to understand, and I'll be hanged if they are not a lying, thieving race of dogs, who don't know the difference between right and wrong. The sooner they are killed off the better it will be for the country. " This was too much for Sarpy. He advanced to the front of the speaker and interrupted him in an excited manner. " Do you know who I am, sir? " he asked with considerable emphasis. " I am Peter A. Sarpy, sir! If you want to fight, sir, I am your man, sir! Choose your weapons, sir! Bowie knife, shotgun, or revolver, sir! I'm your man, sir! " Here the speaker, by way of emphasis to his remarks, snapped his pistol at the lighted handle on the table, about three paces away, and all were left in total darkness. The stranger availed himself of this opportunity to make his exit by the side door, being unwilling to serve as a target for the unerring marksman, who would probably have extinguished him in a similar manner - New York Herald

A Musical Crab - Among the animals Doctor Alcock has specially observed is the red ocypode crab which swarms on all the sandy shores of India...

Small-Pox In Wall Paper - " Many years ago a person was sick of small-pox in a farm house in the country town of Groton, and after the patient recovered the dwelling was fumigated and repapered. Ira Chester and family now dwell in the house. The paper was removed a week or so ago, and presently Mr. Chester's daughter was stricken with small-pox. In the opinion of the physician the germs of the disease were dormant in the walls of the room. "...

The Banner, Vol. 1, Clanton, Ala., Thursday, April 13, 1893, No. 23

Claus Spreckles, of the sugar trust, and his little scheme to annex Hawaii have been turned down. It is said President Cleveland had much to do with the defeat of the scheme...

HON. THOS. E. WINN TALKS - Hon. Thomas E. Winn, ex-member of congress from the ninth district of Georgia, in an interview with a representative of the press, made the following terse statements in regard to the political situation: " Everything is in an unsettled condition now, and it will be until the end of this administration develops itself.

AN INCOME TAX - ... Now, on what lines and these reforms the effected? Edmund Burke never made a truer or more important statement than he did when he said, " that the lines of liberty and equal rights were laid on the lines of taxation, and that every battle of freedom had been fought out on that parallel...

SUCCESS OF REFORM - The following communication was addressed to the editor of the National Economist by Mr. L.F. Livingston: " From a recent issue of your paper I gather that your intention in the future is to vote your columns to the accomplishment of the legitimate reforms demanded by the masses of the people of this country from a strict non-partisan standpoint. "...

Will Be Sold - Judge Lacombe has authorized Wm. C. Lane as permanent receiver of the United States Rolling Stock Company to sell all securities, land and patent rights belonging to the company and now in its possession. Several suits are now pending in Illinois, Ohio, Alabama and other states for the foreclosure and mortgage bonds of the company. The value of the securities set forth in the application of the receiver is $578,353, besides fifteen patents, several lots of real estate at Hedgewisch, Illinois, 1,554 acres of land at Ball Play, Ala., and cars and barges.

Board Of Pension Examiners - A Board of Pension Examiners has been established in Montgomery by the Pension Commission at Washington. Drs. L.L. Hill, president; M.L. Wood and J.R. Jordan constitute the board by appointment, and hold examinations four times a month - every Wednesday...

Senator McCormick, who was elected as a Republican state senator in the Wyoming legislature, withdrew from a Republican caucus some time ago and declared that he was no longer a Republican, but hereafter would act with the People's party.

At a special election to fill a vacancy in the Georgia house of representatives, the People's party of Forsyth county elected their man, B.H. Brown, by 135 majority. Many counties were carried in the state in the county elections last month and satisfactory gains were made in others. In Screwen county the Republicans and Democrats combined, defeating the Populists by 200 majority.

Wichita, Kan., March 29, 1893. To the People of 7th Congressional District - Hon. Jerry Strupson authorizes me to say to those designing Federal appointments that he has nothing whatever to do with the distribution of patronage and that it is useless to write him in regard to Federal positions Mr. Simpson says: " This is a Democratic administration, and persons desiring office will have to seek it through Democratic sources, and I am not a

Democrat. " Fred L. Bailey, Chm. 7th Cong. Dist. Com....

Tax Assessor Rollins says that a great number of the tax payers of the county have failed to meet him on his rounds; his deputies will all be busy by the 20th getting up the delinquent assessments...

Jemison Gems - The district singing at Rocky Mount was a success, well attended and so forth. The President Mr. A. Glasscock was scarcely able to preside, otherwise the meeting would have been much more enjoyable.

Leroy Campbell who was recently so ill, is out at work with a vim beyond his present strength.

Mr. D.L. Langston and bride are stopping at the Jemison hotel.

Mrs. Garner of Oxford, Ala., has taken charge of the Jemison hotel.

DR. B. W. GROCE ON THE PRINCIPLES OF THE ALLIANCE - Last Monday morning a numerous audience gathered at the Court House, Clanton, for the purpose of hearing an address upon the Alliance and its principals delivered by Dr. B.W. Groce, our beloved State President. At precisely eleven o'clock ex-County President Brother Honeycutt, in a few well-chosen words, introduced the Doctor to the audience. In expressing his obligation to Brother Honeycutt for the introduction he took occasion to say he hardly needed any introduction to Alliancemen, and talking as a farmer to farmers he was more hopeful today than ever before...

OUR COUNTY OFFICERS, SUPERINTENDENT MOORE - Education is the basis upon which civilization is constructed; its influence extends through every degree of life, and happy is the child who in his early years has the opportunity of receiving instruction at the hands of a duly qualified preceptor. In closing this series of " Our County Officers " we are proud to do so with one of Chilton county's own progeny born in the county, of which both his parents were also natives, raised and educated in the county, his life's work - the noble work of teaching the youthful mind - performed in the county. Chilton may well be proud of its County Superintendent. Superintendent J.W. Moore, son of Lundsford and Elizabeth Moore, was born within two miles of Coopers station, April 2, 1859. As he grew up he assisted his father on his farm for a time, but the desire for knowledge proving irresistible he entered the academy at Verbena, where, under the careful instruction of Professor Acree, he commenced a scholastic life. Unceasing study has since brought him to the front ranks of the profession, and his method of teaching, and his pleasant but firm manner, have endeared him to his pupils, while the success they attain renders him deservedly popular with their parents. Brother Moore became a member of the Missionary Baptist church at Verbena in 1886. He joined the Alliance in 1889, and at the present time is a member of Evergreen Alliance. In 1887 he was a member of the Board of Education, and was elected County Superintendent in August, 1892. Brother Moore sought and found his charming wife among the fairest daughters of Alabama - the unrivaled belles of Chilton county. He was married, May 30th, 1889, to Miss Mary Eliza Thompson, daughter of Mr. Albert Thompson, of this county, and two sweet little girls have blessed their union. Superintendent Moore is yet but a young man and bids fair by the advance he has already made to make for himself a place of distinction in the state, and has proved to be one of the most valued of " Our County Officers ".

Lily Lyrics - Mrs. W.H. Foshee and Miss Jessie Jones, of Clanton, are visiting relatives and friends near Lily.

.

Prof. Jack Hicks, Bibb's efficient county superintendent, and sister, paid a visit to relatives near here last week. Mr. Geo. Jackson, of Autauga, is the guest of Mr. Deshazo.

.

Many of the young people of Lily attended Prof. Durham's cantata at Macedonia on Sunday. The Professor is becoming a very popular instructor in vocal music.

TOWN ITEMS - Mr. E.C. Worns, Birmingham's popular plumber, paid a visit to friends in Clanton last Saturday.

.

Mrs. Kicker, an old and highly respected inhabitant of our city, departed this life on Monday last at Duke's mill. To our esteemed friend, Mr. Newt Kicker, and other sorrowing relatives, we offer our sincerest sympathy, and beg to remind them she is " Not lost, but gone before. "

.

Rev. J.S. Gill, of Birmingham, gave and interesting lecture on " The(?)ts and Shadows of Home Life, " (?) Tuesday, the proceeds being for benefit of the Baptist church

.

Mr. C.H. Abbot, the well-known contractor, has finished at Messrs. Gullahorn's saw mill at Verbena, and has gone to fix the new of the Pratt Saw Mill Company at Saginaw.

.

Mrs. B.H. Chesnut is paying a visit to relatives at Anniston, accompanying her brother, Mr. G.R. Evans who has been visiting here.

.

(?)day last Jim Ellis, a negro, was (?) Judge R. Honeycutt for (?) Jim acknow-(?) with a switch (?)

.

There will be preaching at the Congregational church on the first (?)nday in each month Rev. J.L. Busby, pastor.

.

Near Bozeman Mrs. R.F. Sugar's family has been visited with a remarkable fatality, no less than seven members having been stricken with (?) suddenly within the past week, and the only surviving sister his not expected to live at last hearing the doctors pronounce the ma(?) be pulmonary disease.

.

In Beat one, near McKee's grocery, last Saturday night, Tom Martin seriously cut Mr. Mat Davis on the left side of the head, extending from the top down the neck, narrowly missing the jugular vein; his arm was also cut. Martin, who was under the influence of liquor, deliberately walked up to Davis and cut him. Mr. Davis is doing well, but is not yet out of danger. Martin has disappeared.

Lightwood Listenings - Mr. Wadsworth has completed his railroad to the river and will be fetching logs from Coosa soon.

.

Our beloved pastor, Brother A.C. Wells, who has been serving us for four years, a sermon last Sunday on " Love, " from Job; it was the most interesting he has ever delivered at this church; everyone who heard it was much interested.

There will be a lecture by Major Harris and others, on Sunday school, the third Sunday in this month, near this place, at Friendship church.

There was a very sad circumstance occurred near Bicks a few days ago. The mother of Dr. W.N. Surle was burned to death. The wood was on fire, and Mrs. Surl went to look at it. Finding she did not return her daughter went in search of her, and was horrified to find the poor lady burned to death beyond recognition.

Verbena Views - Several of the young people near Verbena attended preaching last Sunday at Bethel, Rev. J.M. Dykes preached an interesting sermon.

Rev. McCord and family have gone to Six Mile to attend the marriage of Miss Stella Pratt.

Miss Georgia Thompson has returned home from a visit to Strasburg. Mr. General Norrell has returned home, Louisiana was too tough for him. The farmers seem to be planting in hope of good crops.

Dr. Ivey, of Montgomery, was in town the other day, en route to his mica mine in Coosa.

Collins Chapel Chirpings - Assistant Lecturer L B. Pounds will deliver a lecture at Collins Chapel Alliance, on Saturday, April 22nd, at 2 p.m. and will preach a sermon at night. The Rev. J.M. Dykes will also be present.

Lomax Liltings - Miss Willis Marlar has returned home after a pleasant visit to friends and relations in Shelby.

Dr. A.J. Marlar has returned to Stanton after a pleasant visit to his family near Clanton.

Mr. A. Smith, of Clanton ford, moved his family to Lomax.

Four Physicians Failed, A Running Sore Five Years - Hoods Sarsaparilla Perfectly Cured...I was troubled with a running sore on my ankle, the doctors pronouncing it salt-rheum. For 5 years (during which time I employed 4 different physicians), I received very little, if any, benefit, and it continued to increase in size. I then commenced taking Hood's Sarsaparilla, and using Hood's Olive Ointment, and at the end of 2 years I was completely cured, and have had no trouble with it since." Simeon Staples, East Trenton, Mass.

TROTTERS AND PACERS - ...Moonbars, 2.11 1/4, will go back into George Starr's stable aft a season in the stud. Matt Maloney thinks he will have one of the sensational campaigners this year in Manager, 2.09 1/3, by Nutwood...

Horace Laudon, of Eden Center, N. Y., has a promising colt by Fieldmont, out of the dam of Fanny Wilkes, 2.24 1/4...

L.A. Davis will campaign Roy Wilkes, 2.074 1/4, this season and will enter him in the $10,000 free-for-all pacers at Washington Park....

Speaking of prices, L.V. Baker, of Comstocks, N.Y., says:"Maud S. only brought a little over $200, but the sale was worth a quarter of a million to Woodburn."...

J.E. Turner has taken charge of Nyanza, 2.30, by Quartermaster; and Nutshell, by Bayonne Prince, two four-year-old fillies handled last year by W.E. Weeks...

The dam of the Jewett Farm sire, Bonnie Boy, was killed by a rattle snake when that horse was but a few weeks old, and like his illustrious grandsire, George Wilkes, he was brought up on a bottle...

The black gelding Midnight, 2.18 1/4, by Peacemaker, died at Lakeland Farm, Wickliffe, O., early this winter. He was owned by John D. Rockefeller and was turned out in 1892. At the time of his death he was 20 years old....

The stallion Highland Gray, 2.28, one of the representative sires of the Black Hawk family, died at the home of his owner, G.H. Davis, Hubbardston, Vt., last week....

E.D. Wiggin last year measured Martha Wilkes' stride, with these results....

The Banner, Vol. 1, Clanton, Ala., Thursday, April 20, 1893, No. 24

Will Help Build Our Towns - D.G. Edwards, the general passenger agent of the Queen and Crescent line, with his customary enterprise, his issued a circular to connecting lines, which if concurred in will do much toward advertising the rescues of our Southern country and at the same time afford Southern visitors to the World's Fair an opportunity of seeing the towns on the different railroads...

The people throughout the State are anxiously awaiting Col. Willis Brewer's reply to the Alliance Herald's letter addressed to him in which some pertinent questions were asked as to the failure of the committee of which he was a member to act. It is due to Gov. Jones and to the citizens of Alabama that these questions be answered.

Gen. Black, who was commissioner of pensions in 1885-9, is a pensioner. He receives a pension of $100 per month for being "mentally and physically incapacitated for work." He has been receiving this pension for more than twelve years. Yet he got $5000 a year as pension commissioner because he could work and at the same time $1,200 a year because he couldn't work. Now he has been elected to congress, and this "mentally and physically democratic wreck" still gets his pension. This is a case which the democrats will hardly investigate - Pickens County News.

Coosa County Alliance met recently. J.W. Cooper, secretary pro tem, writes as follows: -...

THE JUDGES - Following is a list of the Grand and Petit Jurors for the Spring Term of the Circuit Court, 1893, Chilton County, commencing May 15.

GRAND JURORS

Name	Beat
J.T. Cobb	2
B.H. Chestnut	4
G.L. Speer	3
R.E.R. Hicks	8
Z.J. Jones	3
Jasper Gentry	7
W.M. Price	8
B.N. Martin	1
W.H. Shaw	2
Moses Mims	4
W.F. Claughton	5
H.A.J. Harris	5
I.W. Middlebrooks	6
W.F. Nix	7
J.C. Walker	8
J.A. Logan	4
T.W. Wellden	6
W.A. Mims	1
James Cooley	3
I.K. Mullins	6

PETIT JURORS - First Week.

W.J. Brown	2

J.J. Hicks 7
W.A.G. Logan 4
Aaron Littleton 4
H. Henry 2
I.J. Littlejohn 7
J.S. Atchison 8
L.S. Sammons 2
Wylie Littlejohn 4
W.D. Nix 3
W.H. Wells 5
H.M. Butts 8
J.T. Mims 1
I.S. Eaves 8
H. Hardy 4
A.F. Childers 3
G.W. Littleton 1
Isaac Littleton 3
L. Moore 5
T.J. Robinson 1
James R. Harris 8
H.Z. Barnes 2
John Roberts 8
Ed Smitherman 7
J.M. Honeycutt 3
W.T. Hayes 7
Wm. Callaway 5
G.W. Mims 1
Thos Lawrence 7
N.J. Maddox 1
D.A. Friday 8
A.Z. Bean 1
C.I. Glasscock 1
PETIT JURORS - Second Week.
L.H. Reynolds 2
W.D. Goss 5
J.B. Killingsworth 2
John A. Strock 5
J.G. Burkhalter 5
J.T. Mullins 5
J.K. Driver 5
J.W. Sorrell 1
Elijah Mims 4
J.C. Callaway 5
E.M. Bean 1
Thomas Mims 4
Joseph Ray 5
N.F. Easterling 5
P.E. Harris 8
S.E. Waldrop 3
J.H. Sexton 8

A.J. Adkinson	2
H.W. Houlditch	2
W.N. Johns	1
R. Killingsworth	2
Elijah Jones	4
John Patterson	5
W.E. Lowry	2
J.P. Haley	8
J.S. Jones, Jr.	5
G.W. Askins	5
Henry Cox	8
J.H. Aldridge	4
W.J. Millstead	2
J.M. Thacker	4
George Gore	4
J.E. Domining	4

Clear Creek Clippings - Rev. W.B. Chamson will preach at Oak Grove school-house on the fourth Sunday in April, and the Rev. R.M. Honeycutt will preach at Providence church on the third Saturday and Sunday in April.

Kincheon Ketchings - I am sorry you published in your valuable paper the marriages of Messrs. W.D. Burnett, Monroe Askins and J.T. Middlebrooks; I would have sent the news to you, but I knew it would make the hearts of some of our young men harder and faster: if you never saw a crowd of young men with sick hearts, come down here and take a smile.

Mr. B.G. Boles' daughter, Miss Sallie Boles, is quite sick: we hope she may soon be restored to her wanted health.

Mr. R.N. Wilkins, of Vine Hill, paid a visit to his father recently. Mr. W. H. Wilkins visited his son, G.W. Wilkins, last week.

TOWN ITEMS - Mrs. Bowden has moved her school from Dudley's mill to her home and re-opened last Monday with fifteen pupils.

Rev. A.C. Wells held a largely attended meeting at Mrs. Bowden's school-house on Tuesday night.

Mr. Patrick Smith and Mr. Henry Culver paid a visit to their old homes in Coosa this week.

Mr. T.H. White has rented Mr. Tom Gullahorn's residence, and moved his family from Birmingham to Clanton.

There will be a prayer meeting on Friday night, and Sunday-school at (?) o'clock, Sunday afternoon, at Mrs. Bowden's school-house, under the direction of Rev. A.C. Wells.

Mrs. Crew and Miss Emma Bent(?) have returned home to Goodwater after a pleasant visit to Mrs. (?)olen.

Squires Nolen and Baldwin come to Rockfort to attend circuit court at town this week.

(?) Ola McDaniels has (?) after a visit to South Calera.

Little Bill Dawson went fishing Saturday and as he could not catch any fish he put himself on the hook and Dr. Johnson had to unhook him.

Our accommodating and genial de(?) agent Mr. W.W. Dunkin, is off for a visit to Atlanta this week, Mr. Hester is officiating by day an his absence. Mr. Butterworth, of (?)ville, acting at night.

Tax collector Gentry was in town today.

John Bailey and family have return after five weeks visit to Montgomery.

Preparing for Circuit Court which convenes Monday May 15th, has caused Sheriff Moore and Circuit Clerk J.P. VanDerveer to be quite busy this week.

Bro. Ben Wells, of Coopers paid us a pleasant call today.

Preaching at the Baptist Church on the third Sunday in each month. Rev. J.L. Busby, pastor.

Collins Chapel Chirpings - Last Saturday a very distressing and tragical accident happened in the neighborhood of Collins Chapel by which the wife of Mr. W.D. Martin was burnt to death. Being unwell Mrs. Martin had laid down on a quilt before the fire when by some means her clothing caught on fire, and running out to her husband who was working in his garden he endeavored to put out her burning clothing, she fell down as she reached him and Mr. Martin himself was severely burnt trying to extinguish the flames. She was carried in doors and medical attendance was at once sent for, but was unavailing she was perfectly conscious up to the time of her death which took the following morning about 4 o'clock, she made disposition as to where she would like to be buried and said she was perfectly willing to die. She leaves her husband and one son, their only child, to mourn her loss. The interment took place at Collins Chapel on Monday, the services were conducted by the local Alliance with Alliance ritual, the Revs. R.M. Honeycutt and W.N. Riggins officiating by special request.

Ad - DENTISTRY, DR. MASSEY & DR. SANDEFUR are extracting teeth daily by the use of ODONTUNDER without the least pain or bad effect.

ENGLISH LANDLORDISM - A tract of 80,000 acres of land in central Wyoming was purchased several years ago by Loinel Sartoris, a cousin of the Englishman who married and then deserted Nellie Grant. Sartoris failed in the range business, but has now found profitable use for his acres. He has bought water rights and built an irrigation plant, and will colonize his tract with English tenant farmers. He announces that he intends to " farm on a large scale. " Yes, he will farm the farmers. And the small farmer, who tills his own acres with help hired at the market rates for American labor, must compete in the market where produce is sold with this English landlord, whose laborers are ground serfs. This is what English landlordism and tenant farmers in the United States means - the economic destruction of the loftiest type of the republic's citizen, the American farmer. " Alien ownership of land should be prohibited, " says the Omaha platform. The Western Farmer recognizes his danger. The People's party takes up his cause. So does not any other political party. - The Vanguard

MR. WATSON'S VIEWS - Hon. Thomas Watson, in a lengthy interview in the Atlanta Constitution, gives by request, his opinions in regard to the great issues of the day and the attitude he will unofficially assume in regard to them...

EMIN PACHA DEAD - The Great African Explorer Given Up For Lost.
A letter received at Zanzibar, Africa, from Tippoo Tib's son confirms the report of the death of Emin Pacha, the great explorer, and all his people...

Ad - Hood's Cures, After The Grip It Restores Health and Strength.
Mr. Dexter Curtis is well-known in Wisconsin as a manufacturer of collar pads and boots for horses, and is a reliable business man...."I cannot speak in too favorable terms of the good qualities of Hood's Sarsaparilla. I have had a bad cough for 2 years, coming on after the grip. I tried physicians, went twice to the Hot springs of Arkansas, but all did no good. I got a bottle of Hood's Sarsaparilla and it gave me relief at once. The second dose seemed to go to the right spot. I afterward got 6 bottles, and have taken nearly all of it, and know I am much better every way. So many medicines are advertised that do no good. I would not say anything in favor of Hood's Sarsaparilla any unless I was fully satisfied it was good and worth trying. I believe Hood's Sarsaparilla is good." Dexter Curtis

The Banner, Vol. 1, Clanton, Ala., Thursday, April 27, 1893, No. 25

Rogue's Gallery For The Fair - Wilson McLaughey, son of Chief of Police McLaughey of Chicago, returned recently from a trip which has occupied him for several months. He was sent all over the United States to procure pictures of every crook of any notoriety for the rogue's gallery here in anticipation of the fair. It was realized by the chief of police that with the fair there, crooks from all quarters of the United States would flock to that city to prey upon the hundreds of thousands of strangers. The trip has been successful. Over 4,000 likenesses of crooks have been secured for the guidance of the Chicago police. The work done by Wilson McLaughey is regarded as one of the most important character.

Prohibition Organ Reappears - The Mississippi Leader, a prohibition party paper which suspended publication at Jackson in November, made its appearance again Wednesday. Its plant has been considerably increased, and it will hereafter be owned and published by a stock company, at the head of which is Mr. Henry Ware, chairman of the State prohibition executive committee. Mr. B.T. Hobbs, former editor and proprietor, continues as editor and business manager. It announces its unswerving allegiance to the principles of the prohibition party, and proposes to keep up the fight along that line.

From a recent interview with Governor Jones, the Editor of The Living Truth gives the following:... "Kolb is not a Democrat, and has no right to call himself a Democratic; the great bulk of his are Republicans, and he is to all intents and purposes a Republican "...

Jemison Gems - On the 19th inst., at the County Hospital, near Jemison, after a short illness Mr. Joe Busby died. He was an old blind man and leaves no family to mourn for him. The keepers of said institute kindly cared for him in sickness, and his remains were decently laid away.

Lomax Linings - We are glad to hear Mrs. H. Stewart, who has been quite sick, is better: we hope to see her out soon.

.

Miss Mary Roebuck, one of Clanton Ford's fairest young ladies, spent Saturday and Sunday with friends at Lomax: Miss Mary gained many friends by her genial manners.

.

Mr. Wiley Foshee spent Sunday with his mother at this place. Mr. Aurelias Attaway left on Sunday for Leesdale, Ala., where he will engage in business with L. & N. bridge crew; success to him.

.

Dr. A.J. Marlar spent Saturday and Sunday with his family at this place.

.

Miss Willis Marlar, one of Lomax's most charming young ladies, has returned home after a delightful visit to friends at Ruddick.

.

Mr. Lee Wells, of Walnut Creek, spent Sunday with his best role at this place; look out, boys!

Pleasant Grove Pleasantries - We are glad to note that Mr. Thomas Franklin and family, who have been very sick, are all much better.

.

We learn that Professor Durham, of Jemison, is to sing at Pleasant Grove church on the fourth Sunday in May; hope there will be a good attendance.

We are sorry to note that Mr. Davis Davenport is very sick at present, but hope he will soon recover.

TOWN ITEMS - Mr. O.A. Dukes gave a farewell dance on Monday night, and has removed his family to Bainbridge, Ga.

Judge Callen has, we understand, purchased the residence of Mr. Dukes.

Mr. Jim Smith, of Coosa, and Mr. (Tom?) Smith of Mountain Creek, paid a visit to their parents here this week.

Deputy-sheriff Will Hayes has gone home to recuperate and to assist his father, ex-Sheriff Hayes, on his farm.

Mary Carter, a colored woman, was charged before Judge Honeycutt with assaulting little Yancey Bivings, and was fined $1.00 and costs.

(?)sday morning a funeral pro(?)on wended its sorrowful way (?)gh our town, conveying to its (?)resting place the mortal remains (?)he infant child of Mr. and Mrs. (?) Johnson, of Birmingham. The little spirit flew heavenward last (?)sday, and the mourning parents and friends laid the body to rest in (?) cemetery.

Mr. Thomas W. Smith will wed the beautiful Miss Mary Martin at Macedonia next Sunday. May success and happiness always go with them.

Major Thomas Keyes was in town Saturday morning on his way to (?) the County Alliance at Re(?) South. Full account of the (?) next issue.

Plantersville Pickings - Mr. G.M. Robertson of Huntsville, who has just completed a course in stenography at the Birmingham Business College, has accepted a position with the Jackson Lumber Company at this place.

The following was published in the Selma Mirror last week: " Contributions to the fund for hunting down the negro Shelton have been offered the Mirror. It is reported that he was caught and attended to one night last week. The dead tell no lies. " We presume this refers the negro Shelton who shot and killed Mr. James Harris near here on the 3rd instant. So far as we can learn the report is incorrect, and Shelton has not yet been captured.

Collins Chapel - RESOLUTIONS OF SYMPATHY. At a regular meeting of Collins Chapel Alliance the following resolutions were unanimously adopted, respecting the death of Mrs. Angeline Martin. The deceased was for several years a member of the Alliance; by the noble qualities of her life she endeared herself to all who knew her; noble in her nature, generous in all her acts, she won for herself the unsought esteem, admiration and love of this entire community. Therefore be it resolved: First, that in her removal from us we deeply mourn the loss we sustain, yet bow with submission to Him is " too wise to err, too good to be unkind. " Second, that we tender to the heart-stricken family our most sincere sympathies and pray God that He may sustain them under his mysterious dispensation of His providence, which has brought so much sadness and sorrow to their hearts. Third, that a copy of these resolutions be sent to the afflicted family and also a copy to The Banner for publication. G.W. Pate, Sec.

Preaching at the Baptist Church on the third Sunday in each month. Rev. A.A. Hutto pastor.

There will preaching at the Congregational church on the first Sunday in each month. Rev. J.L. Busby, pastor.

Ad - Hood's is the Best, The Judgement of Long Experience
" Myself and my wife have taken several bottles of Hood's Sarsaparilla with gratifying results. For years I have had kidney trouble and also heart difficulty. I was unable to sleep on my left side for years. Hood's Sarsaparilla has done me a great deal of good. I am free from kidney trouble, and can sleep on either side now thanks to Hood's Sarsaparilla. My wife has had a chronic sore throat for more than 20 years. It always troubled her more or less, but the last 6 months, since taking Hood's Sarsaparilla, she has not had a sore throat except once when she took a slight cold. We cheerfully recommend Hood's Sarsaparilla as a good reliable medicine for the blood and to build up the system; I consider it the best medicine in use. " Grant W. Barnes

REFORM NEWS AND NOTES - Current Comment Concerning The Great Crusade Against Oppression
...The bill introduced in the House last session by Representative Clover, Populist, of Kansas, which proposes to levy a graduated income tax to be expended in pensions, public works, and the employment of labor, has found former endorsement by the Legislature of Kansas, which by resolutions laid before the Senate by the Vice-President, has urged Congress to enact it into law.
... The politicians having failed to lie, legislate or prosecute the Populist party out of existence; have dropped everything and are now trying persistent lying again. The latest is colored quotations from what Congressman Watson and Congressman Wynne, of Georgia, are quoted as saying; " Politicians in all parts should learn honesty is the best policy. The dishonest course may succeed for a time, but like all things, there is a disastrous ending. " - Progressive Farmer
... Through the preference of Bro. J.H. McDowell, of Tennessee, to tape but connecting rooms have been secured in the city of Chicago for Alliance headquarters..
... The first purely and distinctive Populist measure became a law under the post office appropriations. Hon. Tom Watson tacked an amendment on to that appropriation bill which granted $10,000 as a fund for experimenting in free rural postal delivery...

Remains Of Mr. Davis. - By order of J.B. Gordon, general-commanding, an order has been issued from headquarters of the United Confederate Veterans, which directs that commanders of camps will at once notify all the members of their respective camps of the request contained in a letter dated Richmond, Va., April 14, to Gen. George Moorman, from Col. Thomas Elliott, secretary of Lee Camp, which says; " I am instructed by the executive committee of Lee Camp who are making arrangements for the reception and re-interment of the remains of President Jefferson Davis, to write and ask you to notify all camps in the United Confederate Veterans that they are invited to the ceremonies, which will take place on Wednesday, May 31, in New Orleans...

The Doctors In Session - The doctors convened in Selma, Ala., Tuesday in annual session with a large attendance, and President J.T. Searcy in the chair. Mayor Stewart made a speech of welcome, as did Dr. Gay, president of the Dallas county association. Routine proceedings followed till adjournment, an at night Dr. Glen Andrews delivered the annual address. Wednesday was consumed in the regular routine business of the session, including reports of officers. Selma's hospitality is being extended in boundless profusion.

The Banner, Vol. 1, Clanton, Ala., Thursday, May 4, 1893, No. 26

Strange Breed Of Hay-Eating Hogs - " One of the curious things we have taught our hogs to do at Klamath Falls, Oregon, " said G.W. Smith, a merchant of that place, " is to eat hay like horses. They will do it, too, and thrive on it. In fact, in winter they get nothing else. It is alfalfa hay we have taught them to eat. It is put in a rack that is not too high and they can reach up to, and they pull it out just like horses and cattle...

United States Marshal Walker of Brooklyn, is making arrangements for the appointment of a couple of hundred deputies to arrest all Chinamen who persists in refusing to register themselves in the revenue office.

Frank S. Beedleson, of Mechanicsville, N.Y., is the champion one-legged bicycle rider. Monday he will leave Mechanicsville for San Francisco, Cal., from whence he will ride a wheel to New York, starting May 22, with the expectation of making the trip in 100 days.

William Townsend, the man arrested in London on suspicion of having designs upon the life of Gladstone, has been pronounced insane and will probably be placed in an asylum. The police, however, attach importance to the arrest and hope to be able to discover that someone was behind Townsend inciting him to the assassination.

Zulus Take A Train - A train load of Zulus bound for the World's Fair, gave a railroad crew and a squad of Chicago police a lively experience. The first heard of the affair was when Police Lieutenant Creighton received a telegram saying that two hundred Zulus had captured an inbound train near Grand Crossing, and had imprisoned the trainmen. A wagon load of bluecoats met the train at Sixty-first street. They found Conductor Throne and his brakemen imprisoned in the baggage car, while two hundred Zulus had possession of the train. The savages claimed that one of their number had lost some property, and they were holding the conductor responsible. Lieutenant Creighton, after much excited palaver, quieted the Zulus and rescued the imprisoned railway employee. The Zulus were then quickly transferred to the fair grounds.

Bootlicking Barred - Secretary Carlisle has, because of recent violations, issued a circular letter to treasury officials calling their attention to the law which provides that no officer, clerk or employee in the United States government's employ, shall, at any time, solicit contributions from other officers, clerks, or employees in the government service for a gift or present to those in superior official positions; nor shall any such officials or clerical superiors receive any gift or present offered or to them as a contribution of persons in government employ receiving a salary less than themselves, nor shall any officer or clerk make any donation as a gift or present to any official superior. The law further provides that those who violate it may be discharged, and Secretary Carlisle enjoins strict compliance.

Called Calvin A Scoundrel - A meeting of the Troy Presbyterians was held in Troy, N.Y., to discuss the overtures handled by the General Assembly. During the discussion Rev. T.P. Calvin said he did not wish to be known as a Calvinist, and said: " I do not like the idea of Calvinism. Calvin was a murderer and a scoundrel. He said many good things, and those by will accept, but the church should be an exponent of the gospel, and not of Calvinism." The Presbytery adopted a resolution overturning the General Assembly in Washington to prepare a new short creed, clear, concise and Scriptural in its wording, to be used by the church in harmony with the existing doctrines come expressed by the Westminister confession of faith.

A call has been issued by President George F. Gaither for a meeting of the State Executive Committee of the Peoples Party, to take place at the Acme Hotel, Birmingham, Thursday, May 11th.

Those who regard government control of the railroads as an impracticable visionary idea of cranks only, will perhaps be surprised to learn from the following associated press dispatch, that our government has already control to some extent of at least one railroad. " Washington, April 26, - The President today announced the following appointments: Government Directors of the Union Pacific Railway Company, Henry F. Cimock, of New York, Don M. Dickinson, of Michigan; J.W. Deane, of Illinois; Fitghugh Lee, of Virginia; Joseph W. Paddock of Nebraska. "

Sir D.E. Colnaghi, the British Consul-General stationed at Florence, Italy, in his report to the British Government in regard to the condition of the Italian working class, states that the workmen of Italy have given up the strike as a futile weapon to defend their interests, on account of its failure, and has decided that independent political action is the only method by which they can better their condition. The men have already elected a number of their fellow workmen to official in the larger cities. - Journal of K. Of L. Sensible workmen, the most effective strike, is the strike through the agency of the ballot box. Especially so is this the case when their vote is counted as cast.

COUNTY ALLIANCE NOTES - Last Wednesday your editor in company with Major Thomas Key of the Southern Agriculturist visited the County Alliance; on arrival we found a goodly company gathered; shortly after dinner was announced, we gathered around the table to do justice to the very bountiful repast spread before us. Our brethren and friends have reason to be proud of their helpmates and are certainly fortunate mortals in every sense of the word; after dinner all gathered in the house to hear Major Key who discussed sheep, grasses, corn, in an able and exhaustive manner. Lecturer L.H. Reynolds followed and he convinced the minds of all who heard him of the material benefit the Alliance has been to the people of this section. The second day Ex-President Honeycutt dwelt upon the excellence of the Alliance and its principles Bro. L.A. Logan spoke at length, dwelling the benefits the farmer had derived from the organization. Bro. L.R. Vinson then spoke in their favor of the Alliance Exchange; his remarks were instructive and received with marked attention. The claims of the Alliance Herald, that staunch champion of reform was ably advocated by Ex-President Honeycutt. The Banner was substantially remembered. Editor Batzell owing to a misunderstanding was not present, greatly to the regret of all.

THE COUNTY ALLIANCE - The Chilton County Farmers' Alliance convened on Wednesday, April 26th with the brethren of Reform South, at Bethsalem church the Alliance was called to order at 10 a.m. by President Moses Robinson. The proceedings were opened with singing and prayer. Brothers J.A. Logan and J.M. Scott, Committee on Credentials, fifteen Alliances represented: the report was received, and after discussion, Brothers L.H. Reynolds, Lee Hayes and J.A. Logan were appointed a committee to wait upon Major Thomas Key, of the Southern Agriculturist, to ascertain when it would suit his convenience to address the Alliance... The committee having returned, announced Major Key was ready whenever called upon; on motion. Major Key was invited to address the Alliance at one o'clock, and County Lecturer L.H. Reynolds would follow him...At one o'clock the

Major commenced his address, speaking for two hours on Agriculture. He was followed by Bro. L.H. Reynolds, who discussed the Alliance, its aims, objects and benefits. Editor T.H. White, of The Banner, concluded the day's proceedings by impressing upon the brethren the necessity of making the Alliance meeting attractive and instructive to the young in order to keep the organization in a healthy and vigorous condition... On a vote being taken, Liberty Hill Alliance was unanimously chosen as the next meeting place of the County Alliance, Bros. Lee Hayes, W.H. Shaw and T.H. White being appointed as a committee to invite speakers thereto...

MULBERRY BAPTIST ASSOCIATION - ... The religious services were conducted very effectively by Bro. G.W. Freeman. Bro. A. Glass delivered the welcome address in a plain and forcible manner which made all present feel at home. Organization being next in order; Bro. R.M. Honeycutt, Moderator, took the chair. The Secretary being absent, on motion Bro. J.E. Jones was requested to act in his place... Some short but pointed talks were made by Bros. R.M. Honeycutt, J.M. Langston and W.A. Wood on the Sabbath-school work... Discussion of subjects.1st What is the purpose of holding a Sabbath school convention? Opened by Bro. J.M. Langston, followed by Brothers A. Mimms, J.E. Jones, R.M. Honeycutt, W.A. Wood and Z.J. Jones, which we believe gave much needed information on the subject. 2d. What is the duty of a Sabbath school superintendent at home and with his school? Discussed by Bros. Z J. Jones, W.G. Riggins, J.M. Langston, A. Glass and R.M. Honeycutt, in it various lights...3d. What is the best to awaken the people to the Sabbath school work? Discussed by Bros. A. Glass, Moore, Freeman, Riggins, Mimms and Honeycutt very heatedly in its various lights and forms... A motion was made and carried for the chairman to appoint a committee to get up a programme for the next convention. Committee, W.G. Riggins, Z.J. Jones and J.E. Jones... At 9:30 the Sabbath school mass meeting began, which was conducted by Bro. Z.J. Jones, who is a faithful worker in the cause. There were some able and spirited discussions upon the second school cause by Brothers Adams, Langston, Riggins and others, and the writer feels confident that good and lasting impressions were made many. At 11:30 Brother Riggins proceeded, according to previous arrangements, to preach to a large and attentive congregation, and from every appearance the people were greatly interested and benefited; after which the convention adjourned to meet with New Salem church on Saturday and Sunday (embracing the fifth Sunday) in July, 1893. J.E. Jones, Clerk...

A PEOPLES PARTY CALL - The Executive Committee of the People's Party of Chilton County is hereby called to meet at Clanton, Thursday, May 25th, at 12 o'clock. There will be very important business to be transacted by the committee and the presence of every member is desired. O.M. Mastin, Chairman

Lomax Linings - Rev. Moore delivered an excellent sermon Sunday eve.

.
Mrs. A. Smith and son are quite sick.

.
Miss Lizzie Lodge, one of Clanton Ford's charming young ladies, has been visiting here, much to the delight of her many friends. We regret to learn that Mr. George Tidwell will move his family to Saginaw; some of our young men are looking very sad; a box of the prettiest flowers ever seen in Lomax arrived here Sunday evening from Leesdale for Miss Willis Marlar.

.
Our young friend Mr. George Lodge has just returned from a pleasant visit to Clanton Ford

he is looking very sad this week there surely must be some one who is very attractive down there. Mr. G. don't grieve, we hope you will get to go again soon.

Dixie Doings - Mr. W.H. Cox and family are visiting Mr. H. Cole and his family near Plantersville. On the 22nd of April, at the residence of Mr. T.G. Letcher there was a large sociable where the young people enjoyed themselves very much. Hurrah for Mr. W. Price, he made a raid on Mr. D.H. Mitchell's bees to get a start of bees. We were glad to see Uncle Sap over at Valley Creek he came over to see his best girl: hurrah for Uncle Sap! Mr. J.W. Letcher shot and killed a turkey April 25th, his wife had to sit up all night, for he has the turkey fever bad, he will have to try the virtue of turkey pills before the can get rid of it.

Mr. Dave Rodgers, the jug peddler, came through this county, and Mr. Letcher challenged him for a horse swap, a swap was made and now he has two good mules and both parties are well pleased. Mr. H.L. Cole's hogs are dieing very fast, he is giving them poke root to make them poke off and to keep from having them to drag off.

PROGRAMME OF CHILTON COUNTY TEACHERS' INSTITUTE
... FRIDAY 9:30 a.m. Opening Exercises, Welcome address, G.L. Speer.
1. " Vocabulary Development ", W.C. Robinson and L.B. Pounds.
2. " The Grube Method in Arithmetic. " H.L. Davis, S.J. Jennings
3. " Discontents of a Teacher. ", Miss Lafarice Deadwilder, General discussion.
4. " Uniform course of study. " David Moore and J.M. Scott
5. " How to secure regular attendance. " Miss O.M. Garner
SATURDAY...
1. " English Grammar. " E.C. Jones and A.B. Harwood
2. Report of Book Committee.
3. " Local Taxation. " General discussion.
4. " Ideal High School. " W.L. Pruette
Isabella church is situated in the Mulberry community, 5 miles north east of Maplesville. Teachers wishing conveyance from railroad should write to G.L. Speer, Lily, Ala.
R.E.R. Hicks, G.L. Speer, J. Alex Moore, Committee

NOTICE TO DELINQUENT TAXPAYERS - The State Of Alabama, Chilton County The Tax Collector of said county has filed in my office a list of delinquent taxpayers and real estate upon which taxes are due and unpaid. You are reported as delinquent, and the following lots of land are reported as assessed to you, as will appear hereinafter. This is to notify you to appear before me on Monday the 29th day of May, 1893, to show cause why a decree for the sale of said land should not be made for the amount of the taxes, costs and charges due thereon, as follows:
BEAT NO.1. - J.D. Atkinson, F.M. Atkinson, J.H. Cannon, S.W. Jones, Mrs. E.A. McClanerhan, R.G. Walker
BEAT NO. 2 - Brierfield Ore Co., John Duke, Mrs. Bettie Ebron, Mrs. Mary Elison, Joseph Goeter, J.L. Graham, P.H. Mack, John T. Milner, Thomas Purvis, Mrs. Ella Stroup, T.P. Shanklin
BEAT NO. 3 - Jeff Baker, Silas Campbell
BEAT NO. 4 - R.C. Duke, J.T. Cain, James Atkinson, J.H. Gullespie, Jesse Foster, A.B. Hill (estate of), G.W. Powell, T.G. Robinson, Anderson Thomas, E.T. Gullahorn & Bro.
BEAT NO. 5 - John Anderson, Stewart Thomas, Sam Evans, Lucinda Bryant, Gordon Frederick, J.S. Jones, W.B. Jones

BEAT NO. 6 - Charley Jackson, Dan Martin
BEAT NO. 7 - Mrs. M.A. Foshee, Thomas Foshee, G.W. Chambers, T.E. Callier, L.J. Moore
BEAT NO. 8 - W.H. Anderson, B.F. Abbot, N.L. Broadhead, Burl Bailey, (?)C. Cosby, Thomas Cook, Mrs. Margaret Friday, Mineral Land Co., A.B. Williams (estate of), Wm. E. Walles, Wm. Walles, H.J. Young, Mrs. S.J. Marshall
...R.M. Honeycutt, Judge of Probate

TOWN ITEMS - It is with great pleasure that we welcome the return of Mr. R. Ehrman and family to our neighborhood.

Preaching at the Baptist Church on the third Sunday in each month. Rev. A.A. Hutto, pastor.

There will be preaching at the Congregational church on the first Sunday in each month. Rev. J.L. Busby, pastor.

Verbena Views - The ladies of Verbena did not forget to prepare flowers for the graves of the Confederate dead, as is their custom, and several went to Montgomery on Memorial day. Several Verbenians went to the District meeting at Salem. Professor Holloway will sing at Canaan on the 4th Sunday in May. The gold and mica miners pass through our town occasionally.

NATIONAL LECTURER TERRELL - ... The national lecturer, Hon. Ben Terrell, has a long and intimate acquaintance with the old guard of the Alliance in every state in the Union..

THE FARMER NO LONGER LEADS - Agriculture is supposed to be the foundation of our progress and prosperity, writes R.H. Edmonds in an article in the Engineering Magazine on modern progress... In a pamphlet recently published by Mr. C. Wood Davis, it is shown that the area cultivated in staple food crops increased from 1875 to 1880 on and average of 6.8 per cent a year, and since then has steadily declined, having been 3.9 per cent from 1885 to 1890... Mr. James R. Dodge, the statisticians of the agricultural department, estimated the value in 1890 at $3,800,000,000 - a gain of $100,000,000 - notwithstanding a heavy average declined in price and very short crops, owing to bad weather...

PIONEER ALLIANCEMEN - Following we give notify a brief history of some of the early workers in the Alliance, who are well known and to whose indefatigable efforts the successful organization and of our order is to a great extent due:
Isaac McCracken - Born in Huntington, Canada, East in the year 1846, he is of Scotch-Irish parentage. At eight years of age his parents moved to Lowell, Mass. He shipped as a common seaman before the mast in 1860 come and followed the sea for three years. Upon returning home he learned the trade of machinist. He married Miss Allen in Sparta, Wis. He moved to Arkansas in 1870 and settled upon the farm where he has since lived. He first organized the farmers and laborers of his section under the name of " Brothers of Freedom. " which, when it had 643 subordinate organizations and a membership of 4,300 consolidated with the Agricultural Wheel in the fall of 1885. He was president of his county and state organization of the " Brothers of Freedom. " Then president of the State Wheel of National Agricultural Wheel, and when the National Farmers' Alliance and Cooperative Union agreed to consolidate as the Farmers' and Laborers' Union of America,

he was chosen as vice-president.

COL. ROBERT BEVERLY - Virginia may well be proud of having furnished the order with a Col. Beverly. He is one of the oldest and best workers. He even commenced on this line long before the Alliance reached his State. He was for years president of the National Farmers' Congress, and it is largely due to his efforts that the South was ripe for the introduction of the Farmers' Alliance. He embraced the Alliance at the first opportunity and has been a valiant soldier ever since. He has refused almost every office in the order and prefers to be an efficient worker in the cause to holding any position. He always attends the national and State meetings, and is an able counselor and advisor. He is the true type of the old Virginia gentlemen - able, honest, sincere, honorable, courteous, and hospitable to a fault.

C.M. WILCOX. - Was elected secretary of the Farmers' State Alliance of Texas in August, 1881, at the meeting held in Parker county. He held that office without any change until August, 1886. During this time the order was built from a small Alliance to over 2,700 strong and active working bodies. Brother Wilcox then for two years acted as assistant to the national secretary. He is fully devoted to the cause, and has made many sacrifices for it.

J.W. McFARLAND -Brother McFarland filled the office of State Secretary of the Farmers' Union of Louisiana for several years. He is one of the ablest and most efficient workers in that State. He has attended every national meeting since the national order was organized. His home is at Homer, and he is one of the old line workers in the good cause that can be depended upon in the coming struggles of the order.

COTTON EFFORT ABANDONED - The following correspondence is self-explanatory: Memphis, Tenn., March 16, 1803. Hon. H.D. Loucks, President: Dear Sir and Brother: Receiving no reply to my letter of the 4th, I am directed by the Cotton Cooperative Bureau to hand you the enclosed communication, and request that you publish the same as a matter of information to the brethren and justice to the bureau...B.G. West, Secretary.

To Members of the Alliance in the Cotton States: Brethren - It appearing from the minutes from the National Council, held in Memphis, Tenn., November, 1892, as enrolled by the secretary, that no authority was delegated to the Cotton Cooperative Bureau by that body, and our attention having been called to this fact by the presiding president of the National Alliance, we hereby notify the of the several cotton states, that notwithstanding the progress made, we will make no further effort to put the enterprise in operation as a part of the work authorized by the National Council, but will, in accordance with the minutes as enrolled, refer the matter to the several state alliances of the cotton states for their consideration and action. Fraternally, Jas. R. Maxwell, Fiscal Agent; R J. Sledge, President; B.G. West, Secretary

STATE NEWS - Dr. Bow has accepted the call to the First Baptist Church, of Eufaula, and will take charge on the 20th of May.

The dwelling house and all contents of John Owen, living near Hokes Bluff, Etowah county, was destroyed by fire last Friday, entailing a heavy loss.

Secretary Cross of the Epworth League expects 500 delegates to be present at the meeting of the State Epworth League in Gadsden May 9. Gadsden will entertain them.

Jim Morrison, the escaped convict and outlaw, who was caught near Greensboro a few

weeks ago, was taken from the jail to Pratt mines, his wound having sufficiently healed for his removal.
.
T.J. Wilder has entered suit against the city of Gadsden for $10,000 damages for injuries received last October in a runaway. About the middle of last October T. J. Wilder and his brother were driving down Locust street, when they encountered a train, and the horse, becoming frightened, reared up and fell backward on the occupants of the buggy, breaking Jeff Wilder's thigh and bruising him up.
.
The late Federal grand jury have found indictments against J.V. Allen, W.S. White, Joe H. Nathan, Murphy Hill and W.H. Sadler, all of Colbert county. These gentlemen are charged with intimidating voters at the late Presidential election. They are all well known and highly respected citizens of their county, and the charged comes in the nature of a great surprise.
.
Whitman & Son warehouse at Boaz, a small town sixteen miles from Guntersville was struck by lightning by and totally destroyed by fire, together with 300 bales of cotton, 275 bales of which belonged to Whitman & Son, and was a total loss. No insurance. The firm will probably suspend business at Boaz, their loss being so heavy.
.
The Queen & Crescent Route will, on the occasion of the Southern Baptist Convention at Nashville, May 12th to 19th, sell tickets at one fare for the round trip, selling daily, May 9th to 12th inclusive, good to return until May 23rd. This low rate will enable many to attend the convention who would not otherwise do so. The Queen & Crescent run solid vestibuled trains. Further information regarding this excursion can be had by addressing D.G. Edwards, G. P. A., Cincinnati, O.
.
The incorporators of the Mobile and West Alabama Railroad, the line from Mobile via Tuscaloosa to Florence on the Tennessee, met at Mobile last week, according to the terms of the charter, and elected John T. Milner, president; W.J. Wood, vice-president; J.H. Tindall, treasurer; and George B. McKnight, secretary. The directors, the present incorporators, formally resolved to open books of subscription, and the president was authorized to subscribe for the $50,000 worth of stock which must be subscribed to before the company may commence operations, and the president was further authorized to enter into negotiations for raising money for building the road and to enter into contracts for building the road subject to the approval of the board.

Ad - " German Syrup "
Two bottles of German syrup cured me of Hemorrhage of the Lungs when other remedies failed. I am a married man and, thirty-six years of age, and live with my wife and two little girls at Durham, Mo. I have stated this brief and plain so that all may understand. My case was a bad one, and I shall be glad to tell anyone about it who will write me. Philip L. Schenck, P. O. Box 45, April 25, 1890. No man could ask a more honorable, business-like statement.

The Banner, Vol. 1, Clanton, Ala., Thursday, May 18, 1893, No. 28

Electrocuted - Carlyle W. Harris, charged with the murder of his wife, was electrocuted at Sing Sing, N. Y., this week. The death warrant was formerly read to Harris at 8:30. He displayed indifference, and its reading did not noticeably affect him. He showed no signs of breaking down and appeared cheerful after the reading of the death warrant. Harris was brought into the execution chamber looking pale. He was entirely alone, and when the guard pointed to the chair, without even a look of curiosity at the thing which was to end his career, dropped into the seat. As he did so, he said he had a word to say if the warden would permit. The warden asked what he wished to say. Harris, in a weak voice, as though each word cost him a powerful effort, said: " I have no further observations to make. I desire to say that I am absolutely innocent. " These were his last words. The helmet containing the other electrode was placed on his head, and the wires were attached to the two electrodes. There was an instant's pause, while every man in the room held his breath, a sharp click from the lever, and the form in the chair straightened up till the straps creaked. It was just 12:40 1-2 as the current 1,760 volts passed through the body of Carlyle W. Harris.

Slew the Salvation Lass - Daniel W. Haskins walked into the Salvation Army barracks at Spokane, drew a revolver, fired two shots into the heart of Capt. Ida Bennett and then fired two more into his own brain. They fell within a few feet of each other and immediately expired. Haskins had made repeated threats on Captain Bennett's life because she refused to marry him. The affair got into the papers some time ago. Haskins declaring that Miss Bennett had played the part of a coquette with him, while the captain declared that Haskins was insane, that he had threatened her life and that she felt only a feeling of sorrow for his delusions. Captain Bennett is a native of San Bernardino, Cal., and has been connected with the Salvation Army for about two years. She is widely known over the Pacific coast, and was beloved by all members of the army with whom she came in contact. Haskins came here several years ago from Arkansas, where he had been a sheriff and deputy United States marshal. He was about 43 years of age. Since coming to Washington he has been a laborer. His wife died a few years ago, and some of his children are in the Sisters' Orphanage. It is thought Haskins was demented.

Matters of Moment Called at Random from the Reform Press - Miss Maude Brown, of Lampasas, Texas, is the owner of the old cottage where the first Alliance was organized in the United States, and proposes to have it carried to the World's fair and placed on exhibition at our National Alliance headquarters - if money can be raised to transport it. It would be a great honor to the Lone Star State - the mother of the Alliance.

Every state, county, and subordinate Alliance in the nation should cooperate with Chairman McDowell in furnishing any relic of the Wheel or Alliance showing origin and progress, and history of these two great organizations now blended into one, for exhibition at Alliance headquarters at Chicago. The oldest charters of both orders from every state should adorn the walls of the rooms; also pictures of prominent workers in each state. Chairman J.H. McDowell's address is, "Englewood, Ill, near World's Fair.

NOTICE FROM THE NATIONAL SECRETARY TREASURER - National Secretary-Treasurer Duncan has issued the following notice: " There seems from my correspondence to be some misunderstanding as to the location of the Secretary-Treasurer. Therefore I desire to give notice that the office is now located at Columbia, S.C. ...

J. HUGH McDOWELL - J. Hugh McDowell is one of the oldest Wheel and Alliancemen in the South. He entered the Agricultural Wheel in Obion county, Tennessee, in 1886, and in 1887 was sent as a delegate by the State Wheel of Tennessee to the National Alliance, which met at Shreveport, La., for the purpose of concern the question of uniting the two orders under one name. The National Alliance who received McDowell and delegates from the Kentucky and Ark State Wheels, and after initiating them as members of the Alliance, appointed a committee of three from the Alliance to confer with these Wheel brethren. J. H. McDowell was chairman of this committee, and brought in a report recommending a union of the Wheel and Alliance into one organization. The report was unanimously adopted by the National Alliance and referred back to the State Wheels and State Alliance for approval, which later resulted in the union of the two bodies. At this national meeting of the Alliance J. H. McDowell was elected vice president of the National Alliance, and returned to Tennessee, and soon organized the Tennessee State Alliance and was also state secretary, which position he held for two terms, and was then elected president. He held the office of state president until last August. He was sent as a delegate by the State Wheel to the National Wheel twice and until its union with the National Alliance. He has been a delegate to every annual National Alliance meeting since 1887, taking an active part in every movement looking to the advancement and upbuilding of the order. For five years he edited the *Toiler*, the official organ of the Tennessee State Wheel and Alliance, speaking nearly half his time organizing and educating in the Alliance work. A chairman of a committee of three, he secured from the World's fair managers two rooms in the stock pavilion of the agricultural department of the World's fair, and will be in charge of National Alliance headquarters at and during the World's fair.

The World's Fair and American Railways - The Queen & Crescent Route, widely known as the road running the " Finest Trains in the South, " is in the field to carry everybody from the South to the World's Fair at Chicago. No part of the Southern county is left uncared for by this great railway and its connections.. Any of the agents of the company named below will cheerfully give all possible information and assistance: R.H. Garrett, New Orleans, La, I. Hardy, Vicksburg, Miss. J.R. McGregor, Birmingham, Ala. E.T. Charlton, Chattanooga, Tenn. W.D. Cozart, Junction City, Ky., or D.G. Edwards, Cincinnati, O.

Death of Emin Confirmed - An indirect confirmation of the death of Emin Pasha has come form Bagamojo, German East Africa. All his manuscripts and collections have, by order of the German government, been shipped to his native town, Heisse, Silesia, where also his 12-year-old daughter is soon expected to arrive.

H.L. Loucks, Nat. Pres. of the Farmers Alliance, is a member of the Industrial League.

Mr. Manning claims that the members of the meeting at Birmingham on Thursday were bolters from the People's Party. Great Scot! Read their names: Populites, Sam Adams, Philander Morgan, Shackleford, our Alliance Exchange Manager, Whitehead of the Living Truth, Powell of Cullman, Mastin of Chilton, and several others to numerous to mention.

Mr. Manning seems surely exercised about the call for a convention of our party....

The State executive committee of the Jeffersonian democratic party, at the meeting of that body on the 11th, endorsed Mr. R. Seymour of Sumter for United States marshal of the Northern district; W.E. Richardson of Montgomery, for United States district attorney of the middle district; J.H. Gardner of Dallas, for register of the land office in the Montgomery district.... If William C. Oates is nominated for governor, and mourners are called for, it seems now that the entire time and our the feasts will be consumed by the experience of backsliders asking for.

THE MEETING OF THE STATE EXECUTIVE COMMITTEE OF THE PEOPLE'S PARTY

at Birmingham, Ala., May 11, 1893 - The meeting was called to order at noon by Mr. G.F. Gaither, chairman of the State Executive Committee of the People's Party. T.H. White, of The Banner, was requested to act as Secretary pro tem, in the absence of Mr. Manning. The question being raised as to a quorum being present. Chairman Gaither ruled that a quorum was present. The following committee was appointed to draw up a for organization: Philander Morgan, J.M. Whitehead, Wood, Shackelford, and S.M. Adams. The meeting then adjourned for dinner....

Following will be found a clipping from the Progressive People, edited by Chairman G.F. Gaither, of the State Executive Committee of the Peoples Party, adverting to that body at Birmingham on the 11th inst. Mr. Gaither evidently don't agree with the Birmingham News in its alleged in the early dissolution of the People's Party in this state...

A Splendid Showing for Chilton - To the Honorable N.D. Denson, Judge of Fifth Judicial Circuit: We the Grand Jury, empanelled by your honor for the Spring Term, 1893, of Chilton County Circuit Court, beg leave to submit the following report:...W.F. Claughton, Foreman

Jemison Gems - Mrs. R(?), the talented of the Jemison High School, and her scholars enjoyed the pleasure of a picnic at the ford of Yellow Leaf creek on Saturday. About 40 children participated. Mr. and Mrs. B.M. Gentry accompanied the party.

Lomax Linings - Miss Geneva Jones, one of Lily's fairest young ladies, is visiting friends and relatives at this place.

.
Mr. Aurelius Attaway spent Sunday with friends and relatives here.

.
Miss Mary Lowe has returned home to Jemison after a pleasant visit here.

.
Mr. G.W. Lodge and Miss Willis Marlar attended the marriage of Miss Lizzie Lodge at Clanton Ford last Thursday.

.
Married at the church at Clanton Ford, Thursday night, May 11th, Mr. Henry Gregg to Miss Lizzie Lodge. After the ceremony all were invited to the bride's home, where a bountiful supper was spread; everything went off nicely and all seemed to enjoy themselves better than they had in a long time. We wish the happy couple much success in life, and after life a happy home in heaven.

.
We are glad to see our young friend, Mr. Charlie Marlar, out again after a serious attack of measles. The children of Mr. William Lodge are confined to their bed with measles. Measles are preventing us from holding Sabbath school; we hope all will be well by next Sunday.

Pleasant Grove Pleasantries - We are glad to note that Mr. (Name Blacked Out) will wed the beautiful Miss (Name Blacked Out) on the fourth Sunday in this month at Pleasant Grove church at nine o'clock in the morning; may peace and happiness go with them.

There will be singing, conducted by Professor Durham, at our church all day on the fourth Sunday in May.

Clear Creek Clippings - Mr. W.H. Parr is wanting hands on his farm very bad; he will pay a fair price to good hands. Also W.E. Skipper is wanting a hand; work is plentiful with the farmers now.

One of H.N. Beasley's boys has left home, not liking the treatment he received there; his father is trying to prevent him from working in the settlement, but is not succeeding very much.

Jumbo Jumbles - Rev. R.M. Honeycutt preached quite an interesting sermon at Mt. Zion last Sunday, which pleased all very much.

A stray copy of the View we saw last week, and noticed a paragraph to the effect that "Hon. P. McKee, from Jumbo, a manufacturing town in Chilton county, was in Clanton last week, " and we would very much like to know what the editor means by calling Jumbo a manufacturing town.

(C?).R. Mullins went to Clanton last Sunday to see his best girl.

Professor Joseph Gore is visiting friends in the Lily neighborhood.

Mr. C.T. Bates of Shelby, came down Sunday and spent the day with friends in our neighborhood.

Kincheon Ketchings - Mr. R.N. Wilkins has moved his family from Vinehill near this place; we welcome them to our community.

Messers John Culp, J.P. Culp, James Moore and H. Herrod's families were the guests of Mr. John Moore last Sunday. Mr. Wiley Letcher and family, Miss Mattie Cole, Miss Jennie Letcher and Richard Letcher, of Plantersville, attended the picnic at Billingsley on the 13th inst.; we hope they enjoyed themselves while among their friends in Autauga.

Misses Manda Vinson and Sallie Vinson, of Energy, paid a visit to their Uncle in Autauga last week.

NOTICE, The State Of Alabama, Chilton County, Probate Court, May 6th, 1893, Special Term
In the matter of the Estate of Nancy Sims, deceased. - Notice is hereby given that Mrs. Drusilla E. Tilton, Administratix of said estate has filed in this office her application, asking for the correction of a mistake in the numbers of the land sold, viz.: e 1-2 of nw 1-4, nw 1-4 of e 1-4 and n 1-2 of sw 1-4 and w 1-2 ne 1-4 of section 11, and sw 1-4 of sw 1-4 of section 11, all in township 23 of range 12, and lying and being in Chilton county, Ala.; said lands having been properly advertised and sold. In reporting said sale the following

numbers were given, which were erroneous, viz.: e 1-2 of nw 1-4, nw 1-4 of ne 1-4, w 1-2 of ne 1-4, w 1-2 of se 1-4, s 1-2 of sw 1-4, of section 11, and sw 1-4 of sw 1-4 of section 11, all in township 23, range 13 lying and being in the county of Chilton, state of Ala. It is therefore ordered by the court that Monday, the 5th day of June, 1893, be and the same is hereby appointed the day for the hearing of said application and passing upon the same, at which time all persons interested may appear and contest if they see cause to do so. Given under my hand this May 6, 1893. R.M. Honeycutt, Judge of Probate.

The law requires teachers to attend these Institutes. If they fail to, with out a plausible excuse, their names will be sent to the Superintendent's office to be dealt with. J.W. Moore, County Supt.

Verbena Views - Tuesday night, about 8 o'clock, (?) Norrill shot Bud Allen with (?) shot, wounding him badly in the head and back. The shooting occurred near K(?) W(?) place in this neighborhood.

Prof. J.W. Moore, and wife and babies are visiting relatives near Verbena.

TOWN ITEMS - Circuit court convened on Monday at 10 a.m., Judge N.D. Denson, presiding, and was adjourned today. During this time some 50 cases have been disposed of, twenty by continuance and thirty by trial. Some cases which it was expected would be tried this term were settled outside, the most important of these being a suit involving $40,000 damages. Criminal court convenes on Monday, there being upwards of forty cases on the docket, the most serious being that of John Harvell charged with carnal knowledge of a child. The following is a list of visiting attorneys this term: Peters Lyman, Wilson, Brown, McMillan and Leeper from Columbiana; J.T. Ellison, Centerville; Ball, and Pearson, Montgomery; Bush, Ward, and Jorns from Birmingham; Bass and Holmes, Wetumpka.

The concert last Tuesday night for the benefit of the Baptist church was a decided success in every way, intellectually and financially. Considering the short time the various performers had for rehearsal the result was highly gratifying and reflects great credit upon all concerned, more especially the lady managers, Mrs. Sampey, Mrs. Rainey, and Miss Inez Collier, upon whose fair shoulders the hard work fell. Want of space precludes our going into details, but we must mention the historic ability displayed by Miss Jessie Jones and Miss Inez Collier as being of a far higher order than could be naturally expected from the little opportunity they have had studying their parts... The rendition of Miss Callie Watts was remarkably clear and good, and the dialogue of (?) Watts and Mr. Henry Honeycutt was very diverting. Mr. Os(?) Middle(?) is great at recitation and Scott Chestnutt brought down the house with his capital performance...

The Methodist church last Sabbath (?)orn presented a spectacle of happy (?)owing youth crowned with flowers (?) material and spiritual, long to be (?)membered. The programme for Children's Day was happily conceived and well carried out: all did their part so well it would be invidious to particular-(?), but the clear enunciation of Miss Pearl Parker and Master Scott Chestnutt especially attracted our attention. Mr. (?)ate Wilson did admirably announcing the programme and to Mesdames Garner, Middleton and , Chestnutt's efforts is due the completed success of the undertaking the amount realized was $8.48.

Tour week has brought many visitors (?)our city this week. Amongst the many friends of the Banner who called on us were: Tax Collector Gentry, Y. (?) of Randolph, J.J.L. Stewart of Verbena, Ed. O'Neal Pres. Evergreen Alliance, J.W. Middlebrooks Kincheon, (?) Mims Collins Chapel, Lee Hayes (?)ry, R.J. Langston Jemison, J. E. (?) Energy, J.W. Letcher Plantersville, (?).J. Hicks Shoultz, T.J. Robinson Collins Chapel, County Commissioner (?) Robinson, W.H. Shaw Clear Creek

Ad - All Run Down, A Puzzling Case - How Health Was Restored, Gained From 135 to 176 Pounds
A few years ago my health failed me and I consulted several physicians. Not one could clearly diagnose my case and their medicine failed to give relief. After much persuasion I commenced to take Hood's Sarsaparilla. Have taken several bottles and am much improved. From an all run down condition I have been restored to good health. Formerly I weighed 135 pounds, now I balance the scales at 176 pounds. Hood's Sarsaparilla has been a great benefit to me, and I have recommended it to friends, who realized good results by its use. Geo. W. Twist, Coloma, Wis.

A Great French Prison - " Mazas Prison, in which the French Panamaters are incarcerated, " said P.G. Fouse of Philadelphia, " is one of the meanest and dreariest on the face of the earth...

Befriended a Tramp - As a reward for giving a meal and helping him on his way, C.L. Kreissing, of the Home Dressed Beef Company, Pittsburgh, Penn., has been bequeathed $12,000. A year ago Kreissing, while walking Carson street, was accosted by a stranger, who told a harrowing story of hard luck. Kreissing was on his way to a restaurant, and taking the man with him, bought him a meal. The tramp refused to drink liquor and that caused Kreissing to take additional interest in him. After the meal, Mr. Kreissing gave the tramp his address, some change to help him buy a ticket to his home in Kittaning, and left him. A few days ago Mr. Kreissing received word from a firm of lawyers in Kittaning, stating that the stranger whom he had helped had died and left him $12,000 that he had come in possession of a few weeks before his death. A singular part of the story is that mother C.L. Kreissing, living at Lock Haven, has put in a claim for the money.

A WORD TO THE BOYS - Charles Dudley Warner, a famous writer, once wrote the following: " If I owned a girl who had no desire to learn anything, I would swap her for a boy...

The Banner, Vol. 1, Clanton, Ala., Thursday, May 25, 1893, No. 29

NEWS OF OUR GREAT ORDER - Matters Of Moment Which Concern The Order And Its Members
National Lecturer, Ben Terrell, is doing good work in Tennessee and Kentucky. He goes to Texas early in June, and will push the good work throughout the season. Bro. Terrell is so deeply interested in the Alliance cause that nothing can stop him.

HON. BEN TERRELL TALKS - The following are brief interesting extracts from a speech delivered at Henderson, Ky., recently by Hon. Ben Terrell, National Lecturer: He said that the good allianceman is free and will vote against the demands of the Alliance if they are contrary to his honest convictions of right, but he will study to inform himself so that his convictions will be in accord of the truth...

OFFICIAL LETTER - President Loucks has prepared a letter for publication in regard to the national organ matter. In it he says: I had hoped to avoid any controversy during my term of office, believing that the advocacy of our principles was of much greater importance than the calling of hard names. But the course being by Dr. McCune, in the *National Economists*, demands an answer. Silence might be misconstrued, I regret exceedingly that any man who has been so highly honored in our ranks could so far forget our teachings as to issue such a tissue of unfair, misleading, and untrue statements he has guilty of in the *Economist* of March 18,-25, and April 1...

Ignatius Donnelly Sued - The war between the two factions of the Minnesota Farmers' Alliance reached a culmination when Dr. Everett W. Fisher of the Great West brought suit against Ignatius Donnelly for $25,000 for defamation of character, and against George L. Stoughton, editor of the Representative, for criminal libel. In the issue of the Representative published recently, Senator Donnelly said, over his own signature: " I plainly, distinctly, and unequivocally charge Everett W. Fisher, while editing a newspaper called the Great West, with having, at different times, and especially during the political campaigns of 1890 and 1892, while pretending to support the Republican ticket, taking sums of money, amounting to thousands of dollars, from officers of the Republican State Central Committee. I make this charge deliberately, and invite Everett W. Fisher to begin proceedings against me for libel ".

We have before us the initial number of the Alabama Pioneer, published at Lowndesboro, by that able single tax advocate, S.M. Dinkins, in which he asks the question: " Will the populist party in Alabama permit itself to be swallowed be Jeffersonians? " No the People's party is - as its name implies - the party of the people, who would not let it, even if it's leaders so desire, be swallowed by a faction.

Oak Grove Openings - We had a very good singing last Sunday conducted by Bro. N.A. Dobbs; the old brother sings delightfully and we hope to have him with us again soon.

Mr. R.T. Atkinson paid his girl near Wayside a visit last Sunday.

Miss Fannie Deason of Deatsville, is visiting relatives and friends here.

Mr. George Askings and wife paid a pleasant visit to the family of Mr. James Chambers last week.

Energy Events - Mr. J.W.G. Kicker and wife, of Coopers, visited relatives near this place Sunday. Hope to see them again soon.

Mr. James A. Hathcock and the charming Miss Jennie Tarver (better known as Davis) jumped the broom and tied the everlasting knot last Thursday evening; we wish them a long and happy life and much success.

Mr. Alpheus Dennis, our young doctor, visited his best girl at this Sunday; we agree with you, Doctor, she is a sweet girl.

Mr. Newton Vinson, one of our handsome young men, went with his best girl to church at Maple Springs last Sunday. Look out, boys, or you will get meet sure.

Mr. Newton Burkhalter has been seeing some bears near Verbena, but is not very frightened; we are expecting he will catch one for his pet

Mrs. Clinton Driver, of Bozeman, visited her father, Mr. G.B. Gray, last Saturday, but had to return home on account of her husband being taken very sick.

Clear Creek Clippings - Last Saturday and Sunday we had preaching at Providence church by Rev. R.M. Honeycutt. Saturday after preaching we had communion and foot washing. A large congregation attended each day; we had a good time, I think the lord was with us.

Mr. H.N. Beasley's boy has hired out to Mr. W.H. Parr.

CIRCUIT COURT CRIMINAL CASES - Circuit Court reconvened on Monday for the trial of criminal cases with the following results: Cases continued. James Davenport, charged with violating revenue law; William Bean, forgery; Henry Hawkins et als, malicious mischief to stock, Willie Martin assault and battery with a weapon; William Jones, grand larceny and resisting an officer; George Mims, selling liquor without license; John Harvell, carnal knowledge of a child, continued on account of absence of witness in Perry County. Not processed, George Buckner, false pretense. Defaulting witnesses, Thos. Caton, Sanford Smitherman, Jack Langston. Ed. Lavinsky and Will Deramus for refusal to work public roads, the fact was established that Coopers was Incorporated for 200 yards around a certain oak tree (facetiously termed Cooper's Capital by Solicitor Brewer) within which limit the defendants resided, they were discharged; Bill Shelton charged with burglary, was discharged upon his own recognizances; T.F. Jackson, bastardly, this case was settled between the parties; Aaron Welsh, charge carrying concealed weapons failing to appear forfeiture taken against his bondsmen; Dock Wilkins, for sheep stealing, defendant appeared at Court until a few minutes before his case was called when he skipped, forfeiture was taken against his bondsmen. Convictions, Wm. Headley, carrying concealed weapons, $50 fin; Burrel Bailey, selling whiskey to minors and without license; $50 fine in each case; Chas. Lee, hog stealing, 13 months in penitentiary; Jeff Narrell, assault with intent to murder, four years in penitentiary (the crime, shooting Bud Allen, was committed on the night of the 16th and on the night of the 23rd about the same he was convicted. Swift justice.) Sam McCann, assault to murder, $10 fine and six months imprisonment. Wm. Jones, burglary 5 years in penitentiary. Court adjourned 11:30p.m. Tuesday.

Plantersville Pickings - Miss Susie Harris and Miss Polly Latham are visiting friends near Alpine.

Preaching by Rev. Adkin Perry at Plantersville on the first and third Sunday in the month, and by Rev. L.B. Pounds on the second Sunday; the have preaching here every Sunday.

A new school-house, known as the Bluff Spring academy, has been built by the people near here; they have a very nice young lady, Miss Mollie Reynolds, daughter of Mr. John Reynolds, for a teacher.

Collins Chapel Chips - Thursday last as Messrs. W.A. Mims and B.M. Martin were returning home from Clanton, where they had been attending Court, when nearing the Marlar place a turkey running out in the road scared the mule they were driving, causing it to run away and over-turning the buggy. The occupants were thrown out; Mr. Mims escaping with a severe bruising, but Mr. Martin was so unfortunate as to have both arms broken just above the wrists. Dr. S.J. Johnson,Jr. was called and set the broken bones and the patient is progressing favorably. Both gentleman would much enjoy making a meal off the turkey, the cause of the accident, that is all the harm they wish it.

Valley Creek Visitings - Brother L.B. Pounds delivered an excellent sermon here Sunday morning.

Mr. Harry Mead and his young bride made a visit to the latter father on the 13th inst.

Mr. Morgan Campbell and wife, from Dallas, visited Mrs. Campbell's father here last Saturday and Sunday.

Mr. R.L. Mitchell and wife, accompanied by their daughter Mrs. Ada Gay, visited relatives and friends at Six-mile last week. Another daughter, Mrs. Jennie Hayes, returned with them to spend a week here.

Mr. W. did not get as good a start of bees as he thought he would, for Mr. Willie Marshall made a raid and took them from him. Hurrah for Willie!

Mr. Newt Latham, of Bibb county, visited his best girl here on Sunday.

Mr. Tobe Terry, of Perry, visited his best girl last Sunday.

Mr. Shelby Barnes paid a pleasant call to his best girl Sunday, I think he wont have to make any more calls judging from appearances.

Miss Alice Mitchell and Miss Nettie Smith, of Bibb County, visited relatives and friends at Valley Creek Saturday and Sunday we were all glad to meet them.

Wessington Whisperings - Mr. O. Killegraw, who lives near this place, happened in have bad luck; he lost his mare, we all sympathize with him on that account.

I am sorry to say that J.D. Hardy has shut down for more than three weeks, but we hope he will start up again soon.

The Wessington saw mill is running now, but the foreman quit the other day and we think the mill will soon stop.

Calera Cuttings - On the 15th inst. Mrs. Minnie Gist became the mother of twins, but ere life began the little pair were separated. One rose to heavenly bliss, while the other was left to battle with life's rough mixture of fates

TOWN ITEMS - Mr. Dave Cooley and sister, Miss Sallie Cooley, of Lily, paid a visit to relatives in Clanton last Sunday.

Mr. Eugene Evans store is being beautified with a new shed in front.

Mr. O.K. Mullins is the happy father of a little girl baby. Mrs. Mullins' mother is attending on her daughter and granddaughter.

Lawyer Ally Smith, of Bozeman, has, we understand, bought the Marsh place, and will shortly move his family here.

Dr. Bivings and family have gone to Talladega Springs for the benefit of the Doctor's health.

Mr. John Sexton and child, of Dixie, are visiting relatives here.

We are sorry to learn Brother Knight's four children are down with measles.

Mr. Tom Smith and Mr. John Wil(?) of Mountain Creek, paid a visit (?) Clanton on Tuesday.

Mrs. Nolen is on a visit to Goodwater and Squire Nolen joins her (?) week.

Mr. Broadhead, of Blocton, is in town on business.

Mr. Henry Randall, of Marion, was in town last week.

STRAYED - From the possession of Mr. J.W. Collins, living in the Collins Chapel settlement near Strasburg one light camel glass-eyed filly aged about 20 months has three white feet and white on side. Any information that will lead to its recovery will be thankfully received by Bro. Collins.

FINAL PROOF NOTICE, NOTICE NO, 13,650. LAND OFFICE AT MONTGOMERY, ALA., May 24, 1893Notice is hereby given that the following named settler has filed notice of his intention to make final proof in support of his claim, and that said proof will be made before The Clerk of the Circuit Court at Clanton, Ala., on July 15th, 1893; viz.: Benjamin Brown, Homestead Entry No.18,168, for the w 1/2 of n w 3/4 of Section 20, Tp.21, n of Range 14 e. He names the following witnesses to prove his continuous residence upon who and cultivation of said land, viz.: Madison Popwell, Charles Jackson, Daniel Martin, all of Kincheon, Ala., and Joseph Williams, of Clanton, Ala.,J.H. Bingham, Registrar

Ad - FREE COURSE BY MAIL WITH THE LEAVENWORTH BUSINESS COLLEGE

To Advertise Our College we will give a thorough course of instruction and Double and Single entry bookkeeping and commercial arithmetic by mail free of charge to a limited number of persons... Professor F.J. Vanderberg, President

Chronicled In A Woman's Album - Pierre Loti's likes and dislikes were chronicled by him lately in a lady's album...

QUIET LIFE OF AN EX-EMPRESS - The widowhood of ex-Empress Frederick of Germany is in sem(?)tirement and in the performance of acts of charity...

A PROPOSITION FOR REUNION - Submitted To The Organized State Democratic Executive Committee
Hon. A.G. Smith, Chairman of the Organized Democratic State Executive Committee of Alabama: By a resolution of the state executive committee of the Jeffersonian democracy of Alabama, I have been instructed to present to the state executive committee of that organized democratic party of Alabama the following proposition, to-wit:... Very Respectfully, A.T. Goodwin, Chairman of the State Executive Committee of the Jeffersonian Democratic Party of Alabama.

The Banner, Vol. 1, Clanton, Ala., Thursday, June 1, 1893, No. 30

GENERAL NEWS - Current Events of General Interest Epitomized And Grouped At Des Moines, Ia., Judge Woodson, in the Federal Court, has sentenced Prof. R.A. Vanngelback for using the mails to sell fraudulent diplomas. The penalty imposed was one year in jail an a fine of $400.

Robert T. Lincoln, ex-minister to Great Britain, was at the State Department Friday. He had a long call with Secretary Gresham, and they afterward went to the White House, where Mr. Lincoln had an interview with the President.

Surgeon-General Wyman, of the marine hospital service, received a cable dispatch from Surgeon Irwin, who is stationed at Marseilles, announcing that cholera has appeared at Nimes and Cetto, in Southern France. These places are situated within 75 or 100 miles of Marseilles. Cette is directly on the coast.

Secretary Gresham has received official notice of the of the Italian government to raise its diplomatic representative at Washington to the grade of an embassy. It is presumed that the present Italian minister, Baron Fava, will succeed to the new office. Our minister to Italy will now be an ambassador.

At Duluth, Minn., the Minnesota Blast Furnace Company, composed of Chicago people, with Charles Himrod at the helm, assigned Thursday to W.H. Stowell, president of the Duluth Iron and Steel Company, from whom the blast furnace company leased the furnace plant at Duluth nine days ago.

At Pittsburgh, Pa., Col. W.D. Moore, representing the plaintiffs in a suit of a number of Johnstown people against the South Fork Hunting and Fishing Club for damages to persons and property by the Johnstown flood will ask for a mandamns on Judge Rayburn to compel him to set the time for the trial of the case.

Secretary Herbert has given his approval to the findings and recommendations made by Capt. Matthews, as a result of his inspection of the Mare Island, Cal., navy yard. The secretary is gratified at the nature of the report, as it enables him to carry out a plan which he has cherished as in the line of economy, and as calculated to build the important naval interests on the Pacific coast.

President Cleveland has approved the deeds of the Choctaw and Chickasaw nations for their right and title to the leased lands, in the Indian Territory, formally occupied by the Cheyennes and Arapahoe Indians, but now constituting a portion of Oklahoma Territory, for which the sum of $2,991,450 was appropriated by the Indian appropriation act March 3, 1891.

The president has commuted to imprisonment for life the death sentence of Edward Pickens, a full-blooded Chicasaw Indian, who was convicted of murder in the district of Kansas. The ground for the commutation his that Pickens is of a very low order of intelligence, whose surrounding have not been favorable to the development of moral sense, and there was some provocation.

At Pittsburgh the outlook for an early settlement of the miners' strike is gloomy. The operators have made no overtures for a conference with the men, and have not to the latter's request for a conference. In less than 30 days President Walters, of the miners' union, thinks the mining of commercial coal in Kansas, Missouri, Indian Territory and Colorado will be stopped.

The National Prison Congress meets this year in Chicago, and the opening session will be in the new Art building Wednesday evening, June 7, and will be devoted to memorial addresses in honor of its late president, Gen. Rutherford B. Hayes. Gen. Brickerhoff, who succeeds Gen. Hayes, as the presiding officer of the association for the current year, in place of the annual address, will deliver a eulogy upon Gen. Hayes.

Chauncey M. Depew, president of the New York Central and Hudson River Railroad Company, says: " The idea that the business of the railroads in 1893 is going to be disappointing is a mistaken one. The outlook for the roads, in my opinion, is better than for years. Trunk line rates have not been so well maintained in ten years, and the increase in gross earnings, therefore, means a greater increase in net earnings.

At San Antonio, Texas, in the Federal Court, Wednesday, fifteen of the Mexican revolutionists were sentenced to terms of imprisonment for violation of the United States neutrality laws. Col. Prudencio Gonzales was given two years and nine months, Peblo Gomez two years and four months and Estevan Bonivides and Santos Candena ten months in the state penitentiary at Anomosa, Ia. The reminder were given jail sentences ranging from two mons. to one year.

F.C. Pearson, of the West End Railway system, of Halifax, N.S., is reported to be the head of a syndicate of Boston capitalists who have purchased the blast furnaces and iron mines at Ferrona and the forge and steel works at New Glasgow. They propose to revolutionize the iron industry of Nova Scotia, and to place themselves in a position to supply the New England markets with pig iron in case the United States duty is removed or lowered.

At Wilkesbarre, Pa., last February, private banker E.V. Rockafellow closed the doors of his bank on 840 depositors. The report of the assignee showed that the depositors would get 4 per cent. Heretofore it was impossible to get warrants of arrest on the ex-banker, as he remained in bed, his physician testifying that he was unable to leave his bed. Thursday evening Constable Bauer, disguised as a delivery man for a grocery store, got access to Rockafellow's kitchen. He made his way upstairs and served nine warrants on the banker charging him with embezzlement.

OFFICIAL, To the officers and members of the various State Farmers Alliances:
Brethren - By the unanimous action of the executive committee of the National Farmers' Alliance and Industrial Union, Brother D.P. Duncan has been chosen as secretary-treasurer of the National Farmers' Alliance Industrial Union, and all business pertaining to that office, including remittances, should be addressed to him, at Columbia, S. C....Fraternally yours, H.C. Demming, Secretary Executive committee, Washington, D. C.

Alexander Stephens - The monument to Alexander Stephens, vice-president of the Confederacy, congressman and governor of Georgia, was unveiled at Crawfordville last Thursday afternoon. The imposing ceremony was witnessed by hundreds gathered to do honor to the memory of the statesman and public benefactor. The exercises at Crawfordville were begun with prayer by Rev. Mr. Barnett of Atlanta. Hon. Geo. T. Barnes, president of the monument association, followed with a speech introducing the orator of the day, ex-Senator Thomas M. Norwood.

Foster's Finances - J.B. Gormley, assignee of Ex-Secretary Foster, states that further investigation shows the affairs to be in even worse than at first thought. The liabilities will reach $800,000 and possibly $1,000,000, with assets much less.

Hon. S.M. Adams will be with us on the 28th, he has accepted an invitation to address the Populites of Chilton county on that day. All are invited to come out and hear this true and tried champion of reform.

We publish a request from the State Master Workman W.S. Barefield, of the order of Knights of Labor, for all Local Assemblies to make preparations for the meeting of the State Assembly in July.

If there was any faint hope in minds of Alabamians that Grover Cleveland was the friend of the masses it must have been dissipated by the appointment of Wallace Screws as postmaster at Montgomery. Mr. Cleveland was respectfully petitioned by organized labor not to appoint Mr. Screws, without effect. As a political partisan Mr. Screws, as editor of the Advertiser, has been so offensive to the people of this state, his own political colleagues requested him to forbear in the last campaign.

J.C. Manning is making himself ridiculous. He contended at Birmingham that the committee had no power to supply vacancies in its own membership, because it had no quorum. To satisfy him, the convention was called to accomplish this work. Now he says the convention is called without authority. It follows that there is no power anywhere according to Manning to do anything. Members of the committee having resigned and declined till it is reduced below a quorum, the party is eternally dead and can not be revived. Manning's parliamentary law may be good but we don't believe it. If the will send properly accredited delegates to Calera, we think the committee will be filled up, and some other useful work done, preparatory to this great battle of next year. Manning is a very smart young man - but not smart enough to kill the party with a wag of his limber elastic tongue. We need more good hard sense and less flippant, foolishness - wiser heads and stiller tongues.

Chairman H.E. Taubeneck, of the People's Party National Executive Committee, in a letter to the National Watchman, says " It is the duty of every patriot to organize for the coming conflict. The People's Party local committees in every county and school district ought to make arrangements to hold picnics on July Fourth, not only to celebrate the anniversary of the adoption of the Declaration of Independence one hundred and seventeen years ago, the greatest calamity howling document ever issued by man, but also in commemoration of the Omaha Convention of last year. "...

Strasburg Straws - The measles are raging in this community. We are sorry to note the death of Brother Richard Price's daughter last week, and also that of old Brother James Collins.

I want to say I am always glad to get my Banner: I love to hear from the brothers, especially Bro. Providence. I think he hit the key-note; we want a Tom Watson in Alabama without so much Jeffersonianism. The time has come to get off the fence so that we may know where they are at. I am in hopes that we have got plenty of Tom Watson's in Alabama.

Swift Creek Swishes - We are sorry to note that Mr. Hy. Sewell's dwelling-house, smokehouse and the contents therein, were destroyed by fire a few nights ago and one of his mules was badly burned.

Mrs. Alice Burnett is on a visit to her father, J.M. Askins, to see her little sister who is very sick.

Prof. David Moore was to lecture last Saturday at Culp's schoolhouse on the duties of a school teacher; we hope he had a good and appreciative audience.

Pleasant Growth Pleasantries - Captain Farmer and General Green have been having quite a combat for the past two or three weeks, but as the weather has been favorable the former is about to come out victorious. The crops are looking nicely and bid fair for a rich harvest.

Mr. J.W. Thomas has the nicest melon patch in the settlement; from all appearances he is growing them for himself and best girl.

Mr. Martin Franklin will recommence work in his gold mine in July.

Mr. W.R. Maddox is death on cats; this is verified by his killing all that come about his premises.

Little Lizzie Hubbard, daughter of Mr. T.J. Hubbard, who has been quite ill for several days, is convalescent.

We are sorry to say that Aunt Susan Hubbard who has been confined to her room, and the greater part of the time to her bed, for the last eight years, is no better.

Mr. Thomas Franklin has been very feeble for some time past, but we are glad to say he is now improving.

Rev. W.G. Riggins preached one of his plain and instructive sermons to a large and attentive congregation at this place last Sunday. Prof. Durham, the well-known musician, was on hand, and led in singing, to the great delight of all present.

Wessington Whisperings - Last Sunday we had at Oak Grove at Rev. W.B. Crumpton; we have a fine time and I think God blessed us. Rev. W.B. Crumpton will preach at Oxmoor on the first Sunday in June.

Mr. H.N. Beasley's son is home at his father's house, sick with typhoid fever and is very low.

Miss Jennie Parker is visiting her brother at this place, and we hope she will enjoy herself while with us.

Miss Sally Hooper and Mr. Broghton were married last Thursday night; we hope they will be happy and live according to the laws of God.

Mr. Tom Fletcher and Miss Prissy Webb are to be married on Sunday at Jemison, at 10 a.m..

Ruddick Ripple - Mr. Henry Sewal lost his house by fire a few nights back.

Mr. S.B. Batcliff, who was crippled by a falling derrick some time ago, is getting well fast.

Mr. W.R. White, who has been almost hopelessly sick for a year, is recovering, and we hope will soon be able to visit her many friends.

Union Unities - Prof. Jennings, who recently finished a ten months school session, has decided to teach again for the same number of months, and already has the names of 72 scholars enrolled. Union stands high educationally.

KNIGHTS OF LABOR - ATTENTION BRETHREN! Please make preparations for our July State meeting; we want every local in the state represented...W.S. Barefield, S.M.W.

TOWN ITEMS - A.J. Gullahorn & Bro. want five or six good lumber teams at Verbena, Ala..

We are glad to welcome the returned of Mr. W.H. Merritt's charming family to Clanton.

Captain Middleton's genial presence will be missed from the court (?), he having retired from the legal field.

Mr. Joe Chandler has return to (?) town after several months absence.

Three prisoners, convicted at last circuit court, were carried to Pratt mines by Mr. Connell, agent of the Tenn. Coal Co., last Friday; the remaining prisoners, destined for Coalburg, are still awaiting transportation.

Mrs. P. Moore has gone on a visit to Plantersville to attend on her estimable son-in-law, Mr. Frank Harris, who, we are sorry to say, is very sick.

Next Tuesday, at 4 p.m., at the Methodist church, our society folks will have the pleasure of attending the wedding of one of the most charming of their number, Miss Leah Watts, to Mr. W.C. Satterwhite of Virginia. Miss Watts will be greatly missed by her many friends, and The Banner unites with them in wishing in advance a life of happiness and felicity to the young pair.

There was no service at the Episcopal church, Tuesday, and it is possible the Rev. J.F. Smith's engagements will preclude any further sermons until July.

Mr. C.H. Abbot has returned from Saginaw where he has been erecting a mill at the Pratt Saw Mill Co.

Tax collector B.M. Gentry paid us a pleasant visit this week.

Mr. J.E. Wilson and Miss Annie Wal(?) marry at Verbena this evening.

Died on the night of the 25th May, (?) Collins, aged 75. His death was quite sudden, occurring about 11 (?) after he had been working in the fields all day. He was a member of the Methodist church and also of the Alliance. He was buried at Cedar Grove, May 27th, Rev. F. A. (?) officiating. He leaves a wife, seven children, 100 grandchildren and 2(8?) great children to mourn his loss.

False Teeth Not Chattels - Judge Kelly, of St. Paul, has decided that a dentist does not have a lien on a set of false teeth after they have been attached to the mouth and the dentist has parted with the possession thereof. This decision is reached in the case of Charles A. Vauduce against William J. Woolsey. It had been claimed that the Sheriff could take possession of the teeth and disposed of them at public sale, but judge Kelly decides that so long as the teeth are in the defendant's mouth they are part of his body an cannot be seized as " chattels. " The case has been before the courts for some time and has attracted much attention. - (New York Advertiser)

Ad - Profoundly Grateful For Help Derived From Hood's Sarsaparilla, I am profoundly impressed with the medical virtues of Hood's Sarsaparilla. I was threatened with cancer, and disagreeable eruptions on my back and other places. The cancer was appearing on my lip. Providentially I obtained a bottle of Hood's Sarsaparilla, and by the time it was gone, the symptoms had nearly all disappeared. I have used four bottles, and I believe it has saved me from premature death. I am now almost 73 years of age and I work like a tiger. And I know that Hood's Sarsaparilla has had much to do with my tiger strength. Rev. O.H. Power, 2924 Hanover Street, Chicago, Ill.

The Banner, Vol. 1, Clanton, Ala., Thursday, June 8, 1893, No. 31

GENERAL NEWS - Current Events Of General Interest Epitomized And Grouped
Edwin Booth is said to be dying at his home in New York.

Dr. Briggs, after a long-winded trial, as been suspended.

Jim Hall knocked out Slavin in seven rounds at London. The inducement was glory and better $25,000 time.

The Prohibition State convention of Iowa has nominated Capt. K.W. Brown for governor and a full state ticket.

T.M. Scruggs has been appointed Judge to fill out the unexpired term of DuBose, who has just been suspended from the bench at Memphis.

President Cleveland has returned to Washington from his fishing trip to Hog Island, and it is reported will at once take the cases of the Internal Revenue collectors.

Col. Logan H. Roots, an Arkansas millionaire, who died a few days sinse, left $700,000 to be used for a hospital and park for Little Rock. A portion of the hospital is to be set side for old and destitute masons.

At the national session of the Federation of American Mechanics recently held in Indianapolis, John J. Lamb, of Scranton, Pa., failed of re-election and absconded, it is alleged, with all the funds in his possession, commenting to about $5,000. Lamb has returned to Scranton and has been arrested.

Dr. T.P. Bell, well known to all Southern Baptists and who has been for a number of years connected with the Boards of the Southern Baptist Convention, has been tendered the position of Corresponding Secretary of the Foreign Mission Board. Dr. Bell has not given his answer to the invitation.

All the charges of murder, etc., against N.C. Frick and others, of the Carnegie Steel Company officials, as well as the Pinkerton detectives, have been dropped in court. In turn, all of the strikers who had been arrested and as yet untried have been released their own recognizances. This virtually ends all homestead cases in connection with the big strike of last year.

A.S. Waters, president of the Kansas Miners' Union, is at Osage, where he will organize a strike among the coal miners of that district to act in sympathy with the strike in Southeastern Kansas. When this district has joined the fight there will be 10,000 miners out in Kansas, 9,000 men in the six camps in Missouri and 9,500 in the Indian Territory. In the meantime, the president of the Colorado Union, which has charge of the Atchison, Topeka & Santa Fe mines, at Trinidad and Rockville, will have convinced the 4,000 men now working under his jurisdiction. By July 1, President Waters says all the work will have been accomplished. In round there will be 30,000 miners out west of the Mississippi river. There are 10,000 members in the union, and Waters expects the remaining 70,000 to assist the strikers in carrying on the fight. He makes the boast that the union has so effectually fortified itself that it can hold out for two years.

A Fortune for $2 - Lee Stanton, an English painter, bought a leather valise at the Grand Trunk Railroad sale of unclaimed baggage for $2. On opening it he found 107 shares in the Western Gas Improvement Company, of Chicago, fully paid of and worth $107,000. The valise was the property of Louis Halberstadt, who died at Brockville,Ont., in October, 1891, of Alcoholism. He went to Brockville from Napierville, Ill. A large sum of money and some jewelry which he was known to have just prior to his death, were missing, and it was generally believed at the time that he had been robbed.

Sentiment in Hawaii - The secretary of state has received several reports from Minister Blount in regard to the sentiment of the people in Hawaii on the subject of annexation. The reports will be made in few season, as the desires to sound the sentiment of his own country before he makes recommendations to Congress regarding the future relations of the United States with Hawaii.

Judge DuBose Impeached - Judge J.J. DuBose, of Memphis, of whom so much as been said and written in the past few weeks, has been impeached by the Tennessee Legislature and removed from office and forever disqualified from holding any public trust again.

THE FINANCIAL PROBLEM - In an extended interview in regard to the solution of the financial question, Senator Stanford, of California, gives his opinion on the subject and offers some good suggestions...

JOB LOT OF WAIFS - The late Samuel E. Adams, of Richmond, Ind., was fond of telling of a remarkable coincidence which happened several years ago. During a severe thunder storm a canary bird flew into the house. Within a few minutes a shivering and badly frightened spaniel was found begging for admission. The dog was let in. Less than an hour afterward a child was heard crying on the outside and the door opened to admit the little tot scarcely 2 years old. The child, dog and canary were never claimed. Mr. Adams found a comfortable home for the little one, while he continued to care for the dog and bird.

We disliked personal controversies believing them to be of little benefit to any cause. Sometimes, however, they become necessary on that very account. Mr. Manning, writing to the Living Truth, says: " The Calera racket is a scheme to throw dissension in the ranks of our party. "...

We publish this week the call for a mass meeting of the People's Party of this county to take place Wednesday, June 28th, for the purpose of selecting delegates to the State Convention which will convene at Calera, July 4th. Hon. S.M. Adams will be present and make an address...

Our correspondent at Washington amongst other items of news in his communication last week, stated that Mr. Broughton had married on the Thursday night previous. We are in receipt of a card from Mr. Broughton informing us that this statement was incorrect. We desire to apologize to Mr. Broughton and the lady for making such publication, and take this opportunity to request of our correspondents not to forward us news that they can not personally vouch for.

NOTICE - MASS MEETING OF PEOPLE'S PARTY OF CHILTON COUNTY, The members of the People's Party in Chilton county are hereby requested to meet in mass at Clanton at 12 a.m., on Wednesday, June 28, 1893, for the propose of selecting delegate to the State Convention of the party called to meet at Calera, July 4, 1893, and to transact such other business may be brought before the meeting., O.M. Mastin, Chm. P.P. of Chilton Co.

Oak Grove Openings - Mr. Henry Sewell happened to the bad luck of having his dwelling-house, kitchen, and everything else except two bedsteads and a sewing machine burned on the ninth of the 22d ult.

A bright little daughter about two years old of Mr. J.M. Askins died on the 1st inst., much lamented by its relatives and friends; we extend our heartfelt sympathy to the bereaved ones, and hope they will meet the little one in that world where all is peace and love.

The little babe of Mr. I.M. Deason is very sick, but we hope it will recover soon.

Mr. W.L. Gray visited relatives and friends at Energy last week.

Miss Etta Chambers, one of our most charming girls, who has been visiting her sister, has returned home, much to the delight of her many friends - especially the boys.

Dixie Dots - Parson Perry was to have preached at Valley Creek on the second Sunday in June, but failed to attend.

Mr. Ross Barnes is very fond of going over to Bibb county; there is a very great attraction there.

Mr. Caruth, of Six-mile, paid a pleasant visit here, and says he is going to attend school at Valley Creek academy; we welcome him to our community.

On June 4th,, H.W. Cole received the prettiest bouquet you ever saw; he appreciated it very much because such a pretty girl gave it to him.

We are glad to know that Mr. Frank Harris is better and hope he will soon be able to work.

West Chilton - Mr. John Haley will begin teaching school at Chestnut Hill church.

Mr. P.W. Barnes happened to some more bad luck the other day; his buggy horse was kicked on the head by a mule and was instantly killed.

Mrs. O'Neal is up and about again after an eight weeks sickness with slow fever.

Dr. Little, of Stanton, is getting an extensive practice, he is called for from far and near. Rev. Mr. Longcryer will soon take charge of the school at Valley Creek.

Harriet Landslide, a colored woman, while fishing, a few days ago, got a large fish-hook fast in her hand, and was obliged to get Mr. W.M. Price to cut it out.

Northwest Chilton - Mr. I.L. Walldrop visited Montgomery the other day.

Mr. Sutton Smitherman, of Bibb, is expected to preach at Macedonia next Sunday, the pastor, Mr. Langston, expecting to preach in Mississippi at that time.

Mrs. F.C. Crumpton is sick.

There is a new arrival at Mr. Zeke Nix's - a son.

Prof. J.E. Jones, of Bibb, is teaching at Pleasant Grove.

Mrs. Samanthra Walldrop visited Clanton the 29th ult.

Lomax Linings - Mr. J.H. Foshee spent Sunday with friends and relatives at this place.

Miss Willis Marlar will open her school here next Monday.

Mrs. Sarah Lodge, of Clanton Ford, spent several days with her daughter, Mrs. A. Smith.

Dr. A.J. Marlar, who was at home on the sick list, is able to be at his post again at Clanton Ford.

Mr. Aureilus Attaway paid a pleasant visit to relatives and friends here last week.

Mrs. A. Smith and children are confined to their beds with measles.

Mr. John Wilkins, of Shelby, spent a couple of days last week with Dr. A.J. Marlar's family.

Rev. Brother Gibson delivered an interesting sermon the last Sunday in May.

Rev. — Henley will preach at this the second Sunday in June at 3 o'clock.

Mr. D.B. Lowe made a visit to Clanton Ford last Sunday week.

Mrs. Mattie Bruce and children spent a day last week with Mrs. Mary Marlar.

We are glad to see Mr. Wm. Lodge's children up again.

Mulberry Musings - Mr. J.T. Farley paid a visit to his son near Mulberry church last Saturday.

Mr. W.E. Farley has a stalk of mustard in his garden three feet across.

Dr. Dennis paid a visit to a fair lady the other Sunday; we think it will be a match.

Jumbo Jumbles - Mr. Eddie Giles, of Clanton, has been visiting his church at Cane Creek, and had a large turnout and a good meeting.

There came a woman to our neighborhood a few days ago, claiming to be an Indian, hunting for gold which was buried by the Indians many years ago. Mr. John Littleton and Mr.

Henley Clecker and many others are helping to hunt for the gold, but have not found any yet.

Verbena Views - Miss Lizzie Gardner, one of Evergreen's most heroic young ladies, killed a traveling mad dog with a stick.

Montgomery, Verbena, Energy, Kincheon, Clanton, Swift Creek, Oak Grove, Wayback and Grassy Hill were well represented at Coopers last Sunday.

Mr. John Estes, of Texas, arrived at Verbena, his former home, with three little children.

Miss Sadie Bentley, of Rockford, is visiting friends there.

Mr. W.G. Gibson, of Washington, D.C., has been on a visit to his brother, Major J.C. Gibson.

Miss Mary Carr Gibson is visiting relatives in Georgia.

FROM OUR READERS - Wessington, Ala., June 5, 1893, Editor Banner - Will you be so kind as to allow me space in your paper to contradict the announcement of the marriage of myself and Miss Hooker. I most emphatically say that there is no foundation whatever for the erroneous statement. By publishing the same, your kindness will be appreciated. Yours very respectfully, Madison Broughton

NOTICE - To trustee stockholders of the Primary Alliance of Chilton county owning stock in the state exchange, Please meet me at the Court House at Clanton on the 24th day of June, for the purpose of attending to the business of the trustees. Be sure to come, as there is business of importance. Jno. R. Vinson, Chairman

Programme of Sabbath School Convention
To be held with New Salem church, on Saturday before the fifth Sunday in July, 1893.
SATURDAY
10 a.m. Devotional Exercise conducted by L.B. Pounds; alternate, A.L. Foshee. Address of welcome by W.A. Wood
SUBJECTS
1. " Have we any scriptural authority for carrying our children to the Sabbath School? " Opened by J.P. Gentry, followed by J. Bice, W.G. Riggins and others.
2. " How can the Sabbath School be made a safeguard against the spiritual dangers that surround them? " Opened by G.W. Freeman, Alex Glass, D.H. Hudgeons and others.
3. " What will be the final results of a well-conducted Sabbath School? " Opened by R.M. Honeycutt, J.A. Moore, W.D. Martin and others.
SUNDAY
9 A.M. Sabbath School mass meeting conducted by W.A. Mimms; alternate J.E. Jones. Preaching at 11 o'clock by Sutton Smitherman; alternate, D.A. Seal.

TOWN ITEMS - $200 REWARD. The above amout is in the Commercial Bank of Selma, Ala., and offered as a reward to the person arresting and delivering Alex Shelton to the Sheriff of Chilton county, Ala.. Alex Shelton is a dark mulatto about 5 feet 10 inches high, weighs 180 to 200, slightly stooped, very broad chested, rather drawling speech, small dark brown eyes, small mustache, about 35 years of age. Wanted for the killing of James

Harris, near Plantersville, April 3rd, 1893. The above reward will hold good until June 1, 1894.

Mr. E.C. Worns and family, of Birmingham, are spending their summer vacation in our town.

At the Congregational church last Sunday morning and evening the Rev. R.M. Honeycutt filled the place of J.L. Busby who was unable to come. This is the more interesting as being the first occasion on which our reverend brother has occupied the pulpit in Clanton.

Dan Harris, charged with selling liquor without a license, was arrested and jailed by Sheriff Moore on Wednesday.

Mr. Frank Harris, son-in-law of our esteemed Sheriff, is recovering from a severe attack of illness.

The Clanton post office cannot be said to be, from an architectural point of view, a thing of beauty, but our highly efficient postmaster, Mr. B.H. Chestnut, makes amends for the ugly external appearance by the cleanliness and neatness on the inside, and the way in which he handles the mail gives perfect satisfaction to all.

Mrs. W.B. Nolen has returned home from a visit to relatives at Goodwater.

Miss Amelia Dawson has gone on a visit to her sister at Oxford.

Mr. Abram Smith, of Coosa, paid a visit to Uncle Paddy last week.

County Court convened Monday, R.M. Honeycutt presiding. The following cases were disposed of, J.M. Abrams, George Chambers, failure to work on public road, each were fined one dollar and costs, John Chambers, Martin Hester and George Patrick, the same charge, were found not guilty.

Prof. W.C. Robinson paid us a pleasant call this morning and certainly looks well. The season of vacation has been of great benefit to our esteemed friend. We were glad to learn from him that his father, Bro. Moses Robinson, President of the County Alliance, has recovered from his recent attack of sickness.

Genial Supt. Moore, paid the Banner a pleasant visit this week.

Ad - Misery Turned To Comfort ",Kidney Troubles, Sleeplessness, Distress - ALL CURED, I can truly say that Hood's Sarsaparilla has done more for me than all the prescriptions and other medicines I have ever taken. For 14 years, I have suffered with kidney troubles; my back being so lame at times that I could not raise myself up out of my chair. Nor could I turn myself in bed. I could not sleep, and suffered great distress with my food. I have taken 4 bottles of Hood's Sarsaparilla with the most gratifying results. I feel like a new person, and my terrible sufferings have all gone. Life is comfort compared to the misery it used to be. I can now go to bed and have a good night's rest; can eat heartily without any distress. I am willing this should be published for others good. Mrs. Theresa Hartson.

STATE NEWS - A Careful Summary Of The Week's Doings In Briefest Form

N.T. McCorkle has been appointed postmaster at Waterloo.

Judge John Irvin, of Jasper, has been stricken with paralysis.

At Opelika, Ed Austin, convicted of robbery, got ninety-nine years in the pen.

V.O. Hawkins, of Decatur, has been granted a patent on a cast metal monument.

The preliminary trial of the Hueys for the killing of Capt. J.B. Cocke, has been under way the past week at Marion.

The Bibb county grand jury has indicted Dr. G.B. Crowe, for the murder of B.F. Glass, at Brierfield, July 1, 1891.

There will be ten contests before the House of Representatives next winter. In Alabama the seat of Jas. McComb will be contested by Martin W. Whatley.

Dr. J.R. Phillips, a prominent citizen of Pickens county, was shot and fatally wounded by his brother-in-law, William Mustin. The trouble was the outcome of a family quarrel.

Congressman Wheeler's wife and daughter, Birdie Wheeler, jumped from their carriage at Wheeler, Ala., just in time to see a freight train demolish it, kill the horses and hurt the driver badly.

A.H. Smith, of Anniston, was attacked by a negro while in company with his wife, while en route to church on Sunday, and knocked senseless by being struck on the face with a piece of slag.

Henry D. Clayton, the new district attorney for the middle district, and J.C. Musgrove, the new United States marshal for the northern district, have both filed their bonds and taken the oath of office.

William Upchurch, tax assessor of Greene county, committed suicide a few weeks since. It is thought that his mind became unbalanced in trying to straighten out his books, which were in a tangled condition.

A little daughter of Mr. T.D.L. Wilson, of Coosa county, poured some kerosene on a fire she was building to make it burn quicker. An explosion followed and the child was burned so badly as to cause her death in a few days.

Brooks Story, an express robber, who escaped from the Mississippi penitentiary at Jackson three times, and who was recently captured at Americus, Ga., made his escape from a fast train on the Alabama Great Southern road by jumping from a car window. He was manacled at the time.

Col. Gibbs Gardiner, who for a time was editor of the Birmingham Argus, is missing, and there is some mystery surrounding his disappearance. While in Alabama he took the Keely Cure at Fort Payne and again at Mobile, but afterwards fell into his old ways, and when last heard of was in New Orleans. His family have instituted a search for him.

TRADE REVIEW - Condition and General Outlook of The Prospects of the Country R.G. Dunn and Co's weekly review of trade says: More disheartening conditions have prevailed during the last week, and those who saw the beginnings of a permanent recovery and better tone a week ago are disappointed. Money has been closer, especially in the interior, and manufacturers and trade are more affected than before...

SACRED DEER IN JAPAN - Tame Creatures to Be Found in a Queer Mountain Town, Humphrey B. Kendrick, a former resident of Santa Barbara, Cal., who has just returned to San Francisco after a residence of several years in Japan, gives the Examiner an interesting description of a little mountain town named Nara in that county: "Everyone, or almost everyone in Nara has a deer, " said Mr. Kendrick, " and they are as plentiful there as dogs in an American town, while around the temples are great numbers, all sacred to the Japanese...

The Banner, Vol. 1, Clanton, Ala., Thursday, June 15, 1893, No. 32

THE ALLIANCE GROWING - President Loucks, in a special letter to *The Progressive Farmer* (Raleigh, N.C.) writes encouragingly of the outlook and gives some timely suggestions for the future...

The Extra Session - President Cleveland has announced and he will call an extra session of Congress not earlier than the 1st nor later than the 10th of September.

A Few Late Items - George Potter, a labor agitator of London, is dead.

Printing Office Blown Up - The greatest excitement exists in Breathett county, Kentucky, over the blowing up of the Hustler office by unknown parties. The Hustler is a weekly paper edited by Rev. J.J. Dickey. Dynamite was placed under the door of the building and wrecked the entire structure. The Hustler is credited with carrying the local option law recently passed in that county.

Lomax Linings - Masters Mack Marlar and Lloyd Marlar are confined to their beds with an attack of measles.
.

Mr. Henry Gregg and Misses Maggie Lodge and Elvie Smith spent Saturday and Monday with relatives at Clanton Ford.
.

Rev. Henley delivered an interesting sermon, Sunday evening, to a large congregation.
.

Mr. A. Smith says his corn patch has got the measles, and would like to know what to do for it; the writer would suggest that the call Dr. Hoe and Dr. Plow to assist him. I think they would be of great benefit to his corn.

Coopers Cuttings - Mr. Whit Kicker, of Birmingham, came down to Coopers and carried the fair Rose out to ride, and Uncle John is looking pale.
.

Mr. J.N. Mims, of Kincheon, visited friends near here, Friday.
.

Mr. Virgil Courtney, one of Energy's handsome young men, spent the past week with his best girl at this place.
.

Mr. Alpheus Dennis went out to Handline's fish pond, fishing, Saturday, and had grand success finding birds' nests, and reports a jolly time.
.

Mr. Harry Cook, of Montgomery, is visiting relatives at this place.
.

Mr. John Dennis and Mr. Joe Downs attended singing at Cannon.
.

Mr. John Connell spent Friday in Verbena. Mr. Harry Cook and Mr. James Goodson had a nice time with their girls last Sunday.
.

Miss Emma Goodson, one of our fairest flowers, is visiting friends near Mountain Creek.
.

Mrs. Emma Bland visited relatives at Energy, Tuesday.

Lily Lyrics - Boys, when you go hunting, see that you have good wadding. Mr. R.J. Williams and myself went squirrel hunting the other morning, he had the Banner for gun wadding and I had the View; he killed two owls at one shot, and also killed four squirrels, while I killed nothing because my wadding was no good.

Mr. Doc Jones paid his best girl a visit last Sunday. She is the best girl of several of the boys.

Mr. Hammond has missed some of his chickens; perhaps this can be accounted for; he has made application for the county register's office, and the governor loves chickens, you know.

Mars Hill Murmurings - Miss Fannie Woolly began teaching school here the 12th inst.

Verbena Views - Eagles are frequently seen in this community. Mr. John Dennis, Jr., has killed nine hawks this Spring.

Prof. S.J. Strock, of Harpersville, is visiting at home.

Dixie Dots - Rev. L.B. Pounds preached an eloquent sermon at Valley Creek church last Sunday. Prof. J.P. Haley will open school at Chestnut Hill church on the 19th inst. Prof. H.L. Davis was in our neighborhood a few days ago on business.

Miss Nettie Haley is visiting relatives in Verbena, and some of our young men are wearing sad faces.

J.M. Brennan, John Wyly and W.M. Price will leave in a few days for the World's Fair.

FROM OUR READERS - Lincoln, Ala., June 5th, 1893, Editor Banner: - I would like to say to your readers we cannot afford to compromise the principles of our organization to insure the success of a fusion with any party, or even to advance the political interest of our own... Respectfully, Philander Morgan

Notice to Non-Resident, The State of Alabama, Chilton County, J.W. Weldon, Complainant, vs. Lula Weldon, at Clanton, Seventh District North-eastern Chancery Division - In this cause it is made to appear to the Register by the affidavit of J. W. Weldon that the defendant, Lula Weldon, is a non-resident of the State of Alabama, and that her place of residence and post office is unknown to affiant. It is therefore ordered by the Register that publication is made in The Banner, a newspaper published in the town of Clanton, once a week for four consecutive weeks, requiring her, the said Lula Weldon, to plead, answer or demur to the bill of complaint in this cause by the 17th day of July, 1893, or in thirty days thereafter a decise pro confesso may be taken against her. Done at office in Clanton this 13th day of June, 1893, W.E. Stewart, Register

TOWN ITEMS - U.C.V. All Soldiers who were Volunteers in the Army of the Confederate States, and who were honorably discharged from the service, are invited to join us on Saturday, June 24th, at Clanton, for the purpose of organizing a Camp of United Confederate Veterans.

James M. Stanfield, 1st Ala. Cavalry
James A. Dudley, 7th Texas Infantry
Solomon Parker, 1st Ala., Infantry
J.M. Dawson, 5th Ala., Infantry
(?).B. Wells, 34th Ala., Infantry
(?).A. Thornton, Waddell's Battery
Robt. H. Knox, 2 Co., Wash ton Artl'y
(?).R. Kemp, 1st Ala. Cavalry
J.D. Maxwell, 6th who Ala. Infantry

.

The Episcopal church was well attended on Tuesday night, when Rev. J.F. Smith preached a most interesting sermon.

.

Mr. E.C. Worns and family have returned to their home in Birmingham.

.

Mr. W. Mullins was called out to his father's home on Wednesday. Mr. Mullins Senior being we regret to say very sick.

.

Sheriff Moore has gone on a business trip to Birmingham.

.

The Sheriff went over to Plantersville on Monday and returned with Mrs. Moore who has been nursing their son in law Mr. Frank Harris, who we are glad to say is rapidly recovering.

.

The Banner had a fishing frolic and picnic party last Friday and Saturday out at the river at Higgins lower ferry. Mr. and Mrs. E.H. White, Mr. and Mrs. E.C. Worns, Uncle Paddy and Miss Annie Smith, Miss Nellie White and Mr. Frank Crichton composed the party. Fishing was good (for the fish, as they didn't bite) but fish or no fish we had a real good (?).

.

Mr. Abbot has gone for a trip to Plantersville.

.

Brother Knight's children are recovering from an attack of measles.

.

Miss Louisa Hill, relict of the late Rev. A.B. Hill, has been visiting Judge Honeycutt's family this week.

.

Miss Kate Sampey, of Greenville has been visiting her cousin Mr. (?) Sampey. Miss Sampey (?) home tomorrow, Mrs. Sampey will accompany her.

Judges Couldn't Agree - The judges in the World's Fair opening suit could not agree. Judge Wood thought the injunction should be granted and the fair close. Judge Jenkins agreed on the main points, but Judge Grosscup held that the fair may be kept open.

The Banner, Vol. 1, Clanton, Ala., Thursday, June 22, 1893, No. 33

GENERAL NEWS - Current Events of General Interest Epitomized and Grouped" Blount has resigned as minister to Hawaii.

President Cleveland has been reported somewhat under the weather, so to speak.

Judge John L. Sneed, of Tennessee, has been appointed as consul-general to Honolulu, Sandwish Islands. He has accepted.

Joseph Mavtublev, a full-blooded Choctaw Indian, has been awarded the highest honor for oratory at the Trinity College (Durham, N.C.) commencement.

D.B. Loveman & Co., of Chattanooga, Tenn., who made an assignment last week, have perfected a settlement with their creditors and resumed business.

D.E. Barnum, of Amsterdam, N.Y., has just made the cheerful discovery that he was left $58,000 by the will of the late Phineas T. Barnum, who was his cousin.

Captain J.L. Rider has left Denison, Tex., for the World's fair. He takes with him a rifle which was once the property of the celebrated hero of the Alamo, Davy Crockett.

Mad dogs are running wild in Emanuel county, Ga. The little son of Judge Henry R. Daniels was recently bitten by a pet dog which was suffering from hydrophobia.

The baptism of Mr. J.W. Massey, of Walker county, Ga., after he was dead, has created a sensation throughout that section. It is the only and queerest case of the kind on record.

It has been publicly announced that Secretary of the Navy Herbert will be wedded to Mrs. Manning, widow of the late Secretary of the Treasury under President Cleveland eight years ago.

The Piedmont Phosphate company, located at Rock Springs, Fla., and of which H. Miller is manager, is now busy filling an order for $100,000 worth of phosphate. This is said to be the largest order ever received by any company.

Gen. A.W. Campbell, of Jackson, Tenn., died at his home in that city the past week. He was a brigadier general in the Confederate Army and a member of the constitutional convention of 1870 and a prominent candidate for governor on several occasions.

L.F. Gurrard, representing H.H. Eping and the trustee bondholders of the Mobile and Girard railroad, has filed a petition in the United States court at Montgomery, Ala., to foreclose a mortgage of $1,000,000 on the bonds issued in 1877. $800,000 of the bonds are at 2 per cent and $200,000 at 6 per cent.

George R. Lombard has under serious consideration a project which contemplated making his employees the owners of his extensive iron works in Augusta - that is, the formation of a co-operative stock company to which will be given titles and the duty of operating the Lombard Iron Works, the stockholders therein to be the men who are now employees of the big enterprise of which Mr. Lombard is the head, they to share the profits accruing from the concern.

Some Late Items - Wm. B. Copeland has been made postmaster at Birmingham.

The Joseph Bumis chemical works, in Williamsburg, N.Y., were destroyed by fire; loss $100,000.

Eutaw papers have this item: "Captain Duncan Jew,Jr. of Eutaw, has brought suit against Messrs. J. Gid Harris and Alonza Hill, executors of the estate of his sister, Mrs. C.H. Taylor, involving over $200,000 or $300,000 - almost an entire county in Texas and several thousand acres in Alabama.

Southern Boys at West Point - The graduating class at the United States Military academy consists of fifty-one members. Charles W. Kurtz of Pennsylvania head the list; George P. Howell of North Carolina, second; Meriwether Walker of Virginia, third; Robert P. Johnston of North Carolina, fourth; Edward J. Timberlake,Jr., of Tennessee, sixth; William Bates of Georgia, twenty-fifth; Matthew C. Smith of Alabama, thirty-second; Robert E.L. Spence of Georgia, forty-first; George H. Jameson of Virginia, forty-fifth; Hamil A. Smith of Georgia, forty-seventh; Hunter B. Nelson of Tennessee, forty-ninth.

Prominent Lawyer Dead - Reuben C. Shorter, a prominent attorney of Montgomery, died while sitting in his chair a few days since; cause heart failure.

STATE NEWS - A Careful Summary of the Week's Doings Served in Briefest Form. Hon. Gaylord B. Clark, on of the most prominent citizens of Mobile, is dead.

Rev. W.L. Culberson of Oneonta, has been elected principal of Hoke's Bluff high school.

John C. McLeod, of Barber county, is missing, and his absence is causing his family much uneasiness.

Professor T.N. Coleman, of Texas, has been chosen as president of the Scottsboro College and Normal school.

Professor C.L. McCartha of the State Normal college at Troy, will spend several weeks in Ohio on a lecturing tour.

Capt. H.W. Lightfoot, the newly appointed Chief Justice of the Texas court of Appeals, is a native of Jackson county, Ala.

The Third Congressional Teacher's Institute will be held at Eufaula June 25-30, with Prof. E.M. Shackleford, of Troy; presiding.

Rev. John J. Beeson has been appointed county treasurer of Jackson county, to fill the unexpired term of Dr. J.M. Dicus, dec'd.

At the last meeting of the Board of Trustees of Howard College, the degree of D.D. was conferred on Rev. A.W. McGaha of East Lake.

Colonel Clarke has announced that the next encampment of the Second Regiment will be held at Birmingham from the 11th to the 18th of July.

The faculty and trustees of the Southern University, at Greensboro, conferred the degree of D.D. upon J.O. Keener, V.O. Hawkins and S.M. Hosmer.

Wm. Mustin, the man who shot and killed Dr. J.R. Phillips at Millsport a short time ago, was acquitted on his preliminary trial on the ground of self-defense.

F.A. Hopkins, of Philadelphia, has been appointed receiver of the Birmingham, Sheffield & Tennessee River railroad. Hopkins is president of the company.

The contract for building the Abbeville Southern railroad has been let to S.G. Pruett of Montgomery. The road will be constructed from a point three miles west of Dothan on the Alabama Midland to Abbeville.

Isaac H. Vincent, ex-state treasurer of Alabama, who was pardoned by Gov. Jones a few weeks since, has accepted a position as soliciting agent for the Equitable Life Insurance Co., E.L. Simonds & Co., of Birmingham, employed him.

Draper Pope, colored, while digging near an old cabin at Merrelton, Calhoun county, unearthed $41 in old gold an silver coin. The oldest date on the silver coin was 1817, and on the gold was 1834 to 1856. It is supposed that an old negro miser, Shaw Prater, had buried the treasure there years ago.

The following are the replies received from the Alabama members in answer to the New York World's enquiry as to their position relative to the repeal of the Sherman silver law: R.H. Clarke, Mobile, "I favor repeal of Sherman act with accompanying legislation for coinage of silver bullion in the treasury and for coinage of a reasonable amount of silver bullion to be purchased monthly."
J.E. Cobb, Tuskegee, "I favor the repeal of the Sherman silver law by a law providing for free coinage of silver."
W.H. Denson, Gadsden, "I am for free coinage of silver. Oppose repeal Sherman law unless the law repealing it gives security for free silver."
Senator Morgan is in Europe. He is on record against silver repeal. Senator Pugh favored repeal on March 5. Representative Wheeler, of Wheeler and Oates of Abbeville, live in towns where there are no telegraphed offices, and could not be reached. Representative Robbins was said, at Selma, to be in Washington, but he could not be found there.

Jemison Gems - Prof. S.J. Jennings, one of Chilton's rising young men, was married on the 12th inst. at Talladega court house by Judge G.K. Miller to Miss Fannie Idel Archer, one of Talladega's fairest daughters. The Banner wishes for both bride and groom much happiness, health and prosperity.

Mr. James Hand, of this town, and Miss Mattie Webster, late of Washington city, D. C., were happily married here, Tuesday night. We wish them all happiness.

The many friends of Mrs. Ira Campbell will learn with concern that this estimable lady and friend of reform is quite sick.

On Saturday last the mortal remains of Mr. Miner Woolley, of this place, were consigned to the grave by the members of Clanton Lodge with the impressive solemnity which characterizes the Masonic ritual, Mr. Woolley being a reverend and beloved brother of that order. The interment took place at Isabella church, Rev. Mr. Ruddick officiating. The deceased gentleman has been paralyzed for over two years and was released from pain on Friday.

Lomax Linings - Mr. G. Foshee's baby is quite sick.

Mr. Wiley Foshee is at home again for a couple of weeks, his many friends welcome him - especially his best girl.

Mr. Aurelius Attaway spent several days at home this week, much to the delight of his many friends.

The Lomaxians spent Friday and Saturday out at Mimms mill, fishing, and report a most enjoyable time. Mr. and Mrs. John Cox, with their charming daughter Miss Bessie Cox, and Mrs. Mattie Rose, of Birmingham, came down for the fishing.

We are glad to note that Mr. A. Smith's baby, who has been quite sick with an attack of measles, is somewhat better, hope it will soon recover.

Miss Willis Marlar is, we are sorry to learn, confined to her bed with measles. We hope the attack will be very slight and that this charming and accomplished young lady will soon be out again.

Dixie Dots - Mr. M.J. Cole and wife, and Mr. John W. Reynolds have gone on a visit to Mr. Jasper Wylie; we wish them a merry trip.

Mr. Wyley Mitchell has gone to Six-mile to attend the commencement exercises of the school.

Mr. Willie Marshall not long since turned his buggy over with his best girl, but no one was hurt.

The Hustler and Old Mike wonder what is the banner with Uncle Sap, never see anything from him now-a-days, and we would like to hear from the Mayflower again, we think she did mighty well before.

Mr. C.G. Barnes is standing a big hand with the Dallas county girls. Hurrah for Charley!

Our Sunday school and prayer meetings are progressing very fast. Mr. M.H. Barnes will lead in prayer meeting next Sunday.

Pleasant Grove Pleasantries - Prof. J.E. Jones' school is having a vacation this week; the Professor is attending the Six-mile exhibition. Miss Alice Ward and Miss Lizzie Crompton are attending the Six-mile exhibition this week, hope they will have a fine time.

Mr. J.P. Cost and wife paid a pleasant visit to her brother last Sunday.

Mr. A.M. McCary was out buggy riding with his best girl last Sunday, think he means business.

Wessington Whisperings - Mr. Campanes little boy, Ellis Campanes, happened to bad luck last week; he was driving a horse and wagon and the horse got scared and ran away; the boy was thrown out of the wagon and broke his arm; he was taken to Jemison where the doctor set the broken limb, and he is getting on all right.

Prof. E.B. Deason commenced his school at Oak Grove, near this place, last Monday.

Mr. J.B. Martin says he is having plenty to eat. Mrs. Thomas asked him the other day why he said I killed a jay bird.

Clear Creek Clippings - Prof. J.M. Scott re-commenced his school again last Monday after a vacation of a month; we learn he has a very good school at present, which we think will be much larger soon.

Reform South Alliance - Reform South Alliance met last Saturday evening, and their was a goodly number present. It being the time to elect new officers the following were elected: J.S. Popwell, President; P.C. Moore, Secretary; G.H. Pierce, Treasurer...

Providence Alliance - Providence Alliance met on June 3d, and after going through with the regular business he proceeded to the election of officers for the ensuing year, with the following result: W.R. Houlditch, President; J.J. Mote, Vice-President; W.H. Shaw, Secretary; Jno. M. Brantley, Treasurer; W.W. Melton Chaplain; L.H. Reynolds, Lecturer; R.M. Honeycutt, Assistant Lecturer; J.T. Martin, D. K; O.C. McGraw, Ass't D. Mack.; Bros. B.M. Gentry, G.N. Honeycutt and Z.W. Langston, Executive Committee; W.H. Shaw, Trustee Stockholder... I am fraternally yours, W. H. Shaw, Sec. P.A.

Union Alliance - The following resolutions were passed at the last meeting of our Alliance, held June 16th. Resolved: That we meet on Saturday before the third Sunday in July, 1893, at nine o'clock, for the purpose of public speaking, and Resolved further: That the Secretary correspond with Brothers L.H. Reynolds and W.G. Riggins, inviting them to be with us on that day. Resolved further: That we respectfully invite Collins Chapel and Rocky Mount to be with us on that day. Resolved further: That the chair appoint a committee of three on order of the day. Committee appointed, J.W. Sorrell, T.J. Dorming and Wm R. Robinson. Resolved further: That these resolutions be sent to the Banner for publication. J.M. Robinson, Sec. U.A.

TOWN ITEMS - Mr. B.W. Groce, President of the State Alliance, paid Judge Honeycutt a visit last Monday.

A shocking tragedy took place in (?) neighborhood of Ehrman and Merritt's mill on the evening of the (?). About 8 o'clock Mr. James Riggins was sitting in his house opposite the back doorway resting (?) the arduous toils of the day. (?) the report of a gun rang out in the still night air and Mr. Riggins fell from his chair, mortally wounded, his abdomen and bowels (?) literally riddled with squirrel (?). Melvin Williams, a young negro, with whom who Mr. Riggins had difficulty at the mill earlier in the (?) was the perpetrator of this (?). It appears that during work Riggins allowed a plank to slip, (?)ing Williams to curse him, Riggins (?)emonstrated with him, whereas Williams struck Mr. Riggins (?) the head twice,

Riggins ran (?) gun and returning met Williams (?) the road, Williams escaped (?) and in his turn got a gun, (?) returned to the mill with it in (?). Mr. Ehrman disarmed (?) returning it to him at the close of the day, the negro declaring the (?)wms at an end. However (?) appears Williams made (?) he was going to kill Mr. Riggins and his threat has most (?)lessly executed. At time of (?)ting pursuit is being made of the perimeter by the Sheriff and posse. (?) Johnson says the wounded man (?) live for five or six days but (?) his recovery is hopeless. Mr. Riggins is a young single man living with his aged mother whose sole support he has been. He has been (?)ing at the Ehrman and Merrit's mill for several years past and was (?) liked by all who knew him. Ehrman and the mill hands has (?)ed a reward of $100 for the apprehension of the murderer.

That enterprising firm, the Messrs. (?)llins have purchased the Merritt (?)cuse to accommodate their rapidly increasing business. They will move their stock of goods in at once.

Our esteemed friend and brother, (?) Natty Dobbs, chaplain of the County Alliance, paid us a visit last Wednesday.

Jim Goodson, colored, was arrested and jailed, Wednesday, charged with being an accessory in the murder of Mr. Jas. Riggins

Last Saturday evening a runaway mule knocked down the shed (?) of Mrs. Phillips' millinery store, (?) as if the mules and (?) had affected a combine to knock them all the old sheds.

Mrs. Patrick Smith paid a visit to her son, Mr. Thomas Smith, at (?) Creek last week.

We regret to hear that Mr. Mullins, Senator, is still seriously ill, and that there is no improvement to report in his condition.

Mr. F.W. Lenty's mother is very (?) at Vincent, Shelby county, she is afflicted with consumption.

Mr. W.L. Sampey is one of the (?) of Clanton's merchants. (?)y close attention to business and (?) the interests of his customers he has built a fine trade. As an (?) of this Mack one he handled up-(?) bales of cotton and (?) about $50,000 worth of merchandise last year.

Mr. (?). T. Gullahorn, of Verbena, was visiting friends in town (?) week.

Knew Too Much - About four weeks ago, near Day's Gap, one night some persons went to the house of old man Higgins, a well known citizen, and threw rocks on his house. He came out, and was shot down and killed. The assassins were unknown at the time. Now comes a story from Day's Gap which says that Charles Morris has since confessed to having fired the fatal shot. Morris is said to be a son-in-law of George Davidson, tax assessor of Walker county, and it is stated that he confessed the crime to Davidson. In the confession it alleged that Morris implicated John Bonner and Bogue Bonner, Sam Key and one Bell. All five of the men went to Higgins' house and threw the rocks. When Higgins appeared Morris did the shooting. All of the men have fled, but vigorous efforts are being made to apprehend them. An old feud, which had existed for some time Higgins and John and Bogue Bonner, is given as a cause for the killing.

The Banner, Vol. 1, Clanton, Ala., Thursday, June 29, 1893, No. 34

STATE NEWS - A Careful Summary of the Week's Doings, Served in Briefest Form"
Capt. James W. Bryant, editor of the Choctaw Herald, is dead.

Tuscaloosa furnishes Texas with a young lady dentist in Miss Annie Hayes.

Hinton E. Carr, the of the defunct Tuscumbia bank, was arrested and released during the past week.

Mrs. Angeline Troupe, postmistress at Carpenter, and Bayless E. Ladd, dealer in liquor have been bound over on the charge of poisoning I.L. Hembree.

A singular accident occurred to Cobb Harris near Oneonta, Ala., lately. He was riding a mule, when the animal suddenly threw his head up, striking Harris on the chin and breaking his jawbone.

Hon. E. Spencer Pratt of Alabama, has been appointed Consul General to Singapore Straits settlements and Benjamin D. Williams, commissioner to negotiate with Chippewa Indians in Minnesota, act approve January 14, 1889.

Patents have been issued the past week suffering to Alabamians as follows: Geo. B. Herndon, Birmingham, preserving can; Thomas J. Missildin, assignor, one-half to S.C. Turnipseed, Ramer, churn; George W. Swartz, Florence, electric signal.

Dr. B.F. Riley, the president of Howard College, has been elected to the chair of English and Belles Letters in the University of Georgia. Dr. Riley is comparatively a young man, stands high in the Baptist Church of this State, and has many friends all over Alabama who will regret that he has consented to go elsewhere.

Mr. D. Stevenson, who lived about 5 miles from Selma, died a few days since. He was worth about $65.000 and had made a will bequeathing a large sum to St. Paul's Episcopal Church of Selma. He had sent to the city for a justice, in whose presence he was to sign the will, when death came, thereby depriving the church of the legacy. The deceased's sole heir is a brother, who lives in Baltimore.

While shoveling ore from a platform into the Bluffton ore washer, which was running at full speed, the platform gave way, throwing Will Cameron, a young white man, into the washer. The lugs on the log, which revolves like a sausage mill, caught his feet, dragging him into the same, tearing the flesh and breaking the bones into a horrible mass. The washer was stopped and the body pulled out, which was crushed into a jelly. He leaves a wife and four small children.

Jacob Williams, a farmer of Marshall county, had heard that his nephew, Robert Williams, had connected him in some way the recent burning of a barn in the neighborhood. He took his shotgun and loaded it with slugs and went in search of his nephew. The farmer found him, near his house and halted him and told him what he had heard. Robert told him to wait a minute, and he would go with him to the parties. Jacob said, "No I'll settle with you here by shooting your head off." This he did.

An Electric Boy - A correspondent writing to the Mobile (Ala.) Register, from Wager, Ala., tells of a strange phenomenon at that place in the person of a colored boy 10 years old living near Carson. He is so thoroughly electrified that he is a perfect conductor of electricity. It has been known for two years by the colored people that he possessed unusual power, but their superstitious nature led them to believe he was endowed with some divine power, or filled with some disturbing element from the evil one. The correspondent tells of several incidents in which the boy figured as an electric curiosity, and among others said: " When his hand was placed on a set of wires leading into the telegraph office, it would shut the current from the instruments, making a complete circuit through his hands... The next experiment with him will be the incandescent electric light. Mr. Van Vlick an electrician, thinks if he can get a suitable negative he can get current enough from him to light one small lamp.

GENERAL NEWS, Current Events of General Interest Epitomized and Grouped - Lizzie Borden has been acquitted of the murder of her father and step-mother.

.

California's many times a millionaire, Senator Sanford, is dead. His death was very sudden and unexpected.

.

William Mutchler, of Easton, Pa., Democratic member of Congress from the Eighth District of Pennsylvania, is dead.

.

Minister to Liberia, W.D. McCoy is dead. This is the fourth of Uncle Sam's ambassadors to succumb to the Liberian climate within the past twelve years.

.

Miss Julia Force is on trial in Atlanta, charged with killing her two sisters, Minnie Force and Florence Force. Miss Force is connected with some of the best blood of Georgia. The defense will try to save their fair charge on the ground of lunacy.

.

Thomas G. Sample of Pennsylvania, has been elected supreme treasurer the Knights of Pythias, to succeed S.J. Willy, resigned. It is believed the order will get back very little if any of the $70,000 deposited in the Washington bank.

.

As the result of the snapping of a governor belt on an engine of the electric light works, in Chattanooga, a fly wheel burst. H.B. Sweet, an employee, had a leg broken, and $3,000 damage was done the machinery. Heavy pieces of iron flew hundreds of yards, and several miraculous escapes happened.

.

George W. Vanderbilt has just concluded the purchase of 20,000 acres of land in the "Pink Beds" section of Anderson and Transylvania counties, North Carolina. The purpose of the purchaser is to make one of the finest game preserves in the world. Game keepers are already in charge of the property, and every farm house on the estate has been torn down. The property is only a few miles from the Vanderbilt residence.

.

Paymaster-General Stewart has completed the statement of the expenses of the navel review. The total expense of the review was $76,800 and the appropriation was $350,000, leaving a balance of $273,200, of which $250,000 will be covered into the treasury June 30, leaving the department in a balance of $23,000 to meet any contingent expenses which may be reported later.

Eighty-seven special examiners of pensions have just been reappointed. The law has always limited these appointments to one year and the salary is reduced for the next fiscal year from $1,400 to $1,300. The following are among the appointments: Thomas A. Broadus, James S. Vowles, Robert S. Coleman, Virginia; John M. Foote, James A. Graham, North Carolina; Edward B. Hammer, Alabama; Harlem P. Maxwell, Tennessee; William S. Roudenuth, Mississippi.

White Cappers in Blount - The Oneonta (Ala.) News - Dispatch says white-cappers visited the home of Florida Smith in Blount County insulted him and abused him and his family, and made them move from the neighborhood.

Tales Briefly Told - The first seizure of American fishermen this season in Nova Scotia waters occurred on Sunday. The American fishing schooner Lewis H. Jiles, Captain Judson Warren, became a prize to the Canadian fishery protection cruiser the Vigilant, Captain Knowlton.

At Indianapolis, Indiana, on the test case in the circuit court, Tuesday, or State ex rel. Stout vs. Henderson, auditor of State, Judge Brown decided the fee and salary law of 1891 unconstitutional. This is the law that placed nearly all the State and county officers of Indiana on salaries and reduced their compensation more than one half.

Isaac Hembree, a prominent farmer of Carpenter, in Jackson county, now lies at the point of death, caused from drinking a solution of whisky and arsenic. Recently he received through the mail a package containing a quart bottle with the label of, and purporting to be from, a prominent whisky dealer in Chattanooga, as a sample of a very fine whisky. Mr. Hembree drank freely from the bottle and shortly became very ill. A physician of Chattanooga was summoned, who pronounced Mr. Hembree in a very dangerous condition. The whisky was sent to Chattanooga and analyzed, and contained two ounces of arsenic. Various theories are advanced as to the probable cause of the attempt on Mr. Hembree's life, which may come to light very soon.

People's Party Mass Meeting at Clanton - The meeting was called to order at noon by Hon. O.M. Mastin, Chairman of the County Executive Committee. On motion, L.B. Pounds, of Maplesville, was elected chairman of the meeting; and T.H. White, Editor of the Banner, was elected secretary...J.J.L. Stewart, of Verbena, said that it would be proper to ascertain if all present propose to act with the People's Party and to let the same be known by rising to their fee...On motion of O. M. Mastin it was ordered that each beat elect two delegates and that the meeting elect two delegates at large. The following delegates were elected: Beat 1, Sam Pate, T.J. Robinson; 2. L.H. Reynolds, W.H. Shaw; 3. J.W. Foshee, Newt Riggins, 4. J.A. Miller, O. Mastin, 5. B.H. Wells, J.M. Dykes; 6. E.H. Smith, J.R. Vinson; 7. L.B. Pounds, W. Nix, 8. E.W. Bailey, W.A. Weaver; At large, B.M. Gentry, J.J.L. Stewart, J.M. Dykes, delegate for beat 4,. asked for instructions for the delegates....On motion, W.R. Bean, of Beat 1, was appointed by Chairman Mastin of the County Executive Committee to serve on that committee from that beat...All business having been transacted, the meeting adjourned to beat State Alliance Lecturer S.M. Adams, who made an able and exhaustive address on reform issues, especially calling attention to the Sayre election law and explaining its purpose, methods and enormities...He was followed by L.H. Reynolds, J.J.L. Stewart, L.B. Pounds, J.M. Dykes, J.A. Logan and others. The following resolution offered by L.H. Reynolds was adopted...

West Chilton - Miss Mattie Carroll has returned home after a long visit to Birmingham, which makes the hearts of some of our young men beat with great joy, especially one who looks as pleasing as a basket of white oak chips.

Mr. Ross Barnes visited relatives at Woodlawn on the 18th inst.

Mr. Wiley Mitchell is visiting relatives and friends at Six-mile.

Rev. Jas. Longcrier will preach at Valley Creek on the first Sunday in July.

Mr. Willie Chandler had some very bad luck the other day; he was very badly cut with the oat mower.

Mr. Duffy O'Neal, one of our popular young men, has returned home after a long visit to Florida.

Bro. J.W. Dunneway preached an eloquent sermon at Fellowship church on Sunday the 18th inst., it being Children's Day there was a large number of sweet little girls and boys present, altogether there was upwards of 500 people there.

Old Brother Leroy Friday, one of our land marks, is in very bad and feeble health, we regret to say.

Hon. Sam Young, better known as the New York farmer, residing near Dixie, says he had a cotton blossom June 5th, another the next day, and two more the day after. Bully for the New Yorker! He can bind oats as fast as three men can cut with cradles.

It seems that there is some great attraction for widowers at Valley Creek church; we met there the other Sunday our good old friend, Thomas Mitchell, neatly dressed, looking out for his third bride; he says he can jump as high as ever he could, but not quite so often. So look out boys, we saw him casting a sheep's eye at the girls; some of you are going to be too late, for you know what great success the widowers have at Valley Creek.

Where are you Uncle Sap? I would be very glad to see you over this way again, as your best girl over here wants to see you.

Dixie Dots - Married last Monday at the residence of the bride's father in the Weaver settlement, Mr. Lee Onsley to Miss Clara Hull, the ceremony being performed by J.E. McCullough, J. P. May happiness and prosperity be their portion.

Welchville Winnowings - Miss Claughton, of Verbena, is visiting her brother, Mr. A.B. Claughton, at this place.

Misses Sallie Welch and Daisie Welch have returned home after a pleasant visit to relatives in Brewton.

Miss Mamie Sanderson, of Shearerville, is visiting the family of Mr. J.C. Sanderson here.

Mrs. Eaves, accompanied by her little brother and Miss Mary Harris, of Selma, are visiting

Mr. D.H. Martin.

Miss Minnie Culverhouse is visiting her aunt's family.

Lily Lyrics - Mr. Bill Dunlap is the happy father of a little baby girl.

Mr. John Foshee, of Maplesville, visited his best girl near this place last Sunday.

The Misses Sallie Collins, Maggie Maddox, Ada Mimms, Cora Hill, and Mr. Walter Hill, all of New Calera, have been visiting friends near this place.

We had a delightful singing at Liberty Hill church last Sunday by Mr. Natty Jones, we are always glad to have Mr. Jones with us. There was also as noble a sermon as man can deliver by the Rev. R.M. Honeycutt, we were glad to hear him.

Jumbo Jumbles - We are sorry to have to report the death of our esteemed fellow citizen, Mr. Henry K. Cleckler, which sad event occurred after a very short illness caused by congestive chills, at four o'clock last Monday morning at his residence near Wax hatchie creek, about three miles northeast of Jumbo. The deceased gentleman was a young man not quite thirty three years old, and leaves a widow and three children to mourn his loss. He was well liked and respected by all in this community where he has lived for the last two years, having moved here from Yellowleaf Creek. He was a member of the Baptist faith at Corinth church, and was buried at Mineral Springs on Tuesday.

Reform South Alliance - The weather is fine and farmers are getting on with their work; the oat and wheat crop is good in this section. That thorough going energetic farmer, J.A. Hathcock, has twenty five acres of the finest corn in these parts.

Rev. T.E. Taylor preached to a large audience at Enterprise last Sunday.

Jemison Gems - The school at Union, four miles east of Jemison, which was taught under a subscription of 62 scholars last year, and enrolled 135 pupils, under the efficient management of Professor S.J. Jennings, opened again on June 26th for a new term of his second year with a subscription of 80 scholars. Mr. Jennings is a good teacher who works on the principle of "move up", and with his handsome bride, who is to be his lifetime assistant, he starts into his second years' work with the brightest of prospects. Prof. Jennings asks the patronage of all persons who can't do better than patronize him, which we are persuaded does not mean everybody. May the brightest laurels crown all his efforts in the educational work, and much happiness attend his and her pathway through life.

TEACHER'S INSTITUTE - First Day,The second session of the Chilton County Teachers' Institute was called to order by Supt. J.W. Moore at 10 o'clock, Friday morning, June 16th, the place of meeting being Isabella church, Mulberry community. The exercises were opened by prayer. Prof. G.L. Speer, in his able and impressive manner, welcomed the teachers on behalf of the community. Supt. J.C. Hicks, of Bibb county, was present and invited to take an active part in the Institute. "Vocabulary development" discussed by Messrs., Robinson, Speer, Hicks and Supt. Moore....Since our worthy and honored State Supt. Jno. G. Harris has requested the various county superintendents of the state to hold more meetings in their respective counties, and since we, the teachers of Chilton county in Institute assembled, regard this as an important measure...."Discontents of a Teacher,"

was the theme of a paper read by Miss Lafarice Deadwilder. "How to Secure Regular Attendance," was the theme of a paper by Miss O.M. Garner....
Second Day, Exercises opened with prayer by Rev. L.B. Pounds. "English Grammar", discussed by Messrs. Harwood, Hicks, Speer and Pounds....A motion to recommend to the teachers of the county the books selected by the committee was discussed by Messrs. Hicks, Pounds, Speer, Robinson and Harwood...J. Alex Moore, Sec. Chilton Co. Teachers' Ins.

TOWN ITEMS - (?) Thomas J. Haney, of Talla-(?) arrived in town this morning, and will assist the Rev. Mr. Busby, who will be here tomorrow in a (?) of meetings at the Congregational church, commencing Friday (?) Mr. Haney will remain with Rev. A.C. Wells for probably some (?) time and will assist him in his work. Everyone is invited to come and hear the boy preacher, he is but twenty-one years of age.

The Masons had a most enjoyable time last Saturday night, and ani-(?) by music and singing the installation of officers took place as followed: W.D. Sartor, W. M.; J.M. Stanfield, S. W.; B.H. Chestnut, J. W.; W.A. Middleton, Treas; J.W. Stanfield, Sec.; W.H. Sartor, S. (?), L.A. Miller, J. D.; P. Smith (?)

Rev. J.E. McCane, of Verbena, has been holding a protracted meeting at the Methodist church. Our local preachers of every denomination (?) and assisted in the services.

The Birmingham Age-Herald con-(?) muddled and incorrect ac(?)pecting the supposed capture of Alex Shelton the negro wanted for the killing of Mr. James Riggins. The A-H, as usual, drew largely from its imagination. A deputy sheriff fancied he had caught Shelton telegraphed to Sheriff Moore to come to Birmingham to identify him, our Sheriff went up twice for this purpose, the deputy with his (?) managed not to be there and discovered he had got the wrong man. As Sheriff Moore never had a (?) of either deputy or prisoner it is hard to see how he could closely (?)ble them; he would have been (?) to have had the chance.

(?) A.T. Clarke, of Shelby, and (?) J. Stallings, of Troy, were (?) today on business connected (?) the Congregational Church.

Miss Jessie Jones has returned to her home in Arkansas after a long visit to her sister Mrs. Hugh Foshee.

A meeting will be held either at the house or some other convenient (?), Friday night, for the purpose of entertaining what can be done in the matter of erecting a new school house. Prof. M.Y. Morris, of Snowden, Ala, will be present and if proper encouragement is given he will move here and establish a school, erecting a building for that purpose. The Professor comes (?) recommended, beside being well known to many of our citizens.

Tuesday morning, Melt Williams, the negro who shot Mr. Jim Riggins on the night of the 26th last, was delivered to Sheriff Moore by Deputy Sheriff (?) Young was promptly (?) reward of $100 offered by (?) Ehrman and Merrit and their employees for the capture of this criminal. On Wednesday Sheriff Moore delivered Melt Williams to Montgomery where he will be kept until the fall term court at Clanton. Sheriff Moore (?)med it advisable to take this step (?) threats have been made of lynching Williams.

Wednesday night, Wm. Henry, colored, was charged with carnal knowledge of (?)ley, a child of tender years (?) from Lomax by the (?) and jailed. On Tuesday he (?) preliminary trial before Judge Honeycutt and was committed to jail to (?)tion of the grand jury.

Edwin Booth's Will - The will of Edwin Booth has been filed. He leaves the bulk of his property to his daughter, Elina Booth Grossman. The value of the personal estate is estimated at $605,000. He gives to his brother, Joseph A. Booth, $10,000 and niece May Booth Douglas, $10,000; other nieces and nephews $5,000 each. Cousins Charlotte Mitchell Baltman and Robert Mitchell of North Carolina, each $10,000 and to several friends $5,000 and $10,000 each. Actors fund and other actor's societies $5,000 each.

Declared Unconstitutional - Judge Hanford of the United States Circuit Court of Washington, has rendered a decision declaring the anti-cigarette law unconstitutional, The decision says: "The law of the State of Washington prohibiting the sale of cigarettes is in contravention of article 1. section 8, or the constitution of the United States, and null and void in so far as it prohibits, or attempts to prohibit, selling, giving or furnishing to anyone by an importer.

The Banner, Vol. 1, Clanton, Ala., Thursday, July 6, 1893, No. 35

Mrs. Laura Armstrong of Huntsville presented her husband with three sons the other day.

Mrs. Sarah Willis has been paid $10,000 by the Western Railroad of Alabama for killing of her husband.

The Alabama Press Association presented the retiring president, Mr. John C. Williams, a very handsome gold-headed cane appropriately engraved.

Lieutenant E.N. Jones,Jr., of Wilcox county, now stationed at Fort McKinney, Wyoming, has recently passed a successful competitive examination and will be promoted.

Secretary Herbert has appointed Miss Letitia C. Tyler of Alabama and daughter of ex-president Tyler, to a clerkship in the bureau of supplies and accounts in the navy department.

Manuel Williams, a notorious character, has been rearrested and confined in the Montgomery county jail. He is wanted in Covington county, but has been carried to Montgomery for safe keeping.

Some one dug into the grave of Charles Kelly, one of the men lynched for the murder of Tax Collector Armstrong of Butler county and threw the remains out on top of the ground. The motive for the act is not known.

The Anniston Evening News has been suspended, and Editor McKay has taken charge of the Hot Blast. Milton A. Smith, editor of the Hot Blast, assumed his duties as Anniston's postmaster on the 1st, but still owns the paper.

Prof. F.M. Peterson of the Southern University has been appointed presiding elder of the Greensboro District, Methodist Church, in place of Dr. O.R. Blue, deceased. Dr. Peterson has entered upon the discharge of his duties.

President Cleveland has appointed J. Courtney Hixon of Alabama to be consul at Nigpo, China, and Henry C. Smith at Sautos, Brazil. Mr. Hixon is only 29 years of age, and the position to which he has been assigned is one of considerable importance. H.C. Armstrong,Jr., has been appointed to Grenable, France.

Uncle J.G. Rollo and his wife, Mrs. Charity Rollo, died in Pike County within one week of each other. They were one of the oldest couples in the county, having come to this State from South Carolina in 1836. They first settled in Montgomery county and afterwards moved to Pike, where they were married.

The contract for the construction of the big lock on Colbert Shoals Canal on the Tennessee river has been awarded to M.V. Henry of Birmingham at $345,000.

Impending Trouble With Miners - ... Secretary Tracey, of the United Mine Workers Association, stated the other day that inside of ten days the miners of Missouri, Arkansas and Indian Territory will be out, and word has been received that the miners in Colorado are willing to strike in aid of their Kansas brethren...

Good Advice - Mr. Chauncey M. Depew has written for Donahoe's Magazine an article in answer to the question, "Should young men go into politics?" Mr. Depew answers no - that is, he strongly advises young men not to adopt politics as a career...

The way of the organized democratic news (?) paper in Chilton county appears to be hard. Again there is a change of proprietors, making the third editor of that paper in three months. Mr. Frank Baldwin having quit the journalistic field has sold out the View to Mr. C.W. Hare, of Montgomery, who announces himself as loyal to the principles (when they can be found) of the Democratic party.

Adjutant-General Moorman, by order of J.B. Gordon, general commanding United Confederate Veterans, has ordered the postponement of the confederate reunion at Birmingham until Friday and Saturday, Sept. 15 and 17, 1893. This postponement makes no change in arrangements or dispositions already made and all delegates appointed will remain for the date now set.

Lomax Listings - Mrs. Ella Jones and children, of Blocton, is visiting her mother, Mrs. Foshee, of this place.

Dr. A.J. Marlar was called to the bedside of his son, Mackey Marlar last Wednesday who was dangerously ill from relapse of the measles.

We are sorry to note Mr. Ogilvie Foshee's baby is no better.

Mr. T.J. Marcus' baby is quite sick.

Mrs. E.H. Lowe and children, of Jemison came down last Thursday to spend the Fourth; their many friends welcome them.

Misses Mattie Lowe and Mary Lowe, of Jemison, and Miss Willie Marlar, of this place attended picnic at Coopers the Fourth; they report a most enjoyable time.

One of our charming young ladies was very badly disappointed Monday evening, when Mo. 3 passed and did not bring her long looked for Male; don't grieve, he will come soon.

Miss Willis Marlar opened school last Monday, success to her.

Mr. E.H. Lowe, of Talladega Springs, came down on Saturday last to join his family and take in the picnic at Mim's mill on the Fourth' his many friends welcome him.

Messrs. G.W. Lodge, and D.B. Lowe, of this place, left Saturday for parts unknown, and did not get back until Sunday evening, it is supposed they went to see their best girls.

Verbena Views - Mrs. A.J. Brooks and Miss Lucas visited Verbena recently.

Mr. John Moody will spend a few weeks in Tenn. for his health.

Rev. Mosely, of East Lake, preached last Sunday at the Baptist church, the present pastor is sick.

Prof. Holloway will teach a singing school at Canaan and Coopers; it commences the 17th July.

Pleasant Grove Pleasantries - Mr. A. Patterson, of this place is visiting relatives and friends in Elmore and Coosa counties this week.

Misses Monty Davenport and Ora Davenport two of Mulberry's fairest belles paid a pleasant visit to relatives and friends near this place last week.

Little Herma Hudgens, son of J.D. Hudgens, was on his way to school attacked by a dog at Mr. Smitherman's, and was badly bitten; we learn he is better. Mr. Hudgens killed the dog.

Our Alliance is getting along all O.K., everything is lovely and harmonious about Pleasant Grove. We met on the first day of July and elected officers for the ensuing year as follows: J.T. Blow President; J.B. Childress, Vice-President; M.C. Childress, Secretary; H. Driver, Treasurer; A.J. Lee, Lecturer; A.L. Thomas, Assistant Lecturer; T.M. Driver, Chaplain; W.M. Gibson, Doorkeeper; and J.L. Thomas, trustee stock holder Exchange; so we are not dead, neither are we sleeping; but alive and ready to show our hand for Justice or any Reform movement.

We have a good Sabbath School with an average attendance of thirty-students, also a good literary school conducted by that noble and energetic young man J.E. Jones.

Brother White we feel grateful to you for the noble stand you have taken in battling for the right.

Mrs. D.C. Hubbard, accompanied by her little son Vernon Hubbard, spent several days last week visiting friends and relatives in Pinehill.

Mr. R.C. Jones, of Six Mile, was over Saturday and Sunday to see his brother and sister Mr. J.E. Jones and Miss Ella B. Jones.

Mr. H.L. Hicks, of Bibb, passed thro' our neighborhood a few days ago, en route to Jemison to see his best girl. Come again, Harvie, it is absolutely necessary for you to see her sometimes.

Miss Ella Sellers, of Randolph, opened her school at Macedonia last Monday.

Rev. R.M. Honeycutt delivered one of his instructive sermons from the subject "How is it that we are saved?" in a plain and forcible manner to a large and attentive congregation at Macedonia last Sunday, while Brother Honeycutt is one of the highest officials in the county he is improving every opportunity of working for the spiritual interest of his fellow man, O that the world were full of such men as R. M. Honeycutt and S.M. Adams.

Jemison Gems - Mr. J.P. Allen, who has been quite sick is now improving.

Mr. J.W. Langston, had the misfortune to dislocate his ancle and break the small bone of his leg a few days ago while getting out of his buggy.

Mr. J.W. Holly was married to Miss Dora Bristow at China Grove, Pike county, last Thursday evening. We wish them long life and happiness.

Mrs. S.J. Heath has returned home after a long visit to friends in Texas.

Miss Mattie Hand is visiting friends at China Grove, we hope she will not stay long, as we miss her charming presence so much.

Miss Minnie Wells, of East Lake, is visiting relatives and making lots of friends here.

Mr. H.T. Bevels and Miss Sarah E. Varden were married on June 23d, near Jemison, the Rev. S.J. Jennings officiating on the happy occasion.

Dixie Dots - Mr. J.B. Cox and Mr. J.P. Haley caught four coons last Saturday morning, as are each keeping one for a pet.

Mr. James McKinney found two bee trees about twenty feet apart, he cut one and got seventy-five pounds of honey from it, and will cut the other soon.

Rev. J.H. Longeryer preached an excellent sermon at Valley Creek last Sunday.

Mr. C.G. Barnes paid a visit to a pretty little girl last Sunday when he enjoyed himself very much, and he is going back soon. Hurrah for Charley!

Messrs. D.H. Mitchell, R.P. Barnes, H.W. Cole, W.A. Marshall, W.T. Mitchell and W. Ready visited Friendship on the Fourth when they had a nice time with the girls.

Mr. W.A. Gandy and wife, of Billingsley, paid Mr. T.G. Letcher and family a pleasant visit on the 2d inst., remaining until the 4th.

Mr. W.M. Price and Old Mike say if they do not get off to the World's Fair this time they will go to the next one. Hurrah for them!

TOWN ITEMS - Clanton Camp, United Confederate Veterans, held a meeting on (?)day at the Court House, they (?)urned to meet again on the (?) Saturday in August, when arrangements will be made for at(?)ing the reunion at Birmingham in September. The following ((?)he the officers of Camp Clanton: J. Stanfield, Commander; Jas. A. (?)lley, Lieut Commander; O.H. Cook, Chaplain; J.P. Givhan, (?)on; W.A. Middleton, Sec(?)

(?)im Goodson, accused of being (?)ssory to the shooting of Mr. (?)s Riggins, will have his ad(?)ed preliminary trial Tuesday.

(?)e Honeycutt and family (?)ly escaped death by light(?) last Sunday afternoon at the (?)s plantation. The Judge (?) Honeycutt and their son (?)e were sitting conversing to(?) on the piazza of the redi(?) when a flash of lightning (?)uck a tree in the yard within (?) feet of the house; the frag(?) of bark from the stricken tree being showered over Mrs. Honeycutt as she sat. It was indeed a narrow escape. The Judge says they (?) shock distinctly, that it made them feel quite sick, in fact the Judge was feeling quite unwell (?) consequence on

Monday.

Misses Maggie Moore and Bamma Moore (?) on a visit to their old home in Plantersville.

Last Sunday evening about 4 o'clock, Mr. Jerem(?)an passed away at his home about three (?) east of Clanton (?) where he resided for about fifty years. The deceased gentleman, who was the father-in-law of our esteemed and ex-Sheriff Lee Hayes, was between 90 and 100 years old and he enjoyed perfect health until about the last five weeks.

Mr. Matthew's household is graced with the presence of Miss Tilden, of (?), she is engaged in teaching the Doctor's children.

Mr. Wiley Davis Moore, brother of our sheriff, was taken ill on Monday morning with congestion and expired Wednesday night. The deceased was in his 33rd year; he leaves a wife and four children to mourn his death.

Jumbo Jumbles - About three weeks ago Mr. Jas. Connell left the house of Mr. Wm. Willis on Waxalatchie creek in Shelby county at about 4 o'clock on Saturday evening to go to the house of his son Mr. H.M. Connell about a half mile distant, and has not been seen or heard from since. It is supposed he lost the way and by some means or other got into the Coosa river.

Mr. Albert Gore, aged 18, and Miss Theodora Cox, aged 17, were married near this place on the 4th.

We have a prosperous Sabbath school at the Kilgore school house; we feel that God's spirit has been with us. Superintendent, J.B. Sellers; Rev. W.S. Cox; teacher.

Mountain Springs - Perhaps no more pleasant and profitable way of spending the Fourth could have been devised than that taken at Mountain Springs, five miles north east of Clanton. A pleasant drive, followed by a coming (?) of the people in Christian fellowship, then a basket dinner and picnic in the cool shade of the leafy woods under the blue canopy of heaven, and an inspiring and instructive sermon by the popular boy preacher, Rev. T.B. Hainey, assisted by Rev. A.C. Wells and the Pastor of the Mountain Springs church, the venerable Father Wells. There was a large number of people present, including several from Clanton, and all thoroughly enjoyed this manner of spending the day.

Stanton Sayings - Wednesday evening a shooting affray took place here, the result of too much liquor, it is said. Minion White, of this place, shot Peter Jones in the mouth, inflicting a serious wound.

Dr. J.S. Johnson is building an addition to his store.

Mr. R.H. Crew, of Goodwater, paid a visit to Squire Nolen, and Mrs. Hulda Crew returned home with him.

Mr. E.O. Boyd and wife have returned to their home in Birmingham, after a short but pleasant visit to relatives here.

Dr. A.E. Bivings and family have removed back from Talladega Springs.

. Supt. Moore was in town last Saturday, attending to the monthly payment of teachers, and gave us a call. We always rejoice to see his genial face in the office.

. Mr. James Riggins was much improved in the early part of the week, but this morning it is rumored he is not quite so well.

SOMEWHAT STRANGE, ACCIDENTS AND INCIDENTS OF EVERYDAY LIFE - Mrs. France Shelton, who penetrated 500 miles into the Dark Continent, last set up a booth at the World's Fair to exhibit African curiosities, and to sell her book about Africa. She told an Indianapolis reporter a curious story of African customs...

. Charles H. Price, a seven-year convict, sent from Detroit September 20, 1890, for forgery, has made the cleverest escape from the prison within the history of the institution. Price was engaged in packing snacks in boxes to ship to Australia. He left out half of one lot, made a false top for the box, which he fastened in by means of wooden buttons on the inside, and had himself carted to the car platform outside the prison. When the coast was clear he opened the box and escaped. He had made two other attempts and was caught in the act.

. A coatimondi, a species of ant-eater, which is owned by Joseph Wallace, of Brunswick, Ga., does not confine itself to destroying ants, but has committed several robberies of jewelry, money, and other articles of value. All the articles, however, have been recovered in out-of-the-way places, where the animal had hidden them.

. Morris McDaniel, of Madison County, Ind., caught recently a half-grown rat with a gold ring round its neck which cannot be removed. Three months ago, Mr. McDaniel's daughter lost the ring, and it is supposed that the rat got his head through it while very young. Now it is a tight necklace.

. Clare May Kivlan, an infant child born at Leominster, Mass., has the distinction of having been photographed seven minutes after birth. This is a development of the snap-shop idea in photography such as is likely to appeal to the heart of every fond mother..

. The youngest telegraph operator in America is little Euphra Dunn, the five-year-old daughter of Mr. and Mrs. E.N. Dunn, of West Point, Ga. The child has been about the office a great deal and quickly picked up the Morse alphabet. She can call up other operators, and receives messages with remarkable accuracy.

. Mrs. Soar of Ambaston, England, has a loaf of stale bread of which she is extremely proud. It is 600 years old, and was originally given to one of Mrs. Soar's illustrious ancestors by King John, who accompanied it with a grant of land.

The Body And Its Health - Cause of Human Rumination.-In narrating his observations of several cases of rumination in man-three of which occurred in man and two in a mother and child of three and one-half years - M. Decker states that in three instances the complaint was congenital, nor is there any reason for believing that rumination is due to any paralysis of the cadia, but that the latter opens at the time of each regurgitation; only in one case was there any evidence of cardiac weakness...

Death From A Broken Heart. - Do people in trouble ever really die of "a broken heart?" The late Sir George Padget, in one of his lectures, acknowledges that in the vast majority of cases thus popularly described there is nothing like an actual rupture of the heart; yet he admits that mental affections will not infrequently cause real disease of the body, and he mentions an actual case of broken heart cited by Dr. J.K. Mitchell of the Jefferson College, Philadelphia, in lecturing to his pupils. In an early period of his life Dr. Mitchell accompanied, as a surgeon, a packet that sailed from Liverpool to one of the American ports. The captain frequently conversed with him respecting a lady who had promised to become his bride on his return from that voyage. Upon this subject he evinced great warmth of feeling, and showed some costly jewels and ornaments which he intended to present as bridal gifts. On reaching his destination he was abruptly informed that the lady had married some one else. Instantly the captain was observed to clasp his hand to his breast and fall heavily to the ground. He was taken up and conveyed to his cabin on board his vessel. Dr. Mitchell was immediately summoned, but before he reached him the captain was dead. A post-mortem examination revealed the cause. His heart was found literally torn in twain. The tremendous propulsion of blood (adds the narrator) consequent upon such a violent nervous shock, forced the powerful muscular tissues asunder, and life was at an end.

Mrs. Sarah Hawn, the mother of seventeen children, died recently at Okland, Ill., at the age of 105. At the time of his death, a few years ago, her husband had attained his 97th year.

Charles Henry Pearson, an Englishman, has written a book in which he claims to have proved that the great races of the world are losing ground and that the Chinese, Hindoos, and South American half-breeds are the coming leaders of civilization.

The Banner, Vol. 1, Clanton, Ala., Thursday, July 13, 1893, No. 36

GENERAL NEWS - President Cleveland is confined to his room at Buzzard's Bay.

Associate Justice Samuel Blatchford of the United States Supreme Court is dead.

J.B. Nicklin, of Chattanooga, has been elected President of Southern Base Ball League, in place of President Hart, who resigned.

Judge Hudson, of South Carolina, has rendered a decision that the new dispensary law of that State is unconstitutional. The old dealers are much encouraged.

The marriage of the Duke of York and the Princess Victoria Mary of Teck, an event which all England has looked forward to with deep interest, has been consummated.

Rev. J. R. Graves, D. D., Dead - Rev. J.R. Graves, D. D., died at his home near Memphis, Tenn, during the past week, aged seventy-three years. Dr. Graves, since 1885, has been a heroic sufferer, having been sorely afflicted and in a state of comparative helplessness ever since. The life of this great man has been marked by Singular ability, great industry and prodigious enterprise as a preacher, editor and author. Perhaps no man in the Baptist denomination, or in any other denomination, has done so much and accomplished results upon the same lines as he. He was the oldest editor among the Baptists, having assumed editorial control of the Baptist, afterwards the Tennessee Baptists, in Nashville, as far back as 1845. It was in Memphis before the war in that he founded the Baptist Publication Society and from which issued his first great work, "The Great Iron Wheel", and other productions from himself and others of a kindred literary character.

ALABAMA CROPS - The Condition of the Crops as Reported by the Agricultural Department"
The condition of the crops during the past month is of very great importance to enable the formation of an opinion as to the aggregate yield. Commissioner of Agriculture H.D. Lane has just issued the monthly bulletin of the department for June, which will be found of great interest....

Late State Items - "The Business League" of Florence is now fully organized and ready for business, with the following officers: M.P. Camper, president; John T. Ashcraft, vice-president; H.B. Lee, secretary and treasurer.

A Healing Salve - Fifty thousand dollars, the largest sum ever paid by an American railroad company for injuries to a single person, will be paid by the New York Central Railroad to Mrs. Homer R. Baldwin, of Yonkers, within a few days, in settlement for the injuries she received in the disaster at Hastings on Christmas Eve, 1891. The accident was a rear-end collision and the result of carelessness in signaling. The World's exposures immediately after the accident caused the Central to put in a block signal to prevent the occurrence of a similar accident.

Fourth of July Rallies - There never has been a more auspicious time in the history of the People's party for a general revival of interest and enthusiasm. There never has been a time when our speakers could present our principles with greater effect, and vanquish our enemies with so much ease...Invite your neighbors of every political faith and order to come out and hear the truth. Let this Fourth of July be not only a celebration of the declaration of 1776, but also a celebration of our second Declaration of Independence as proclaimed at Omaha on the 4th of July, 1892...H.E. Taubeneck, Chairman National Committee of People's Party; J.H. Turner, Secretary National Committee of People's Party; Lawrence J. McParlin, Secretary National Committee of People's Party; M.C. Rankin, Treasurer National Committee of People's Party; Geo F. Washburn; Ignatius Donnelly.

A National Convention - Gen. A.J. Warner, president of the American Bi-metallic league, today issued a call for a national convention of that league to meet in Chicago August 1, to continue as long as the convention may direct...

Hon. R.F. Kolb, vice-president of the American Bi-metallic League, will attend the meeting of the Silver League which has been called to meet at Chicago on August 1.

The People's Party of Ohio met at Columbus at that state on July 4th and nominated a state ticket. There was over 200 delegates in attendance and H.E. Taubeneck, chairman of the national Peoples Party was present. The platform adopted reaffirms the principles of the Omaha convention.

Lomax Linings - Mr. E.H. Lowe and family have returned to their home in Jemison, after a pleasant visit to relatives and friends near here.

Mrs. Ella Jones and children have returned to their home in Blocton, after a most delightful visit to her mother at their place.

We are sorry to note that the beautiful Miss Annie Walker, of this place, is quite sick; we hope the attack will be light and that we may soon see her out again.

Mr. J.W. Foshee has returned to his work with the bridge crew after a protracted visit to his mother and friends at this place.

Rev. - Wells preached an interesting sermon to a large congregation last Sunday night.

Rev. - Henley delivered an excellent sermon, Sunday night.

Mr. John Kemp's house caught fire from the stove flue last Monday, but the fire was put out before any damage was done.

Dixie Dots - We regret to learn of the death of Mr. W.D. Moore after a very brief illness. He died on the fifth day of July, and leaves a widow and four children to mourn his loss, but we hope they will so live as to meet where there is no more sorrow or parting.

J.E. McCullough has a mush melon 23 inches long in his patch, and a ruttabegga turnip measuring 17 inches in circumference; they are of the Kolb seed of 1893.

Wessington Whisperings - We expect to have preaching at Oak Grove once a month by Rev. W.B. Crowson. There is a nice Sunday School at Providence, near this place, and preaching there every third Sunday by Rev. R.M. Honeycutt. Quite a large crowd comes out every time.

Jumbo Jumbles - The old school house here has been closed, and two new schools have taken its place. Both opened up last Monday. Miss Ada Goodgame is teaching one near to Mt. Zion church, commencing with twenty-six subscribed scholars, and Miss Sophie Mullins is teaching about one mile south of the church, commencing with about thirteen scholars.

Reform South Alliance - Mr. Dawson Davis will commence work on his new mill and gin in a few days.

Mr. Henry Culp, I understand, is to put up a steam gin near Mr. John Vinson's.

Well, the glorious Fourth has come and gone; the children, both old and young, met and spent the day at Mr. J.A. Hathcock's and enjoyed themselves with him and his charming young wife.

A word to Old Mike. You ask where is Uncle Sap. He has strayed off, but is still in the right road, his post office is Vinehill, Ala.

The good people met at Mr. George Bowles on the Fourth and had one of the best times possible; it was a day of thanksgiving; there were two sermons, one by Elder C.C. Billingsley, and one by Elder Culp. There was dinner in abundance, and all enjoyed themselves. What a satisfaction it is to meet our friends at such a feast.

On Sunday next there will be preaching and singing all day at Maple Springs, three miles south of Clanton. Preaching by Brother Thomas. Singing led by Brother Riley Robinson.

Poplar Springs Sprigs - The Fourth at this place was passed in a delightful way. There was a large crowd present, and some excellent talks by Brothers Riley Robinson and John Wells. We had a capital dinner and plenty for all. The singing was quite a treat and was led by Brothers Riley Robinson, Robert May, Joseph Goss and Tillman Robinson. The second lesson, which was led by Miss Jennie May, was unanimously declared to be the best effort of the day, and was highly appreciated by all who had the pleasure of hearing it.

Programme of Chilton County Teachers' Institute
An Institute for the white teachers of Chilton county will be held at Concord, September 8 and 9, 1893.
FRIDAY 10a.m. Address of welcome. Joseph Green, Response, Supt. J.W. Moore.
 Miscellaneous Business. 1. Plans of introducing uniform text books, R.A. Roscoe and W.J. Martin. 2. Model school, Miss Etta Moore and Clement Mullins.
RECESS.
1:30p.m. The importance of classifying students. N.W. Wilson and T.F. Sessions
Advantages of a true education, Miss Geneva Jones and E.J. Hayes.
My Difficulties: how to overcome them. S.J. Jennings and John Lebron.
SATURDAY
9a.m. School Examinations. H.T. Estes and P.M. McKee
Vocal Music. Miss Fannie Woolley and J.P. Haley.
Education Address. G.L. Speer.
RECESS
1:30p.m. Are the studies prescribed by law sufficient for common school training? J.E. Jones and J.P. Gore.

School law discussed. D.S. Robinson and W.J. Popwell.
Closing Speeches.
Concord is situated in Dry Valley, five miles south of Montevallo and five miles west of Wessington. Teachers wishing conveyance from L.&N railroad will go to Wessington and from the E.T.N.&G. railroad will got to Montevallo. Those who expect conveyance from railroad free of charge should write to J.B. Moore,Jr., Montevallo. This is the last Institute of this school year and all the teachers are urged to attend.
R.E.R. Hicks, G.L. Speer, J. Alex Moore, Committee

Programme Of Sabbath School Convention
To Be Held With New Salem Church, on Saturday Before The Fifth Sunday in July, 1893
SATURDAY
10a.m. Devotional Exercises conducted by J.B. Pounds; alternate A.L. Foshee
Address of welcome by W.A. Wood
SUBJECTS
1. "Have we any scriptural authority for carrying our children to the Sabbath School?" Opened by J.P. Gentry, followed by J. Bice, W.G. Riggins and others.
2. "How can the Sabbath School be made a safeguard against the spiritual dangers that surround them?" Opened by G.W. Freeman, Alex Glass, D.H. Hudgeons and others.
3. "What will the final results of a well-conducted Sabbath School?" Opened by R.M. Honeycutt, J.A. Moore, W.D. Martin and others.
SUNDAY
9a.m. Sabbath School mass meeting conducted by W.A. Mimms; alternate J.E. Jones.
Preaching at 11 o'clock by Sutton Smitherman; alternate D.A. Seal

Programme of Exercise of 2d District Meeting
To be held with Valley Creek Church of Unity Association on Friday and Saturday before fifth Sabbath in July.
FRIDAY
Opening Exercise . Reading and Prayer by Bro. J.(? maybe H.) Longcryer.
TOPIC FOR DISCUSSION
1. "What constitutes the true church of Christ, and what is its mission?" - Rev. W.J. Rudle and Dr. W.B. Crumpton, at 10 o'clock a.m.
2. "Duties of Pastors to churches." - J.W. Michael and L. L. Hicks, 1:30p.m.
3. "Duties of Churches to their Pastors." - Rev. J.W.D. Desnaway and E.W. Bailey 2:30p.m.
SATURDAY 9:30a.m.
Reading and prayer by Rev. L.L. Hicks
1. "What is most conductive to a growth in grace, and what are its signs of growth?" - Capt. R.H. Pratt and J.H. Longeryer. 10:30a.m.
2. "Is it not the duty of Pastors to instruct their congregations in regard to their duty concerning Pastors' salary. Home Foreign and State Missions, ministerial education, etc." - David Moore and J.W. Price. 11:30a.m.
3. "Is it a Christian duty to support missions, and what amount of our means should we use to that end?" Rev. L.B. Pounds and J.G. Gay 1:30p.m.
4. "Sunday school work." - Rev. J.W. Michael and R.J. Michael 2:30p.m.
The churches of the District are requested to send full delegations. All are cordially invited to attend by the church and community of Valley Creek; those desiring conveyance form the railroad (Plantersville, nearest station) will be accommodated by writing Bro. Thos. Gay, P. O. Plantersville.
L.B. Pounds, R.J. Michael, J.G. Gay, Committee on Programme

TOWN ITEMS - Bricks For Sale. Good hard bricks for sale cheap. Purchase at once at your own (?)ce. C.H. Abbot, Clanton

The luscious water-melon ha(?)rip on Clanton now, and the Banner is (?) it. Brother (?) Smith, (?) presented (?)th a fine specimen last Wednesday.

Mr. C.H. Abbott is engaged in making some alterations to Messrs. (?)ins store.

Mr. T.H. White spent a few days visiting friends in Birmingham this week.

Mr. Tom Smith, of Mountain (?) is paying a visit to his parents (?).

The 5th was a great day for census taking. Mr. Rufus Littlejohn, Mr. (?)hn Collins, and Mr. W.R. King became happy fathers on that day.

Mr. and Mrs. Patrick Smith paid a visit to Birmingham last week.

Our genial depot agent Mr. W. W. (?)kin gave us a pleasant call the other night, we are always pleased to see our friends come in. The Banner door is always wide open, don't wait for a special invitation, (?) walk right in, you are always welcome.

Prof. McMorris' offer has been accepted and he is to be provided with a lot upon which to build his school house. We shall be glad to (?) the school house build and the school flourishing.

Mr. and Mrs. W.L. Sampey have gone on a two weeks visit to (?)elle Springs, Tenn.

Rev. A.C. Wells gave us a call (?) morning on his return from (?) church, Elmore county, where he reports a good meeting (?) Sunday. He says crops in that neighborhood are looking (?)y well and the people are happy.

Notice to Delinquent Taxpayers, The State of Alabama, Chilton County - The Tax collector of said county has filed in my office a list of delinquent taxpayers and real estate upon which taxes are due and unpaid. You are reported as delinquent and the following lots of land are reported as assessed to you, as will appear hereinafter. This is to notify you to appear before me on Monday, the 14th day of August, 1893, to show cause why a decree for the sale of said land should not be made for the amount of the taxes, costs and charges due thereon, as follows:
(Land descriptions given)
Beat No. 4. E.T. Gullahorn & Bro., J.H. Gallaspie
Beat No. 8 N.L. Broadhead, Burwell Baile

The heaviest man in the United States is John H. Craig, of Danfille, Ind. At birth he weighed 11 pounds; at 2 years of age his weight was 200; at the age of 37, two years ago, he weighed 907 pounds. His height is 6 fee 5 inches. It takes 41 yards of cloth to make him a suit of clothes.

Wild Hogs in Velasco Texas, pursued a young hunter named James Weems and he sought refuge in a tree where he was compelled to remain all night. Two sportsmen discovered him, and they had to shoot all the hogs before Weems could descend.

E.A. Rood, Toledo, Ohio, says; "Hall's Catarrh Cure cured my wife of catarrh fifteen years ago and she has had no return of it. It's a sure cure." Sold by Druggists.

AD - Suffered Every Minute. Since I came out of the war, with catarrh in my head, chronic diarrhea and rheumatism," says Mr. J.G. Anderson, of Scottsdale, Pa. "I had pains all over me, my sight was dim and there seemed to be floating specks before my eyes. The food I ate seemed like lead in my stomach. The rheumatism was in my right hip and shoulders. Hood's sarsaparilla and Hood's Pills did me more good than anything else. All my disagreeable symptoms have gone."

AD - I am seventy-seven years old, and have had my age renewed at least twenty years by the use of Swift's Specific. My foot and leg to my knee was a running sore for two years, and physicians said it could not be cured. After taking fifteen small bottles S.S.S. there is not a sore on my limbs, and I have a new lease on life. You ought to let all sufferers know of your wonderful remedy. Ira F. Styles, Palmer, Kansas City.

Justice Blatchford Dead, A Peaceful End, in the Presence of His Wife and Son. - Justice Samuel Blatchford, of the United States Supreme Court, died at his cottage on Greenough place, at Newport, R. I. a few evenings ago. Death had seemed probable for three days, but it was not till 3 p.m. that the family realized that it was at hand. From that hour Judge Blatchford sank rapidly passing away as if asleep. Mrs. Blatchford and Mr. Appleton Blatchford, the deceased jurist's only son, and Doctor F.H. Rankin, his physician, were with him when he died. Three weeks before he received two slight paralytic shocks, which his physician described as partial loss of motion. The shock affected his system generally, and left him very weak, but in full possession of his faculties. Justice Blatchford had been a Newport cottager for twenty-five years and was regarded as one of the most distinguished of its summer residents. Samuel Blatchford. born in New York City on March 9th, 182(?). He entered Columbia College very young and graduated at the age of seventeen, showing promise of what his future career would be. He received the degree of L.L. D. from Columbia College in 1867. Judge Blatchford then became private secretary to Governor William H. Seward for three years. In the year 1842, he was admitted to the Bar, and began practicing in New York City, removing to Auburn in 1845. He then entered into a law partnership with Governor Seward, and came back to the city in 1854. About this time Judge Blatchford began publishing his decisions in the United States Circuit Court, which won him a great deal of fame in legal circles. His career was established from that time, first he was appointed Judge of the district Court of The Southern District of New York in May, 1867, by President Johnson, and on March 4, 1878, President Hayes showed his appreciation of the brilliant lawyer by appointing him Circuit Judge of the Second Judicial court. His last promotion occurred on March 22, 1892, when President Arthur made him Associate Justice of the Supreme Court of the United States. Judge Blatchford was one of the ablest jurists in this country, and his loss will be deeply deplored by the entire American Bar.

FATAL FLAMES, Five Persons Burned to Death on a Steamboat - The big steamboat Bethel, anchored at the foot of Sibley street, St. Paul Minn., and used for the past three years as a lodging and boarding house for about 203 poor people, was burned to the waters edge at eleven o'clock p.m. Five lives were lost and seven persons were injured. Fifty persons were asleep on the Bethel. So rapid was the progress of the flames that those aboard the boat had to jump for their lives in their night clothing. The steamboat Sidney was tied to the Bethel, but by quick work in cutting her hawsers she was floated down stream uninjured. The loss on the Bethel is $10,000. At 1 o'clock in the morning five bodies had already been recovered, those of Mrs. Meak, matron of the Bethel, O'Shaughnessy and two unknown men. Lulu Morgan, a girl of twelve, daughter of the Rev. David Morgan, pastor of the Bethel, was taken to the City Hospital in a dying condition. The bodies of two women were then still in the hull of the boat. When the second story of the boat fell in they were seen to fall, clasped in each other's arms, into the flames. The fire was caused by the explosion of a lamp in the wash room.

OFF FOR POLAR REGIONS, Peary's Ship Starts On Her Northern Voyage - The Bold Arctic Explorer, Accompanied by His Wife, Sails Away From Brooklyn on His Second Attempt to Solve the Mystery of the North Pole.
After laying in New York Harbor for three days Lieutenant Peary's Arctic ship, the Falcon, cast off her moorings and backed off into the middle of the East River from the foot of Dock street, Brooklyn, bound for the North Pole...The exploring party will consist of Lieutenant Peary, his wife and her maid, his colored servant, Matthew Henson; S.J. Entreken, of Westchester, Penn., who belonged to the party which went to Peary's relief on his first expedition; Edward Astrup, a Norwegian who accompanied him before; Doctor Vincent, F.W. Stokes of Philadelphia, artist of the expedition; George H. Carr, Chicago; J.W. Davidson, of Austen, Minn.; E.B. Baldwin, of Nashville, Tenn; Hugh J. Lee, Meriden, Conn., and George H. Clarke, of Brookline, Mass....

THE NATIONAL GAME -Pittsburg has released Pitcher Gastright.

"Pete" Browning, of Louisville, is batting well.

The St. Louis Club has canceled the release of Catcher Buckley.

Stein and Kennedy have so far done about all of Brooklyns' winning pitching.

George Davies, the pitcher of the Cleveland Club, has been released to New York.

Milligan is catching finely for New York, which would have been in a bad hole without him.

With Nichols, Stivetts and Staley all in good form, the Boston team is well equipped for pitchers.

Hoy, Washington's deaf and dumb centre fielder, is playing a great game. He is hitting the ball hard, too.

Stein, of Brooklyn, still leads the League pitchers in point of effectiveness, he having had fewest runs earned off his pitching.

It is now assured that Catcher MacMahon, of New York, whose third finger on the right hand was so badly shattered, will not play again before 1894.

There isn't a right fielder in this country who has cut off half as many base hits this year as Treadway, of the Baltimores. He has seventeen assists to his credit.

Rusie and Milligan, of New York, weigh 435 pounds, constituting the heaviest battery in the league. Carsey and Cross, of Philadelphia, make on the lightest batteries in the League.

Ward points out as evidence of hard luck that New York lost eleven games by one run and won only one by that narrow margin, besides, the club has not been able to win an extra-inning game.

The three men who are regarded as the greatest baseball leaders on the ball field - Anson, of Chicago; Comiskey, of Cincinnati, and Ward of New York - are heads of teams away down in the race.

PROMINENT PEOPLE - Jules Verne has written seventy-four novels.

Samuel Minturn Peck, the Alabama poet, is running a turkey farm at Tuskaloosa.

Governor Flower, of New York, is one of the best amateur trap-shooters in America.

W.A. Deharity, the Mayor of Elwood, Ind., is only twenty-two years old, and is probably the youngest mayor in the country.

The Army of the Potomac, encamped at Boston, elected Major-General Nelson A. Miles, United States Army, President of its organization.

Rev. W.H. Furners, pastor emeritus of the First Unitarian Church in Philadelphia, was ninety-one years old a few days ago. He is the oldest living graduate of Harvard University and is the only survivor of the class of 1820.

Senator Sherman has moved into his new residence, which is one of the finest in Washington. It is said to have cost $150,000. Senator Sherman has made a great deal of money in Washington real estate and still has large holdings there.

Miss Emma Sickels, the Indian philanthropist, has three proteges, who are wonders in the musical world. They are the Misses Bluejacket, and they sing like nightingales. Of real Cherokee origin, they have the richest of copper-colored skin, brightest of black eyes an reddest of lips.

The new United States District Attorney for Eastern Wisconsin is a knight and may properly be called Sir H.H.M. Wigam. On June 14, 1885, he received the official notice that he had been made a knight of the Order of St. Gregory the Great, receiving the brave seal the Pope's seal, the fisherman's ring. and signed by Cardinal Ledochowski.

Scrubbing the Floor - An incident is told by Dr. Scoffern which illustrates in a pleasant way the good humor and geniality which belonged to Michael Faraday as much during his later as his earlier years. Professor Brande, during the year 1851, was lecturing at one time on a newly discovered method of purifying sugar by sugar of lead; while they were in the laboratory Scoffern accidentally let fall a retort of corrosive liquid. In an instant, he tells us, Professor Faraday threw some soda on the floor; then down on his hands and knees he went, slop-cloth in hand, like any humble housemaid. "Laughing, I expressed my desire to photograph him then and there; to demurred at the pose, begged me to consult his dignity, and began laughing with a childish joyousness." Hilariously boyish upon occasion he could be, and those who knew him best knew he was never more at home and never seemed so pleased at when making an "old boy" of himself, and he was wont to say, lecturing before a juvenile audience at Christmas time.

The Banner, Vol. 1, Clanton, Ala., Thursday, July 20, 1893, No. 37

STATE NEWS - Prof. Charley B. Gipson of Mobile has accepted the Presidency of the A. C. F. College at Tuscaloosa.

Burch who was on trial in the city court at Selma the past week, for the killing of Mr. McConnell, was acquitted.

Hendree Simpson, son of E.E. Simpson, of Montgomery, has been promoted in the Navy Department for merit.

John Walker murdered William Campbell, near Huntsville. No facts are known, except they were both drunk.

On the farm of J.M. Lawrence, Cherokee county, there is an oak tree which measures twenty-nine feet eight inches three feet above the ground.

Jeff Williams, colored, of Hayneville, cut Jane Mead's throat from ear to ear, and then tried carving his own. She is dead, but it is thought he will recover.

Dr. B. Dudley Williams, of Oxford has accepted a position as Commissioner to the Chippewa Indians in Minnesota and is now en route to his post of duty.

Tom Watson, a brakesman on the Mobile and Birmingham railroad was knocked from his train and killed. The accident occurred at the Cahaba river bridge.

W.J. Chadwick the young man who shot and killed Sylvester Corcoran at Faunsdale some four years ago, has surrendered to the authorities and given bond in the sum of $5,000.

Pruet Hodges, twelve years old has been granted a certificate to teach school by the Morgan county Board of Education. The Enquirer says he passed a very successful examination.

Charlie Robinson of Lowndesboro was burning a hole in an empty whiskey barrel with a piece of iron when an explosion occurred, which resulted in Robinson having two ribs broken.

Col. S.D. Howe, of Wilkesbarre, Pa., an experienced mica miner, owns some valuable mica property in Cleburne county and will open and operate the same. He says Cleburne has the finest mica he ever saw.

Mrs. George Mingo died at her home between Faunsdale and Dayton the past week. She was very old and was before her marriage, a Miss Harrison, of Virginia, an immediate relative of ex president Harrison.

James O. Lacy, a young man living in North Alabama took his pistol a few days ago, went out into the field and shot his horse three times and then blew out his own brains. Both he and the horse are dead. The only reason he gave for the rash act was the he wanted to get out of trouble. He has succeeded so far as plowing in new ground goes.

At Lawrenceville in Henry county, Tom Craddock, a negro, was arrested by Deputy Sheriff Dalton, on a warrant sworn out by Hatcher Vicker. The officer carried Craddock to Vicker's house and the two were standing a short distance from the prisoner, when to their surprise he grabbed the deputy's valise, wrenched it open, took therefrom a pistol and ran. Both gentlemen were then unarmed, but gave chase to the fleeing man. The negro turned and fired four shots at Mr. Vicker in rapid succession, killing him almost instantly.

A few days ago Deputy Sheriff J. Wesley Thomas, of Mobile, in an attempt to arrest the notorious desperado, Mike Fincher, had to kill him. Fincher's friends swore vengeance against the Deputy and on Tuesday morning his body was found near his home, mutilated in a horrible manner. Deputy Thomas was a one-armed man, but from all evidences made a desperate fight for his life. Every effort will be made to arrest the murderers, who, in such event, will no doubt be summarily dealth with, as great excitement prevails. Since the above was placed in type it has been decided that other parties for whom the deputy held warrants, are the parties to the killing. The facts bear out the latter supposition.

A Slick Trick - Annie Taylor, alias Annie McDowell, of Cincinnati, has been arrested and is now languishing behind the bars because on one would make for her a $2,000 bond. She is charged with using the mails for the purpose of fraud. It was her scheme to advertise for a husband in the matrimonial papers and having received an offer, fall in love with her correspondent and send a photograph of a beautiful young girl as that of herself. She would then offer to come to her lover if he would advance railroad fare and the price of a few trinkets needed. Having received the money she would drop the correspondence. She has practiced this for more than two years and has victims in all parts of America, from Texas to Canada. Thirty victims have been definitely located.

Grange and Alliance Combine - A movement is on foot in Texas to unite the two farmer organizations - the State Grange and Farmer's Alliance. B.J. Kendrick, the originator of the movement has called a meeting of the two organizations to take place in Franklin on the 8th proximo and to continue in session until the 10th. This meeting is to complete the work of uniting the two Texas agricultural organizations which shall have for its object the promotion of the interest of the farmers.

General News - Peary has decided to take carrier pigeons with him on his arctic expedition. Perry is off on his arctic expedition, and the question will soon be who will go after Peary.

Superintendent Porter, of the Census Bureau, has tendered his resignation which will take effect July 31st.

The Florida Agricultural College has conferred the degree of L. L. D. on Hoke Smith, Secretary of the Interior.

Howard Mutchler, of Bethlehem, Pa., has been nominated for Congress to fill the unexpired term of his father, the late Wm. Mutchler.

Yellow fever at Santos is depopulating the entire city. This is encouraging news no doubt for H.C. Smith the newly appointed consul from Alabama.

Secretary Hoke Smith has visited fort Tetten, Indian agency. He was met by 200 pupils of the Indian Industrial school, led by an Indian band. The Indians made known their grievances. Chief Wannatan presented the Secretary with a pipe of peace.

Secretary Carlisle has decided that foreign exhibitors shall be allowed to sell their exhibits for delivery after the exposition. This decision upsets the calculations of the managers of the Fair, who have been counting on a big revenue in the shape of per centages from the sale of exhibits.

The Fish Commission has dispatched one of its cars to Florida to make collections of interesting and economic specimens of marine life of the Atlantic and Gulf coasts for exhibition in its aquarium at the Columbian exposition. James E. Benedict, a prominent naturalist is in charge of the work.

Great excitement prevails in and around Bristol, Tenn. over an effort which is being made to capture the Fleming gang. The Sheriff with a posse of sixty men are after them and hundreds of shots are being fired on both sides whenever they are located. Two of the Flemings have been mortally wounded and one of the Sheriff's party.

Ex-Alderman John D. Crimmins, of Chattanooga was killed on Chickamanga battlefield Sunday by a falling tree under which he had taken refuge from a storm. Chief of Police Mitchell was also badly injured. He was taken home and given medical attention by a Doctor Johnson recently moved to the city, who in treating him gave him a dose of morphine and shortly afterwards he died. Johnson has been arrested and place under $1,000 bond, under the charge of involuntary manslaughter.

Signal officer Sherry, at Cape Henry has wired the signal officer at Norfolk Va., that the British brig Darma, bound from Havana to Saint Johns, N. S. had come to the capes and anchored off quanantine, Fisherman's Island, thirty miles east from Hampton, Roads, reporting that she had lost her captain who died with yellow fever, and three of the crew are down with the disease. United States quarantine officials have the vessel in charge.

He Likes Good Neighbors - In the southwestern portion of Vanderbilt's estate of 9000 acres Asheville, N. C. is a little track of land of 14 acres which the millionaire does not own, and, though it is entirely surrounded by his possessions, is a tract that he has in (?)ied to buy. The little p(?) owned by a negro named Collins, who makes his living by hauling on Asheville's streets. When Mr. Vanderbilt commenced to purchase the land he now owns he struck a snag when he came to Collins. The negro stubbornly refused to sell and finally named a price that was $600 more that the highest figure offered him by Vanderbilt. The millionaire at first refused to pay it, and when he finally did agree to give Collins the amount he asked, then Collins backed down and refused to sell at any price. In vain the money king pleaded and threatened; the negro, who, it is believed, was encouraged by outside parties, remained firm, and Vanderbilt could not buy. Collins cooly remarked that what he wanted in this life was good neighbors, and now he had the chance for the first time. He said that he especially liked Mr. Vanderbilt, and believed he would be a nice neighbor. Then Vanderbilt fenced in the negro's property, being compelled, of course, to allow him an outlet, but this had the opposite effect. Collins was tickled, and expressed his delight in unmeasured terms. "Now, I'm fixed," he declared. "I have good fences without any cost to me, and I can let my stock run loose without being worried about bothering neighbor Vanderbilt." An so this state of affairs exits. Some day Vanderbilt will give him an immense sum, and Collins will be "well fixed" for the remainder of his life, and somebody else will likely get a bit out of the purchase money also.

A Pugilistic Preacher - Dr. H.C. Neal, a minister of the Methodist church at Kirkpatrick, had just concluded a temperance sermon a few evenings since, when O.P.C. Evans, one of the leading prohibitionists of Indians, arose and began a speech denouncing all the laymen and ministers not belonging to his party as hypocritical knaves and rascals. Dr. Neal called upon him to desist, when Evans started abusing him. Neal finally came down from the pulpit and threw the disturber bodily out the doors, while the congregation cheered enthusiastically.

Action for Damages - It is now reported that the National Citizens Rights Association has interested itself in the case of C.J. Miller, who was hanged and burned at Brawl, Ky., Backed by this organization Mrs. Bertie Miller, widow of the negro, will bring an action for damages against the city marshal and his bondsmen at Sikeston, Mo., the Sheriff of Carrels county, Ky., his bondsmen, and members of the posse individually who aided in the capture of Miller, all citizens of Illinois, Missouri and Kentucky who participated in the affair which it occurred. Suit will be commenced in the United States court for the Southern district of Illinois.

Rigid Prohibition - If Judge Hudson's decision is sustained South Carolina will have the most rigid prohibition in the world, for then liquor could not be obtained in case of sickness, nor alcohol for druggists' prescriptions nor wine for the communion table. The celebrated Evans act opens with the prohibition of the sale or manufacture of liquor save through a State dispensary. Judge Hudson decides the prohibition feature to be constitutional and the dispensary feature unconstitutional.

A Fatal Duel - Two young men of prominent families of Sandersville, Ga., became engaged in a street fight and both were killed. They were Richard P. Broughton who was shot through the head and Fred Rawlings who was shot through the heart. They both died within a few minutes.

PROMINENT PEOPLE - President Cleveland is still suffering from rheumatism.

.
The late Duke of Bedford was one of the richest and most miserly men in England.

.
The Duchess of Teck, mother-in-law of the future King of England, is fair, fat and sixty.

.
Sir George Tryon was the fourth British Admiral who lost his life by disaster unconnected with warfare.

.
General Nelson A. Miles was a clerk in a Boston store and familiar with a yardstick before he took hold of a sword.

.
Doctor Guzman, the Nicaraguan Minister at Washington, has presented his letter of recall, his Government having abolished his post.

.
Attorney-General Hendrick, of Kentucky prides himself on the fact that he rose from a farm laborer to his present place of dignity and honor.

.
Charles Nordhoff, the New York Herald man, who has returned from Honolulu, says Minister Blount wouldn't stay in the islands for $60,000 a year.

Jay Gould's sons, George Gould, Edwin Gould and Howard Gould, do not frequent any of the big New York fashionable clubs, but confine their attendance to athletic clubs.

Chew Shu Sum has landed at San Francisco. He is the agent of the Six Companies of China, the combination which controls millions of dollars and practically owns several hundred thousand Chinamen.

Miss Ella Knowles, who was the Populist candidate for Attorney-General at the last election in Montana, has been selected by the Republicans in that State as counsel in their effort to secure control of the Legislature.

The death of Guy de Maupassant, the French author at the age of fifty-three, removes a genius who in his was the equal of Edgar Allen Poe. His short stories are remarkable for their brilliancy, but it is the brilliancy of insanity.

Admiral Tryon, who was lost on the Victoria, was a descendant of Governor Tryon, the English Colonial Governor of New York, who assisted at the burning of Norwalk, Conn., watching the conflagration from a safe distance.

The Duke of Veragua has recently lost his entire fortune. President Thomas W. Palmer, of the World's Fair, has started a subscription for him and the people of the United States, South America and the West Indies will be appealed to for contributions.

Ex-Senator Hill, of Colorado, has made a fortune by smelting gold and silver by a secret process of his own, by which his big refinery in Denver is able to do some of the best refining in the world. He is said to be one of the best judges of metals in the United States.

Secretary Smith is making a tour of all the important Indian agencies and will also visit the Yellowstone National Park. The land grant railroads will likewise receive his attention, and he intends, as far a possible, to investigate all the details connected with his department. He will probably make a few speeches along the route, especially in the far Northwest. He will be absent three or four weeks.

C.W. Macune has sold out his interest in the National Economist. Exit Macune.

Our Jeffersonian friends have been called upon to organize in each county and beat in the state by Chairman Goodwyn.

The People's Party of New York will hold a state convention, August 18th, at Sylvan Beach, Lake Oneida,. Gen. Weaver, Senators Stewart and Peffer, Representatives Simpson and Pence, Hon. Ignatius Donnelly and H.L. Loucks will be present.

STATE ASSEMBLY K. of L. - The Assembly was called to order by S. M. W. W. S. Barefield. Brothers E.J. Grove of Mobile and H. Herrington of Castleberry were appointed as a committee on credentials, they reported all present as entitled to admission. In the absence of Bro. Ira Campbell, Bro. T.H. White was requested to act as secretary. After some discussion it was decided to go into the election of officers resulting as follows: State Master Workman W.S. Barefield, of Bertha, Dale county; State worthy Foreman, E.J. Grove, of Mobile; State Secretary Treasurer, T.H. White, of Clanton, Chilton county; State

Worthy Inspector, S.M. Franklin, of Brewton, Escambia county; State Statistician H. Herrington, Castleberry, Conecuh county...Bro. McGugin, an old steamboatman, fairly surpassed himself as a successful barbecuer of meat...We desire to return especial thanks to Bros. Lowery, Schell, and Franklin for courtesies received.

Lomax Linings - Dr. A.J. Marlar paid his family a flying visit last Monday, he reports a great deal of sickness at Clanton Ford.

Mr. John Lodge of Clanton Ford spent Saturday and Sunday with his brother, Mr. W.M. Lodge of this place.

Mr. George Lodge paid the Magic City a flying visit last Sunday.

There was a most enjoyable ice cream supper given for the young people of this place at the residence of Mr. W.M. Lodge on the night of the 15th inst; the young people were delighted with the music by Mrs. Markee and Mrs. Lodge and Miss May Lowe; all seemed to have a most delightful time and thank them very much for their hospitality, especially Mr. George Lodge. Mr. Henry De La Rue, of Birmingham, and Miss May Lowe of Jemison, came down to attend the ice cream supper and spent Sunday with Miss Willie Marlar. Mr. John Wilkins of Shelby spent Saturday night with Mr. D.B. Lowe near here, he intended spending Sunday but finding his best girl had gone back on him he returned home Sunday morning.

Miss Cora Smith of this place is visiting her grandfather Mr. David Lodge at Clanton Ford.

Welchville Winnowings - Misses Callie Cunningham and Vesta Welch are visiting relatives in Calera.

Miss Annie McGrier has been visiting in Selma the past week, and some of the young men are wearing long faces.

Messrs. W.H. Reynolds and Ernest Welch went to Jones' switch today to see their best girls.

Bro. Starr preached an excellent sermon at this place Sunday night.

Mr. H.D. Landrum of Plantersville, has been coming to see his best girl right often up this way. Hurrah for Houston!

Mr. J.H. Cox and family of Dixie, have been visiting relatives at this place.

Mrs. Benjamin, of Selma, is visiting Mr. Martin's family.

Vinehill Varieties - We are glad to note that Mr. Johnny Herrod's family are better after a serious attack of slow fever. Mr. Huey Herrod's hogs are dieing with the cholera. I advised him to try Mr. H.J. Coles plan, give them poke root so they will poke off to keep from having to drag them off.

Miss Ida Weaver has been quite sick but is better now.

The famous shoemaker, Mr. Carrie Herrod, has begun his old trade again; we know shoes are reasonably cheap but I think we had better make our own shoes at home.
.

Miss Alice Weaver paid Miss Mary Tidwell a pleasant visit this week.
.

We are glad to note that our esteemed friend H.D. Davis has a splendid school in Autauga.
.

Rev. A. Perry preached at Bethel Church on the fourth Sunday, and the Saturday before.
.

While Mr. Nat Reid was on his way home from Prattville, his mules ran away with his buggy and came very near killing him, it is very likely he will die yet.
.

Mr. Jim Warren paid a pleasant visit to relatives in Perry county.
.

Mr. Ben Warren of Perry county is visiting his mother Mrs. Herrod, and he reports that his brother cut his foot nearly off with an axe a few days ago.
.

Maple Springs Music - We had a very nice time at our church last Sunday. The crowd began to gather about nine o'clock and singing commenced directly afterwards. A committee was appointed to arrange the singing: M. Popwell, Arch Foshee and W.L. Price. The singing was led by Bros. Joe White, Downs and Thomas. Then prayers by Bros. Price, White, Thomas and Riley Robinson. The meeting was continued throughout the evening.

Verbena Views - A negro prisoner jumped from the mail train just below Mountain Creek, the train was running about 40 miles an hour he jumped out of a window with handcuffs on.
.

Mrs. A.W. Carter and her daughter Miss Jessie Carter, of Shelby, are visiting the family of Mr. Perry Daniels.

Shady Grove Shadows - Rev. Ritch preached at Shady Grove, Sunday night.
.

Miss Lily Bates, of Selma is visiting her grandmother here.
.

Miss Georgia Thompson, of Birmingham, is visiting her cousin, Mrs. Gray, at this place; she spent a few days this week with Miss Beulah Cooper.
.

Prof. Headley has a very good school of thirty pupils at this place and we hope it will soon increase.

Mulberry Musings - Robert Fox and John Fox, of Stanton, spent the Fourth with friends and relatives; we think Mr. Robert is about to get us a case in this settlement.
.

Mr. Lee has been quite sick, be we are glad to hear he is improving.

Energy Events - Prof. R.J. Eiland's school opened at Enterprise last Wednesday.
.

C.N. Dennis and many friends seined out his pond last Thursday and caught a great many nice fish.
.

W.A. Sleighton spent the past week here. T.E. Taylor will preach at Enterprise school house on the fourth Sunday.

Robert May, of Bozeman, will commence his singing school at Bethsalem on the 18th inst.; we hope to have a large attendance.

Miss Etta Moore has returned home after a pleasant visit to relatives at Oxmoor.

Jumbo Jumbles - Professors Joseph Gore and E.G. Smith have gone down to Mulberry to see their to see their best girls.

Rev. James H. Mullins, we are glad to say, is somewhat better.

Rev. - Dobbs, of Texas is this week holding a series of meetings at Mt. Zion church.

Prof. W.S. Garner, of Dry Valley, was down last Sunday to see his best girl. O.K. Mullins and family are visiting relatives and friends in this neighborhood.

J.S. Jones went to Clanton on business last Saturday, and reports water-melons plentiful.

There was a lively meeting at Limesprings church, near Jumbo, last Sunday; Pastor Isaac Rutherford preached both morning and evening.

Rev. - Gibson will preach at Kilgore school house, near Jumbo, on Friday night before the second Sunday in August.

TOWN ITEMS - Miss Maggie Reeder, of Atlanta, Ga., a niece of O.M. Mastin, will spend the summer here with friends and relatives.

Sen. A.T. Goodwyn and Hon. R. Kolb will address the County Alliance at Liberty next Wednesday.

Miss Mollie Parker's many friends will be sorry to learn she is suffering from an attack of typhoid fever.

Henry Honeycutt has been visiting his old home this week; he reports having a good time.

Bro. W.R. King and family are visiting relatives in Coosa county.

Rev. R.M. Honeycutt held an interesting meeting at Providence, on Sunday.

Miss Ella Gartman has closed her school at Duke's mill and returned (?)e.

(?) H. Abbott has been making some improvements to Uncle Pat(?) Smith's residence.

(?)emp and Culp have rented the (?) store and removed into it.

(?).L. Sampey and lady have returned from a pleasant visit to (?)stle Springs, Tenn.

(?).W. Adams, manager of the (?)nce store at Jemison, paid us a pleasant call on Wednesday.

(?).N. Jones, our popular assistant depot agent, has gone on a (?) to Hanceville. During his absence James Hester will officiate.

(?) Clayton came in from the (?) last Saturday, and reports (?) in that direction as being in (?) condition.

CARNEGIE'S DREAM - Andrew Carnegie, the iron king, thinks the time is not far distant when the United States and most of the British domain, including England, Ireland, Scotland and Canada, will be united in a governmental union, and he is so enthusiastic over it that he even now speaks of the new nation as the "British-American Union."...

The Banner, Vol. 1, Clanton, Ala., Thursday, July 27, 1893, No. 38

STATE NEWS - Jim Sullivan, the Selma murderer, was found guilty and got a life sentence.

Sam Bush escaped prison at Pratt Mines. A reward of $50 has been offered for his arrest. Monroe C. Herstein, a popular young merchant of Gadsden, committed suicide by shooting himself with a pistol.

Sy Blythe, a young man of Cherokee county, was struck by lightning and instantly killed near Rock Run furnace,

A four-year old son of Mr. Dave Jones of Florence was struck by a stone thrown by a girl and his skull fractured.

J.L. Jay of Albany, Ga., has the contract to build the $50,000 addition to Eufaula's cotton mills, and will commence the work at once.

Deace and Ryan, the two men who so brutally murdered Deputy Sheriff Thomas at Mobile, have been arrested. One of them confesses his crime.

Hon. Willis G. Clarke of Mobile has been selected by Governor Jones for the railroad commissionship, made vacant by General Holtzclaw's death.

Hardy Rice has been arrested in Etowah county charged with the murder of Sam Powell during the Christmas holidays of 1890.

John W. Walker of Huntsville, was killed by William Campbell. The murderer is out on a bond of $1,000. The court admitting him guilty of voluntary manslaughter.

While trying to arrest a negro, who was stealing his corn, Mr. Joseph Menshew of Pickens was stabbed and died in a few minutes after the occurrence. The negro was arrested.

Jim Andrews, colored, resisted arrest near Burnsville, Dallas county, and was shot and killed by Constable, W.K. Campbell. He was suspected of robbery and attempt to murder.

A liberal reward is offered for the arrest and delivery to the Sheriff of Henry county of Tom Craddock, colored, who murdered Mr. H.J. Vickers near Lawrenceville on the evening of the 11th inst.

Claud Pridgin, a section boss, on the Mobile and Birmingham railroad, was knocked on the head by a negro man named Gus Daniels, and death resulted in two hours. A long handle shovel was the weapon used.

GENERAL NEWS - Col. C.C. Jones,Jr., historian of Georgia, is dead.

Vice-President Stevenson and party received a royal welcome at San Francisco.

George C. Perkins, of California has been appointed United States Senator.

Joseph Jefferson the great tragedy actor, is not expected to live longer than a few days.

A negro Lee Walker was hung afterwards burned, at Memphis. The same cause as usual.

Gen. James T. Holtzclaw, late commander of the United confederate Veterans, died at Montgomery, Ala., the past week.

President Cleveland tips the beam at 300 pounds. This is 75 pounds more than his usual weight. No wonder it hurts when he sits down "on a feller."

Congressman Breckenridge, from the blue grass regions of Kentucky, is fixing to fly - at least has taken unto himself a wing. He was married a few days since to Mrs. Louise Scott Wing, a most estimable lady of that state.

Henry Singleton, who is serving a life sentence in the penitentiary at Jackson, Miss., killed Lula Payne. He will be tried for the murder, and it is believed will be hung. His case will be the only one on record where a life convict has ever before been tried before the courts.

Mr. Henry E. Gladstone, nephew of the English Premier, who has been making a tour of this country, is now in Baltimore, much pleased with his trip thus far. He is 23 years old and was graduated at Trinity College, Dublin, two years ago. He intends to sail for home within two weeks.

The State department has received advices from Minister Baker at Managua confirming the news that a revolt has broken out again in Niaragua and that the president of the republic and his minister of foreign affairs are held prisoners at Leon. There was no battle, but the minister regards the situation as critical.

A sensational tragedy occurred in a court room at Tabasco, Mex. An outlaw, named San Francisco Rodrigues, had been tried, and found guilty, and the judge had just finished reading the sentence when the prisoner drew a pistol and discharged it at the magistrate. The bullet took effect, killing the judge instantly.

Not In Practice - A most remarkable case of attempted lynching took place at Beamon's Station, Va. Within the past twelve months Mr. Cartright, who lives near Beamon's Station, has had twelve horses killed by some person. About three weeks ago his house was burned to the ground. Suspicion rested upon a negro named Isaac Jenkins. He returned to the neighborhood yesterday, was arrested and while being taken to jail by a constable was captured by a party of twenty-five men, who hung him to a tree and shot and left him for dead. After the lynchers left he took his knife from his pocket, cut himself down and made his escape. As soon as it became known that the lynchers had failed, there was made up a crowd and the woods were scoured, but the man could not be found.

Didn't Hear of The War - Boomville Correspondent St. Louis Chronicle: Edie Hickam, an old negress, is the plaintiff in perhaps the most remarkable case ever tried in the courts of this county. She is an ex-slave, and brought suit against her master. Joseph Hickman of this county, for $5 a month's wages as a family domestic for twenty-four years, during which time she claims to have been kept in ignorance of her emancipation. The suit was instituted here in 1889 for $1,400, and resulted in a judgment in her favor for $700. Defendant appealed to the Kansas City court of Appeals, which remanded the case to the Circuit court of this county, which now renders a decision for the defendant. A motion for a new trial has been filed, and public sentiment is in favor of the old negress, who has toiled for her master for a quarter of a century without remunerations.

Colored Catholic Congress - James A. Spencer, Chairman of the Executive Committee of the Colored Catholic Congress of the United States has issued a call from Charleston, S.C., for the fourth National Catholic Colored Congress to be held in Chicago, Sept. 4 next. The basis of representation for the election of delegates is: To societies of fifty members or less, one delegate and for each additional twenty-five one delegate; but not to exceed three delegates to any society. Parishes that have no societies may form temporary organization and send one delegate. Accompanying the call is a letter of approval from Archbishop Frehan of Chicago.

Farmers' Institute - Hon. Hector D. Lane, Commissioner of the Agriculture, assisted by Major Thos. J. Key, of the State Agricultural Department, and Professors Bondurant and Stedman, of the A. and M. College, Auburn, Ala;, will hold "Farmers Institutes" at the following named times and places...

And now it appears that Tommy Jones didn't have sense enough to get out of the wet.

Morgan and Pugh, Denson, Bankhead and Turpin are for Free Silver. The manipulatives of the gold conspiracy will find them a hard team to down.

The County Alliance met yesterday, and with the brethren of Liberty Alliance. Hon. R.F. Kolb and Tyler Goodwyn, editor of the Reform Advocate, were present and addressed the audience, which was composed of over one thousand of Chilton's citizens who greeted the speakers with frequent bursts of applause...Mr. Goodwyn dwelt upon the cause of free silver most eloquently and forcibly and was listened to with close attention from commencement to finish. Rev. J.M. Dykes closed the speaking with a short talk replete with good advice and full of wit and description of which would but lead circumstance....Bro. Lee Hayes' vaunt, that Liberty's meeting would be a great success has been amply sustained....

Swift Creek Siftings - The singing convention was opened Saturday by R.D. May, chairman. First was "How sweet the name of Jesus sounds"; then prayer by W.L. Price. First lesson by Prof. Durham, second by R. Robinson; recess for dinner; there was plenty of dinner for all and it was thoroughly enjoyed. Lecture by Prof. Holloway; first lesson by J.S. Jones, second by R.T. Grant. Your correspondent was not there when services opened; after I got there, first lesson by R.D. May, second by James Gulledge; recess for dinner; first lesson by Tillman Robinson, second by John Hatchet. By request, Prof. Durham, and R.T. Grant, led the singing to last lesson which was closed by Prof. Holloway. To meet with Salem July next. Officers elected, N. Dobbs, chairman; as't, James Pyran; sec. Joe Goss; visitors, three Hatchets, Gulledge, Grant, Noral, from Coosa, Thomas from Elmore. DAD'S BEST BOY

Lomax Linings - Mr. W.M. Lodge and family are visiting friends and relatives at Clanton Ford.

.

Mr. J.W. Foshee is at home on the sick list; we hope to see him out again soon.

Mr. Aurelius Attaway spent Sunday with friends and relatives.

Mr. George Lodge and Miss Willis Marlar spend Sunday in Jemison with her cousin Miss Mary Lowe.

Rev. Mr. Gibson preached an interesting sermon, Sunday evening at this place.

Mr. C.H. Abbot spent Sunday with Dr. A.J. Marlar's family near here.

West Chilton Warblings - Mr. Ed. Bell, a fine, and well to do farmer, residing near Plantersville, on the morning of the 18th was awakened about daylight by the weak crying of a young baby; he at once arose from his bed and went out and was shocked to find a child lying in a small goods box placed on a lumber pile at his yard gate, and no mother to be seen anywhere about. On examining the box he found it to contain a poor little forsaken boy baby and a cup, teaspoon and a phial of soothing syrup and a few articles of clothing. The child is supposed to be about two weeks old, it had evidently been placed there by some unknown persons from a long distance. Mr. Bell found near by, marks where a buggy had stopped, and tracks of a man and a woman had passed to his house and back to the buggy; he pursued them and gave them a close chase; he tracked the buggy on the Selma road 5 miles below Plantersville and there the parties left the big road and took an old by-road and bore across west to the new market road and turned north and traveled that road 15 miles, to near Chestnut-hill church, there the fleeing parties turned back east in the direction of Maplesville, and struck the Selma road again and turned down it south. Mr. Bell chased them about 30 miles and was only 8 hours behind them. During this chase the woman dressed three different times, first in men's clothing, in order to fool the pursuing crowd. They were in a buggy with a big mule pulling them. If they are caught a will be punished to the fullest extent of the law; there are detectives at work on every side after them. The baby will be turned over to the orphans home at Summerfield, Ala., in a few days if no owner is found. No wonder we are having droughts and other disasters and cyclones sent upon us.

Capt. Ellis Mixson, an old land mark of Burnesville, Ala., dropped dead with heart disease on the morning of the 14th; he had walked out to his farm and was dead when he was found; he was 75 years of age and the only brother of Dr. Wm. Mixson, of Plantersville.

Mr. Nat Reid, of Vinehill, happened to some bad luck a few days ago; he was driving a span of young horses to his buggy when they became frightened and run away with him tearing up his buggy and crippling him for life.

Dixie Dots - On the 15th of July Mr. W.M. Price, F.J. Wylie, Willie Marshall and others went fishing; they had the success of catching 400 fish.

F.J. Wylie, the champion of the wilderness, enjoyed his part of the fish very much.

Prof. R.J. Mitchell and wife spent the day at Captain Price's, on the 7th, better known as Texas field.

Mr. Martin, of Sixmile, this going to school at Valley Creek academy.

Mr. J.F.T. Letcher, of Texas, says he has a good crop, and also a good time with the girls.

Miss Mollie Olive, of Texas, is a pretty girl; the Hustler would like to see her very much.

Mr. Charlie Barnes, one of our handsomest young men, paid the girls a visit in Dallas county; he was on a wooing tour.

The convention of Trustee Stockholders of the Farmers Alliance Exchange, is called to meet at Talladega, August 8th, by President Joseph Shackelford.

TOWN ITEMS - The wind storm of Thursday took off the roof of Ely Williams and a (?)amed Dan Dansbys houses (?) miles north east of Clanton.

Rev. A.C. Wells gave us a pleasant call last week but to late for this week's paper, and reported a right good meeting at Shady Grove church all last week, with seven new converts to the church and an (?) revival in the cause of Christ.

Clifford Cook, son of John Cook, fell from a tree out at Ehrman, and Mullins mill last Monday, breaking (?) bones of his right arm. Doctor (?) set the broken bones, and the little sufferer his progressing favorably.

Mrs. Bozeman and Mrs. Blackmore of Coosa are visiting friends at Mulberry.

There will be a public discussion at the Court House Saturday August (?)h of the Sayre election law. Mr. (?) Logan will open the discussion.

Bishop Jackson of the Episcopal church will visit Clanton, August (?).

Next Monday a mathematical (?) will be opened in the hall of Mullins store by that scholastic veteran Prof. J.M. Corderie.

(?) Miller has returned home after a pleasant visit to friends at (?).

We regret to announce the death of James H. Mullins on Wednesday (?) his home in the Jumbo neighborhood. The deceased gentleman had been very sick for some time at last reports, it was hoped departing would be deferred some while longer.

(?)mes McKee is visiting Mrs. (?)game.

Sheriff Moore arrested a negro at (?)ation to day supposed to be Shelton, but he proved to be (?) else, and the Sheriff turned (?).

S.D. Smitherman was arrested at Jemison charged with grand larceny and was brought before Justice Harrison and then liberated on bond.

The county Alliance elected the following officers for the current year: Moses Robinson, President; B.H. Wells, Vice-President; H.L. Honeycutt, Secretary-Treasurer; L.B. Pounds, Lecturer; J.A. Logan, Ast. Lecturer; Wm. M. Wood, Chaplain; Thomas Driver, Doorkeeper; Lee Hayes, Asst Doorkeeper; T.J. Dorminy, Executive committee; Moses Robinson, Delegate to State Alliance.

Mr. E.W. Boyd, of Coosa county visited relatives here this week.

Programme Of Clanton District Conference
To meet with Kingston church, Autauga county, August 4-6, 1893.
Friday, August 4
9 a.m. Devotional Exercises, led by Bro. A. Baker.
10 a.m. Organization and Report of Business Committee.
11 a.m. Introductory sermon, by Rev. J.L. Busby.
2 p.m. Report of Officers and appointment of Committee.
3:30 p.m. Report of Pastors and Delegates on the State of Religion.
7:30 p.m. Devotional Exercises, led by Brother T.R. Busby.
8 p.m. Sermon, by Rev. Wm. Crowson.
Saturday, August 5
8:30 a.m. Devotional Exercises, led by Rev. C.W. Culver.
9 a.m. Business.
10 a.m. " Power of the Gospel to Overcome Worldliness, " by Rev. W.A. Wells.
11 a.m. Sermon, by Rev. J.J. Stallings, General Missionary for Ala.
2 p.m. Business and Reports of Committee.
3 p.m. " The Best Method to Educate Our People To A Higher Standard Of Cheerful Giving To Support The Gospel. ' God Loves A Cheerful Giver.'" Led By Rev. A.C. Wells and others.
4 p.m. " The Advantages Of Sabbath Schools, " by Rev. Wm. Shaw.
7 p.m. Prayer and Praise Service, led by Rev. T.J. Rutherford.
8 p.m. Sermon, by Rev. W.R. East.
Sunday, August 6
9 a.m. Sunday School, conducted by Rev. Wm. Shaw.
10 a.m. Experience Meeting, by Brother Wm. Davis.
11 a.m. Sermon, by Rev. S.E. Bassett. Followed by the Lord's Supper.
2:30 p.m. Holiness Meeting, left by Rev. S.E. Bassett.
7:30 p.m. Prayer and Praise Service, led by Rev. J.F. Gaylor.
8 p.m. Sermon, by Rev. A.T. Clarke.
Delegates will meet at Bozeman, (L.& N.R.R.) on Friday morning.

The People's party of Ohio met at Columbus recently in state convention with over 200 delegates in attendance. H.E. Taubeneck, of Illinois, chairman of the national committee, was present. The following ticket was named: For governor, J.E. Brack, of Columbus; lieutenant governor, M. Bookey, of Vinton county; treasurer, William H. Taylor, of Champaign county; attorney general, J.H. Rhodes, of Sandusky; judge supreme court, C.T. Clark, of Columbus; dairy and food commissioner, Thomas N. Hickman, Morrow county; member of board of public works, for Matthew Baber, of Clark county.

THE VIRGINIA POPULISTS - General James G. Field, of Albamarle county, Va., who last year was a candidate for vice president of the People's party, made a speech a few days ago at Midlothian, which is parted as outlining in part the plan of the campaign of the Virginia Populists in the fall election for governor and members of the legislature...

WHERE DOES HE STAND NOW - It is a matter of regret that men so often forget to defend the interests of the masses when, through the suffrages of their country men praises, they have been placed in office... Below we give a few extracts from a patriotic speech delivered by Governor Elias Carr, at Asheville in 1890, while he was president of the State Alliance. In speaking of the National meeting held in St. Louis, in 1889, he said: " The most important meeting ever held in this county has been the assembling of the farmer and labor organizations in December last, the necessity for which was foreshadowed by that eminent statesman and jurist, the late Judge David Davis...

A Change in Postal Cards - Postmaster General Bissell last decided to abandon the three sizes of postal cards now in use, and to substitute one size for both single and reply cards...

Saved From Death By Gum - Bibles, pocketbooks and many others of the like have all been the means of saving people's lives from bullet wounds, but probably be first time for a package of gum to act in that role occurred at Carey, Idaho, one day recently, where the life of Dave Evans was saved by a package of gum, the bullet lodging in the package.

Ad - Life and strength are given to weak and frail children in wonderful manner by Hood's Sarsaparillas. Mr. Edward Hilbert, Lawrence, Mass., says: " Our daughter, Etta Hilbert, had little strength when a baby. When two and one-half years old she had frequent fainting spells, caused by heart trouble. We gave her Hood's Sarsaparilla. Her general health improved until she became healthy and rugged. We give her Hood's Sarsaparilla occasionally now, whenever she complains of that tired feeling in spring and summer.

Wine Worth Its Weight In Gold - The champagne drank at the Martin Craven wedding in New York City last week was a vintage which had never been served in this county before. Bottles of this wine are worth their weight in gold. Bradley Martin bought 200 of these from the Cafe Royal in London, paid $50 a bottle. Connoisseur as like Mr. McAllister were delighted at this part of the entertainment which, to those who appreciate rare wines, was a royal feast.

The Banner, Vol. 1, Clanton, Ala., Thursday, August 3, 1893, No. 39

ALABAMA ITEMS - Emanuel McCauley fell through an elevator in Huntsville and will die.

Dr. E.T. Taliaferro, one of Madison county's most prominent citizens is dead.

Harry Heath an ex-editor of Mobile has been placed in the asylum at Tuscaloosa.

Robert Hudson is on trial at Mobile for a murder committed twenty-four years ago.

By the capsizing of the schooner Charles A. Swift at the entrance to Mobile Bay, Capt. James Johnson was drowned.

James H. Baldwin has retired from the editorial chair of the Sheffield Reaper and will be succeed by E.O. Comstock,Sr.

A man called himself Pickard on Pickerel is doing Alabama towns in the interest of the Y.M.C.A. He is advertised as an impostor.

Miss Julia Woodruff, a prominent society young lady of Eufaula, ran away with a Mr. Busch, of New York, and were married in Georgia.

A negro woman named Caroline Lee, living in Sumter county, beat an orphan boy who was under her charge so that he died from the effects.

Charley Davis, colored was shot at Brookside, while helping himself without leave to W.J. Early's watermelons. The wound is painful but not dangerous.

Carbon Hill has elected new City officers. A. McDonald was elect Mayor and with E.W. Goss, D. McDonald, Lewis Lillick, John Townley and R.G. Cary as Alderman.

Joseph H. Parker, a lineman in Mobile, received a shock from crossed wires while on top of an electric light pole. He fell headlong to be ground and was almost instantly killed.

The police department officials are trying to get possession of the pistol with which Guiteau shot Garfield to add it to the museum of such articles already collected and on exhibition.

Deputy Sheriff Bush shot and killed a negro by the name of Chaney at Galloway. Bush was trying to put a man out of a store when Chaney interfered and tried to strike him with a large stick.

Sam Bailey, colored, convicted in the city court of Etowah county and sentenced to two years in the coal mines, has been given his liberty by Judge Morague on a writ of habeas corpus, owing to a misunderstanding with the lessees of the convicts and the county commissioner.

The property of the Woodstock Iron Company at Anniston, has been sold by A.H. Shepperd, the commissioner. There was only one bid and that was $400,000 made on behalf of the bondholders. The sale includes four furnaces as and 50,000 acres of land. The bonded indebtedness of the company is $1,000,000.

At Russellville during the progress of a divorce trial Leslie Richardson was shot and John Ligon, who did the shooting had his throat cut from ear to ear. John Ligon had married the mother of Richardson. It is alleged that he had treated her badly and she sued for a divorce. It was during the trial Ligon gave some testimony very damaging to the lady, whereupon Leslie Richardson called him a liar, and he drew a pistol and shot Richardson in the shoulder. Just then Clark Richardson rushed to his brother's rescue and cut Ligon's throat. It is thought both will recover. Clark Richardson had a preliminary trial and was acquitted.

Preparing For War - An interesting fact in regard to the strike among the coal miners of Kansas has been made public. It is that negroes from Alabama, Tennessee, and other States to take the places of the strikers had been placed under military discipline. They are confined to a well-built stockade and whenever one becomes a mutineer he is thrown verified the breastworks. Captain Cleary, of St. Louis, is in charge of the negroes. Captain Cleary is famous for his services in protecting property during the gray Burlington strike, and also during the Southwestern strike, led by Martin Irons in 1886. His experience in this line is very great, and his nerve is unquestioned. He is now engaged in going the negroes in the stockade.

GENERAL NEWS - Governor Fishback, of Arkansas is quite low.

James T. Kilbreth has been appointed Collector of Customs of New York.

Miss Etta Rabbitt of New Bedford, Mass., has had her name changed by the Probate Court to Ella Rabbitt.

James Gordon Bennett is thought to the in danger of blood poisoning from wounds received some months ago in Paris.

It is now rumored that John G. Carlisle will in all probability be appointed to the vacancy upon the Supreme Bench.

Con. Sheehan, one of the latest men in and around Meridian, Miss., is dead.

It is currently reported that T.V. Powderly is going to resign as Grand Master Workman when the general convention of Knights is held in October. It is believed that T.H. McGuire will be his successor.

Wm. J. Taylor was electrocuted at Albany, New York. The first attempt was a failure, the dynamo burning out. Lieutenant connected the prison apparatus with a street electric light plant and after an hour's delay the second attempt was made which proved successful.

Miss Kate C. Cantwell, of Wilmington, N.C., has been elected to represent the Tarheel State in the tableau of beautiful women at the Confederate Veterans reunion to be held in Birmingham, Ala., September next. Miss Cantwell is the daughter of Colonel Cantwell, a brave veteran and prominent citizen of her State. She is a wonderfully handsome woman.

A Constitutional Amendment - The Alabama Educational Association at its recent session

passed the following resolutions... In accordance with the forgoing the following committee has been named:
First District - A.G. Iron, Demopolis
Second District - F.M. Shackleford, Troy
Third District - O.D. Smith, Auburn
Fourth District - J.B. Graham, Talladega
Fifth District - G.R. McNeill, La Fayette
Sixth District - T.C. McCovey, University
Seventh District - Douglass Allen, Collinsville
Eighth District - Jas. K. Powers, Florence
Ninth District - I.W. McAdory, Birmingham

Items of Interest - Miss Kirby Smith, daughter of the famous Confederate leader, was only a fourth-class postmistress when she was given the office at Sewanee, Tenn., but she has managed it with such tact as to carry it into the Presidential class, and she now gets $1,300 a year out of it.

Mr. Louis Cheney of Chelsea, Mass., claims to be last surveyor of the men who built the railroad for granite transportation purposes at Quigley, Mass., which was the first railroad constructed in the United States. The road was built in 1826, from the quarries to the Neponset River, and was first used to carry stone for the construction of Bunker Hill Monument.

Indignation at Memphis - There is a great deal of indignation at Memphis, Tenn., against Sheriff McLendon, for allowing a mob to hinch Lee Walker. McLendon has been suspended from office pending an investigation. Several of the parties to the lynching have been arrested and Judge Scruggs avows his determination to bring all the parties to justice.

Indictments Found - At Washington, D. C., the grand jury found true bills against Col. Frederick C. Ainesworth, Chief of the Record and Pension Division of the War Department; George W. Dant, the contractor employed to make the excavation for the electric light plant; William E. Covert, superintendent, and Francis Sasse, engineer of the building, holding down responsible for the Old Ford's Theater disaster of June 9 last, in which twenty-three persons lost their lives, and a large number of others were injured. It is understood that the defendants will not be arraigned for some days yet, as their trial can't take place before the September term of court.

Must Pay Up - Secretary Carlisle has replied to the request of Kentucky distillers for an extension of ninety days in which to pay their Internal Revenue taxes upon their whiskey which has been held three years in bond that the law is imperative and leaves him no discretion in the premises. So these distillers when the three years are up, which will be this month, will have to pay a tax of ninety cents a gallon or subject themselves and their stock of whiskey to the penalties prescribed by law.

A Close Call - A dispatch from Queens Ireland, says: The passengers on board the Gulon line steamer Arizona, report that the vessel had a very narrow escape from a collision with an unknown Red Star Line steamer during a thick fog on the 17th instant. The Red Star steamer crossed the Arizona's bow not fifty yards distant. Mr. Lucien J. Walker, of Alabama, U. S. Consul at Cork, was a passenger on the Arizona, and says the escape of the steamer was providential. With the passengers realized the peril they had escaped, round after round of cheers were given on both vessels.

No Tobacco Users - There is no Tobacco-user in Lieut. Perry's crew. The explorer barred the users of nicotine, not because he considered the weed debilitating, but because of the distress and discontent that is sure to prevail when the supply runs short, as it is liable to do in the course of an excursion such as he has undertaken. A tobacco-user out of tobacco is lonesome anywhere. In the Arctic regions, with an ocean of ice between himself and the nearest wooden Indian, his case is desperate.

Free silver gained a victory at Birmingham. On Tuesday, an effort was made, by the gold-bug element to commit the Commercial Club, an association of the business men of that city, to the passage of a resolution, demanding the immediate repeal of the Sherman law unconditionally. The resolution was sinally defeated, in spite of the fact that Rufus Rhodes of the News, introduced the resolution...

The Chilton County Farmers Alliance met in regular quarterly meeting at Liberty Hill on Wednesday the 26th day of July and had a pleasant and harmonious session....The election of officers for the next year was quietly and quickly done, and seemed to give the utmost satisfaction, every one seemed well pleased with the result which was as follows: Bro. Moses Robinson was re-elected President by acclamation, every one knowing he was a good man, and in the right place so they could not afford to give him up. The other officers elected are as follows: B.H. Wells, Vice-President; H.L. Honeycutt, Secretary-Treasurer; L.B. Pounds, Lecturer; J.A. Logan, Ast. Lecturer; W. Wood, Chaplain; Thomas Driver, Doorkeeper; Lee Hayes, Ass't Doorkeeper; T.J. Dorminy, Executive Committee; Moses Robinson, Delegate to State Alliance...Capt. R.F. Kolb and Mr. Tyler Goodwyn were with the people the first day, and made instructive and entertaining speeches to a large and attentive audience, composed of both Alliance people and persons who belong to the opposition, and every one seemed to like their speeches very much. H.L. Honeycutt, Sec. Chilton County Alliance

Shady Grove Shadows - A series of meetings will begin here next Saturday, conducted by Rev. Ritch and our pastor Rev. Henley.

Mr. and Mrs. Hampton and two daughters of Birmingham, and Mr. Robert Cooper and family of Stanton, paid a flying visit to their Father Mr. E.M. Cooper, arriving Saturday and staying over Sunday they spent a pleasant time Sunday enjoying peaches melons and apples. Mrs. Albert Headley treated the merry party to a nice supper Sunday night.

Mr. Morgan, who formally lived near here, is we are glad to know moving back again soon.

Mr. James Headley lost a valuable horse last Sunday morning whilst being watered another horse kicked it causing it to jump over some sharp palings which tore its entrails out, causing its death instantly, we sympathize with our friend in his loss.

Dixie Dots - Miss Alice Mitchell, Miss Nettie Smith and Mr. E.W. Mitchell, of Oakmulgee, paid a visit to Valley Creek last Saturday.

Little Arthur Cole has a little pet goat, he thinks there is nothing like it.

Mr. Dan Mitchell had better mind how he goes with the Hustler's s girl, or he might get into trouble.

Rev. Longcryer will preach at Valley Creek next 2nd Sunday in Rev. Pound's place.

Miss Susie Harris was well pleased by her best fellow coming to see her.

Mr. C.G. Barnes and H.W. Cole will take a pleasant trip before long.

The outlook is that we are going to have some new buildings in our community; Mr. W.A. Weaver, M.E. Johnson, John Herod, and J.E. McCullough are making preparations to build new dwellings.

Mr. C.W. Klener and H.P. Weaver have their new houses most completed.

Mr. L.W. Johnson speaks of building a new smoke house; go ahead, Mr. Johnson, I am afraid you won't need it.

Mr. H.P. Weaver has his brick yard in full force now.

Mr. J.N. Chandler and family, of Billingsley, visited relatives and friends here last week.

Miss Ella Weaver is having a pleasant visit to Mr. L.W. Johnson.

Pleasant Grove Pleasantries - Mr. R.W. Maddox has just returned from a business trip in Bibb county, he reports having had a fine time. We guess he was talking in the interests of Tommy Jones; we glory in his spunk, but somewhat doubt his judgment.

Vinehill Varieties - Mr. Richard Moore's wife is quite sick; we hope she will soon be restored to her wanted health.

Mr. Albert Onsley's dwelling and store house were burned down on the 25th inst.; it is not known how the fire broke out.

Mr. Bill Hunt's wife, of Birmingham, is visiting friends here.

Mr. Ben Warren, of Perry county, is going to move to this place.

Mr. William Herrod and wife are spending this week in Perry county. Miss Sarah Herrod paid the Misses Weaver a visit on the 27th inst.

The charming daughter of Mr. John Motley, Miss Betty Motley, was apparently in perfect health on the night of the 24th inst., and when the family arose the next morning they found her nearly dead and by seven o'clock she passed away, which threw the whole community in mourning. She was highly respected and loved by all who knew her. We deeply sympathize with the family in their bereavement, and hope their sorrows will be turned into joy.

Cane Creek Alliance - We met at Cane Creek church on 29th July; there was a good attendance, and the following officers were duly elected for the ensuing year: William Lambert, president; H.B. Rodgers, vice-president; Alex G. Daie, secretary; Isaac Littleton, treasurer; H.M Mahan, lecturer; Joseph Goer, assistant lecturer fellow Wm. G. Davis, chaplain; — Stevens, doorkeeper; William Wagner, assistant doorkeeper. After a very pleasant meeting we adjourned, to meet on Saturday before the second Sunday in August at 10 o'clock a.m..

Union Point - Rev. A.C. Wells preached here last Sunday, and acting on his earnest exhortation the congregation humbly offered a petition to the Almighty for rain, and strange to say almost before the prayer was ended a loud clap of thunder was heard and this was immediately followed by a copious rain, of which our people stood greatly in need, as crops were almost ruined for want of it.

West Chilton Warblings - J.H. O'Neal has bought land near Stanton from Dr. Little, and will move there this Fall.

W.M. Price has got as fine fruit as there is in Chilton county.

D.A. Friday has got as fine a watermelon patch as there can be found round here.

F.J. Wylie went fishing and caught three turtles the other day; if anyone is bothered with turtle send for him, and he will catch'em.

Will Friday and wife were down on a visit last week; he has worked his crop.

D.H. Mitchell and Will Martchell carried a cow home today.

Joe Wylie started to school last Monday.

W.M. Price the other day killed a dog that was killing sheep. Hogs are dieing yet.

Ross Barnes visits Bibb county a heap; there must be some strong attraction over there.

Albert Ware and Bill O'Neal are soon going on a visit to Texas.

Mrs. Wylie has been very sick, but is better now.

D.C. Gandy and wife, of Stanton, visited his father-in-law this week.

Mr. Mitchell and wife visited Mr. Price this week.

D.A. Friday set out some potatoes the 15th day of May, and the 22nd day of July, he got a mess, they were as big as my arm, who can beat that?

Shelby Shoutings - Mrs. Arch Carter and her charming daughter have just returned from an extended visit, and some of the boys are happy.

Miss Annie Marlar is on a visit to Mr. and Mrs. Teal's.

Miss Ella Martin is visiting her sister, Mrs. F. M. Bruce.

From Our Friends - Editor Banner - We take this method of extending to Bro. W.S.

Barefield, S.M.W. of K. of L., our warmest thanks for the manner in which he speaks of us in a complimentary letter we received from him a few days since...Ira Campbell

TOWN ITEMS - Mr. Isaac Davenport died at his home on Mulberry Monday the 31st, after an illness of five weeks duration, he was buried at Pleasant Grove church on Tuesday, Rev. R.M. Honeycutt officiating. Mr. Davenport leaves a wife and several children all grown to mourn his loss, he was the uncle of Mrs. R.M. Honeycutt.

Miss Victoria Franklin of Mulberry, is visiting Judge Honeycutt's family this week.

There will be services next Sunday morning at the Episcopal Church, Ven. F.B. Ticknor of Georgia officiating. Bishop Jackson will be unable to be here on the 7th as previously announced, but will visit Clanton some time in the near future.

Rev. A.C. Wells, Rev. J.L. Busby, and Hon. O.M. Mastin, are attending the Congregational District conference at Kingston Church this week.

Handsome Will Hayes was in town Tuesday.

Mr. Jean Salter has secured the contract to build the new school house.

Dr. A.J. Massey requests us to announce that he will be at Clanton (?) three days: Tuesday, Wednesday and Thursday August 8th, 9th and 10th, to demonstrate how teeth are extracted painlessly by the use of Odontunder. The Doctor will also be prepared to do all classes of fine dentistry.

Ike Hunter a negro who had been employed as a section hand on the L. and N. R. R., attempted to commit an assault on Mrs. Edner of South Calera last Thursday night her screams awakened her husband who fired at Hunter as he jumped out of the window. Hunter was captured next day near Montevallo and brought before Mrs. Edner, who fully identified him. The posse who had him in charge, started with him for Clanton, but on the way Hunter was taken from them and swung up near the scene of his crime, he confessing the same. Sheriff Moore who was reported by the Age-Herald as the office having Hunter in charge, was in Clanton at the time and had no connection whatever with the affair.

SOMEWHAT STRANGE, Accidents and Incidents of Everyday Life, Queer Facts and Thrilling Adventures Which Show That Truth is Stranger Than Fiction - Advices just received from Umtali, say that the two Umtali Hospital of Mashonaland's mission, Miss R.A. Blennerhassett and Miss Lucy Sleeman, have recently had a escape. Both sisters were seriously ill with malaria fever, lying for helpless in a hut, waited on by native boys, there being no native women available. One night they were so bad that Doctor Wilson decided on sitting up with them. In the middle of the night a strange sound as of an animal bounding on the roof of the hut was heard. Shortly afterward the door of the hut, the upper half of which was partly open, rattled, and Miss Blennerhassett called out that there was " a great black thing " on the top of the door. The doctor went hastily to be door and slammed the top rather violently. He easily persuaded the sisters that nothing was there, as Miss Sleeman was nearly dissensible, and Miss Blennerhassett delirious. A large leopard had tried to get through the roof and not succeeding, had sprung upon the open upper half of the door. The creature's head and claws were on the top of the door, and he was drawing himself up to drop into the hut when the doctor's presence of mind prevented him. The women are recovering.

One year ago Charles Boger, of Morrisons, Penn., was married. Nine months later he was a widower. He became crazed with grief eventually, and as a result his affliction produced a dementia pronounced incurable. He raved continually about his wife and entertained the idea that she had been foully dealt with. So strongly did he believe in this that friends decided to disinter the body. They did so, and the body was found face downwards and all the evidence which goes to show that the woman had been buried alive was plainly apparent. The glass in the men of the coffin was broken to atoms. The shroud enveloping the form was torn to shreds. The limbs were twisted and distorted, the hair matted, and in her hands she clinched a bunch of it. Those who were engaged in disinterring the body fell back, entirely overcome. The most composed man in the party was the departed husband. He assumed an air of complacency and assisted in the work of rearranging the body. He has shown no signs of mental aberration since, and from all appearance his mental powers have been restored.

Lieutenant H.R. Sayce, of Bristol, has succeeded in crossing the English channel in a miniature boat, which he has patented as the Midge pneumatic collapsible lifeboat, and is designed for fishing, shooting, or sailing. The weight is under thirty-five pounds, and the length is 8 1/2 feet, with thirty-two-inch beam. The boat is decked with canvas, with an opening for the owner's body, an is fitted with inflated air tubing. The boat is fitted with a topsail about the size of a woman's apron, and a still smaller mizzen. Mr. Sayce was accompanied by a small sailing lugger. There was a light wind and a course was steered straight for Cape Grisnez. Mr. Sayce was provided with a double paddle, which he kept in constant use. The little craft entered Boulogue harbor at 5 p.m., having started at 3 o'clock a.m. Mr. Sayce was somewhat benumbed by sitting so long in one position. The lugger returned to Dover with the little boat folded up on board. The boatmen remarked that she had skimmed over the waves " like a duck. "

Mr. Frank Fields, who resides at Mount Tabor, Or., reports that a great scheme has been hit for the for extermination of caterpillars in that neighborhood. He says that at the corner of West avenue and the railway a toboggan slide has been fixed from the corner of the fence to the ground, on which is placed a bucket containing kerosene oil. The caterpillars all make for this corner and slide down into the bucket, where they perish. Mr. Fields says over twenty bushels of caterpillars have been trapped and killed in this way, and the work goes on.

There is now to be seen in the midway Plaisance in Chicago Herr Pollak, who claims to be the fastest talker in the world. He has a repertory of 20,000 words, which he repeats in forty minutes being at the rate of 500 words a minute. These words are in no way connected and make no sense, the rapidity of their enunciation being the sole feature of Herr Pollak's performance. He places himself other bonds to repeat no words, and offers 40,000 florins, which he carries with him, to any stenographer who can take down what he says.

A Shorthorn Devon steer, eight years old, weighing about 5,000 pounds, and a 2,780 pound Norman gelding are among the curiosities at the Chicago stock yards. The horse stands twenty-one hands high and the steer nineteen hands. The steer is supposed to be the largest in the county, and his owner, W.W. Crandall, of Crandall, Kan., challenges the world on three points: Weight, style and color. He values him at $1 per, pound or $5,000.

Moses Williams, colored, lives on a farm about five miles east of Fayetteville, Texas. He is 65 years old, but no one would take him to be more than about 50. He was married twice and had born to him forty-five children. By the first wife he had twenty-three children - three boys and twenty girls - and by the second twenty-two children - two boys and twenty girls. He says he has about 40 grandchildren.

Charles Burson, an employee at the mills of the Andrews Brothers' Company, at Youngstown, Ohio, has developed into a veritable curiosity. His hair is naturally white, but after working in the mill a few hours and becoming heated it turns a brilliant red. When Burson leaves the mill and cools off his hair resumes its natural color.

The Chinese Minister's Baby - The member of the Chinese legation at Washington, who monopolizes popular interest, is the minister's daughter, Miss Tsui, a young lady of about two summers, who, for a Celestial of high station, has the unusual distinction of having been born in this county. Miss Tsui, except for her bright, almond-shaped eyes, and her queer clothes, impressed me as being very much the same kind of baby as our own babies are...

Skirts Of A Late Date - One of the handsomest skirts, a new Empire in shape, is of three widths of material at least forty-four inches wide, writes Emma M. Hooper in the Ladies Home Journal...

Ad - Students, Teachers (male or female), Clergymen and others in need of change of employment, should not fail to write to B.F. Johnson & Co., Richmond, Va. Their great success shows that they have got the true ideas about making money. They can show you how to employ odd hours profitably.

Ad - W.H. Griffin, Jackson, Michigan, writes: "Suffered with Catarrh for fifteen years, Hall's Catarrh Cure cured me." Sold by Druggists, 75c

The Banner, Vol. 1, Clanton, Ala., Thursday, August 10, 1893, No. 40

Silver Bullion Depository - Attorney-General Eugley of Colorado, has rendered an opinion to the affect that it is within the power of the legislature to enact appropriate legislation for the establishment of a statuary depository of silver bullion and the issuance of certificates thereon, assignable by delivery, and receivable by the State in the payment of State taxes.

GENERAL NEWS - John Dan, of Palatka, Fla, suicided in Augusta, Ga., by taking chloroform.

John Carter, a negro, was struck and killed by lightning near Wilmington, N.C.

John Stevenson, the well known car builder, died at New Rochelle, N.Y., aged 84 years.

Martin Reed, wanted in Cincinnati on an old charge, has been captured after twenty years.

Officer J.A. Harvey, of Syracuse, N.Y., was shot to death by a prisoner named George A. Barnes.

Ex-Secretary of the Treasury Foster is in trouble. As President of his bank he managed to overdraw his account $136,000.

The Populist party of Virginia have held their State convention and nominated a full State ticket. Hon. E.R. Cocke, is their candidate for Governor.

At Parkland, a suburb adjoining Louisville, the Marshal Andrew Blunk was shot and killed by Edward Grim, whom he was trying to arrest, and Murry Blunk, son of the Marshal's in turn killed Grim.

Mayor Harrison of Chicago asked that the poor children of the city be shown the sight's of the World's Fair and 15,000 boys and girls from the slums of Chicago marched in procession through the streets, became guests of the Illinois Central Street Railway and were royally entertained by Buffalo Bill, who gave them the most glorious day in all the history of Chicago waifdom.

The Reunion Again Postponed - The southern Confederate Reunion, which was originally to have been held at Birmingham in July, and was then postponed until the 15 and 16 of September, has again been postponed to take place on Monday and Tuesday, October 2 and 3....Adjutant General Moorman his issued a general order announcing the postponement, and stating that the reunion would positively take place at Birmingham on the last named dates, and that the unveiling of the Confederate monuments at Chicago would occur on October 17....General John B. Gordon, appeals to all comrades to form clubs and take advantages of the cheap excursion rates secured for the occasion. Hon. W.C.P. Breckenridge will be the orator of the day.

Officers Indicted - the grand jury at Memphis, Tenn., indicted Sheriff McLendon, Deputy Sheriff J.A. Perkins, Jailor Harold and Police Captain O'Hara and Captain Hackett for failing to do their duty in permitting Lee Walker to be taken from the jail and lynched and burned two weeks ago. Several members of the mob were also indicted.

ALABAMA ITEMS - Joseph May, one of the oldest and best known citizens of Selma, is dead.
.
Chief Justice Stone celebrated the fiftieth anniversary of his judicial career on the 4th inst.
.
Mr. J. Baumhauer of Whistler is under bond of $100 for sending threatening postal cards through the mails.
.
Colonel Lum Duke has resigned as Register in Chancery at Lafayette and J. Thomas Heflin has been appointed in his place.
.
Thursday night of last week and unknown party called Lem Howze of Clark county to the door after night and shot him to death.
.
Rev. Dr. Hale and Dr. Whittle pastors of churches in Birmingham, have gone to Chicago and other points with a large party of pleasure seekers.
.
About a year ago a little son of Mr. James Bryant of Lowndes county was bitten by a mad dog, and last week the little fellow died with hydrophobia.
.
A stranger named Street dropped dead among strangers in a Montgomery saloon. He was a Mason and Odd Fellow, and had evidently seen better days.
.
Jules Levy, the World's greatest cornetist, and Stella Osta, the wonderful Belgian Cantatrice, gave an entertainment in Birmingham the past week.
.
Robert Hudson was tried at Mobile for a murder committed twenty-four years ago, found guilty of manslaughter and sentenced to five years in the penitentiary.
.
Mr. Robert Skipper of Midland City, has been arrested upon the charge of embezzling funds belonging to the Southern Express Company and burning the depot at Midland City.
.
The Huntsville Argus claims that the pistol with which Guitteau shot President Garfield is now owned by a citizen of Huntsville, and proof can easily be made as to its identity.
.
Last week a negro girl was found hanging to the limb of a tree on Mr. Harmon Gay's place in Randolph county. There are a number of rumors as to the cause of her death and some arrests will be made.
.
Hon. H.C. Smith, United States consul to Sautos, Brazil, and President Cleveland's first colored appointee in this term, was given a farewell banquet and reception by his colored friends at Birmingham.
.
Mallinda Goggins, a white woman committed suicide in the Anniston jail by taking morphine. At police court she was sentenced to three months in the stockade. She left a letter stating that she preferred death to imprisonment.
.
News has been received from Blockville, that an unsuccessful attempt was made by J.H. Morgan, to burn up the town. Morgan is a former railroad ticket agent of Opelika, and a

man well thought of in that city. He has been arrested and placed in jail.

Gilbert J. Dease and John Ryan, the two Mobile & Ohio railroad engineers, charged with the murder of Deputy Sheriff J. Westly Thomas at Mobile have had a hearing and were remained to jail without bail, to await the action of the November grand jury.

Death Preferred - A special from Antigo, Wis., says: William Nunemacher, a farmer killed his wife and babe and two boys, age 5 and 3 years, by dashing out their brains. He then plunged head first from a window in an attempt to kill himself. He is still alive, but paralyzed. The cause of the quadruple murder and suicide is said to be a fear that his family would die from starvation.

AN AMENDMENT - To the Constitution of Alabama, to be Voted Upon at Next General Election.
At the next general election for Representatives in Alabama, the following proposed amendment to the Constitution will be voted upon. That our reader may familiarize themselves with the same we publish in full:...Official: J.D. Barron, Secretary of State

A Horrible Crime - Near Montgomery, Tex., three negroes attacked the house of Mr. M. Marsh, killed Mr. Marsh, brutally assaulted his wife, murdered his infant and cut out the tongue of his 7-year old child. One of the negroes was caught and lynched. The Sheriff and posse are searching for the others, who will certainly be lynched if caught.

She Horsewhipped Her Slanderer - Lula Balknap, a farmer's pretty daughter, horsewhipped Thomas Connolly, a popular young merchant, (?) the postoffice at Lamette, Jackson county, Ia., because, as she announced to the crowd, Connolly slandered her after she refused to marry him.

Mr. Crisp has been elected speaker of the fifty-third congress.

The governor hasn't appointed a registrar of election yet for Chilton county, but he has not entirely forgotten us. Last week he graciously returned to our midst a distinguished citizen by pardoning Charley Lee, late cook to Mr. H.A. Wilson, of Lomax, who was convicted of hog stealing at the spring term of court and sentenced to thirteen months imprisonment with hard labor. The governor evidently appreciated Mr. Wilson's efforts in the past in his behalf and does not forget them, he would have been ungrateful indeed to have allowed Mr. Wilson's cook to have remained a moment longer in durance vile than he could help, especially in view of that famous barbeque last year.

The Banner is under ligations to Ven. F.B. Ticknor and to Messrs. F.W. Denty and W.L. Price for assistance kindly given in getting out last week's issue, during the unavoidable absence of Mr. F. Crichton.

Next Wednesday the first issue of the Helper, a religious denominational semi-monthly, devoted to the interest of the Congregational Churches, will be published by this office. The Helper will be edited by the Rev. A.T. Clarke, of Shelby, this state, an able and eminent writer of more than ordinary ability who has successfully edited a similar publication in the past, which gives ample guarantee for the excellence of the present venture, and having as well the entire support of the ministry and members of this denomination throughout the state will without doubt succeed, and become in fact as in name a helper indeed in the Master's cause.

Jemison Gems - On the 6th inst., Miss Fannie Muse, after a lingering illness, crossed over the last river. Her sister and relatives have the sweet assurance that her new home above is bright and permanent. May tender sympathy help soothe the bereaved family till one by one they join the loved one in the sweet bye-and-bye.

Jumbo Jumbles - We are sorry to say that our esteemed friend, J.F. Goodgame, is quite sick with marlarial fever, but we hope he will soon recover and be able to meet with us at our Alliance meeting next Saturday.

Miss Ada Goodgame has a thriving and most prosperous school at this place.

Dixie Dots - C.P. Barnes and H.W. Cole went to Elbethel last Sunday, and saw a lot of pretty girls there.

R.P. Barnes is going back to Bibb county next Saturday to see his best girl.

Miss Mamie Sanderson went home with her brother Jim Sanderson, who lives at Welch's mill.

Collins Chapel Chirrupings - Our Alliance met last Saturday, and was called to order by President Pate. We had an interesting meeting, about twenty-five being present. The visiting committee having failed to do their duty, we heard reports form the brethren present. Having been blessed in this neighborhood with good rains they reported good crops.

SABBATH SCHOOL CONVENTION - The Sabbath School Convention within the bounds of the Mulberry Association met with New Salem at 10 a.m., July 29, 1893. As neither Brothers L.B. Pounds or A.L. Foshee were present, the devotional exercises were conducted by Rev. W.D. Martin. Brother W.A. Wood delivered the welcome address, taking for his subject; "The Importance of Organization, "in such forcible manner that all present were constrained to realize that in union there is strength; in concluding, he made both delegates and visitors feel they were not among strangers but friends, and that they had met together for noble purpose...At two o'clock, after a song, organization being next in order, Rev. R.M. Honeycutt, moderator, took the chair. The secretary being absent, J.E. Jones was requested to act in his place....Discussion of subjects: First, "Have we any scriptural authority for carrying our children to the Sabbath school?" Opened by Bro. W.G. Riggins, followed by Bros. J. Bice, — Flowers, W.M. Wood and W.A. Wood...Second subject "How can the Sabbath school be made a safeguard against the spiritual dangers that surround them?" Discussed by Bros. G.W. Freeman, Alex Glass and R.M. Honeycutt. Bro. Z.J. Jones, being unable to attend in person, sent in a well gotten up paper on this subject, which was read and listened to with special interest...A motion was made and carried for the Chair to appoint a committee to get up a programme for the next convention; committee appointed J.A. Moore, A. Glass, J. Bice, W.A. Wood and J.E. Jones...The Sabbath school mass meeting was conducted by Bro. J.E. Jones, who read the 27th Psalm. Some logical and feeling speeches were made by Bros. J.A. Moore, R.M. Honeycutt, W.D. Martin and V.H. Caine...At 11 o'clock there was preaching from the stand by Rev. Sutton Smitherman...At 2 o'clock the people re-assembled in the house, and the class led by Professors B. Riggins and C.L. Glass made some good vocal music for about forty minutes which was highly appreciated by all present...J.E. Jones, Clerk pro tem.

First District Mulberry Association - The meeting of the first district of Mulberry Association was held with Mars Hill church, near Jemison, August 4th and 5th. The introductory sermon was preached on Friday at 11 a.m. by Sutton Smitherman of Six Mile. In the evening the meeting was organized by electing W.A. Wood chairman, and G.W. Gothard sec. then engaged in discussing "What constitutes a call to the ministry?" which brought out some interesting speeches from L.B. Pounds, G.W. Freeman, Sutton Smitherman, S.D. Posey, J.P. Gentry, A.J. Lee and others. Bro. Freeman's address describing the difference between ministers called of God and those called of men, was particularly interesting. Saturday morning, engaged in discussing the duty of christians to the church financially. On this question Bro. Pounds and several others delivered interesting addresses: at 11 a.m. Bro. Pounds preached an impressive sermon on the high calling in Christ Jesus...The community and Pastor (W.A. Wood) nobly did their duty in entertaining the congregation and delegates. Z.J. Jones

Swift Creek Siftings - Mr. Albert Brown, one of the most charming young men of this place, fell from a swing last Friday and injured his back, but is up again.
.
Jessie Holland is very sick with chills, but we hope to see him out again soon.

In Memory Of Brother Minor Woolley - Whereas it has pleased the Grand Master of the universe to call from labor below to refreshment above, our much loved brother Minor Woolley, who was made a Master Mason at Benson Lodge No. 103, and affiliated with the Lodge April 2nd, 1887, and departed this life June 16th, 1893. And whereas he demonstrated daring his life as a man on such great love for the Mystic brotherhood, therefore be it Resolved, That with sad hearts we humbly bow to the divine mandate, knowing that our loss is his great gain, that he who doeth all things well is too great to do wrong, and two wise to err. Resolved. That we as members and brethren of this Lodge, whilst we bow in humble submission to the will of the great Architect of the universe, do indulge the hope that when our brother's work was called to pass the test of an unerring square it was found well framed, true and trusty, as perfect ashlar, worthy a place in the temple above, whose maker and builder is God, and that we will strive to emulate his virtues, covering his faults with the mantle of charity, remembering that is human to err but devine to forgive. Resolved. That in the death of Bro. Minor Woolley, his wife has lost a kind and affectionate husband, the children a loving and indulgent father, and this Lodge a much loved brother, and to all the relatives and friends of the deceased, we tender our sincerest and heart-felt sympathy, and in this hour of our sad bereavement would suggest that we all look to our Heavenly Father for comfort, who alone is able to soothe our sorrows. Resolved. That a copy of these resolutions be spread upon our minute book, and one presented to the beloved widow of our deceased brother, and that a copy be sent to the Banner for publication. J.M. Stanfield, B.H. Chesnutt, W.H. Wright, Committee, Clanton, Ala., August 5, 1893

Programme of Chilton County Teachers' Institute
An Institute for the white teachers of Chilton county will be held at Concord, September 8 and 9, 1893.
FRIDAY
10 a.m. Address of welcome. Joseph Green, Response, Supt. J.W. Moore
Miscellaneous Business. 1. Plans of introducing uniform text books, R.A. Roscoe and W.J. Martin. 2. Model school, Miss Etta Moore and Clement Mullins.
RECESS

1:30 pm. The importance of classifying students, N.W. Wilson and T.F. Sessions.
Advantages of a true education, Miss Geneva Jones and E.J. Hayes.
My Difficulties: how to overcome them, S.J. Jennings and John Lebron.
SATURDAY
9 a.m. School Examinations, H.T. Estes and P.M. McKee.
Vocal Music, Miss Fannie Woolley and J.P. Haley
Education Address, G.L. Speer.
RECESS
1:30 p.m. Are the studies prescribed by Law sufficient for common school training? J.E. Jones and J.P. Gore.
School law discussed, D.S. Robinson and W.L. Popwell.
Closing Speeches.
Concord is situated in Dry Valley, five miles south of Montevallo and five miles west of Wessington. Teachers wishing conveyance from L. & N. railroad will go to Wessington, and from the E.T.V. & G. railroad will go to Montevallo. Those who expect conveyance from railroad free of charge should write to J.B. Moore,Jr., Montevallo. This is the last institute of this scholastic school year and all the teachers are urged to attend. R.E.R. Hicks, G.L. Speer, J. Alex Moore, Committee.

TOWN ITEMS - There was quite a romantic wedding in town Tuesday afternoon. Of course it was a runaway couple. Mr. G.W. Lodge, of Lomax, and Miss Willie Marlar, of that place, were the contracting parties. Dr. A.J. Marlar, the father of the bride, was the objecting party. But they were not to be outdone on such an important matter so they waited until the Doctor was away. Then with a few selected friends came to Clanton and procuring the necessary papers, they repaired to the Duke house, and listened to the few words said by Bro. B.E. Feagin that made them one forever. They spent the night at the home of the bride's mother, leaving next morning for Ohio and other Northern points. May much pleasure ever be theirs.

Bro. E.H. Smith, of the Kincheon neighborhood, who by the bye brought us some very fine peaches this week, informs us that he finds no trouble in selling at good prices, and also that he finds ready sale for vegetables; he has sold $25.00 worth of onions alone out of his garden this spring.

Mrs. W.S. Sharbutt, living on the Lane place, placed on our table a sweet potato measuring nine inches in circumference, which he grabbed in his patch Tuesday. Next!

Work is progressing briskly on the McMorris school house. Mr. Sorter is a hustler.

Rev. S.E. Bassett preached at the Congregational church Monday night, to an attentive audience.

Mr. J.S. King's storehouse at Clanton Ford was burnt down last week. It was occupied by Mr. Davy Lodge, who kept a commissary store. The fire is supposed to have been incendiary in its origin.

We regret to chronicle the death of Mr. Will Farley, of Mulberry, from typhoid fever on Tuesday evening, the 8th inst. His wife, Solenna Farley, also succumbed to the fell destroyer last week. These young people had been married scarcely more than a year, their marriage having taken place in December 1891 Loving and affectionate in their lives, in death they were not divided. Both are interred in Mulberry cemetery. To the sorrowing relatives and friends we tender our condolences.

This morning at Jumbo, Mr. Joe Cox was thrown from his mule, resulting in a broken shoulder. Dr. Johnson has been called to attend him.

On Monday, the following cases were disposed of by the county court: Steve Pate and E. Whatley were each fined $20.00 and costs for disturbing religious worship.

Messrs. Ehrman and Merritt have advertised for $10,000 worth of stock of the First National Bank of Birmingham. This is a striking evidence of their confidence in the stability of this institution.

Judge R.M. Honeycutt and Pres. Moses Robinson of the County Alliance are both attending the State Alliance at Talladega this week.

Secretary Brock is quite sick.

SHERIFF'S SALE - Under and by virtue of an execution issued out of the Clerk's office of the Circuit Court of Chilton county, Alabama, against the Clifton Iron Company, a corporation, and in favor of G.W. Lodge, for the use of officers of Court, I will proceed to sell at the Court House door in Clanton, Ala, between the legal hours of sale, at public outcry, to the highest bidder, for cash, on MONDAY, SEPTEMBER 11, 1893, the following described property to wit: E 1/2 of SW 1-4, and NW 1-4 of Section 32, Township 20, Range 12; and NE 1-4 of NE 1-4 of Section 20, Township 24, Range 13, and lying and being in Chilton county, Alabama. This, the 7th day of August 1893. P.M. Moore, Sheriff Chilton County.

THE REFORM MOVEMENT - Senator Peffer, on being interviewed recently on the silver question, said: "The Sherman law will be repealed the first thing. The effect of this will be to destroy both of the old parties, and build up the new one. That will be followed by a new alignment of parties."

No more Knights of Labor, no more Federation of Labor, but a vast central council, representing all the workmen in the United States by their trades - such is the plan for the labor union of the future as proposed by General Master workman T.V. Powderly, of the Knights of Labor. In line with this plan is a movement in the west for the erection of a great central labor temple, where representatives from every state in the United States can assemble for conference at stated periods of the year. In speaking of the plan Mr. Powderly says: "In the first place I believe that the labor union of the present and past has seen its day of usefulness. It can win no great strikes; it can accomplish no great reform. In the future, the power of the labor union will be its great strength as a political factor. The man who, with the lessons of the past to guide him, says that labor unionism without politics can be a success is a fool."

THE SECRET OUT - Senator Sherman, the author of the Sherman silver law, is telling secrets. He says his law was passed to prevent the passage of a free coinage bill...

THE SUB-TREASURY ADOPTED - The Christian Patriot, Morristown, Tenn., edited by Rev. James B. Converse, makes the following able argument in favor of the Sub-Treasury, taking the recent issue of clearing house certificates for a text:...

It is now known that ex-Secretary Foster, who failed in business a few weeks ago, had overdrawn his bank account to the amount of $36,000. "Lack of confidence" may have caused the failure, but to a man up a tree, it looks like a plain case of lack of money in bank.

Libby Prison Survivors - During the latter part of August there will be a reunion at the Libby prison war museum of the survivors of the famous tunnel escape from this prison on the night of February 9, 1864. This event will be marked by the attendance of Col. Thomas E. Rose of the Seventy-seventh Pennsylvania infantry, the projector of the celebrated escape, and Capt. A.G. Hamilton of the Twelfth Kentucky calvary, his companion in the undertaking. Colonel Rose is now in the United States army and stationed at Fort Ringgold, Tex., and Captain Hamilton is living at Reedyville, Ky. The are the most prominent members of the tunnel party, and will meet for the first time since the close of the war. Among others that will be present are Capt. L.N. Johnson, Sixth in Kentucky infantry, Pleasantville, Ky., Capt. Terrence Clark, Seventy-ninth Illinois infantry, Paris, Ill., and Gen. H.C. Hobart, Twenty-first Wisconsin infantry, Milwaukee.

Founded by a Numismatist - George W. Becker, of Dover township, exhibits a number of coins which he found in the Conewago Mountains. There are fourteen pieces in all. They are all brass except one, which is composed of nickel or lead. Five of the coins are about the size of a twenty-dollar gold piece, while the balance are the size of a cent. They are all round except one of the large ones, which is eight-cornered. On one side of the large coins are the English letters "N,P,V,A", and the figures "8" and "728", the former at the top and the latter at the bottom of the coin. On the reverse side is an "N", with strange figures and hieroglyphics in the spaces between the "X". On the lead piece the hieroglyphics are the same, but the letters are different, viz.: "S, V. L, T." A large number of persons have examined them, but no one has been able to tell to what nation or country they belong. The coins are not tarnished and are in a good state of preservation. The brass coins appear to be galvanized. Mr. Becker says he found them on the surface of a rough strip of land in the Conewago Mountains, where he had planted strawberries. He also found near the same place a number of Indian relics. The coins will be sent to the Smithsonian Institution at Washington. - (Baltimore America)

The Banner, Vol. 1, Clanton, Ala., Thursday, August 17, 1893, No. 41

GENERAL NEWS - Minister Blount denies the rumor that he is to be the administration candidate for governor of Georgia.

President Cleveland has gone to Buzzard's Bay, where it is said he will remain until the 1st of September.

C.W. Wickstone of Bridge, Ga., fifteen miles from Lyons, was shot and killed by the accidental firing of a gun he had set in his store for burglars.

Rev. Robert J. Willingham, D. D., pastor of the First Baptist Church of Memphis, Tenn., has been chosen as Corresponding Secretary of the Foreign Mission Board of that denomination.

Robert H. Coleman of Lebanon, Pa., the iron millionaire, has made an assignment. His liabilities will approximate $3,500,000, and it is asserted that they exceed his assets. Coleman's interest in the Jacksonville, Tampa and Key West railroad has brought him to the verge of financial ruin.

An Ex-President's Relation Suffers - Some weeks ago a fine-looking old man, nearly 80 years of age, with snow white hair and beard, applied to the county commissioners at Denver, Col., for aid and was sent to the county poor farm, where he still remains. The old man gave his name as William Harrison and said he was the first cousin of the ex-president. The officials smiled at the pauper's story, but the secretary of the humane society, quietly decided to investigate, he has now received letters confirming the old man's statements in every particular. George S. Cunningham of Lancaster, O., formerly Mr. Harrison's attorney, gives the facts, and his daughter, Mrs. Rebecca Williamson, of the same place, has been written to. Mr. Harrison charges his daughter and his former attorney with ingratitude, but says Benjamin, his cousin, does not know of his sad straits. The old man's resemblance to his distinguished relative is striking.

Whitecaps Came to Grief - A party of whitecaps came to grief in West Virginia a few nights since in a manner similar to the experience of the Indiana avengers. A mob went to John F. Wiler's boarding-house at Sweet Springs to tar and feather him because he had not left the country as ordered. When the mob attempted to break down the door Wiler stepped out, shot and killed Powell Beckner and probably fatally wounded Thomas Coyne. Coyne is a well-to-do farmer and was respected in the community. Beckner had been employed in connection with the management of the hotel at Sweet Springs. Wiler surrendered to the authorities.

Killed His Family - While suffering from delirium, the result of a severe attack of bilious fever, John Finn, of St. Louis, murdered four of his children and then cut his own throat. He declared he was inspired of God. Finn still lives.

Man-Eater Said to be Insane - Alfred Packer, the man-eater, who ate five of his comrades in a mining camp, some ten years ago, and who is now in prison under cumulative sentences of forty years, is reported to have become insane and investigation has been ordered. Packer's attorneys recently tried to break the cumulative sentence, but failed.

ALABAMA ITEMS - Joseph May, on of the oldest and best known citizens of Selma, is dead.

Prof. L.A. Cockrell has been chosen principal of the Livingston Male Academy.

Chief Justice Stone celebrated the fiftieth anniversary of his judicial career on the 4th inst.

Eugene Harrison is running a poultry farm near Athens. He is succeeding very satisfactorily.

Gilbert Hudgins, a lumberman at Eulaton, received injuries from a falling tree which caused his death.

The libel case brought by Governor Jones against editor Baltzell of the Alliance Herald has been nol prossed.

Deputy Marshal Perry Griggs was killed in Cleburne county in a fight with a band of white cappers, for whose arrest he had a warrant.

H.M. Hall,Jr., of Florence, has been appointed by the comptroller of the treasury, temporary bank examiner of the First National of Decatur.

J.W. Harris shot Will F. Collins at Kennedy. Collins only lived a few hours. The cause of the shooting was and old feud. The deceased leaves a wife and three children.

Clark, Choctaw, Wilcox and Marengo counties are excited to the highest pitch, and armed men are in Meacham's beat to avenge alleged wrongs. Troubles growing out of the sale of whiskey had led to many disturbances, and the best element of the community is determined to be rid of the desperadoes. Among the tragedies which have grown out of the affair, at the bottom of which lies illicit distilling, were the killing of John A. Hare, Ernest McCorquadales and others. The latter indicated that one James (?), his assassin, and on Monday he (?) death at the mouth of four Winchesters. Others will be similarly punished.

(?)ien A. Holmes, a lineman for (?)ell Telephone Company, was killed by an electric shock. He was climbing a pole when some wire he was carrying came in contact with a guy wire fastened to the pole. This guy wire was heavily charged with electricity and Holmes was involved instantly in a blaze of fire. He fell to the ground dead. Investigation shows that the guy wire was connected with the electric trolley wire by a piece of wire, which had been tied round the two wires. The object of the tying was to keep the trolley wire away from a fire alarm which was in proximity to the trolley wire. It is not known who tied the wires together. This is the second lineman who has lost his life by a shock at Mobile within the past two weeks.

Officers Indicted - The grand jury at Memphis, Tenn., indicted Sheriff McLendon, Deputy Sheriff J.A. Perkins, Jailor Harold and Police Captain O'Hara and Captain Hackett for failing to do their duty in permitting Lee Walker to be taken from the jail and lynched and burned two weeks ago. Several members of the mob were also indicted.

Orange Blossums Budding - The report is being circulated through the daily press that Secretary Herbert, of Alabama is soon to wed Miss Sallie Brown, daughter of ex-senator

Joseph E. Brown.

Yellow Fever - A few days since Surgeon-General Wyman notified Dr. H.T. Inge, president of the quarantine board of Mobile bay, that the British barkentine Glenora, Captain Morris, which had sailed from Havana for Mobile, had three cases of yellow fever on board while in the harbor of Havana. The health authorities consequently kept a sharp lookout for the vessel, which on its arrival was immediately ordered into quarantine. Dr. George Fowler's inspection disclosed that she was still infested, one of the crew having died at sea, and there were two cases of sickness on board. The man who died at sea had yellow fever, and the sick men were suffering with the same disease. They were transferred to the quarantine hospital for treatment. The vessel was moved to the quarantine docks and is now undergoing fumigation. The Glenora will be kept at the docks until all danger from the disease has disappeared. Dr. Inge will detail another physician to assist Dr. Fowler, so that while he attends to the sick in the hospital the other physician will board all vessels, thus preventing any contact with the disease.

Makes Its Appearance at Brunswick - John W. Branham, assistant surgeon of the Marine hospital service, is reported to down with the fever at Brunswick, Ga. He has been isolated and every precaution taken to prevent the spread of the disease. The city is in excellent condition and no serious results are anticipated. About 300 timid people left the place as soon as the alarm was sounded, but the great majority of the citizens will remain.

Startling Statements - A remarkable declaration has been made by Mayor Carter H. Harrison of Chicago. In an address of welcome to the annual convention of the military surgeons of the national guard of the United States, he said: "There are 200,000 people in Chicago today unemployed and almost destitute of money. If Congress does not give us money we will have riots that will shake the country."

PROMINENT PEOPLE - The Sultan of Johore eats from a dinner service worth at $750,000.
.
George Washington Murray, of South Carolina, is the only colored member of Congress.
.
Ex-Senator J.J. Ingalls, of Kansas, predicts a great financial upheaval and a general redistribution of wealth.
.
English scientists are rejoicing over the visit of Professor E.E. Barnard, of Lock Observatory. They speak of him reverently as "The discoverer of the fifth satellite of Jupiter".

Mr. Gladstone is one of these incautious people who do not destroy letters. The venerable statesman is said to have a collection of 60,000 letters deposited in a strong room at Hawarden Castle.
.
Admiral Humann, the French naval commander at Bangkok, Siam, is fifty-five years old. He was promoted to his present grade in 1889. He is now third on the list for promotions to Vice-Admiral's rank.

Miss Martha Washington Stoddard, of Marthatown, Ill., claims to be a relative of the first President. She is ninety-two years old, and has twenty-eight descendants, the eldest of whom is a son, seventy-four years old.

The oldest living chaplain of the war is now being sought by those curious in such matters. Rev. John Walworth, of Wisconsin, is claimed to be the man. He was chaplain of the Forty-third Wisconsin Volunteers, and is now eighty-nine years old.

Sarah T. Bolton died in Indianapolis, Ind., a few nights ago. Mrs. Bolton was known as the poetess of Indiana, and has written verses that are well known, among them being "Paddle Your Canoe" and "Indiana," a glowing tribute to that commonwealth.

Governor McGraw, of the State of Washington, "went West" eight or ten years ago, arriving in San Francisco with $42 in his pocket. He sent $10 home to his wife, and began his western life, as a horse car driver. He made his way to Seattle, where he became sheriff, hotel-keeper and lawyer, and finally one of the most prosperous and popular men in the new State. He is about forty years old.

We are glad to note that an effort made at Talladega to make Mr. J.R. Manning chairman of the People's Party Executive committee failed. One who would cause the publication of a statement reflecting upon another knowing it to be false is not fit to be placed in such a position.

The Populists of the House are made up of the following: Jerry Simpson, John Davis, William Baker, William A. Harris, and T J. Hudson, of Kansas; Lafe Pence and J.C. Bell, of Colorado; O.M. Kem, and W.A. McKeighan, of Nebraska; Marion Cannon, of California; F.G. Newlands, of Montana; H.E. Boen, of Minnesota. The Populists of the Senate are W.A. Peffer of Kansas; J.H. Kyle, of South Dakota; W.V. Allen, of Nebraska.

The best People's Party paper in the country is undoubtedly the National Watchman, edited by N.A. Dunning, and published weekly at Washington, D. C., under the directions of the congressional committee of the People's Party. The subscription price is only fifty cents yearly.

Alliance brethren throughout the state will be glad to learn of the re-election of esteemed brother B.W. Groce; this was a well merited tribute to our brothers untiring zeal in the Alliance cause.

James G. Field, candidate for Vice President on the People's party ticket last year, in a recent speech made at Midlothian, declared that: Cleveland had not dealt fairly with the people in calling an extra session of congress when, he said, the present perilous condition of the country is largely the result of a financial policy which the executive branch of the government finds embodied in unwise laws which must be executed until repealed by congress...

The State Alliance convened at Talladega on Tuesday 8th inst. at 1 p.m. At the first roll call fifty two counties responded. Dr. B.W. Groce was re-elected president; J.W. Jones of Marengo, Vice-President; L.L. Brock re-elected secretary; J.H. Harris, of Chambers, Lecturer; S.M. Adams, of Bibb, Delegate to National Alliance....

Pleasant Grove Pleasantries - Rev. S.M. Adams delivered one of his able and instructive sermons to a large and attentive congregation last Sunday at Macedonia.

We believe a good and lasting impression was made, Oh, that the world was full of such men! Bro. Pounds, we would be much pleased to have you with us at our alliance. We need some good alliance talk at our alliance; please give us an appointment some time shortly.

Dixie Dots - Mr. T.G. Letcher and A.B. Davis, had a fight a few days since; both were hurt very seriously; however matters have been satisfactorily adjusted between them.

R.C. Barnes did not get off to Bibb last Sunday; he must sure go the next.

All the Dallas boys were over at Valley Creek church last Sunday to see their best girls.

Energy Events - All performers, lovers of sacred music, both vocal and instrumental are earnestly solicited to meet at Shilo church, the 16th and 17th of September, 1893, and assist in completing the organization of the Chilton County Singing Convention. Prof. H.J. Showalter, of Dalton, Georgia, has been invited, Respectfully, J.E. White, Robt. D. Durham, R.D. May, Committee

ATTENTION TEACHERS, Congressional Institute to White Teachers, Childersburg, Aug. 21-23 - The teachers of the fourth congressional district and especially of Talladega and adjoining counties are earnestly urged to attend this institution. The following experienced educators have been engaged by the State Superintendent as Instructors:
Prof. J.W. Morgan,Jr., State Normal College, Florence, Alabama
Prof. J.A. Liner, State Agricultural School, Evergreen, Ala, Supt. H.C. Gilbert, City Public Schools, Florence, Ala. These will be assisted during the week by eminent co-laborers...J.B. Graham, Supt. Education Talladega County.

Pages Missing

The Banner, Vol. 1, Clanton, Ala., Thursday, August 24, 1893, No. 42

ALABAMA ITEMS - John Foster, colored, of Montgomery climbed up in a tree and caught over 500 martins.

United States Marshal J.S. Musgrove was married to Miss Susie Neal, of Georgetown, Ky.

Editor W.H. Shropshire, of the Coosa River News, died the past week from an overdose of morphine.

W.A. Andrews, of Montgomery, committed suicide by shooting himself through the heart with a pistol.

George S. Livingston of Prattville has been appointed trustee for township entries of lands in the Territory of Oklahoma.

Harvey Spreck, a notorious character and murderer, has been arrested near Newburgh. Some three years ago he killed a bank boss at one of the coal mines in Walker County.

At Mobile William Lawshe and Zack Therrel, two M. & O. engineers, came together on account of an old feud. Lawshe may die from gunshot wounds Therrell is under arrest.

Dr. C.J. Clark, one of Selma's oldest physicians, died in Jacksonville, where he had gone hoping to be benefited. Dr. Clark has been an invalid for years. His friends had hoped for his recovery, but death claimed him for his own. The funeral will take place at Selma.

The committee appointed to examine the banking firm of Josiah Morris, who recently made an assignment at Montgomery, report that the assets of the company are $3,351,483.91, while the liabilities are $1,641,298.90. The bank will probably soon resume business.

For several weeks past a gang of horse thieves have infested the counties of Marion, Winston, and Franklin. Two of the gang have been captured by Jas. Madison, who unexpectedly encountered Jessie Turner and Lee Quinn. The two men are now in jail at Russellville. It is thought the capture is an important one and will lead to the arrest and breaking up of the entire gang.

Mr. Vest has offered in the Senate bills fixing the compensations of United States district attorneys, marshals and clerks of circuit and district courts....

Mr. W.C. Harris,Jr. chief consul of the League of American Wheelmen, Mr. Eugene Ware, C.W. Burney and George S. Brown are on an extended bicycle trip through the (?) of the state. They will reach Tuskaloosa, Greensboro, Uniontown, Demopolis, Marion, Selma, Montgomery, Troy, Union Springs, Eufaula and Opelika in the order named. The object of the trip is to secure information regarding the condition of the roads in that section. This is the first of a series of tours which will be made during the fall with the above object in view, and the information gained will be condensed and published by the Alabama division of the league for the benefit of tourists. The entire trip will be made awheel.

OFFICIAL REPORT - Of the Proceedings of the Last State Executive Committee of the

People's Party
Birmingham, Ala., Aug. 19 - The State Executive Committee of the Peoples party of Alabama held its most successful meeting of any up to date, at Talladega, on the 9th and 10th of this month. The sessions was resided over by Chairman Gaither. The first important procedure was the supplying of vacancies that existed upon the committee. This being done, the committee is now organized as follows: Geo. F. Gaither, Walnut Grove, Ala., chairman. Joseph C. Manning, Birmingham, Ala., secretary; 1st District, Chas. E. McCall, Desotaville; Chas. Spies, Mobile.
2nd District, Z. Terry, Red Level; J.B. Townsend, Pine Level.
3rd District, W.S. Bell, Echo; Edward Roach —.
4th District, J.H. McIlwain, Selma; Jno. W. Pitts, Creswell.
5th District, M.W. Whatley, Idaho, Joseph Shackleford, Coosada.
6th District, Samuel Snoddy, Jasper; L.F. Burks, Tuscaloosa.
7th District, W.M. Wood, Cullman; G.F. Gaither, Walnut Grove.
8th District, J.J. Stutts, Green Hill; David Cook, Lacon.
9th District, S.M. Adams, Randolph, L.C. Litesey, Marion
The state at large, A.P. Longshore, Columbiana,; Philander Morgan, Lincoln; J.M. Whitehead, Greenville; T.W. Powell, Cullman.
The next step taken was the formation of a campaign committee, which is as follows: A.P. Longshore, chairman; Jno. W. Pitts, secretary; C.E. McCall; J.M. Whitehead; W.S. Bell; Philander Morgan; M.W. Whatley; Samuel Snoddy; T.W. Powell; L.C. Coulson, Scottsboro; J.C. Manning...A.P. Longshore presented a resolution calling for the circulation of "Politics of Alabama", by J.C. Manning, as the author had tendered the profits to be derived from its sale to the Campaign Committee...The name of A.P. Longshore was suggested for national committeeman of the People's party to succeed J.B. Ware. The suggestion was adopted. The session then adjourned. J.C. Manning, Secretary.

NEWS OF OUR GREAT ORDER - Matters of Moment Which Concern the Order and Its Members
The union of the two branches of the Farmers' Alliance in Ohio - the open and secret branches - is being advocated, and it is expected that their interests will be blended in the early winter. The State Secret Alliance has 22,000 members. L.L. Pegg is president of the secret Alliance, and also president of Franklin County Alliance.

A National Farmers' Encampment - Thousands and thousands of farmers from all parts of North America will meet at Mount Gretna, Pa., August 19th to 26th...Hon. John S. Dore, of Fresno, California, perhaps the wealthiest and most extensive farmer of the Golden State, has been elected president, Col. James Young, of Middletown, Pa., Hon. M.D. Davie, of Beverly, Ky., and Hon. C.B. Matthews, of Buffalo, N.Y., vice-presidents, with and advisory board composed of a leading farmer from every state and territory in the Union, an executive committee of eminent farmers. Col. J.R. McFarland, of Harrisburg, president of the Agricultural Implement Exhibitors' Union, will be the superintendent of exhibits, assisted by E.E. Kent, Esq., Syracuse, N.Y. The general direction of the whole encampment will be under the National Farmers' Alliance summer encampment committee, of which Col. H.C. Demming, of this city is chairman, Dr. S.P. Heilman, of Heilmandale, Lebanon county, serving as secretary...

READS LIKE ROMANCE - A Moonshine Still Captured in a Jail Running In Full Blast
A still was captured in the county jail at Birmingham, Ala., during the past week. It was found in the cell of Charles E. Welborn, who awaits trial in the Federal court for forgery.

The raid was made by deputy collector Carl Tutwiler and deputy marshal A.L. White. After a conference with Sheriff Morrow the trio entered the white ward of the jail and commenced a search. They finally reached Welborn's cell. Here, under an improvised table, they found a bucket, in which a piece of gas pipe was curled. This was the flake stand. In one corner of the cell were three tin candy boxes. These were fermenters. Under the bed was a spittoon full of grease. This was the furnace. The still proper, a tin oil can, had been destroyed. The capacity of the plant, said the officers, was a gallon a day. Welborn was summoned. He took the matter easily and went to pains to show the officers the originality of the worm. The government's informant was Bud Parker, of the celebrated Cherokee county whitecap band. He gave the thing away en route to prison, describing the situation of the plant and stating that a sort of rum was the output. The material used, he said, was the molasses given as food to the prisoners. Welborn's furnace, the spittoon, and his worm, flake stand and fermenters were carried off by the officers to be used in evidence, if necessary. Welborn had a trial before Commissioner Hunter for illicit distilling. The miniature still found in his cell was produced as evidence and he was bound over in the sum of two hundred dollars. He was sent back to jail but will be closely watched to see he makes no more moonshine whiskey. His life reads like a dime novel, but his latest exploit takes the cake. Two years ago he was arrested for using the mails fraudulently in that he advertised himself as the representative of a big syndicate and had consignments of goods sent to him for which he never paid. After being arrested he got out of jail by forging his bond. He turned up next in New York, where he stole a yacht and sailed to Florida, where he robbed a railroad ticket office, and was sent to the chain gang, but escaped and was captured a few months ago in New Orleans. He had made several thousand dollars by fraudulent methods in Texas. Since then he has been in jail at Birmingham.

Alabama Alliance - The Alabama Farmers' Alliance, which met at Talladega, was attended with great success. It was said to be one of the most representative sessions held in the history of the order. Among the prominent reform leaders present were R.F. Kolb, P.G. Bowman, J.C. Manning, A.T. Goodwin and others of less note. Speeches were made during the meeting by these visiting champions of alliance (?).

Surgeon Branham Dead - The dread disease yellow fever, from which Surgeon John W. Branham was suffering last week, has claimed him as its own, and he who would have saved others has himself been taken from earth. He died at Brunswick last Sunday and was interred to the cemetery at that place. Those who were with him when he died have been placed in strict quarantine, where they will remain until all danger is passed.

Alliance State Secretary I.L. Brock is still very ill.

We take the following from President Loucks letter to the Farmers Alliance: "Our chief magistrate realizes that our nation is in peril. Our business interests are paralyzed. The great Shylock Juggernaut is rolling his merciless wheels over every industry of the nation."...

We clip the following from an expression of opinion on the President's message by Col. Joseph F. Johnston, president of the Alabama National Bank, Birmingham: "If our silver is such a menace to the country, why is it that Wall street bankers are now advertising to pay $750 per $1,000 premium for standard silver dollars in certified checks of the great banks there?...

Read President Louck's and Banker Johnson's utterances regarding Cleveland in this issue.

The one a Populite, the other a Democrat; they seem to be pretty closely together in their views as regards Cleveland's policy.

Chairman Goodwyn of the Jeffersonian Democratic Executive Committee has is issued a call for the committee to meet at Montgomery, Sep. 7. The call states that "matters of importance will be considered and acted upon by that committee."

Congressman Cathings of Mississippi, has been deservedly catching it from the Vicksburg Herald, for misrepresenting his district, by opposing free silver; and explanation has bee demanded of him.

County assistant lecturer, J.A. Logan, is doing work for the Alliance cause; he makes it his practice to answer every call, at no matter what personal inconvenience it may entail.

Verbena Views - Verbena Baptist church had a series of meetings held by Rev. J.G. Lowrey, of Calera.

Miss Ula Rollins, one of Bikeville's most charming young ladies is visiting Mrs. Short and friends.

Mrs. A.J. Brooks and her daughter Miss Lucas are visiting friends in Verbena.

Mr. McGuire, of California, is visiting his daughter Mrs. McCan.

Prof. S.J. Strock will teach at East Lake next year.

Mr. Clarence Moody is spending the summer at home.

Mr. Harris Askins has vacated his clock business in Georgia and is spending awhile at home.

Mount Zion Alliance - Mount Zion Alliance re-organized on Saturday, August 19th 1893, and elected the following officers: W.J. Collins, President; J.A. Murphy, Vice-President; J.W.E. Wells, Secretary; John Ellison, Treasurer; J.F. Goodgame, Lecturer; James Vines, Chaplain; John Ellison,Jr., Door Keeper; James Wagner, Assistant Door Keeper. We were highly entertained by that indefatigable alliance worker J.A. Logan; his theme was the Sayre election law and the silver purchasing clause in the Sherman Act and also sowing how congress could benefit the people if disposed to do so...

Jumbo Jumbles - Mr. J.F. Goodgame who has been quite sick is convalescent.

Mr. Abb Glasscock is teaching a singing school at Mount Zion church.

Rev. R.M. Honeycutt, of Clanton, filled his regular appointment here last Saturday and Sunday.

Mr. T.H. Williams and C.F. Williams have been attending the protracted meeting at Bay Springs, in Shelby county.

Mr. V.H. Vines and sister, Miss Venecia Vines, of Clanton, visited friends and relatives here this week.

Miss Janie Goodgame, of Clanton visited her cousin, Miss Emma Williams, last Saturday and Sunday.

Mr. Mard McKee visited his best girl near Jumbo last Sunday.

Miss Roberta Marcus, of Clanton, is attending school here.

Mr. Eddie Giles and Pink Giles, brothers, visited relatives here last Sunday.

FROM OUR READERS - Editor Banner - I wish to write a few more lines for your paper, the champion of Chilton county. Mr. Editor, I have been thinking upon the line which has been drawn between the world and Christians. You remember the disciples of Christ were first called Christians at Antioch. Now, we take it for granted that there was a reason for the name given them, and the reason was, the disciples were so much like Christ. The Christians had been brought from nature's darkness into the marvelous light and liberty of the Gospel of Christ, being born again with the love of Christ planted within their hearts; this love creating in them a desire for that is right and good and makes to the glory of God and the salvation of the souls of the people and for doing the will of God in carrying out the mission of Christ on earth denying themselves of the deeds of darkness and self, and going about doing good; therefore, they were called Christians. Now, Mr. Editor, don't you suppose if that preacher that J.E. Jones, of Jemison, in his letter in the Alliance Herald heard say in Marion, "Yes, we counted them out; we did just what we ought to have done." had been a Christian, that he would have given his consent for the ballots to have been counted any other way than right?...

Cane Creek Alliance - Cane Creek Alliance held a very pleasant meeting on the 12th, a great many being present. Assistant county lecturer J.A. Logan addressed the Alliance by invitation, his subject being the Good of the Order, his address was greatly appreciated. Bro. Logan is a fluent speaker and indefatigable in the Alliance cause. Dinner was enjoyed on the grounds close to the big spring the next meeting will be held Saturday, 26th, the subject set for discussion, the Sayre election law.

Goose Pond Dots - Mr. James Littlejohn is one of the happiest fathers in our town; it is a boy.

Mr. Blanton Riggins, of Birmingham, visited his brother R.C. Riggins, and sister Mrs. James Littlejohn, last week.

Mr. James Littlejohn treated the ladies of this neighborhood to a nice lot of watermelons one day last week.

Mrs. Holmes visited Mrs. Littlejohn last week.

The dogs are paying havoc with the sheep in this neighborhood. Mrs. W.Q. Childress would have laid one of them in the shade if the gun had not failed to fire.

COMMITTEE IN CONGRESS, How Alabamians Are Placed. - Washington, August 21. - The committees of the house were announced today, and the greatest surprise was the fact that the chairmanship of the ways and means committee did not go to Mr. Springer, who was tucked away in the chairmanship of the committee on banking and currency, a place for which Mr. Springer had no particular longing. Alabama has secured the chairmanship of three committees: Gen. Wheeler securing that of the committee on territories; Mr. Bankhead that of public buildings and grounds; while Mr. Oates is given that of expenditures in the post office department. Mr. Denson, who is a new member, appears as eighth on the committee on elections. Oates, in addition to the chairmanship of the committee on expenditures in the post office department, is named second on the committee on judiciary. Bankhead, in addition to the chairmanship of the committee on coinage, weights and measures. Cobb, is seventh on the banking and currency committee. Clarke, of the first district, is fourth on the rivers and harbors committee, and second on the committee on expenditures in the department of justice. Robbins, of the fourth district, is fourth on the committee on merchant marine and fisheries, and seventh on the committee on patents. Chairman Wheeler, of the committee on territories, is second on the committee on military. Turpin, is fifth on the committee on postoffices and post roads, and third on the committee on Indian affairs. Mr. Stallings is seventh on the committee on education, and eighth on the committee on election of president and vice-president.

Program of Sunday School Convention to be held at Collins Chapel Oct. 28 & 29, 1893
SATURDAY
10 a.m. 1. Devotional exercises, Z.J. Jones; alternate J. Bice
Address of Welcome, W.A. Mims
SUBJECTS.
1. "Is it the duty of every church member to take an active part in Sunday school work?" W.G. Riggins, J.M. Scott and J.J. Hicks
2. "Is it necessary to have a Sunday School where that is preaching every Sunday?" Jno. E. Jones, David Johnston, A.L. Foshee and Thos. Harrison.
3. "What can we do to induce people to attend Sunday School?" W.N. Johns, Dr. V.H. Caine, David Wallace, Alex Glasscock.
SUNDAY
9 a.m. Mass meeting. "Mark the perfect man and behold the upright of the end of that man is peach." J.C. Hicks; alternate, J.N. Flowers
11 a.m. Preaching, Rev. R.M. Honeycutt; alternate, Rev. W.A. Wood.

AD - University School, Clanton, Alabama, E.Y. McMorries, Ph.D., Principal...

AD - W.I.R. Thompson & Co., Montgomery, Alabama...

TOWN ITEMS - Louis A. Decater, a negro, was committed to jail on Saturday charged with assaulting his wife with a weapon; the crime was committed near Jemison. Decater was tried before Justice Thos. Harrison, of that town.

Mr. R.C. Middleton, of Birmingham, visited relatives in Clanton last Saturday.

Mrs. Oscar Mullins, is visiting her mother near Mount Zion.

Mrs. John Goodgame is visiting Mrs. James McKee near Jumbo.

Mrs. Dr. Marlar has returned from a visit to relatives at Clanton Ford.

Mr. Wm. Lambert, of Cane Creek, was in town Tuesday.

Mrs. Judge Callen is visiting relatives at Selma.

Rev. T.B. Haynie will not be able to preach at the Congregational church on the first Sunday in September.

Miss Gamma Middleton is visiting friends and relatives at Springfield, Tennessee.

Charming Miss Maggie Reeder, who has been spending the summer with the Hon. O.M. Mastin's family, returns home to Atlanta tomorrow, much to the regret of her may friends here.

Widow Gullahorn's house is undergoing repair for the occupancy of (?).W. Dunkin, whose mother and sister (?) make their (?) here.

There was a private ball held at Mullins' hall last Tuesday night, and a most enjoyable time was spent. Mr. Leonard Gullahorn was floor manager.

Dr. A.E. Bivings has returned home considerably improved in (?).

(?).O. Ward who has been (?) his family for the past two (?)urned to Sistrunk Wed-(?)

(?) any friends of Mrs. R. Q. (?) be glad to learn that (?) improving in health.

(?)oneycutt's aged mother (?) him this week.

(?)W.C. Robinson paid us a (?) call. He has a fine school, (?) attendance averaging over (?).

(?) Moore reports that cot-(?)ing the rust very badly.

Mr. John W. Connell of Verbena (?), traveling salesman for a pat-(?)gon tombstone, was in town on Saturday.

Last Friday night ex-sheriff Lee Hayes had the misfortune to lose a mule. On Thursday morning Mr. Hayes met a negro man who asked him for work. He worked that day and the next. About midnight the dogs awoke Mr. Hayes who at once found the negro was missing and also discovered a mule with saddle and bridle was also gone, likewise a quantity of clothing from the room in which the negro had slept. Mr. Hayes at once summoned a posse and went in pursuit and about ten miles from home he found the mule loose near Maplesville. Securing the mule he continued in chase of the negro and finally caught him about twenty miles from home. When captured, the negro was wearing the clothes belonging to Mr. Hayes, who at first hardly recognized him. He was taken before Justice Robt. Martin and sent to jail at Clanton in default of bail. The negro gave his name as Jim White.

Mr. G.W. Goodgame of Miss., was shot dead by a man named Hopper last week. He had whipt Hopper for insulting remarks regarding his sister and was leaving him when Hopper fired upon him three times, killing him. This will be sad news to Mr. Goodgame's many friends.

Mr. Hugh Foshee is, we are sorry to learn, suffering from an attack of fever.

Mr. Wm. Lodge, of Lomax gave us a call this morning and renewed his subscription for a year. Come thou and do likewise.

Mr. Givhan and Miss Inez Collier have returned from a trip to the World's Fair.

AT THE CAPITOL, A Full Synopsis of What Has Been Done at Washington the Past Week - SEVENTH DAY - Less than half the members were present when the Senate was called to order at noon today, but the galleries were full...Mr. Voorhees, chairman of the committee on finance, introduced and had referred to that committee a bill to provide for the issue of circulating notes of national banks. Mr. Vest introduced a bill for the coinage of silver bullion. Mr. Hill of New York offered a resolution declaring it to the be sense of the senate that no legislation other than legislation pertaining to the finances shall be considered at the present extraordinary session of congress...At the close of his speech, Mr. Hoar obtained the floor, and then, after a short executive session for reference to the committees today, the senate at 4:30 o'clock adjourned.

EIGHTH DAY - In the Senate today a bill to repeal so much of the act of July 14, 1890, as directs the purchase of silver bullion, was introduced by Mr. McPherson, democrat, of New Jersey. Mr. Gordon of Georgia, introduced a bill to suspend for six months the operation of the law which now imposes a tax of 10 per cent, upon State banks, in his speech advocating the bill he asserted that if it should become a law it would end the panic in fifteen days. Mr. Voorhees, chairman of the finance committee, reported back the bill introduced by him yesterday to enable National banks to issue circulation to the amount of the par value of their bonds. An objection of Mr. Cockrell sent the bill over till tomorrow. Speeches were made by Messrs. Hunton, Lodge, Walcott, Hoar, Stewart, Cockrell, Aldrich, and Sherman, and 5:10 the Senate adjourned.

NINTH DAY - Mr. Vest's bill appropriating $300,000 for a site and building in Washington, to be known as the "Hall of Records" was passed. Then the bill to increase the circulation of national banks was taken up and postponed til tomorrow. But before it was laid aside an important amendment was proposed by Mr. Cockrell, to authorize the redemption (at par and accrued interest) of such 2 per cent bonds (over $25,000,000 in all) as may be offered, and to authorize the issue of new treasury legal tender notes in payment therefor. Another amendment to the bill was offered later on by Mr. Allen of Nebraska for the cessation of interest on the bonds on which the increased national bank circulation should be based. Mr. Berry of Arkansas addressed the Senate in favor of the double standard of gold and silver. The Lodge resolution was taken up with the Gallinger amendment to it, to the effect that is would be unwise and inexpedient to make any radical changes in the tariff prior to March 1897 and Mr. Gallinger addressed the Senate...

TENTH DAY - The only new proposition in that direction was an amendment offered by Mr. Gorman to the bank circulation bill prohibiting nation banks from withdrawing circulation without a previous sixty days notice to the comptroller of the currency and without the approval of the secretary of the treasury, and limiting the aggregated amount of such withdrawals to $3,000,00 within any calendar month. Mr. Vest made a vigorous protest against its passage. Messrs. Hoar, Vilas, Pasco and Call supported the resolution. Mr. Peffer moved it indefinite postponement and demanded the yeas and nays. The death of Representative Chipman of Michigan was announced.

ELEVENTH DAY - The finance committee, however, through its chairman, Mr. Voorhees, presented a bill to repeal the purchasing clause of the Sherman act, and making a declaration that it is the policy of the government to maintain the parity between gold and silver coins. The minority of the party, through its spokesman, Mr. Vest, presented a substitute fixing the grains to be contained in the dollars, half dollars and quarters... There was a long discussion on the amendment offered by Mr. Allen (Pop.) of Nebraska, providing for the cessation on the bonds upon which the increase is to be based and an amendment to the bill by Mr. Cockrell (Dem.) of Missouri, for the redemption in greenbacks of the 2 per cent bonds that may be offered. Mr. Allen's amendment was rejected (?) to 11 - and Mr. Cockrell's amendment was not acted upon before the Senate adjourned...

HOUSE

SEVENTH DAY - ...Mr. Boatner of Louisiana was accorded the floor...Mr. Layton, democrat, of Ohio, was the next speaker; he favored the bill to repeal the purchasing clause of the Sherman act. Mr. Patterson of Tennessee also favored the bill. Mr. Bailey of Texas followed Mr. Patterson in a speech advocating Mr. Bland's free coinage substitute. Mr. Pendleton of West Virginia said that upon this question all democrats could differ without surrendering their convictions...Mr. Lacey, republican, of Colorado, spoke in favor of amendment which he proposed to offer, if he had an opportunity, providing that the Wilson act should not take effect until the silver circulation should be increased to $7,00,000,000. Mr. Warner, democrat, of New York, spoke in favor of the repeal of the proposed cause of the Sherman act, and was followed by Mr. Hutchinson, democrat, of Texas, who made a humorous speech in favor of free coinage, but before he concluded the House, at 5 o'clock adjourned.

EIGHTH DAY - ...Mr. Hutchinson concluded his remarks from yesterday in favor of free coinage. Mr. Blanchard spoke in favor of free coinage. Mr. Grosvenor of Ohio opposed free coinage, Mr. Hall of Missouri spoke in its favor, while Mr. Snodgrass, democrat, from Tennessee, made a bitter assault upon his colleague, Mr. Patterson, on account of the position taken by the gentleman against free coinage...

NINTH DAY - ...It was staffed by Mr. McCall, republican, in favor of the purchasing clause of the Sherman bill and was closed by Mr. Moses of Georgia in opposition thereto. Sandwiched between these two speeches were remarks by Mr. Coombs, democrat, of New York; Mr. Bryan, democrat, of Nebraska, and Mr. Henderson, republican, of Iowa...Mr. Bryan made the speech of the day, and although he occupied more than two hours in its delivery, he commanded the earnest attention of his colleagues throughout. He was one of the apostles of bimetallism and his sympathizers regarded his arguments as unanswerable, but the same thing was said of the speech of Mr. Henderson by the opponents of free coinage, and taken altogether the day's debate might be put down in the category of a drawn battle.

TENTH DAY - ...Mr. Daniels of New York was the first speaker. He declared himself in favor of the purchasing act of the Sherman law. Mr. Cooper (Dem.) of Florida said that he would vote for the Wilson bill and against each and every one of the propositions presented by the silver men. Mr. Cooper is a new member, and the attitude taken by him was somewhat of a surprise to his friends. He is a young man with a strong voice, a ready flow of language, a quickness for repartee, and a pleasant manner. He bids fair to join the ranks of the rising young members of the House. Mr. Goldzier (Dem.) of Illinois spoke a favor of the repeal of the Sherman bill and raised his voice in support of the creditor class, which did not, he said, consist of the bankers and brokers of Wall street, but of a great mass of people. At the conclusion of Mr. Goldzier's remarks Mr. Weadock announced the death of his colleague, J. Logan Chipman, of Michigan. The usual resolutions were adopted and the speaker appointed the following committee to take action in the premises: Messrs Caruth, Cannon of Illinois, Powers, Haugen and Atkin...

ELEVENTH DAY - The silver debate was resumed immediately after the reading of the journal, and the floor was accorded to Mr. Sibley (Dem.) of Pennsylvania, who is in favor of the bimetallist standard. He spoke in support of the proposition suggested by Mr. Johnson of Ohio, providing that the holders of United States bonds might deposit their securities with the government, receiving therefor treasury notes. The debate was then suspended in order to allow Mr. Catchings (Dem.) of Mississippi to report from the committee on rules a resolution authorizing the speaker to appoint the various committees of the House...Mr. Haines (Dem.) of New York taking the floor...Mr. English (Dem.) of New Jersey took the same ground...Mr. Everett (Dem.) of Massachusetts, in old-fashioned and courteous manner, raised his voice in favor of the repeal of the Sherman law. Mr. Simpson (Pop.) of Kansas spoke in favor of free coinage...Before Mr. Simpson had concluded his remarks the House took a recess at 5 o'clock until 8:30...Mr. Simpson, resuming his remarks, denounced the gold standard and predicted that such a standard would produce a revolution that would shake the government to its very foundation...After some discussion by Messrs. Morgan and Talbert, the House, at 10:30, adjourned.

THE MINING BUILDING, A Striking Feature of the World's Fair - ...An industrious collector of crystals, A.B. Crim, Middleville, N.Y., makes a most charming display.

A Sinecure - Sir Boyle Roche was a fine, bluff soldier-like old gentleman, holding some post at the viceregal court, sitting for a government borough, and always voting faithfully for the "Castle". The debate one night was on sinecures, which Curran had indignantly denounced, and twitted by one of the opposite side on some personal inconsistency in the matter, he replied, hotly; "Sir, I am the guardian of my own honor." To which Sir Boyle neatly rejoined; "Then the gentleman himself has got a very pretty sinecure."

The Banner, Vol. 1, Clanton, Ala., Thursday, August 31, 1893, No. 43

Dr. Keely in Memphis - Dr. Keely, the founder of the Keely Institutes, was in Memphis the past week, and that city did itself proud in the ovation given the world famous doctor.

YELLOW FEVER, The Latest News About the Dread Scourg Which is Now Causing Consternation" - At Brunswick, Ga., it had been hoped that the precautionary measures taken, when it was discovered that Dr. Branham had yellow fever, would prevent any further cases, but these hopes have been futile, for hardly had the clay settled over the remains of Dr. Branham before it was announced that Peter Harris was ill with the disease at the Presbyterian parsonage. He was immediately carried to quarantine headquarters at City Physician Branham's home. Mayor Lamb issued a proclamation as soon as the case was announced, urging every one to leave the city at once. His instructions were obeyed by thousands. The Brunswick & Western road sent the mayor authority to issue free passes to deserving poor and hundreds accepted the opportunity thus given to leave the stricken city. Later reports from Brunswick state one more case of fever, an infant of Mrs. Bertha Cox. The distress is said to be terrible. The following message has been sent to Washington signed by the relief committee, the same being addressed to the Senators and Representatives from Georgia: "The situation here is distressing. We are shut off from the entire outside world. Starvation stares the poor people in the face. The refugees, the poor ordinary bread winners, with their families, have left the city without means. About 4,000 are left in the city unable to procure supplies. Immediate provisions and money are needed. Time is an important element. We appeal in behalf of a starving people for immediate aid and confidently rely upon the heart of a great American people and the government to respond." The marine hospital service has made arrangements for the establishment of a probation camp twenty-five miles from Brunswick, Ga., on the road to Waycross. The site of the camp, which will be under the command of Surgeon W.H. Sutton, is high and dry, with good water. Two hundred tents were shipped there from St. Louis. Atlanta welcomes all refugees from yellow fever districts. Several thousand are already there and so far no suspicious cases have developed. The disease has never taken foothold in Atlanta and the people are not at all afraid of it. Quarantine regulations have been issued by the board of health of Augusta against Tampa, Fla., Pensacola, Fla., and Brunswick, Ga. Jacksonville, Fla., sent $1,000 in cash and $500 worth of provisions to Brunswick. Mobile has raised her quarantine against Pensacola.

ALABAMA ITEMS - A.R. Dodson has sold the Cleburne Plowboy to A.P. Taylor.

.

Mr. J.M. Lunsden, of Key, Ala., has a kettle in his possession that has been in the family since 1775.

.

Dave Clark and J.R.J. Waldrop are in the Huntsville jail charged with whitecapping in Winston county.

.

A.B. Brooks has assumed the editorial management of the Rutledge Wave, P.A.W. Keel having retired.

.

The Confederate veterans of Alexandria Valley, Calhoun county, have formed a camp with Charles Martin as commander.

.

(?) Carr, the ex-bank president (?) been brought back to Tus-(?)bia, and is now in jail to answer to thirty-three indictments.

Ralph Richardson, a prominent young man of Goodwater, shot himself accidentally, from the effects of which he died a few hours later.

Charles Ezell, a negro, on trial in Montgomery, for the murder of his wife, Hattie Ezell, has been convicted of murder in the first degree and sentenced to death.

Thursday of last week, Johnny Pitts, son of Mr. L.B. Pitts of Alston, started hunting. In crossing a fence he put his gun over first and then climbed on the fence, when the rail broke, the gun struck a lower rail and was discharged, the load striking young Pitts in the heart, killing him instantly.

Isaac Davis, an ex-convict, was killed near Elyton by J.T. Alley. Some one had been stealing from Alley's corn field and garden. He and son watched for the thief and after several nights caught Davis in the act. He was arrested by them, but broke loose and ran and was shot and killed.

A deplorable accident occurred near Selma the past week, which has cast a gloom over the entire community. Garner Scott, the 14-year-old son of E.A. Scott, went out hunting with some boys about his own age. He was walking behind Frank Scott, his cousin, when in some mysterious manner the latter's gun went off, the entire load entering the boy's breast just below the shoulder. With a groan Garner sank to the ground, while, almost frantic, his two companions stood over him. Finally one hurried back to the city on horseback in search of a doctor and the boy's father, but before he returned death had come to the little fellow.

Late State Item - Governor Jones is in Chicago.

A ten-months-old son of J.P. Hickey, of Anniston, has a head twenty-four inches in circumference.

The trial of Robert Skipper on the charge of burning the depot at Midland City resulted in an acquittal.

The dry kiln, containing over 20,000 feet of lumber, belonging to Mr. G.S. Kelley, of Geneva, was burned Thursday of last week.

While the family was at supper a thief entered the residence of Chancellor Williams at Clayton and stole a sum of money from a trunk.

In a fight over a game of craps at Point Clear last Sunday, Thomas Badgett was shot and fatally wounded by J.R. Jones. Jones escaped in a boat had not been arrested at last accounts.

An Editor Dropped Dead - Dr. William H. Williams, editor of the Central Baptist of St. Louis, dropped dead on the platform while waiting for a train at Alexandria last week. He had been attending the Baptist convention for at Kahokia, and the day before preached a sermon before the association. It is supposed his death was caused by heart disease.

Will Return - President and Mrs. Cleveland will, it is understood, return to the White House on the last day of this month.

NEWS OF OUR GREAT ORDER - When the mortal remains of Rothschild, John Sherman and Cleveland are placed in the grave the monument should be inscribed: " Sacred to the Memory of Three Twins. "-Pioneer Exponent.

In a communication in the National Watchman Jerre Simpson says: " You have asked me for my views on the future of the People's party. Broadly stated, I believe the People's party should keep its " ear to the ground " and listen to the wishes and needs of the people, and at all times seek to direct legislation to meet their demands...

Three Of A Kind - A cable line in Washington claims its third victim from among the members of Congress the past week. A few months ago Representative Hooker, of Mississippi, was thrown from a cable car and injured so seriously that he was confined to the hospital for several weeks. About ten days ago Senator Oates, of Alabama, was injured and is still suffering from concussion of the brain. And now Representative Shell, of Alabama, was knocked down and trundled along the fenders of a cable car for some time, and sufferers with confusion of the chest. He was removed to his suite at the Arlington. At 9 o'clock he was resting comfortably and his physician is hopeful of his immediate recovery.

A Large Verdict - In the United States Court at Norfolk, Va., a verdict was rendered in the case of Walter G. Oakman, receiver of the West Point Terminal Railway and Warehouse Co., vs. the Richmond and Danville Railroad Co., in a suit to recover an indebtedness. The case having gone by default the jury rendered a verdict in favored of the plaintiff for $2,756,074.

THE REFORM MOVEMENT - President Ellington, of the Georgia State Alliance, has adopted the policy of keeping the Alliance meetings separate from the People's party rallies.

1878 John G. Carlisle, now secretary of the treasury, said: "The movement to totally demonetize silver is a stupendous conspiracy conceived by the moneyed interests of all countries to increase the value of one-half of the world's metallic money by destroying the other half. The successful consummation of that conspiracy would be more disastrous to the people of this world than war, pestilence and famine.

There will be public speaking at the Court House at 11 a.m., Saturday, September 9th. County Alliance Lecturer L.D. Pounds is expected to be present.

The Alabama members, with the exception of Clarke, Oates, Turpin and Wheeler, voted against the Wilson bill.

Gov. Jones claims that the Sayre election law is much more careful of the rights of electors than the, as he terms it, "unperverted Australian" system. We are glad the Governor used the term unperverted in speaking of the Australian system, for there never has been a perversion of a system more flagrant than that of the Australian by the enactment of the Sayre law in its stead...

The position of Senator Morgan on the all aba(?)ing silver question he sums up as follows:

"My views upon the financial question will be given in the Senate, and before that it might not be well for me to anticipate..."

Goose Pond Dots - Mr. W.Q. Childress is down with fever we are sorry to say.

Miss M.J. Riggins, of Talladega county, has been visiting her brother, Mr. R.C. Riggins; she was accompanied by Miss Naomi Farris and Miss Sidera Riggins.

Swift Creek Swishes - The son of Mr. W.A. Aldridge is very sick with brain fever.

Mr. Rhodes' little son is suffering from congestion of the bowels.

Mr. L.E. Price's family have been under the doctor's hands for quite awhile.

Nine and a half pounds was the weight of the latest arrival, a bouncing baby girl born on the 29th instant to Mr. W.H. Hicks.

On the night of the 22d instant the shaving house at Ehrman and Meritt's mill caught fire; but was soon extinguished.

Jumbo Jumbles - Mr. W.W. Jones has been visiting relatives at Okemulgee for the last few days. He says crops in that neighborhood are fine, and that the people are in a very prosperous condition in every respect.

There was a lively protracted meeting being held at Friendship church under the direction of Brother Luther Hick.

Poplar Springs - The citizens of beat 5, bet at this place, and after some consultation Bro. J.B. Wells was called to the chair, who stated the purpose of the meeting; on motion J.J. McDowell was elected secretary. On motion the following resolution was passed, to wit: Resolved that the chair appoint a committee on resolutions, J.H. Jones, E.G. Rollins, J.J. McDowell, J.J. Armstrong, Aaron Dennis, B.H. Wells, Moses Mims...J.B. Wells, Chairman, J.J. McDowell, Secretary

West Chilton Warblings - We have just closed a protracted meting of five days at Fellowship church in north Dallas. It was conducted by Bro. Dunaway, of Plantersville, and the Rev. Mr. Samuel, of Clarke county. We had a great revival. There were eleven additions to the church. The little cotton is opening rapidly and cotton picking is the order of the day. Crops are very short in this portion; every body should sow large turnip crops as soon as it rains to help out the short corn crop. Albert Barnes, son of Old Mike, killed a large rattlesnake on the 25th ins. in his fathers' field, it was four feet and three inches long and had twelve rattles and a button.

We are very sorry to learn that Dr. Little, of Stanton, is going to move to Piedmont, Alabama.

We regret to learn our esteemed young friend Prof. Dave Moore is very sick, we truly hope he will soon be able to take charge of his school again. Prof. J.W. Bearden has taken a nine months school at Welch's Mill, he is an experienced teacher.

New Salem - I have just returned home from a protracted meeting at New Salem Baptist church. We had a good time; great interest was manifested and the manifestation of the presence of the spirit of the Lord was seen and felt. Notwithstanding the busy time with fodder, the people attended the meeting; the congregations were large. The preaching was with power and demonstration of the spirit of God. Accessions 14, Baptized 4, 8 awaiting baptism. May the good work go on. Attending ministers: W.A. Wood, W.G. Riggins, John Hewit, Editor of the View, and the writer, W.M. Wood

Lincoln, Ala., Aug. 25, 1893, Editor Banner - I am pleased to learn that the action of the Executive Committee of the People's Party taken at Talladega meets with such universal favor with our people...Yours very truly, Philander Morgan.

Liberty Hill - We have just closed a few days protracted meeting at Liberty Hill Baptist church, conducted by Rev. L.B. Pounds and A.L. Foshee, both untiring workers in the cause of Christ. I think they did all in their power for the salvation of sinners; may the Lord bless them and their efforts in His cause. We had four accessions, three by baptism and one by letter. W.M. Wood

Program of Sunday School Convention to be held at Collins Chapel, Oct. 28 & 29, 1893
SATURDAY
10 a.m. Devotional exercises. Z.J. Jones; alternate J. Bice
Address of Welcome, W.A. Mims
SUBJECTS.
1. "Is it the duty of every church member to take an active part in Sunday school work?" W.G. Riggins, J.M. Scott and J.J. Hicks
2. "Is it necessary to have a Sunday school where there is preaching every Sunday?" Jno. E. Jones, David Johnston, A.L. Foshee and Thos Harrison.
3. "What can we do to induce people to attend Sunday School?" W.N. Johns, Dr. V.H. Caine, David Wallace, Alex Glasscock.
SUNDAY
9 a.m. Mass meeting. "Mark the perfect man and behold the upright for the end of that man is peace." J.C. Hicks; alternate J.N. Flowers.
11 a.m. Preaching. Rev. R.M. Honeycutt; alternate Rev. W.A. Wood

TOWN ITEMS - Mr. Amos Baker, of Montgomery, is visiting relatives in Clanton this week.
.
Mr. John D. Maxwell has opened up a meat market near Dr. Johnson's house and will supply only first-class meats.

Squire and Mrs. Nolen left last Saturday night for a visit to relatives in Goodwater. The Squire returned home Wednesday.
.
We are sorry to say that Mr. Ben Wells had to be carried home last Saturday morning, suffering from an attack of rheumatism. He is now much better and able to attend to business again.
.
Mr. W.D. Sortar is going to move out to Ehrman & Merritt's mill.
.
Mrs. Mary Smith has returned home after a pleasant visit to relatives in Coosa.

Mr. T.H. White occasioned (?) friends considerable alarm (?) evening, when Mrs. (?) him insensible. Dr. (?) who was hastily summoned (?)ounced him suffering (?)on of the brain. We (?) he has almost re(?).

Rev. A.C. Wells will preach next Sunday at Kingston church, Autauga county.

The first bale of cotton was brought into Clanton last Monday by Mr. James Edwards, it weighed (?)2 pounds and was purchased by our enterprising friends Messrs. Mul(?) Bros. for 10 cents a pound. Come on with the next!

Capt. W.A. Middleton is again with the Probate Judge's office assisting in making out the Tax ab(?)act for the Collector.

Little Marion Matthews, daughter of Dr. E (?) Matthews, left us on the 25th for Dickson, Tenn., where she en(?) the Dickson Normal School (?) nine months in company with Miss Mary P. Ross, of Opelika, who has been employed as assistant teacher in the musical department. (?) miss Marion's bright little (?), but hope she will return next (?)ing much improved.

Mrs. Evans, of Anniston, is visiting relatives in Clanton this week.

Rev. A.J. Briggs paid Clanton a (?)ing visit last Tuesday.

There was a smash-up just across (?) bridge last Tuesday. Mr. Rob(?) who was driving a wagon with (?) ladies, Mrs. Johnson and Miss (?)es of Montgomery, collided with a mule ridden by Mr. T.J. Robin(?). The wagon was upset but fortunately all escaped without serious injury.

Mr. Will Callen has built a new (?)le at his residence.

Mr. Ray is completing Mr. Stan(?)l's new house, which will soon be ready for renting.

Mr. Frank Goodgame has rented the Biving's gin and is now ready to gin all your cotton at the rate of 1/16th or 40 cents per 100 pounds.

The Baptist church is now being furnished with the pews. Mr. Oates is doing the work.

Mr. Dick Edwards has just had the roof of his store house re-shingled.

Mullins Bros. are improving their store house and will soon lay a brick pavement in front of it.

The Churches - Preaching at the Baptist Church on the third Sunday in each month. Rev. A.A. Hutto, pastor.

There will be preaching at the Congregational church on the first Sunday in each month. Rev. J.L. Busby, pastor.

AT THE CAPITOL, A Full Synopsis of What Has Been Done at Washington the Past

Week
TWELFTH DAY - The Senate was not in session today.
THIRTEENTH DAY - In the Senate this morning a large number of petitions and memorials were presented, relating to the questions of finance. They were referred. Mr. Peffer offered a substitute for the bill to increase the national bank circulation. Mr. Morrill delivered a speech from the text, " Sound Money Cheats Nobody. "...
FOURTEENTH DAY - In the Senate this morning Mr. Allen offered an amendment to the Voorhees repeal bill in the form of a provision for the coinage of silver at the present ratio of 16 to 1 under the same conditions enforced as to the coinage without unnecessary delay of the silver bullion now in the treasury. It was referred to the finance committee, as was also a bill introduced by Mr. Peffer for the reduction of the salaries of all government officers, from $1,000 upwards, by 15 and 20 percent. Mr. Voorhees addressed the Senate in favor of his bill and was followed by Mr. DuBois, republican, of Iowa, in opposition of the same, who in turn was followed by Mr. Palmer in an address favoring the bill. At the close of Mr. Palmer's speech the bill was laid assigned and the Montana senatorship taken up. Mr. McPherson moved this matter be laid aside informally and to proceed to the consideration of the bill to increase the national bank circulation. This motion provoked much colloquy, in the course of which Mr. Voorhees gave notice that if it should turn out at the national bank bill was to be used to delay action on the bill to repeal the Sherman act he should move to sidetrack it. Mr. McPherson's motion close agreed to and the national bank circulating bill was accordingly taking up, the question being on the amendment offered by Mr. Cockrell for the redemption of such 2 percent bonds as may be offered and for payment in a new issue of treasury notes. The amendment and the bill itself were discussed by Messrs. Stewart, Faulkner, Cockrell, Hawley, Allison and Carey...
FIFTEENTH DAY - Mr. Pasco gave notice of his substitute to Mr. Vest's minority bill for silver coinage at the ratio of 20 (?)...The resolution offered yesterday by Mr. Peffer of Kansas, inquiring of the secretary of the treasury as to the conduct of national banks on refusing to pay promptly in currency the checks of their depositors was taken up, and a motion to refer it to the committee on finance was made by Mr. Hoar... The discussion of Mr. Hoar's motion was cut off by the expiration of the morning hour, and the resolution went over without action. The report of the committee on privileges and elections in favor of seating Lee Mantle as Senator from Montana was taken up. Arguments against the adoption of the report and admission of Mr. Mantle were made, and at 5:15 o'clock a vote was on the substitute offered by Mr. Vance declaring Mantle not entitled to the seat. The vote resulted-yeas 35, nays 20. Mr. Manderson changed his vote from nay to yea in order to make a motion to reconsider, which he did, and a motion to lay the motion to reconsider on the table was made...
SIXTEENTH DAY - Mr. Peffer of Kansas made a three hours' speech today upon the silver question he was followed by Mr. Allen of Nebraska, in support of his amendment to Mr. Voorhee's bill, a proviso for the free and unlimited coinage of silver at the ratio of 16 to 1...
SEVENTH DAY - The Senate today listened to Mr. Hill of New York, on the silver question... At 2 p.m. his speech was interrupted, and the Lee Mantle case was laid before the Senate as the regular order of business. It was, however laid aside informally and Mr. Hill proceeded. Senator Stewart followed Mr. Hill in a speech on the silver question...
EIGHTEENTH DAY - The Senate was not in session today.
HOUSE
TWELFTH DAY - The silver debate was resumed after reading of the journal, and Mr. McCreary (Dem.) of Kentucky took the floor in advocacy of the repeal of the purchasing clause of the Sherman act. Mr. Catchings (Dem.) of Mississippi said he would vote for the

unconditional repeal of the purchasing clause of the Sherman act and he would vote against any proposition directly or indirectly looking to the free coinage of silver in this county at this at any ratio that should be suggested... Mr. Livingston (Dem.) of Georgia said there was no reason why men should not rise above partisanship and discuss the disposition of the pending question as sensible men and patriots... Mr. Richards (Dem.) of Ohio believed that President Cleveland was right in attributing the purchasing clause of the Sherman silver bill the present depression. Mr. Curtis (Rep.) of Kansas spoke in support of the Wilson bill, but in a conservative manner... Mr. Broderick (Rep.) of Kansas spoke in favor of bimetallism in prosperity in terms which he regarded almost synonymous. Mr. Clark (Dem.) of Missouri addressed House in favor of free coinage of silver...

THIRTEENTH DAY - After reading of the journal, Mr. Powers republican of Vermont, took the floor in support of the repeal of the purchasing clause of the Sherman act. Mr. Hooker, democrat, of Mississippi, opposed the unconditional repeal of the purchasing clause... Then on motion of Mr. Bland, Saturday next was set apart for several debates on the Wilson bill, instead of debate under the five minute rule. Mr. Cooper, democrat, of Indiana, spoke in opposition to the free coinage of silver. Mr. Alexander, democrat, of North Carolina, advocated free silver coinage and spoke for a larger currency. Mr. Sperry, democrat, of Connecticut, opposed free coinage and advocated the Wilson bill. Mr. Cox, democrat, of Tennessee, argued against the pending bill. Mr. Settle, republican, of North Carolina, said that in his canvas he had opposed the free coinage of silver...

NIGHT SESSION - At the evening session Mr. McLauren, democrat, addressed the House in opposition to the Wilson bill and in favor of the free coinage of silver. Mr. McDonald, democrat, of Illinois, said that he was in favor of free coinage of gold and silver at any ratio that might be acceptable... Mr. Bartlett, democrat of New York, said that with the message of the President he was in thorough accord... Mr. Stockdale, democrat, of Mississippi, argued that the Sherman bill had little to do with the present stagnation of business, but that it was attributable primarily to the tariff...

FOURTEENTH DAY - ... Mr. John Johnson, of Ohio, introduced his incontrovertible bond bill and had it referred to the banking and currency committee, with leave to report at any time after the silver debate. The silver debate was then resumed, and Mr. Brickner, democrat, of Wisconsin, addressed the House in favor of the repeal of the purchasing clause, Mr. Mallory, of Florida, was opposed to the unconditional repeal of the purchasing clause of the Sherman act, and he was also opposed to the free coinage of silver at the present ratio of 16 to 1... Mr. Hopkins, republican, of Illinois, argued against the Bland amendments to the Wilson bill and in support of the repeal measure. Mr. Lane, democrat, of Illinois, spoke in support of free coinage, attending that a silver dollar was the equal of a gold dollar. Mr. Newman, populist, of Nevada, voiced the demand of his region when he vigorously advocated the free coinage of silver. Mr. Bynum, in advocating the Wilson bill, said that unquestionably the vast majority of people believed that the Sherman law was responsible for the evils described by the president. Mr. Hepburn opposed the repeal of the Sherman law. Mr. Jones, democrat, of Virginia, opposed the unconditional repeal of this purchasing clause, and favored free coinage...

FIFTEENTH DAY - ... Mr. C.W. Stone, republican, of Pennsylvania, was the first speaker this morning on the silver bill... Mr. Ryan, democrat, of New York, announced his intention to vote against each and every substitute offered by the gentleman from Missouri (Mr. Bland), and to cast his vote for the unconditional repeal of the purchasing clause of the Sherman act. Mr. Covert, democrat, of New York, spoke generally commending the good temper in which this debate has been conducted, referring to some of the slurs cast upon New York in the speeches, and vigorously resented now... Mr. Fitch, democrat, of New York, believed in party platforms, but between the democratic and other political platforms

made before the present emergency arose and demands of the workingmen and starving people, if he had to take his choice, he would let the platform drop...
SIXTEENTH DAY - ...
SEVENTH DAY - ... Aside from the speeches delivered by Messrs. Burrows and Springer, their were none that commanded the attention of the members, and indeed these two speeches were not listened to with the interest they deserved...
EIGHTEENTH DAY - ...

NEWSY GLEANINGS - In smoking out wasps John B. Perrin, a farmer of New Brunswick, N. J., destroyed all his buildings, worth $10,000.

Condy McGroarty, a mine boy, thirteen years old, fell 280 feet down a mine shaft. His dog aroused the neighborhood. The boy was found at the bottom of the shaft, badly bruised, but he was still alive. At daylight he was brought to the surface.

SOMEWHAT STRANGE - Queer Facts and Thrilling Adventures Which Show That Truth is Stranger Than Fiction
George Wiley, son of a well-known colored man living in Pearl River swap, Jones county, Miss., left home on a recent morning to go on a fishing excursion, taking with him a long, stout rope line, such is generally used among the natives for catching large catfish. A shepherd dog accompanied him. Early the same evening the dog came back to that house alone and whined and jumped about the old man in such an unusual manner as to attract his attention. The old man ran out into the yard and the dog sprang out in front of him, running off a few yards and then coming back and pulling on his clothes. Convinced that something was amiss, Wiley followed the dog and was led to a point on the river about five miles from the house, where he found the lifeless body of his boy suspended by one leg from an overhanging limb by a line which ran over the bough and extending far out into the river. Investigation showed that the boy had thrown his line over the bough to give his catch better play, and then, for greater security, had tied the end around his leg. A 150 pound catfish had seized the bait and hauled the lad up to the bough and wrapped the line fast around the willows in its struggles to escape.

Dr. Knox, of Danbury, Conn., has possessed for a year, two big African snakes, Adam and Eve. He has kept them in a cage in the back office. When the doctor opened his office on a recent Monday, he examined his snake collection. He saw what he supposed were several new potatoes under the python snake. He opened the cage door to remove the supposed potatoes. Going close to the snake it hissed at him. This made him pause. He took a second look and was surprised to see about one hundred snake eggs under her. The eggs vary in size and are rather heavy. They are soft to the touch, oval in form, and of ashy gray color. The smallest of the eggs and the size and shape of a of a duck's. The largest one is no thicker but about six inches long. They are slightly speckled. It is said that the shell will become hard. Pythons before have laid eggs in this country, but there is no record of any snakes having been hatched. At the Paris geological garden in 1811, a python hatched out a number of young. That is the only record of a python in captivity hatching out young.

A highly respectable Indian gentleman, a member of the Bombay Anthropological Society - Mr. Sarat Chaudra Mita - has come forward with an apparently well authenticated story of a girl who has been discovered in Jalpaiguri in the den of a bear. The young person's habits were decidedly bearish, for she tried to bite and scratch those who came near her, went down "on all fours" for locomotion, and "growled at meals". The orphanage of the new Dispensation Church in Calcutta could make nothing of the ferocious foundling, who has consequently been removed to Bas Aram, a refuge founded and supported by Brahm gentlemen in that city. Nor is this all. A Bhagl Gemindar has captured in the jungle a wild boy, whose only approach to speech is the utterance of chattering sounds like those of a monkey. Col. Sleeman and the Rev. Mr. Lewis, of the Secundra Church Mission, have vouched for similar stories. Mr. Mitra is of the opinion that when as sometimes happens, an infant child is abandoned in the bush, there is nothing absurd in the idea that it might be adopted by a female wild animal that had lost her young.

The ruins of a prehistoric city have just been discovered by a party of prospectors from Yuma, Cal., on the Colorado Desert while in search of the Peg Leg mine. The wind had laid bare the walls and the remains of stone buildings. For a distance of 420 feet in length by 260 in width gigantic pillars, quaintly carved to represent dragon heads and rattlesnakes, still stood in the sand of the deserts, supporting on their tops huge slabs of granite. The frieze ornamentation resembled Egyptian sculpture and exhibited a greater degree of skill than is possessed by the Indian artisans of the present day. Fragments of pottery were found underneath the debris and, together with parts of the crumbled piers of the frieze, were taken by the prospectors to San Diego, Cal,. Prospector Ferguson called the matter to the attention of H.C. Gordon, who interested John F. Gay,Jr., wealthy man of San Diego, and in company with four others, they went to the desert to explore the ruins. They were driven back by a sandstorm. They will make another start and make a careful investigation of the ruins.

"We are not much troubled with snakes down our way," said Capt. Lapeyre, of Galveston, "for we have a bird which keeps 'em pretty well cleared out. This is the chaparral cock, or 'roadrunner,' as it is commonly called, and we all protect it on account of its snakekilling propensentries. The bird is about the size of an ordinary guinea fowl and is stoutly and compactly built. It wanders all over the country and its chief object in life appears to be the killing of snakes. The 'road-runner' approaches its enemy cautiously and circuitously, and as it gets near stretches one wing down as a shield, after the fashion of a turkey gobbler strutting in a barnyard, and waits for the snake to strike. The wing is thrown to catch the bite, and as quick as a flash and before the snake can recover, the 'roadrunner' with unerring aim sends its long bill, which is as hard as ivory, through the head of its antagonist, which puts in the time from thenceforth until sunset is dying."

A prehistoric relic of exceeding rarity has been unearthed near Bluff Springs, Ill., by Leslie Vail and Lew Conner and George Conner, who were fishing in a stream which runs through the bank of the stream which runs through the County farm. Projecting near the bank of the stream was a large bone which excited their curiosity, and the work of unearthing it was soon done. It proved to be a monstrous jawbone of a mastodon, containing four huge teeth, weighing 103 pounds, and measuring 3 feet 8 inches in length by 21 inches in width. The foothills and bluffs in the vicinity are rich with antediluvian relics, this being but one of several valuable finds made within the last month.

An example of the mutation of fortune occurred several days ago when the Supervisors of Sonoma, Cal., made a special order placing Jonquin Carrillo on the poor list at $10 a month. He was once one of the richest men in California.

FIRST TO SAIL TO CHICAGO, It Was the Schooner Tracy, Which Arrive There Ninety Years Ago - The first vessel that arrived in this port was the schooner Tracy, in the year

1803, with a man named Dorr as master, says a writer in the Detroit News. This vessel was either owned or chartered by the government, and conveyed Captain John Whistler, U. S. A., and his command, together with supplies and material for the construction of a fort at the mouth of the Chicago River. He built Fort Dearborn, which was located at the point which is now the corner of Michigan avenue and River street. Captain Whistler remained at this post, I think, until 1809 or 1810, when he was relieved by Captain Heald and ordered to report at Detroit, and was with General Hull at the time of the surrender in 1812. Captain Whistler was the father of the late Mrs. Judge James Abbott, Mrs. Major Hamilton, and Mrs. Captain Phelan, all old residents of Detroit. Mrs. William R. Wood, another daughter, was well known in the early society of Detroit as a young lady. She was born in Fort Dearborn about the year 1805. Colonel William Whistler, son of the Captain, will also be remembered by many old Detroiters, having been stationed there with his regiment for several years. General U.S. Grant was a lieutenant in his regiment at the time. The judge and Mrs. Abbott were married at Fort Dearborn, and their bridal trip was made from Chicago to Detroit on horseback. They camped out at night and followed the Indian trail, which was afterward know as the Territorial road, through Michigan. The steamers Sheldon Thompson and William Penn were the first steamers that stirred the waters of Chicago harbor. They arrived here together on July 8, 1831, having on board General Winfield Scott and soldiers for the Black Hawk war. At this time (eighteen years after Captain Whistler and his troops first set foot upon Chicago soil) the city of Chicago could boast of only five houses, and three of these were built of logs. - Chicago Herald

The Banner, Vol. 1, Clanton, Ala., Thursday, September 7, 1893, No. 44

NEWS AND NOTES - SENATOR VOORHEES'S BILL. Senator Voorhees has introduced a bill in the senate authorizing the issue of national bank notes up to the full value of the bonds deposited. He claims that his measure would put nineteen million dollars more in circulation at once. There are several objections to this bill...Nineteen million dollars would be considered only pocket change for a millionaire like Vanderbilt or George Gould. Jay Gould would have made that much clear profit in one day and then considered it a bad day for moneymaking....Thomas Jefferson, J.C. Calhoun, Andrew Jackson, Abraham Lincoln, and all honest men who know the difference between a cow and a piano will testify to the truthfulness of this. We thank Senator Voorhees for his efforts, but hope he will not compromise on such a tiny thread when it ought to be a rope as large as your waist. Progressive Farmer.

TO THE N. F. A. AND I. U. President Loucks has issued the following timely address to the order throughout the country. It contains food for much serious thought and every Allianceman in the land should read it:...

NEWS OF OUR GREAT ORDER - General Weaver very truthfully remarks; There hasn't been a change of administration in this country in 28 years - except postmasters."

GENERAL NEWS - Current Events of the Day Boiled Down Into a Few Lines For Busy People.

Susan B. Anthony, Mary Lease and others of their ilk will begin a campaign in Kansas on woman's suffrage.

.

Surgeon-General Wyman, after a visit to Jersey City, has returned to Washington and officially declares cholera has existed in that city.

.

W.C. Rinearson has been appointed as general passenger agent of the Queen and Crescent route to succeed D.G. Edwards, who has accepted a position with the Cincinnati, Hamilton and Dayton railroad.

.

The senate has rejected the nomination of Henry C. Stuart, of Denver, Col., to be Secretary of Legation in Guatemala and Honduras and Consul General to Guatemala. Stuart was nominated on Aug. 16 to senate.

.

Henry D. Ellis, general agent of the passenger department of the Kansas City, Memphis and Birmingham railroad at Memphis, has resigned, and John A. Scott, district passenger agent of the Louisville and Nashville in Memphis, is appointed to succeed him.

.

Fred A. Hull, president of the Long Mountain coal, coke and timber company of Kineville, Ky., has made an assignment. His Kentucky property is valued at $1,000,000, and he owns extensive interests in Danville. Hull is prostrated at his home and not expected to live.

.

George Walter, a young bicyclist of San Antonio, Texas, has just arrived home from a trip to Chicago and Milwaukee and return, every mile of which was made on his wheel. He left San Antonio June 11. The total distance as shown by the cycle meter, was 3750 miles.

.

Outlaws held up the 'Frisco passenger train at the little town of Mound Valley, Ks., shot and killed Express Messenger Chapam and robbed the passengers. They secured nothing from the express car, but not a passenger escaped. Even the women were relieved of their money and jewels.

The city council of Little Rock, Arkansas, has passed a resolution suppressing the Little Rock Tribune, a weekly paper, published and edited by Kellogg O. Gould. The paper started three weeks ago, since which time it has ceaselessly waged war against Mayor Hill and the entire city administration. Gould will now take the matter before the courts,.

The Nashville, Chattanooga and St. Louis employees presented to Major Thomas, the president, a signed agreement, accepting the 10 per cent agreement for ninety days, saying among other things: "We are willing to bear our share of any burdens fallen on the railroad interests of the company and in view of the present financial conditions agree to receive for ninety days 10 per cent less than our regular wages."

The trouble between the striking miners and the imported negroes in Kansas has not abated. The situation is critical and may result in a collision at the slightest provocation. Mayor D.W. King has issued a proclamation calling on all good citizens to assist him in enforcing the law and forbidding all persons to carry arms within the city. This is thought to be directed as much against the negroes as the strikers. It is said that 400 Winchesters have been shipped to points near there within the last week. Sheriff Arnold and Deputy Sheriff Douglass have called to their aid a large force of citizens who will respond at a moment's notice.

William D. Smith, A Massachusetts envelope manufacturer, estimates that about 300,000,000 envelopes are used in this country annually.

A probable unique instance of the power of a ruling passion was evidenced by George Turner, who was executed for murder at Spartanburg, S. C., last Friday. During his confinement in jail he gave is attention to money making and accumulated, it is said, about fifteen thousand dollars by real estate transactions.

The County Executive Committee of the People's Party of Elmore county met and re-organized at Wetumpka, Saturday, Aug. 26th. R.M. Bennett, of Wetumpka, was elected President, and S.D. Oliver, of Elmore, Secretary of the body, to serve for the term of two years. The committee asserted its faith in the Omaha platform and its full determination to follow the lead of the state committee.

Senator Lodge, author of the famous force bill, was the first senator to endorse and commend the financial policy of Mr. Cleveland in a speech in the senate. Last fall Lodge was the fullest embodiment of tyranny, oppression and meanness at whom democratic oratures could let fly their invective and vituperation. Today he is one of Mr. Cleveland's "old reliables" in the senate; and a much stronger reliance than any democratic senator from the South - Alliance Herald.

Farmers and planters should understand, if the present silver law is repealed and the price of silver thereby forced down, as it would be, that wheat and cotton will go down with it...A.J. Warner, Pres. Amer. Bi-metallic League.

Monday was Labor Day, a legal holiday in this state. At Birmingham, in spite of the prevailing hard times, it was celebrated with great ecla(?). Our old time friend and representative workingman Jno. C. McNulty, of the Boiler Makers Union, was Grand Marshal of the day, and another old friend and veteran, Jno. W. Callahan, of the Typographical Union, was orator of the day...

Jemison Gems - Jemison High School opened last Monday, with Professor J.L. Ruffin as principal. Knowing Professor Ruffin's efficiency along that line, the people feel satisfied that he will make a success of his school.

Dr. J.P. Givhan is now convalescent after a long case of "blood poison" inoculated while performing an operation.

Misses Ray Mauchline, Benie Mauchline and Minnie Wells, from Birmingham, are visiting friends and relatives here.

Miss Annie Smith, after a long visit to friends in South Alabama, has returned home.

Mr. S.J. Heath is visiting relatives at Sloss this week.

Mrs. B.W. Silsbee gave the young people an entertainment last Friday night. It was well attended and greatly enjoyed.

J.R. Hill and family are visiting relatives in Columbiana.

Rocky Mountain Alliance - ...While in session it was resolved that under the eighth question, are any sick or in distress, Bro. W.G. Atkinson was reported in distress on account of the death of his two children...After this song was sung, prayer was offered by Rev. W.M. Green, after which several spoke in sympathy with the bereaved, and we all tender our sympathy to the bereaved parents, and as it has pleased the good Lord to take their loved ones it makes them the father and mother of angels. Jno. A. Green

Pleasant Grove Pleasantries - The church at Pleasant Grove has just enjoyed a glorious series of meetings beginning Aug. 26 and closing Sept. 1 The congregations were large both day and night. A deep interest prevailed through the entire meeting. The pastor, W.G. Riggins, worked with real faithfulness.

Rev. R.M. Honeycutt was with the pastor, and added much to the interest of the meeting. His discourse on Monday was pronounced one of his grandest efforts, being mainly on the evils of intemperence; he held his audience spellbound as it were, while his earnest appeals rang out in behalf of temperence; his denunciations of the evil of strong drink, and uncompromising attitude toward the evil, we think surely added more jewels to the crown.

Brethren Gothard and Waldrup also assisted in the meeting. Prof. J.E. Jones added much to the interest of the meeting. There were added to the church by baptism 25, by letter 3.

On Tuesday Bro. N.L. Maroney and family arrived with the remains of their little son for interment here. Bro. Honeycutt conducted the funeral services. Bro. Maroney and family have many friends here who would gladly alleviate their distress if possible.

Dixie Dots - We were glad to hear from Old Mike again. Well, Old Mike, W. Price may be good to cut fish-hooks out of old Harriet Landslides finger, but if you don't want to see the seven stars you had better not get him to pull a tooth for you. I have just returned home from Dr. Todd, he pulled my tooth, I thought of everything but living.

W.W. Price goes every two of three days to hunt his sheep, but I think he has quit advancing.

Dr. David Moore's friends of Valley Creek are glad to learn that he is better and hope he will be over soon.

S.R. Letcher and H.W. Cole will start to school at Welch's mill soon. We would like to have R. P. B. with us.

Robert Molten met his fatal doom. A few nights since he was swung to a tree by unknown parties.

Central, Ala., Sept. 1, 1893
The farmers in this vicinity are putting forth all their energies gathering cotton, which has proved about three-fourths of a crop. Several parties in this vicinity have recently received warm and disagreeable visits from a crowd of distinguished men who called themselves White Caps. A series of revival meetings have proved a grand success at Equality Congregational church. The meeting was conducted by Rev. A.C. Wells, who effected much good by his powerful and impressive sermons. Many thanks to you, Brother Wells, for your earnest and faithful and Christian efforts during your stay with us. Brother Wells left for home last Thursday. The meting was continued till last night by the Rev. T.B. Haynie. He leaves this morning for his appointment in Tallassee, accompanied by a number of people who reside at this place who have become wonderfully enthused about their soul's salvation.

TOWN ITEMS - Mrs. Lamar, of Deatsville, is visiting Miss Nannie Dukes this week.

Mr. Tom Gullahorn and family will shortly return from Verbena to their old home here.

Mr. T.H. White has rented the house vacated by Mrs. Rainey and will remove there shortly.

The old store house next to the Messrs. Mullins store has been pulled down this week.

We desire to call attention to the advertisement of the Union Warehouse, which appears in this issue. Mr. F.H. Merrit, general manager is a gentleman of experience in handling cotton, he will give his personal attention to all business entrusted to his care.

Professors Lindsey Smith and Mard McKee, of Jumbo, were in town last Saturday.

Professor Joseph Gore is about to open a store in the Lowe settlement.

(?)sday night, Walter Vin-(?) (?) Green, and Flem Mickay (?)d, convicted of gambling (?)day, were taken from jail (?) their sentences in the coal (?) Coalburg. They were (?) on the night express in (?) officer C.C. Colman.

(?)gret to announce the death (?)h Moore, the two year old (?).M. Moore and grandson (?)end Sheriff Moore. The (?)erer passed away last Sat-(?) and was laid to rest (?) on Sunday.

The venerable Mrs. Honeycutt, mother of our esteemed Probate Judge, returned home Wednesday.

Genial county Supt. Moore paid us his customary pleasant visit last Saturday - teacher's day.

Rev. J.F. Smith will preach at the Episcopal church next Tuesday night at 8 o'clock.

Mrs. (?)aynie has removed to the (?)rm house opposite Mr. Parker.

Mr. (?).Clair Thornton of Bangor, (?) paying a visit to his father here.

Owing to delay in getting all the material for the new school building, Professor McMorris is compelled to postpone opening from Wednesday the 13th to Tuesday the 19th ins.

A fair congregation attended the services at the Congregational church on Sunday, when Rev. J.L. Busby preached in the morning from Hebrews iii, 19. "For we see they could not enter because of unbelief;" in the evening from St. Matthew (?)-5, "Judge not that ye be judged."

(?)s. Mary Denty, the aged mother of F.W. Denty, ex-(?) suddenly Tuesday morning at home at Vincent, Shelby County. She was in her 71st year. We (?) our sympathies to the bereaved members of her family.

(?) S.J. Johnson,Jr.'s practice is steadily increasing. So much so that it taxes the Doctor to the utmost to keep up with it.

Cards are out announcing the marriage of Mr. W.H. Sartor and Miss Belle Watts next Tuesday the (?) at the residence of the bride's (?).

ESTRAY NOTICE - Lost from the Charles Watson place one yoke of steers, one being five years old, yellow brialled, small white spot on forehead, ring around his tail; the other being seven years old, solid black, with the exception of some white under the (?)ank in from of hind legs; and white hair half an inch above both hind hoofs, white marks on back. Both are marked. They have been missing for the past four months. Any information regarding them will be thankfully received by Oscar Mullins, Clanton, Ala.

FINAL PROOF NOTICE, Notice No. 13,905, Land Office At Montgomery, Ala, September 6, 1893 - Notice is hereby given that the following named settler has filed notice of his intention to make final proof of his claim and that said proof will be made before The Clerk of the Circuit Court at Clanton, Ala., on Oct. 30, 1893; viz.: William I. Mullins, Homestead Entry No. 19,673, for the ne 1-4 of Section 33, Tp. 21, n of Range 16 e. He names the following witnesses to prove his continuous residence upon and cultivation of said Land, viz.: John W. Scott, Robert S. Owens, J.J. Owens and J.T. Williams, all of Kincheon, Ala. J.H. Bingham, Registrar

Frank Goodgame reports his gin is ready for operation.

AT THE CAPITOL
NINETEENTH DAY - ...Mr. Platt, from the committee on Indian affairs, reported a bill authorizing certain Cherokee allottees or claimants to purchase lands held by them. The bill was passed...The final vote in the two cases from Montana and Washington, deciding Messrs. Mantle and Allen not entitled to seats, was 32 to 29...The amendment was offered by Mr. Cockrell and discussed at great length...
TWENTIETH DAY - Mr. Voorhees, chairman of the finance committee reported back the House bill repealing a part of the Sherman act with an amendment in the nature of a substitute...A resolution offered yesterday by Mr. Stewart was then laid before the Senate...Senator Gordon of Georgia, then addressed the Senate favoring the unconditional repeal of the purchasing clause of the Sherman act...Mr. Teller in a speech then proceeded to show that the Sherman law was not responsible for the financial troubles...
TWENTY-FIRST DAY - ...Mr. Pugh offered a resolution, which was referred to the committee on privileges and elections, to pay $(?),000 to Lee Mantel in full compensation for his time and expense in presenting his claim to a seat in the Senate form the State of Montana. Mr. Stewart offered a resolution for a comparative statement for the present fiscal year. Referred. At 12:35 p.m. the bill to repeal the Sherman act was laid before the Senate, and Mr. Sherman addressed the body for two hours in favor of the bill. When he had concluded his remarks the bill was laid aside and the national bank circulation bill was taken up to allow Mr. Teller to finish his speech begun yesterday...
TWENTY-SECOND DAY - Mr. Cockrell introduced a concurrent resolution directing the Secretary of the Treasury to issue certificates not to exceed 20 per cent of the amount of gold coin and bullion in the treasury and to be the same in payment of interest in that public debt, or any other demand, liabilities or obligation of the United States. It was laid on the table for the present. The repeal bill was again taken up and Mr. Wolcott, of Colorado, opened the debate in a speech opposing the bill. Then the floor was taken by Mr. Caffery of Louisiana, in his maiden speech the resolution previously offered in reference to national banks refusing to pay checks of depositors in currency was taken and again was referred to the finance committee by a vote of 35 to 21...
TWENTY -THIRD DAY - In the Senate today the repeal bill was taken up to allow Mr. Vance to speak upon it, which he did for an hour and forty minutes...Mr. Vance concluded his speech by the declaration that he was for the free and unlimited coinage of silver..
TWENTY-FOURTH DAY - ...Having thus disposed of the silver bill, the Senate devoted the remainder of the day's session to a discussion of Mr. Dolph's bill, appropriating $500,000 for the execution of the Chinese exclusion act.
HOUSE
NINETEENTH DAY - ...The Wilson bill having been read, Mr. Bland offered his first amendment that of free coinage at the present ratio of 16 to 1, and it was amid applause from the anti-silver men, who received one more majority than they expected...After Mr. Cathings gave notice that he would call up the house rules tomorrow, the house at 3:30 o'clock adjourned.
TWENTIETH DAY - ...Mr. Catchings called up the report of the committees on rules. Mr. Reed made a few remarks and Mr. Crisp replied to him...Before adjournment, however, Mr. Springer introduced a bill to provide for the coinage of the seignorage silver in the treasury department.
TWENTY-FIRST DAY - Mr. Talbot asked unanimous consent to introduce a bill repealing the statutes authorizing the appointment of marshals and supervisors of elections...Mr. Breckinridge from the committee on appropriations reported the urgent deficiency

appropriation bill...
TWENTY-SECOND DAY - ...
TWENTY-THIRD DAY - ...

A Telescope Worth Having - James M. Neal, one of the most enterprising and prosperous farmers in Washington county, Georgia, while in Sandersville was informed by the express agent that the telescope that he had been expecting had come, with the privilege of examination and immediate trial. As soon as convenient Mr. Neal went to the express office and received the telescope, and in company with his friend, Colonel Fleming, climbed to the top of the city hall, the highest building in the city, to try the power of the telescope to see the rounding country. They viewed the landscape o'er and took a bird's eye view of Tennille, Davisboro and Warthea, and all the points of interest within the range of the instrument. When Mr. Neal drew a focus on his plantation, which is five miles north of Sandersville, he remarked to his friend, Colonel Fleming, that he was satisfied with the telescope. He then shifted it to this pasture, where there were fine Jersey cows, improved breed of hogs and varieties of live stock in abundance. He observed a great commotion among his cows and upon adjusting the focus to a nicety he noticed that a tremendous rattlesnake was the cause of the commotion. He quickly handed the telescope to Colonel Fleming, descended the iron steps, mounted his horse and in a short while reached his place, where he found two of his cows lying dead from the effects of the serpent's bite. He searched diligently for the serpent and found him coiled under a mullein plant. Mr. Neal rushed to his house, got his gun, returned to where the rattler was and emptied both barrels into his body. Mr. Neal came to town that afternoon bringing with him the rattles, which numbered fourteen and one button. He says "there is not enough money in the United States to buy his telescope." - Atlanta Constitution.

Thirty-Two years ago, John Bahler of Battle Creek, Mich., became blind and his eyeballs were removed. Now it is said, that new eyeballs are growing in the sockets, and he is already able to distinguish colors.

NOTES AND COMMENTS - The inconvenience created in Italy by the scarcity of silver coins, will be alleviated by a measure just taken up by Signor Grimaldi, the Finance Minister...

.
The election of Miss Ella M. Grubb to be Superintendent of Schools for Adams County, Ill, has aroused great interest there, for next to Cook county, the head city of which is Chicago, Adams is the most populous county in the State, and this is the first time in its history that a woman has been elected to office. Miss Grubb is only twenty-eight years old. As an instance of her pluck and high character it maybe said that she has already paid back from her earnings as a teacher the money she was compelled to borrow to secure a college education.

.
Lt. Hung-Chang has intimated, according to a Daily Dew Shanghai correspondent, that a new treaty between China and the United States will be necessary in view of the present condition of the Chinese immigration question, and that the new Minister will probably be charged with the task of arranging one.

.
Mme. Tel Sexo, a Japanese lawyer, is said to be the only feminine member of the bar in the land of the Mikado. She was educated in this country. She takes a great interest in the welfare of her sex, and has founded a training school for women.

SLAVERY DAYS IN NEW YORK, The Captain of a Successful Trader in Live Freight Was Four Times Mayor. - On the turn from the seventeenth to the eighteenth century slave-dealing was an important and well-thought-of industry, or, in the more elegant phrase of one of the gravest of New York historians, "a species of maritime adventures then engaged in by some of our most respectable merchants." The Dutch are credited with having brought the first cargo of slaves to the northern part of America - from their possession on the Guinea coast to the Virginia plantations - and according to Harper's, a regular part of the business of the Dutch West India company was providing African slaves for use in the American colonies. The profits of the business, even allowing for the bad luck of a high death rate, was so alluringly great that it was not one to be slighted by the eminently go-ahead merchants of New York, and the fact must be remembered that as a business slave-dealing was quite as legitimate then as is the emigrant traffic of the present day. Young John Cruger has left on record a most edifying account of a voyage which he made out of New York in the years 1698-1700, in the ship Prophet Daniel, to Madagascar for the purchase of live freight, and the sentiment of the community in the premises is exhibited by the fact that the slave-dealing Mr. Cruger was elected an Alderman from the Dock Ward continuously from the year 1712 until the year 1773, and that subsequently he served four consecutive terms as Mayor. In addition to the negro slaves there were many Indian slaves held in the colony. For convenience in hiring, the law was passed November 30, 1711, that "all negro and Indian slaves that are let out to hire within the city do take up their standing in order to be hired at the market house at the Wall street slip." Probably the alarm bred of the so-called negro plot of 1741 was most effective, in checking the growth of slavery in this city. Certainly the manner in which the negroes charged with fomenting this problematical conspiracy were dealt with affords food for curious reflection upon the social conditions of the time. After a trial that would have been a farce, had it not been a tragedy, Clause was condemned to be "broke upon a wheel," Robin to be hanged in chains alive, "and so on to continue without any sustenance until he be dead;" Tom to be "burned with a slow fire until he be dead, and consumed to ashes," and so on. However, everything depends upon the point in view. In that strong, stomached time judicial cruelty to animals met with universal approval, and, as to slavery, the worshipful Sir Edward Coke but a very few years earlier had laid down the doctrine that pagans properly could be held in bondage by Christians, because the former were bond slaves of Satan, while the latter were servants of God.

The Banner, Vol. 1, Clanton, Ala., Thursday, September 14, 1893, No. 45

THE NATIONAL GAME - McCarthy and Duffy lead Boston in stolen bases.

Twitchell, Of Louisville, leads the League in batting.

Boston is especially fortunate in having hard hitting catchers. Bennett, Meritt and Ganzel have all been batting well this season.

Gastright, of Boston, has won eleven out of twelve games in which he has pitched for the team, and the other one was tied when he was succeeded by Nicholas in the ninth.

Captain Pfeffer, of the Louisville, is a warm advocate of the double umpire system. He says the new rules have added so much to the umpires' work that they are unable to accomplish it satisfactorily, no matter how able or well disposed.

NEWS BOILED DOWN - Sadie Wood of Riverdale, S. C., tried kerosene on a slow fire. She is dead, and her mother, who rushed to her rescue is badly burned.

At Washington District Commissioner John W. Ross was knocked down by a cable car and dragged thirty feet before the gripman could stop the car. His head was badly hurt, one rib broken. Mr. Ross says the accident was due to his own carelessness.

A NEW PROPOSITION, Which the Jeffersonians Have Made to Organized Democracy. - Headquarters of the State Executive Committee of the Jeffersonian Democratic Party of Alabama, Montgomery, Ala., Sept. 7, 1893. - Hon. A.G. Smith, Chairman of the State Executive Committee of "Organized" Democratic Executive Committee of Alabama - Dear Sir: The state executive committee of the Jeffersonian party of Alabama has instructed me to submit the following proposition to the "organized" democratic party of Alabama, to-wit:...Very respectfully, A.T. Goodwin, Chairman of the State Executive Committee of the Jeffersonian Democratic Party of Alabama.

Emin Pasha Dead - Rev. A.J. Swann, a missionary, who has returned from Ujiji, on the east shore of Lake Tanganyika, says that it is impossible to doubt honestly that Emin Pasha is dead. "There is no question as to his death, " said Mr. Swann. "In February a letter came to me while I was at Ujiji, asking what should be done with Emin's effects. This inquiry naturally prompted me to make investigations. I did so, and the result was information which is authentic, to the effect that Jacob Schneltzer, or Emin Pash, as he was better known, had been killed by a native chief in the Manyema country. This was sufficiently startling information, but it was not the worst nor most startling. I ascertained that Emin's guard of thirty Nubian warriors had not only been slaughtered, but they had subsequently been eaten by the cannibalistic natives who had overcome the expedition."

Big Iron Combination - The associated press has just published to the world the facts that the finishing touches to the last agreement which make an accomplished fact of the Lake Superior Consolidated Iron mines, a combination controlling nine-tenths of all iron ore produced in the United States, with a capital of $30,000,000 and a reserve of $100,000,000 more in aggregate property. These statements are made on the authority of Leonida Merritt, one of the Merritt Bros.., who control the

Meseaberage iron mines. Mr. Merritt came to New York city more than three months ago to bring about the agreement by which the syndicate was sprung into existence. He as well as his brother in Duluth, have created themselves trustees to represent one interest, while C.W. Wetmore and F.T. Gates, Private Secretary of J.D. Rockfeller, represents the other. In an interview Mr. Merrit said the company has made an agreement to maintain in a standard of prices. "These prices will be such as preclude the possibility of competition by the hard ore mines of the older range. This consolidation will mean such a saving in shipping, both by rail and water, insurance and in office and other sundry expenses that will insure us a profit of $2.95 on the ton...

Big Rumpus Over Sheep - There is trouble on the Mexican border over the attempt of Mexican officers to drive a flock of 3,000 sheep from the United States to Mexico. A telegram received at the war department from Gen. Wheaton, commanding the department of Texas, states that two troops of the Fifth calvary with scouts will march from Fort Ringgold for Havana, the scene of the trouble, to support the twenty men under Capt. Furbush, who have the Mexican officers and sheep in charge. The telegram also states that the commanding officer at Fort Ringgold has received unofficial information that Col. Mictro of the Mexican army is coming up the Rio Grande to Havana from Reynosa with a force of men. The war department is making an effort to secure detailed information as to the ownership of the sheep and its action will depend upon the result. Should the claim of the Mexican authorities that the flock belongs to a Mexican citizens be proved, the sheep will be allowed to cross over the Mexican line. Pending a settlement of the military aspect of the affair, the state will hold the matter in abeyance and then demand of the Mexican government an explanation of the action of its custom officials in sending an armed force to make a seizure on United States soil. The question of whether the strip of land on which the sheep are located is in Mexico or the United States by reason of a change in the direction of the Rio Grande, will also be subject to diplomatic arrangement.

Pauper Becomes Rich - Mrs. Amanda C. Riddle, an inmate of the alms house at Norfolk, Va., has just won a suit in the courts of that city, awarding her real estate valued at $70,000. Mrs. Riddle has been an inmate of the alms house constantly since May 23, 1891. The suit was for the purpose of recovering real estate near Norfolk, and has been in the courts for several years. Mrs. Riddle is about 65 years old, and has one brother. Several of her sister's children are also living.

Trying to Suppress a Newspaper - K.O. Gould, editor of the Little Rock Tribune, and the city authorities of Little Rock, are at daggers points The Tribune has been very free in its criticisms of the city officials and an attempt was made to suppress the publication of the paper; but this failed as Gould carried the matter to the courts and was given a verdict. Gould is now under arrest charged with publishing obscene and scurilous literature, and the authorities say they will make a case against him for each paper issued. Public sentiment is with the paper.

THE REFORM MOVEMENT, Current Comment Concerning the Great Crusade Against Oppression - Still Fighting. By their great haste to secure authority to issue their notes at the par value of the bond, they have openly conceded the necessity for a material increase in the volume of our money; and the secretary of the treasury in approving the Voorhees bill, has certified to the overshadowing necessity for the increase....J.B. Weaver

Cold Water Candidates - The Prohibitionists of Virginia held their State Convention at Richmond the past week. There were in all about sixty delegates present, including one colored man. After the organization, Maj. D. Humphrey of Norfolk named Col. J.R. Miller of Pulaski county for governor, and he was nominated by acclamation. The nominee then addressed the convention. Later the ticket was completed by the nomination of J.S. Tylor of Accomac county, for lieutenant governor, and W.B. Gagley of Wytheville for attorney general.

Another girl was born to President and Mrs. Cleveland last, Saturday; born in the purple at the White House.

Congressman Stallings writes the passage of the Wilson bill will seriously affect the success of the party in Alabama. Wise man, Stallings!

Senator Kyle has introduced a bill providing for postal savings banks; the passage of this bill would ensure the absolute protection of poor mens savings. But this would be paternalism, besides its a populist measure, the plutocrats will object. Poor people's interests had better be sacrificed rather than we should sanction such measures as these.

THE JEFFERSONIANS AGAIN TENDER THE OLIVE BRANCH TO THE ORGANIZED - The State Executive Committee of the Jeffersonian Democrats met at Montgomery on the 7th, and submitted another proposition to the Democratic State Executive Committee which proposes, as in the first proposition, a joint primary to be held by both parties...Every white man who voted for Kolb or Jones in 1892, or who would have so voted had circumstances permitted, who is a qualified voter, or who being disqualified to vote at said election, will be eligible to vote in the August election of 1894, and who will support the candidate so chosen, shall be eligible to vote...

.
J. Sterling Morton, Cleveland's Secretary of Agriculture, repeats that old error that only three farmers in a hundred fail, while 95 business men out of a hundred fail. The inference is that the poor business man is much to be pitied and the farmer much to be envied...

Strasburg Stray-Shots - J.M.W. Pierce and Miss Julie Thacker were married at the residence of the first named on the 6th inst..

.
Prof. J.W. Moore has removed his family to the residence formerly occupied by J.M. Collins.

.
There is now only one store in our city, Mr. Collins having moved to Shelby.

.
Mr. J.R. Swinford has a new grist mill which aids much to the convenience of the community. It is said the shortening is already in the rocks. Dr. McNeal, of Jemison, also has one 2 1/2 miles west of this place.

.
Green Collins says he wants to sell his place.

Coopers Cuttings - We suppose that Mr. T.S. Kicker and Mr. J.T. Eiland are feeling greatly relieved since Wednesday as they were seen riding with their best girls.

.
Mr. Jessie Holland has been visiting Coopers very often of late; we don't know what he

means by it, but we guess it means something very important by his coming every Saturday.

We hope to see a large audience at our church on the third Sunday night. Preaching on the first Sunday in each month by Rev. A.C. Swindle.

Verbena Views - Verbena Academy opened Sept. 10th with 45 pupils. Prof. Slaten is an efficient teacher and has been able to obtain some boarding pupils.

Mrs. Nix and her beautiful and accomplished daughter, Miss Fannie Nix, have moved to Chicago.

Miss Georgia Thompson is visiting her sister Mrs. Moore, of Strasburg.

Mr. John Moody has returned from Tennessee much improved.

The bell buzzard seen recently is not the one seen in Georgia a few years ago, but one belled by Mr. Noah Gardner recently.

Mr. K. Wells soon will have his mill and gin on Sandy completed.

Mr. Will Caffey has returned from a trip to Atlanta.

Valley Creek Visitings - We are glad that Mr. David Moore is well and I expect his best girl would be glad to see him; I think he had better come over soon to see her for some one else is swinging her.

Mr. Newt Latham and Miss Belle Barnes tied the everlasting knot Sept. 3rd; we wish them a long and happy life.

Mr. John Martin, of Jemison, is standing a good chance with some of the young ladies here.

The two Misses Campbell will visit relatives and friends at this place, this week; we are glad to have them with us.

Mr. T.H. Gay was out hunting the other day and run upon a gang of wild turkeys and killed one.

We had the pleasure of witnessing the marriage between Mr. Newton Latham and Miss Bell Barnes on the 3rd inst.; we wish them a long and happy life and at death a happy home in heaven.

Poplar Springs - At a regular meeting of Poplar springs Alliance. On motion it was decided to endorse the action of the County Alliance, and invite County Lecturer L.B. Pounds around as soon as he can possibly come. W.H. Wells, President; J.J. McDowel, Secretary.

AD - Union Warehouse Co., Cotton Factors and Commission Merchants, Montgomery, Ala., F.H. Merritt, President; H.E. Quillian, Secretary.

TOWN ITEMS - (Top half of this column was missing), The first inquest on a lynching ever held in Chilton county took place this week at Dixie on the body of the negro that was found hanging in the woods near that place on the 1st. The verdict rendered was that the deceased was taken from the officers having him in (?)ly masked men and that he was shot and hung by parties unknown.

Chancery court is in session today. Chancellor S.K. McSpadden presiding. The following decisions have been tendered: - J.D. Pitts vs. Susan Pitts, divorce granted to complainant. J.W. Weldon vs. Lula Weldon, divorce granted to complainant. Susan Jane Headley vs. Headley divorce granted to complainant; there were other cases to be disposed of.

Uncle Sam has changed postmasters at this thriving town. Mr. B.H. Chestnutt who for the past two years has served so faithfully and well, retires on the 1st in favor of Mr. John Garner.

On Tuesday evening Mr. W.H. Sutton and Miss Belle Watts united their cestimies for life; it was the groom's natal day, and of all the prayers breathed for his future wel-(?) on its first advent none had (?) fulfillment than the evening on Tuesday. We wish the happy pair much happiness.

Divine service was held at the Episcopal church last Tuesday night, Re. J.F. Smith officiating.

AT THE CAPITOL, A Full Synopsis of What Has Been Done at Washington the Past Week.
SENATE
TWENTY-FIFTH DAY - The House joint resolution making the 18th of September, 1893 a holiday within the District of Columbia was, passed. The corner stone of the United States was laid on that day one hundred years ago. Mr. Galinger of New Hampshire introduced a bill supplemental to the pension act of June 27, 1893. The most important provision contain these words: " except in cases of established fraud no pension shall be suspended or without until after notice of ninety days given to the pensioner, and after a full and impartial investigation. " Mr. Butler of South Carolina, offered an amendment to this bill repealing the Sherman act... Mr. Kyle of South Dakota, offered a free coinage amendment to the repeal bill. Mr. McCullom of Illinois addressed the Senate in favor of a bill to repeal the purchasing clause of the Sherman act. Mr. Coke of Texas, was the next speaker. He was in favor of free silver. After the close of Mr. Coke's the Senate went into executive session... Mr. Peffer addressed the Senate until the hour of adjournment.
TWENTY-SIXTH - Mr. Morgan introduced a concurrence resolution for the appointment of a joint committee of the two houses, consisting of seven Senators and members... Mr. Peffer finished his speech of yesterday and was followed by Mr Stewart in a speech opposing the repeal bill...
TWENTY-SEVENTH DAY - Among the bills introduced and referred was one by Mr. Collum to repeal all acts providing for the creation of the maintenance of the sinking fund. Mr. Morgan addressed the senate at considerable length in favor of special committee resolution. The repeal bill was brought before the senate again and Mr. Stewart resumed his speech of yesterday...
TWENTY-EIGHTH DAY - Among the numerous resolutions presented and referred was one by Mr. Wolcott (Rep.) of Colorado, for the immediate repeal of the McKinley tariff bill. At 12:45, after several unimportant resolutions had been read and referred, the repeal bill was called up, and Mr. Stewart yielded the floor to Mr. Walthall of Mississippi, who

had previously signified his intention to address the house today... At the conclusion of Mr. Walthall's speech Mr. Stewart again took the floor and proceeded with the third installment of his speech. He held the floor until 4:15, when Mr. Daniel of Virginia went over and whispered a word in his ear, when, to the astonishment of all, he announced that he would now close his speech...

TWENTY-NINTH DAY - Speeches from democratic senators in the senate today on the repeal bill were made by Mr. Faulkner of West Virginia, Mr. Turpie of Indiana, Mr. Jones of Arkansas...

THIRTIETH DAY - The first two hours of today's session in the senate were consumed in discussing a resolution offered by Mr. Peffer, to inquire into the refusal of the banks of New York, Boston and Philadelphia to pay the checks of their depositors in currency. The remainder of the day was occupied by Mr. Teller in a speech, most which was devoted to a denunciation of the newspaper press of the country, especially the metropolitan part of, for its impudence and mendacity...

HOUSE

TWENTY-SEVENTH DAY - ... Mr. Henderson of Iowa, who was standing beside the petition, dropped in the first petition. After the adoption of the rules, Speaker Crisp announced that it would be in order for the members to hand in their bills and resolutions to the Speaker's desk for active and reference...

TWENTY-EIGHTH DAY - ... The only action worthy of mention was a report from the committee on elections by Mr. Paynter, of a resolution granting the right to Mr. Belknap, claiming a seat from the Fifth Michigan District, to file notice of contest against Mr. Richardson the sitting member. Mr. Paynter said that this was the unanimous report of the committee and the resolution was adopted without objection...

Over A Cob Pipe - At Rocky Comfort, Ark., an old man named W.F. Crow and a neighbor named J.B. Barke had a difficulty over the ownership of a corn-cob pipe, which ended in Barke's shooting Crow through the body, killing him. Clint Crow, son of the old man, then shot Burke, fatally wounding him. The latter shot and killed Clint Crow and died five minutes later.

ALABAMA ITEMS - Mr. W.A. Derring has been appointed express agent at Russellville.

A little child of Mr. John Hughes of Calhoun county pulled a harrow over on itself and received wounds that may be fatal.

Mr. M.H. Rulland of Barbour county was seriously bitten by a pony one day last week. The pony and a mule were fighting, and when Mr. Rulland interfered the pony bit a piece out of his face just over the right eye.

R.E.L. Neil, of the Selma Journal, has been appointed assisted librarian of house of representatives at Washington. The position is a responsible and remunerative one. He will leave in a few days for his new post of duty.

The store of Mr. S.H. Dobbs at Blauche, Cherokee county, together with all its contents, was burned last week. The postoffice, telegraph and express office were located in the building and were all a total loss. It is supposed the store was robbed and set on fire to hide the robbery.

Mr. John Yarbrough of Beulah, is a somnambulist, and this misfortune came near costing him his life a few nights since. Being sixteen miles from home Mr. Yarbrough decided to spend the night in Opelika. He engaged a room and retired at 9 o'clock. About 10 o'clock he got out of bed and while asleep walked deliberately out of the window and fell to the brick sidewalk, some 30 feet below. Fortunately no bones were broken. It will be several weeks before he can leave his room.

Reports come from Troy that Chas. Bowden killed ex-sheriff Folsom near Elba. Folsom was drinking and Bowden, as a friend, endeavored to get him off home. They got in a buggy and started. When they had gone some distance, when Folsom ordered Bowden to get out of the buggy. He did so, and very soon Folsom made at him with a knife. Bowden, seeing his own fate, hit him across the head with a board. He died a few hours after. Bowden went at once to the sheriff and surrendered, claiming he acted in self defense.

Caught In The Act - A train was held up on the St. Louis and San Francisco road the other night, with the unique accompaniment of the capture of one of the robbers. The robbers flagged down the train and when it came to standstill two men held the engine crew at bay, while a third went to the express car, and demanded admittance. The messenger refused to open the door. The order then came from one of the engine guards to " blow her open. " This order almost instantly followed by a deafening report and the woodwork of the car was wrecked. Then the three highwaymen joined forces and tried to enter the car, but was impeded by the wreckage. The conductor and brakeman rushed up to the robbers with pistols drawn and commanded them to surrender. The robbers answered with a poorly directed fusillade, which the two brave trainmen gave back with interest. Such unexpected resistance unnerved the robbers; two of them took to their heels. The third was overpowered and made a prisoner. So far as known no one was hurt. The prisoner gave his name as Lenox. He is a son of a farmer at Newberg.

WEIGHT OF A CROWD, Experiments Show It is from 140 to 150 Pounds Per Square Foot. - The load which is produced by a dense crowd of persons is generally taken at 80 to 100 pounds per square foot, and is considered to be the greatest uniformly distributed load for which a floor the to be proportioned. That this value may be largely exceeded in an actual crowd was pointed out by Prof. W.C. Kernot, of the Melbourne University, Austria, in a recent paper before the Victorian Institute of Engineers... Prof. Kernot also quoted from Stoney, who placed fifty-eight Irish laborers, averaging 145 hounds each in weight, in an ship deckhouse measuring fifty-seven square feet floor area...

Lady Colin Campbell says that kissing ruins the complexion. Lady Colin ought to try shellac on her complexion, and then it wouldn't come off when kissing.

The Banner, Vol. 1, Clanton, Ala., Thursday, September 21, 1893, No. 46

ALABAMA ITEMS - John the Baptist is the Bible-historical name of a negro arrested in Mobile and wanted in North Alabama for highway robbery.

Judge Denson of the Circuit Court held court at Lafayette last week. He is a hustler, opening court at 8 o'clock a.m. and not adjoining until 6 p.m. except a short time at noon hour.

Rev. Sam Jones is to lecture in Birmingham September 19th.

Mr. J.A. Roberts, of White Pond, accomplished the wonderful feat last week of picking 609 pounds of seed cotton in a day.

Some sneak thief or thieves entered the larder of M.M. Hooks at Selma a few nights ago and robbed it of a quantity of pickles.

Miss Jessie Newman, an employee of the Matthews Cotton Mills at Selma, got one of her hands caught in some of the machinery and very badly mashed.

Tom Armour, a noted crook, who broke jail in Cedartown, Ga., about twelve months ago, was arrested near Cedar Bluff, Cherokee county, a few days since and safely lodged in jail at Centre.

A freight train on the Central railroad was wrecked near Troy a few evenings since. Fireman George Wright was killed instantly. The engine was a total wreck. A spike was placed on the track just where a curve was made. No one has any idea as to who did the placing of the obstruction.

E.M. Reid, a prosperous farmer and justice of the peace of Calhoun, was held up and robbed of $318 on the road about four miles north of Anniston. The highwaymen were a white man and a negro, with masks, but with hands uncovered. Mr. Reid was on his to the city to deposit the money. As soon as he gave up his roll he was allowed to leave unhurt.

GENERAL NEWS - Baby Ruth's little sister and its mother are doing nicely.

Frederick L. Ames, of New York, vice-president of the old colony railroad and a millionaire, was found dead lying on his face on the floor in a state room of the steamer Pilgrim He died of heart disease.

Uriah Huff, of Wabash, Ind., got scared of the banks and drew out his little roll of $2,000 and hid it for safe keeping. A few days afterward his team ran away with him and he was killed. Relatives are now searching for the money.

LIKE A TORNADO, A Hundred Thousand People Settle Upon the Cherokee Strip - One good thousand people settled upon the Cherokee strip the first day it was opened to settlement... Dr. Gallagher of the General Land Office, has received instructions from Washington to the registration booths open until further orders and to issue certificates to all who were unable to obtain them before noon today.

Heroism Rewarded - As a car on the Lookout Mountain incline at Chattanooga was ascending a man named Moore was crossing a trestle and did not see the danger. The electric signal wire was broken and the car could not be stopped and a tragedy seemed certain. At this juncture Charles M. Willingham, a young man who was a passenger, threw himself down flat upon the front platform of the car and grabbed the man around the body and succeeded in going him up from the track. If Mr. Willingham had not acted as quickly as he did, Moore would have been ground to pieces under the wheels of the car. As a reward for his courage he received a life-time pass on the incline which reads: " Presented on account of an act of personal bravery in saving a human life. "

White Caps Burn A Gin - The large gin house and cotton sheds belonging to E.D. Jones, at Carlisle, Claiborne county, Miss., on the branch of the Yazoo and Mississippi Valley, was burned Sunday night by a band of white caps. The gin house was posted about three weeks ago by white caps, who threatened its destruction if any cotton should be ginned there before the price of the staple with to 10 cents per pound. A number of gins in adjoining counties have been posted this way, but this is the first that has been fired.

Big Revenue - Secretary Carlisle has made public a letter received from David A. Wells, the well-known Democratic tariff reformer. The letter recommends the imposition of the maximum internal revenue rates on distilled spirits, malt liquor and tobacco. Mr. Wells' table shows that the revenue from these articles for the year ending June 30 was $180,000,000 and that this revenue would be about $245,000,000.

Practical Philanthropy - Augustus Hemenway, of Canton, Mass., has a practical philanthropist room. He has invited all the school teachers of his town, twenty-six in number, to visit the World's Fair at his expense, and it is hardly necessary to say that they have all accepted. They will travel in regal style in two weeks to do the curiosities of the Midway and other features of the exposition.

MEAN BUSINESS - A Call for a Convention of Those Favoring Bi-Metalism at Denver. ...Mr. Olney Newell, secretary of the Denver chamber of commerce and board of trade, has been authorized to conduct the correspondence, to who communications may be addressed.

Senator Morgan's proposition for a committee to investigate the cause of the present financial depression before final action on the repeal of the Sherman act was a just one, and for whom that reason it has been unanimously condemned by the plutocratic press.

The plutocratic press has suddenly changed its note. A few short days ago, disaster and gloom; today, returning prosperity and happiness. The reason for this change is thus given by a Washington correspond:-" the truth about the matter is this: Soon after Senator Peffer introduced his resolution of inquiry concerning the unlawful doings of the Wall St. ring of banks and its reference, in direct violation of the custom of the senate, by the request of senator Voorhees, to the Committee on Finance, where it was buried, certain citizens of New York, who had been robbed of hundreds of thousands of dollars by being forced from three to five percent, to get their own money out of the banks, where they had deposited it resolved to take the matter into their own hands and not wait for Secretary Carlisle and the Comptroller...

Jemison Gems - Miss Mattie Hand will leave for a visit to relatives in California about the first of next month.

Mr. J.A. Butler and wife had returned home from a visit to relatives in Sterett, Ala.

Mr. John Jenkins moved his family to Elmore, Ala..

Mr. Bennie McNeal will leave for Auburn College next Monday.

Mr. F.W. Bandy, from New Orleans, is visiting relatives here.

Mr. John Henly is very sick, and has been for several days.

Oak Grove Openings - Peoples party met at 7:30 p.m. for organization, with Bro. Ira Campbell as temporary chairman. On motion Bro. I.B. Martin was elected as permanent chairman with W.J. Martin secretary. The house then proceeded to business.

On motion Bro. Campbell read and explained part of the Sayre election law, after which he read the Omaha platform.

Believing a knowledge of the law before us to be necessary to our success; it may contribute largely to our political interest as citizens, and to our mutual happiness as common supporters of this commonwealth. It was agreed to elect one of our members as lecturer, whose duty it shall be to study and explain the law in a series of lectures. W.J. Martin was elected.

Mrs. Ira Campbell presented a good paper carefully prepared, under the title " Your vote is your weapon " nothing further calling attention, the house adjourned to meet Thursday 21st inst.., I.B. Martin Chairman, W.J. Martin Secretary

Dixie Dots - H.W. Cole has left W.H. Cox and is going to school at Welch's mill.

Mr. Willie Marshall was thrown over by a mule and got hurt very bad, but is better now.

Mr. Bennett Edwards, the great horse swapper, was in this country last week; he challenges everybody for a swap.

While Mr. J.B. Cox was hunting a few days since one of his dogs took the cramp, and he was obliged to get down and rub her; she got well and is now ready to tree another squirrel.

Mr. S.P. Barnes will take a school at Little Bethel in a short while.

Providence Pickings - Bro. George B. Armstrong, who was severely hurt by a runaway horse team last June, is again able to go to work.

Mr. James Watson has rebuilt his gin house which was burned two years ago and is again ready to accommodate the public in the line of ginning.

TOWN ITEMS - There was a dance given at Mr. R. Ehrman's last Monday night.

Mr. Roberts has removed his family from Stanfield's mill into the Marsh house, opposite Mr. Stanfield.

Mr. J.P. Allen, of Jemison, was in town this week.

Mrs. May, of Montgomery, is visiting Mrs. Hester.

Amongst the pupils who at arrived to attend Prof. M. Morries' School are Miss Katie Bradley, of (?)pine; and Miss Allen, of Birmingham.

Prof. W.C. Robinson was in town last Saturday.

The friends of Mr. Hugh Foshee will be glad to hear that he is up again after several weeks illness.

Miss Bulger has returned to her home in Birmingham after a pleasant visit to relatives in Clanton.

Sheriff Moore and his little son Harvey Moore visited Birmingham last Saturday.

Mr. Charlie Merritt has returned (?) after a pleasant visit to relatives in Montgomery.

(?)nry Dupree died from (?)ver last Sunday night (?)me near Clanton. Mr. (?) very sick with the same (?) We tender our sincere (?) to the afflicted family.

Sam Catts visited Verbena Sunday.

Miss Minnie Weaver returned to Montgomery after a pleasant visit (?) the family of Mr. T.H. White.

Dr. Johnson has improved his (?)g store by removing a partition and taking in a room at the back.

Squire Nolen retires from the (?) Solicitorship on Oct.1st, Mr. (?).W. Hare having been appointed Solicitor Brewer as his deputy.

Tuesday afternoon a horse came galloping through our town with a broken harness attached to him, it was known to be the property of W.H. Merritt in a party at (?) went out to find what was the matter. It is with much regret we have to say they found Mr. Merritt unconscious about a mile from town. He was carried home and Dr. Stewart was summoned. It appears the horse became frightened and the buggy overturned dragging Mr. Merritt for some distance. He is (?) cut and bruised but fortunately he has escaped any very serious injury.

Mr. McMories opened his school this morning with 58 pupils.

Mr. Tom Gullahorn is very sick at the house of his brother-in-law, (?) McDaniel.

(?)melia Dawson has returned from a long pleasant visit to her (?) Oxford.

Rev. A.C. Wells has been off on a ten days trip to Union and Shady Grove and reports glorious meetings at both places; he says he believes the spiritual world is reviving in our county.

Brother Fonza DuBose died of typhoid fever at his home a few miles east of Coopers Station Saturday morning and was buried at Chestnut Creek churchyard on Sunday at 11 o'clock. He leaves a wife and family to mourn his loss. The little son of his is also lying at the point of death from the same complaint. We sympathize with the afflicted one and family.

Bro. J.A. Logan will be with the brethren of Providence (?) Alliance Sept. the 30th, at one o'clock p.m. to discuss and explain the Sayre election law. All who feel an interest in this matter are invited to attend. W.H. Shaw, Secty, Providence Alliance

THE REFORM MOVEMENT - The most extensive cotton grower in the world, Col. Richardson, of Louisiana, says that with all his skill, tact, and business ability, his cotton costs him more than 6 cents per pound net to raise it. Where is the smart Aleck who says cotton can be grown for 2 1/2 cents?-Southern Mercury.

Thomas A. Edison, the greatest inventor of the age, and to whom we owe much for all the latest electrical appliances, spoke a parable the other day when forced to close his great factory at Orange, N. J., he wrote the following notice and posted it on the door: " The phonograph works are shut down because we have nearly completed all orders on hand an the proprietor, seeing that the county had resolved itself into a national lunatic asylum, has decided to wait until the wave has subsided somewhat. "

A QUESTION OF MORE MONEY - The following address of President W.D. Evans, of the Farmers' State Alliance of South Carolina, is self-explanatory: " I have been requested by State Lecturer J. William Stokes to call an extra session of the State Alliance to consider the propriety of petitioning the governor to call an extra session of the legislature to give such relief to farmers as lies in its power, as well as to petition congress to issue $300,000,000 of government notes to be distributed throughout the south for the purpose of moving the cotton crop...

The Sun's Light - It is now many years since Doctor Johnstone Stoney, F. R. S., published his important paper in which he propounded what seems to be the most rational explanation sunlight yet afforded, says Sir Robert Ball...

Watering A Crop With An Engine - Fortunate in having his farm intersected by one of the arterial trains of the district, Mr. Young, of Swineshead Abbey Farm, in the neighborhood of Boston, England, determined to utilize the water provided, and arranged with Messrs. Merryweather & Son, Limited, to send down one of their most powerful fire engines. With this engine about eighty tons of water per hour have been pumped onto crops of mangold seed and potatoes, and land is now being drenched preparatory to cauliflower active...

Female Pirates - Two of the most extraordinary of the pirates who formerly scourged the waters of the West Indies were women. One of them was Mary Read. She was a native of England, and had been dressed as a boy from childhood for the purpose of hiding a family secret. At one, she served on a British war vessel, where her sex was not suspected. Finally she took passage on a ship bound for Cuba, which was captured by a pirate. Having nothing better to do she conducted the piratical trade. One of her cut-throat shipments was

Annie Bonny, who was likewise disguised as a man. Anne, not imagining that Mary was a female, fell in love with her, revealing her own sex. Mary was thus obliged to make a similar revelation. These two extraordinary persons took their part with the men in every conflict. The facts regarding them are perfectly well authenticated. While fighting bravely, their ship was at length taken by a war vessel. They were tried for their lives at Jamaica, where Mary died in prison. It is not served what became of Anne, but she was not executed.- Globe Democrat.

The Banner, Vol. 1, Clanton, Ala., Thursday, September 28, 1893, No. 47

THE REFORM MOVEMENT - Cleveland is right, then John Sherman and the Republican party are right. - Atlanta Constitution.

Congressman Bryan, of Nebraska, strikes the nail squarely when he says: " There are two classes of gold bugs, one for what there is in it and the other on account of ignorance. The first cannot be helped, the others are to be pitied. "

The Iowa State Populists convention at recently at Des Moines and nominated the following state ticket; Governor J.M. Joseph, of Creston; lieutenant governor, E.O. Otto Weeks of Des Moines; supreme judge, A.W.C. of Winterest; railroad commissioner, J.A. Gray of Muscantine. There was no contest for places on the ticket.

A FORCIBLE ADMISSION - In a recent issue, the Chicago Inter-Ocean, a staunch Republican paper, which has since the opening of congress banking a conservative position on the silver question, startled its readers by admitting editorially the justice of the fight for free silver, of and dealing a scathing rebuke to the eastern bankers, who, it claims, are responsible for the present trouble. It said among other things: ... " Colonel Ingersol early in the session of disturbance properly called this a banker's panic...

To Restrict Immigration - Representative Oates, of Alabama, has introduced in the House a bill designed to restrict immigration. It provides that no criminal, anarchist, polygamist or any person unable to read the Constitution of the United States shall be naturalized, who has not continuously for five years next proceeding his application resided within the United States...

Mexican Congress Convenes - The Sixteenth Mexican congress was formally opened in the city of Mexico last Monday morning at 5 o'clock, Hon. Jose de J. Lopez presiding. Nearly all the members in their seats when President Diaz entered the chamber of deputies and read his annual message, which was an able document and well received.

A Paper Correspondent In Trouble - The sensation of the day in Brunswick, Ga., is the enforcement of martial law, and the punished up Mike J. Eagan, a newspaper correspondent, by his banishment from the city on account of slanderous statements made by him in a recent article.

AT THE CAPITOL
THIRTY-FIRST DAY - Senate - Mr. Stewart of Nevada stirred up a hornet's nest today when he offered a resolution of inquiry into the fact of senators being stockholders in national banks. Mr. Hill bitterly opposed the resolution, as being unnecessary, unprecedented and a gross reflection upon the Senate. The resolution went over. The bill for the repeal of the purchasing clause of the Sherman law was taken up and Mr. Pugh of Alabama, a member of the finance committee, made a two and one-half hour speech against it, declaring at the close that it was the determined and unalterable purpose of the of repeal to oppose it until their physical strength was exhausted and their power of speech gone. The remainder of the session was occupied in a continuation of Mr. Teller's speech against the bill.
House - The session of the House today was brief... Mr. Murray, the colored representative

of South Carolina, attempted to get consideration for a joint resolution, appropriating $20,000 for the relief of the cyclone sufferers along the Atlantic Coast, but there were objections and the resolution had to go over...

THIRTY-SECOND DAY - Senator Mitchell of Oregon occupied the attention of the Senate today for three hours in an argument against the repeal bill. After he got through there sprung up between Senator Teller of Colorado and Senator Hawley of Connecticut, quite a spirited discussion...

House - The attendance was even smaller today than yesterday... The matter was referred to a committee, Mr. Richardson of Tennessee, from the committee on printing, reported a bill providing for public printing and binding for the distribution of public documents. The other proceedings were of even less interest than the foregoing.

THIRTY-THIRD DAY - Senate - In the absence of the vice-president the senate was presided over today by Mr. Harris, president pro tem. A bill for a bimetallic money system was introduced by Mr. Peffer by request. Mr. Stewart's resolution for a committee of inquiry as to senators owning stock in national banks was laid before the senate and Mr. Stewart proceeded to argue in favor of it. Mr. Allen of Nebraska, also made a speech in its favor... Mr. Voorhees, chairman of the finance committee and champion of the bill made some suggestions as a date for closing the debate and taking the vote, but not liking the tract of the discussion his remarks called forth, he withdrew his propositions. Mr. Shoup, republican, of Idaho, then took the floor for the unconditional repeal of the purchasing clause of the Sherman law. He was followed by Mr. Dolph who opposed free coinage...

House - ... Over the printing bill reported by Mr. Richardson yesterday there was a lively discussion, that gentleman asking for its immediate consideration. After much maneuvering Mr. Richardson carried his point and the bill was read, pending action upon the same in detail the house adjourned.

THIRTY-FOURTH DAY. - Senate - The great event of today's session of the senate was a speech by Mr. Daniel of Virginia against the passage of the repeal bill... No other senator desired to speak after Mr. Daniel and the senate adjourned.

THIRTY-FIFTH DAY. - Senate - In the senate today speeches were made by Senator Lindsay of Kentucky, and Senator Higgins of Delaware, and Mr. Allison of Iowa, took the floor, but postponed speaking until tomorrow... A number of petitions were presented in the forenoon, among them one by Mr. Collum of Illinois, signed by a large number of ex-soldiers, residents of his state, alleging that they were beset by detectives of the government traveling in disguise, and asking for protection against them.

NEWS BOILED DOWN - A.J. Goldstone, of Chatham county, N. C., took his gun and went to the house of a neighbor to shoot a dog. Becoming involved in a quarrel with the neighbor he struck the latter with the butt and of the gun, the gun was discharged and the charge entered Goldstone's body, killing him instantly.

Near New Orleans Judge Victor Espinal was shot to death while trying Rosolins Julian. August Espinal, a son of the murdered official, was also badly wounded. The shooting occurred in the courtroom and the murderer continued firing until the judge, who followed to close in upon him, fell mortally wounded immediately outside and to the left of the building. The brutal negro then stood over the prostrate form of his victim and fired the fourth shot, which is supposed to be the one that past through the heart. The negro then made his escape to the swamp. Posses were organized and a search made for fugitive, but without avail. The mother, three brothers and two sisters of the negro were arrested and taken to jail. All were charged with assisting the fugitive. Later a mob of twenty-five men came and took the three brothers and hung them. They whipped the three women and told them to leave the parish.

New Minister To Hawaii - Albert S. Willis, our new minister to Hawaii, has had no experience in diplomacy, but is said to possess the wisdom of discretion necessary for his duty at Honolulu. He is a Kentuckian by birth, breeding and education, patent was born in Shelby county in 1843. He was in congress four terms and could have been there now if he had not declined a renomination. He is a lawyer by profession.

The First of the Kind - Bertha Clark of Atlanta, Ga., a native of Germany, has applied for naturalization papers. She is said to be the first woman to be naturalized in the South. She has a promise of a clerkship in Washington.

Attention Ex-Confederates - General J.B. Gordon, commanding United Confederate Veterans, is anxious that the information showing progress made in organizing camps in this benevolent association, be given to the public, with the hope and belief that it will stimulate and encourage those veterans who have not yet organized to do so at once, and send their applications for necessary papers for membership immediately, into these headquarters, so as to be represented at Birmingham at the great reunion... Very Respectfully, George Moorman, Adjutant General and Chief of Staff.

A mathematical problem. If it took Grover six months to give Clanton a new postmaster, how long will it Tommie Jones to give Chilton an election registrar?

Editor Baltzell's editorial in the last issue of the Alliance Herald on the situation and the relief that would be afforded by sub-treasuries, should be read by all. It was a fine effort, worthy of the writer.

The Montgomery Journal's Washington correspondent confidently states that the unconditional repeal will never be accomplished without a revolution, more to be feared than that attempted to be foisted upon the people than by the passage of the force bill... Such men as Teller, Stewart, Walcott, Morgan, Pugh, Harris, Bate, George, Butler, Cockrell, Daniel, Call, the two Joneses, Berry, Vest, Vance, Coke and Walthall are stirred to the bottom of their soul, and they alone can and will prevent the consummation of unconditional repeal. Teller has called it a " damnable bill " and so they all say...

Marion Cannon, congressman from the sixth congressional district of California, has been denounced by the people of Los Angeles in mass meeting assembled as infamous and he held up to the scorn of all right minded and liberty loving as a second citizen of Benedict Arnold for voting for the unconditional repeal of the Sherman act, he having declared previously to his constituents his unswerving loyalty to free silver and his opposition to the repeal of the Sherman act without a free coinage of silver clause thereto. Clark, Oates, and Turpin of Alabama, might well be included in the same category.

" I had a talk, unsought by me, with a bank official of New York. He wanted an autograph, and he readily confirmed the editorial statements of the Constitution to the effect that the banks in that city, while refused either to loan money to businessmen or to the checks of the depositors, had made a pretty little sum by selling currency at a premium through their brokers"... The above written by Joel Chandler Harris in a letter written by him from Washington, shows how the New York bankers acted during the panic. Comment is unnecessary.

In Virginia the Populist campaign is being vigorously pushed. Jerry Simpson has wiped up the so called democratic cyclone Congressman Marshall of that state each time he has met him in joint debate.

Jemison Gems - Dr. Givhan is out and about once more attending to his practice, much to the delight of his many friends.

The Alliance store, under the able management of Bro. W.W. Adams, has been a great assistance to the farmers of this section.

Kincheon Ketchings - We are glad to see our esteemed friend J.W. Mims at our old haunts again; his school closed at Sardus, Friday. Also we are glad to have him with us again to help us smoke.

Mr. W.P. Headly and his old chum Walter went hunting Friday and had quite a success, they killed quite a number of squirrels, and something else I will not say.

We are glad to see our old friend J.H. Anderson home again; he states he has been having a good time and plenty fun; he has a flourishing school at Alpine church 5 miles east of Plantersville, though he has vacated it till the 10th of October; he also says if the boys want to see pretty girls and good people go to that community. No more but hurrah for W.C. Roper, and P.A. Vance both fine girls.

Valley Creek Visitings - Mrs. Jennie Hayes, of Sixmile, Ala., is visiting friends and relatives at this place.

J.T. Martin left for home last Saturday at Jemison.

Rev. J.A. Carruth left his morning for Sixmile; his friends were sorry to see him leave.

Mr. S.R. Letcher will start school at Welch's mill soon; I hope they will learn fast.

Last Friday night Mr. David Ellis and Mr. Walter Ellis, east of Vinehill, were cutting down a tree to get it out of the way, Mr. Walter Ellis was found dead under the log; he was bruised up. It was supposed that when the tree fell it caught on another tree and slid back over the stump and caught Walter. A piece of sap fell on David Ellis and hurt him very bad. Walter was buried last Sunday. We hope that David will soon recover. The morning after these men were hurt, their family cooked breakfast, then they went to hunt for them, and found David in his mill house, he could not speak, and they went to hunt Walter and found him under the log dead.

Mrs. Jennie Hayes and son will return to their home at Sixmile, Ala., Thursday; they will see their friends whom they love, and are loved by. Mrs. Hayes' baby has been very sick, but is better.

Mr. Shelby Barnes made a young lady's heart glad by visiting her home.

Mr. J.W. Mitchell paid his Uncle a visit, and went to friendship and saw some pretty girls.

Plantersville Pickings - Bad accident happened the 23 inst. Mr. Dave Ellis and Mr. Walter Ellis were cutting down a tree, it lodged on some timber, in getting it down it caught them, killing Walter Ellis and hurting Dave very badly.

Mr. J.H. Gaydy has got his shop about complete, he is now ready to do any kind of wood and iron work; all people wishing anything of the kind should call on him.

Little Maudie Letcher had eight pe chickens, they are first in the morning and last thing at night with her.

Dixie Dots - Mr. Walter Ellis, who met with the fatal accident, as reported elsewhere, was to have started to Arkansas on the 26th inst. Oscar Harris and a lot of others.

We were glad to see the Misses Bamma Moore and Nannie Moore, of Clanton, with us during the Alpine meetings.

Mr. H.H. Burchfield, of British, Ala., attended the Alpine meetings to see his best girl; we hope he enjoyed himself and will come again.

West Chilton Warblings - Capt. Robert Prayer,Sr., of East Perry, and Miss Ida Stewart, of Stanton, were married Sep.20th, at the Methodist church in Stanton. We wish the good couple great luck and success in life.

Rev. J.C. Longcryer's school at Valley Creek closed the 23rd, he will start at Howard J. College in a few days, and Mr. J. Carrouth will return to Sixmile.

T.W. Barnes and Duffy O'Neal will start for Palmetto, Florida, the 26th.

Jumbo Jumbles - Mr. Carter Willis, of Jumbo, and Miss Martha Marcus were married last Sunday afternoon at the home of the bride's father. Rev. W.S. Cox officiated.

J.P. Gore closed his school on last Friday, and had a good time generally. Everybody was pleased - teacher, pupils and parents. The Prof. will open his school in the Lowe settlement the 16th of October.

Providence Alliance - Bro. J.A. Logan will be with the brethren of Providence sub Alliance Sept. the 30th, at one o'clock p.m. to discuss and explain the Sayre election law. All who feel an interest in this matter are invited to attend. W.H. Shaw, Secty. Providence Alliance

MULBERRY ASSOCIATION - The Mulberry Baptist Association was in session at Providence, on Saturday, Sunday and Monday last. Eld. Job Langston, Moderator, and Eld. R.M. Honeycutt, Secretary... On Sunday, Elders L.B. Pounds, Sutton Smitherman and Elder Martin delivered discourses...

COUNTY SINGING CONVENTION - Convention called to order at 11 a.m., by Bro. J.E. White reading a chapter. Congregation singing "Down at the Cross" then Rev. Rich of Coosa led in prayer. J.E. White was elected temporary chairman. The object of a County singing convention was discussed, permanent organization was deferred, committee on services Rev. N.A. Dobbs, and Bros. Joe Billingsley and B.F. Atkinson. Lessons in music led by Bros. White, Patrick and Dobbs. Arrangements for next annual session left with the chairman.

TOWN ITEMS - Mrs. Nolen, accompanied by her little niece, has returned home from a very pleasant visit to her (?) home in Goodwater.

Miss Lafarice Deadwilder, of Mulberry, after visiting friends has returned home last Monday.

Mr. Tom Smith has frantic the (?) house and removed his family here from Mountain Creek.

Professor J.P. Gore is on a visit to friends in town this week.

Mr. Potts has purchased the Marsh house and is making extensive alterations and repairs there, for the occupancy of Mrs. Raynie, who, as we understand, has rented it.

Mrs. Ed McDaniel of Sylacauga and family, are visiting relatives here.

Miss Lou Norris has closed her school.

We are very sorry to hear that (?) Judge Callen is seriously ill.

Mr. Ned Duke of Bainbridge, (?) is in town looking up his old (?)s.

Mr. R.C. Crosswell was in town this week.

Mr. May, of Montgomery, visited relatives in Clanton last week.

Mr. Hugh Foshee who was on (?)ek after his severe sickness (?) say, had a re(?) confined to his (?).

Miss Lafarice Deadwilder and Professor J.P. Gore are to be married at Mulberry church on the se(?) Sunday in October. We (?) the young couple a long, prosperous and happy life.

Mr. W.H. Merritt can stand a (?) deal of knocking about and (?) heartily glad to see him again after his narrow escape (?) week.

(?) Adams, colored, was arrested at Lomax last week for using obscene language, and as a consequence was lodged in the jail.

(?) Honeycutt has, we very regret to say, been seriously (?)sed since his return from Mulberry Conference.

Professor McMorries has made a (?) start with his school, and (?)ing promises fair for a prosperous career for the University.

(?) T.B. Haynie, the popular crusader from Tallassee will be at the Congregational church the first Sunday in October.

Commissioner H.A. Wilson, (?), in a letter addressed by members of the U S. Grand (?) Birmingham addressed to (?) Attorney General, is charg-(?) having charged per claim (?)

Lee Foster, colored, (?) is alledged, that per diem (?)dy been charged in another (?) were several other U. S. (?) charged with offenses of like (?) in the same letter.

FINAL PROOF NOTICE, Land office at Montgomery, Ala., September 24, 1893. - Notice is hereby given that the following named settler has filed notice of his intention to make final proof in support of his claim, and that said proof will be made before the Clerk of the Circuit Court at Clanton, Ala., on November 10th, 1893; viz.: Oliver C. McGraw. Homestead Entry No. 18,779, for the s w 1/4 of n w 1/4 of Section 32, Tp. 21, n of Range 13 e. He names the following witnesses to prove his continuous residence upon and cultivation of said land, viz.: William H. Shaw, William A. Sims, John A. Lowery and W.J. Watson, all of Clear Creek, Ala. J.H. Bingham, Registrar.

SOMEWHAT STRANGE - Peter Phillips, a colored man, lost the power of speech in McDade, Texas, some fifteen years ago. He says he knows no reason for it. The most curious part of all is that he talks away from town as plainly as any man. He runs his farm in an intelligent way, always making as good crops as his neighbors, and even when unable to talk his trades with the merchants or others are as economically and sensibly made as the average man of his race. For years some people have doubted his statement and thought he could talk if he would, but for more than twelve years no man has ever heard him speak a word in any town or at any public gathering.

Miss Patt Lyle Collins, of Mississippi, is an invaluable worker in the Dead-Letter Office in Washington, where she is known as the "blind reader" - not that she is blind by any means, for she is wonderfully keen sighted. She has a remarkable facility in ascertaining the intended destination of letters that are "blind" because of incomplete or imperfect or incorrect addresses. The Ladies Home Journal gives fax simile reproductions of many such that she has deciphered. One is "Rickbier Stiejt Kanedika" which she correctly read Roxbury, Conn.

On John Kreutzer's forty-acre farm in Portsmouth, Ohio, there was recently a terrible fight between a bull and a stallion. The latter tore "great quivering chunks of flesh" out of the bull with his teeth and pounded him with his forefeet, and the bull gored the horse to death. Then the bull was shot. Cause of the ruction: a blacksnake wound around the bull's hind leg.

John Bonner, a Georgia farmer, who died the other day at the age of 87 years, was the father of twenty-three children, all by one mother, and as they grew up and married all settled on farms adjoining his own.

NOTES AND COMMENTS - James Mooney, of the Ethnological Bureau in the Smithsonian Institution, is one of the leading authorities on the North American Indians. For twenty years he has been traveling among them and living with them, studying their characteristics. His work, indeed, antedates the ethnological work of the United States Government. Mr. Mooney and Miss Alice Fletcher are said to be the only whites in whom all the Indians throughout the West place implicit confidence.

Quinnemore, formerly chief of the Coeur d'Alen Indians, has a fine farm of 167 acres on the south side of the Spokane river, about a dozen miles above Spokane, Washington, and the other day the tax gatherer thought it would be a very proper and desirable thing to tax it a good round sum. So he came smilingly with his bill. But Quinnemore was prepared for him even on such and unexpected mission. He brought forth a paper which in part read thus: "This patent is issued upon the express condition that the title hereby conveyed shall not be subject to taxation of any character, but shall remain inalienable, and not subject to taxation for the period of twenty years from the date hereof, as approved Jan. 18, 1881." The assessor apologized and withdrew, not smiling.

Reports from Illinois indicate at least the partial success of recent attempts to replace prairie chickens and quail with other birds. Two years ago Mr. George Simpson of Alexis, Warren county, Ill., liberated in a small park a few pair of Chukor partridges and pheasants. The former were imported from India and the latter from China. The first two nests, of twenty pheasant eggs each, hatched thirty-eight birds. The pheasants like the open country, and their flight is short and quick to the nearest cover. Fleetness of foot and ability to hide are more depended upon for safety than the wing. The adult male is two feet tall and twenty inches long. The female is a quarter less in size. The experiment, says the owner of the pheasants, "now depends for success solely on the protection and forbearance of hunters for the next few years." The Chukor partridge has not done as well as its Chinese comrade.

A party of Americans will start next spring to explore a portion of the Arctic regions that has never been visited before. The expedition will be led by Robert Stein of the United States Geological Survey, and its purposes will be to trace the west coast line of Ellesmore Grinnell land as far north as possible. A great mass of land faces the northwest coast of Greenland, and is separated from it by the narrow waterways of Smith Sound and Kennedy and Robeson Channels, says the New York Sun...The eastern coast of this land has been fairly well mapped by the explorers, who have pushed along its edge toward the North Pole. The southern Coast has been followed through Jones Sound, and the northern coast was traced by Aldrich, of the Narez expedition. But no one has ever seen the western coast except Lockwood and Brainard of the Greely expedition, who looked out over the sea from the west shore of Grinnell land and discovered the great fiord penetrating far inland, which they named after their leader...

The Banner, Vol. 1, Clanton, Ala., Thursday, October 5, 1893, No. 48

ALABAMA ITEMS - Mr. J.M. Gay of LaFayette lost the end of one of his fingers while trying to mend his bicycle.

The slaughter house belonging to Mr. Morris Koenigsthal in the outskirts of Selma was burned last Tuesday.

Mr. and Mrs. D.J. Strickland of Barbour county have a baby that is two months and ten days old and it has five teeth.

Bob Procise, the 18-year-old son of Ambrose Procise of Tupelo, Jackson county, was choked to insensibility and mutilated with a knife. He says a negro tramp did it.

In trying to reach his appointment at Geneva, Rev. Mr. Morgan had a narrow escape in crossing a creek, and as it was one of his mules was drowned and he missed his appointment.

At Mobile Jim Anderson shot Tom Mitchell with a load of squirrel shot because he wanted him to apologize for insulting his sister. This might be said to be adding injury to insult.

In a creek near Tuscumbia the body of a white man named Bynum was discovered. The crushed condition of the head indicated that he had been murdered and thrown into the creek.

R.L. Hembree has been acquitted of the murder of J.C. Murphree in Jackson county. It will be remembered that Murphree was poisoned some months ago by drinking whisky sent to him through the mails.

Some Added Items - Mrs. M. E. Patterson of Clay county, lost two children by death last week.

In East Florence, Catherine Swinney, was cut in four or five places by Claud Lamar.

A little son of Mr. John Wright of Pike county, was smothered to death in a pile of cotton seed last week.

Mr. S.P. Lovelady has held the position of Worshipful Master of the Danville lodge of Masons for eighteen years.

A dispatch from Russellville says Charlie Nelson, a carpenter, ran away with Miss Roddy, his wife's niece, leaving the latter and four children to shift for themselves.

John W. Coppock, superintendent of the ice plant at Jacksonville, was horsewhipped, so a correspondent from that city says, by a young man because he had deceived his sister into a promise of marriage, when he was already married.

Chairman A.G. Smith, of the State Democratic Executive Committee, in compliance with the wishes of a majority of the members of that body, has called the committee together for October 12th, at Montgomery, to consider the latest proposition of the Jeffersonian

Democracy.

Ayres Jones a notorious moonshiner of Frog Mountain, has been murdered by his son. Ayres Jones and a brother led a crowd of moonshiners, a few years ago in a battle with a detachment of regulars. The moonshiners ambushed the regulars and in the fight killed Lieut. McTyre.

Bent On Bloodshed - Alfred Griffith, a well to do colored farmer living fourteen miles southwest of Brookhaven, Miss., had his cotton-house and three bales of seed cotton set on fire and burned by Whitecaps. His fence was also set on fire, but was extinguished by the leading white citizens, who hurriedly came to his rescue and have stood guard all day. The only cause that can be accepted for this wholesale destruction of property is that he lived on land owned by a Jew. On last Friday night the water mill and cotton gin owned by Dan Sasseer, in the southern portion of Lincoln county, was burned to the ground, without a dollar of insurance. Sasseer was one of the few farmers outside of the city of Brookhaven who shouldered his gun and marched to the courthouse with the Brookhaven boys led by the gallant Judge J.B. Chrisman when the Whitecaps sympathizers stormed the court and attempted to rescue the Whitecaps confined in jail. There is a great deal of suppressed indignation among the better classes of farmers on account of these outrages, and speculation is rife at to what steps will be taken in the next few days. It is publicly asserted that unless Judge Chrisman gives the forty-seven men who pled guilty to storming the courthouse in the recent Whitecap uprising the full penalty of the law, that a reign of terror and bloodshed will prevail, which nothing short of armed troops can subdue. While the assertion of the Whitecaps is undisguised that the Jews must go, these outlaws have not regard for color, creed or nationality, but are bent of the destruction of life and property.

Yellow Fever Theorist - Dr. J.J. Knott of Atlanta, Ga., believes he has discovered a true cause of yellow fever and the remedy for it. He says it is nothing more nor less that phosphoric poison. He has prepared a pamphlet in which his ideas are given, and he is now in Washington to present his ideas to Surgeon General Wyman and ask to be sent to yellow fever sufferers there. In his pamphlet the doctor says his theory is based on observation made by him during the epidemic in 1878 in Chattanooga, Tenn.

Uncle Sam's Officers Indicted - The Federal court grand jury in session at Birmingham, Ala., turned loose a bomb shell in the camp of the Federal office-holders last week, when they returned true bills against six officers of the government. The charge is that they have sent in fraudulent accounts or bills for service to Uncle Sam. Those indicted are Commissioners Hunter, of Birmingham, Wilson, of Clanton and Charlson, of Attalla; Deputy Marshals Nuckles of Tuskaloosa county and Reid and Osborn of Jefferson. A letter signed by sixteen members of the jury was forwarded to the Attorney General.

AT THE CAPITOL
THIRTY-SIXTH DAY - Senate - A second effort on the part of Senator Voorhees today to reach an agreement to the time for closing debate on the repeal bill, and proceeding to vote on the bill and amendments had better results than his previous one, except that there was a sort of intimation by Mr. Teller that as no speeches had been made for delay, none would be; and that the question of closing debate might lie over for the present at least. Mr. Allison made a three hours' speech in order to prove that the true way to rehabilitate silver was to repeal the silver purchase law, and thus force England and the nations of Europe to come to an international agreement on the subject...

THIRTY-SEVENTH DAY - Senate - ...Senator Stewart offered amendments to the Wilson-Voorhees silver bill, and they were ordered printed, inviting Mexico, and south and Central American republics, Hayti and San Domingo to join the United States in a conference, to be held within four months, for the purpose of adopting a common silver dollar of not more that 383.13 grains, which shall be legal tender for all debts, public and private...At 12:15, on motion of Senator Harris, the senate went into executive session, but for a few minutes, and then Mr. Peffer called up a resolution offered a week ago directing the committee on Interstate commerce to investigate the recent train robberies. Senator Peffer took the floor in advocacy of his resolution...

THIRTY-EIGHTH DAY - Senate - ...Mr. Voorhees then took the floor and made lengthy explanations of certain rules of the senate. He was followed by Dubois of Idaho along the same line. Mr. Hoar also took a hand in the debate, and Mr. Platt of Connecticut presented an amendment to the rules, after which Mr. Teller and Mr. Mills took a hand in the discussion...

FORTIETH DAY - Senate - ...After which the repeal bill was taken up and Mr. White of California took the floor and argued against the unconditional repeal of the purchasing clause of the Sherman act...After parleying over yesterday's journal, Mr. Catchings from the committee offered a resolution setting a day for the consideration of the Federal election bill and also a date upon which a vote should be taken...

FORTY-THIRD DAY - Senate - ...Mr. Stewart was the first speaker and occupied two hours in discussing a resolution offered by him on Saturday as to the coordinate departments of the government. He yielded the floor to Mr. Cameron of Pennsylvania, who spoke in opposition to the repeal bill. Mr. Cameron was followed by Mr. Bate also in opposition to the bill...

House - ...Mr. Hudson, populist, of Kansas, asked consent for the immediate consideration of a resolution for the appointment of a committee of five members to investigate the recent killing of settlers in the Cherokee strip by United States troups...

FORTY-FOURTH DAY - Senate - ...One of which was offered by Mr. Dubois, to the effect that all legislation relating to Federal election laws, the tariff and financial matters be postponed until January 15, 1894, to enable the states of Washington, Montana and Wyoming to be fully represented. At 12:10 the repeal bill was again taken up and Mr. Stewart continued his speech. For a time he yielded the floor to Mr. Dubois, who in turn yielded to Mr. Perkins of California...Mr. Stewart again took the floor but was not able to finish his speech. Senators Morgan and Voorhees both made talks in defense of President Cleveland who was arraigned by Mr. Stewart, and as they claimed misrepresented by certain newspaper articles.

Fire in the Strip - A special to the Republic from Guthrie, O.T., says: A disastrous fire occurred in the west part of the Cherokee strip yesterday, and scores of settlers lost their property and narrowly escaped with their lives. Mrs. J.S. Kennedy and her two children were badly burned. John Baker and a Mr. Thompson and family were burned to death. The children of Mrs. George Harrison are also missing; it is fear they also perished. Mrs. Thompson and two children were fatally burned. Most of the men were absent at the land office to register their claims, and the women and children struggled against the fire alone.

Our county alliance lecturer Brother L.B. Pounds has just finished a series of meetings of appointments extended through the month of September; he now announces another series of appointments, commencing at Valley Creek on the 16th. Brother Pounds is an indefatigable worker in the Alliance cause and an able exponent of reform. Brother Alliancemen will be repaid for attending the appointments. Emulate your lecturer in performance of duty to the Alliance.

Gen. Warner, of Ohio, who has been a prominent leader of the democratic party of that state, has abandoned his allegiance to democracy and joined the peoples party, on account of the adoption of the republican policy on finances by the democracy. He objects to following John Sherman and Czar Reed as much now as when their policy was labeled republican...

Jemison Gems - Saturday was a fine day for business, the Alliance store was crowded from morning till night. Bro. Adams, his genial son Johnnie had their hands full all day waiting on the crowd.
.

Detective Barnes got a bad fall last week from a moving train, however he escaped with slight injuries.
.

Clever Buck Chestnutt was here Tuesday, every one is always pleased to meet Buck.
.

J.R. Warren, of Montgomery was in town Tuesday. Editor White of the Banner, Rev. W.G. Riggins and County Commissioner Glasscock.
.

The camp meeting at Rocky Mount has been in progress since last Thursday, P.E.J.S. Freeman, of the Anniston district delivered an able discourse on Sunday morning to an immense concourse of people, his subject was based on the following text...

At night P.E.J.A. Webb, of the Birmingham district preached, his subject being the death and resurrection of the Savior. Many came forward and much interest was manifested, during the afternoon P.E. Freeman administered the rite of baptism to five infants...Your scribe had the pleasure of dining with Bro. Mason Northcutt and family and well and kindly was he treated.

Bethel Babblings - The citizens of this community have got up a petition asking the commissioners to grant a public road, leaving the Cooper and Dixie road near W.D. Courtney's and running a northerly direction and intersecting with the Cooper and Clanton road about one mile south of Clanton on W.H. Merritts's land.

A.B. Dennis and B.L. Dennis each gathered and weighed one acre of corn on the 29th of Sept. the former made 44 bushels and 5 pounds, the latter made 43 bushels and 47 pounds on common piney woods land, which had not been built up until this year.
.

Mr. H. Anderson from Plantersville paid his friends a visit at this place last week.
.

Prof. H.L. Davis' school will begin at this place on the 16th inst.

West Chilton Warblings - Died, recently, near Macedonia. Mr. F.C. Crumpton, an aged and highly respected citizen of that community; his funeral was conducted by Elder Elam, and was attended by a large number of people.
.

Rev. W.G. Riggins has been called to the pastorate of Macedonia church for the ensuing year.
.

Died not long since, very suddenly at her home near Paragould, Ark., Mrs. Paratine Jones, who was born and raised in this part of Chilton County; she leaves a husband and six children.

Rev. Sutton Smitherman has accepted a call to Mars Hill church for next year.

Mr. F.M. Davenport, of Blocton, is visiting relatives here.

Prof. Jones' school at Pleasant Grove has closed. Mr. Jones is an ornament to society wherever he goes.

The Messrs. Cofer are making business lively around their gin and mill.

Dixie Dots - We are sorry to learn of the death of little James Monroe Campbell, son of J.M. Campbell, of Autauga Co., who met his death by smothering in cotton, it seems that the elder children while playing in the cotton made a hole in the cotton 15 inches in diameter 3 feet deep and so left it on Friday the 29th Sept. he went in there and by some means got head first into the hole, he was found about 3:30 p.m. quite dead. He was interred at Bethel, Saturday the 30 of Sept. we tender our heart felt sympathy to the bereaved family.

Mr. C.H. McBride begins a singing school at Alpine on the 2nd of Oct. We hope he will have success.

We are sorry to learn that Mr. W.D. Ellis is not doing so well.

Mr. H.P. Weaver is at work on his Mill Dam, we hope he will soon be able to mash our bread corn.

New Salem - A meeting of the leading citizens of this community was held at the church house here last Friday and it was unanimously decided to have a school here. There is a fine opening for a real good teacher and we invite any such to make a start and open a school the beginning of next month and we promise our hearty support and influence. Mr. Aaron Littleton will be pleased to give any teacher further information on the subject.

Mr. W.H. Merritt has recently purchased between nine and ten thousand acres of land in the neighborhood of Clanton. These lands are well and conveniently situated near the Louisville and Nashville railroad, and are about equi distant from the great cotton markets of Montgomery and Selma both being about forty miles distant. Situated in a district that affords good school facilities, with established churches of all denominations, good society, a healthy climate, abundance of good freestone water, productive soil plentifully timbered no other locality offers better inducements to those, who desire a home where they can enjoy the comforts and blessings of life. These lands can be bought on easy terms, their value is from two to five dollars per acre and when desired can be bought on long time with easy payments in lots to suit purchasers.

TOWN ITEMS - Mr. H.W. Strock, of Verbena, will enter Howard College on Monday.

Mr. Joe King of Montgomery, visited his best girl Sunday.

We are sorry to learn that last week, Mr. Gast was called to the bed side of his son in Birmingham but glad to know that he is improving.

Uncle Paddy Smith will open a meat market at his old stand next week.

Mr. Hugh Foshee's health is steadily improving.

Mrs. R.C. Croswell is visiting relatives in Clanton this week.

We are glad to inform Judge Honeycutt's many friends, that his health is improving.

Capt. W.A. Middleton now has charge of the post office which has been moved into Kemp and Culp's store.

Whilst kneeling at a spring, Sheriff Moore narrowly escaped death last Friday, his pistol falling from his pocket to the ground exploded, the ball passing through the side of his coat.

Rev. B.H. Chastine, of Elmore County, a Presbyterian minister and also Tax Collector of Elmore County paid a visit to Rev. A.C. Wells last Friday and Saturday on his way to his Conference Meeting at Birmingham.

Mr. Frank Crichton has been seriously unwell since Saturday last, suffering from a severe bilious attack, he is we are glad to say improving in health and we hope will be at his post again in a few days time.

Last Sunday evening all of our people gathered at Gods acre to witness the interment of Mrs. H.J. Callen who was called to her rest early that morn, universally beloved and universally mourned by all who knew her. A noble christian soul, whose charities were freely given without ostentation, she will be sorely missed by those she aided and befriended. In these remembrances she leaves a priceless legacy to those who called her theirs. To the sorrowing family who mourn and irreparable loss, we tender our sympathies.

REGISTER'S SALE, James T. Cooley, Complainant Vs J.C. Sewell, Et a.s. Defendants, Chancery Court. - By virtue of a decree rendered at the Fall Term, A.D. 1893, of the Chancery Court at Clanton, Chilton County, Alabama, in said cause, I shall proceed to sell to the highest and best bidder for (?), at public auction at the Court House door in Clanton within the legal hours of sale on Monday the 6th day of November, A. D., 1893, the following deserted Real Estate to wit...W.E. Stewart, Register, Clanton, Oct. 3, 1893

Our revolutionary sires threw the British tea overboard. We are now in favor of throwing the whole British outfit overboard - trade and all. We could teach John Bull a lesson if we had half the independence of our fathers. - Coming Crisis

Senator Gordon, of Georgia, says he doesn't endorse the Alliance "since it has fallen from grace." Neither does the Alliance endorse Senator Gordon since he has fallen from grace. The Senator will not play football with the farmers of Georgia after his present term expires.

During the proceedings of the Chicago silver convention Ignatius Donnelly delivered an address in which he said: "The silver question is but an incident in the great struggle that covers the world. It is the battle of plutocracy against the people. They have stricken down silver because it was one movement to the end they sought...

SHOULD BE IMPEACHED - One of the first acts of the house of representatives should be the impeachment of Secretary Carlisle. The Sherman law, so called, requires the secretary to purchase 4,500,000 ounces of silver monthly at the market price, and to issue in exchange therefore legal tender treasury notes...

A Matter of Health - ...Dr. Edson, Commissioner of Health of New York, in an article in the "Doctor of Hygiene," indicates that the advantages of a good baking powder and the exemption from the dangers of bad ones in which the harsh and caustic chemicals are used, are to be secured by the use of Royal Banking Powder exclusively, and he recommends this to all consumers...

Sir William Outwitted Him - Mrs. Kipling, Rudyard Kipling's mother, once hit off a very clever but extremely garrulous and persistently talkative official by saying that he was essentially a clever man, but he ought never be allowed to talk; he should be used as a dictionary, and consulted when required. This man was once a guest at a dinner in company with Sir W.W. Hunter. the conversation began by going general, but the Lahore talker and Sir W. W. soon monopolized it. A duel or a duologue suited neither, and at last Sir William said down the table: "Excuse me one moment, Mr. —, and allow me to finish my remark." And Mr. — did so; but the remark lasted until the company rose from the table, and Mr. — never had a chance of getting in another word edgeways.

NEWS BOILED DOWN - At Atlanta, Charles Herring, a 19-year-old husband, killed his 16-year-old wife and then suicided. Jealousy was the cause.

.
G.M. Beard a prominent citizen of Robertson county, Tex., was killed while in bed with his wife and baby. It is thought the motive for the deed was revenge as there was no attempt at robbery.

THE NATIONAL GAME - Hoy, the deaf mute, has been signed to play center field next year by Cincinnati.

.
Nelson, the old Metropolitan short stop, is manager of a milk route in Brooklyn.

.
Fuller is at the very foot of New York's batting list, even the pitchers proceeding him..

.
Kelly caught but eight full games for the New Yorks during the season and six of them were defeats.

.
Captain Comiskey, of Cincinnati, says the playing rules this year have been so satisfactory there is not apt to be any change in them.

.
It is not likely that Pinckney will cover third base for Louisville next season. He seems to have lost his nerve in facing hard hit balls.

Unlucky Gems in America - ...Thousands of stones were obtained during the last two years, according to Mr. Kunz, many of them fine blue color, quite equal to the best Persian.

The Banner, Vol. 1, Clanton, Ala., Thursday, October 12, 1893, No. 49

THE REFORM MOVEMENT - Tom Watson takes every inch of hide of the Atlanta, Ga., authorities for preventing freedom of speech by arresting J.B. Osburn, whose only (?)ne was that he started to make a speech, Osborn was fined $100 and costs. Atlanta is noted for that and the day of retribution is near at hand.

A committee of the Texas State Alliance, who had been instructed to ascertain where was the birthplace of the Alliance in Texas, reported that Lampasas county was entitled to the honor, and that the sub-Alliance was organized by John R. Allen. This report was adopted by the Alliance in session. This the question is settled officially.

Tax Collector Missing - A dispatch from Russellville, Ala., says that R.A. Tompkins, tax collector, who was recently found several thousand dollars short, is missing.

GENERAL NEWS - F.L. Greenhagle has been nominated by the Republican party of Massachusetts, for Governor.

Henry Lack, of Savannah, asserts that he can certainly cure any and every case of yellow fever without the use of disinfectants or drugs, but he declines to say what his remedy is.

Miss Sarah Carmichael, a poor, dependent young lady of Ripley, O., advertised for a well-to-do husband and as a result is now the happy bride of Arthur Nelson of St. Peter's Minn., a farmer with 500 acres of rich land. It pays to advertise.

A breach of promise case of Mrs. Anna D. Van Houten vs. Asa P. Morse in the Boston courts had ended and a verdict for $40,000 has been returned. This is the case of which the Judge ordered that no newspaper report should be made until the conclusion of the trial.

The latest move of the whitecappers is to post notices that they will kill any one found picking cotton for less than a stipulated price which they name in their notices. A special from Grenada, Miss., states that a negro at work "picking cotton on Capt. Curt. Gay's place, ten miles of Grenada, was shot from ambush with buckshot. He had been guilty of nothing," so the dispatch continued to read, "but gathering cotton and whitecaps is the only explanation."

Deceived His Looks - Senator Allen, of Nebraska, is a big, burly man who looks like a prosperous dealer in live stock. Shortly after his arrival in Washington he was stopped at the door of the senate chamber by a new doorkeeper, who informed him that no one save senators were allowed on the floor. Mr. Allen smiled sadly, waved his hand and said: "Very well, sonny. I'm a senator. I don't look like it, I know, but I am, just the same, " and he passed into the (?) precinct.

ITEMS OF INTEREST - The tronomter is a device of Dr. Quintard, a Frenchman, for gauging the trembling of a nervous person.

NEWS BOILED DOWN - Walter H. Rhett, a prominent young lawyer of Atlanta, Ga., committed suicide the past week. No cause is known for the rash act.

Lewis Stranz, a jewelry drummer, killed himself at Memphis. He checked his baggage from Birmingham to Memphis and it was lost. Efforts to secure the value of it, $380, were fruitless, and, being out of funds, Stranz cut his throat with a razor.

Dr. Lesseps, the builder of the Suez canal is reported dying.

Roswell Beardsly of North Lansing N. W. is said to the oldest postmaster in the United States, he was appointed in 1823 and has been in actual service ever since.

Congressman Robbins declined to express an opinion on the latest Jeffersonian proposition when requested by a reporter to do so. Well we are not surprised at his declining. Congressman Robbins is not apt to regard with any particular favor a proposition, which if agreed to would do away with the occupation of the black belt hero.

The Referendum again. Congressman Cooper, of Texas, has introduced a resolution providing that the governor of each State shall call a special election for the purpose of affording the people an opportunity to express their sentiment either for or against free coinage...

We call special attention to our clubbing arrangement with the great southern weekly, The Atlanta Constitution, which enables us to offer both papers for the remarkable low sum of $1 and fifty cents a year...It is essentially a farmer's paper and at the head of the weekly press in this country. It's agricultural department alone is worth the subscription price of the paper, while it numbers among its contributors such well known names as Bret Harte, Mark Twain, Joel Chandler Harris, Sarge Plunkett, Bill Arp, and a host of others whose reputations are world wide...

ROCKY MOUNT - The camp meeting closed Wednesday morning with very good results in spite of the wicked one and his forces...We had Brother J.L. Freeman the P. E. of the Anniston District, Bro. T.J. McCain and Brother Hay from Birmingham visiting us with Brother Webb our P. E. they preached with power and many were deeply convicted and several converted there were 13 tent holders and there are some who say they will have them a tent next fall.

Coopers Cuttings - We regret to announce the death of Mr. G.B. Gray, which took place at his home near Coopers, on the 3rd. Mr. Gray had long been suffering with lung disease, his death occurred quite suddenly. He left a large family to mourn the loss of a devoted loving husband and father. He was a consistent member of the Baptist church, and a staunch Allianceman, he died regretted by all.

LAST CHANCE FOR CHICAGO - You will only regret it once, and that will be all your lifetime, if you miss seeing the great Columbian Exposition at Chicago which closed October 31st...See the L. and N. Agent for any further information or write to C.P. Atmore, G. P. A., Louisville, Ky

TOWN ITEMS - Died in Birmingham on Tuesday, October 10th, Dr. John P. Robinson in the 80th year of his age. His remains were interred here on Wednesday.

At the beat meeting here last Saturday, the following delegates were elected the county convention of the People's Party T.H. White, O.M. Mastin, Ab Eiland, Wm. Lambert and Wiley Littlejohn,Jr.

Tax Collector B.M. Gentry left here last Tuesday to visit his brother in Texas.

Whils't Mr. Crichton is far from being well, his health is still improving.

Mr. Sampey Davis has opened a confectionery store on the corner next to Depot.

Miss Gamma Middleton has returned home after spending the summer months with relatives and friends in Nashville and Springfield Tennessee.

Dr. A.J. Massey the popular and well known dentist desires to inform the public that he will be at Clanton Oct. 17th, 18th, and 19th.

Divine service will be held at the Episcopal church on the fifth Sunday Oct. 29, Rev. J.S. Smith officiating, the probability is that Bishop Jackson will be present on this occasion.

Mr. Geo. W. Langston of Bibb county and Miss Ophelia Merchant of the Cox's Chapel neighborhood are to marry to-day.

T.P. Crossin was lodged in jail on Saturday, to await the action of the grand jury; having had a preliminary examination before Justice Harrison of Jemison, charged with attempting to rape his niece, he contends that he is innocent.

Prof. J.P. Gore and Miss Lafarice Deadwilder were happily married last Sunday at Mulberry church. The Banner extends its congratulations to the fortunate couple.

George Edwards a young white man was arrested on Wednesday near Clear Creek by Sheriff Moore and posse. A true bill was found against him at the Spring term of court 1891, for assaulting with intent to commit murder Mr. Smith living near Jemison; until now Edwards has been successful in evading arrest, although several attempts have been made to capture him.

FINAL PROOF NOTICE, NOTICE NO. 14,079, LAND OFFICE AT MONTGOMERY, ALA., October 4, 1893 - Notice is hereby given that the following named settler has filed notice of his intention to make final proof in support of his claim, and that said proof will be made before The Clerk of the Circuit Court at Clanton, Ala., on November 18th, 1893; viz.: John M. Robinson, Homestead Entry No. 20,383 for the w 1-2 of s e 1/4, s e 1/4 of s e 1/4 Section 30, Tp 21 n, Range 13 e. He names the following witnesses to prove his continuous residence upon and cultivation of said land, viz.: Henry M. Mahan, John Giles, James F. McKee, and James M. Davis, all of Clanton, Ala. J.H. Bingham, Registrar.

FINAL PROOF NOTICE, NOTICE NO. 14,121, LAND OFFICE AT MONTGOMERY, ALA., October 11, 1893 - Notice is hereby given that the following named settler has filed notice of his intention to make final proof in support of his claim and that said proof will be made before the Clerk of the Circuit Court at Clanton, Ala., on Nov. 18th, 1893; viz.: Martha S. Chandler for the heirs of Millie Chandler Homestead Entry No. 19,099, for the E 1-2 of N W 1-4 of Section 36, Tp. 20, n of Range 12 e. He names the following witnesses to prove his continuous residence and cultivation of said land, viz.: John F. Roberts, Thomas

Roberts, Ed. J. McCollough, and George W. Frith, all of Chilton, Ala.   J.H. Bingham, Registrar

AD - "Little Paint Store", The Merchants and Farmers Friend, W.K. Harwell & Co., No. 23 South Court Street (Yellow Front), Montgomery, Ala.

Brave Hannah Snell - There have been many women warriors in the world, but it must be admitted that there have been very few whose deeds were such as to claim the admiration of the country for any great length of time. In the annals of woman's warfare there are generally stories of over-zealousness, leading to fanaticism and subsequent punishment and disgrace. Seldom, indeed, has a woman warrior been gratefully recognized by the government of her county. Within the memory of our grandparents there lived in England a woman named Hannah Snell, who, when but a girl, took the strange resolution of enlisting as a soldier. She served as a marine on one of the vessels of a fleet bound for the West Indies, and showed so much courage that she was repeatedly promoted. Her sex was unknown, and therefore it could never be claimed that Hannah Snell's success was due in partiality or favoritism. Once, when dangerously wounded, she extracted the ball herself, fearing that she might be discovered and discharged. After long service she returned to her native house at Worcester, England, where her adventures soon became spread abroad. The government, on investigation of her really great career, granted her a pension of 20 pounds. She died full of years and laden with honors in an inn near Wapping. - Philadelphia Inquirer

Who Were Darby and Joan? - The names Darby and Joan are now synonymous with man and wife. They originated in a popular ballad called "Darby and Joan, " written by Henry Woodfall in the last century. It is not generally known as the two characters of the ballad were real personages. John Darby and his wife lived in Bartholomew Close, and died in 1730. In the poem Joan gets dissatisfied with being a household drudge, and declares that her work is harder than her husband's labors in the field. He offers to exchange places with her, and she consents. The result is that both are quite content to go back into their legitimate spheres.

The Banner, Vol. 1, Clanton, Ala., Thursday, October 19, 1893, No. 50

THE REFORM MOVEMENT - President Cleveland, in his message said: " Our government cannot make its flat equivalent to intrinsic value. " John C. Calhoun said: " I undertake to affirm, without fear that I can be answered, that a paper issued by the government, with the ample promise to received it for all its dues, would be as uniform in its value as the panels metals themselves. " If Cleveland is a Democrat, what was John C. Calhoun, brother?-Cotton Plant

IMPORTANCE OF FREE COINAGE - The roxboro Courier refers to sufficient assertion made in a speech by Col. Polk some years ago when he said that the passage of a free coinage bill would not be sufficient financial legislation, as it would only put some 30 odd cents per capita in circulation annually...

Major Mann Page, of the National Alliance Executive committee, has been nominated for the State Senate in Virginia. He is one of the most popular citizens in the State.

HOW VANCE WILL COMPROMISE - A few days ago Senator Vance was asked if he would agree to a compromise on the silver question. He said he would provided the bill called for the coinage of a thousand million dollars, for we could probably get along with that amount of silver coin...

Horse and Bicycle - At Paris, W.F. Cody, familiarly known to the old and new world as " Buffalo Bill, " has challenged M. Terront, the bicyclists, who has just completed his trip across Europe, to a two hour's race, Cody to ride a horse and Terront a wheel. It is designed to test the merits of the two mounts, each rider being allowed a change if desired. The challenger places the stakes from 10,000 to 20,000 francs at the option of the bicyclist.

He Was Found Guilty - The second trial of Wesley G. Ripper for shooting Millionaire J.W. Mackey last February has been concluded. The jury after being out three hours, returned a verdict, finding the defendant guilty of assault with a deadly weapon, and recommended him to the mercy court. His defense was temporary insanity.

LATE STATE ITEMS - Will Lacy, colored, was hanged at Jasper for a rape committed some six months ago.

Otto Von Koenitz, a German portrait painter living in Huntsville, who accidentally fell from a porch and was killed.

Near Gold Hill, an old man named Broughton threw himself across the bed saying he did not feel very well, and in a few minutes he was dead.

John Davis, colored, was killed by a posse who had captured him for entering the room of J. T. Farmer's daughter at Shortville, Henry county. He undertook to give the party leg for bail, but Winchester bullets overtook him.

READABLE ITEMS - Paynter Frame, a farmer of Sussex county, Delaware, has shipped to President Cleveland a watermelon weighing 72 pounds and measuring 40 inches one way around an 60 inches the other. It is in Mr. Frame's region that watermelons are varnished and kept to grace the Christmas dinner table. It is here, too, that the watermelon is boiled and preserved in sugar as a winter delicacy.

Harry Tracy and J.A. Davis are whooping up the People's party cause in Texas.

Senator Morgan, characterized the Voorhees substitute for the Wilson bill, as " very ridiculous, very injurious and very cowardly. "

Tom Watson of Georgia, has just finished the " People's Campaign " in that state, for the year 1893; he has met thirty-seven different meetings, addressing an advocate of 425,000 people, since July 4th, the enthusiasm manifested at these meetings is unprecedented. Wherever Tom met the enemy they were his. Hurrah for gallant Tom Watson.

PEOPLES PARTY CONVENTION - The convention was called to order by O.M. Mastin at 11 a.m. who appointed T.H. White editor of the Banner Secretary. The chairman then appointed the following delegates as a committee on credentials, L.B. Pounds, Lee Hayes, and W.A. Green who reported as follows: Beat 1. Samuel Pate, J.W. Sorel and F.J. Robinson. Beat 2. J.B. Martin, W.M. Green, T.M. Driver and Ira Campbell Beat 3. Lee Hayes Beat 4. T.H. White, O.M. Mastin, Wm. Lambert, Ab. Eiland and Wiley Littlejohn,Jr. Beat 5. J.B. Wells, H.M. Strock, N.N. Vincent, Joe Jones and J.M. Robinson Beat 7. L.B. Pounds, W.A. Green and W.B. Green Beat 8. Dan Mitcheal and D.N. Martin. Beat Six not being represented...On motion the resolution were adopted as read. The chairman then declared that nominations for county executive committee men were in order Beat 1. L.W.A. Mims, J.W. Sorrel. 2. Ira Campbell, L.B. Martin. 3. Lee Hayes, S.E. Waldrup no 5. B.H. Wells, H.M. Strock no. 6. J.R. Vinson, John Middlebrooks no. 7. W.G. Nix, W.A. Green no. 8. E.W. Bailey, W.A. Weaver...The chairman then declared nominations in order to delegates to the state convention, the nominations being made, election was held for delegates and alternates resulting as follows, Delegate O.M. Mastin, Alternate Ira Campbell, Delegate B.H. Wells Alternate Samuel Pate, Delegate L.B. Pounds Alternate H.M. Strock, Delegate T.H. White Alternate R.M. Dykes...

AUTAUGA ATOMS - Mr. and Mrs. J.P. Clements have a sad bereavement, caused by the death of their eldest child Pearlie Clements, who died Oct. 11th. Their friends all join them in mourning their loss.

Mr. Askew is talking of moving back to Chilton county, where he was raised near Clear creek, he will move 1st Nov. his wife's bad health is the cause of his moving; he thinks probably it will be an advantage to her.

ROCKY MOUNT - Bro. E.W. Honeycutt will be on hand next Sabbath.

Mr. Ben Veas(?) and wife are visiting relative at Oxmore and West Birmingham, he is talking of making his home in these parts, we wish him good luck.

Hurrah for Messrs. Will Shelby and Tom Burnett, both fine girls.

We are sorry to hear of the death of one of Jim Dubes twins and that the other one is very sick and expected to die.

CLANTON FORD OR PINGS - There was a negro run over by Mr. Coes log engine today, he had to have his leg amputated.

OAK MULGA OUTCRIES - Messrs. D.A. Friday, Joe Wylie and Wm. Marshall went Opossum hunting the other night, and caught a very happy one. Mr. W.M. Price and his little boy also went hunting the other night and caught two very nice ones; Hurrah! for Price. If anybody is bothered with opossum, send for Mr. Price and he will catch them, and eat them too.

D.H. Mitchell went to see his best girl last Sunday. I think he will soon marry.

Brigham Young moved his steam mill home last week, and (?) it last Tuesday.

Mrs. Margaret Friday has had a carbunkle for the last six weeks, she is getting better now.

ENERGY EVENTS - I think Mr. J.W. Billingsley and Miss Obie Smith will jump the broom and tie the everlasting knot yet.

TOWN ITEMS - H.E. Culver, will hereafter entertain a gentleman stranger, as a regular boarder, who arrive at his residence at sunrise Tuesday morning.

Mr. W.L. Sampey, we regret to learn is lying at his residence quite sick. We hope his recovery will be speedy.

We hear that Mr. Will Kemp and Miss Sallie Woolley, of Montevallo are to marry next Tuesday.

Mrs. R.—. Smith, of Key West, Fla., has been holding union services at the Court House, the past two nights, we understand the services are to be continued.

Rev. Wm. Shaw, State Superintendent of the Congregational Sabbath Schools, is visiting Clanton today.

Mr. Massey pulled six teeth in succession, from Dr. J.S. Johnson,Jr.'s mouth this morning. Our friend the Doctor says he suffered no pain whatever during the operation, this is certainly a great triumph for Odontunder.

Mr. Frank Crichton, we are glad to say is fairly convalescent.

The Marsh residence is being repaired by Mr. Potts, the present owner, and Mrs. Carroll is having her residence completed

Assistant agent F.M. Jones, has returned, to the great pleasure of his many friends.

A number of our citizens left to take in the World's Fair this week: W.W. Dunkin, J.W. Stanfield, Tipton T. Mullins, Col. and Mrs. Go(?)er and daughter Alice, and Dr. W.E. Stewart and wife.

Divine service will be held at the Episcopal church on the fifth Sunday, Oct. 29, Rev. J. S. Smith officiating, the probability is that Bishop Jackson will be present on this occasion.

A GIRL "TELEGRAPH BOY" - Up in Easthampton, Mass., the people receive their telegrams with a promptness that makes the neighboring towns green with envy. The reason is that the "telegraph messenger boy" is a girl, and that baseball, marbles, and dog fights have no charms for her. She is a ten-year-old girl, named Elsie Gough, and she works in order that her big brother may go to school. She is also saving up earnings to buy a bicycle, and her present ambition, aside from the bicycle, is to become a telegraph operator.

AN UNUSUALLY LIVELY CHOIR, Among the Singers Put the Parson to Flight. - Perhaps if the Rev. Lamb Agnus of Weeping Canon, N. M., knew as much about church choirs as he does now he would not have attempted to start a male choir at that place. If the reports of the Weeping Canon experiment are correct, Mr. Agnus had but recently left a theological school and had more enthusiasm than practical knowledge, but there can be not doubt that his intentions were the best...

The "Gatored Mule" - "Did you ever hear of a gatored mule?" asked Mr. William G. Thompson of New York, who is on his way home, after a year spent in Florida for his health. "A gatored mule" as he is called in Florida, is one of that stubborn race which has been driven partially insane from an alligator fright. In fact, while a mule will stolidly wait to be thrown off a railroad by a locomotive before he moves, he goes into a wild state of terror at a single glimpse of a saurian monster...

The Banner, Vol. 1, Clanton, Ala., Thursday, October 26, 1893, No. 51

THEY CAN NOW RESUME - During the prevailing money stringency, among the thousands of business failures that have taken place, have been a large number of national banks. These were probably banks that were endeavoring to comply with the laws established for their government. Senator Gorman, Senator Hoar and several other good democratic and republican senators say that such foolishness would break every national bank in the United States.

ADVISED TO HOLD THEIR COTTON - W.D. Evans, President of the Farmer's State Alliance, of South Carolina, has issued the following address: To the Cotton Planters and Members of the Alliance of the Cotton States: This has been a bad year for cotton...

THE REFORM MOVEMENT - A goldbug paper recently said that Senator Peffer would never be satisfied until the government printed enough greenback money to fill bedticks...

The People's Party Paper, Atlanta, Ga., owned and edited by Hon. T.W. Watson, is now two years old...

ODDS AND ENDS - Sir Arnold White, an English lawyer who died recently, was the private soldier of Queen Victoria and other members of the royal family, as well as the king and queen of Belgium.

The following clippings does not appear to tally with a recent utterance of the View regarding Bro. Adam's position: "Rev. S.M. Adams, ex-state president of the Alliance and late candidate for commissioner of agriculture on the Kolb ticket, has been elected chairman of the populist committee of Bibb county." - Selma Mirror

The county Alliance met at Evergreen on Wednesday, concluding the session the same day. Dr. B.W. Groce our honored and beloved State President was present and addressed the Alliance. We will publish a full report of the proceedings in our next issue.

Some of our contemporaries to this state, are very fond of asserting that the People's party is dead...Yesterday, Congressman W.J. Bryan, of Nebraska, In Colorado, The Hon. T.M. Patterson of the Rocky Mountain News and ex-governor Routt, then there are Senators Stewart and Jones of Nevada; State Senator B(?) of Iowa, for sixteen years Democratic leader in the Iowa State Senate...

From the information of our readers we give the following summary of the action taken, during the past week on the silver question: - The situation last Friday night, worn our physically and mentally by the champions of the people's money; the cuckoos majority of the majority of the Senate, the would -be (?) Cleveland's sycophantic henchmen, confessed their defeat Senator Voorhees moving for adjournment in these words...On Monday morning Dan Lamont, his whilom secretary, came in post haste from New York bearing the commands of Wall Street to Cleveland that the compromise should not be allowed. Then came John Sherman, and to his arguments, backed by Wall Street's demands, the President of the United States yielded, and rescinded his assent to the proposed compromise, and caused a message to be written for the press associations announcing that the President still held to his message, and was determined to have unconditional repeal, this acted like a bomb shell under the proposed compromise in the senate and blew it all to atoms.

West Chilton Warblings - Charley Barnes, my oldest son, left Plantersville on the 19th for Palmetto, Florida, to make that place his future home, and his cousin, Leroy Barnes, will leave in a few days for the same place.

Capt. R.W. Little, of Morrowsville, Ala., is having a fine residence erected upon his lot in Maplesville, and will in the near future open up a large dry goods and grocery store in his large store house that he had built there last year. Capt. Little is a whole soul gentleman and is a true reform man.

Mr. Ed. Potter, Of Sherrershill, visited friends near Valley Creek (?) the 22nd and made his best girl glad one more time.

Our good old friend, E.G. Sanderson, and wife visited Valley Creek the 22nd from Sherrershill; we were very proud to meet with them again.

Dallas County Alliance was in session at Fellowship church on the 16th and 17th, and our State Lecturer, Mr. Harris was there, and addressed about 800 people, and everybody returned home rejoicing, full of renewed Alliance principles, determined to stick to the order. We met at Valley Creek church on the 21st and organized a reform club, and elected Capt. R.J. Mitcheal president, E.W. Baily Secretary, T.A. Gay, treasurer, determined to stand, to the Third Party rack fodder or no fodder.

Mr. H.W. Cole and P.W. Haley were returning home from (?) church in east Perry, a few Sundays ago, and night closed in upon them and they became lost near Chestnutt Hill; they traveled and wandered around all night, they say they went over hills and bluffs, logs and trees.

On the night of the 15th the only daughter of Mr. Walter Jones of East Perry, Melissa Jones, 16 years of age, ran away from home in her night clothing and met her bet fellow, Mr. Hermon Rush, nearby, and she dressed and they were married at 2 o'clock at night by Capt. R.W. Little who was on hand a waiting for their arrival.

South Calera - On the 7th, Mr. J.E. Edwards was in the woods hunting. Near, the close of day he came within half a mile of Wessington, when he saw an unusual number of sweeps gathering around a hollow gum stump. His curiosity was aroused, he went home, and returned the next day in company with his sons, and Alfred Pate and Jim Pate. They proceeded to investigate, kill and count with the following result: Killed 308, (?) 201, making a total of 512....

Dallas County Dots - Mr. J.P. Stricklin, our noted Dallas County farmer, (?) hauled 20 bushels at a load in a one horse wagon. Hurrah for J. P, don't you say so?

Kincheon Ketchings - Mr. John Alerga and family spent Sunday last with Mr. John Edwards.

We are sorry to learn that Mrs. Matilda Hewit is dead; died last Sunday night, She had been suffering for twelve years with her throat and lungs, she left word that she was going to rest. Now, my friends, let us not grieve after her body, but try to meet her in heaven, where parting is no more. Mrs. Hewit was a kind woman and a friend to all.

AD - Charles W. Hare, Attorney-At-Law, Clanton, Alabama

FINAL PROOF NOTICE, NOTICE NO. 14,177, LAND OFFICE AT MONTGOMERY, ALA., October 18, 1893 - Notice is hereby given that the following named settler has filed notice of his intention to make final proof in support of his claim and that said proof will be made before the Clerk of the Circuit Court at Union, Ala., on December 4, 1893, viz.: Asbury Gibson, Homestead Entry No. 20751, for the N W. 1-4 of Section 10 Tp 2(?) North of Range 14 East. He names the following witnesses to prove his continued residence upon and cultivation of said land. viz: George Pearce, James Moore, Henry Wilkins, and J.L. Vinson, all of Kincheon, Ala. J.H. Bingham, Register.

TOWN ITEMS - Dr. W.E. Stewart and family have returned from a visit to the World's Fair. The Dr. can interest anyone by the hour with his vivid descriptions of the sights he saw and the pleasures he enjoyed.

Clanton Alliance met in regular session last Saturday and elected Bros. A.D. Massey and T.H. White delegates to the county Alliance.

Rev. Wm. Shaw, Superintendent of the Sabbath Schools, delivered an interesting address to the pupils of Prof. E.Y. McCorries' school last Friday afternoon; in the evening he delivered an able discourse to a large audience at the Congregational church his subject being the Tabernacle.

Mr. Patrick Smith has re-opened his restaurant at his old stand in store house nearest the court-house where he will supply you as of old with meals and lodging at moderate prices.

Prof. J.P and Mrs. Gore have rented Mr. Will Callens residence. They are a welcome addition to Clanton society.

Mr. W.L. Sampey's health is improving, he is able to be out once more.

We take pleasure in calling attention to the law card of C.W. Hare, which appears in this issue, careful and prompt attention will be given all cases with which he may be entrusted.

Mr. W.B. Nolen, whose law card appears elsewhere, will give careful attention to all business entrusted to him. In criminal cases where parties are in embarrassed circumstances, Mr. Nolen will be as indulgent as possible.

Mr. Will Callen had removed his family to the home of his father ex-Judge Callen.

Mr. A.C. Smith has rented Mr. Patrick Smith's residence, and removed his family from Bozeman to our town. We are glad to welcome them to our midst.

Our popular young merchant Mr. Will Kemp, was happily married to Miss Sallie Wooley of Montevallo. The young couple will make their home here and we wish them all happiness and prosperity.

Another wedding took place in Clanton last Tuesday. Mary E. Parker was united to Mr. W.E. Skipper, may their future be all bright and happy.

Dr. B.W. Groce, President of the State Alliance made a visit to Judge R.M. Honeycutt this week, the many friends of Dr. Groce will be glad to know he is well in health.

SOMEWHAT STRANGE - A.P. Hinton, of Oklahoma is a "boomer". So is S.S. Slowson, likewise of Oklahoma. They were bosom friends, and one day Hinton traded Slowson a revolver for a watch. When the Cherokee Strip excitement began they boomed along amicably for awhile, but finally quarreled over a jumped claim or something. The Slowson pulled out the revolver and blazed away at Hinton. The bullet struck the watch and Hinton's life was saved. The incident affected Slowson to tears, and he apologized. They took a drink and then boomed along together again.

The Vienna (Ga.) Progress tells this remarkable story: Messrs. J.R. Duncan and Joe T. Collier were speaking of war reminiscences a few days ago, when one of them told a remarkable circumstance. A company of one hundred men, of whom the above named gentlemen were, which was formed at Perry. The night before they left for the scene of the war they met at this church, and a good old minister by the name of Talley was called upon to pray. He prayed very earnestly, and among other things prayed that not a single yankee bullet might strike one of these men. This company of one hundred men went through the war, being in many fierce battles, and not one was killed or wounded, and about sixty of the one hundred men are now living.

O.L. Wilhott, of Warrentown, Ga., comes to the front with a very intelligent act of young pigs. For some time he has noticed that his milk cows would give but little, in fact almost no milk, every morning, and he was unable to account for this. It was at first thought that they were being milked by some one, so a watch was placed at the end of the pen to catch the miscreant. Instead of his catching a supposed two-legged offender he caught about a dozen little pigs. While the cows were lying down resting the pigs would go up beside them and getting hold of the teat would take all the milk, leaving them perfectly dry. The pigs are no longer allowed the privileges of the cowpen, and the usual quantity of morning milk is being obtained.

Mr. Christman, of Pottstown, Pa., was very much surprised the other day at the behavior of his large herd of cows. They were all staggering about like so many drunken hoodlums. They bellowed, threw up their heads and tails, and pranced around like a lot of circus horses performing for a brass band. Very anxious about his stock, he hurried off to summon a veterinary surgeon. The doctor, after a brief examination of the patients told him that his cows were all drunk. He was puzzled for a time to tell how they came so, but presently it came out that they had broken into a corn field and filled themselves full of green corn, and the doctor decided that the corn had fermented in their stomachs and produced alcohol enough to account for their condition.

Judge E.W. Cunningham, of Emporia, Kan., has a good deal of nerve in an emergency. He heard a noise in his house the other night, and getting out of bed went down stairs to ascertain the cause. Half way down the stairs he came suddenly on a masked burglar crouching in a corner. The burglar rose to his feet remarking: "I guess I'll shoot you." "I guess not," replied the judge, "but I will shoot you, " and he raised his empty hand as though to point a pistol at the burglar. In an instant the latter turned and, running down the stairs, fled out the open window, by which he had entered, while the judge who says that he was as fully scared as the other, ran in the opposite direction to get hold of the gun which he keeps in his room. Hereafter he will look up unusual noises in the night with the gun in his hands.

The latest from the sea serpent comes form the upper Ottawa river. Mrs. Lahey, a farmer's wife, according to the Ottawa Free Press, went down to the river to do her washing. Going to dip a bucket of water out of the river, she found a great log on the way. She took a pole and undertook to push the log out of the way, and to her horror found that the side of the log sunk inward under the force of her efforts, but the log itself would not give an inch. While she stood considering what to do suddenly the log rolled over and about ten feet from her the head of a hideous monster rose five feet above the surface of the water, hissing in a snakish way, and then with another roll and splash of its tail, which was fully twenty feet from where the head appeared, the animal plunged toward the middle of the river and disappeared. The lady was so terrified by the sight that she fainted, and was confined to her bed for several days.

James Smithers, of Haliburton, Ontario, while moose hunting in that vicinity not long ago, made a singular discovery. Walking across the country in an unfrequented place, he was suddenly astonished to find himself sinking. He fell about six feet, but, owing to the descent of the loose earth with him, sustained no injury. He was amazed to find the bottom of the pit composed of solid ice of a brackish taste, and evidently of untold age. Walking about the pit Smithers made out an object protruding from the icy foundation, and, with his short hunting axe, cut away the surrounding material, until he saw that the object was a human hand holding a spear. Further excavation revealed the entire figure of a man clad in fur garments and perfectly preserved in his cold bed. Near at hand were also the remains of a deer, which the hunter had doubtlessly lost his life in pursuing to this treacherous spot. The frozen man was an Indian of noble build and wore a chief's amulet about his neck. That he died by cold was to be plainly seen by his expression, which was the placid one of persons who die thus. The skin of his face and hands was drawn and like parchment, but that protected by his clothing was firm and natural, as if death had come within the hour. When thawed and exposed to the air, the body speedily crumbled away.

A Sioux Squaw's Prudence - "One day Flying-by's wife came to our tent and asked us to lend her a small hand mirror which we possessed. We gave it to her, and then watched her to see what she would do with it. About a mile and a half or two miles away a horse race was in progress, watched by three or four hundred mounted Indians. The squaw took the mirror, stood in front of the tent, and reflected a beam of sunlight from the glass along the ground in line with the group of Indians. It was only two or three minutes before a solitary horseman left the band and came tearing over the prairie toward us. It was Flying-by who sprang off his horse at our door and looked inquiringly around. His wife had gone back to her cooking and was apparently quite heedless of his coming. To his question whether some one had not sent for him, we could only reply that we had seen his wife playing heliostat with our mirror, whereupon he went over and spoke to her. In a moment he returned, and with a grin, told us that, knowing he had money, his wife had called him home for fear he might be tempted to gamble it away. He chuckled over her prudence, and told us that he might have made a lot of money if he had stayed, and not a cross word was spoken."

A NOTED FRONTIERSMAN, An Incident in the Career of King S. Woolsey - King S. Woolsey, the noted frontiersman, and one of the white men most dreaded by the Apachees, lived the latter part of his life in this county, and died in this city, says a Phoenix (Arizona) correspondent of the St. Louis Republic. She originally settled and reclaimed Agua Calient, now a fine ranch in the western part of the county, and near the scene of the Oatman massacre. He lived there during the days of overland travel to California, and many stories are told of his dealings with rough men and with the Indians. His place was a resting spot for those going over the trail, and in 1866 two Texans stopped a few days to rest their teams. While there they talked a great deal in a kind of braggadocio style, remarking that " Apaches were nothing, anyway; " that " a boy could kill them; but for a good hard Indian fight a man must meet Comanches, such as grew down in Texas." Finally Woolsey got tired of it, and told them that he did not believe they would fight Indians, anyway, but if they wanted to try, he was going to some mines he had in the Bradshaw mountains, and if they would accompany him they might meet some. Now, Woolsey knew that every canyon swarmed with Indians and he had no idea of going, thinking that the Texans would back down from his offer, but, instead, they accepted, and a few days later, with three pack animals, they began the journey. It so happened that they were not molested till they reached Pine Creek, well up in the Mongollous, but one morning they were attacked by a large band. The white men replied with such an effect that the Indians would not crowd them, but lay behind the rocks waiting for one to expose himself, when they would shower a handful of bullets at him. Finally one of the burros was killed, and knowing that something besides fighting must be done, else they would all perish when darkness fell and the Indians could creep up, Woolsey signaled for a talk. Of course, the chief had no idea of letting them out, but words did less harm than bullets, and knowing that ever minute brought night nearer, he granted it. Every prospector has a bottle of poison in his kit, and this part of Woolsey's outfit was a bottle of strychnine. The remaining burrow was packed with a pinole, a roasted meal made from mesquite beans, very nutritious and a favorite dish of the Indians. Before going up to the place designated for the "talk" he poured the ounce of strychnine into the meal and thoroughly mixed it. Pretty soon the animal wandered off and some of the Indians stole it. Woolsey pretended not to see it, but this was just what he wanted them to do. When the beans have been roasted before grinding the Indians eat the meal raw, and being hungry from their day's fast the load was no sooner taken off than they began eating it. The immediate guard of the chief kept slipping away one at a time until only three or four were left, and knowing full well what was going on the whites continued the "talk", waiting for the poison to take effect. In a little while the warriors began to double up and die in great agony before they had time to tell what was the matter or how they suffered. Finally the survivors began to run, thinking that witches had attacked them in great force. The chief saw the maneuvers and stood it as long as he could, but without saying a work in excuse to the white men, he slipped into the brush and was gone. This was one time that the Indians did not carry off their dead, and at sundown sixty-three corpses were found lying among the rocks. About a year afterward Woolsey met the chief at Fort Whipple and asked him how many of his band died. He replied very sadly: "All dead; can't fight white man any more till warriors grow up."

Sent Them About Their Business - Ferdinand Hassler, the father of the United States coast survey system, was once waited upon by a committee of Congress sent to inquire into the progress of the work. The committee reached New York and wended their way upstairs to the room where Hassler was drilling his classes and preparing them for work. Hassler, who allowed no intruders, met them at the door and inquired their business. The answered that they had come to investigate. "What part of the work do you wish to inspect?" inquired

254

the Swiss mathematician. Congress had no definite idea on the point. "Then you had better go and find out," returned Hassler, as he shut the door in the face of the astonished committee. The committee looked at each other, and, on second sober thought, concluded that Hassler was about right, and quietly wended their way downstairs and back to Washington.

John Wesley's father was a country clergyman.

The Banner, Vol. 1, Clanton, Ala., Thursday, November 2, 1893, No. 52

CURRENT NEWS - John H. Craig of Danville, Ind., only weighs 907 pounds, but hopes to pick up a few hundred as soon as the weather gets cooler.

Governor Flower has had a lake named after him. It is a body of water near Saranac lake and has just been cleaned by the state authorities.

Miss Jane Kane of Chicago, who is going to run as in independent candidate for judgeship of a superior court, has secured over 3,000 names to the petition she will file with the election commissioners.

Miss Mary Hamilton, a lady noted for her good looks, has just started on horseback, en route to St. Petersburg, a distance of nearly 2,000 miles. She is accompanied by a groom, her coachman following by a train with the luggage. This enterprising equestrian feat was once performed by a lieutenant of dragoons, who came from Pottowa to Paris in thirty days.

Very few people know anything of the Indians in western North Carolina - the Cherokees. There are 1,200 of them, and they are increasing in numbers. They own 73,000 acres of land, and very fine land it is. Their chief is Still Sounooke. He cannot speak English at all. There are some native preachers and four schools, the government maintaining the latter. There are other Cherokees, but these are not included in the 1,200, as they live elsewhere than on the reservation.

GENERAL NEWS - It has been announced that the Corbott - Mitchell fight is off.

Secretary Carlisle has furnished a statement which announces the startling information that the treasury will be behind at least $73,000 at the end of June, 1894, unless something is done to divert such a calamity.

Judge Broom, of Orlando, Fla., has issued orders forbidding any one to publish or report for publication any of the evidence given on an important murder case now on trial. The Judge says he will send any one to jail for contempt to court who disobeys his orders.

Miss Nellie Bullard, of Waycross, Ga., a pretty young lady 17 years of age, has until recently been dumb. The cause of her being speechless was a cleft palate, a misfortune from birth. The change has been wrought by means of an artificial palate (?)duration, made of vulcanite and rubber.

Dr. McCoy, of Alabama, caused an excitement in Chicago by pronouncing the death of Marcus Conant to have been from yellow fever. Conant is a Massachusetts soldier who went from Mayport, Fla., to visit the Fair and who died suddenly after a visit to Libby prison. Other physicians were called in who disagreed with the Alabama doctor.

Bill Wade, a notorious desparado, rode into the town of Webb, Miss., armed with a rifle, a brace of revolvers and a butcher knife. He soon cleared the streets of everybody but J.M. Evans, a quite citizen who was sitting in front of his store. Wade opened fire on Evans, but the latter refused to be bluffed and returned the fire with such angering aim that when the smoke cleared away Wade was found with six bullet holes through his heart. Evans is seriously but not fatally wounded.

A sensational article is going the rounds of the press that Dr. Graves, the famous poisoner, was not himself poisoned as per statements made a the time of his death, and in fact that he did not die at all, but that he is now at liberty in a land beyond the waters. The report goes on to charge high officers, who were members of certain secret organizations with Dr. Graves, of "fixing up" a dummy and passing it off and to the grave for the wily doctor. The rumor is strengthened by the fact that no one was allowed to view the remains and Mrs. Graves refusal to allow the body embalmed.

ITEMS OF INTEREST - Two clocks that have been in the possession of the Webster family, of Hartford, Conn. for the past century, are still keeping good time, never varying a second, it is claimed.

A wedding ceremony that took place in Washington City Tuesday contains romance involving James (?) Baxter, an architect of Chicago and the designer and builder of several of the buildings at the World's Fair and Mrs. Nellie N. Metcalf. Seventeen(?) years ago this couple was first married. One child was born to them, then they were divorced and each re-married. Within a few years their second partner in life and the children that were born to the latter unions were dead. Now they are again bride and a groom and have left for their future home in Chicago.

A Munificent Offering - One million dollars cold money will be given by Marshall Field to the museum, which is to be the outcome of the World's Fair. Mr. Field names conditions which be easily complied with. They are simply that $500,000 more be subscribed and that the stockholders of the World's Columbian Exposition subscribe to the fund $2,000,000 of their holdings, which represent an investment of $5,000,000, but they are worth much less. The biggest stockholders never expected to realize anything on their investment, and they have already expressed a willingness to turn over all the stock they have. The trustees of the museum have no doubt that a majority of $5,000,000 of the World's Fair stock will be turned over to them, as also the $500,000 to be raised before Mr. Field's munificent offering is secured; $100,000 of it has been unconditionally subscribed by Geo. M. Pullman. The balance it is said will be raised in a few days.

Chaplain Dead - Rev. Samuel W. Haddaway, chaplain of the House of Representatives and pastor of Marvin Chapel M. E. (?) South, is dead.

Compressed Air - Mr. Ferris, he of the wheel, proposes to make Chicago a seaport. He says that the chief item of cost in canals is the building and maintenance of locks, and that this can be avoided by the use of compressed air. "There is no reason why a box could not be constructed into which the largest ocean ships could be floated, the box closed, and the whole box - water, ship and all - raised by compressed air as easily as you lift an elevator." We have no doubt this is true. Dr. Gatling, who invented the compressed air drill, but was not allowed to patent it, has always claimed that there was practically no limit to the work that could be done by means of compressed.

Overtaken By Fire - Mr. James W. Whitehead and daughter, while on a claim in the Cherokee strip Tuesday, were overtaken by a prairie fire near H(?)sey. The mother placed her daughter on a pony. Before Mrs. Whitehead could mount her own the flames reached her and she was burned to death. The daughter escaped.

ASSASSINATED, Carter Harrison, Mayor of Chicago, Shot down at His Home. - Another crazy crank has done his dirty work and Carter Harrison, five times Mayor of Chicago, and one of the best known men in the West, is dead. The murder was committed by Eugene Patrick Prendergast, a paper carrier, who declared that Mayor Harrison had promised to make him corporation counsel and had not kept his word. This, he said, was the only reason for committing the crime. The only person in the house besides Mr. Harrison was his son, William Preston Harrison, 25 years of age, and the servants. About 8 o'clock the door bell rang and when Mary Hanson, the domestic, opened the door, she was confronted by a man about five feet, five inches high, smooth shaven, his rather keen cut features lit up by a pair of dark eyes. "Is Mr. Harrison in?" asked the man in a quiet, pleasant voice. "Yes sir," responded the girl as she threw the door open wider to permit his entrance. "I would like to see him please," said the man as he walked toward the back end of the hall. Mr. Harrison was in the dining room. Hearing the man ask for him he rose and stepped into the hall, walking toward Prendergast, who by the time he caught sight of Mr. Harrison had advanced about ten feet from the door. Without saying a word, Prendergast drew his revolver and commenced to fire. He pulled the trigger three times, and every time hit the mark. One ball shattered Mr. Harrison's hand, another passed into the lower right side of his abdomen making a wound that would have been mortal within a few days; the third bullet entered the chest slightly above the heart. This bullet was the immediate cause of death. Mr. Harrison lived about twenty minutes. The murderer made his escape from the house and made his way directly to one of the police stations and gave himself up. When questioned why he did the shooting, he would only say it was because the Mayor had promised to make him corporation counsel and had not done so. Prendergast is crazy beyond all question.

The vote on the Peffer free coinage amendment in the Senate was as follows: For free coinage 23 democrats, 10 republicans and 4 populists: total 37. Against free coinage, 21 democrats and 27 republicans; total 48. Six southern senators, Ransom, of North Carolina; Gordon, of Georgia; White and Gaffrey, of Louisiana; Mills of Texas, and Lindsay of Kentucky were against free coinage. If these six southern senators had voted for the amendment it would have carried, they all represent free silver states.

A correspondent asks who is this General Rosser? - General Rosser belongs to the class of '61 at West Point, the same to which belonged Col. Chas. P. Ball, of our own state. General Custer and many others whose names belong to American pride. The official record of the Union and Confederate armies are full of his deeds of gallantry. No soldier rose more rapidly, not even our gifted and mourned Pelham. From the time of his first exploit at the battle of Bull Run, when he commanded a battery of the famous, Washington Artillery to the very close of the h(?) war. His name amongst the soldiers who served under Lee Longstreet, A.P. Hill and Stewart Butler were synonyms of chivalry and valor.

Brother (?).L. Brock better known as Warwick has commenced the publication of a newspaper at Centre, Cherokee county. We wish him success.

THE COUNTY ALLIANCE MEETING AT EVERGREEN - ...After the opening services, conducted by brother Monroe Green the president announced the body ready for business. The committee on credentials composed of Brothers E.G. Rollins and J.A. Logan, reported twenty delegates present representing fourteen alliances. Before commencing the regular order of business a motion was made to adjourn until after dinner, and listen to a lecture by President B.W. Groce of the State Alliance, which was very interesting and instructive and appreciated by every one present...The following resolution by Brother Dake was read and after considerable discussion was adopted unanimously by motion of Samuel Pate as follows:...The following resolution by H.I. Honeycutt, was adopted by motion of Brother Dake, and from the discussion by the brethren it seemed that it was the expression of the sentiments of the people of the county...Resolution by Brother T.H. White as follows was adopted by motion of Brother Powell:...Vice-President B.H. Wells in a short speech dwelt upon the necessity of supporting the Banner, calling attention to the fact that those subscriptions that were made when this enterprise commenced would expire with the coming week, and requested all delegates to use their best efforts to get them renewed...H.I. Honeycutt, Secy Chilton Co. Alliance

SUNDAY SCHOOL CONVENTION - ...The convention called together by singing at 10 a.m. J. Bice conducted the devotional services, the Moderator and Secretary being absent. Nominations were in order: M.A. Wood was elected M. D. Pro tem; Sam Pate, Secretary pro tem. After which W.A. Mims, gave the welcome address...Morris Hill: J.P. Gentry, W.B. Scott; Pleasant Grove: A.J. Lee; Providence: H.W. Haldwick, J.M. Scott; Cedar Hill and Liberty Hill not represented. Misses Katie Crosbie, Ada Collins, Nettie Burse, Nettie Ogletree, Nancy Ogletree, Emma Ogletree, J. Bice, New Salem; M.D. Martin, T.J. Robinson, Miss N.J. Mims, Miss Mattie Green, Collins Chapel. Mineral Springs not represented. R.M. Hubbard, A. Glasscock, Macedonia. J. Bice appointed a Reading Committee. Moved to adjourn for dinner.
AFTERNOON SESSION - The convention convened at 1 p.m, opened by music and prayer by Rev. R.M. Honeycutt. Is it the duty of church members to take an active part in Sabbath school work, opened by W.G. Riggins, followed by J.M. Scott and others...Is it necessary to have a Sabbath school where there is preaching every Sabbath? Opened by R.M. Honeycutt, followed by W.A. Wood, W.A. Mims and others. What can we do to induce people to attend Sabbath School? Opened by W.N. Johns, followed by Alex Glasscock, W.G. Riggins, R.M. Honeycutt and others...
SUNDAY - The Convention was called together by music; W.A. Wood continued the services by reading a portion of scripture; Bro. Champ(?)y led the prayer "mark the perfect upright man for the way of that man is peace":, Opened by Bro. Riggins and others...
ESSAY ON WHAT CAN WE DO TO INDUCE PEOPLE TO ATTEND SUNDAY SCHOOL - "We can go ourselves, carry our children, have good lesson, make our school interesting, and its influence will reach out over the community and others seeing our faithfulness, will perhaps join in with us and help to carry on the good begin working we can get those in who claim to be Christians, if they have any religion at all, they will be interested, and will help to reach out after the sinner and the ungodly...Maggie Houlditch

GRAND JURY
Beat 1 - J.W. Sorrel, T.J. Collins, W.P. Cleckler.
Beat 2 - L.M. Langston, Thomas Harrison, S.A. Curry
Beat 3 - A. Patterson, Chas.J. Coburn
Beat 4 - W.C. Robinson, G.W. Jones
Beat 5 - L. Patillo, Riley Robinson, J.L. F(arr?), G.O. Logan
Beat 6 - E.(?). Smith
Beat 7 - George Patrick, Goodman Smitherman, John Letcher
Beat 8 - D.M. Martin, T.M. Cook, O.H.P. Wright
PETIT JURY - FIRST WEEK

Beat 1 - J.M. Mims, H.C. Young, G.T. Cleckler, W.L. Littleton
Beat 2 - D.B. Watts, W.H. Martin, John J. Green, J.L. Rasberry, G.B. Armstrong, W.W. Adams, J.A. Watson, J.M. Brantley
Beat 3 - Robert Williams, J.D. Glasscock
Beat 4 - Noah Littlejohn, W.A. Chandler, N.A. Kicker
Beat 5 - John Robinson, Benjamin Popwell, B. McGhee, Andrew Wilson, Elijah Robinson, J.H. Burkhalter, J.B. Wells, J.C. Alred, F.M. McCary, Andrew Howard, J.M. Robinson,Sr.
Beat 6 - James Popwell
Beat 7 - Robert Walker, Monroe Ramsey
Beat 8 - J.O. Butler, R.T. McGuire
SECOND WEEK
Beat 1 - T.J. Robinson, G.W. Mims, J.T. Mims, N.J. Maddox, (?).J. Bean, C.L. Glasscock, G.W. Littleton
Beat 2 - W.J. Brown, J.Henry, H.Z. Barnes, L.S. Sammons
Beat 3 - James S. Adehison, J.M. Honeycutt, A.F. Childress, W.D. Nix
Beat 4 - Aaron Littleton, Isaac Littleton, Wylie Littlejohn, H. Hardy
Beat 5 - L. Moore, William Callaway, Will Wells
Beat 7 - J.J. Hicks, T.J. Littlejohn, E.D. Smitherman, W.T. Hayes, Thomas Lawrence
Beat 8 - John Roberts, H.W. Butts, L.A. Friday, James R. Harris, (?).S. Eaves.

MORTGAGE SALE - Under and by virtue of a Mortgage deed executed by Mary A. Gibson to Bartley Martin on the 11th day of November 1890, and recorded in Book 23, page 221 of Mortgage Records in office of Judge of Probate of Chilton county, I will sell to the highest bidder for cash on the 2nd DAY of DECEMBER 1893, at the Court House door in Clanton, Alabama the following real estate to wit 85 and 81-100 acres of land in Fractional Section 12, Township 23, Range 12. This Nov. 1st, 1893, Bartley Martin, Mortgagee

TOWN ITEMS - Squire J.H. Gibbons of Randolph was in town Tuesday on business, he gave us a pleasant call and subscribed for the Banner; said he could not do without the county paper.

.
C.R. Bruce brought us some Rutabaga turnips and large potatoes planted the last of July at his place 1 1/2 miles north of here.

.
Saturday afternoon last the streets of our quiet town witnessed an affray between Mr. Wm. Connell and Mr. Wm. Headley, brought about by a difference regarding a debt due, so Headley claimed, by Connell. In the course of the dispute, Headley accused Connell of stealing some corn from him thereupon Connell cut him in his right side with his knife, before any further blows could be exchanged the parties were separated. Dr. Matthews was called in and dressed Mr. Headley's wound, which whilst painful was not of a dangerous character and he was able to proceed to his home on Sunday. Connell surrendered and had his trial on Tuesday, when he plead guilty to an assault with a weapon acknowledging he was somewhat under the influence of liquor at the time of the difficulty; he was fined $10 and costs which amounted to $26,25

.
Sometime in September at Mr. Joe Kicker's who lives two miles west of Coopers, one of his children a seven year old boy, fell with an open knife in his left hand, resulting in the point of the knife sticking in his left temple, which hurt him just a little while and then cured up and was supposed to be healed, about two weeks later, took with pain in that side of the head accompanied with fever, death ensuing in a few days. Death resulted from inflammation of the internal lining of the skull which was only slightly injured, but being

secreted internally probably excitement overheat or worry developed the fever and inflammation. No medical aid could have given the sufferer relief even at the first onset of the cut, as the bone is too thin over the part injured to protect the brain.

Last Sunday morning about 4 o'clock R. Ehrman's commissary was destroyed by fire, and owing to the fact that the fire had made too much headway before it was discovered all efforts to extinguish it were unavailing. The commissary and stock of merchandise were entirely destroyed out of the latter. Mr. Ehrman saved only eleven barrels of flour and some tobacco. The origin of the fire is unknown. Whilst the commissary was insured for $1,000 Mr. Ehrman will suffer a material loss, this amount failing to cover the value of the property destroyed.

Mr. Ira Campbell of Jemison paid us a pleasant call yesterday.

Prof. Gore has opened a school in the Lowe neighborhood.

We are under obligations to Mr. J.A. Logan for some very fine turnips of his own raising, Mr. Logan is one of the most progressive farmers of Chilton county.

Postmaster Garner is having his office filled up with lock boxes; when finished it will afford great convenience to the public.

Rev. J.S. Smith held morning and evening service at the Episcopal church last Sunday.

Mr. Potts is converting the old Marsh house into one of the prettiest residences in town.

APPARITIONS IN HISTORY - List of a Few Connected with the Names of Famous Men
Goethe states that he one day saw the exact counterpart of himself coming toward him.

Pope saw an arm apparently come through the wall, and made inquires after its owner.

Byron often received visits from a specter, but he knew it to be a creation of imagination.

Dr. Johnson heard his mother call his name in a clear voice, though she was at the time in another city.

Count Emmanuel Swedenborg believed that he had the privilege of interviewing persons in the spirit world.

Loyola, lying wounded during the siege of Pampeluna, saw the Virgin, who encouraged him to prosecute his mission.

Descartes was followed by an invisible person, whose voice he heard urging him to continue his search after truth.

Sir Joshua Reynolds, leaving his house, thought the lamps were trees and the men and women bushes agitated by the breeze.

Gilver Cromwell, lying sleepless on his couch, saw the curtains open and a gigantic woman appear, who told him that he would become the greatest man in England.

Ben Johnson spent the watches of the night an interested spectator of a crowd of Tartars, Turks and Roman Catholics, who rose up and fought around his armchair til sunrise.

Bostock, the physiologist, saw figures and faces, and there was one human face constantly before him for twenty-four hours, the features and headgear as distinct as those of a living person.

Benvenuto Cellini, imprisoned at Rome, resolved to free himself by self-destruction, but was deterred by the apparition of a young woman of wondrous beauty, whose reproaches turned him from his purpose.

Napoleon once called attention to a bright star he believed he saw shining in his room, and said: "It has never deserted me. I see it on every great occurrence urging me onward. It is my unfalling omen of success."

Nicolai was alarmed by the appearance of a dead body, which vanished and came again at intervals. This was followed by human faces, which came into the room, and, after gazing upon him for a while, departed.

NEWS OF OUR GREAT ORDER - Matters of Moment Which Concern this Order and Its Members

By securing a good cotton tie at a reduced price, Col. Duncan has saved the members of the Alliance in South Carolina $100,000 this season.

The great metropolitan newspapers which have been urging hotly the repeal of the Sherman bill are able only clumsily to conceal their contempt for their new and important allies, Carlisle and Voorhees. This is natural. The English people never did and never will really like that very distinguished American citizen, General Benedict Arnold, who undertook to render a great service to England. Even the beneficiaries of treason hate a traitor. - Pennsylvania Farmer

REFORM NEWS AND NOTES - Current Comment Concerning the Great Crusade Against Oppression

Uncle Sam will have to give Miss Columbus some plain talk. She has in three months spent $20,000,000 in excess of the old man's income. She may have to do without new clothes this winter. - Kansas Tribune

It seems the people of Nebraska made no mistake when they elected Senator Allen. A few days ago he spoke exactly fourteen hours and forty-five minutes in the senate against the unconditional repeal of the Sherman law. When he sat down his voice was clear and he seemed as fresh as ever. The roll was called several times during the speech, but he stood quietly waiting for the end of the roll call. The only nourishment he took was an occasional sip of tea. This is believed to be the longest speech ever made without intermission and for a wonder was a good one clear through.

ALABAMA ITEMS - A Careful Summary of the Week's News Served in a Brief Form
Master Robert Cowan, of Opelika, got his foot caught in the chain of a bicycle and three toes were very near severed from his foot.

The North Alabama Conference of the Methodist Episcopal church South will convene in the city of Talladega on the 15th of November. Bishop Duncan will preside.

Saturday of last week while Adeline Crittenden, colored, and her five children were crossing Claybank creek near Clayhatchie, Dale county, they in some way fell in and three of the children were drowned.

Commissioner of Agriculture, H.D. Lane and his clerks are preparing for the fertilizer season, and the tags are ready for delivery to dealers. It is anticipated that more fertilizers will be used in Alabama this year than ever before.

Congressman Oates, Capt. Joseph F. Johnston of Birmingham, Mayor J.C. Rich of Mobile, and Judge Wm. Richardson of Huntsville, are all prominently spoken of in connection with the next gubernatorial election in Alabama.

At Pine Apple the steam mill and ginnery belonging to J.N. Stafford was burned to ashes. The entire city came near being destroyed. The loss to the proprietor is about $10,000, without any insurance. The fire originated from the engine room.

Chairman A.T. Goodwyn, of the Executive Committee of the Jeffersonian Democrats, has issued a call for a convention to meet in Birmingham on the 16th of November. He urges a full attendance. The object of the meeting is for the purpose of naming the time and place for holding the State convention to nominate a candidate for governor and other state house officers.

Mark Montgomery, a negro mail rider between Alberta and Camden, this state, disappeared last week and search was made for him. The searchers found the mail bags in the woods, cut open. A day later Montgomery was found. He had been terribly beaten and was unconscious. His mind is clear at intervals and he says he knows who robbed and beat him. He says a white man did it, but he has not told yet who the white man is. If he continues to get better he will be able to tell all about the wiple affair. He says others were there besides the man to struck him. The mail bags were rifled.

The Banner, Vol. II, Clanton, Ala., Thursday, November 9, 1893, No. 1

THE REFORM MOVEMENT - Current Comment Concerning the Great Crusade Against Oppression

Horace Greely wrote more than 21 years ago: "We have liberated four million slaves, but we have fastened on the American people a monetary system that in its bondage is none the less cruel than chattel slavery."

"Shall we wait until there is an armed guard at every door?" said Patrick Henry in old Virginia's halls and the same question comes to us with equal force today. Shall we arouse and throw off the yokes from the people by the ballot, or shall we slumber on in financial security until all of liberty is lost? - Bulletin of Reform

Hon. Thomas E. Watson is still on the war path. The democrats of the state of Georgia are aghast at the enthusiasm of the people over his speeches. It is estimated that the number of people who have heard him at the last eighteen meetings would aggregate 60,000. His meetings are almost always opened with prayer, which is followed by the entire audience singing, "All Hail the Power of Jesus' name," or "Glory Land," and then Mr. Watson speaks for two hours or more. It is claimed that accessions amounting to thousands have been made to the cause in the last six weeks. - Ex.

Seven years ago Roger Q. Mills, of Texas, was a member of congress. In a speech on the 3rd of February, 1886, he said: "The agricultural states have suffered eighty times more than the silver states by the demonetization of silver, and would be benefited eighty times more by free coinage, and sir, by this infamous crime of 1873, the farmers are now suffering a yearly loss of $1,300,000,000." Now we understand that Roger Q. Mills is on the goldbug side. He was elected to the U. S. senate two years ago. Like John G. Carlisle, he has tasted of the Wall street fleshpots and is no longer on the side of the people. How much longer will the American people tolerate traitors? - Progressive Farmer

THE SITUATION IN TEXAS - The political warfare goes bravely on in Texas. Joint debates between Populists and democrats are going on in every part of the state, Harry Tracy and J.H. Davis being always ready to defend the People's Party platform against all comers, and the papers all admit that the majority in attendance at these meetings are Populists. The democratic papers admit that the next time Judge Nugent runs for governor on the Populist ticket he will be elected. A reporter attending the recent state convention at Waco says: " If any politician in Texas has been hugging the fond delusion that the Populists compose an insignificant party of malcontents, led by a game of demagogues, he might as well turn the phantom loose, for the state convention just closed has demonstrated to the satisfaction of every observer that the rank and file are honest, earnest workers for what they believe to be a great and noble cause. "—Virginia Sun

ALABAMA ITEMS - Careful Summary of the Week's News Served in a Brief Form
Mr. Hignett, of Limestone county, fell dead while laying brick on a chimney.

The Sheffield Standard will be issued about the 10th so says Mr. E.M. Ragland.

An East Tennessee passenger train was wrecked near York a few days since, Jim Everett, a colored fireman, was killed.

John Hutchinson, a Calhoun county citizen was held up in the public road near Anniston and relieved of coat, hat, boots and suspenders.

Will Blanton, a trusted employee of Drs. Davis & Davis' Infirmary, at Birmingham, was sent to the bank to make a deposits of $150 for the firm. He took the money and skipped.

Daniel Weymath, a young engineer at Coalburg, while returning home from a ball about 4 o'clock, accidentally fell into a heated coke oven. The oven had just been emptied, but the heat of it burned his clothing off and fairly cooked his flesh. He managed to get out and dragged himself home, only to die a few hours later.

At Troy, Charles Towles, a well known young man, while drunk, went to the house of Mr. Stallings, and tried to enter. The woman screamed and Prof. John Watson, living next door, rushed in and encounter followed which ended in Watson shooting Towles twice in the abdomen. Towles is expected to die. Towles says he thought he was entering his own house and did not know the difference until he was shot. Mrs. Stalling's husband is a minister and was absent from home.

R.H. Hughes shot and killed John H. Smith at Springville. The parties had a difficulty over a wagon and Smith told Hughes he was going to kill him. Afterwards, went into a store and got a shot gun, loaded with buckshot and went out through the store. When he got to the door he threw the gun to his shoulder with an oath and told Hughes that he had him. Hughes pulled a 44 Smith & Wesson revolver from under his coat, lying on his wagon. Holding his mules with one hand he shot Smith in the center of the forehead. Smith fell in the doorway and expired a few minutes later. Hughes fired two more shots, which struck the pavement. Hughes was released at preliminary trial. Both men were respected citizens of the community.

Wanted to See the Fair - Roy Longwell, who was serving a six months sentence in the county jail at Creston, Ia., and made his escape about ten days ago, has returned to the jail. He says after his escape he went to Chicago. After seeing the sights at the world fair he returned to serve out his term.

CRIMES AND CASUALTIES - John C. Poston, a well-known Smythe county, Va., man, fell into a hole of water and broke his neck.

The Alabama representatives who voted against repeal were Messrs. Bankhead, Cobb, Denson, Robbins, Stallings and Wheeler.

Senator Manderson has introduced a bill to protect the interests of the United States in the Union Pacific railroad... Next let us note what an Assistant Postmaster-General has to say regarding government ownership of the telegraph: " James W. Clarkson, Assistant Postmaster General during Harrison's administration, says: " The idea of private ownership of telegraph plants is as absurd as private mail service, " and asserts that under a postal telegraph 10 cents for 10 words to any of the entire country, and 5 cents for 10 words within a 500 mile limit would yield a handsome profit...

Rockymount Ripple - Mrs. L.M. Thames is visiting Oxmoor to see her new granddaughter, hope she will bring her home with her.

.

The little infant of C.L. Glasscock was buried yesterday; their loss was its gain.

.

Miss Metha Shannon, of Anniston, is visiting relatives in this community; she made the young men smile at her arrival, tho' there are not more young men in this community than are needed here, we don't want her to take any of them off, though we will let her stay with us.

Elbethel Echoes - Mr. S.R. Letcher, of Valley Creek, visited his best girl here on the 3rd and 4th.

.

Miss Mollie Reynolds and Miss Mattie Reynolds have been visiting friends.

.

Mr. James Sanderson and family of Welch's Mill, have been visiting relatives here.

Programme of Chilton County Teacher's Institute
A teachers institute will be held at Verbena on the 24th and 25th of November, 1893.
FRIDAY
9 a.m. Opening exercises. Music
9:30 a.m. Welcome address, C.C. Slaton
10 a.m. Benefits of Systematic teaching in the school room, J.L. Davis. Music.
11 a.m. Best method of training children in primary branches, Miss Lela Dawson
11:30 a.m. Advantages and disadvantages of classing pupils. W.M. Askins., Music. Recess.
2 p.m. Benefits of evening exercise on Friday., H.S. Estes.
2:30 p.m. School entertainment, Miss Geneva Jones. Music.
3:30 p.m. The art of writing, J.L. Ruffin.
SATURDAY
9:30 a.m. Punctuality on the part of teachers and pupils, H.L. Davis
9:30 a.m. Music.
10 a.m. History and Geography, H.L. Hicks.
10:30 a.m. Graded Schools., E.Y. McMorries.
11 a.m. Co-Operation of parents and teachers, J.W. Connell
11:30 a.m. The New Education, C.C. Slaton. Music . Recess.
2 p.m. Manner of conducting recitations, G.L. Spear
2:30 p.m. How to secure and retain the pupil's interest, W.C. Robinson. Music
3 p.m. The Word vs. A B C method. All the teachers.
The law requires all the teachers to attend the institutes held in the county.
J.W. Moore, Supt
R.E.R. Hicks, Chm.

TOWN ITEMS - Sheriff Moore paid a visit to (?)ewton on Wednesday and brought back Doc Wilkins, who walked out (?) court room during the last term of court before his case was called. Doc has a liking for wool, especially when on foot. Our opinion is that Doc will be pretty (?)ectually shorn before Judge Brew(?) gets through with him.

.

The Hotel Moore is being liberally patronized, several vocalist's (?) spending a few days with Sheriff Moore, they will probably go north 'ere many days.

.

The County Commissioners were in season this week. There was considerable discussion over public (?)ds, several petitions being prepared however but one was granted, (?)it runs through the Wilson neighborhood south of Clanton. The Maplesville, Hays and Clanton road has been continued. Mr. O.M. Mastin was appointed county surveyor. Several claims were passed upon, among them being three new pauper claims. By an unfortunate (?) the list of petit jurors drawn for the second week of fall term was a repetition of that drawn for the spring term for the same week. This error will not however entail any additional expense on the county.

.

The patrons of the public school are very generally desirous that Prof. W.C. Robinson be awarded the school.

.

Last Monday night a young lady made her appearance at Bro. A.L. Foshee's house near Goosepond, and insisted that hereafter she would make his abode her home. Our brother, hospitable and gallant like all of his name, took the young lady at her word and henceforth she will be known as Miss Foshee.

.

Mr. Hugh Foshee has succeeded in raising the hoss radish; he brought one into our office, grown from seed planted in August, that measured nine inches around and sixteen inches in length.

.

Mr. Frank Davis has returned from a visit to Coosa.

.

Mr. Ben Davis, of Beat 1 underwent a successful operation at Montgomery on Wednesday. The operation was performed by Dr. L.L. Lill of Montgomery, assisted by Dr. J.S. Johnson,Jr. of Clanton and was the removal of a fungous growth covering nearly the entire right side of his face. Mr. Davis is doing well.

.

Bro. W.A. Mims paid us a visit this week; we are sorry to say that his esteemed lady is still quite sick.

.

Our friends the county Commissioners Messrs. Robinson, Bailey, Glasscock, and Pate, have enlivened the Banner office this week by their frequent calls; we know they have been well cared for and they in their turn have well cared for the interests of all.

HONORING A GREAT POET, The Best of William Cullen Bryant to Be Mounted in New York - There is no sweeter name in the range of American literature than that of William Cullen Bryant, and in erecting a monument to him in Central park, New York, the people of the republic's metropolis are alike paying tribute to genius and doing a work that will call out expressions of admiration throughout the land. Before Mr. Bryant's death, which occurred in 1878, the sculptor-artist, Launt Thompson, executed a bust of the poet which was acceptable to him and his family. Since his death the bust has occupied a niche in the Metropolitan Museum of Art. It is now proposed to mount the bust upon a handsome monument in Central Park, New York. The monument and pedestal have been designed by Architect Ernest Flagg, of New York, and will be erected from the purest Italian marble. The cost of the monument and pedestal will be $30,000. On the monument will inscribed the titles of the poet's greatest works. The name of the poet will be carved on the pedestal, and underneath it will be the word "Thanatopsis," the title of his greatest poem. The life of Mr. Bryant was exceedingly sweet and pure. He was true to nature, and nature's simplicity is reflected in his verse. Between him and the great Milton a not unfavorable comparison could be instituted. While American literature shall endure the name of William Cullen

Bryant will shine side by side with those of Washington Irving and Famed Fer(?) (?)oper.

NOTES AND COMMENTS - Forty years ago a mulatto boy of Chatham County, N.C., was sold into slavery and was taken to Georgia. A few days ago he returned, a venerable-looking man and worth more than $500,000. His name was Nathan, and he was sold to a man named Toomer, who made him his body servant. He proved himself honest and faithful and enjoyed his master's full confidence. He served Mr. Toomer until his death, shortly after the war. His unusual intelligence, quick perception and good judgment gained Nathan the respect and esteem of all the white people, and he acquired considerable property. He then married the daughter of Dixon, the big cotton planter, and it is well known that Dixon left his large estate to this daughter. Last month Nathan's' wife died, and she left all her property to her husband. Nathan recently converted all his Georgia property into money, and will, it is said, make New York city his future home.

.

A New York exchange notes the fact that the treatment of cholera invented by Dr. Elmer Lee, of Chicago, and triumphantly demonstrated in the hospitals of St. Petersburg last year, has robbed the dread disease of most of its terrors. The process is the simplest thing possible. It consists merely in flooding the intestinal canal of the patient with warm soapsuds at frequent intervals, and thus washing out and rendering harmless the cholera germs, whose ravages are carried on in the intestines. By the use of this method Health Officer Jenkins of New York, has been able to save no less than nineteen of the twenty-two cases that have developed at Quarantine, reducing the mortality to 15 per cent. This is a wonderful achievement, considering that the ordinary death rate of cholera runs from 50 to 75 per cent, according to the violence of the plague. Since this discovery a person fortified with soap and water and a good syringe need dread the cholera no more than an attack of pneumonia or bilious fever. The disease has been vanquished and an American doctor did it.

.

The alligator business in Florida, Dr. Hugh M. Smith, of the Fish Commission, informs us, is on the decline for want of alligators. Formerly the capture of alligators brought many a dollar to the state. Hunting was as systematic as it was relentless. "It is within bounds to say," writes Dr. Smith, "that since 1880 not less that 2,500,000 alligators have been killed in the state, and it is not surprising that the supply has been greatly reduced in view of the more migratory habits, the remarkably slow growth of the animal, and the sacrifice of large numbers before they had reached the reproductive age." According to the observations of those who have studied the alligator, it is not more than a foot long in a twelvemonth. He is ten years old before he is two feet long. When he is twelve feet in length he has lived three quarters of a century. On the St. John's below Palatka alligators are rapidly diminishing. In the Indian River hunters are today at Cocoa, Melbourne, and Fort Pierce. Ten years ago 5,000 alligator skins in the season were thought to be a fair business. Today not half this number are taken. Kissimmee, on Lake Tohopekaliga, is the centre of the alligator hide business. In 1880 33,600 hides were taken there. It was not unusual for a hunter to kill a dozen alligators in a day. The business in hides seems to be centered in Jacksonville, but the receipts are rapidly diminishing.

Some Curious Superstitions - "Say," said Colonel Peter Sweeney of the Union Pacific the other evening to the Omaha Bee, just after the man he was walking up with stopped and picked up a pin that lay shining close to the curbstone, "Did you ever notice how many cranks there are in the world? Of course, I don't refer to present company - oh no, certainly. But I was just remarking on the curious superstitions that people get into their hands.

Now, for instance, you stopped just now and picked up that pin, from which I infer that you are in the habit of doing so whenever you see one. "Well, I know of lots of men who never fail to pick up a pin, the same at you do. Then there are the sidewalk cranks, who always step on each third or fourth crack, according to the width of the boards, or, if they are walking on a pavement, they step between and on the cracks. "After these come the stair cracks. They wouldn't tell it to anyone if they were asked about it, but the fact is that these persons always start upstairs left foot first, and feel badly if the right foot doesn't strike the top of the stairs first. These persons, I may remark, are usually those who have been afflicted with a seminilitary education, as are those sock and shoe cranks who put their hosiery and footwear on the left foot first...

T.T. Bell of Independence, Mo., while chopping down a large walnut tree a few days ago found a tenpenny nail nearly ten inches beneath the surface. Mr. Bell says he remembers driving it there while fixing a swing the beginning of the war - thirty years ago.

ANDREW MARVEL AND THE BRIBE - Andrew Marvel, a poet of some little fame, was chosen as a member of Parliament for the borough of Hull, in the reign of Charles II. He was a man of integrity and spirit, and such persons seem to have been rare in that reign. The Government, wishing to bring over to their side so important a person, and believing that a man of no fortune could readily be bought, sent the lord treasurer, who had been his school fellow, to see Marvel Danby, at parting, slipped into his hand an order for $5,000, and then went to his carriage. Marvel called the treasurer back to the garret, and then summoned Jack, his servant boy. "Jack, what had I for dinner yesterday?" "Don't you know, sir? The little shoulder of mutton you ordered me to bring your from the market." "Quite right, child; and what have I for today?" "Don't You know, sir, that you bid me lay by the blade-bone to boil?" "Tis so; very right, child; go away." Then turning to the astonished treasurer, he said: "My lord, do you hear that? Andrew Marvel's dinner is provided. There is your piece of paper; I want it not. The ministry must seek other men for their purpose; I am not one."

The Chocolate Tree in Trinidad. - We learn that J.H. Hart, Curator of the Royal Botanic Gardens, Trinidad, has recently returned from a visit to Central America, after having successfully transported thither no less than twenty-five thousand plants of Trinidad cocoa. In return he has conveyed to Trinidad two highly desirable varieties of the Theobroma Cacao, and two species new to that colony, and already numerous plants of each are thriving well. One of the varieties is a purely white-seeded one, producing white pods and splendid beans, which require only forty-eight hours' fermentation instead of the ten days usual in Trinidad. The second variety, known in Nicaragua as "alligator cacao" is peculiar from the soft covering of its pod and the raised instead of indented sectional ribs. The new species are Theobroma bicolor and Theobroma sp(?), the latter known as "cacao meco" "cacao mono" or "monkey cacao." - Scientific American

He Hadn't Changed. - Dr. Berrian, a former rector of Trinity Parish, in New York City, was an indifferent preacher, but a fine executive officer and a man of great personal kindlings. Whithal he was very simple-hearted. A country clergyman, half starved on a salary of five hundred dollars a year, came to Dr. Berrian asking his influence to get him a better charge. "Dear me!" answered the good old man; "I don't see why you young clergymen want to change so often. Why, I have been here in Trinity Church for forty years and never have thought of leaving."

An Ignorant Singer. - Catalani, a gifted songstress and a lovely woman, was the idol of society and the favority of fortune. But she had neither knowledge or culture, and her ignorance sometimes made her stumble into ludicrous mistakes. One of her greatest triumphs in London was the singing of "God Save the King." The town went mad over her rendering of the national anthem. Two hundred guineas were paid her for singing it once. But she always sang it "God Shave the King." At the court of Saxo-Welmar, she noticed the marked attention paid to a gentleman of majestic appearance. "Who is that?" she asked. "That, madam, is the celebrated Goethe," was the reply. "Goethe - Goethe?" asked the puzzled singer, to whom music was the only profession that brought celebrity. "on what instrument does he play?" "he is the renowned author of the 'Sorrows of Werther'," madam." "Oh, yes, I remember." Then abruptly addressing the great man, she said with fascinating vivacity: "Oh, sir, what an admirer I am of Werther!" Goethe, always sensitive to woman's praise, bowed, profoundly. "I never, " she continues, "saw anything so laughable in my life. What a capital farce it is?" "'The Sorrows of Werther' a farce, madam?" exclaimed the poet, coldly, annoyed that the most sentimental of his books should be thus spoken of. "Oh, yes," added Catalani, laughing loudly, "never was there anything so ridiculous." She was referring to a burlesque of the story, which she had seen acted. Goethe did not recover himself for the whole evening. Catalani's husband, a handsome Frenchman, was even more unintellectual that his wife - he was stupid. Once having found the pitch of the piano too high, she said after the rehearsal to her husband: "The piano is too high, will you see that it is made lower, before the concert?" When the evening came Catalani was annoyed to find that the piano had not been altered. Her husband sent for the carpenter, who declared that he had sawed off two inches from each leg, as he had been ordered to do. "Surely it can't be too high now, my dear!" said the stupid husband, soothingly.

The Banner, Vol. II, Clanton, Ala., Thursday, November 16, 1893, No. 2

ALLIANCE READING - Hamlin V. Moore, a veteran Alliancemen, is stumping Minnesota in the interest of the Alliance.

The Banner Alliance of Sacramento county, Cal., is located at Florida, and probably is the only Alliance in the state that owns the hall in which it meets. It has a membership of eighty. L.M. Landersborough writes; "We have gathered in everybody except those beyond redemption." - Golden State

We think that Mr. Bissell is wrong when he comes to the broad conclusion that because a man belongs to the Alliance therefore he is not a Democrat. We believe that a man can be a good Democrat and at the same time be an Allianceman. There are some Alliancemen who are not Democrats. Some of them are Republicans and some are Thirdpartyites, but there are some who are Democrats. - Newberry S.C. Herald and News

Postmaster-General Bissell made a decision that he would appoint no Alliancemen to office, but after an interview with Mr. Livingston, of Georgia, he has decided to reconsider his action. His is a very foolish move as there are just as good democrats in the alliance as there is anywhere, and no member of the cabinet should be so narrow-minded and prejudiced as to think otherwise, and we are sure that Mr. Bissell will so conclude. - Tuscaloosa, Ala., Gazette

Wanted to be President - Elmer E. Raub, a young farmer from Finney, Henry county, Mo., was arrested on his arrival in Kansas City, a dispatch having been received to the effect that he was crazy and had announced his intention of going to Washington to see President Cleveland. Raub was not violent and made not threats, but he said he had as good a right to be president as Cleveland had, and he wanted to talk with President Cleveland about the matter. If he could not be president of the United States, he said he ought at least to be president of Henry county, Mo. A police officer remarked to Raub, "There have been a good many men like you running around of late," and the would-be president replied, "Yes, and one of them shot Mayor Harrison in Chicago the other day."

The Queen to be Restored - Uncle Sam says that Queen Lillonkaloni's throne shall be restored to her. Hawaii, bye-bye.

A Very Old Coin - Levi Kinsley, of Ohio, it is said, has just unearthed a copper coin dated 1250, making it 613 years old.

CURRENT NEWS - Upon several occasions last week policemen were required to stand guard at the door to prevent admittance to the Sam Jones' services at Memphis, the house being packed to its utmost capacity.

Wm. E. Carlin, son Gen. W.P. Carlin, of the United States army; his brother-in-law, John Harvey Pierce, and A. Himmel Wright of New York, are snowed in at head of Clearwater river, in the Bitter Root mountains, and grave fears are entertained for their safety. Captain Louis M(?)iam has organized a searching party and are now looking for them.

Andrew Warren of Chicago, 80 years old, and said to be worth $360,000, has sued for divorce from his wife. He alleges that she tried to kill him with both knife and poison, and that she has been very cruel and has a passion for speculating on the board of trade. Warren alleges that his spouse has stolen money from him, sold his clothes, hay from his barns, trees from his yard; in fact, everything she could find to secure money from speculation.

Judge Parker Dead - Judge Richard Parker, who presided at the trial of John Brown, the noted abolitionist, and his accomplices at Charleston, now in West Virginia, and who sentenced Brown to be hanged, died at his residence at Winchester the last week.

ITEMS OF INTEREST - Samuels Gammel and Simms Gammel, of Hickory Flats, Simpson county, Ky., are probably the largest twin brothers in the United States. Their combined weight is 542 pounds.

Mayor Harrison's Will - The text of the will of the late Carter Harrison, of Chicago, has been made public. The value of the personal estates is given at $250,000, and that of real estate at $600,000, and the whole value of property bequeathed does not exceed $950,000. The sum of $10,000 is to be divided between two or more charitable institutions in Chicago for the purpose of endowing funds in perpetuity in such institutions in the name of his wife, Sophanisbe Preston Harrison. The estate is to be kept together and managed as a whole for two years. At the expiration of that period the estate is to be divided into four equal shares and distributed among his four children, Carter H. Harrison,Jr., William Preston Harrison, Mrs. Caroline Dudley Owlsey and Sophy Harrison.

Senator John P. Jones, of Nevada, has decided to cast his lot with the Populists. Mr. Jones is a strong man, and earnest in every undertaking. - National Watchman

The fourth number of Bro. Brocks paper, the Sentinel, reached us on Friday. It is bright and forceful and hews square to the line. Cherokee county is to be congratulated on it possession of such an able advocate of the reform cause.

Oates made a fine speech in Congress in favor of free silver, but filed to back it up with his vote. It is not to be wondered at therefore that the gold-bugs are willing to make him their candidate. They won't care how a man talks so he votes with them. - Alliance Herald

The View has mast-headed Tommie Jones; this will be bad on Tommie this cold weather. Whether the View thus punished Tommie because he spent the surplus left in the treasury by Governor Seay, increased the tax rate, or for sending the troups to Decatur, we are unable to tell.

Bro. Whitehead, in the Living Truth, sets forth the self-evident fact that there will be a fight between the administrationists and the an(?)s in this State for the control of the legislation which will elect Senator Morgan's successor...

West Chilton Warblings - Prof. E.H. Hayse has opened his school at Macedonia.

Prof. John S. Waldrup will leave for the "Lone Star" State.

Mr. Jasper Greene has located near Macedonia.

Mr. Monroe Nix, of Macedonia, has moved near Pleasant Grove.

Rev. L.B. Pounds, of Maplesville, has opened a school at Pleasant Grove.

The Pleasant Grove community is on a real boom; one tract of land there that recently sold for $500 has jumped to $2000. Mr. W.R. Dawson has recently moved to that community. Others are wanting homes there. Mr. J.L. Waldrup,Jr. is preparing to move to Texas.

Mr. S.N. Waldrup recently took a business trip to Boston.

Mr. John Atcheson has considerably improved his residence.

Mr. J.P. Gentry is preparing to build a new dwelling house.

Mr. Mat Rasberry has returned from Etowah county.

Verbena Views - Mr. Singleton Posey died on the 5th of Nov. He was 81 years old. He was one of the first settlers of this community.

Mr. John Short reports potatoes that weigh six pounds.

Mr. Lewis Jones has a hog two months old that weights 6(?) pounds.

Energy Events - The many friends of Miss Jessie Gray are sorry to learn that she is quite sick with an attack of slow fever.

Mr. W.W. Grey and his charming sister, Miss Alice Grey, spent Thursday night with relatives near Energy and afterwards went to see his best girl at Big Springs; wish him much success.

Misses Georgia Thompson and Mary Johnson spent last Monday with Mr. Henry Daniels' family, and Mr. James Downs paid them a visit on some important business.

We are glad to see Mr. Virgil Courtney visiting Coopers' again very often. I guess he is reviving his case with his little Emma.

Mr. Ed Ganes and Eula Eardmus are renewing their old cases again. We hope to get some wedding cards soon.

Mr. Rufus Harrell and Noah Gardner paid their best girls a visit last Sunday. We are expecting to see them jump the broom.

There was quite a delightful party at the residence of Mr. Morgan Durden Wednesday night.

Miss Havana Burkhalter spent Thursday night with the charming Miss Ollie Stewart.

Mr. W.S. Gray visited relatives near this place last Sunday, and as it happened he got to see his best girl.

Hurrah for Wesley Billingsley and his best girl. I see wherein he is right in going to see her.

Home Hints - If there are any girls or widows that want to marry just come down, Mr. J. P. wants somebody to cook him one more ash cake. Mr. P. is a fine grass widower. When Mr. Edwards gets him a sulky he can sure ride, then look out boys.

Mr. Nestor Carter opens his school Monday next at Mr. John Atkins' old house.

Mr. E.M. Pitts is going to leave us all in a few weeks; he is going to move to the Cansie place, two miles west of Verbena.

Mr. P. is not the only one who wants to marry; Mr. T. D. would like to be happy one more time. I think he will have to call on some of the girls that have been riding with him in his buggy to help him fix it up, and somebody will have to furnish him a good old blind ox or something to pull his buggy; if they don't you will see him pulling it before much longer.

Announcement - In addition to the already interesting program of the Teachers' Institute, to be held at Verbena on the 24th and 25th inst., Dr. E.R. Eldridge, of Troy, Ala., will be present to delight the teachers with his able and instructive lectures. All the teachers of Chilton, as well as those visiting from other counties, will do well to be present. The teachers living at a distance are requested to come to Verbena by the evening of the 23rd. Much care is being had for the comfort and entertainment of all who respond to this call of our worthy county superintendent, and strive to make the Institute a success. Respectfully, C.C. Slaton

TOWN ITEMS - Mrs. Amanda Smith, residing near Kincheon, sent to this office on Monday a mess of bunch yams of her own growing. From four pounds of seed she gathered seventeen bushels. These yams grow without running vines or strings and bear from eight to sixteen potatoes to the hill. They are smooth skinned and are of fine flavor and color, somewhat mealy, and are altogether very desirable variety to cultivate. We understand Mrs. Smith will have seed for sale.

Sheriff Sedberry, of Elmore county, arrested on Monday night near Wetumpka Wm. Lodge, who was indicted at the full term of court, 189(?) for grand larceny. Sheriff Moore, being notified, went to Wetumpka and brought him in the county jail. Our readers will remember the abortive attempt to capture Lodge last July near Stanton, which was thwarted through the instrumentality of his wife.

Dr. Johnson has bought the St. Lambert Jersey full-blooded bull. This animal is only three years old. The doctor thought it from Major Gibson, of Verbena. Doc is nothing if not progressive and enterprising.

Saturday last the school trustees met and after an animated discussion on the part of citizens interested in their decision gave the public school to Prof. W.C. Robinson. In the discussion our friend and fellow citizen, Mr. J.R. Kemp, took the manly and public spirited position, putting aside all considerations whether personal or political, that the interests of the citizens and children of the township entitled them to the very best ability that could be secured. He set an example that all would do well to emulate.

We had the pleasure of spending a day recently at the residence of Assistant Lecturer Bro.

J.A. Logan. His farm bears abundant evidence of care and good management and progressiveness. Bro. Logan has been experimenting with various varieties of cotton and secured thereby some valuable data which will be of great service to his friends and fellow citizens of Chilton county. In the course of his experiments he has produced a very fine variety by crossing with the (?). He will have a specimen (?) thereof on exhibition at this office in a few days time. Bro. Logan's motto is "Excelsior".

We regret to chronicle the sad accident that befell Mr. Henry Wells last Friday whilst bird hunting. By the accidental discharge of his gun his (?) was badly wounded and it was somewhat doubtful if amputation would not have to be resorted to however thanks to Dr. Johnson this was averted. We are glad to say Mr. Wells is doing as well as could be expected.

Dr. J.S. Johnson went to Montgomery on Tuesday last and brought back with him Mr. Ben Davis, who is now under Dr. Johnson's care at his private hospital. Mr. Davis is progressing very favorably after his operation.

Final Proof Notice, NOTICE NO. 13,328, Land Office at Montgomery, Ala, November 11, 1893 - Notice is hereby given that the following named settler has filed notice of his intention to make final proof in support of his claim, and that said proof will be made before the Clerk of the Circuit Court at Clanton, Ala., on December 30, 1893, viz.: Nancy M. Culp, Homestead entry No. 21,808, for the n 1-2 of nw 1-4 of Section 36, Tp 21, north of Range 13 e. He names the following witnesses to prove his continuous residence upon and cultivation of said land, viz.: John Edward, Albert Wilson, Abram C. Mims, John L. Smith, all of Kincheon, Ala. J.H. Bingham, Register.

Final Proof Notice, NOTICE NO. 14,338, Land Office at Montgomery, Ala, November 14, 1893 - Notice is hereby given that the following named settler has filed notice of his intention to make final proof in support of his claim, and that said proof will be made before the Clerk of the Circuit Court at Clanton, Ala., on December 23, 1893, viz.: Isaiah L. Hicks, Homestead entry No. 21,727, for the S E 1-4 of N E 1-4 Section 2(?), Tp 21 north of Range 11 east. He names the following witnesses to prove his continuous residence upon and cultivation of said land, viz.: Thomas N. Lawrence, Jake Lawrence, John Lawrence,Jr., Charles Walker and all of Shoults, Ala. J.H. Bingham, Register.

SOMEWHAT STRANGE, ACCIDENTS AND INCIDENTS OF EVERYDAY LIFE - J.W. Garrison, of Flat Creek, N. C., boasts of a pig which has two heads, two sets of teeth, three eyes, two tails and six legs.

A woman named Marm Smeaton, residing in the suburbs of Cincinnati, although past the age of ninety-one, has within the last year cut four new teeth.

After a separation of sixty-four years William Shaw, an inmate of the Binghamton, N.Y. county farm, has been restored to his family. Mr. Shaw is reputed to be 105 years old.

A living curiosity is in the possession of Henry Gerbending, of Fort Wayne, Ind. It is a freak of nature in the shape of three kittens which are inseparably joined at the hips. There are three heads, six fore feet and only three behind.

Samuel Leffers, an aged resident of Moraine, N(?), who has been a great sufferer from rheumatism for over twenty years, has been entirely, and, it is thought, permanently cured by a slight stroke of lightning.

A horse fell down a well on the Bailey farm, in Polk County, Oregon, recently and was rescued in a novel manner. Straw was thrown down the well, and the horse tramped it and rose until he was able to climb out.

Three years ago, William Brown, of Lost Creek, Pa., walked down a mountain path to the Philadelphia Reading Railroad tracks just in time to have his leg cut off by a passing train. A few weeks ago he was on the same mountain, walked down to the same path, and at the spot of his former misfortune, he tripped and fell and had his remaining leg taken off by the same train.

The English papers tell the following story of a badly malformed lamb: Mr. W. Hewitt, of Harrington Mills, has a ewe which this spring yeaned a lamb that is certainly curiously and wondrously made. It has two eyes, both in the centre of the forehead and in a single socket, both covered with one eyelid. One ear is situated at the back of the head and the other directly under the lower jaw, near the hinge. It has no tail, but in the place of that very necessary appendage a fifth leg almost as long as the other four, fully equipped with hair, hoofs, etc. It was living at last accounts, being almost three months old.

A few days ago William Bell was released from prison at Birmingham, Ala., after having been convicted or murder, and sentenced to hang. He managed to get a new trial and proved an alibi through a Memphis man, for whom he was working when the crime was committed. It appears that the murder was committed by a man named William Bell, who very much resembled his innocent namesake. This man moved to Memphis after the crime, and joining the church, got so much reputation for piety that he became a deacon. The other night Mr. Persica, of Memphis, found a burglar on his premises and blew off his heard with a shotgun. It turned out to be William Bell, and the facts, which came out at the inquest, proved that he was the wanted murderer.

Edward Lane, a painter employed in painting the smokestack of a flouring still in San Diego, Cal., recently passed through a thrilling experience. He had painted half of the stack, 120 feet high, and had just been drawn to the top when the hook holding his platform gave way. He fell twelve feet, striking a guy rope with his legs, which he wound around the rope in a twinkling, but without effect. He fell again, dropping forty feet further, where he struck another guy wire, luckily catching it with both hands and feet. He held on pluckily, although considerably bruised on the breast and shoulder, until help reached him, and he was lowered to the ground. It was a narrow escape, but he did not appear to be especially disturbed over his accident and was at work next day as usual.

Mind-waves which strike separated friends at the same time and make each sit down and write to the other after six months or six years of silence are common enough. But the case of two brothers living in the South comes a little nearer the rarity of cases placed high in the investigations of the Psychical Research Society. It appears that recently Mr. McCrory of Oglethorpe decided at a certain hour on a certain night to visit his brother. who lived in Florida. It had been a long time since the two brothers had seen each other, and the strange part of it is at the very hour on the same night the Florida man had decided to visit his brother in Georgia. They both started about the same time and were both eminently successful, for each reached the home of the other about the same time and was much surprised to find the other gone.

A correspondent witnessed a strange duel on one of President Crespo's big cattle ranches in the interior of Venezuela. Two vanqueros, or cowboys, were enamored of the same dark-eyed Indian girl of the great Orinoco plains, and they decided to settle by a duel with the lasso which of them should take her to wife. A dozen fellow vanqueros assembled to witness the fray - The lovers soon appeared mounted on mettlesome mustangs, each with a long powerful lariat of tough cow hide. The were both experts with the lasso, and their horsemanship was a marvel. They approached to within forty and fifty yards of each other and then began to maneuver for a deciding cast. After several feints the lariat of the younger of the rivals, a handsome, sun-bronzed fellow from Carabobo, went whizzing through the air so swiftly that the eye could scarcely follow it. The other sank his spurs deep into his mustang. The animal sprang forward just in time to save his master from the noose, and as he did so the second lasso rose in the air and settled around the shoulders of the man who missed, pinning his arms to his sides as in a vice. He was jerked headlong out of the saddle. His successful rival drew him along hand over hand, half lifting him from the ground by the tenacious thong, and put a bullet square between his eyes. He then turned and rode directly to the camp where lived the cause of this barbaric scene. She mounted behind him and he came galloping back swinging his sombrero.

Career of a Famous Detective - Vidocq, the great French detective, was born in Arras in 1775. He began life as a baker and early became the terror of his companions by his athletic frame and violent disposition. At the same time he was a notorious thief, and after many disgraceful adventures he enlisted in the army. In 1796 he returned to Paris with some money, which, however, he soon squandered. Next he was sentenced at Lille to eight years' hard labor for forgery, but repeatedly escaped, and in 1808 he became connected with the Paris Police as a detective. His previous career enabled him to render important services, and he was appointed chief of the safety brigade, chiefly composed of reprieved convicts, which purged Paris of the many dangerous classes. In 1818 he received a full pardon, and his connection with this service lasted until about 1828, when he settled at St. Mande as a paper manufacturer. Soon after the revolution of 1830 he became a political detective, but with little success. In 1848 he was again employed under the republican government, but he died penniless in 1857. - Commercial Gazette

Pennsylvania Forests Disappearing - Dr. Joseph T. Rothrock, the botanist of the State Forestry Commission has been working for two weeks in the Licking Creek region in Mifflin and Center Counties, and finds that there are only about twenty-two cubic feet of merchantable timber to the acre in all that district of 180 square miles, which was once a great forest. Dr. Rothrock believes that his surveys and estimates will result in bringing the people at large to their senses regarding the destruction of timber and lead to better arrangements for taking care of the woodland. One of his favorite ideas is the plan of establishing forest sanitariums, such as the Adirondack region in New York, where the public may go for the health-giving rest. - Philadelphia Press.

The Banner, Vol. II, Clanton, Ala., Thursday, November 23, 1893, No. 3

GENERAL NEWS - Van Robert, a hotel keeper at Rush Till, Mo., has fallen heir to $600,000, left him by John Bennett, who died recently. Van Robert saved Bennett from drowning in the Sangamon river twenty years ago.

Capt. Tom Ryan, of Memphis, ran a line of steamers on the Mississippi. He was converted at one of Sam Jones' meetings, and ordered the bars on his boats turned into chapels. In one of these chapels he hung up Sam Jones' picture as his guardian saint.

At Memphis C.H. Van, an advertising solicitor, and his wife retired for the night in a folding bed. The bed, by some movement, began to close up. Mrs. Van started to leap out but was caught. Van was crushed so badly that it is thought he will die; at the least will be a cripple for life. His spinal cord was strained, and he is paralyzed in the lower extremities. The wife is also badly bruised.

Full returns, which will be but little changed by the official figures from all counties of Nebraska, give Harrison (republican) for supreme court, 72,597; Holcomb (populist) 65,307; Irvine (democrat) 37,654; Bittenbender (prohibitionist) 7,450. Harrison's plurality is 7,242; the populists last year carried 41 counties, the republicans 40 and the democrats 9. This year the populists carried 57 counties, the republicans 25, and the democrats 8. Nebraska's total vote is 17,500 less than last year, the democrats losing most heavily; only the prohibitionists gain.

A few days since, three robbers rode into the town of Milton, Oregon, and dismounted at the door of the Bank of Milton. Two of them entered the bank, while the third stood guard outside and held the horses. President A. Hopson, Cashier, N.A. Davis and Assistant Cashier William Hopson were in the bank at the time. The first intimation of the coming of the robbers was when two shots were fired by the intruders before making any verbal demands. Both shots took effect in President Hopson's body, inflicting painful flesh wounds. The revolver was held so close to the head of Cashier Davis that the concussion knocked him down. The robbers then demanded money of William Hopson. He handed them a tray containing $944. Taking this they left without attempting to get the cash in the vault. The noise of the shots spread the alarm, and within five minutes an armed mounted posse was in pursuit, but all traces were lost after a short distance.

Love versus Money - Douglasville, Texas, was the scene of a double tragedy Saturday night. Trinidad Romer, a Mexican, 30 years old; Julius Larinsky, a Polish settler, and the latter's daughter, were the principals. Romer was desperately enamored of the only daughter of Larinsky, and his suitor was favored by the father, but she had her choice in another of her own race in the person of Sorowski. Sorowski had little to offer other than his love, while Romer had much wealth. Not long ago Larinsky informed Romer that he looked upon his suit with favor, and that if he could arrange to put Sorowski out of the way he would give him the hand of his daughter in marriage. Shortly after Sorowski disappeared as if swallowed up by the earth. All was then smooth sailing for Romer, who yesterday was wedded to Miss Larinsky. At the wedding feast Romer became intoxicated and boasted of the fact that he had killed Sorowski and that he was abetted in his crime by Larinsky. This so enraged the newly wedded Mrs. Romer that she attempted to cut the throat of her husband with a butcher knife, and was only prevented by her father slipping forward and wrenching it from her. Believing that all were leagued against her, she turned her wrath from her husband upon herself and plunged the knife into her throat, which she cut from ear to ear. This crazied Larinsky, and, looking upon Trinidad Romer as the sole cause of the tragedy, he emptied both barrels of his shotgun into his body. The strangest part of all is that Sorowski, who was supposed to have been murdered by Romer, returned yesterday morning just after the double killing. He made the statement that he was hired about a month ago to go to Eddy, N. M. to see a man about a projected cattle deal.

PROMINENT PEOPLE - Ex-Governor Charles H. Bell, of New Hampshire, is dead.

Rudyard Kipling has applied for membership to the Society of American Authors.

Judge Richard Parker, of Virginia, who presided at the trial of John Brown in 1859, is dead.

Governor Russell, of Massachusetts, says he will resume the practice of law when his term expires.

Baron Koenigswarter, the Vienna banker, is dead. He was a popular philanthropist and leaves a fortune of $20,000,000.

"Mark Twain" looks old. His fuzzy hair is almost white and he stoops more than ever. But he can crack a joke with his usual grin.

Dwight L. Moody, the evangelist, is to conduct a series of revival meetings in Washington this winter at the invitation of several ministers of that city.

Senator Sherman's real estate holdings at Washington are rated on this year's tax list at $400,000. He is the heaviest individual taxpayer at the Capital.

William D. Howell, the novelist, is about to come out as an advocate of radical changes in the social system. He is even accused of decided leanings toward Anarchy.

Mr. Greenhalge will be the first Governor of Massachusetts born a British subject since governor Eustis, who was elected in 1823, and served until his death, in 1825.

The oldest officiating clergyman in the city of London, the Rev. James Jackson, Vicar of St. Sepulchre's, who took deacon's orders in 1825, is about to resign his living.

L.Z. Leiter, the Chicago millionaire, has notified the directors of the Columbian Museum that he will contribute $100,000 to the fund, provided the museum is built and retained in Jackson Park.

Geronimo, the once powerful Indian chief of the West, who made a great deal of trouble for the United States Army, is now a quiet and peaceful prisoner at Mount Vernon Barracks, an army post on the Alabama River, a short distance above Mobile.

The present Mayor of the town of Molliens Vidame, in the Department of Somme, in France, has held the office continuously since 1839, or for fifty-four years. His name is M. Trancort, and he is ninety-two years old. He possesses the vigor of a well-preserved man of fifty.

The will of the late historian, Francis Parkman, gives all his printed books relating to history, voyages, and travels, also his printed books in Greek and Latin and all his maps, to Harvard College. His historical manuscripts go the Massachusetts Historical Society.

NEWSY GLEANINGS - John D. Rockefeller has given another $500,000 to the Chicago University.

Rockymount Ripples - Sorry to say that Mrs. Candice Glasscock is very sick with fever.

Last Sunday week Mr. Tom Harrel starting down in a new well, fell and broke his leg and he is so badly injured that is not certain whether he will recover or not.

Mr. S.M. Avory, of Tennessee is visiting relatives in this community, we are very glad to have him with us, hope he will stay with us and hope he will stay some time.

Mr. J.A. Green's wife is better; her sore foot has got so, she can walk on it some, after suffering nearly four months.

Mr. C.M. Northcutt paid his best girl a visit the second Sunday.

Mr. A. C. is carrying the day with the Anderson girl, it is a case, hope to get an invitation to the wedding. I think there are several that would like to jump the broom especially the grass widows, look out boys that some of the old widowers don't beat you.

A.F. Northcutt and J.N. Northcutt carried their best girls home last Sunday, I see where they are right.

Messrs. George Moore and Charles Walker, residents of this county, were arrested on Monday on a warrant sworn out by one, T.N. Vallins, charged with conspiring together unlawfully to post and then to threaten to burn gin houses, so reads the warrant. The case was called for trial before Judge R.M. Honeycutt; but owing to the absence of county solicitor Hare it was late in the evening before proceedings could be commenced. Messrs. Moore and Walker both of whom are well known and highly respected citizens were very anxious for a speedy trial and declared their innocence of the offense charged. Solicitor Hare on his arrival had the charge against Mr. Walker dismissed for the purpose of using him as a witness against Mr. Moore. Thereupon Mr. Moore through his attorney Mr. W.B. Nolen's requested that the case against him be dismissed, on the ground, that, it being impossible for him to be guilty as charged, of conspiracy, necessitating the participation of two or more persons, hence, there was no complaint. The Judge held that this was correct and ordered the case dismissed. In this case no witnesses were examined or testimony taken, all the witnesses summoned, with one exception were present and Mr. Moore's attorney offered to admit his written evidence. We learn that Mr. Moore states that on the evening said conspiracy was alleged, that he was prepared to prove that he was in his wife's company the whole time. Thoughtful and absent minded persons will be cautious hereafter, for, if discovered in an abstracted condition, they might possibly be charged with conspiracy in Chilton county.

I have been a sufferer for the past fifteen years from headache, hardly ever missing a week until about two months ago Dr. Johnson gave me a powder while I was suffering which relieved me in a few minutes. I have not had the headache since. F.W. Denty This medicine is for sale at the Clanton Drug Store.

Call the Clanton Drug Store and make it your headquarters when you come to town. Dr. Johnson has bought out all the Drugs and Patent Medicines in town, and they can not be had only at the Clanton Drug Store.

TOWN ITEMS - Married on Tuesday, Nov. 21st at the home of the bride's parents Mr. Floyd Wilson, of Clanton, to Miss Lucinda Power, also of Clanton. Rev. A.C. Wells officiated.

The friends of Mr. Henry Wells will be pleased to learn that he is getting all right.

Mr. J.F. Sewell was released under a peace bond last Sunday.

County Superintendent Moore at Strasburg on Monday, after hearing the facts in the case regarding the public schools in this township, decided that the public school money be divided pro rata according to the number of scholars between the schools taught by Professor W.C. Robinson and Mrs. Bowden.

When you are visiting Clanton and get hungry call at Smith's restaurant near the Court House and get what you want good and reasonable.

Dr. A.J. Massey, the Birmingham Dentist will be at Clanton the second week of court. Office at Dr. Johnson's Drug Store.

Rev. James Henley, of the Protestant Methodist church died at his home on the night of the 17th in the 28th year of his age, his death was caused by an attack of malarial typhoid fever.

Mr. John W. Baker has made 2220 gallons of molasses this season working one mill. The children in his neighborhood will be amply provided with long sweetening this winter.

Mr. Jesse R. Jones formerly of Autauga county and a resident of this county for the past twenty years died on the 21st, aged 8(1?).

Prof. Robinson has 37 scholars attending his school this week, an increase of nine from the commencement.

All parties who wish to have their cotton ginned at Dr. Biven's gin are respectfully requested to bring in their cotton not later than next week. F. R. Goodgame.

Dr. J.S. Johnson's household has been enlivened by the advent of a charming little daughter. The happy event took place last Tuesday.

Dr. Johnson has bought a fine covered buggy. It is a model of comfort and convenience.

Will Hayes gave us a pleasant call Wednesday. Will looks happy and feels so. We think there is a young lady to credit for this.

Mr. James A. Dudley has been appointed deputy United States marshal for this district.

Mr. J.H. Gibbon and Mr. R.L. Davenport, of Randolph, were in town Monday and paid us a pleasant visit.

The dwelling house at Ehrman's mill, occupied by Mr. Charley Motes, was destroyed by fire today.

We learn that wages have been reduced at Bozeman mill to 80 cents per day, and at Wadworth mill 75 cents.

SOMEWHAT STRANGE, ACCIDENTS AND INCIDENTS OF EVERYDAY LIFE. - Farmer Cushman, of Chenango County, N. Y., thinks we are going to have a very severe winter, for the following reasons: Corn husks are very thick; hog's melt runs jagged; the breastbone of a May goose shows spots resembling the canals of Mars; the ducks are flying in U-shaped instead of V-shaped flocks, and green frogs are changing their skins and seeking springs for winter quarters.

A terrible ballooning accident is reported from Piedmont. An aeronaut named Charbonnet, who was married on a Wednesday, subsequently ascended in a balloon with his bride, with the intention of making a wedding trip in this manner across the Alps. The pair were accompanied by another aeronaut to assist in the navigation of the balloon, and the start was made under favorable circumstances, but in the evening, when in the vicinity of Ceres, north of Turin, something went wrong with the balloon. It descended with great velocity and finally struck the ground with terrible force. Charbonnet was killed, and his wife and the assistant were both seriously injured.

A mysterious affair is reported from Chillicothe, Mo. Judge Johnson died at that place the other day, at the age of 88 years. He was one of the pioneer citizens, and a man of great influence in the community. Before his death he had lain in a state of unconsciousness for a considerable time. Saturday night he roused up and said to those standing by that his eldest son Samuel Johnson, who resided in Colorado, was standing by his bedside, but would not speak to him. Several times the old man spoke into vacancy, as though some one was beside him, and finally turned over in his bed and died. The next day a telegram arrived saying that the son had died at the very hour that his father claimed to see him at his bedside.

Basgoa Guzuella is a Zulu who was on exhibition at the World's Fair. He left for his own country a few days ago, taking with him as his wife a fair American girl, who he had become acquainted with at a soda fountain over which she presided at the fair. He met the girl only a few times until he found himself head over ears in love with her, and she reciprocated the attachment. In a few days more they were duly married. The young lady has no relatives in the world except a brother in Texas. She is said to be thoroughly infatuated with her dusky husband, and is very anxious to get back to his native land with him. He has nine other wives there, but he intends to give them all to his brother without delay. He claims to be an aristocrat and of the immediate family of the king of the Zulus. His young wife will probably have plenty of time to repent of her choice after she has lived awhile in a Zulu hut and learned how women are treated in that county.

The Banner, Vol. II, Clanton, Ala., Thursday, November 30, 1893, No. 4

MEAN BUSINESS, A Business System Inaugurated by State Officers of the Alliance in Mississippi - State officers of the Mississippi Farmers' Alliance met at Tupelo last week continuing in session three days... The officers visited Verbena and were assured by the Commercial Club of that city, 600 strong, of their earnest cooperation. Agencies similar to that managed by B.G. West in Memphis are planned at New Orleans, Mobile, Atlanta, Birmingham and other suitable points...

DR. TALMAGE, The Famous Brooklyn Preacher to Preach in Birmingham - Rev. T. DeWitt Talmage, the world's most famous preacher, will lecture in the Winnie Davis Wigwam in Birmingham Saturday night, December 9th and will preach there the following night. The price of admission to the lecture has been put at the low figure of 50 cents. Every purchaser of a ticket to the lecture is given a free ticket to the sermon. This arrangement has been found necessary as there are fully 50,000 people who are anxious to hear Dr. Talmage preach. Rev. W.A. Whittle, 2030 First avenue, has the matter in charge. The subject of Dr. Talmage's lecture is " Bright and Happy Homes ". When the famous orator was in Birmingham before $1.50 was charged for admission to the lecture alone. Excursions will be run on all roads entering Birmingham. It is estimated that the Winnie Davis Wigwam will hold 8,000 people and it will doubtless be packed on this occasion.

Proclaimed a Prince - Prince Pedro has been proclaimed Prince emperor of Brazil.

Extract from Senator Morgan's speech on repeal: " The President of the United States will not have driven a majority of the Democrats in this chamber into this corner and have compelled them into this unfortunate condition - where the Senator from Ohio has exercised the power, it seems, of marking out what we shall do or what shall be done by the majority of this body - that would not have occurred, if the president did not have his face set cast free silver...

The General Master Workman of the Knights of Labor, Terence V. Powderly, has resigned. Bro. J.R. Sovereign, State Master that Workman, of Iowa, has been elected in his stead. The members of the order throughout the world will learn with regret of Brother Powderly's action, mingled with feelings of gratitude to the brother who has so ably for the past fifteen years espoused their cause and administered his office. His administration has been characterized by honesty of propose and he has won the esteem and admiration of all men without distinction of class, by his constancy to the cause of labor, his sincerity and conservatism.

GRAND JURY REPORT - To the Hon. N.D. Denson Judge of the Fifth Judicial Circuit: We, the Grand Jury empanelled by your Honor at this term of the court, beg leave to submit the following report: We have inquired into the violations of the law in county, and as a result of our investigations have returned eighteen true bills; the books of our county officials we find well kept generally, those of the circuit clerk especially neat... There are ten inmates of our county poor house, nine white and one black, it affords us much pleasure that investigation shows that these unfortunate ones are made comfortable in every way by the efficient manager Mr. Quigley. Having discharged our duties to the best of poor one ability, and thanking your Honor for the clear charge given us, Solicitor Brewer, for his able cooperation and Mr. Chesnutt our bailiff, for his prompt and courteous attention, we now respectfully ask to be finally discharged. Thomas Harrisson, Foreman.

REPORT OF TEACHERS' INSTITUTE - At 10 a.m. the Institute was called to order by county Superintendent J. W. Moore. Prayer by Rev. S J. Jennings. H.F. Estes was elected secretary. Teachers in attendance were, C.C. Slaton, W.N. Askins, B.F. Calloway, J.W. Connell, H.L. Davis, M.S. Garner, S.J. Jennings, J.B. Knight, J.L. Ruffin, R.Q. Headley, R E.R. Hicks, W.C. Robinson, C. Mullins, A.N. Wilson, R.J. Anderson, J.L. McDonald, D.S. Robinson, Miss Etta Moore, Miss C.M. Slaton, Miss Evelyn Caffee, Miss Lela Dawson and Mrs. M. Bowden. At 10:20 a.m. C.C. Slaton delivered the address of welcome. At 10:45 Advantage and disadvantages of classing pupils. W. N. Askins followed by J.W. Moore, H.L. Davis, C.C. Slaton, H.F. Estes and S.J. Jennings. Adjourned to 2 p.m. 2 p.m. Benefits of evening exercises on Friday. H.F. Estes followed by J.N. Moore.1:30 p.m. Best methods of training children in primary branches, essays by Miss Lela Dawson, followed by J.W. Moore and C.C. Slaton. 3 p.m. Punctuality on the part of teacher and pupil. H.L. Davis followed by C.C. Slaton. 3:30 p.m. Old time school K. Wells. 3:45 p.m. Teachers institute and education, Lonnie Beard. Adjourned until 9 a.m. Saturday. Saturday at 9 p.m., the proceedings commenced with prayer by Professor J.L. Ruffin, R.E.R. Hicks and C.C. Slaton as executive committee, also J.L. Ruffin, R.E.R. Hicks and W.C. Robinson as committee on resolutions.8:30 p.m. Systematic teaching in the school room, R.E.R. Hicks, followed by J.L. Ruffin, C.C. Slaton and H.T. Estes. 10 p.m. J.L. Ruffin on teaching geography, 10:30 a.m. Cooperation of teachers and parents, J.W. Connell, followed by C.C. Slaton, J.L. Ruffin and B.T. Callaway. An adjournment was then taken until 2 p.m. when the subject of How to secure and retain the pupils interest was discussed by W.C. Robinson, followed by J.L. Ruffin, R.E.R. Hicks, C.C. Slaton and C. Mullins.2:30 p.m. The New Education, C.C. Slaton, followed by J.L. Ruffin...J.L. Ruffin, R.E.R. Hicks, W.C. Robinson, Executive Committee; J.W. Moore, Chairman; H.T. Estes, Secretary.

TOWN ITEMS - Rev. A.C. Wells has been compelled to forgo his appointments on account of the serious accident which befell his son Henry who is getting on favorably.

Last Friday Rev. A.C. Wells was called to officiate at the burial services of Mrs. Heflin, a daughter of Bro. Sidney Weldon, who died at Birmingham and whose remains were brought to Mountain Springs churchyard for interment. She leaves a husband and three children to mourn her loss.

The concert given by Mrs. Rainey and her pupils on Tuesday was well attended. The rendition of the very lengthy programme was excellent, and respected great credit on Mrs. Rainey. Where all did so well, it would be invidious to particularize but Miss Gamma Middleton's song " Pretty as a picture " literally brought down the house. She was bewitching in the part. Messrs Dunkin, Honeycutt and Wilson added greatly to the enjoyment of the evening, by their capital rendition of the parts assigned them. The concert will be repeated on Tuesday.

Dr. Johnson has established an infirmary, where those who need surgical and medical treatment can be accommodated. The Dr. has made arrangements with Dr. Stewart to have him attend to patients during his absence. The advantages of an infirmary are obvious, especially so in the treatment of cases involving extreme care in nursing, the dressing of wounds and other cases, which will readily occur to the reader. Knowing that the services of a skilled surgeon is always attainable, will enable many to avoid waiting for assistance in case of accident, for where practicable the sufferer can be brought to town and immediate treatment had.

Owing to the illness of Judge Denson, but few cases of importance were disposed of this week in our Circuit Court. Those cases unlitigated were postponed that the instance of the bar. Amongst the lawyers in attendance were ex-Judge Craig, of Selma; Col. C.S.G. Doster and Z.C. Abney, Esq. of Prattville; Messrs. Crum and Ray Rushton, of Montgomery; Hon. Walter L. Oliver, of Calera; Messrs. Peters, Wilson and Brown, of Columbiana, and W.W. Lavender, Esq., of Centreville, J.L. Beard of Verbena. The Court, immediately after the receipt of the report of the Grand Jury on Wednesday evening, adjourned over to meet next Monday, when the criminal docket will be taken up. The following judgments were rendered: FOR PLAINTIFFS: W.H. Merritt vs. Thos. Baker; Sarah Jane Myers vs. J.T. Bland; R.L. Sawyer vs. Louisa Crawford; G.O. Foshee vs. J.O. Rutherford; R. Ehrman vs. H.M. Mohan; Goetter, Well & Co., vs. E.T. Gullahorn; Henry Gentry vs. L &N.R. Co; W.M. Wilson & Bro. vs. W.H. Lowe; W.M. Wilson & Bros.. vs. W.S. Mims and Francis D. Mims; Gregory & Co's Lumber Company vs. William Walker FOR DEFENDANT: Moses Moore vs. L.&N. R. Co.

AD - Jas. L. Beard, Attorney-At-Law, Verbena, Alabama, Will practice in all the State and Federal Courts of Alabama.

MEDICINE COMPANIES AT LAW, Sued for Using a Trade Mark - An Important Case Decided - The trade mark lawsuit to enjoin the Chattanooga Medicine Co. from using the name of M.A. Thedford or M. A. Thedford & Company in connection with their liver medicine or Black-Draught has been decided by Judge Newman in the U.S. Circuit Court in Atlanta, Ga., and the suit dismissed. One branch of the case in which the Court was asked to enjoin the Rome Company from manufacturing a medicine said to be an imitation of the Chattanooga Medicine Co.'s medicine, has been appealed, and will be argued before the U.S. Appellate Court in N. O. in a few months...

The Banner, Vol. II, Clanton, Ala., Thursday, December 7, 1893, No. 5

FOREIGN AFFAIRS - The president in his message first alludes to the condition of affairs as he found them and their present condition and our relation with Brazil, Chili, China, the Congo State, France, Germany, Great Britain, Hayti, Honduras Liberia, Mexico, Nicaragua, Guatemala, Samoa, Spain, Turkey, Venezuela, Hawaii... This treaty I withdrew for examination, and dispatched Hon. Jas.H. Blount, of Georgia, to Honolulu as a special commissioner to make an impartial investigation of the circumstances attending the change of government and of the conditions bearing upon the subject of the treaty...

Hawaiian Imbroglio - A special from London says: Hawaii looms up here as a disturbing ailment. The Foreign Office is agitated over an appeal said to have been received from ex-Queen Lilloukalani. The dusky ex-Monarch asks for protection. She declares her restoration will probably be vouchsafed, and then that her relations with the United States will be restrained. Princess Kaiulani professes not to know of Queen Lil's appeal to Great Britain, but hopes it is true. Her opinion is, however, that it is the Provisional Government, headed by Dote, which has requested British aid in case American protection is withdrawn. There is anxiety over the Hawaiian appeal, from whomsoever it may have come. It is understood that very important communications have been sent to the commander of the British squadron on the Pacific, which may prove of momentous interest to the United States. Ambassador Bayard has certainly in informed of the affair, and has probably notify the Administration at Washington.

Powderly Resigns - At a meeting of the Knights of Labor delegates in Philadelphia the other day Grand Master Workman Powderly's resignation was accepted by a practically unanimous vote after that gentleman had stated to the convention that he had tendered it in good faith and that his action was final. J.R. Sovereign of Iowa, was elected to succeed Mr. Powderly, the vote being Sovereign 23, James Campbell of Pittsburgh 8, T.B. McGuire 1, Powderly 2. The vacancies on the general executive board were filled by the election of the following: C.A. French of Boston, H.B. Martin of Minnesota and J.I. Kenny of Omaha, all anti-Powderleyites.

A Republican Resigns - Secretary Carlisle has received the resignation of William Davis, the collector of customs at Natchez, Miss.

Another Political Party - W.F. Rightmire has issued a call for a conference at St. Louis, March 20, to organize a new political party. Rightmire called the conference in 1890 at Cincinnati, which gave birth to the People's Party. He was, until last year, a leading populist, but since then has opposed Governor Lewelling and his administration. He says Chairman Taubeneck and many leading Populists are with him in this movement.

A Liberal Proposition - Maj. R. Milsap, of Jackson, Miss., who has already given Millsap College, located there, $64,000, at a recent meeting astonished the friends of the college with another proposition of steel greater liberality. He proposes to duplicate annually any amount the people and church will raise, the only limitation being that he will give no more than $25,000 in any one year.

The article treating of gin burning which appeared in the View last week unwarrantably reflected upon our Probate Judge and upon the people of our county. For the purpose of refutation we here give a copy of the warrant: " George Moore and Charles Walker did conspire to postand to threaten to burn gin-houses. " This is verbatim et literatim a copy of the basis of the charge embodied in the article of referred to against Judge Honeycutt. What lawyer or what layman has not known that the above charges no offense? What Christian but would hesitate before he sought by inuendo thus to create a wrong and erroneous impression. In the matter referred to, doubtless Judge Honeycutt had more in mind his oath of office than the pleasing of the recently self-appointed censor, who for the nonce controls the View

Jumbo Jumbles - Mr. Eddie Giles of Jumbo spent Sunday with his best girl in the Poplar Spring neighborhood.

Mr. John McDowell, of this neighborhood built him a new rock chimney the other day, since its completion all of his cats have been missing, he suspects that they have been drawn up the chimney; the chimney has such a draft, that Mr. McDowell is afraid to light a fire in it. He is afraid the draft will draw all the children up the chimney.

Rockymount Ripples - Mr. P.B. Northcutt is clerking for P.N. Langston of Jemison.

Mr. Ben Veasey is building his new house near this place.

Preaching next Sunday by Bro. Crowson, on the third Sunday by R.M. Honeycutt; on the fourth W.A. Green, prayer meeting every Wednesday night.

Hurrah for W.H. Conway, a fine girl.

Died at Shelby, Alabama, November 10, 1893, Nalda O'Neil, daughter of Mr. and Mrs. Wm. M. O'Neil; aged three years and five months.

Editor Living Truth: - The egotism so salient in the life and character of Mr. Manning is no where so emphasized as in his letter to the Alliance Herald of November 24th, where among other things, he says: " In my opinion, no higher tribute could be to me than the general recognition of the fact, a fraction of our reform forces in Alabama was crystallized through our direct efforts. " It is true that Mr. Manning was among the first to organize the People's party in Alabama, and it is equally true that he had nothing to do with the origin of the party and presumes upon the ignorance of the people when he claims to have crystallized that sentiment in the state! And we are not aware that any tribute has been paid to him by a " general recognition " of his claims to this honor! His youth and vanity, perhaps, should be taken in mitigation of Mr. Manning's unwarranted claims! Mr. Manning now desires to repudiate his own pretended offspring by calling this child of his fertile imagination " a faction of the reform forces in Alabama " who are vitalized by the true principles of Jeffersonian Democracy! Mr. Manning certainly forgets. In his great hatred for the organized democracy he seems unmindful of the fact that Jeffersonians are but a mere offshoot of the parent organization professing the same creed and particeps criminis to the same class of frauds they now condemn. This party estrangement resulted from alleged efforts on the part of one faction to defraud the other in the conduct of a Democratic State Convention, and the only real issue developed was as to choice between democrats. Fraud was charged then and Mr. Manning says that fraud is now the supreme issue and the only one. Was fraud in elections the supreme issue when Mr. Manning placed Gen. Weaver in nomination? Yet Mr. Manning denounces as traitors men who where he stood in the fall of 1892. POPULITE

A JEFFERSONIAN CALL. - Headquarters State Executive Committee Jeffersonian Democratic Party, Montgomery, Ala., November 20, 1893.
In compliance with instructions of the State Executive Committee of Alabama, a State Convention is hereby called to meet in the city of Birmingham... A.T. Goodwyn, Chairman.

TOWN ITEMS - The criminal cases in the Circuit Court were as follows:
James Davenport, white, violating revenue law, forfeiture taken against bail.
William Bean, white, forgery continued..
Aaron Welch, col., carrying concealed weapon; forfeiture..
John Harwell, col., carnal who knowledge of a child, life sentence. An appeal was taken in this case to the Supreme Court.
Doc Wilkins, white, grand larceny, 2 cases, sentenced to 4 years imprisonment in each case.
Peter Jones, col., assault and battery, dead.
Dan Harris, col., selling liquor with license, not prosse.
Doc Wilkins, and other, forfeiture of bail in two cases $5 each.
George Edwards, white, assault in battery with a weapon, $250 fine.
Will Shaw, white, selling liquor to a minor, not guilty.
Willie Lodge, white, grand larceny, continued. Welch et als forfeiture of bail; continued.
Henry Hawkins and others, injuring domestic animals, nolpross.
Willis Martin, col., assault and battery with a weapon, nol pross.
William Jones, grand larceny, indictment withdrawn and filed, resisting an officer, same order.
George Mims, white, selling liquor without license, not guilty.
Willis Young, col., burglary, 3 years in penitentiary.
John Gibbons carrying concealed weapons, fined $50 and costs.
Dick Gaines, col., injury to animal, not guilty.
John Wilson, white, assault and battery, $50 and costs.
Jim White, col., Louis Love, col., George Reed, col., grand larceny 2 years in the penitentiary.
Louis Love carrying concealed weapons carrying concealed knuckles, two cases continued.
Melton Williams, col., assault to murder, 10 years in penitentiary.
Jim White, temporary use of property, continued.
Shugg Smitherman, white, G. Lacy, forfeiture of bail.
Joe Adams, col., grand larceny, continued.
Thomas Dungan, concealed weapon, not guilty.
Anderson Davis, public drunkenness, $10 fine.
Thomas McCullough, the court adjudged insane.
.
Bishop Jackson will visit- D. V. and officiate at the Episcopal church, Tuesday next.
.
A good butter cow - Mr. W.J. Gentry recently sold a cow to Mr. Joseph Gore, living near Cane Creek church, the cow milked three quarts producing half a gallon of good fine butter. Next!
.
An oyster supper will be given on Friday, December 15th, for the propose of raising money to a wire fence around the cemetery, this has long been needed and attention thereto, has often in called in these columns. In a case like this, we are assured every citizen assist, so let everyday attend the supper. The following ladies have the matter in charge, Mesdames

Hannen, Hester, Garner, Matthews, Merritt, W.H. Phillips and Stewart.

Married today, at the home of the bride's parents Mr. Louis Easterling to Miss Mahala Baker. Rev. A.C. Wells officiating.

Mr. J.B. Sellers visited his brother at Fayetteville last week.

Last Sunday morning Miss Mary Riggins residing at the home of Mr. J.M. Maddox, 4 miles west of Clanton, was found by the family to be speechless and in an apparently dying condition. Miss Riggins had retired to rest the evening before, apparently in the best of health.

LATE STATE NEWS - Jules Loie, of Mobile, drew $600 from the bank to pay a bill. After walking two and one-half blocks he discovered he had lost the money.

M. Echols, a medical statement at Mobile, had a diamond pin stolen from his necktie while standing in a crowd, a few days since.

The Birmingham Railway and Electric Company has been sued for $15,000 damages by Annie Clay, administratix of Jerry Clay, who was killed by one of the cars of the company.

Near Union Springs fire destroyed the gin house of J.L. Moultrie.

Will Farmer is to hang at Tuscaloosa for murder.

Mayor Joseph C. Rich, of Mobile, has announced that he will be a candidate for Governor.

Bridgeport's mayor-elect, Mr. Kilpatrick, has resigned. The office for the present is filled by R.A. Jones.

Albert Huffman, a young and well-to-do farmer of Autauga county, was cleaning out his well a few days since, when a bucket filled with water fell from near the top, a distance of forty feet, directly on the young man at the bottom. He was horribly crushed and lived only a short while after being taken out. Mr. Huffman was engaged to the well-known authoress, Alice Vivian Brownlee, and they were to have been married in the near future.

Samuel J. Anderson, of Sulphur Springs, lost $50 while in Chattanooga a few days since, no trace of which has been found.

Some excitement has been created in colored circles, in Birmingham, by an individual who has recently circulated among them as an Indian chief and has cost some of the credulous some money. Felix Drew is the name he is said to have given. He was a dark skinned man, such as a Mexican might look like. He told the negroes that an Indian chief had given him $50,000 with which to export free to the Cherokee strip any Alabama colored folks who felt like going and did not like the bad treatment they were getting at home. In this manner Felix circulated around and picked up several dollars. He told his victims that he was arranging a grand excursion to carry them all at once. Eventually his game played out and he left.

The sheriff of Greene county has offered a reward of $100 for the arrest of Armistead Rice, who killed Burrell Kimbrough in that county in November.

M.H. Stewart, a conductor on the Georgia Pacific railroad, was killed while coupling cars at Corona. He was caught between the bumpers.

Geo. M. Yielding, a citizen of Blount county, was badly injured by being run over by a wagon.

Miss Hettie Bradley, of Oregon, was thrown from a wagon and quite badly bruised.

E.L.C. Ward is now sole proprietor of the Bridgeport News.

The following officers were elected at the late election in Midland City: Mayor, J.E. Peters; councilmen, W.W. Preston, W.H. Gilbert, G.W. Kelley, Sheperd Kennedy, H.C. Copeland; clerk and treasurer, R.H. Walling; marshal, J.W. McKinney.

Fire destroyed the gin, five bales of cotton and about 500 bushels of cotseed, on what is known as the John Cross place, near Huntsville. It is supposed republic was caused by a match in the cotton.

Dave Jones, a citizen of Florence, sold his saloon, and put between $1,600 and $1,700 in his coat pocket, hung his coat up in the rear of the bar. He still has the coat, but is wondering who has the money. He was on a trade for a farm, but will for the present have to forego the pleasure of making such purchase.

Two gins were burned in Marshall county during the past week. One was set on fire by drunken rowdies. The other originated from a pistol cartridge, which passed through the gin.

A little son of Mr. and Mrs. S.V. Bynum of Blount county, drank some lye through mistake a few weeks since, and was so badly injured that he has since died.

Henry Pope Taliaferro, of Mobile, was accidentally shot with his own gun, while out hunting a few days since, from the effects of which he died.

The little village of Orrville, twenty miles from Selma, is shrouded in gloom over the death of Miss Maggie Lou Mosely, one of the brightest young ladies of Dallas county. On last Friday evening Miss Mosely and a young friend passed so close to a burning fence that the dress of her friend caught on fire. Miss Mosely attempted to put the fire out when her own dress became ignited and she was burned almost to a crisp before assistance could reach her. She lingered for several hours before death relieved her of her sufferings.

About five weeks since three barns belonging to A.H. Simpson, of Calhoun county, were burned and his gin house was saved only by heroic efforts. All this was the work of the incendiaries. A week or two later the gin house of Tom Clements in the same neighborhood was fired, but was discovered in time to save from destruction. Of late hogs, cows, corn, potatoes and many other things have been made only with and numerous residences broken into and robbed. Suspicion pointed to a family of negroes make Bush as the guilty parties, and a detective was put to work on the cases. Abundance of evidence was secured, and Mitch Bush and his two sons, Mackey Bush and Fate Bush, were arrested under warrants charging them with setting fire to Mr. Simpson's barns and gin house. Sam, another of old man Mitch's sons, was wanted, but he escaped. There is believed to exist an organized gang of negro thieves and house burners, of which Mitch Bush is the leader, and their depredations have been going on for many years. The Bushes and their allies are threatening to burn every house in the valley if not left alone, and serious trouble may result.

Charles A. Patterson, a prominent citizen of Selma, is dead.

Mr. Thomas Weathers, one of the most highly respected citizens of Barbour county, was almost instantly killed the past week. Mr. Weathers was standing by his buggy when his horse became frightened and he was thrown against a tree with the above stated result.

Mitchell H. Marshall, a forger who bores with a big anger, and wanted in Cincinnati has been arrested in Huntsville. The facts appear to be as follows: a telegram was received from the office at Nashville giving a description of the man and placed in the hands of the policeman. In the meantime a letter was received at Cincinnati from Marshall, postmarked Huntsville giving his plans of operation, which was forwarded to Huntsville, by this time the policeman having located his man, and at once made the arrest. The charge is that on November 20th Marshall wired from Cincinnati to B.H. Hudson at Birmingham, Ala., for $1,500, signing Norman Thornton to the message. The money was wired him on what seemed satisfactory identification. Later it appeared that the money had been paid to the wrong party, hence the finale as above stated.

The depot of the East Tennessee, Virginia & Georgia railroad at Vine Hill, a small station in Autauga county, was burned a few nights since. Adjoining the depot was the office of the Vine Hill Lumber Company. In it F.M. Frederickson, president of the company, had a room where he slept. Before he could be aroused from his slumber the office was in a sheet of flames and he was burned to death. The origin of the fire is unknown. Mr. Frederickson was a prominent and wealthy man.

In Chambers county, ten members of one family, that of Mr. Early Teall, were sick at one time. They all reported as improving now.

Dan Green, of Pike county, lost his gin house and twenty-two bales of cotton.

Miss Maggie Lou Mosely, of Dallas county, was so badly burned that death resulted in a short time. She and some of her schoolmates were standing around a burning fence when the clothes of one of her companions caught fire and in her attempt to put out the fire her own caught with the above results.

At the Galloway mines in Walker county, a young man by the name of Herron was killed by falling slate.

It is reported upon good authority that Stephen W. Noble and associates, of Anniston, will buy a controlling interest in the blast furnace at Bristol and will start it up in a few weeks.

Benjamin Micou of Anniston, has received notice of his appointment as chief clerk of the department. He is a son-in-law of Secretary Herbert, and one of the most popular and promising young lawyers in the State.

G.W. Tucker lost his dwelling house at Notasulga by fire a few nights ago. With it all his provisions. The loss is about $2,500; insurance $800. Mr. Tucker was a good farmer and a hard working man.

.

Dr. Wesley D. Wiggins died Monday morning at 10 o'clock at Oneonta. This will be sad news to his numerous friends as he was a splendid young physician, highly esteemed by all. He leaves a wife and one child to mourn his death.

.

Fire destroyed eleven cottages near Alabama Midland shops at Montgomery at 11 o'clock Monday morning. Three of the houses belonged to Mr. Booth, one to Mr. Lewis and the seven others to Mr. Nathan Alexander. All were occupied by negroes. A little negro boy is supposed to have burned in the fire. The department were powerless to extinguish the flames on account of low water pressure and the combustibility of materials in the building.

.

Troy was partly destroyed by fire Sunday morning, entailing losses aggregating between $50,000 to $65,000, upon which there is an insurance of between $12,000 to $15,000. It is thought that the fire resulted from sparks from an engine of the Alabama Midland railroad, which made their way into fodder in the warehouse of Joseph Bell, near the depot. The new Parker House was totally destroyed, with all its contents; loss $9,000, partly covered by insurance. The Court house was also badly damaged.

.

The market committee of Mobile general council met the other day for the propose of opening bids for the construction of the new market building at the intersection of Spring Hill avenue and Scott street. There were six bids opened as follows: M.T. Judge, $2,540; C.A. Chamblin, $3,197; Houston & Richards, $2,752; John McAdory, $3,100; Fincher & Fairlay, $2,870; Henry Teel, $3,325. A tower and the clock now in the guardhouse tower is to be removed to the new market building.

.

The residence of Mrs. Lazarus B. Parker, widow of the late Hon. L.B. Parker was burned last Friday night. It was located in the western part of Autauga county, and was a typical old-time family residence. Mr. Wm. Parker, son of Mrs. Parker, and family, besides a daughter of Mrs. Parker, occupied the dwelling with their mother at the time. The loss was complete, nothing being saved from the old home which had stood for many years a notable landmark in the community. Mr. L. Pattillo who was a guest of the Parker family for the night, lost his gold watch and other valuables in the devouring flames. The cause of the fire is not reported.

.

Mrs. R.L. Disharoon, living near Cedar Bluff, was burned to death a few nights since. She left the lamp burning on a bed post, it was overturned in some way, the bed clothes caught and she was so badly burned that she died from the effects.

NEWSY GLEANINGS - George Shorter, colored, died from the effects of a quart of gin, swallowed on a bet, in Washington, D. C.

.

Mrs. Mary Crosby, a poor seamstress, living at Springfield, Ill., has won a suit which entitles her to land in North Carolina worth $75,000.

.

The New Hampshire World's Fair building has been bought by General Charles Williams, who will present it to the city of Manchester.

.

President Cleveland's Thanksgiving turkey this year did not weigh so much as White House turkeys usually do. It weighed twenty-seven pounds and was shipped from Westerly, R. I., by Horace Vose, who has had the selection of a New England turkey for the White House ever since President Grant's time. The largest turkey he ever sent to Washington was to President Grant. It weighed thirty-six pounds.

HE ROBBED THE MINT, Henry S. Cochran, Who Stole Over $100,000 From The Government - Henry S. Cochran, who confessed that he stole over $100,000 worth of gold bullion from the government, has for forty years been employed as Weighing Clerk in the Philadelphia Mint. The vault from which the bullion was extracted was sealed in 1878, and not until it was opened recently was the theft discovered. Ever since the vault was sealed Mr. Cochran has been engaged in taking the gold. By means of a crooked wire he pulled the bullion bars from the top of a pile where they were placed crosswise like railroad ties. When they fell on the floor he would, by means of his little hook, pull the bars to the iron latticed door, the bottom of which was a little lose on one side. As the gold bars only weigh from twelve to fifteen pounds each, he could carry them home secreted in his lunch basket. His later stealings Mr. Cochran hid in a ventilator loft of the mint, and here the gold was discovered after his confession. Some of the gold he sent to himself at the net by express, and when it arrived he had it coined. When Secretary Carlisle's order was received ordering the coinage of the gold bullion in the mint, Cochran manifested great uneasiness, and even went to Washington and begged the mint authorities there to persuade the Secretary to countermand his order. This, they told him, was impossible, and Mr.. Cochran returned home. Suspicion was aroused by Mr. Cochran's course of actions and a detective was sent to Philadelphia from Washington. To him Mr. Cochran confessed his crime. $13,003.40 is the exact value of the bullion taken.

MRS. SARAH MINK, The Newly Elected President of the Women's Relief Corps. - Mrs. Sarah Mink of Watertown, N. Y., was elected President of the National Women's Relief Corps at the convention in connection with the encampment of the G. A. R., at Indianapolis, lately. Mrs. Mink is well known throughout New York State, having formerly resided in Syracuse, and latterly in Watertown, and having for many years been active in G. A R. affairs. Her husband is Major Charles F. Mink, who was commander of Mink's Battery.

Mexico's Ingenious President - President Diaz of Mexico is a hard worker, and has a hobby for collecting fire-arms of all ages and nations. He is a practical mechanic, having constructed all the furniture in his bedroom with implements of his own make, and many implements, including a new-fangled corkscrew.

The Banner, Vol. II, Clanton, Ala., Saturday, December 16, 1893, No. 6

LATE STATE NEWS - Geo. R. Cather, Alabama's weather prophet predicts a very severe winter.

Governor Jones has appointed Miss Laura C. Spaulding of Anniston, a Notary Public.

Miss Bessie Tarrant has been appointed Secretary of the Blount county Board of Education.

Mr. J.S. Dean of Monroe county, lost his dwelling and a part of its contents by fire last week.

A. Johnson shot and fatally wounded Charles Ellis, at Lim Rock. The shooting was in self-defense.

Mr. Eli Lide while returning to his home from Selma, was shot from ambush. It is believed he will recover.

It is reported that W.H. Cartwright, a revenue officer, was killed in a battle with moonshiners in labor Cleburne county.

Mr. Dave Munn of Florence has made a table which is certainly a curiosity. It contains twelve kinds of wood and 4,000 pieces.

Geo. Jones shot and killed Tom Hartsfield at Troy. Both colored. This was the fourth shooting scrape within one week in Troy.

Messrs. Whittle and Berger of Nashville will be in Birmingham this week to ride their bicycles against race horses for the world's record.

Capt. F. Watkins of Opelika killed four hogs a few days ago, which netted him 1,243 pounds of meat. These hogs were raised on his lot in the city.

J.F. Thomason, City Marshal, and E.W. Goss of Carbon Hill got into a fight a few nights since, in which Thomason received several severe cuts.

Mr. Henry W. Drake of Anniston was elected Vice-President for Alabama of the National Association of Letter Carriers, which met recently in San Francisco.

Mr. John A. Yother of Clay county, while trying to unwrap a belt from a moving shaft had his hand caught and his arm was torn from his body and thrown into the river.

Mr. Charles Fay of Prattville while attempting to clean a running gin, had his left hand cut off and his arm so lacerated that it had to be amputated just below the elbow.

The life of Governor Jones has been threatened by anonymous letters of late. The writer of one of those letters has been located and the Governor writes him a merited rebuke.

Mr. Dan Bradley of Russell county, lost his barn and stockade by fire a few nights since.

He lost 1,000 bushels of corn, and a large lot of fodder and oates. He saved his stock.

A few days ago Mr. Delaney Sanford, living near Maysville, Madison county, while running after a hog was seen to fall, and when his friends got to him, it was found that he was dead.

The saw and grist mill of Mr. Bell Harper, in Geneva county, was burned Tuesday night of last week, together with a lot of lumber, twelve bales of cotton and a large amount of cotton seed.

Charlie Davis goes to the penitentiary for life of assaulting a woman, and Marion Crowder's murderer, Rufus Reaves, gets a similar sentence. Both are from Tuscaloosa county.

Mrs. Mary McLendon of Henry county has received the sum of $1,868 as back pay on a pension claim, her husband having served in the war of 1812, and being entitled to a monthly pension of $12.50 during life.

On last Sunday Wm. Montgomery, an officer at Bessemer, in an attempt to arrest Wm. Sweeney, for disorderly conduct, was met with resistance and struck Sweeney on the head with his club, fracturing his skull. Two days later the wounded man died. Montgomery is under arrest.

Deputy Sheriff A.G. Gordon at Pensacola, Fla., shot and fatally wounded Alex Shelton, a negro desparado, who is wanted in Prattville, for the murder of a deputy sheriff of that place. Gordon held a warrant for the negro and attempted to arrest him. The negro resisted and the officer was compelled to use his pistol to protect himself.

Wm. Bankhead son of Congressman Bankhead has been honored by being elected President of the law class of Georgetown University, Washington, D. C. This is the second time since the war that this honor has fallen upon a Southern young man. The other time, two years ago, it was John H. Bankhead,Jr. The same family twice honored.

A hand-car on the Kansas City, Memphis and Birmingham Railroad was struck by a freight train in a cut near Adamsville, fifteen miles west of Birmingham. Three of the colored laborers on it escaped just in time. James Nelson got off, too, but got in front of the car, which, when hit by the engine, struck him and knocking him on the track the train ran over him Death resulted immediately.

Mr. W.T. Smith, of Richmond, killed a negro who had entered her bedroom Friday night. The fellow attacked her with a knife, when she made an outcry, but she secured her husband's revolver from under her pillow and killed him. It is said that the negro had three accomplices, who have been arrested. Unless they prove their innocence they will doubtless be lynched.

Monday night at Daleville, near Ozark, a house occupied by Mr. P. Beckham, his wife and seven children was totally destroyed by fire. At one time all of the family were safely out of the burning building except Mr. Beckham's little daughter Lizzie Beckham, 10 years of age. The oldest daughter, Miss Lura Beckham, 17 years old ran back into the building to rescue her little sister, when both perished in the flames.

In the circuit court at Bessemer, James Jenkins has been awarded $1,300 damages for the loss of the body of one of his children. The defendants were S.E. Jones, undertaker and the

Bessemer Land and Improvement Company. The company bought the graveyard property at Bessemer for the location of the Bessemer Pipe Works. The bodies were dug up by Undertaker James and removed to another place. In making the transfer the body of Jenkin's child was in some way lost - hence the suit.

Pension Frauds - The Pension Bureau has been notified that Dr. T.N. Thompson who was appointed examining surgeon of the Bureau at Sobetha, Kansas, has been for several months engaged in swindling operation in the neighborhood of Chattanooga, Tenn., and has suddenly left that section. The Bureau telegraphed that Thompson was dropped from the Board in 1890. Pension Bureau officials believe that another nest of pension frauds has been discovered at New Orleans. The character of the operations, it is believed is identical to that of the frauds at Norfolk, Va., and the newly discovered cases at Buffalo. A special examiner is now at work on the investigation.

A Man Is Sawed in Two - Robert Wyman, of Merrimac, Warren County, while engaged in sawing logs, was the victim of a horrible fate. A heavy piece of timber slipped from his grasp and threw him upon the carriage of the mill. Before he could recover his balance the carriage had taken his body against the big circular saw and he was cut in to, the saw (?).

GENERAL NEWS, Wholesale Summary of the News of the Week Gathered from Every Quarter - It is stated that Corbett will be arrested as soon as he arrives at Jacksonville.

Mitchell, the pugilist, will train near Jacksonville, beginning about December 28th.

The latest news from Honolulu is that Queen Lil can never be restored except by force.

Two hundred and seven men were examined before a jury was secured for the Pendergast trial.

Sidney B. Wood, a wholesale grocer of San Antonia, Tex., has sued the Bradstreet Commercial agency for $20,000 damages for the rating that agency gives him.

Joseph Jefferson and Stuart Robson will give a benefit for the starving poor of Chicago in that city next Friday. They will be assisted by all the dramatic talent in the city.

Morris Green was arrested in Chicago charged with running a lottery, and a bogus one at that. He claimed to be representing an Austrian concern and was reaping a harvest of $2,000 per month.

A Mexican named Pancha, 113 years old, and totally blind, was burned to death in his home near San Diego, Cal. He was left alone in the house with some cigarettes and matches, and it is supposed he set the place on fire.

D.K. Perkins, of Chicago, has offered to give $25,000 to Dary college, at Springfield, Mo. providing $75,000 can be raised from other sources, and he will increase the gift to $50,000 if an additional $150,000 can be secured.

Horace G. Allis, expresident of the First National Bank of Little Rock, Ark, and who has been on trial for several days, charged with violating the United States banking laws, has been found guilty and sentenced to the penitentiary for five years.

A bomb was thrown in the chamber of deputies at Paris, but happily without fatal results. The fiend who threw the bomb was a noted French anarchist, named Vaillant, who glories in his crime, and said after arrest, that he only regretted that his hand swerved and that the bomb did not explode nearer his mark. He claims to be the only guilty party, but it is believed he has at least three accomplices. The bomb-thrower lost his nose when the explosion occurred.

Striking it Rich - The new gold district in the Orgon mountains, fifty miles north of El Paso, Tex., is beginning to turn out some rich gold ores from nine different properties. Two ten-stamp gold mills have been ordered by Ernest Waid, who had purchased the Alabama Belle for a Birmingham, Ala., syndicate, and the other by G.W. Wood and W.R. Fall, of Las Cruces, N. M., owners of the Sunol. The camps now numbers about 200 souls and considerable development work is being done.

STRANGE STORY, A Freak of Nature by Which the Child Cannot Speak to the Father - Dr. George R. Hallewood of Birdseye, Ind. relates the story of a 10-year-old child of one of his parents, who cannot speak to its father, though perfectly glib with every one else. The cause assigned may be gathered from the following: Previous to the child's birth a difference arose between the parents, and for several weeks the mother refused to speak to her husband. the offense, whatever it was, was condoned, but not till after the child was born. In due time the little boy began to talk, but when with his father was invariably silent. It continued thus until the child was 5 or 6 years old, when the father, having exhausted his power of persuasion, threatened condign punishment for its stubbornness. This was inflicted, but without eliciting a word, though his groans told too plainly he could neither cry nor speak and that he vainly tried. Those present joined in the opinion that the prenatal effect of the parental quarrel made it impossible for the boy to speak to his father. Time has proved the correctness of this theory. Though on perfectly friendly relations with his father, attempts to speak to him elicit nothing but sighs.

Virginian's Election Returns - The vote cast for governor and lieutenant governor at the elections held last November in Virginia was canvassed before the legislature the past week with the following results: For governor - O'Ferrall, 127,940; Coke, 81,239; Miller, 6962; Scattering, 16. for lieutenant-governor - Kent, 128,526; Beverly, 78,916; Tyler, 6,658.

Waite on State's Rights - Governor Waite of Colorado in a recent address says that every State has a right to make its own legal tender and he recommends that Colorado enact a law making every dollar a legal tender, no matter where such dol-(?)

FROM JUDGE HONEYCUTT - Editor Banner - If you will allow me a little space in your esteemed paper I will give an explanation which I feel to be my duty to my friends and to the people of Chilton county... I remember while the Committee of the Grand Jury was in my office, examining the office and my books, that the contract which I had made with the Sloss Iron & Steel Co. was examined by the honorable solicitor Mr. Brewer and that committee... The reason why no money has yet been paid is on account of a debt contracted by the county under the contract made by Judge Callen with the Sloss company, by which the company was required to pay all the costs in the cases in advance...R.M. Honeycutt, Judge of Probate

RINGING LETTER FROM GRAND MASTER WORKMAN SOVEREIGN - At this time it seems eminently proper that some expression from me should be given to the members of our Order... At the recent session of the General Assembly, at which I was not president and at which I did not seek official position, I was elected to succeed Bro. T.V. Powderly as General Master Workman of the Knights of Labor...J.R. Sovereign, General Master Workman

Energy Events - That enterprising farmer, Mr. E.H. Smith, made 45 gallons of syrup, 300 pounds sugar and dripped 15 gallons molasses; this was the product of a half-acre of ribbon cane.

Rev. J.M. Dykes held services at Bethel church last Sunday when there was a large congregation present to hear the venerable preacher.

West Chilton Warblings - Married recently Mr. George Dawson and Miss Collins.

Married near Pleasant Grove by Elder W.G. Riggins, Mr. Clarence Childress and Miss Alice Dawson.

Mrs. Susan Davenport, Miss Bessie Davenport, and E.D. Davenport have gone to Texas.

Married on the 10th inst., by Rev. W.G. Riggins, Mr. Zeke Atchinson and Miss Victoria Franklin.

Messrs. Bud McCary and Jase Hayse have gone to Texas.

Mr. Jonathan Jones of Paragoned Ark., has permanently located here.

Elder Sutton Smitherman of Six Mile has recently been visiting here.

Dr. R.S. Jones of Six Mile was visiting here last week.

Elder L.B. Pounds preached a good sermon at Macedonia on the 10th inst., his discourse was timely and was delivered with great earnestness. Oh! for a ministry that will stand up bravely for the truth, regardless of popular opinion, titles or salary.

Miss Lena Moore, of Perry, will make that part her home for the future.

Mr. G.S. Rasberry will locate near Pleasant Grove.

Rev. L.B. Pounds has moved his family near Pleasant Grove.

Bozeman Bits - Bozeman saw mill is somewhat wrecked, they have cut mens wages to 80 cents which in August was $1.25.

We regret to announce the death of Mrs. Ivey who died last Monday at the residence of Mr. William Hayes.

Mr. James Connell and his two little daughters, of Birmingham, have moved to our flourishing little city.

To the regret of our young men in Chilton, Miss Jane May and Mr. Houston Glenn jumped the broom at the residence of the champion singer Mr. Robert May, on the 30th of November and spent Friday night in our town with Mr. H. Connells family on their way to their new home in Coosa.

Mr. Sam Gray and Mr. Newton Burkhalter spent last week with relatives and best girl here.

We regret to hear that Mr. John Lewis is very ill with an attack of la grippe.

TOWN ITEMS - FOUND - One pair of child's shoes. Owner can get them on identification by applying to Mr. J.B. Mar-(?)

Last Sunday morning the horse belonging to Mr. Pate Wilson took (?)ght and ran away with the buggy; the vehicle was smashed, but fortunately no one was hurt.

We are sorry to say that Mr. (?)ill Callen is seriously sick, and under the care of Dr. Johnson.

Married on the 7th inst, at the residence of Mrs. A.C. Ward, the mother of the bride, near Jemison, Mr. Geo. N. Honeycutt, to Miss Alice Ward, the Rev. W.G. Riggins officiating. The Banner (?)es for the happy couple a pleasant and prosperous journey through life.

The Right Rev. Henry Melville (?)son D. D. Assistant Bishop of the Diocese, preached a confirmation sermon at the Episcopal church Tuesday evening to a very large and attentive congregation. The sermon was impressive and (?) delivered. At its conclusion, (?)dministered the rite of confirmation to Mesdames R. Ehrman (?) Rainey. Rev. J.F. Smith, the (?)mbent assisted in the services.

Alex Shelton, who shot and killed (?)r. James Harris near Plantersville, the 3rd of April last, and for whom a reward of $200 was offered has been captured and lodged in jail at Pensacola, Fla.. Shelton, we learn, was badly shot before his capture was effected.

Senator Goodwyn, chairman of the Jeffersonian State Executive Committee, was in town last Saturday and paid us a pleasant call. The Senator says that the state convention called to meet at Birmingham, Feb. 8th will be the largest held in the state.

(?) Saturday night last, Messrs. (?)deus W. Wright, John Wright (?) Mr. Blunt Bazemore were (?) out of house and home; they (?) their entire all, nothing what-(?) being saved save the clothes (?) wore. On their behalf we ask (?)ance in this their time of dis(?). contributions can be forwarded to T.J. Lenoir, Lily or to Wm. (?)er of Maplesville.

Non-Resident Notice, State of Alabama, Chilton County, In Chancery, T.W. Robbins vs. S.J. Robbins, at Clanton, Seventh District North-eastern Chancery Division - In this cause it is made to appear to the register, by the affidavit of T.W. Robbins, that the defendant, S.J. Robbins is a non-resident or the state of Alabama, and that her place of residence is unknown to affiant, and further, that in the belief of said affiant, the defendant S. J. Robbins is of the age of twenty-one years. It is therefore ordered by the Register that publication be made in the Banner a newspaper published in the town of Clanton, once a week for four consecutive weeks, requiring her, the said S.J. Robbins, to plead, answer or demur to the bill of complaint in this cause by the 15th day of January 1894, or in thirty days, thereafter a decree pro conpreso to be taken against her. Done at office in Clanton this 12th day of December, 1893. W. K. Stewart, Register, R.H. Knox, Solicitor for Complainant.

ALLIANCE READING - The selection by the Executive Committee of the Maryland State Farmers' Alliance of Brother E.J.C. Parsons, of Longride, for Business Agent, is the best possible that can be made. It is proposed to send Brother Parsons through New York, Pennsylvania and other states to see about marketing our fruits and produce in the principal towns thereof. The plan for this will be printed in a few weeks. This means that the Alliance will now become what it ought to be, a financial help to the members. - Peninsula Farmer

ALL RIGHT, MR. GOULD. - George Gould, elder son of the late Jay Gould, says he will build no more railroads in the West until the people there treat the railroads better. We don't know what he means, but suppose he wants the people to use their bodies for cross ties and then he will have nothing to do but furnish the rails and rolling stock. There are two sides to this question. The people West and everywhere else ought to tell Mr. Gould and his kind that he can build no more railroads until the railroads treat the people better. The American people want railroads, but they don't want to give up both life and liberty to get them. Bankers can learn a lesson here also. If they propose to take all, as they have been doing, corrupt the government and stint the people, it will be "can we build more banks?" - Progressive Farmer

Southern Editress Dead - Mrs. Laura B. Foute, editress of the Gulf Messenger, a monthly literary magazine of wide circulation in the south, published at San Antonio, Texas, is dead. Mrs. Foute had made for herself an enviable reputation as a woman of brilliant mind and brave, self-sustaining character.

They Resolute - At Brunswick, Ga., at a mass meeting resolutions were adopted calling on the relief committee of the recent epidemic for a statement of receipts and disbursements, and exonerating correspondent M.J. Fagan, who had been accused of sending out a false report reflecting upon committee canvassers.

AT THE CAPITOL, Report of the Proceedings of the Fifty-Third Congress
IN THE SENATE
SIXTH DAY - ...Mr. Hill ac(?)escing to the suggestion of Mr. Hoar that the bill should be referred to the committee on privileges and elections...
SEVENTH DAY - The first gun of the inevitable parliamentary battle in the senate upon the question of the repeal of the federal election laws was fired today, and it came from one of the opponents of repeal - Senator Cullom of Illinois. Senator Stewart of Nevada, in a short speech, advocated the repeal of the election laws, and incidentally gave expression to some of his well-known view on the financial question. The resolution calling upon the president for additional information in the Hawaiian matter was laid over until tomorrow, in order that Mr. Frye of Maine might submit some remarks.
EIGHTH DAY - The Hawaiian question was again the subject of animated discussions in the Senate today. Mr. Blount's report was characterized as containing "not one line of unvarnished truth" by Mr. Frye of Maine, while Mr. Vest of Missouri declared that while he was opposed to the annexation of the islands, the restoration of the queen by force

would be an act of war. The resolution offered on Monday by Mr. Hoar, calling upon the president for further information in the Hawaiian matter, was finally referred to the committee on foreign affairs. The senate also listened with attention to a tariff speech from Mr. Morrill of Vermont.

In The House

FIFTH DAY. - ... Mr. Bland of Missouri moved to strike out the enaction clause, thus defeating the measure, and after an excited debate his motion prevailed...

EIGHTH DAY. - The bill for the admission of Utah to statehood was passed without division by the house today at the conclusion of the debate, the only amendments of importance incorporated in the enabling act being one by Mr. Powers of Vermont, prohibiting poligamy forever, and another by Mr. Wheeler of Alabama, reducing one-half of the land granted to the State for common school purposes. Just before adjournment the resolution of Mr. Hitt calling for the correspondence in the Hawaiian affair, amended so as to include an extension of the period to the covered by the correspondence to March, 1889, the beginning of the Harrison administration, was taken up and passed. It was expected that a lively debate would occur when the resolution was reported back to the house, but Mr. Hitt, the author, refrained from criticizing and there was no explosion. Mr. Boutelle of Maine, who manifested a disposition to speak, was taken off his feet by the motion to order the previous question.

Porterfield Gets Ten Years - For the past month Frank Porterfield has been on trial in the United States court at Nashville, Tenn. The past week he was convicted under ten indictments for violating the national Banking act while cashier of the defunct Commercial bank of that city. The judge has sentenced Porterfield to ten years' imprisonment in the Kings county prison, New York. An appeal was asked and granted to the supreme court of the United States, and a bond of $30,000 acquired, the prisoner to remain in the custody of the marshal until the bond is executed. Frank Porterfield was one of the most prominent citizens of Nashville, 52 years old, a prominent church member, of high social standing, a general favorite and had the unlimited confidence, not only of the people of the city, but in all towns of middle Tennessee in financial matters. Therefore when his make went to smash it caught people all over middle Tennessee and was a bad smash.

Distribution Of Pie - Up to date over 18,000 fourth class Democratic postmasters have been appointed by Fourth Assistant Postmaster General Maxwell. He could have made a greater number of removals than this, if Mr. Bissell had given him the full power he wanted. During the same period, Vice-president Stevenson when he wielded the axe had made 30,000 changes. The prospects is good for a great many more changes in the near future, as the time of incumbents expire.

Sugar Bounty Under Discussion - Mr. Harter of Ohio, has been talking to a number of democratic members of the house in regard to a change in the proposed taxation on sugar. " The sentiment, " said Mr. Harter, " is rapidly growing that the statesmanlike treatment of sugar will be to abolish the bounty and put a uniform tax of 1 percent on all kinds of sugar. It would save next year about $10,000,000 to $12,000,000 in bounties alone and put from $30,000,000 to $35,000,000 of revenue in the treasury. In other words, this change is expected to produce a net increase to $47,000,000 a year, which is greatly to be desired. "

Some Cotton Future Figures - Senator Bate of Tennessee, has arrived in the city from New Orleans, where he and Senator George have been acting as a subcommittee of the senate committee on agriculture in the investigation of the present condition of the market for cotton. Speaking of their work, Mr. Bate said the committee had succeeded to a great extent in getting all the history and modus operandi of dealers in cotton futures, and the investigations developed some remarkable facts, extending back to 1872, at which time the dealing in cotton futures was inaugurated in New York and New Orleans, which will be brought to light when the committee's report is presented or in the discussions in the senate...

In A Line Or Two - Vice-president Stevenson, Secretary Smith and Secretary Herbert visited the Augusta Exposition this week.

The contest on Senator Hill's federal repeal bill has been expected to furnish more genuine political talk in any likely to be under discussion during the present congress..

May Prevent Many Valuable Acquisition to the South - Several months ago A.A. Atkinson of Vermont, Ill., bought a small tract of land in Alabama upon which he wished to establish a ranch for raising Shetland ponies. With Mr. Atkinson a number of other gentlemen were coming, some to farm, some to raise stock and others to engage in different occupations, but all useful and desirable citizens, who would add materially to the prosperity of the community where they were to locate. It was Mr. Atkinson's intention to remain in Illinois until this winter, when he hoped to be able to remove his stock to Alabama. A few days ago he sought to arrange with the railroads for transportation, and here occurred the first hitch in the plan he had formulated. He was told by the railroad agent that he could load ten ponies in each car and send them as far as E. St. Louis. South of that point he would be allowed to put only five ponies in car, or pay the local freight rate, which is 68 cents on the 100 pounds. This was more than he had counted on, and he did not feel that it would justify him to pay that rate to remove his stock to the south. In his letter to a gentleman prominently identified with the development of the mineral district of Alabama Mr. Atkinson says that there quite a number of men in his section who will come to Alabama this winter if more favorable freight rates can be secured. The temperate climate of Alabama is much better suited for the stock business than that of the north, and besides, the stock can be kept up with much less expense there than in Illinois.

Statistics are said to show that young men do not, on the average, attain full physical maturity until they arrived at the age of 28 years. Prof. Scheller, of Harvard, asserts, as the result of his observations, that young men do not attain to the full measure of their mental facilities before 25 years of age. A shrewd observer has said that " most men are boys until they are 30, and little boys until they are 25; " and this accords with the standard of manhood, which was fixed at 30 among the ancient Hebrews and other races.

The Banner, Vol. II, Clanton, Ala., Saturday, December 23, 1893, No. 7

THE REFORM MOVEMENT - It was a lively sensation that Senator Stewart created the other day when he proposed a committee to find out how many Senators were interested in national banks. It was like throwing a bomb into that body. - People's Tribune

A press dispatch from Washington says: " President Cleveland is expected to announce in a day or two the appointment of Frederick R. Coudert and J.P. Doane, of Chicago, bankers, as additional receivers for the Union Pacific road. The government it is said, is much worried about the $30,000,000 claim it holds against the Union Pacific and therefore it is that they have taken steps to control a majority of the receivers.

THE LATEST STATE NEWS. - Gen. John B. Gordon is to deliver his former lecture on " The Last Days of the Confederacy " at Birmingham.

Thomas Allison, an old and highly respected citizen of Stevenson, Ala., committed suicide Monday at the home of his mother-in-law, Mrs. Frank Washington, about four miles south of that city. The deed was done with an old and seemingly harmless pocket knife; although the instrument of death was very dull, the determination of the man to die was so pronounced that he, with one slash, severed all of the large veins and arteries of the neck, and also the windpipe. The throat was literally cut from ear to ear. The dead body of Mr. Allison was found about an hour after the deed is supposed to have been committed, lying in a barn. Near to him was the open knife covered with blood. It is thought that the rash act was occasioned by financial troubles of which Mr. Allison had a great deal of during the past several months.

LATEST TELEGRAPHIC TICKS - Three children of John Peterson of Chicago, were buried in one grave, all having died from small pox.

At Dallas, Tex., a damage suit brought by Mrs. E.S. Randall against J.S. Randle for killing her husband last Christmas has been compromised for $10,000.

Fell Into The Grave - At the funeral of Margaret McLure, only child of the late Chief Justice Gibson, while the body was being lowered into the grave in the presence of a large gathering of people the undertaker, Alex Ewing, slipped and fell headforemost upon the casket. He was lifted out of the grave in an unconscious condition, and it is feared he will die.

Chicago's New Mayor - John P. Hopkins, democrat, has been elected Mayor of Chicago, to fill the unexpired term of Carter H. Hardson.

NEWS IN GENERAL - Jas. J. Corbett, has moved with his family to Mayport, Fla.

Gen. Eppa Hunton and Thomas Martin have been elected United States Senators from Virginia.

Robert Adams,Jr., ex-United States Minister to Brazil, has been elected to congress in the Second district of Pennsylvania to succeed the late Cha(?) O'Neill.

Dr. Wm S. Lawton, President of the Augusta and Savannah railroad, and brother of Gen.

A.S. Lawton, died at his home in Savannah a few days since.

The acquittal of Patrick Meehan from the charge of the murder of Robert McBride in the Fulton county, Ga., superior court concludes one of the most exciting trials that has been held in Georgia for a long time.

At a meeting of the Southern Cotton Yarn Mill in Augusta a committee to advance the interest of the industry in the South was organized. Temporary officers were elected as follows: O.H. Franklin, Union Springs, Ala., President; W.B. Moore, Mount Holly, N.C., Secretary.

Henry Dobson, Bridgeport Conn., until within a week an inmate of the alms house, has come into the possession of a handsome fortune by the death of his father in England. Dobson,, it is said, had partially completed a university course at Oxford twenty years ago, when he suddenly left for (?)

Joseph H. Johnston, banker of Birmingham, and Mayor Rich, of Mobile, have announced themselves as candidates for the organized democratic nomination for governor.

On Monday in congress Senator Peffer introduced a bill appropriating $63,000,000 for immediate use in relieving want and destitution throughout the country...

The general assembly of the farmer's Mutual Benefit Association met at Indianapolis Nov. 29, and unanimously voted to consolidate with the other farmers' organizations of the country. The following officers were elected for the ensuing year, and the assembly adjourned: President, C.A. Robinson, of Fountaintown, Ind.; vice president, A.B. Davis, of Garfield, W. Va.; secretary, W.F. Robinson, of Greenville, Ill.; treasurer, S.S. Gause, of West Liberty, Io.; lecturer, John P. Stelle, of Mount Vernon, Ill.; trustees, F.J. Claypool, of Muncie, Ind.; E.B. Parsons, of Marshall, W. Va., and C.F. Marks, of Jackson, Mo.

Mars Hill Murmurings - The school conducted by Mrs. Virginia Palmer is progressing nicely, and will have a vacation next week for Christmas.

Married on the 3d inst. Mr. W.E. Langston and Miss Julia Gentry; we wish them much happiness.

The prospect is good for another wedding about the 24th inst. in the persons of Mr. Ellis Scott and Miss Alice Gentry.

Welcome! Welcome! Hon. J.R. Sovereign, General Master Workman of the Knights of Labor...It is our indispensable duty to uphold this new officer in this grand work, with our prayers, out efforts and all that will give strength to the man who takes the place of T.V. Powderly. While I sorely regret Mr. Powderly's resignation, and feel as if one of the best spokes is out of the great wheel that moves the labor world, let us hope it is providential. Mr. Powderly's work will live for ever...Now let Mr. Powderly rest his tired brain and body...Should he, however, die today it will be an easy task, comparatively, for Mr. Sovereign to keep up with the blazes which Mr. Powderly has so carefully hewn out on labor's road..Mrs. Ira Campbell

SPELLING MATCH - A spelling match will be held at the court-house next Wednesday night, the 27th inst., between the married people and the young people. Admission ten cents, to be given to the cemetery fund. MARRIED PEOPLE. Messrs. & Mesdames W.E. Stewart, Mathews, Foshee, Nolen, Vauderveer, Hare, Mullins, Gore, Kemp, Sampey, Garner, McMorries, White, Merritt, Cestnutt, Evans, L.H. Stewart, T.S. Phillips, Blasingame, Sartor, Ehrman, W.H. Phillips, W.I. Mullins, Middleton, F.J. Davis, J.S. Johnson, W.M. Wilson, W.T. Callen, Mesdames Lillian Rainey, W.C. Satterwhite, J.W. Forsyth and Orrie Robinson. YOUNG PEOPLE. Misses Julia Hester, Mollie Hannon, Minnie Phillips, Gamma Middleton, Lake Phillips, Minnie Hester, Ella Gartman, Callie Watts, Ola McRee, Minnie Pinkard, Norma Thomas, Minnie Lloyd, Kate Bradley, Mattie Sue Chandler, Xyr Hunt French Evans, Mattie Wright, Gussie Allen, Nannie Duke, Venitia Vines, Ada Goodgame, Janie Goodgame, Belle Lowery, Maggie Moore, Bamma Moore, and Miss Delaney. George Lewis, Eugene Sartor, Tipton Mullins, W.W. Dunkin, A.J. Leonard, Tom Gullahorn, John Gullahorn and Sam Gullahorn, Evans Pinkard, P.D. Wilson, Joe Hester, Jim Hester, N.A. Kicker, Durword Foshee, Victor Vines, Henry Honeycutt, Caldwell McMorries, Leroy Watts, John Stanfield, F.N. Jones, Sid Blasingame, Harry Blasingame, W.H. Wright, W.H. Taylor, A. Culp, Frank Crichton and Reese Mullins.

TOWN ITEMS - All parties indebted to J.F. Goodgame for ginning are requested to make immediate settlement of same. In my absence J.W. Goodgame is my duly authorized agent to make settlement. J.F. Goodgame

.

Drs. Johnson and Stewart this week successfully performed an operation on Mrs. J.K. Henley, by opening a cystic tumor on her abdomen and drawing therefrom upwards of a gallon of pus.

.

S.E. Davis has the finest assortment of candies, nuts, fruits and toys for Xmas time to be found in our town.

.

Died Thursday December the 22, Mrs. Fanny Connor, daughter of the late Andrew S. Norris, of Elmore county, the beloved wife of Mr. D. Connor. The deceased was beloved by all who knew her. To the bereaved husband and family, the Banner tenders its sincere sympathy in this heavy affliction.

.

We regret to record the death of Mr. W.H. Brown, step father to our highly esteemed fellow citizen Mr. Hugh Foshee, which sad event occurred last Sunday night in the Lily neighborhood. The deceased gentleman succumbed to an attack of pneumonia, and his demise is mourned by a large circle of relatives and friends.

.

Mr. John Parnell, an old citizen of our county, died last Sunday in the neighborhood of Stanton, from a paralytic attack

.

Married on the 21st inst. Mr. Shelby Barnes, of north Dallas, and Miss Polly Latham, of Plantersville, at Valley creek church.

Tom Moore in Virginia - A correspondent who has been rambling through Eastern Virginia recalls a description given by an old lady at Norfolk of Tom Moore, the poet, who passed some time in his amorous youth in a quaint old mansion near Norfolk and found nothing there except the ladies to please him.

AT THE CAPITOL, Report of the Proceedings of the Fifty-Third Congress

EIGHTH DAY. - ...Mr. Blount's report was characterized as containing "not one line of unvarnished truth"by Mr. Frye of Maine, while Mr. Vest of Missouri declared that while he was opposed to the annexation of the queen by force would be an act of war. The resolution offered on Monday by Mr. Hoar, calling upon the president for further information in the Hawaiian matter, was finally referred to the committee on foreign affairs. The senate also listened with attention to a tariff speech from Mr. Morrill of Vermont.

9TH DAY. - ...Among the bills introduced the most important was one by Senator Voorhees, chairman of the committee on finance, providing for the coinage of the silver seigniorage in the treasury at the rate of $2,000,000 per month, and when that was exhausted the purchase for coinage of a similar amount of silver monthly...The resolution offered some days ago by Mr. Peffer of Kansas to rescind a recent order closing the senate chamber to visitors was considered...

12TH DAY. - ...A request by Mr. Chandler of New Hampshire for the reading of the instructions of Mr. Willis led to a debate of an hour's duration, and they were finally read. The message and accompanying documents are now before the senate, the pending question being on the motion of Mr. Hoar to refer them to the committee on foreign relations.

13TH DAY. - The debate which was expected in the senate today on the president's message as to Hawaii was averted by Mr. Hoar of Massachusetts, whose motion to refer the message and accompanying documents to the committee on foreign relations is the pending question before the senate, yielding to Senator Berry of Arkansas and to Senator Peffer of Kansas. The first named addressed the senate in advocacy of the bill to repeal the federal election laws, while Senator Peffer argued in favor of the bill introduced by him yesterday appropriating money for immediate use in relieving want and destitution throughout the country. Mr. Hoar stated, however, that on tomorrow he would call up his motion to refer the president's message and accompanying documents to the committee on foreign relations, and in all probability he will address the senate at that time upon the Hawaiian situation generally.

14TH DAY. - The Hawaiian question was disposed of for the present in the senate today when; after Mr. Hoar's argument, the message and accompanying documents were referred to the committee on foreign relations...Mr. Hoar presented and unique petition on the subject of good roads...

In The House

8TH DAY. - The bill for the admission of Utah to statehood was passed without division by the house today at the conclusion of the debate, the only amendments of importance incorporated in the enabling act being one by Mr. Powers of Vermont, prohibiting poligamy forever, and another by Mr. Wheeler of Alabama, reducing one-half of the land granted to the State for common school purposes. Just before adjournment the resolution of Mr. Hitt calling for the correspondence in the Hawaiian affair, amended to as to include an extension of the period to be covered by the correspondence to March, 1889, the beginning of the Harrison administration, was taken up and passed. It was expected that a lively debate would occur when this resolution was reported back to the house, but Mr. Hitt, the author, refrained from criticizing and there was no explosion. Mr. Boutelle of Maine, who manifested a disposition to speak, was taken off his feet by the motion to order the previous question.

11TH DAY. - ...Under the lead of Mr. Cannon an assault was made against Mr. Cleveland's pension policy, especially that portion of it which resulted in the revocation of order 164 and the subsequent suspension of thousands of pensioners. Mr. Livingston of Georgia and Mr. Euloe of Tennessee defended the administration, and Mr. Lacy of Iowa and Mr. Morse of Massachusetts opposed it...

12TH DAY. - ...The first skirmish occurred over the question of reading the instructions to

Minister Willis, which was insisted upon by Mr. Boutelle of Maine. The house finally agreed to this, and immediately after the conclusion of their reading Mr. Boutelle renewed the assault by bringing forward a resolution declaring the administration policy inconsistent with the spirit of the constitution and the traditions of the government. Great excitement reigned, and in the confusion Mr. Boutelle failed to follow up his parliamentary advantages and was ruled out of order. The resolution of Mr. Cockran for the appointment of a committee of seven to investigate the alleged invasion by the territorial integrity of the United States of the last administration also went down under a retaliatory objection of Mr. Boutelle...

Judge Alexander White Dead - Judge Alexander White age 78 years, died at Dallas, Texas, a few days since. He was a native of Franklin, Tenn., but spent his maturer years at Talladega and Selma, Ala., each of which he represented in congress before and after the war. In 1874 President Grant appointed Judge White to fill an unexpired term as chief justice of the territory of Utah. After discharging the duties of this office with distinction he went to Texas, settling at Dallas, where he continued to reside until the time of his death.

Senator Hill's Bill. - Senator Hill has completed his bill for the imposition of a collateral inheritance, legacy or succession tax...

Postponed Until January - ...When the committee met Mr. Bland asked to have the time fixed to take a vote. Mr. Kilgore of Texas said that he was a free coinage man and wanted to do all he could, but was not anxious to make any better record than he had. This hint that the bill was being pressed for a record caused Mr. Bland to say that if there was any opposition among the free coinage men he would not pretend to press it, and the bill was then postponed.

New Chinese Treaty - Ly Wing York, Chinese consul general at San Francisco, has been summoned to Washington to confer with the Chinese minister regarding a new treaty soon to be submitted by China to the United States. He left for Washington last night...

In a Line or Two - Wayne McVeigh has been nominated as ambassador to Italy, to succeed James J. Van Alen.

.

The President and Mrs. Cleveland are very much opposed to exhibiting their children to the public.

.

Civil Service Commissioner Chas. Lyman, has resigned as President of the commission, and is succeeded by Mr. Proctor. Mr. Lyman is still one of the board

LATE STATE NEWS - Mr. J.P. Clayton is now connected with the Geneva Mirror.

.

Joseph F. Johnston, of Birmingham, has formally announced that he is in the race for Governor.

.

Constable Childers of Marshall county was shot, while serving some papers, upon Wm. Bell.

.

W.E. Knox, of Anniston, has been appointed superintendent of the Alabama Mineral Division of the Louisville & Nashville railroad.

The house committee on elections has decided the Alabama case of Wheatley vs. Cobb unanimously in favor of Cobb, the sitting member.

It is stated that Captain Frank S. White will, before a great while, resign his office of assistant United States district attorney of the northern division of Alabama.

Selma boasts of what few other American cities can, a Christian Chinaman. His name is Sam Lee. His conversion was brought about by the untiring efforts of some of the good women of that city.

Deputy Collector Tutwiller and posse have just made a successful raid through Cleburne, Clay and Randolph counties, destroying some seven stills and arresting John Rice and Cam Ward, two well known moonshiners.

Dirnberry and Bliss, bicyclists, did some exceptionally fine riding at Birmingham fair grounds the past week. They lowered the world's records in several instances. The cyclists are paid $1,000 for each record breaking run.

The report of Hon. Craig Smith, treasurer of the state of Alabama, has been made public. It shows that the gross receipts of the state treasury for the past year have been $1,724,995.53. The total disbursements were $1,848,134.70.

Little Harry Parker, the 4-year-old son of Mayor George H. Parker of Cullman, climbed up to the bureau where he found a revolver, and while playing with it, it was discharged, the ball entering its head. There is no hope for the child's recovery.

J.L. Glover, a prominent and well-to-do farmer at Quinton, a station on the Kansas City, Memphis and Birmingham road, twenty miles from Birmingham, was killed by a passenger train a few days since. Quinton is a flag station and at night a lantern must be waved to have a train stopped. Glover and his wife were coming to Birmingham. The Quinton depot is just around a sharp curve. In order to signal a train one must walk some distance down the track and around the curve. This fact Glover did not know. Seeing the train coming he got on the track and waved his lantern. The engineer could not see it till twenty feet away. It was too late to stop. The farmer stood on the track and the wheels of the engine ground him to pieces.

Ought to Chew Dynamite - Geo. Huffman, returning from a ball at East Liverpool, O., quarreled with his sweetheart, and fired three shots into her head and three into his own. He afterwards jumped into the river, but crawled out to throw himself before a train, when he was arrested. The girl may die. Huffman's wounds are serious. The small calibre prevented instant death.

CHATEAUBRIAND'S GRAVE, The Great Frenchman Buried on the Lonely Rock Where He Was Born - Chateaubriand, the famous French author who, after dining with Washington at Philadelphia, said, "There is virtue in the look of a great man," is buried at the actual spot where he was born, and probably no one was ever laid in a stranger resting place. It is on a jutting point of rock in a lonely, exposed position. The father and mother, of the Vicomte Chateaubriand were on board a vessel bound for St. Malo. It was night when they neared the coast, and a terrible storm was raging. No boat could venture to the assistance of the crew, and the vessel was wrecked upon a rock not far from the shore. The mother of Chateaubriand passed the night upon the rock, and there he was born. He afterward purchased the rock and built upon it the tomb in which he now lies.

Contagiousness of Leprosy - In a paper giving the result of his careful and prolonged investigations of this subject, Dr. Duncan Buckle(?) declares that it is not proven that any number of individuals have ever acquired the disease from direct contact with others affected, or that it has ever been traced, in any proportion of cases worth mentioning, directly from one person to another. There is strong reason to suspect, he says, that it may first be introduced into the system by the way of food fish being the most likely of all substances to furnish and convey the poison; heredity probably accounts for a share of the cases, but the disease is not necessarily transmitted by inheritance; inoculation with leprous matter may be the means of conveying the disease when all conditions are favorable.

The Banner, Vol. II, Clanton, Ala., Saturday, December 30, 1893, No. 8

REFORM MATTERS - To say that the gold bug Republicans are pleased with Mr. Cleveland is to put the case too mildly. They bubble over with enthusiasm and thrill with pleasure when they mention his sacred name. He has fairly cut John Sherman and Ben Harrison out in their affections. - Western Watchman

Messrs. Cleveland, Carlisle, Voorhees and their co-workers, John Sherman, have at last anceeded in demonetizing silver, the money of the common people. They did not want to do it, but had it to do before they could "restore the confidence" of the bankers and monopolists to the administration and the democratic party. - Hickory Mercury

In opening his speech upon the silver question in the senate, Senator Allen, of Nebraska, described himself as a humble member of a new political party which had recently come into public notice. That party had been made necessary by the constant drifting away of the nation from its moorings. It was hourly growing in numbers, courage, intelligence and discipline, and would sooner or later force the two old political parties to administer the affairs of the government in the interest of the people, or would force them into disintegration and death.

The Crop of Cranks - A man giving his name at Timothy Kane, aged 35 years, of No. 1776 Third avenue, called at the East 104th, street police station Chicago and announced that he was going to kill the Rev. Dr. Charles Parkhurst and wished two policemen to accompany him and arrest him after the deed. After a hard struggle Kane was overpowered and locked up. An examination as to his sanity will be made.

Secretary Carlisle's Report - Secretary of the Treasury Carlisle sent in his report to Congress on Wednesday. He says: During the first five months of the present fiscal year, the expenditures of the government have exceeded its receipts to the amount of $29,918,095,66...

Some New Bills - ...Senator Cockrell's bill to promote aerial navigation authorizes the appropriation of $100,000 for payment to any inventor from any part of the world who shall at any time prior to the first of January, 1900, construct a vessel that will demonstrate the safety of navigating the air at a speed of thirty miles an hour and capable of carrying passengers and freight at the extent of five tons.

Individual Income Tax - ...Messrs. McMillan and Bryan reported a plan in favor of an individual income tax. Mr. Montgomery reported against it and suggested the plan of a tax on the incomes from invested wealth. Mr. Montgomery defends his plan and says he could get into any community and combat any argument for the plan suggested by the other members of the committee. "In the first place," said Mr. Montgomery, "If a man has $100,000 and engages in any business enterprises he will give employment to many people and is a benefit to the community...While Mr. Montgomery was talking, Mr. Stevens, of the committee, said in a jocular manner that he believed he would win over members of the committee who disagreed about the income tax to support a proposition to put a duty on sugar to make up the deficit, which was expected to be raised by the tax on incomes. This is only an indication that all the members of the committee are not altogether satisfied with the income tax proposition, and that a duty on sugar is yet a question to be considered.

A Fast Run - Frances J. Dawes, a wealthy Chicago Brewer, received word at New Orleans that his child was dying there and chartering an Illinois Central train, the tracks were cleared and Mr. Dawes and his wife were whirled over the 1,000 miles at the rate of a mile a minute. He paid $1,000 for the trip and broke all records between New Orleans and Chicago, making the run in 25 1-2 hours.

The Advertiser quotes Col. Bowman as saying that there was still a possibility of the organized and Jeffersonian wings of the Democratic party uniting.

We learn that Mr. D.W. Garner of Beat three, has been appointed Registrar for this county under the provisions of the Sayre election law.

Energy Events - A number of the young men from Evergreen came up to go with their best girls bird hunting, Christmas. Mr. J.R. Connell arrived last Thursday from Texas, but much to his regret some one had taken the day with his best girl. I think there will be one girl less when he goes back, but don't know when it will be.

Mr. Shepherd Gardner and Miss G. T. — are renewing their old cases again; some of us regret to hear of it, but nevertheless Christmas comes but once a year.

Mr. Rufus Narrel came up and took his best girl a ride last Sunday.

Miss Mattie Bowdan came out to teach a music school on Mr. White's fine organ. I guess we will have music now.

Mr. James Mims spent Christmas with friends near Energy.

We are looking for cards to announce the marriage of Mr. Willie Burkhalter and one of his best girls. Hurrah for the buddie.

Mr. John Burkhalter has been visiting Evergreen very often of late. It leaves the impression that he is trying to catch Ruth.

We are some at loss to know what Mr. Hooper is going to Gips so much for. If madam rumor is correct the little widow is attracting his attention.

Mr. Willie Burkhalter and Houston Hathcock attended the dance at Mr. Edmund Davis' Saturday night and report a fine time.

We were glad to see Mr. James Adair in the neighborhood last Sunday and I know Osie was, too.

There was quite a delightful dance at the residence of Mr. J.A. Hathcock on the night of the twenty-fifth, and all seemed to enjoy themselves ever so much.

Coopers Cuttings - Mr. E.F. Vinson and Mr. K.W. Vinson escorted their best girls home last Sunday and we see where they are right.

Mr. W.D. Courtney celebrated his birthday last Friday; all report a good time.

Miss Maggie Driver was the guest of Miss Elmira Wilson last Sunday; she has been very ill for the past week, suffering from tooth ache. Miss Maggie is one of the most charming young ladies of Coopers.

Rev. J.M. Dykes filled his regular appointment at Bethel last Sunday.

Mr. J.N. Dennis has a flourishing school at Maple Springs.

President Andrew Jackson in his farewell message made the following statements regarding national banks: "We re not left to conjecture how the moneyed power, thus organized, and with such a weapon in its hands, would be likely to use it...."

Jemison Gems - Detective Barnes of Jemison, met with a sad accident on Christmas day. In firing a miniature cannon a premature explosion occurred, resulting in Mr. Barnes being very badly burnt, especially about the face, we are glad to learn that Mr. Barnes is rapidly recovering from the effects of this accident.

Bozeman Bits - A melancholy accident occurred near Bozeman on Tuesday by which Mr. Marbury's youngest son met his death. He was out bird hunting with some young companions and in some manner his gun was accidently discharged wounding him so badly that he died shortly after.

TOWN ITEMS - The Christmas tree at the Baptist church on Christmas night afforded the juveniles unbounded gratification, as well as being the means of pleasure to those of maturer years. The children, under the able management of Mrs. E.A. Matthews made a charming feature in the entertainment.

We regret to announce the death of Mr. Jasper Smith at his home near Strasburg last Thursday. He leaves a widow and five children to mourn his loss.

Mr. Ben Smith, of Fayetteville, Tenn., is spending his Christmas holidays with relatives here.

We understand Mr. Potts was married at Cullman last Wednesday. We shall be pleased to welcome him and his bride as residents in our town.

Mr. Neal Logan, of Texas, is visiting his brother, Mr. J.A. Logan, and delighting his many friends with his musical abilities.

Alex Shelton was brought up from Pensacola, Fla, by Sheriff Moore on Friday and is securely lodged in Montgomery.

Miss Nellie White gave her young friends a dolls' party on Thursday.

Mr. John Rogers little two-year old child underwent a successful operation for club-foot last week at Montgomery, Drs. Hill and J.S. Johnson,Jr., performing the operation.

Tuesday evening a charming entertainment took place at the residence of Dr. Matthews.

The music scholars of Mrs. Matthews rendered an attractive program. Their performance of the different pieces reflected great credit upon their estimable teacher, and showed plainly the guiding hand of one well fitted to assume the role of preceptor. Mrs. Matthews, who was a member of the graduating class off 1880 at the Marion Female Seminary, is to be congratulated upon the proficiency of her students.

Mrs. Wm. Wright is very unwell, we are sorry to say.

Mr. F.W. Denty paid a visit to Coopers this week.

LATE STATE NEWS - Dr. Wm. Lyman Wells, steward of the Marine Hospital at Mobile, died suddenly of heart disease Monday.

Fire destroyed the bar of Frank Geise of Colbert county. Quite a lot of corn, hay and fodder were lost.

A little child of Mr. W.D. Flinn was caught by a bale of cotton rolling on it, and badly injured about the head.

State mine Inspector J.D. Hillhouse is preparing a report, to be made early in January, showing the location, character and product of Alabama coal and ore mines and coke works.

Mr. T.A. Collier near Brundige, had four bales of cotton piled up when fire was discovered in them and he lost about one bale besides the bagging and ties on the whole lot.

Chief of Police McDonald of Birmingham has just received notice of his appointment to the vice presidency of the National Chief of Police Union of America. The honor is regarded as a very high one.

While attending a dance in Lauderdale county Bill Blackburn and Tom Cauhorn got into a controversy about a pipe during which Blackburn was shot and killed. Cauhorn was not arrested as it was clearly a case of self defense.

At McCarty's ferry on the Tombigbee river in Choctaw county, several days ago, while a flat boat was crossing the river, two negro women named Jane Williams and Dolly Alexander fell overboard and were drowned. Their bodies were not recovered.

Charlie Barksdale dropped dead at Cordova a few nights since. He ran several hundred yards to catch a train and his heart ceased to beat just as he reached the depot. He was bookkeeper for the American Coal Company there. Barksdale came from Scottsville, Va., about four years ago.

Pat Cleaves, of Texas, a son of Hon. A.J. Cleaves, of Randolph county, Alabama, was burned to death in Texas a few days ago. Young Cleave's store was on fire and he, in attempt to rescue some valuables therein, was penned in by the flames and burned to a crisp.

C.H.D. Malstraw, of Utah, has purchased 1,200 acres of land in Walker county, which he will at once put under fence and stock with 3,000 sheep. He is an old sheep raiser and says

Walker county is the best place for sheep he ever saw. He says he will bring others to Alabama from the West.

At Bozeman, Joe Marbury, the 11-year-old son of J.H. Marbury, a wealthy lumber manufacturer, was carelessly handling a gun. The muzzle was near the abdomen, when he accidently struck the hammer with his foot. The gun fired, the entire load going through the boy's body. At last account he was dying.

A posse of the friends of the notorious Sides boys broke into the jail at Russellville and liberated Dock Sides and Lee Sides. They were imprisoned for the alleged murder of Postmaster Kirk, at Guin, and was held in default of $10,000 bonds. No blood was shed in the release of the men. This is the second attempt their friends have made to liberate them.

There has long existed a feud between the two men, growing out of disputes over stock running at large in the range. It is said that Norwood has frequently threatened to kill Englebert, and has several times waylaid him. Englebert also claims that Norwood on one occasion shot at him from ambush.

A few days since at the sawmill of W.C. Nickoll's; about ten miles southeast on Huntsville, the boiler exploded and killed the engineer, Ben Thomas, and the fireman, Amos Banks, colored. Banks was thrown a great distance through the limbs of trees and killed. Thomas was struck by a flying missile and fatally wounded. It is supposed that the steam was allowed to get too high for the capacity of the boiler. Both men leave families.

A serious shooting affray occurred Friday afternoon. Mr. M. Helgren, a country surveyor, was out in the woods tracing some lines. Robert B. Englebert, who lived near, had expressed a desire to have his lines established when the surveyor came up, and word was sent him accordingly to come and join the party. When he came up he saw Henry Norwood sitting by a tree and instantly raised his double-barrel gun and fired on him, shooting him in the left shoulder, neck and head with buckshot. Englebert reloaded his gun, went home and got his horse and came to the station and surrendered.

Town Marshal Phillips of Pratt City, learned that a game was in progress in a notorious gambling den in that town, and summoning five other officers, went to take possession of the place. As his posse entered the room the lights were extinguished by the gamblers and a promiscuous fight commenced. During the fusilade the gamblers raised a window and most of them escaped. When the lamps were lighted, Henry Sherman, one of the gamblers, was found dead on the floor, and Sam Stern and Isaac Milton, two others, were groaning, it is said, with fatal injuries. One of the officers was also seriously wounded. It is thought that others of the gamblers were shot, as blood was found along the road by which they departed.

On Christmas day, Sam Black, the 14-year-old son of Mr. Charles Black of Tuskaloosa, while hunting was killed by the accidental discharge of his gun. The entire load entered his breast, producing almost instant death. The dead boy was a universal favorite.

Montgomery was visited by a disastrous fire the past week. The fire broke out at 1 o'clock in the morning in the store on commercial street occupied by Alexander McKinzie & Co., fancy groceries and liquors, and that store was completely destroyed - loss about $10,000, insurance $4,000. The plant of the Alabama Baptist in the adjoining building was also destroyed. The Excelsior Printing Company had just completed a volume of state supreme court reports which were awaiting binding, and they are in ruins. Another valuable document destroyed was the brief of Col. H C. Tompkins for the United States supreme court in the case of Gilmer vs. Josiah Morris. This suit is for nearly a million dollars, and the brief had just been set up and the proof was read yesterday.

Governor Jones has pardoned Charles Meineke, a German, who has for several years been a convict in the state penitentiary. He was convicted of the murder of an old man - Albert Lyons, of Russell county, Alabama. Lyons was shot while going to a well for some water after dark one night. Meineke, who could scarcely understand English and who had just come over to this country, was employed by Lyons, as a farm hand. He was suspected, tried and convicted of murder. He pleaded innocence and claimed that Lyon's wife, who was young and dashing, had offered him a large sum to murder her husband to that she night get the money he possessed, which was considerable. He claimed that he had declined the proposition but was nevertheless convicted and sentenced to life imprisonment. for the past two years the German citizens of the northern part of the state have been working on Governor Jones. Frank O'Brien, of Birmingham has been largely instrumental in securing his pardon and the German citizens of that city presented him with a solid silver water service in appreciation of his kindly efforts.

The following "special" was sent the Atlanta Constitution from Selma; "A three-year old child of Henry Smith and Millie Smith was carried off over a week ago by an eagle. Today the body was found on a rock cliff about three miles from the boy's home. The child's father is an honest, industrious farmer, who lives at Summerfield, nine miles from Selma. There were two children, one boy of fourteen years old and the other the dead child. One day last week while the parents were absent from the house, the older boy took a gun and went a short distance in the woods in search of game. Returning in half an hour, he saw an eagle flying from the house with the child. A search was made by the neighbors, but it was fruitless. After several days' search in the adjacent woods, a party went to the mountains, about five miles distant. There the remains were found, surrounded by a number of skeletons of small animals. The startling find together with the skeletons of the animals, convinced the neighborhood that the decrease in the herds and flocks has not been caused by worthless curs, but by this winged freebooter. Every man in the section has armed himself and a great bounty is being offered for the head of every eagle. Little children are not allowed to go from the house."

BURNED IT OUT, Details of the Lynching of Sloan Allen in Mississippi. - The particulars about the lynching of Sloan Allen, colored, in Holmes county, Miss., Friday night are as follows: After he was arrested for burning Nabor's body and house, after having hacked him to pieces, a regular inquiry began. It soon became apparent that the negro was guilty, though he strenuously denied it. A fire was built up and the negro was thrown into it for the purpose of extorting a confession. When the flames had burned him terribly he yelled that he would tell all he knew if released. He was promptly taken from the flames. He said he and a white man named Jim Berry were the guilty ones. An investigation showed that Berry was innocent. The negro was for the second time cast into the flames and badly burned. On promising to tell the truth he was again taken out. This time, with himself, he implicated three or four other negroes, who upon investigation, proved conclusively their innocence. For the third time Allen was thrown into the flames, and on promising to correctly tell all about the murder of Nabors he was removed, more dead than alive. He said that only he was guilty. He told where considerable of the money stolen could be found, and where he placed the bloody clothes he had on when he hacked the body of Nabors to pieces and burned the residence. All was found as he had stated. Allen was then turned over to some negroes, who then hanged him and burned his body. The negroes were as greatly enraged over the terrible deed as were the whites, and insisted on burning his body as he had burned Nabors. Nabors was a respectable white man, and old bachelor, who lived alone with the negro youth. The sole motive of the crime was robbery. The amount secured was $5 in gold.

GENERAL NEWS, Wholesale Summary of the News of the Week Gathered from Every Quarter. - Mitchell, the pugilist, has arrived at Jacksonville. He was greeted enthusiastically.

.
President Cleveland and Secretaries Gresham and Lamont spent Christmas in hunting ducks.

.
Gov. Fishback of Arkansas has written a letter to President Cleveland complaining that the Indian Territory is an asylum for dangerous criminals of all kinds.

.
J.L. Beeman an Ex-Congressman from Mississippi was called to his door and robbed of $350 by two masked men. He was brutally beaten and is in a precarious condition.

.
Charlie Mitchell, the pugilist, says that if he win's the fight between him and Corbett, he intends to give $10,000 of his winnings to the poor of Jacksonville, St. Louis, Boston and New York.

.
In addition to the donation which it has been the custom of John R. McLean, proprietor of the Enquirer, to distribute at Christmas, he will this year give $5,000 to the worthy poor of Cincinnati.

.
Jos Dan Jam, who sent threatening letters to President Cleveland, Vice-President Stevenson, Senator Mills and other prominent public men and for whom the police in several cities have been looking, has been arrested.

.
Governor Waite has issued his long-talked-of-call for a special session of the legislature to meet Jan. 10. The call consists of about 5,000 words and mentions over thirty subjects on which legislative action should be taken, in the Governor's opinion.

Will McMillon, of St. Louis, and E.B. Bronson, of El Paso, an authority on prehistoric Indian ruins, have discovered near Eddy, N. M., the remains of five different Aztec towns that formerly contained, according to usual estimates, 15,000 to 20,000 people. Excavations are soon to be made to expose walls of farms and dwellings buried by sand from hills near by.

LIVED WITH BROKEN NECKS, Wonderful Recoveries from Apparently Fatal Injuries. - A recent Republic special entitled "An Unparalleled Case", gives particulars concerning a man who lived nine days with a broken neck, and was even supposed to be on the highway of recovery...One of the first really successful operations on a broken neck in America was by Dr. Bayard, of St. Johns, New Brunswick, some time in the '40s, the patient recovering after a portion of the odontoid process, or second cervical vertebra - the pivotal bone of the neck - has been removed. In 1844 a New York milk dealer was thrown from his wagon and sustained a compound fracture of the neck. He was taken to Dr. Watts, of the College of Physicians and Surgeons, and in less than a year had so fully recovered as to be able to attend to his regular business...In 1850 another New Yorker, Thomas Chalmers, a gymnast, broke his neck in such a way as to split the third cervical vertebra, causing the fourth and second bones to touch. Dr. Sayre was called to see what was supposed to be a dying man. He applied restoratives, caused the patient's neck in a collar of plaster of paris and at the end of six months discharged him perfectly cured. Other noted cases of recovery from fractured cervical vertebra or broken neck are the following: William Stafford, New York City, 1862; attending surgeon, Dr. Sayre, of Bellevue Hospital. Robert Miller, while bathing off Fire Island, New York, July 12, 1875; recovered in two years, Dr. Weiss in attendance. John Collery, San Francisco, June 1882; Dr. Stambaugh, attending surgeon. Barney Baldwin, the broken necked brakeman, who exhibited in the dime museums in 1887, '88 and '89. A.L. Hout, London, England, 1883; recovered after the third vertebra had been removed. Lizzie Hammonds, Brooklyn Hotel, San Francisco, July 25, 1882; Dr. Lord and Dr. McLean. - St. Louis Republic.

AN ENGINEERING FEAT, A Tunnel Nearly Two Miles Long Through the Great Divide. - One of the greatest engineering enterprises of the decade has just been completed in Colorado - an enterprise fully as great as the tunnelling of the Hoosac Mountain, whose completion was celebrated as a great national affair...The man who conceived the idea of this tunnel was Mr. B.H. Bryant, chief engineer of the road. The man who, as engineer in charge, directed the work was Mr. W.H. Leffingwell. The tunnel took three years to build and cost $1,000,000. It is little less than two miles long. The plans of the engineers worked out with great accuracy, and the alignment, when the last partitions were cleared away, was perfect.

Christian King Khama. - King Khama, the firm ally of the British in their South African war, is a Christian, a monogamist and a teetotaler. Khama when a youth, accompanied his father to an old Boer's to sell tusks. The Boer produced a brandy bottle and plied Khama's father with the contents until he induced him to give up a valuable quantity of ivory for a paltry horn of powder and a bar of lead. From that day Khama resisted the temptation to patronize the black bottle. - New York Herald

Index

A

Abbo, C.H. 93
Abbot, B.F. 73
Abbot, C.H. 55, 133, 152
Abbot, Mr. 105
Abbott, C.H. 133
Abbott, Mrs. 201
Abney, Z.C. 289
Abrams, J.M. 100
Acree, Professor 54
Adair, J. D. 3
Adair, James 318
Adam, Bro. 249
Adams 71
Adams, (?) 230
Adams, (?).W. 147
Adams, Bro. 236
Adams, Joe 293
Adams, Robert,Jr. 309
Adams, S.M. 31, 36, 79, 91, 96, 115, 123, 178, 182, 249
Adams, Sam 78
Adams, Samuel E. 96
Adams, W.W. 228, 261
Adehison, James S. 261
Adkinson, A.J. 61
Agnus, Lamb 248
Ainesworth, Frederick C. 159
Albrecht, Duke 16
Alcock, Doctor 51
Aldrich 188
Aldrich, 232
Aldridge, G.P. 30
Aldridge, J.H. 61
Aldridge, John 43
Aldridge, W.A. 194

Aldridge, W.T. 30
Alerga, John 250
Alexander, Dolly 320
Alexander, Mr. 198
Alexander, Nathan 297
Allen 208
Allen, A.A. 22
Allen, Bud 81, 84
Allen, Douglass 159
Allen, Gussie 311
Allen, J.P. 123, 222
Allen, J.V. 75
Allen, John R. 241
Allen, Miss 73, 222
Allen, Mr. 188, 189, 197, 226
Allen, Senator 241, 263, 317
Allen, Sloan 322
Allen, W.V. 178
Alley, J.T. 192
Allis, Horace G. 301
Allison 197
Allison, Mr. 226, 234, 309
Allison, Thomas 309
Almon 15, 21
Almond 21
Alred, J.C. 43, 261
Amason, 29
Amason, S. C. M. 25
Ames, Frederick L. 219
Amison, Mr. 15
Anderson, H. 236
Anderson, J.G. 134
Anderson, J.H. 228
Anderson, Jim 233
Anderson, John 72
Anderson, R.J. 288
Anderson, Samuel J. 294
Anderson, W.H. 73
Andrews, Glen 68
Andrews, Jim 149

Andrews, W.A. 181
Anson, 136
Anthony, Susan B. 203
Archer, Miss Fannie Idel 109
Arledge, C.B. 32
Arledge, E.H. 32
ARLEDGE, S.L. 32
Arledge, S.L. 32
Armour, Tom 219
Armstrong, G.B. 261
Armstrong, George B. 221
Armstrong, H.C.,Jr 121
Armstrong, J.C. 26
Armstrong, J.J. 194
Armstrong, Mrs. Laura 121
Armstrong, Tax Collector 121
Arnold, Benedict 263
Arnold, Sheriff 204
Arp, Bill 242
Arthur, President 134
Ashcraft, John T. 129
Askew, Mr. 246
Askings, George 83
Askins, G.W. 61
Askins, Harris 184
Askins, J.M. 92, 97
Askins, Monroe 61
Askins, W.M. 267
Askins, W.N. 288
Astrup, Edward 135
Atcheson, John 275
Atchinson, Zeke 303
Atchison, J.S. 60
Atkin 189
Atkins, John 276
Atkinson, A.A. 307
Atkinson, B.F. 229
Atkinson, F.M. 72

Atkinson, J.D. 72
Atkinson, James 72
Atkinson, R.T. 83
Atkinson, W.G. 205
Atmore, C.P. 242
Attaway, Aureilus 98
Attaway, Aurelias 65
Attaway, Aurelius 79, 110, 152
Austill 15, 21
Austill, Mr. 21
Austin, Ed 101
Austin, W. L. M. 18
Avery, Zacharaiah 4, 15
Avory, S.M. 283
Aycock, R.M. 32

B

Baber, Matthew 154
Baden, Duke of 10
Badgett, Thomas 192
Bahler, John 209
Baile, Burwell 133
Bailey 268
Bailey, Burl 73
Bailey, Burrel 84
Bailey, E. W. 13
Bailey, E.W. 29, 115, 132, 246
Bailey farm 278
Bailey, Fred L. 54
Bailey, Jason T. 29
Bailey, John 62
Bailey, L.A. 29
Bailey, Mr. 189
Bailey, Sam 157
Baily, E.W. 250
Bainbridge, E.C. 35
Baker, 29
Baker, A. 154
Baker, Amos 195
Baker, Jeff 72
Baker, John 235
Baker, John W. 284
Baker, L.V. 56

325

Baker, Minister 150
Baker, Miss Mahala 294
Baker, Thos. 289
Baker, William 178
Baldwin 61
Baldwin, Barney 324
Baldwin, E.B. 135
Baldwin, F.B. 49
Baldwin, Frank 122
Baldwin, James H. 157
Baldwin, Mrs. Homer R. 129
Balknap, Lula 169
Ball 81
Ball, Chas. P. 259
Ball, Robert 223
Baltman, Charlotte Mitchell 119
Baltzell, Editor 227
Bandy, F.W. 221
Bankhead 151
Bankhead, 266
Bankhead, Congressman 300
Bankhead, John H.,Jr. 300
Bankhead, Mr. 186
Bankhead, Wm. 300
Banks, Amos 321
Barbour, 29
Barefied, W.S. 143
Barefield 143
Barefield, W. S. 3
Barefield, W.S. 91, 93, 162
Barett, R.N. 32
Barke, J.B. 216
Barksdale, Charlie 320
Barmon, M.J. 37
Barnard, E.E. 177
Barnes, Albert 194
Barnes, C.G. 110, 124, 161

Barnes, C.P. 170
Barnes, Charley 250
Barnes, Charlie 153
Barnes, Detective 236, 319
Barnes, Geo. T. 91
Barnes, George A. 167
Barnes, Grant W. 67
Barnes, H.Z. 60, 261
Barnes, Leroy 250
Barnes, M.H. 110
Barnes, Miss Bell 214
Barnes, Miss Belle 214
Barnes, P.W. 97
Barnes, R.C. 179
Barnes, R.P. 124, 170
Barnes, Ross 97, 116, 162
Barnes, S.P. 221
Barnes, Shelby 85, 228, 311
Barnes, T.W. 229
Barnett, J.G. 32
Barnett, Mr. 91
Barnum, D.E. 107
Barnum, Phineas T. 107
Barrett, John 11
Barron, J.D. 169
Bartee, 29
Bartlett, Mr. 198
Barton, Philip Key 8
Bass 81
Bassett, S.E. 14, 20, 154, 172
Batcliff, S.B. 93
Bate 227
Bate, G.W. 32
Bate, Mr. 235, 307
Bate, Senator 306
Bates, C.T. 80
Bates, Martin 50
Bates, Miss Lily 145

Bates, William 108
Batzell, Editor 70
Bauer, Constable 90
Baumhauer, J. 168
Baxter, James (?) 258
Bayard, Ambassador 291
Baynard, Dr. 323
Bazemore, Blunt 304
Beale, General 8
Bean, (?).J. 261
Bean, A.Z. 60
Bean, E.M. 32, 60
Bean, John A. 32
Bean, W.R. 115
Bean, William 84, 293
Beard, G.M. 239
Beard, J.L. 289
Beard, Jas. L. 289
Beard, L.D. 50
Beard, Lonnie 288
Beard, P. D. 18
Bearden, J.W. 194
Beardsly, Roswell 242
Beasley, H.N. 80, 84, 92
Beatty, Robert 16
Beauregard 49
Becker, George W. 174
Beckham, Lizzie 300
Beckham, Lura 300
Beckham, P. 300
Beckner, Powell 175
Beedleson, Frank S. 69
Beeman, J.L. 323
Beeson, John J. 108
Belknap, Mr. 216
Belknap, Secretary of War 9
Bell, Bro. 13
Bell, Captain 35

Bell, Charles H. 282
Bell, Ed. 152
Bell, J.W. 3
Bell, J.C. 178
Bell, Joseph 297
Bell, O.R. 44
Bell, T.P. 95
Bell, T.T. 270
Bell, W.S. 182
Bell, William 278
Bell, Wm. 313
Bellenger, 29
Benedict, E.C. 38
Benedict, James E. 141
Benedict, Miss 38
Benjamin, Mrs. 144
Bennett, 211
Bennett, Ida 77
Bennett, James Gordon 158
Bennett, R.M. 204
Bennett, W.A. 32
Benson, J.M. 32
Bent(?), Miss Emma 61
Bentley, Miss Emma 50
Bentley, Miss Sadie 99
Benton, Oscar 26
Berger 299
Beringer, Morris 27
Berrian, Dr. 270
Berry 15, 21, 227
Berry, Jim 322
Berry, Mr. 15, 188
Berry, Senator 312
Bevels, H.T. 124
Beverly, 302
BEVERLY, ROBERT 74
Bibb, J.M. 26
Bice, J. 99, 132, 170, 186, 195, 260
Biggers, 29
Biggers, Mr. 15
Bilbro, John A. 26

326

Bill, Buffalo 167, 245
Billingsley, C.C. 131
Billingsley, J.W. 247
Billingsley, Joe 229
Billingsley, Wesley 275
Bingham, J. H. 4, 15
Bingham, J.H. 32, 86, 207, 231, 243, 244, 251, 277
Birch, John M. 38
Bissell, General 155
Bissell, Mr. 273, 306
Bissell, Mr. and Mrs. William S. 38
Bissell, Postmaster-General 273
Bittenbender 281
Biven, Dr. 284
Bivings, A.E. 125, 187
Bivings, Dr. 86
Bivings, James D. 14
Bivings, Yancy 66
Black, Charles 321
Black, Gen. 59
Black, Sam 321
Black, William 10
Blackburn, Bill 320
Blackmore, Mrs. 153
Blaine, Alice 10
Blaine, Emmons 9
Blaine, Ephraim L. 9
Blaine, James G. 7, 10, 22
Blaine, James Gillespie 9
Blaine, Miss Harriet 10
Blaine,

Miss Margaret 10
Blaine, Mr. 7
Blaine, Walker 9, 10
Blanchard, Mr. 189
Bland, J.T. 289
Bland, Mr. 189, 198, 208, 306, 313
Bland, Mrs. Emma 104
Blanton, Will 266
Blasingame 311
Blasingame, Harry 311
Blasingame, Sid 311
Blatchford, Appleton 134
Blatchford, Mrs. 134
Blatchford, Samuel 129, 134
Blennerhassett, Miss R.A. 163
Bliss, 314
Block 21
Block, . 15
Blondo, Mrs. Gus 17
Blount 107
Blount, Dr. 28
Blount, Jas.H. 291
Blount, Minister 96, 175
Blount, Mr. 305, 312
Blow, J.T. 123
Blue, O.R. 121
Blunk, Andrew 167
Blunk, Murry 167
Blythe, Sy 149
Boatner, Mr. 189
Boen, H.E. 178
Bogan 49
Bogart 15, 21
Boger, Charles 164
Boles, B.G. 61
Boles, Charley 30
Boles, George 30
Boles, Miss Sallie

61
Bolling, 29
Bolton, Sarah T. 178
Bonivides, Estevan 90
Bonner, Bogue 112
Bonner, John 112, 231
Bonny, Annie 224
Bookey, M. 154
Booth, Edwin 95
Booth, Elwin 119
Booth, Joseph A. 119
Booth, Mr. 297
Booth, Mrs. R. E. 26
Borden, Lizzie 114
Bostock, 263
Bourke, John G. 25
Boutelle, Mr. 306, 312, 313
Bow, Dr. 74
Bowdan,
Miss Mattie 318
Bowden, Chas. 217
Bowden, Mrs. 61, 284
Bowden, Mrs. M. 288
Bowles, George 131
Bowman, Col. 318
Bowman, P.G. 183
Box, Judge 42
Boyd, E.O. 31, 125
Boyd, E.W. 154
Boyd, H. 20
Bozeman 303
Bozeman, Mrs. 153
Brack, J.E. 154
Bradford,
Mrs. Martha H. 23
Bradley 15
Bradley, Dan 299
Bradley, Kate 311
Bradley, Miss Hettie 295
Bradley, Miss Katie

222
Brake, J.L. 26
Brande, Professor 136
Branham, Dr. 191
Branham, John W. 177, 183
Brannen, E.R. 26
Brantley, J.M. 261
Brantley, Jno. M. 111
Breckenridge, Congressman 150
Breckenridge, W.C.P. 167
Breckinridge, Mr. 208
Brennan, J.M. 104
Brew(?), Judge 267
Brewer, 29
Brewer, Mr. 28, 302
Brewer, S.M. 32
Brewer, Solicitor 84, 222, 287
Brewer, T.P. 32
Brewer, Willis 59
Brickerhoff, Gen. 90
Brickner, Mr. 198
Briggs, A.J. 196
Briggs, Dr. 95
Bristow, Miss Dora 124
Broadhead, Mr. 86
Broadhead, N.L. 73, 133
Broadus, Thomas A. 115
Brock, (?).L. 259
Brock, I.L. 48, 183
Brock, L.L. 178
Brock, Secretary 173
Brocks, Bro. 274
Broderick, Mr. 198
Brodgett, Henry W. 28
Brogan, W.N. 37
Broghton, Mr. 92
Bronson, E.B. 323

327

Brooks, A.B. 191
Brooks, A.J. 122
Brooks, Mrs. A.J. 184
Brooks, Phillips 16
Brooks, Walter E. 10
Broom, Judge 257
Broughton 245
Broughton, Madison 99
Broughton, Mr. 96
Broughton, Richard P. 142
Brown 81
Brown, 28, 29, 289
Brown, Albert 171
Brown, B.H. 53
Brown, Benjamin 86
Brown, George S. 181
Brown, Gov. 11
Brown, John 274, 282
Brown, Joseph E. 177
Brown, Judge 115
Brown, K.W. 95
Brown, Miss Maude 77
Brown, Miss Sallie 176
Brown, W.H. 311
Brown, W.J. 59, 261
Brown, William 278
Browning, "Pete" 135
Brownlee, Alice Vivian 294
Bruce, C.R. 261
Bruce, Mrs. F. M. 162
Bruce, Mrs. Mattie 98
Bryan 317
Bryan, Congressman 225
Bryan, Mr. 189

Bryan, W.J. 249
Bryant, B.H. 324
Bryant, James 168
Bryant, James W. 113
Bryant, Lucinda 72
Bryant, William Cullen 268
Buckle(?), Duncan 315
Buckley, Catcher 135
Buckner, George 84
Bulger, Miss 222
Bull, John 238
Bullard, Miss Nellie 257
Bumis, Joseph 108
Burch 139
Burchfield, H.H. 229
Burke, Edmund 53
Burkhalter, J.G. 60
Burkhalter, J.H. 261
Burkhalter, John 318
Burkhalter, Miss Havana 275
Burkhalter, Newton 84
Burkhalter, Willie 318
Burks, 29
Burks, L.F. 182
Burnett, James 32
Burnett, K.R. 20
Burnett, Mrs. Alice 92
Burnett, Tom 246
Burnett, W.D. 61
Burney, C.W. 181
Burrows 199
Burse, Nettie 260
Burson, Charles 165
Busby, J.L. 31, 37, 55, 62, 67, 73, 100, 154, 163, 196, 207

Busby, Joe 65
Busby, Mr. 118
Busby, T.R. 154
Busch, Mr. 157
Bush 81
Bush, Deputy Sheriff 157
Bush, Fate 295
Bush, J. G. 25
Bush, Mackey 295
Bush, Mitch 295
Bush, Sam 149
Butler 227
Butler, J.A. 221
Butler, J.O. 261
Butler, Mr. 215
Butler, Stewart 259
Butt, C.W. 22
Butterworth, Mr. 62
Butts, H.M. 60
Butts, H.W. 261
Bynum 233
Bynum, Mr. 198
Bynum, S.V. 295
Byron 262

C

C., A. Wells 14
Caffee, Evelyn 288
Caffery, Mr. 208
Caffey, Will 214
Cain, J.T. 72
Caine, V.H. 170, 186, 195
Caldwell, Josiah 7
Calhoun, 29
Calhoun, J.C. 203
Calhoun, John C. 245
Call 188, 227
Callahan, Jno. W. 205
Callaway, B.T. 288
Callaway, J.C. 60
Callaway, N.J. 43
Callaway, William 261
Callaway, Wm. 60
Callen, (?)ill 304

Callen, ex-Judge 251
Callen, Judge 66, 230, 302
Callen, Mrs. H.J. 238
Callen, Mrs. Judge 187
Callen, W.T. 311
Callen, Will 196, 251
Callier, T.E. 73
Calloway, B.F. 288
Calloway, N.J. 43
Callum, R.S. 32
Callum, W.A. 32
Calvin, T.P. 69
Cameron, Mr. 235
Cameron, Will 113
Camp, Lee 67
Campanes, Ellis 111
Campanes, Mr. 111
Campbell, A.W. 107
Campbell, Bro. 221
Campbell, Colin 217
Campbell, Ira 1, 3, 13, 143, 163, 221, 246, 262
Campbell, J.M. 32, 237
Campbell, James 291
Campbell, James Monroe 237
Campbell, Leroy 54
Campbell, Misses 214
Campbell, Morgan 85
Campbell, Mrs. Ira 109, 221, 310
Campbell, Silas 72
Campbell, W.K. 149
Campbell, William 139, 149
Camper, M.P. 129

Cannon 189
Cannon, J.H. 72
Cannon, Marion 178, 227
Cannon, Mr. 312
Cantwell, Colonel 159
Cantwell, Miss Kate C. 158
Carey 197
Carey, Senator 17
Carlin, W.P. 273
Carlin, Wm. E. 273
Carlisle 263
Carlisle, 38, 317
Carlisle, John G. 158, 193, 265
Carlisle, Mr. 38
Carlisle, Mrs. 38
Carlisle, Secretary 69, 141, 159, 220, 239, 257, 291
Carlisle, Secretary of the Treasury 317
Carmichael, Miss Sarah 241
Carnegie, Andrew 17, 147
Carpenter, Professor 37
Carr, (?) 192
Carr, Elias 155
Carr, George H. 135
Carr, Hinton E. 113
Carrillo, Jonquin 200
Carroll, Miss Mattie 116
Carroll, Mrs. 247
Carrouth, J. 229
Carruth, J.A. 228
Carsey 136
Carter, A.W. 145
Carter, J. M. 15
Carter, John 167
Carter, L.P. 32
Carter, Mary 66
Carter, Miss Annie 14

Carter, Miss Jessie 145
Carter, Mr. 2
Carter, Mrs. Arch 162
Carter, Nestor 276
Cartright, Mr. 150
Cartwright, W.H. 299
Caruth 189
Caruth, Mr. 97
Cary, R.G. 157
Case, 29
Case, Mr. 15
Catalani 271
Catchings, Mr. 190, 197, 208, 235
Cate, Representative 2
Cather, G. R. 25
Cather, Geo. R. 299
Cathings, Congressman 184
Cathings, Mr. 208
Caton, Thos. 84
Catts, Sam 222
Cauhorn, Tom 320
Cellini, Benvenuto 263
Cestnutt 311
Chadwick, W.J. 139
Chalmers, Thomas 324
Chambers, G.W. 73
Chambers, George 100
Chambers, James 83
Chambers, John 100
Chambers, Miss Etta 97
Chamblin, C.A. 297
Champ(?)y, Bro. 260
Chamson, W.B. 61
Chandler, J.N. 161
Chandler, Joe 93
Chandler, Martha S. 243
Chandler,

Mattie Sue 311
Chandler, Millie 243
Chandler, Mr. 312
Chandler, Mr. Joe 93
Chandler, W.A. 261
Chandler, Willie 116
Chaney 157
Chapam, Express Messenger 204
Charbonnet, 285
Charles II 270
Charlson, 234
Charlton, E.T. 78
Chase, Gov. 11
Chastian, G.A. 27
Chastine, B.H. 238
Chateaubriand, 314
Cheney, F. J. 5
Cheney, Frank J. 5
Cheny, Louis 159
Chesnut, Mrs. B.H. 55
Chesnutt, B.H. 171
Chesnutt, Mr. 287
Chester, Ira 51
Chestnut, B. H. 3
Chestnut, B.H. 59, 100, 118
Chestnutt 81
Chestnutt, B.H. 215
Chestnutt, Buck 236
Chestnutt, Scott 81
Childers, A.F. 60
Childers, Constable 313
Childress, A.F. 261
Childress, Clarence 303
Childress, J.B. 123
Childress, M.C. 123
Childress, Mrs. W.Q. 185
Childress, W.Q. 194
Chipman, J. Logan 189

Chrisman, J.B. 234
Chrisman, Judge 25, 234
Christman, Mr. 252
Cillum, D.C. 32
Cimock, Henry F. 70
Clamp, J. H. 17
Clark 227
Clark, 29
Clark, Bertha 227
Clark, C.J. 181
Clark, C.T. 154
Clark, Dave 191
Clark, Gaylord B. 108
Clark, J. C. 25
Clark, Mr. 198
Clark, Terrence 174
Clarke, 186, 193
Clarke, A.T. 118, 154, 169
Clarke, Colonel 109
Clarke, George H. 135
Clarke, Willis G. 149
Clarker, R.H. 109
Clarkson, James W. 266
Claughton, A.B. 116
Claughton, Miss 116
Claughton, W.F. 59, 79
Clause 210
Clay, Annie 294
Clay, Jerry 294
Claydon, (?) 147
Claypool, F.J. 310
Clayton, Henry D. 101
Clayton, J.P. 313
Cleary, Captain 158
Cleaves, A.J. 320
Cleaves, Pat 320
Clecker, Henley 99
Cleckler, G.T. 261
Cleckler, Henry K.

117
Cleckler, J.T. 32
Cleckler, W.P. 260
Clements, J.P. 246
Clements, Pearlie 246
Clements, Tom 295
Cleveland, 317
Cleveland, Grover 35, 91
Cleveland, Mr. 2, 37, 47, 204, 312, 317
Cleveland, Mrs. 193, 313
Cleveland, President 28, 35, 41, 42, 53, 89, 95, 103, 107, 121, 129, 142, 150, 168, 175, 198, 235, 245, 273, 298, 309, 323
Cleveland, President and Mrs. 213
Cleveland, President-elect 2
Clover, Representative 67
Cobb, 186, 266, 314
Cobb, J.E. 109
Cobb, J.T. 59
Coburn, Chas.J. 260
Cochran, Henry S. 298
Cocke, E.R. 167
Cocke, J.B. 101
Cockran, Mr. 313
Cockrell 188, 197, 227
Cockrell, L.A. 176
Cockrell, Mr. 188, 189, 197, 208
Cockrell, Senator 317
Cody, W.F. 245
Coe, Miss Emma 18
Coes, Mr. 246
Cofer, Messrs. 237
Coke 227

Coke, 302
Coke, Edward 210
Coke, Mr. 215
Cokiskey, 136
Col, M.J. 110
Cole, Arthur 160
Cole, H. 72
Cole, H.J. 144
Cole, H.L. 72
Cole, H.W. 97, 124, 161, 170, 206, 221, 250
Cole, Miss Mattie 80
Coleman, 29
Coleman, James M. 5
Coleman, Robert H. 175
Coleman, Robert S. 115
Coleman, T.N. 108
Collery, John 324
Collier, Joe T. 252
Collier, Miss Inez 81, 188
Collier, T.A. 320
Collins, 141
Collins, (?) 94
Collins, (?)hn 133
Collins, Ada 260
Collins, Green 213
Collins, J.H. 32
Collins, J.M. 213
Collins, J.W. 43, 86
Collins, James 91
Collins, John H. 3
Collins, Miss 303
Collins, Miss Ada 18
Collins, Miss Carrie 49
Collins, Miss Patti Lyle 231
Collins, Mr. 213
Collins, Mrs. Sara 3
Collins, Sallie 117
Collins, T.J. 43, 260
Collins, W.J. 184

Collins, W.L. 32
Collins, Will F. 176
Collum, Mr. 215, 226
Colman, C.C. 206
Colnaghi, Sir D.E. 70
Comiskey, Captain 239
Compton, President 15, 21, 22, 25
Compton, resident 25
Compton, Senate-President 15
Comstock, E.O.,Sr 157
Conant, Marcus 257
Conley, Colonel 36
Conley, Miss Sadie 17
Conley, William 17
Connell, H.M. 125
Connell, J.R. 318
Connell, J.W. 267, 288
Connell, James 303
Connell, Jas. 125
Connell, John 103
Connell, John W. 187
Connell, Mr. 93
Connells, H. 304
Conner, George 200
Conner, Lew 200
Connolly, Thomas 169
Connor, D. 311
Connor, Mrs. Fanny 311
Converse, James B. 173
Conway, W.H. 292
Cook, Clifford 153
Cook, David 182
Cook, Harry 103
Cook, John 153
Cook, O.H. 124
Cook, T.M. 260
Cook, Thomas 73

Cooley, Dave 86
Cooley, James 59
Cooley, James T. 238
Cooley, Miss Sallie 86
Coombs, Mr. 189
Cooper, Congressman 242
Cooper, E.M. 160
Cooper, J.W. 59
Cooper, Miss Beulah 145
Cooper, Mr. 189, 198
Cooper, Robert 160
Copeland, H.C. 295
Copeland, Wm. B. 108
Coppinger, John J. 10
Coppock, John W. 233
Corbett 301
Corbett, 36, 323
Corbett, Jas. J. 309
Corbin, Austin 10
Corbott 257
Corderie, J.M. 153
Cosby, ?)C. 73
Cost, J.P. 110
Coulson, L.C. 182
Courtney, Virgil 103, 275
Courtney, W.D. 236, 319
Covert, Miss Eva 39
Covert, Mr. 198
Covert, William E. 159
Cowan, Robert 263
Cox, 29
Cox, Henry 61
Cox, J.B. 124, 221
Cox, J.H. 144
Cox, Joe 173
Cox, John 110
Cox, Miss Bessie 110

Cox, Miss Emma 3
Cox, Miss Theodora 125
Cox, Mr. 198
Cox, Mrs. Bertha 191
Cox, W.H. 72, 221
Cox, W.S. 125, 229
Coyne, Thomas 175
Cozart, W.D. 78
Craddock, Tom 140, 149
Craig, ex-Judge 289
Craig, John H. 133, 257
Crandall, W.W. 164
Craven, Martin 155
Crawford, Louisa 289
Creighton, Lieutenant 69
Creighton, Police Lieutenant 69
Crespo, President 279
Crew, Mrs. 50, 61
Crew, Mrs. Hulda 125
Crew, R.H. 125
Crichton, F. 169
Crichton, Frank 105, 238, 247, 311
Crichton, Mr. 243
Crim, A.B. 190
Crimmins, John D. 141
Crisp, Mr. 169, 208
Crisp, Speaker 216
Crittenden, Adeline 264
Crockett, Davy 107
Crompton, Miss Lizzie 110
Cromwell, Gilver 262
Crosbie, Katie 260
Crosby, Mrs. Mary 297
Cross, 136

Cross, John 295
Cross, Secretary 74
Cross, Thomas 26
Crossin, T.P. 243
Crosswell, R.C. 230
Croswell, R.C. 238
Crow, Clint 216
Crow, W.F. 216
Crowe, G.B. 101
Crowson, Bro. 292
Crowson, W.B. 130
Crowson, Wm. 154
Cruger, John 210
Crum 289
Crum, Mrs. 10
Crumpton, F.C. 98, 236
Crumpton, W.B. 92, 132
Cuero, Premier 28
Culberson, W.L. 108
Cullom, Senator 305
Culp 146
Culp, A. 311
Culp, Elder 131
Culp, Fonza 3
Culp, Henry 30, 131
Culp, J.P. 80
Culp, John 80
Culp, Nancy M. 277
Cultice, John 1
Culver, C.W. 154
Culver, H.E. 247
Culver, Henry 61
Culver, I.F. 26, 41
Culver, Mr. 41
Culverhouse, Minnie 117
Cunningham 15, 21
Cunningham, Callie 144
Cunningham, E.W. 252
Cunningham, George S. 175
Cunningham, Miss Jennis 45
Curran 190

Curry, S.A. 260
Curtis, Dexter 63
Curtis, Mr. 198
Cushman, Farmer 285
Custer, General 259
Cutinan, Chas. 1

D

Daie, Alex G. 161
Dake, A. G. 1
Dake, Alex G. 30, 31
Dake, Brother 260
Dalton, Deputy Sheriff 140
Damrosch, Walter 10
Dan, John 167
Danby, Marvel 270
Daniel 227
Daniel, Mr. 216, 226
Daniels, Gus 149
Daniels, Henry 275
Daniels, Henry R. 107
Daniels, Mr. 189
Daniels, Perry 145
Dankin, Dan 23
Dansby, Dan 153
Darby 15, 21
Darby, John 244
Darden, W. C. 22
Davenport, Davis 66
Davenport, E.D. 303
Davenport, F.M. 237
Davenport, Isaac 163
Davenport, James 84, 293
Davenport, Miss Bessie 303
Davenport, Monty 123
Davenport, Mr. 163

Davenport, Mrs. Susan 303
Davenport, Ora 123
Davenport, R.L. 285
Davidson, George 112
Davidson, J.W. 135
Davie 15, 21
Davie, M.D. 182
Davies, George 135
Davis, 30
Davis, A.B. 179, 310
Davis, Anderson 293
Davis, Ben 268, 277
Davis, C. Wood 73
Davis, C.L. 32
Davis, Charley 157
Davis, Charlie 300
Davis, David 155
Davis, Dawson 131
Davis, Edmund 318
Davis, F.J. 311
Davis, Frank 268
Davis, G.H. 57
Davis, H. L. 4
Davis, H.D. 145
Davis, H.L. 72, 104, 236, 267, 288
Davis, H.M. 23
Davis, Henry M. 27
Davis, Isaac 192
Davis, J.A. 246
Davis, J.H. 265
Davis, J.L. 267
Davis, James M. 243
Davis, Jefferson 67
Davis, John 178, 245
Davis, L.A. 56
Davis, Mat 55
Davis, Mrs. Jefferson 15
Davis, Mrs. V. Jefferson 15, 21

331

Davis, N.A. 281
Davis, S.E. 311
Davis, Sampey 243
Davis, T.A. 22
Davis, William 291
Davis, William G. 32
Davis, Wm. 154
Davis, Wm. G. 162
Dawes, Frances J. 318
Dawsey, 29
Dawson 29
Dawson, 29
Dawson, ?)melia 222
Dawson, Bill 62
Dawson, Dr. 44
Dawson, George 303
Dawson, J.M. 105
Dawson, Miss Alice 303
Dawson, Miss Amelia 100
Dawson, Miss Lela 267, 288
Dawson, Mrs. Jim 20
Dawson, W.R. 275
De La Rue, Henry 144
Deace 149
Deadwilder, Miss Lafarice 72, 118, 230, 243
Dean, J.S. 299
Deane, J.W. 70
Dease, Gilbert J. 169
Deason, E.B. 111
Deason, I.M. 97
Deason, Miss Fannie 83
Decater, Louis A. 186
Decker, M. 126
Deharity, W.A. 136
Del Campello, A. G. 17

DeLacey, 29
Delaney, Miss 311
Demming, H.C. 90, 182
Dempsey, Hugh 16
Dempsey, Hugh F. 16
Dennis, A.B. 236
Dennis, Aaron 194
Dennis, Alpheus 84, 103
Dennis, B.L. 236
Dennis, C.N. 145
Dennis, Dr. 98
Dennis, J.N. 319
Dennis, John 19, 103
Dennis, John,Jr 104
Dennis, P.C. 43
Densmore, Capt. 41
Denson 151
Denson, 266
Denson, Judge 219, 289
Denson, Mr. 186
Denson, N.D. 79, 81, 287
Denson, W.H. 109
Dent, 29
Dent, S. H. 25
Denty, (?)s. Mary 207
Denty, F.W. 20, 169, 207, 284, 320
Depew, Chauncey M. 122
Depew, M. 90
Deramus, Will 84
Derring, W.A. 216
Descartes 262
Deshazo, Mr. 55
Desnaway, J.W.D. 132
Dexter, C.E. 41
Diaz, President 225, 298
Dickey, J.J. 103
Dickinson, Don M. 70
Dicus, J.M. 108

Dill, Professor 50
Dinkins, S.M. 83
Dimberry 314
Disharoon, R.L. 297
Doane, J.P. 309
Dobbs 229
Dobbs, N. 151
Dobbs, N.A. 83, 229
Dobbs, Natty 112
Dobbs, Rev. - 146
Dobbs, S.H. 216
Dobson, Henry 310
Dodge, James R. 73
Dodson, A.R. 191
Dole, S. B. 17
Dolph, Mr. 208, 226
Domining, J.E. 61
Donnelly, Ignatius 83, 130, 238
Donnely, Ignatius 143
Dore, John S. 182
Dorming, T.J. 111
Dorminy, T.J. 153, 160
Dorr 201
Dorth, W.R. 27
Doster, C.S.G. 289
Dote, 291
Douglas, May Booth 119
Douglas, W.L. 32
Douglas, William M. 23
Douglass, Deputy Sheriff 204
Downey 21
Downs 145
Downs, Joe 103
Downy 15, 21
Drake, Henry W. 299
Drew, Felix 294
Driskell, T.J. 49
Driver, H. 123
Driver, J.K. 60
Driver, Miss Maggie 319

Driver, Mrs. Clinton 84
Driver, T.M. 123, 246
Driver, Thomas 153, 160
Dryburgh, F. W. 4
Dubes, Jim 246
Dubois 235
DuBois, Mr. 197
Dubois, Mr. 235
DuBose 95
DuBose, Fonza 223
DuBose, J.J. 96
Duchess of Teck 142
Dudley, Felix 50
Dudley, James A. 105, 285
Duffy 211
Duggar, R.H. 26
Duke 172
Duke, (?) 50
Duke, John 72
Duke, Lum 168
Duke, Nannie 311
Duke, Ned 230
Duke of Bedord 142
Duke of Veragua 143
Duke of York 129
Duke, R.C. 72
Dukes, Miss Nannie 206
Dukes, Mr. 66
Dukes, O.A. 20, 66
Dunaway, Bro. 194
Duncan, Bishop 264
Duncan, Col. 263
Duncan, D.P. 90
Duncan, J.R. 252
Duncan, National Secretary-Treasurer 77
Duncan, W.W. 36
Dungan, Thomas 293
Dunkin, 288
Dunkin, (?).W. 187
Dunkin, W.W. 62,

247, 311
Dunlap, Bill 117
Dunn, E.N. 126
Dunn, Euphra 126
Dunn, R.G. 102
Dunneway, J.W. 116
Dunning, N.A. 178
Dupree, (?)nry 222
Durden, Morgan 275
Durham, Prof. 55, 92
Durham, Professor 66, 80
Durham, Robt. D. 179
Dutton, John 32
Dye, George W. 5
Dykes, J.M. 56, 115, 151, 303, 319
Dykes, R.M. 246
Dykes. M.J. 14

E

Eagan, Mike J. 225
Eardmus, Eula 275
Early, W.J. 157
East, W.R. 154
Easterling, Louis 294
Easterling, N.F. 60
Eaves, (?).S. 261
Eaves, Mrs. 116
Ebron, Mrs. Bettie 72
Echols, M. 294
Eddings, Miss Lula 4, 30
Edgerson, J. C. 18
Edison, Thomas A. 223
Edmonds, R.H. 73
Edmondson, R.Q.,Sr. 27
Edson, Dr. 239
Edward, ohn 277
Edwards, Bennett 221
Edwards, D.G. 59, 75, 78, 203

Edwards, Dick 196
Edwards, George 243, 293
Edwards, J.E. 250
Edwards, James 196
Edwards, John 250
Ehrman 311
Ehrman & Merritt 195
Ehrman and Meritt 194
Ehrman and Merrit 118
Ehrman and Merritt 173
Ehrman, Mr. 112
Ehrman, R. 73, 221, 262, 289, 304
Eiland, 29
Eiland, Ab 243
Eiland, Ab. 246
Eiland, Abe 31
Eiland, J.T. 213
Eiland, R.J. 145
Eisley, J.E. 41
Elam, Elder 236
Elam, Mr. 15
Eldridge, E.R. 276
Elison, Mrs. Mary 72
Ellington, President 193
Elliott, Thomas 67
Ellis, 29
Ellis, Charles 299
Ellis, Dave 229
Ellis, David 228
Ellis, Henry D. 203
Ellis, Jim 55
Ellis, W.D. 237
Ellis, Walter 228, 229
Ellison, C.S. 32
Ellison, J.T. 81
Ellison, John 184
Ellison, John,Jr. 184
Ellison, S.L. 32
Ellison, W.T. 32
Emerson, Mrs. Isiah

4
Englebert, 321
Englebert, Robert B. 321
English, Mr. 190
Entreken, S.J. 135
Eping, H.H. 107
Espinal, August 226
Espinal, Victor 226
Estes, H.F. 288
Estes, H.S. 267
Estes, H.T. 131, 172, 288
Estes, John 99
Eugley, Attorney-General 167
Euloe, Mr. 312
Eustis, 282
Eustis, J.B. 41
Evans 311
Evans, 29
Evans, Dave 155
Evans, Eugene 86
Evans, G.R. 55
Evans, J.M. 257
Evans, Mrs. 196
Evans, O.P.C. 142
Evans, Sam 72
Evans, W.D. 223, 249
Evans, Xyr Hunt French 311
Everett, Jim 265
Everett, Mr. 190
Ewing, 29
Ewing, Alex 309
Ewing, Thomas 7
Ezell, Charles 192
Ezell, Hattie 192

F

F(arr?), J.L. 260
Fagan, M.J. 305
Fall, W.R. 302
Faraday, Michael 136
Faraday, Professor 136
Farley, J.B. 50

Farley, J.T. 98
Farley, Solenna 172
Farley, W.E. 98
Farley, Will 172
Farmer, Captain 92
Farmer, Will 294
Farris, Miss Naomi 194
Faulkinbury, H. N. 17
Faulkner 197
Faulkner, Mr. 33, 216
Faunce, S.E. 35
Fava, Baron 89
Fay, Charles 299
Feagin, B.B. 37
Fengin, B.E. 172
Ferguson, 29
Ferguson, Mr. 15
Ferguson, Prospector 200
Ferris, Mr. 258
Ferry, Miss Della 29
Field, James G. 154, 178
Field, Marshall 258
Fields, Frank 164
Fields, M. M. 4
Fincher & Fairlay 297
Fincher, Mike 140
Finley, 29
Finn, John 175
Fischer 11
Fishback, Gov. 323
Fisher, Everett W. 83
Fisher, Warren 7
Fitch, Mr. 198
Fleming, Colonel 209
Fleming gang 141
Fletcher, 29
Fletcher, Miss Alice 231
Fletcher, Tom 93
Flinn, W.D. 320
Flower, Governor

333

35, 136, 257
Flowers, — 170
Flowers, J.N. 186, 195
Flying-by 253
Folsom, ex-sheriff 217
Folsom, W.T. 26
Fontaine, 29
Foote, John M. 115
Force, Florence 114
Force, Minnie 114
Force, Miss Julia 114
Ford, 29
Forman, 29
Forman, Mr. 15
Forsyth, J.W. 311
Foshee 311
Foshee, A.L. 20, 99, 132, 170, 186, 195, 268
Foshee, Arch 145
Foshee, C. D. 14
Foshee, Durword 311
Foshee, G. 110
Foshee, G.O. 289
Foshee, H. 3
Foshee, Hugh 118, 188, 222, 230, 238, 268, 311
Foshee, J.H. 98
Foshee, J.W. 115, 130, 152
Foshee, John 117
Foshee, Miss 268
Foshee, Mrs. 122
Foshee, Mrs. M.A. 73
Foshee, Mrs. W.H. 55
Foshee, Ogilvie 122
Foshee, Thomas 73
Foshee, Wiley 65, 110
Foshee, Wylie 13, 37
Foster, Ex-Secretary 91

Foster, ex-Secretary 174
Foster, Ex-Secretary of the Treasury 167
Foster, Jesse 72
Foster, John 181
Foster, John A. 22
Fouse, P.G. 82
Foute, Mrs. Laura B. 305
Fowler, George 177
Fox, John 145
Fox, Robert 145
Foy, Levi W. 27
Frame, Paynter 245
Franklin 144
Franklin, Martin 92
Franklin, Miss Victoria 163, 303
Franklin, O.H. 310
Franklin, S. M. 3
Franklin, S.M. 144
Franklin, Thomas 65, 92
Frazier, 29
Frederick, ex-Empress 87
Frederick, Gordon 72
Frederickson, F.M. 296
Freeman 71
Freeman, Bro. 171
Freeman, G.W. 71, 99, 132, 170, 171
Freeman, J.L. 242
Freeman, P.E.J.S. 236
Frehan, Archbishop 151
Fremont, F. 7
French, C.A. 291
Frey, J. J. 22
Frick, Chairman 17
Frick, N.C. 95
Friday, D.A. 36, 60, 162, 247
Friday, H.W. 30

Friday, L.A. 261
Friday, Leroy 116
Friday, Mrs. Margaret 73, 247
Friday, Will 162
Frith, George W. 244
Frye, Mr. 305, 312
Fuller 239
Fuller, 29
Fuller, Chief Justice 35
Fuller, M.D. 26
Furbush, Capt. 212
Furners, W.H. 136

G

Gaffrey, 259
Gagley, W.B. 213
Gaines, 29
Gaines, Dick 293
Gaines, R.H. 21
Gaither, Chairman 182
Gaither, G.F. 79, 182
Gaither, Geo. F. 182
Gaither, George F. 70
Galinger, Mr. 215
Gallagher, Dr. 219
Gallaspie, J.H. 133
Gallinger, Mr. 188
Gammel, Sammuels 274
Gammel, Simms 274
Gandy, D.C. 162
Gandy, W.A. 124
Ganes, Ed 275
Ganzel 211
Gardiner, Gibbs 101
Gardner, J.H. 79
Gardner, Miss Lizzie 99
Gardner, Noah 214, 275
Gardner, Shepherd 318

Garfield 157
Garfield, President 8, 168
Garner 294, 311
Garner, D.W. 318
Garner, John 44, 215
Garner, M.S. 288
Garner, Mesdames 81
Garner, Miss O. 4
Garner, Miss O.M. 72, 118
Garner, Mrs. 54
Garner, Postmaster 262
Garner, W.S. 146
Garrard, L.F. 107
Garrett, R.H. 78
Garrison, J.W. 277
Gartman, Ella 311
Gartman, Miss Ella 146
Gast, Mr. 238
Gastright, 211
Gastright, Pitcher 135
Gates, F.T. 212
Gatling, Dr. 38, 258
Gause, S.S. 310
Gay, Curt. 241
Gay, Dr. 68
Gay, Harmon 168
Gay, J.G. 21, 132
Gay, J.M. 233
Gay, John F.,Jr. 200
Gay, Mrs. Ada 85
Gay, T.A. 250
Gay, T.H. 214
Gay, Thos. 132
Gaydy, J.H. 229
Gaylor, J.F. 154
Geeper 42
Geise, Frank 320
Gemindar, Bhagl 200
Gentry, B.M. 31, 36, 79, 93, 111, 115, 243
Gentry, Henry 32,

289
Gentry, J.P. 99, 132, 171, 260, 275
Gentry, Jasper 59
Gentry, Miss Alice 310
Gentry, Miss Julia 310
Gentry, Tax Collector 82
Gentry, Tax collector 62
Gentry, W.J. 293
George 227
George, C.S. 41
George, James Z. 42
George, Senator 41, 306
Gerbending, Henry 277
Geronimo 282
Gewen, J.M. 32
Gewen, Lee 32
Gibbon, J.H. 285
Gibbons, 29
Gibbons, J.H. 261
Gibbons, John 293
Gibson, Asbury 251
Gibson, Brother 98
Gibson, Chief Justice 309
Gibson, J.C. 99
Gibson, Major 276
Gibson, Mary A. 261
Gibson, Miss Mary Carr 99
Gibson, Mr. 152
Gibson, Rev. - 146
Gibson, W.G. 99
Gibson, W.M. 123
Gilbert, 29
Gilbert, H.C. 179
Gilbert, W.H. 295
Gilden, H.B. 36
Giles, Clemmon 32
Giles, Eddie 98, 185, 292

Giles, J.S. 32
Giles, John 32, 243
Giles, Pink 185
Gill, J.S. 55
Gilland, Judge 26
Gillerstedt, L.E. 26
Gillespie, Miss (?)nna 20
Gillespie, Neal 7
Gilmore, J.L. 26
Gipson, Charley B. 139
Gist, Mrs. Minnie 86
Givham, J.P. 124
Givhan, Dr. 228
Givhan, J.P. 45, 205
Givhan, Mr. 188
Gladstone, Henry E. 150
Gladstone, Mr. 177
Glanton, Dollie 26
Glass, A. 71, 170
Glass, Alex 99, 132, 170
Glass, B.F. 101
Glass, C.L. 170
Glasscock 268
Glasscock, A. 54, 260
Glasscock, Abb 184
Glasscock, Alex 186, 195, 260
Glasscock, Alexander 36
Glasscock, Benjamin and Margaret 36
Glasscock, C.I. 60
Glasscock, C.L. 261, 267
Glasscock, Howard 32
Glasscock, J.D. 261
Glasscock, J.N. 32
Glasscock, Mrs. Candice 283
Gleason, A.W. 5
Glenn, Houston 304
Glover, J.L. 314

Go(?)er, Col. and Mrs. 247
Goddard, 36
Godsey 30
Godsey, 30
Godsey, E. G. 4
Godsey, F. G. 4
Godsey, F.G. 29, 30
Goer, Joseph 162
Goetchius, Charles B. 27
Goeter, Joseph 72
Goethe 262
Goetter 50, 289
Goggins, Mallinda 168
Goins, Lawrence 47
Goldsby, 29
Goldston, John Sidney 50
Goldston, Mrs. 50
Goldstone, A.J. 226
Goldzier, Mr. 189
Gomez, Peblo 90
Gonzales, Prudencio 90
Goodgame, Ada 311
Goodgame, Frank 196, 208
Goodgame, G.W. 187
Goodgame, J.F. 170, 184, 311
Goodgame, J.W. 311
Goodgame, Janie 311
Goodgame, Miss Ada 131, 170
Goodgame, Miss Janie 185
Goodgame, Mrs. John 186
Goodson, (?)im 124
Goodson, James 103
Goodson, Jim 112
Goodson, Miss Emma 103

Goodwin, A.T. 87, 183, 211
Goodwin, John W. 41
Goodwin, Mr. 15
Goodwyn 15, 21
Goodwyn, A.T. 48, 49, 146, 264, 293
Goodwyn, Chairman 143, 184
Goodwyn, Mr. 15, 151
Goodwyn, Tyler 151, 160
Goodywn, Senator 304
Gordon, 259
Gordon, A.G. 300
Gordon, H.C. 200
Gordon, J.B. 67, 122, 227
Gordon, John B. 167, 309
Gordon, Mr. 188
Gordon, Senator 41, 208, 238
Gore 311
Gore, Albert 125
Gore, G.W. 20
Gore, George 61
Gore, J.P and Mrs. 251
Gore, J.P. 131, 172, 229, 230, 243
Gore, Joseph 80, 146, 206, 293
Gore, Prof. 262
Gorman, Mr. 188
Gorman, Senator 249
Gormley, J.B. 91
Gorve, E.J. 143
Goss, E.W. 157, 299
Goss, Joe 151
Goss, Joseph 131
Goss, W.D. 60
Gothard 205
Gothard, G.W. 171
Gough, Elsie 248

Gould, Edwin 143
Gould, George 143, 203, 305
Gould, Howard 143
Gould, Jay 143, 203, 305
Gould, K.O. 212
Gould, Kellogg O. 204
Gowan, Geo. A. 3
Gowin, 29
Graham, J.B. 159, 179
Graham, J.L. 72
Graham, James A. 115
Grandy, 38
Grant 151
Grant, Lou 38
Grant, Nellie 62
Grant, President 298, 313
Grant, R.T. 151
Grant, U.S. 201
Graves, Dr. 258
Graves, J.R. 129
Graves, Mrs. 258
Gray, G.B. 84, 242
Gray, J.A. 225
Gray, Justice 38
Gray, Miss Jessie 275
Gray, Mrs. 145
Gray, Sam 304
Gray, W.L. 97
Gray, W.S. 275
Gray, Willlie 30
Greely, Gen. 41
Greely, Horace 265
Green, (?) 206
Green, A.B.,Jr. 26
Green, Dan 296
Green, General 92
Green, J. J. 4
Green, J.A. 283
Green, Jno. A. 205
Green, John J. 261
Green, Joseph 131, 171
Green, Miss Mattie 260
Green, Monroe 259
Green, Morris 301
Green, W.A. 246, 292
Green, W.B. 246
Green, W.M. 205, 246
Greene, Jasper 274
Greenhagle, F.L. 241
Greenhalge, Mr. 282
Gregg, Henry 79, 103
Gregory, H. T. 18
Gresham 323
Gresham, Judge 35
Gresham, Secretary 89
Grey, Miss Alice 275
Grey, W.W. 275
Griffin, W.H. 165
Griffith, Alfred 234
Griffiths, W. E. 16
Griggs, Perry 176
Grim, Edward 167
Grimaldi, Signor 28, 209
Grinlinton, J.J. 28
Groce, B.W. 42, 47, 54, 111, 178, 249, 252, 260
Groce, W.B. 45
Grosscup, Judge 105
Grossman, Elina Booth 119
Grosvenor, Mr. 189
Grove, E.J. 143
Grover, George C. 17
Grubb, Miss Ella M. 209
Gruscha, Cardinal 16
Guice, C.W. 26
Guiteau 157
Guitteau 168

Gullahorn & Bro 133
Gullahorn, A.J. 93
Gullahorn, E.T. 72, 133, 289
Gullahorn, John 311
Gullahorn, Leonard 187
Gullahorn, Messrs. 55
Gullahorn, Sam 311
Gullahorn, T. 112
Gullahorn, Tom 37, 206, 222, 311
Gullahorn, Widow 187
Gullarhon, Tom 61
Gulledge 151
Gulledge, James 151
Gullespie, J.H. 72
Gunter, Bryant 23
Guthrie 17
Guy de Maupassant 143
Guzman, Doctor 142
Guzuella, Basgoa 285

H

Hackett, Captain 167, 176
Haddaway, Samuel W. 258
Haic, Dr. 168
Haines, Mr. 190
Hainey, T.B. 125
Halberstadt, Louis 96
Haldwick, H.W. 260
Haley, J.P. 61, 104, 124, 131, 172
Haley, John 97
Haley, Miss Nettie 104
Haley, P.W. 250
Hall, 36
Hall,
Deputy Collector 47
Hall, H.M.,Jr. 176
Hall, Jim 95
Hall, Mr. 189
Hall, William 10
Hallewood, George R. 302
Hamilton, A.G. 174
Hamilton, Miss Mary 257
Hamilton, Mrs. Major 201
Hammer, Edward B. 115
Hammond, L.W. 27
Hammond, Mr. 104
Hammonds, Lizzie 324
Hampton, Mr. and Mrs. 160
Hamton, Wade 41
Hand, James 109
Hand, Miss Mattie 124, 220
Handley, W. A. 25
Haney, Mr. 118
Haney, Thomas J. 118
Hanford, Judge 119
Hannen 294
Hannon, Mollie 311
Hanson, 29
Hanson, Capt. 38
Hanson, Mary 259
Haralsay, W.W. 25
Harding, Sheriff 25
Hardson, Carter H. 309
Hardy, 29
Hardy, H. 60, 261
Hardy, I. 78
Hardy, J.D. 85
Hare 311
Hare, (?).W. 222
Hare, C.W. 122, 251
Hare, Charles W. 251
Hare, John A. 176

Hare, Solicitor 283
Harold, Jailor 167, 176
Harper, Bell 300
Harrel, Tom 283
Harrell, Rufus 275
Harris 15, 21, 227
Harris, Carlyle W. 77
Harris, Cobb 113
Harris, Dan 100, 293
Harris, Frank 21, 49, 93, 97, 100, 105
Harris, H.A.J. 59
Harris, J. G. 4
Harris, J. Gid 108
Harris, J.H. 178
Harris, J.W. 176
Harris, James 26, 48, 66, 99, 304
Harris, James R. 60, 261
Harris, Jno. G. 117
Harris, Joel Chandler 227, 242
Harris, John G. 4
Harris, Major 56
Harris, Miss Mary 116
Harris, Miss Susie 85, 161
Harris, Mr. 36, 226, 250
Harris, Oscar 229
Harris, P.E. 60
Harris, Peter 191
Harris, Sam 13
Harris, Senator 235
Harris, W.C.,Jr 181
Harris, William A. 178
Harrison 281
Harrison, Ben 317
Harrison, Benjamin 38
Harrison, Carter 259, 274

Harrison, Carter H. 177
Harrison, Carter H.,Jr. 274
Harrison, Eugene 176
Harrison, Justice 153, 243
Harrison, Mayor 167, 273
Harrison, Miss 139
Harrison, Mr. 8
Harrison, Mrs. 9
Harrison, Mrs. George 235
Harrison, President 35
Harrison, Sophanisbe Preston 274
Harrison, Sophy 274
Harrison, Thomas 260
Harrison, Thos 195
Harrison, Thos. 186
Harrison, William 175
Harrison, William Preston 259, 274
Harrisson, Thomas 288
Hart, J.H. 270
Hart, President 129
Harte, Bret 242
Harter, Mr. 306
Hartsfield, Tom 299
Hartson, Mrs. Theresa 100
Harvell, John 81, 84
Harvey, J.A. 167
Harwell, John 293
Harwell, W.K. 244
Harwood 30, 118
Harwood, A.B. 72
Haseltine, E. T. 6
Haskins, Daniel W. 77
Hassler, Ferdinand

254
Hatchet, John 151
Hatchets 151
Hathcock, Houston 318
Hathcock, J.A. 117, 131, 318
Hathcock, James A. 84
Haugen 189
Hawkins, Henry 84, 293
Hawkins, V.O. 101, 109
Hawley 197
Hawley, Senator 226
Hawn, Mrs. Sarah 127
Hay, Brother 242
Hayes, E.J. 131, 172
Hayes, ex-Sheriff 31, 66
Hayes, John W. 14
Hayes, Lee 37, 70, 71, 82, 125, 151, 153, 160, 187, 246
Hayes, Miss Annie 113
Hayes, Mrs. Jennie 85, 228
Hayes, President 134
Hayes, Rutherford B. 90
Hayes, W.T. 60, 261
Hayes, Will 30, 44, 50, 66, 163, 284
Hayes, William 303
Haynie, T.B. 187, 206, 230
Hays, Rutherford B. 1
Hays, Rutherford Buchard 1
Hays, Webb C. 1
Hayse, E.H. 274
Hayse, Jase 303

Headley, C.N. 32
Headley, Elsza 32
Headley, James 160
Headley, Mrs. Albert 160
Headley, Prof. 145
Headley, R.Q. 288
Headley, Susan Jane 215
Headley, Wm. 84, 261
Headly, W.P. 228
Headly, William 32
Heald, Captain 201
Heath, Harry 157
Heath, Mrs. S.J. 124
Heath, S.J. 205
Heflin, J. Thomas 168
Heflin, Mrs. 288
Heilman, S.P. 182
Helgren, M. 321
Hembree, I.L. 113
Hembree, Isaac 115
Hembree, R.L. 233
Hemenway, Augustus 220
Henderson 115
Henderson, Charles 26
Henderson, Mr. 189, 216
Hendrick, Attorney-General 142
Henley, A. J. 13
Henley, A.J. 1, 3, 31
Henley, James 284
Henley, Mrs. J.K. 311
Henley, Rev. 103, 160
Henley, Rev. — 98
Henley, Rev. - 130
Henly, C.D. 26
Henly, John 221
Henry, Ed. 44, 50
Henry, H. 60
Henry, M.V. 121

337

Henry, Patrick 265
Henry, Wm. 119
Henson, Matthew 135
Hepburn, Mr. 198
Herbert, Hillary A. 28
Herbert, Mr. 38
Herbert, Mrs. 38
Herbert, Secretary 89, 121, 176, 296, 307
Herbert, Secretary of the Navy 107
Herndon, Geo. B. 113
Herod, John 161
Herring, Charles 239
Herrington, H. 143, 144
Herrod, Carrie 145
Herrod, H. 80
Herrod, Huey 144
Herrod, Johnny 144
Herrod, Mrs. 145
Herrod, Sarah 161
Herrod, William 161
Herron 296
Herstein, Monroe C. 149
Hester 294
Hester, James 147
Hester, Jim 311
Hester, Joe 311
Hester, Julia 311
Hester, Martin 100
Hester, Minnie 311
Hester, Mr. 62
Hester, Mrs. 222
Hewell 1
Hewit, John 195
Hewit, Mrs. Matilda 250
Hewitt, W. 278
Hick, Luther 194
Hickam, Edie 150
Hickey, J.P. 192

Hickman, Joseph 150
Hickman, Thomas N. 154
Hicks 117, 118
Hicks, (?).J. 82
Hicks, H.L. 123, 267
Hicks, Isaiah L. 277
Hicks, J.C. 117, 186, 195
Hicks, J.J. 60, 186, 195, 261
Hicks, Jack 55
Hicks, L.L. 132
Hicks, Miss 50
Hicks, Miss Fanny 50
Hicks, R.E. 30
Hicks, R.E.R. 4, 59, 72, 132, 172, 267, 288
Hicks, W.H. 194
Higginbotham, James 14
Higgins 112
Higgins, Senator 226
Hignett, Mr. 265
Hilbert, Dr. 1
Hilbert, Edward 155
Hilbert, Etta 155
Hill 319
Hill, 29
Hill, A.B. 72, 105
Hill, A.P. 259
Hill, Alonza 108
Hill, Cora 117
Hill, Ex-Senator 143
Hill Guard, David B. 38
Hill, J.R. 205
Hill, L.L. 53
Hill, Mayor 204
Hill, Miss Louisa 105
Hill, Morris 260
Hill, Mr. 188, 197,

225, 305
Hill, Murphy 75
Hill, Senator 307, 313
Hill, Walter 117
Hillhouse, J.D. 320
Himrod, Charles 89
Hinton, A.P. 252
Hitt, Mr. 306, 312
Hixon, J. Courtney 121
Hoar 188
Hoar, Mr. 188, 197, 235, 305, 306, 312
Hoar, Senator 249
Hobart, H.C. 174
Hobbs, B.T. 65
Hodges, Pruet 139
Hoffman, W. J. 10
Holcomb 281
Holiday, Joseph 25
Holland, Jessie 171, 213
Hollis, 29
Holloway, Prof. 123, 151
Holloway, Professor 73
Holly, J.W. 124
Holmes 81
Holmes, ?)ien A. 176
Holmes, Mrs. 185
Holt, 29
Holtclaw, J. T. 25
Holtzclaw, General 149
Holtzclaw, James T. 150
Honeycut, (?)e 124
Honeycut, R.M. 32, 81
Honeycutt 71, 288
Honeycutt, (?) 230
Honeycutt, Bro. 205
Honeycutt, Brother 54
Honeycutt, E.W. 246
Honeycutt, Ex-

President 70
Honeycutt, G.N. 111
Honeycutt, Geo. N. 304
Honeycutt, H.I. 260
Honeycutt, H.L. 153, 160
Honeycutt, Henry 81, 146, 311
Honeycutt, J.M. 60, 261
Honeycutt, Judge 12, 20, 30, 50, 66, 105, 111, 163, 238, 292
Honeycutt, Mrs. 124, 207
Honeycutt, Mrs. R.M. 163
Honeycutt, R. 55
Honeycutt, R.M. 2, 20, 32, 50, 61, 62, 71, 73, 80, 84, 99, 100, 111, 117, 123, 130, 132, 146, 163, 170, 173, 184, 186, 195, 205, 229, 252, 260, 283, 292, 302
Hooker, Miss 99
Hooker, Mr. 198
Hooker, Representative 193
Hooks, M.M. 219
Hooper, Emma M. 165
Hooper, Miss Sally 92
Hooper, Mr. 318
Hopkins, F.A. 109
Hopkins, John P. 37, 309
Hopkins, Mr. 198
Hopper 187
Hopson, A. 281
Hopson, William 281
Hosmer, S.M. 109

Houlditch, H.W. 61
Houlditch, Maggie 260
Houlditch, W.R. 111
Houston & Richards 297
Houston, S.A. 41
Hout, A.L. 324
Howard, Andrew 261
Howard, M.W. 26
Howe, S.D. 139
Howell, George P. 108
Howell, William D. 282
Howze, Lem 168
Hoy, 135, 239
Hubbard, D.C. 123
Hubbard, Lizzie 92
Hubbard, Miss Perdelia 36
Hubbard, R.M. 260
Hubbard, Susan 92
Hubbard, T.J. 92
Hubbard, Vernon 123
Hudgens, Herma 123
Hudgens, J.D. 123
Hudgeons, D.H. 99, 132
Hudgins, Gilbert 176
Hudson, B.H. 296
Hudson, Judge 129, 142
Hudson, Mr. 235
Hudson, Robert 157, 168
Huey 101
Huff, Uriah 219
Huffman, 29
Huffman, Albert 294
Huffman, Geo. 314
Hughes, John 216
Hughes, R.H. 266
Hull, General 201
Hull, Miss Clara

116
Humann, Admiral 177
Humphrey, D. 213
Hundley 15, 21
Hundley, Mr. 21
Hung-Chang, Lt. 209
Hunt, Bill 161
Hunt, R.H. 26
Hunter, 234
Hunter, Ike 163
Hunter, W.W. 239
Huntington, R.W. 35
Hunton 188
Hunton, Eppa 309
Hutchinson, John 266
Hutchinson, Mr. 189
Hutto, A.A. 30, 67, 73, 196
Hutto, W.J. 23

I

Ingalls, J.J. 177
Inge, H.T. 177
Ingersol, Colonel 225
Inzer 21
Inzer, I. 15
Inzer, Mr. 15, 21
Iron, A.G. 159
Irvin, John 101
Irvine 281
Irving, Washington 269
Irwin, Surgeon 89
Ivey, Dr. 56
Ivey, Mrs. 303

J

J., J. Green 14
Jackson, 29
Jackson, Andrew 203, 319
Jackson, Bishop 153, 163, 247, 293

Jackson, Charles 86
Jackson, Charley 73
Jackson, Dr. 31
Jackson, Geo. 55
Jackson, James 282
Jackson, Mr. 22
Jackson, T.F. 84
Jam, Jos Dan 323
Jameson, George H. 108
Jas. Longerier 116
Jay, J.L. 149
Jefferson, Joseph 150, 301
Jefferson, Thomas 16, 41, 203
Jelks, William D. 27
Jenkins, Health Officer 269
Jenkins, Isaac 150
Jenkins, J.G. 41
Jenkins, James 300
Jenkins, John 221
Jenkins, Judge 105
Jennings 30
Jennings, Prof. 93
Jennings, S.J. 30, 72, 109, 117, 124, 131, 172, 288
Jew, Duncan,Jr 108
John the Baptist 219
Johns, W.N. 61, 186, 195, 260
Johnson 49
Johnson, (?), 66
Johnson, A. 299
Johnson, B.F. 165
Johnson, Banker 183
Johnson, Ben 263
Johnson, Doctor 141
Johnson, Dr. 62, 173, 195, 222, 262, 276, 277, 284, 288, 304
Johnson, Drs. 311
Johnson, J.S. 125,

277, 284, 311
Johnson, J.S.,Jr. 247, 268, 319
Johnson, James 157
Johnson, John 198
Johnson, Judge 285
Johnson, L.N. 174
Johnson, L.W. 161
Johnson, M.E. 161
Johnson, Mary 275
Johnson, Mr. 190
Johnson, Mrs. 196
Johnson, President 134
Johnson, S.J.,Jr. 85
Johnson, Samuel 285
Johnston, David 186, 195
Johnston, Joseph F. 183, 264, 313
Johnston, Joseph H. 310
Johnston, Robert P. 108
Joiner, 29
Joiner, J.A. 15
Joiner, Mr. 15
Jones 29, 227
Jones, 28, 29
Jones, ?).N. 147
Jones and Brothers 19
Jones, Ayres 234
Jones, C.C.,Jr. 149
Jones, Dave 149, 295
Jones, Doc 104
Jones, E.C. 72
Jones, E.D. 220
Jones, E.N.,Jr. 121
Jones, Elijah 61
Jones, F.M. 247
Jones, F.N. 311
Jones, G.W. 260
Jones, G.W.A. 32
Jones, Geo. 299
Jones, Gov. 59, 109, 193
Jones, Governor 18,

339

65, 149, 176, 192, 299, 322
Jones, J.E. 71, 98, 99, 110, 123, 131, 132, 170, 172, 185, 205
Jones, J.H. 194
Jones, J.R. 192
Jones, J.S. 72, 146, 151
Jones, J.S.,Jr 61
Jones, J.W. 178
Jones, Jesse R. 284
Jones, Jno. E. 186, 195
Jones, Joe 246
Jones, John P. 274
Jones, Jonathan 303
Jones, Lewis 275
Jones, M.H. 32
Jones, Melissa 250
Jones, Miss Ella B. 123
Jones, Miss Geneva 79, 131, 172, 267
Jones, Miss Jessie 55, 81, 118
Jones, Miss Martha A. 13
Jones, Mr. 198, 216, 237
Jones, Mrs. Ella 122, 130
Jones, Mrs. Paratine 237
Jones, Natty 117
Jones, Peter 125, 293
Jones, Prof. 237
Jones, R.A. 294
Jones, R.C. 123
Jones, R.D. 26
Jones, R.S. 303
Jones, S.E. 300
Jones, S.W. 72
Jones, Sam 33, 219, 273, 281
Jones, Tommie 227, 274

Jones, Tommy 151, 161
Jones, W.B. 72
Jones, W.W. 194
Jones, Walter 250
Jones, William 84, 293
Jones, Wm. 44, 84
Jones, Z.J. 59, 71, 170, 171, 186, 195
Jordan, H.B. 32
Jordan, J.R. 53
Jorns 81
Joseph, Emperor Francis 16
Joseph, J.M. 225
Joyce, Bishop 26
Joyner, Mr. 15
Judd, Max 41
Judge, M.T. 297
Juggernaut, Shylock 183
Julian, Rosolins 226

K

Kaiulani, Princess 291
Kampe, Jules B. 10
Kane, Miss Jane 257
Kane, Timothy 317
Karney, James 23
Keel, P.A.W. 191
Keely, Dr. 191
Keener, J.O. 109
Kelley, G.S. 192
Kelley, G.W. 295
Kelly 239
Kelly, Charles 121
Kelly, Judge 94
Kem, O.M. 178
Kemp 15, 21, 311
Kemp, (?).R. 105
Kemp, J.R. 276
Kemp, John 130
Kemp, Will 3, 247, 251
Kempster, Dr. 28
Kendrick, B.J. 140

Kendrick, Humphrey B. 102
Kenna, Senator 33
Kennedy 135
Kennedy, 29
Kennedy, Mrs. J.S. 235
Kennedy, Sheperd 295
Kenny, J.I. 291
Kent, 302
Kent, E.E. 182
Kernot, W.C. 217
Key, Mayor T. 13
Key, Sam 112
Key, Thomas 35, 70
Key, Thos. 48
Key, Thos. J. 151
Keyes, Thomas 66
Kicker, (?)ewt 20
Kicker, J.W.G. 84
Kicker, Joe 261
Kicker, Mrs. 55
Kicker, N.A. 261, 311
Kicker, Newt 55
Kicker, T.S. 213
Kicker, Whit 103
Kid 27
Kilbreth, James T. 158
Kilgore, Mr. 313
Killebrew, 29
Killegraw, O. 85
Killingsworth, J.B. 60
Killingsworth, R. 61
Kilpatrick, Mr. 294
Kimbrough, Burrell 295
King, D.W. 204
King, J.S. 172
King, Joe 237
King John 126
King Khama 324
King of England 142
King, W.R. 133, 146

Kinsley, Levi 273
Kipling, Mrs. 239
Kipling, Rudyard 239, 282
Kirby 49
Kirk, Postmaster 321
Kivlan, Clare May 126
Klener, C.W. 161
Knigh, J.B. 288
Knight, 29
Knight, Brother 86, 105
Knott, J.J. 234
Knowles, Miss Ella 143
Knowlton, Captain 115
Knox, Dr. 199
Knox, James 32
Knox, John 32
Knox, R.H. 305
Knox, Robert H. 3
Knox, Robt. H. 105
Knox, W.E. 313
Koenigsthal, Morris 233
Koenigswarter, Baron 282
Kolb, Capt. 42, 47, 48
Kolb, R. 146
Kolb, R.F. 130, 151, 160, 183
Kreissing, C.L. 82
Kreutzer, John 231
Kunz, Mr. 239
Kurtz, Charles W. 108
Kyle, 29
Kyle, J.H. 178
Kyle, Mr. 215
Kyle, Senator 213

L

La Chambra 41
Lacey, James O. 139
Lacey, Mr. 189

Lack, Henry 241
Lackey 15, 21
Lacombe, Judge 53
Lacy, G. 293
Lacy, Mr. 312
Lacy, Will 245
Ladd, Bayless E. 113
Lafliteau, P.H. 26
Lahey, Mrs. 253
Lamar, Claud 233
Lamar, Justice 2
Lamar, L.Q.C. 22
Lamar, Lucius Quintus Cincinnatus 11
Lamar, Mrs. 206
Lamb, John J. 95
Lamb, Mayor 191
Lambert, William 161
Lambert, Wm. 187, 243, 246
Lamont 323
Lamont, Dan 249
Lamont, Daniel S. 38
Lamoreaux, S.W. 41
Landersborough, L.M. 273
Landley, 29
Landrum, H.D. 144
Landside, Harriet 97
Landslides, Harriet 206
Lane, Edward 278
Lane, H.D. 129, 264
Lane, Hector D. 151
Lane, Mr. 198
Lane, Wm.C. 53
Langston 71
Langston, D.L. 54
Langston, Geo. W. 243
Langston, J.P. 19
Langston, J.M. 71
Langston, J.W. 123
Langston, Jack 84

Langston, Job 229
Langston, L.M. 260
Langston, Mr. 98
Langston, P.N. 292
Langston, R.J. 82
Langston, W.E. 310
Langston, Z.W. 111
Lapeyre, Capt. 200
Larinsky, Julius 281
Lary, 29
Latham, Miss Polly 85, 311
Latham, Newt 85, 214
Latham, Newton 214
Laudon, Horace 56
Lavender, W.W. 289
Lavinsky, Ed. 84
Lavretta, 29
Lawler, Levi W. 25
Lawrence, Editor 49
Lawrence, Geo. H. 6
Lawrence J. McParlin 130
Lawrence, J.M. 139
Lawrence, Jake 277
Lawrence, John, Jr. 277
Lawrence, Thomas 261
Lawrence, Thomas N. 277
Lawrence, Thos 60
Lawshe, William 181
Lawton, A.S. 310
Layton, Mr. 189
Lease, Mary 203
Lebron, John 131, 172
Ledochowski, Cardinal 136
Lee, A.J. 123, 171, 260
Lee, Caroline 157
Lee, Charley 169
Lee, Chas. 84
Lee, Elmer 269

Lee, Fitzhugh 70
Lee, H.B. 129
Lee, Hugh J. 135
Lee, Mr. 145
Lee, Richard Henry 16
Lee, Sam 314
Leeper 81
Leffers, Samuel 277
Leffingwell, W.H. 324
LeGrand, M. P., Sr 25
Leibert, A. J. 3
Leishman, A. E. 5
Leiter, L.Z. 282
Leiter, Mr. 8
Lenoir, T.J. 304
Lenox 217
Lenty, F.W. 112
Leonard, A.J. 311
Leopard, Bethany S. 4
Leopard, Bethany S. 14
Leopard, John G. 4, 14
Lesseps, Dr. 242
Lesser & Co. 3
Letcher, J. W. 12
Letcher, J. Wiley 48
Letcher, J.F.T. 153
Letcher, J.W. 72, 82
Letcher, John 260
Letcher, Maudie 229
Letcher, Miss Jeanie 80
Letcher, Mr. 48
Letcher, Richard 80
Letcher, S.R. 206, 228, 267
Letcher, T.G. 72, 124, 179
Letcher, Wiley 80
Levy, Jules 168
Lewelling, Governor 291
Lewis, George 311
Lewis, John 304

Lewis, Mr. 200, 297
Lide, Eli 299
Lightfoot, H.W. 108
Ligon, John 158
Likins, W. H. 11
Lil, Queen 301
Lill, L.L. 268
Lillick, Lewis 157
Lillonkaloni, Queen 273
Lilloukalani, ex-Queen 291
Lincoln, Abraham 203
Lincoln, Mr. 89
Lincoln, President 9
Lincoln, Robert T. 89
Lindsay 259
Lindsay, Senator 226
Lindsey, 38
Liner, J.A. 179
Lippman, Leonard 4
Litesey, L.C. 182
Little, Dr. 21, 97, 162, 194
Little, George 36
Little, John 25
Little, R.W. 250
Littlefield, W.L. 32
Littlejohn, I.J. 60
Littlejohn, James 185
Littlejohn, Mrs. 185
Littlejohn, Mrs. James 185
Littlejohn, Noah 261
Littlejohn, Rufus 133
Littlejohn, T.J. 261
Littlejohn, Wiley, Jr. 243
Littlejohn, Wylie 60, 261
Littleton, Aaron 60, 237, 261
Littleton, G.W. 60, 261

341

Littleton, Isaac 60, 161, 261
Littleton, J.E. 44
Littleton, John 98
Littleton, W.L. 261
Livingston, George S. 181
Livingston, L.F. 53
Livingston, Mr. 198, 273, 312
Lloyd, 29
Lloyd family 11
Lloyd, Minnie 311
Lodg, Wm. 276
Lodge 188
Lodge, David 144
Lodge, Davy 172
Lodge, G.W. 79, 122, 172, 173
Lodge, George 71, 144, 152
Lodge, John 144
Lodge, Maggie 103
Lodge, Miss Lizzie 71, 79
Lodge, Mrs. 144
Lodge, Mrs. Sarah 98
Lodge, Senator 204
Lodge, W.M. 144, 151
Lodge, William 79
Lodge, Willie 293
Lodge, Wm. 98, 188
Logan, (?) 153
Logan, G.O. 260
Logan, Gundy 37
Logan, J.A. 59, 70, 115, 153, 160, 184, 185, 223, 229, 259, 262, 276, 277, 319
Logan, L.A. 70
Logan, Neal 319
Logan, W.A.G. 60
Loie, Jules 294
Lombard, George R. 107
Lombard, Mr. 108

Long, J.L. 43
Long, John 49
Longcryer, J.C. 229
Longcryer, Mr. 97
Longerier, Jas. 116
Longeryer, J.H. 124, 132
Longeryer, Rev. 161
Longshore, A.P. 182
Longstreet, Lee 259
Longwell, Roy 266
Lopez, Enrique 11
Lopez, Jose de J. 225
Lopez, Maud Alexandrina 11
Lord, Dr. 324
Loring 49
Loti, Pierre 87
Louck, President 183
Loucks, H.D. 74
Loucks, H.L. 78, 143
Loucks, President 83, 103, 183, 203
Love, Louis 293
Lovelace, 29
Lovelady, S.P. 233
Loveman, D.B. 107
Lowe, D.B. 98, 122, 144
Lowe, E.H. 122, 130
Lowe, Mary 122
Lowe, Mattie 122
Lowe, Miss Mary 79, 152
Lowe, Miss May 144
Lowe, W.H. 289
Lowery, 144
Lowery, A.G.W. 32
Lowery, Belle 311
Lowery, John A. 231
Lowery, W.R. 4, 32
Lowrey, J.G. 184
Lowry, W.E. 61

Loyola 262
Lucas, Miss 122, 184
Lunny, F.H. 36
Lunsden, J.M. 191
Lurton, H.H. 41
Lyman, Chas. 313
Lyman, Peters 81
Lynch, Thomas 16
Lyons, Albert 322

M

M(?)iam, Louis 273
M., B. Gentry 14
Mack, P.H. 72
Mackey, J.W. 245
MacMahon, Catcher 135
Macune, C.W. 143
Macune, Dr. 83
Maddox, J.M. 294
Maddox, Maggie 117
Maddox, Mattie 14
Maddox, N.J. 60, 261
Maddox, R.W. 161
Maddox, W.R. 92
Madison, Jas. 181
Mahan, H.M 162
Mahan, Henry M. 243
Malachi, Willie 44
Mallory, Mr. 198
Maloney, Matt 56
Malstraw, C.H.D. 320
Manchester, W. A. 18
Manderson, Mr. 197
Manderson, Senator 266
Manning, J.C. 91, 182, 183
Manning, J.R. 178
Manning, Joseph C. 182
Manning, Mr. 78, 96, 292
Manning, Mrs. 107

Mantel, Lee 208
Mantle 208
Mantle, Lee 197
Mantle, Mr. 197
Mar-(?), J.B. 304
Marbury, J.H. 321
Marbury, Joe 321
Marbury, Mr. 319
Marcus, J.J. 32
Marcus, J.L. 32
Marcus, Miss Martha 229
Marcus, Miss Roberta 185
Marcus, T.J. 122
Markee, Mrs. 144
Marks, C.F. 310
Marlar, A.J. 56, 65, 98, 144, 152, 172
Marlar, Charlie 79
Marlar, Lloyd 103
Marlar, Mack 103
Marlar, Miss Annie 162
Marlar, Miss Willie 122, 144, 172
Marlar, Miss Willis 56, 65, 71, 79, 98, 110, 122, 152
Marlar, Mrs. Mary 98
Marler, A.J. 122
Marler, Mackey 122
Marler, Mrs. Dr. 186
Maroney, N.L. 205
Marsh 86
Marsh, M. 169
Marshall, Congressman 228
Marshall, Mitchell H. 296
Marshall, W.A. 124
Marshall, Willie 85, 110, 152, 221
Marshall, Wm. 247
Martchell, Will 162
Martin, B.M. 85
Martin, B.N. 43, 59
Martin, Bartley 261

Martin, Bradley 155
Martin, C.R. 32
Martin, Charles 191
Martin, D.H. 117
Martin, D.M. 260
Martin, D.N. 246
Martin, Dan 73
Martin, Daniel 86
Martin, Elder 229
Martin, H.B. 291
Martin, H.C. 37
Martin, I.B. 221
Martin, J.B. 111, 246
Martin, J.T. 111, 228
Martin, John 214
Martin, Judge 17
Martin, L.B. 246
Martin, M.D. 260
Martin, Miss Ella 162
Martin, Miss Mary 66
Martin, Mr. 31, 85, 144, 152
Martin, Mrs. 62
Martin, Mrs. Angeline 66
Martin, Mrs. David 21
Martin, O. M. 1
Martin, Robert 18, 20
Martin, Robt. 187
Martin, Thomas 309
Martin, Tom 55
Martin, W.D. 62, 99, 132, 170
Martin, W.H. 261
Martin, W.J. 27, 131, 171, 221
Martin, Willie 84
Martin, Willis 293
Marvel, Andrew 270
Mason, D. 30
Massey, A.D. 251
Massey, A.J. 163, 243, 284
MASSEY, DR. 62
Massey, J.W. 107
Massey, Mr. 247
Mastin 78
Mastin, 28, 29
Mastin, O.M. 11, 71, 97, 115, 146, 163, 187, 243, 246, 268
Mathers, T.L. 5
Mathews 311
Mathews, John 26
Matthew, Mr. 125
Matthews 294
Matthews, C.B. 182
Matthews, Capt. 89
Matthews, Dr. 30, 261, 319
Matthews, E (?) 196
Matthews, E.A. 319
Matthews, Marion 196
Matthews, Mrs. 320
Mauchline, Benie 205
Mauchline, Ray 205
Mavtublev, Joseph 107
Maxwell, Harlem P. 115
Maxwell, J.D. 105
Maxwell, Jas. R. 74
Maxwell, John D. 195
Maxwell, Postmaster General 306
May, Joseph 168, 176
May, Miss Jane 304
May, Miss Jennie 131
May, Mr. 230
May, Mrs. 222
May, R.D. 43, 151, 179
May, Robert 131, 146, 304
maybe, J.(? H.)
Longcryer 132
McAdory, I.W. 159
McAdory, John 297
McAllister, Mr. 155
McBride, C.H. 237
McBride, Robert 310
McCain, T.J. 242
McCall, 29
McCall, C.E. 182
McCall, Chas. E. 182
McCall, Mr. 15, 189
McCan, Mrs. 184
McCane, J.E. 118
McCann, Sam 84
McCarron, 29
McCartha, C.L. 108
McCarthy 211
McCary, A.M. 111
McCary, Bud 303
McCary, F.M. 261
McCauley, Emanuel 157
McClanerhan, Mrs. E.A. 72
McCollough, Ed. J. 244
McComb, Jas. 101
McConnell, Mr. 139
McCord, J.M. 43
McCord, Rev. 56
McCorkle, N.T. 101
McCormick, George C. 27
McCormick, Senator 53
McCorquadales, Ernest 176
McCorries, E.Y. 251
McCovey, T.C. 159
McCoy, Dr. 257
McCoy, W.D. 114
McCracken, Isaac 73
McCreary, Mr. 197
McCrory, Mr. 278
McCullom, Mr. 215
McCullough, J.E. 116, 130, 161
McCullough, Thomas 293
McCune, Dr. 41
McDaniel, ?) 222
McDaniel, Morris 126
McDaniel, Mrs. Ed 230
McDaniels, Ola 62
McDonald, 29
McDonald, A. 157
McDonald, Chief of Police 320
McDonald, D. 157
McDonald, J.L. 288
McDonald, Miss Eliza 1
McDonald, Mr. 198
McDowel, J.J. 214
McDowell, Annie 140
McDowell, J. Hugh 78
McDowell, J.H. 67, 77
McDowell, J.J. 31, 194
McDowell, John 292
McEachen, 1
McFarland, J.R. 182
McFARLAND, J.W. 74
MoGaha, A.W. 108
McGhee, B. 261
McGlynn, Dr. 10
McGraw, Governor 178
McGraw, O.C. 111
McGraw, Oliver C. 231
McGregor, J.R. 78
McGrier, Miss Annie 144
McGroarty, Condy

199
McGugin, Bro. 144
McGuin, Eli 32
McGuire, Mr. 184
McGuire, R.T. 261
McGuire, T.B. 291
McGuire, T.H. 158
McIlwain, J.H. 182
McKay, Editor 121
McKee, (?)mes 153
McKee, James F. 32, 243
McKee, Mard 185, 206
McKee, Mrs. James 186
McKee, P. 80
McKee, P.M. 131, 172
McKeighan, W.A. 178
McKinney, J.W. 295
McKinney, James 124
McKinzie, Alexander 321
McKnight, George B. 75
McLane, C. 5
McLaughey, Chief of Police 65
McLaughey, Wilson 65
McLauren, Mr. 198
McLean, Dr. 324
McLean, John R. 323
McLendon, Mrs. Mary 300
McLendon, Sheriff 159, 167, 176
McLeod, John C. 108
McLure, Margaret 309
McMahon, Martin G. 35
McMahon, Mrs. Martha 11
McMath,

Miss Cornelia 2
McMillan 81, 317
McMillon, Will 323
McMories, Mr. 222
McMorries 311
McMorries, Caldwell 311
McMorries, E.Y. 186, 267
McMorries, Professor 230
McMorris, Prof. 133
McMorris, Professor 207
McMurray, J.L. 32
McNeal, Bennie 221
McNeal, Dr. 213
McNeil, G.R. 159
McNulty, Jno. C. 205
McPherson, Mr. 188, 197
McQueen, 29
McRae 15, 21
McRae, Mr. 15, 30
McRee, Ola 311
McSpadden, S.K. 215
McTyre, Lieut. 234
McVeigh, Wayne 313
Mead, Harry 85
Mead, Jane 139
Meador 29
Meador, 29
Meak, Mrs. 135
Meehan, Patrick 310
Meineke, Charles 322
Melton, W.W. 111
Melville, Henry 304
Menshew, Joseph 149
Merchant, Miss Ophelia 243
Meritt 211
Merrit, F.H. 206

Merritt 294, 311
Merritt, Charlie 222
Merritt, F.H. 214
Merritt, Leonida 211
Merritt, Mr. 2
Merritt, W.H. 93, 222, 230, 236, 237, 289
Metcalf, Mrs. Nellie N. 258
Michael, J.W. 132
Michael, R.J. 132
Mickay, Flem 206
Micou, Benjamin 296
Mictro, Col. 212
Middle(?), Os(?) 81
Middlebrooks, I.W. 59
Middlebrooks, J.T. 61
Middlebrooks, J.W. 82
Middlebrooks, John 246
Middleton 81
Middleton, Captain 93
Middleton, Gamma 311
Middleton, Miss Gamma 187, 243, 288
Middleton, R.C. 186
Middleton, W.A. 118, 124, 196, 238
Mike, Old 194, 206
Miles, Nelson A. 136, 142
Milford, Hobert 14
Miller, 302
Miller, C.J. 142
Miller, E.B. 23
Miller, G.K. 109
Miller, H. 107
Miller, J.A. 115
Miller, J.R. 213

Miller, L.A. 118
Miller, Mrs. Bertie 142
Miller, Robert 324
Milligan 135
Milligan, 136
Millins, W. 105
Mills 259
Mills, 29
Mills, Mr. 235
Mills, Mrs. Sarah 21
Mills, Roger Q. 265
Mills, Senator 323
Millstead, W.J. 61
Milner 15, 21
Milner, 21
Milner, John T. 72, 75
Milner, Mr. 15
Milsap, R. 291
Milton, Isaac 321
Mimms 71
Mimms, A. 71
Mimms, Ada 117
Mimms, W.A. 99, 132
Mims, (?) 82
Mims, Abram C. 277
Mims, Elijah 60
Mims, Francis D. 289
Mims, G.W. 60, 261
Mims, George 84, 293
Mims, J.M. 261
Mims, J.N. 103
Mims, J.T. 60, 261
Mims, J.W. 228
Mims, James 318
Mims, L.W.A. 246
Mims, Miss N.J. 260
Mims, Miss Rosa 20
Mims, Moses 59, 194
Mims, Mr. 85
Mims, Thomas 60

Mims, W.A. 59, 85, 186, 195, 260, 268
Mims, W.S. 289
Minge 15, 21
Mingo, Mrs. George 139
Mink, Charles F. 298
Mink, Mrs. 298
Mink, Mrs. Sarah 298
Missidin, Thomas J. 113
Mita, Sarat Chaudra 199
Mitcheal, Dan 246
Mitcheal, R.J. 250
Mitchell 257
Mitchell, 301, 323
Mitchell, Charlie 323
Mitchell, Chief of Police 141
Mitchell, D.H. 72, 124, 162, 247
Mitchell, Dan 160
Mitchell, E.W. 160
Mitchell, J.K. 127
Mitchell, J.W. 26, 228
Mitchell, Miss Alice 85, 160
Mitchell, Mr. 162
Mitchell, R.A. 27
Mitchell, R.J. 152
Mitchell, R.L. 85
Mitchell, Robert 119
Mitchell, Senator 226
Mitchell, Thomas 116
Mitchell, Tom 233
Mitchell, W.T. 124
Mitchell, Wiley 116
Mitchell, Wyley 110
Mitra, Mr. 200
Mixson, 29
Mixson, Ellis 152
Mixson, Wm. 152
Mohan, H.M. 289
Molten, Robert 206
Montgomery, Mark 264
Montgomery, Mr. 317
Montgomery, Wm. 300
Moody & Sons 5
Moody, Clarence 184
Moody, Dwight L. 282
Moody, John 122, 214
Mooney, James 231
Mooney, John 17
Moore 71, 117, 220
Moore, (?) 187
Moore, (?).M. 207
Moore, (?)h 207
Moore, B. H. 13
Moore, Bama 125
Moore, Bamma 229, 311
Moore, D. 30
Moore, Dave 194
Moore, David 21, 43, 72, 92, 132, 206, 214
Moore, Frank 44
Moore, George 283, 292
Moore, Hamlin V. 273
Moore, Harvey 222
Moore, J. Alex 4, 30, 72, 118, 132, 172
Moore, J.W. 4
Moore, J.A. 99, 132, 170
Moore, J.B.,Jr. 132, 172
Moore, J.N. 288
Moore, J.W. 29, 54, 81, 117, 131, 171, 213, 267, 288
Moore, James 80, 251
Moore, John 10, 19, 80
Moore, L. 60, 261
Moore, L.J. 73
Moore, Lundsford and Elizabeth 54
Moore, Maggie 125, 311
Moore, Miss Etta 131, 146, 288
Moore, Miss Lena 303
Moore, Moses 289
Moore, Mrs. 105, 214
Moore, Mrs. P. 93
Moore, Nannie 229
Moore, P. M. 13
Moore, P.C. 111
Moore, P.M. 173
Moore, Pink 13
Moore, Rev. 71
Moore, Richard 161
Moore, Sheriff 12, 20, 44, 48, 62, 100, 105, 118, 153, 163, 207, 222, 238, 243, 267, 276, 319
Moore, Superintendent 284
Moore, Supt. 100, 126, 207
Moore, Tom 311
Moore, W.B. 310
Moore, W.D. 89, 130
Moore. Wiley Davis 125
Moorman, Adjutant-General 122
Moorman, General 167
Moorman, George 67, 227
Morague, Judge 157
Morgan 151, 190, 227
Morgan, David 135
Morgan, J. Pierpont 42
Morgan, J.H. 168
Morgan, J.W.,Jr. 179
Morgan, Lulu 135
Morgan, Mr. 160, 215, 233
Morgan, Philander 78, 79, 104, 182, 195
Morgan, Senator 109, 194, 220, 246, 287
Morries, M. 222
Morrill, Mr. 197, 306, 312
Morrill, Senator 8
Morris, 29
Morris, Charles 112
Morris, Josiah 181, 322
Morris, M.Y. 118
Morris, Major 17
Morrison, Jim 74
Morrow, Sheriff 183
Morse, Asa P. 241
Morse Bros 5
Morse, Mr. 312
Morton, J. Sterling 28, 213
Morton, J.W. 32
Morton, Mr. and Mrs. J. Sterling 38
Mosely, Dr. 47, 48
Mosely, Miss Maggie Lou 295
Mosely, Miss. Maggie Lou 296
Mosely, Rev. 122
Moses, Mr. 189
Moses Robinson 12
Moses Robinson, Bro., 12
Moss, L.K. 26
Mote, J.J. 111

345

Motes, Charley 285
Motley, John 161
Motley, Miss Betty 161
Moultrie, J.L. 294
Mrs. Edner 163
Mulligan 7
Mullins 311
Mullins, (C?).R. 80
Mullins Bros. 196
Mullins, C. 288
Mullins, Clement 131, 171
Mullins, I.K. 59
Mullins, J.T. 60
Mullins, James H. 146, 153
Mullins, Messrs. 206
Mullins, Miss Sophie 131
Mullins, Mr. 112
Mullins, Mrs. 86
Mullins, O.K. 86, 146
Mullins, Oliver 43
Mullins, Oscar 186, 207
Mullins, Reese 311
Mullins, Tipton 311
Mullins, Tipton T. 247
Mullins, W.I. 311
Mullins, William I. 207
Munn, Dave 299
Murphree, J.C. 233
Murphy, J.A. 184
Murphy, Mr. 2
Murray, George Washington 177
Murray, Mr. 225
Murreh, W.P. 32
Muse, Miss Fannie 170
Musgrove, J.C. 101
Musgrove, J.S. 181
Mustin, William 101
Mustin, Wm. 109
Mutchler, Howard 140
Mutchler, William 114
Mutchler, Wm. 140
Myers, Sarah Jane 289

N

Nabor 322
Nabors 323
Nail, W.B. 26
Nakoma 51
Napoleon 263
Narrel, Rufus 318
Narrell, Jeff 84
Nathan 269
Nathan, Joe H. 75
Neal, H.C. 142
Neal, James M. 209
Neal, Miss Susie 181
Neal, Mr. 209
Neil, R.E.L. 216
Nelson, 239
Nelson, Arthur 241
Nelson, Charlie 233
Nelson, Hunter B. 108
Nelson, James 300
NeSmith 15, 21
NeSmith, 29
NeSmith, Jas. E. 15
Newell, Olney 220
Newlands, F.G. 178
Newman, Miss Jessie 219
Newman, Mr. 198
Newman, Robert 27
Nicholas 211
Nichols, 135
Nicklin, J.B. 129
Nickoll, W.C. 321
Nicolai 263
Nisbet, 29
Nix, Miss Fannie 214
Nix, Monroe 275
Nix, Mrs. 214
Nix, W. 115
Nix, W.D. 60, 261
Nix, W.F. 59
Nix, W.G. 246
Nix, Zeke 98
Noble, Secretary 27
Noble, Stephen W. 296
Nolan, Mr. 14
Nolan, Solicitor 2
Nolen 61, 311
Nolen, 29
Nolen, Attorney 50
Nolen, Mrs. 86, 230
Nolen, Squire 86, 125, 222
Nolen, Squire and Mrs. 195
Nolen, W.B. 50, 100, 251, 283
Noral 151
Nordhoff, Charles 142
Norman, J.D. 37
Norrell, General 56
Norrels, Wm. 20
Norrill, (?) 81
Norris, Andrew S. 311
Norris, Miss Lou 230
Northcutt, A.F. 283
Northcutt, C.M. 283
Northcutt, J.N. 283
Northcutt, Mason 4, 14, 236
Northcutt, P.B. 292
Northington, W.T. 25
Norwood 321
Norwood, Henry 321
Norwood, Thomas M. 91
Nuckles 234
Nunemacher, William 169

O

Oakman, Walter G. 193
Oates 193, 227, 274
Oates, Col. 41
Oates, Congressman 264
Oates, Mr. 186, 196
Oates, Representative 225
Oates, Senator 193
Oates, William C. 79
O'Brien, 29
O'Brien, Engineer Pat 1
O'Brien, Frank 322
O'Connell, Dr. R. 3
O'Ferrall, 302
Ogletree, Emma 260
Ogletree, Nancy 260
Ogletree, Nettie 260
O'Hara, Captain 167, 176
Oliver, S.D. 204
Oliver, Walter L. 289
Olney, Richard H. 28
O'Neal, Bill 162
O'Neal, Duffy 116, 229
O'Neal, Ed. 82
O'Neal, J.H. 162
O'Neal, Mrs. 97
O'Neil, Nelda 292
O'Neil, Wm. M. 292
O'Neill, Cha(?) 309
Onsley, Lee 116
Osborn 234
Osburn, J.B. 241
Oscar, Mrs. Mullins 186
O'Shaughnessy 135
Osta, Stella 168
Ott, 29

Ousley, Albert 161
Owen, John 74
Owens, J.J. 207
Owens, Robert S. 207
Owlsey,
  Mrs. Caroline Dudley 274

P

Pacha, Emin 63
Packer, Alfred 175
Paddock, Joseph W. 70
Padget, George 127
Page, Mann 245
Palmer, Mr. 197
Palmer, Thomas W. 143
Palmer, Virginia 310
Pancha 301
Parish, Eliza 43
Parish, J.M. 18
Parker, A. H. 11
Parker, A.H. 27
Parker, Bud 183
Parker, George H. 314
Parker, Harry 314
Parker, John 44
Parker, Joseph H. 157
Parker, L.B. 297
Parker, Mary E. 252
Parker, Miss Jennie 92
Parker, Miss Mollie 146
Parker, Miss Pearl 81
Parker, Mr. 207
Parker, Mrs. 297
Parker,
  Mrs. Lazarus B. 297
Parker, Richard 274, 282
Parker, Solomon 105
Parker, Wm. 297
Parkhurst, Charles 317
Parkman, Francis 283
Parnell, Jeff 14
Parnell, John 311
Parnell, L. C. 4
Parnell, Mr. 28
Parr, W.H. 80, 84
Parrish, J.M. 37
Parsons, E.B. 310
Parsons, E.J.C. 305
Pasba, Emin 78
Pasco 188
Pasco, Mr. 197
Pash, Emin 211
Pasha, Emin 211
Pate 268
Pate, Alfred 250
Pate, Betsy Ann 49
Pate, G.W. 67
Pate, Jim 250
Pate, President 170
Pate, Sam 115, 260
Pate, Samuel 49, 246, 260
Pate, Steve 173
Pate, Steven 49
Patillo, L. 260
Patrick 229
Patrick, George 100, 260
Patterson, A. 123, 260
Patterson,
  Charles A. 296
Patterson, John 61
Patterson, Mr. 189
Patterson,
  Mrs. M. E. 233
Patterson, T.M. 249
Pattillo, L. 297
Pattison, Robert E. 35
Payne, Lewis 9
Payne, Lula 150
Paynter, Mr. 216
Pearce, George 251
Pearson 15, 21, 81
Pearson,
  Charles Henry 127
Pearson, F.C. 90
Pearson, Thomas C. 17
Peary 140
Peary, Lieutenant 135
Peck,
  Samuel Minturn 136
Peffer, 143
Peffer, Mr. 188, 197, 215, 216, 226, 235, 312
Peffer, Senator 173, 220, 235, 249, 310, 312
Peffer, W.A. 178
Pegg, L.L. 182
Pence, 143
Pence, Lafe 178
Pendergast 301
Pendleton, Mr. 189
Penn, William 201
Pepper, W.R. 51
Perkins, D.K. 301
Perkins, George C. 149
Perkins, J.A. 167, 176
Perkins, Mr. 235
Perkins, Senator 17
Perrin, John B. 199
Perry, A. 145
Perry, Adkin 85
Perry, Lieut. 160
Perry, Parson 97
Perry, William 27
Persica, Mr. 278
Peters, 289
Peters, J.E. 295
Peterson, F.M. 121
Peterson, John 309
Pettus, 29
Pettus, Mr., 15
Pettus, Speaker 21, 22, 25
Pfeffer, Captain 211
Phelan,
  Mrs. Captain 201
Philips, Mrs. 112
Philips,
  Town Marshal 321
Phillips, G.I. 30
Phillips, J.R. 101, 109
Phillips, Lake 311
Phillips, Minnie 311
Phillips, Peter 231
Phillips, T.S. 311
Phillips, W.H. 44, 294, 311
Pickard 157
Pickens, Edward 89
Pierce, G.H. 111
Pierce, J.M.W. 213
Pierce, John Harvey 273
Pinckard, Miss Lula 18
Pinckney 239
Pinkard, Evans 311
Pinkard, Minnie 311
Pitts 42
Pitts, E.M. 276
Pitts, J.D. 215
Pitts, Jno. W. 182
Pitts, Johnny 192
Pitts, L.B. 192
Pitts, Susan 215
Platt, Mr. 208, 235
Plummer, Martha E. 11
Plunkett, Sarge 242
Poe, Edgar Allen 143
Polk, Col. 245
Pollak, Herr 164
Poole 29
Poole, 29
Pope 262
Pope, Draper 109
Popwell, Benjamin 261
Popwell, J.S. 111

Popwell, James 261
Popwell, M. 145
Popwell, Madison 86
Popwell, W.J. 132
Popwell, W.L. 172
Portefield, Frank 306
Porter 15, 21
Porter, Mr. 21
Porter, R.M. 32
Porter, Superintendent 140
Porterfield, Frank 306
Posey, S.D. 171
Posey, Singleton 275
Poston, John C. 266
Potter, Ed. 250
Potter, George 103
Potts, Forrest 37
Potts, Mr. 230, 247, 262, 319
Pound, Rev. 161
Pounds 118
Pounds, Bro. 171, 179
Pounds, J.B. 132
Pounds, L. B. 1, 4, 19
Pounds, L.B. 72, 85, 99, 104, 115, 118, 132, 153, 160, 170, 171, 193, 195, 214, 229, 235, 246, 275, 303
Powderly, General Master Workman 2
Powderly, Mr. 291
Powderly, T.V. 14, 158, 173, 303, 310
Powderly, Terence V. 287
Powell 78
Powell, Brother 260
Powell, G.W. 72
Powell, J.S. 45

Powell, Sam 149
Powell, T.W. 182
Power, Miss Lucinda 284
Power, O.H. 94
Powers 189
Powers, Jas. K. 159
Powers, Mr. 198, 306, 312
Prater, Shaw 109
Pratt, E. Spencer 113
Pratt, Miss Stella 56
Pratt, R.H. 132
Prayer, Robert,Sr. 229
Prendergast, Eugene Patrick 259
Preston, W.W. 295
Price 145
Price, Captain 152
Price, Charles H. 126
Price, J.W. 132
Price, L.E. 194
Price, Mr. 162
Price, Richard 91
Price, W. 72, 206
Price, W.L. 145, 151, 169
Price, W.M. 36, 59, 97, 104, 124, 152, 162, 247
Price, W.W. 206
Pridgin, Claud 149
Prince Pedro 287
Princess Victoria Mary of Teck 129
Procise, Ambrose 233
Procise, Bob 233
Proctor, Mr. 313
Prof. Durham 151
Prof. Holloway 151
Providence, Bro. 91
Pruett 30
Pruett, S.G. 109
Pruett, W.I. 30

Pruette, W.L. 72
Pugh 227
Pugh, 151
Pugh, Mr. 208, 225
Pugh, Senator 109
Pullman, Geo. M. 258
Purvis, Thomas 72
Pyran, James 151

Q

Quay, Mr. 32
Queen Victoria 249
Quigley, Mr. 287
Quillian, H.E. 214
Quinn, Lee 181
Quinnemore 231
Quintard, Dr. 241

R

R., W. Lowery 15
Rabbitt, Ella 158
Rabbitt, Miss Etta 158
Ragland, E.M. 265
Rainey, (?) 304
Rainey, Lillian 311
Rainey, Mrs. 81, 206, 288
Ramer 113
Ramsey, 29
Ramsey, Monroe 261
Randall, Henry 86
Randall, Mrs. E.S. 309
Randall, Samuel J. 9
Randle, J.S. 309
Rankin, F.H. 134
Rankin, M.C. 130
Ransom, 259
Rasberry, G.S. 303
Rasberry, J.L. 261
Rasberry, Mat 275
Rather, 29
Raub, Elmer E. 273
Rawlings, Fred 142
Ray, 32

Ray, C.C. 32
Ray, Joseph 60
Ray, Mr. 20, 196
Rayburn, Judge 89
Raynie, Mrs. 230
Read, Mary 223
Ready, W. 124
Reaves, Rufus 300
Reed, Charles B. 41
Reed, Czar 236
Reed, George 293
Reed, Martin 167
Reed, Mr. 208
Reeder, Miss Maggie 146, 187
Reid 234
Reid, E.M. 219
Reid, Nat 145, 152
Reynolds 15, 21
Reynolds, John 85
Reynolds, John W. 110
Reynolds, Joshua 262
Reynolds, L.H. 60, 70, 71, 111, 115
Reynolds, Miss Mattie 267
Reynolds, Miss Mollie 85, 267
Reynolds, W.H. 144
Rhett, Walter H. 241
Rhodes, J.H. 154
Rhodes, Mr. 194
Rhodes, Rufus 160
Rice, 29
Rice, Alex 42
Rice, Armistead 294
Rice, Hardy 149
Rice, John 314
Rich, J.C. 26, 264
Rich, Joseph C. 294
Rich, Mayor 310
Rich, Rev. 229
Richards, Mr. 198
Richards, S.M. 37

Richardson, Clark 158
Richardson, Col. 223
Richardson, Ed 23
Richardson, Leslie 158
Richardson, Mr. 226
Richardson, Ralph 192
Richardson, W.E. 79
Richardson, Wm. 264
Rick, A. 27
Rick, Mrs. 27
Riddle, Mrs. Amanda C. 212
Rider, J.L. 107
Riggin, W.G. 71
Riggins 71
Riggins, (?)s 124
Riggins, B. 170
Riggins, Blanton 185
Riggins, Bro. 260
Riggins, James 111, 118, 126
Riggins, Jas. 112
Riggins, Jim 118
Riggins, Miss M.J. 194
Riggins, Miss Mary 294
Riggins, Miss Sidera 194
Riggins, Newt 115
Riggins, R.C. 185, 194
Riggins, W.G. 71, 92, 99, 111, 132, 170, 186, 195, 205, 236, 260, 303, 304
Riggins, W.N. 62
Rightmire, W.F. 291
Riley, B.F. 113
Rinearson, W.C.
203
Ripper, Wesley G. 245
Ritch, Rev. 145, 160
Roach, 29
Roach, Edward 182
Robbins, 186, 266
Robbins, Congressman 242
Robbins, Representative 109
Robbins, S.J. 304, 305
Robbins, T.W. 304
Roberson, C.J. 32
Roberson, J.W. 32
Roberson, S.W. 32
Roberson, T.J. 32
Robert, Van 281
Roberts, J.A. 219
Roberts, John 60, 261
Roberts, John F. 243
Roberts, Mr. 221
Roberts, Thomas 243
Robertson, G.M. 66
Robin 210
Robin(?), T.J. 196
Robinson 30, 117, 268
Robinson, 30
Robinson, (?) 82
Robinson, C.A. 310
Robinson, Charlie 139
Robinson, D.S. 132, 172, 288
Robinson, Elijah 261
Robinson, F.J. 246
Robinson, J.M. 32, 111, 246
Robinson, J.M.,Sr. 261
Robinson, John 43, 261
Robinson, John M.
243
Robinson, John P. 242
Robinson, M. 32
Robinson, Mordecai 20
Robinson, Moses 43, 70, 100, 153, 160, 173
Robinson, Orrie 311
Robinson, Prof. 284
Robinson, R. 151
Robinson, Riley 131, 145, 260
Robinson, T.G. 72
Robinson, T.J. 60, 82, 115, 260, 261
Robinson, Tillman 131, 151
Robinson, W.C. 4
Robinson, W.C. 72, 100, 187, 222, 260, 267, 268, 276, 284, 288
Robinson, W.F. 310
Robinson, Wm R. 111
Robson, Stuart 301
Roche, Boyle 190
Rockafellow, E.V. 90
Rockefeller, John D. 57, 283
Rockfeller, J.D. 212
Roddy, Miss 233
Rodgers, Dave 72
Rodgers, H.B. 161
Rodrigues, San Francisco 150
Rogers, 29
Rogers, John 319
Rollins, E.G. 37, 194, 259
Rollins, Miss Ula 184
Rollins, Tax Assessor 54
Rollo, J.G. 121
Rollo, Mrs. Charity 121
Romer, Trinidad 281
Rood, E.A. 134
Roots, Logan H. 95
Roper, H.B. 20
Roper, J.M. 32
Roper, W.C. 228
Roscoe, R.A. 131, 171
Rose, Mrs. Mattie 110
Rose, Thomas E. 174
Ross, John W. 211
Ross, Miss Mary P. 196
Rosser, General 259
Rothrock, Joseph T. 279
Rothschild, 193
Roudenuth, William S. 115
Rowell, E. J. 4
Ruddick, Mr. 110
Rudle, W.J. 132
Ruffin, J.L. 205, 267, 288
Rulland, M.H. 216
Runyor, Theodore 41
Rush, Hermon 250
Rushton, Ray 289
Rusie 136
Russell, Governor 282
Ruth, Baby 219
Rutherford, Isaac 146
Rutherford, J.O. 289
Rutherford, T.J. 154
Ryan 149
Ryan, John 169
Ryan, Mr. 198
Ryan, Tom 281
Ryerson, Ex-Gov. 10

S

S.J. Johnson 207

Sadler, W.H. 75
Salter, Jean 163
Sam, Uncle 263
Samford 15, 21
Sammons, L.S. 60, 261
Sampey 311
Sampey, (?).L. 146
Sampey, Miss Kate 105
Sampey, Mrs. 81, 105
Sampey, W. L. 3, 18
SAMPEY, W.L. 20
Sampey, W.L. 112, 133, 247, 251
Sample, Thomas G. 114
Samuel, Mr. 194
SANDEFUR, DR. 62
Sanderson, E.G. 250
Sanderson, J.C. 116
Sanderson, James 267
Sanderson, Jim 170
Sanderson, Miss Mamie 116, 170
Sanford, Delaney 300
Sanford, Senator 114
Santor, William 43
Sap, Uncle 116, 131
Sarpy, Peter A. 51
Sartor 311
Sartor, Eugene 311
Sartor, W.D. 118
Sartor, W.H. 118, 207
Sartoris, Loinel 62
Sasse, Francis 159
Sasseer, Dan 234
Satterwhite, W.C. 93, 311
Sauls, J.W. 20, 21
Savage, Paul A. 22
Sawyer, R.L. 289

Sayes, H.R. 164
Sayre, 29
Sayre, Dr. 324
Sayre, Mr. 15
Schell, 144
Scheller, Prof. 307
Schenck, Philip L. 75
Scheuer, Bert 27
Schneltzer, Jacob 211
Schofield, General 38
Scoffern, Dr. 136
Scott, E.A. 192
Scott, Ellis 310
Scott, Frank 192
Scott, Garner 192
Scott, J.M. 4, 70, 72, 111, 186, 195, 260
Scott, John A. 203
Scott, John W. 207
Scott, R.W. 45
Scott, Representative 8
Scott, W.B. 260
Scott, Winfield 201
Screws, Wallace 91
Scroggins, William 22
Scruggs, Judge 159
Scruggs, T.M. 95
Seal, D.A. 99, 132
Seals Brothers 3
Searcy, J.T. 68
Seay, Governor 274
Sedberry, Sheriff 276
Sellers, J.B. 125, 294
Sellers, Miss Ella 123
Sellers, Mrs. Minnie 44
Sessions, T.F. 131, 172
Settle, Mr. 198
Sewal, Henry 93
Seward,

Augustus H. 9
Seward, William H. 8, 134
Sewell, Henry 97
Sewell, Hy. 92
Sewell, J.C. 238
Sewell, J.F. 284
Sexo, Tel 209
Sexton, J.H. 60
Sexton, John 86
Seymour, 29
Seymour, (?).S. 41
Seymour, Mr. 25
Seymour, R. 79
Shackelford, Joseph 153
Shackleford 78
Shackleford, E.M. 108
Shackleford, F.M. 159
Shackleford, Joseph 182
Shanklin, T.P. 72
Shannon, Miss Metha 267
Sharbutt, W.S. 172
Shaw, Mr. 15
Shaw, W.H. 59, 71, 82, 111, 115, 223, 229
Shaw, Will 293
Shaw, William 277
Shaw, William H. 231
Shaw, Wm. 154, 247, 251
Sheehan, Con. 158
Shelby, Will 246
Shell, Representative 193
Shelton 66
Shelton, 153
Shelton, Alex 48, 99, 118, 300, 304, 319
Shelton, Bill 84
Shelton, Mrs. France 126
Sheperd, A.H. 157

Shepherd, J.M. 36
Sherman 188
Sherman, Henry 321
Sherman, John 193, 225, 236, 249, 317
Sherman, Mr. 33, 208
Sherman, Senator 136, 173, 282
Sherry, Signal officer 141
Shneider, C. A. 5
Short, John 275
Short, Mrs. 184
Shorter, George 297
Shorter, Reuben C. 108
Shoup, Mr. 226
Showalter, H.J. 179
Shropshire, W.H. 181
Shugart, 29
Shustig, S. 22
Sibley, Mr. 190
Sickels, Miss Emma 136
Sickles, Congressman 8
Sides, Dock 321
Sides, Lee 321
Silsbee, Mrs. B.W. 205
Simmons, Jessie 11
Simonds, E.L. 109
Simpson 143
Simpson, A.H. 295
Simpson Brothers 3
Simpson, E.E. 139
Simpson, George 232
Simpson, Hendree 139
Simpson, Jerre 193
Simpson, Jerry 178, 228
Simpson, John R. 22
Simpson, Mr. 53, 190

Simpson, R. T. 25
Sims, Nancy 80
Sims, W.H. 41
Sims, William A. 231
Singleton, Henry 150
Skipper, Robert 168, 192
Skipper, W.E. 80, 252
Slaten, Prof. 214
Slaton, C.C. 267, 276, 288
Slaton, C.M. 288
Slavin 95
Sleeman, Col. 200
Sleeman, Miss Lucy 163
Sleighton, W.A. 146
Slowson, S.S. 252
Smaw, 29
Smaw, William 26
Smeaton, Marm 277
Smith 15, 21, 49
Smith, 29
Smith, (?) 133
Smith, (Tom?) 66
Smith, A. 56, 110
Smith, A.C. 251
Smith, A.G. 87, 211, 233
Smith, A.H. 101
Smith, Abram 100
Smith, Ally 86
Smith, Ben 319
Smith, C.P. 42
Smith, Craig 314
Smith, E.(?). 260
Smith, E.G. 146
Smith, E.H. 44, 115, 172, 303
Smith, Edmund Kirby 42
Smith, Elvie 103
Smith, Florida 115
Smith, G.W. 69
Smith, General 42
Smith, H.C. 140, 168

Smith, Hamil A. 108
Smith, Henry 322
Smith, Henry C. 121
Smith, Hoke 28, 38, 47, 140
Smith, Hugh M. 269
Smith, J.F. 31, 44, 93, 105, 207, 215, 304
Smith, J.S. 243, 262
Smith, Jasper 319
Smith, Jim 66
Smith, John H. 266
Smith, John L. 277
Smith, Lindsey 206
Smith, Matthew C. 108
Smith, Millie 322
Smith, Milton A. 121
Smith, Miss Annie 105, 205
Smith, Miss Cora 144
Smith, Miss Kirby 159
Smith, Miss Nettie 85, 160
Smith, Miss Obie 247
Smith, Miss. Annie 20
Smith, Mr. 243
Smith, Mr. A. 103
Smith, Mr. and Mrs. Patrick 133
Smith, Mrs. 45
Smith, Mrs. A. 71, 98
Smith, Mrs. Amanda 276
Smith, Mrs. Mary 195
Smith, Mrs. Patrick 44
Smith, Mrs. R.—.

247
Smith, Mrs. Tom 44
Smith, O.D. 159
Smith, P. 118
Smith, Paddy 238
Smith, Pat(?) 146
Smith, Patrick 44, 61, 112, 133, 251
Smith, Secretary 143, 307
Smith, Thomas 112
Smith, Thomas W. 66
Smith, Tom 20, 44, 86, 133, 230
Smith, W.T. 300
Smith, William D. 204
Smitherman, E.D. 261
Smitherman, Ed 60
Smitherman, Goodman 260
Smitherman, Mr. 123
Smitherman, S.D. 153
Smitherman, Sanford 84
Smitherman, Shugg 293
Smitherman, Sutton 98, 99, 132, 171, 229, 237, 303
Smithers, James 253
Sneed, John L. 107
Snell, Hannah 244
Snoddy, Samuel 182
Snodgrass, Mr. 189
Soar, Mrs. 126
Soghie, Marguerite 16
Sorel, J. 22
Sorel, J.W. 246
Sorrel, J.W. 246, 260
Sorrell, J.W. 60, 111
Sortar, W.D. 195
Sorter, Mr. 172

South, D.F. 26
Sovereign, J.R. 287, 291, 303, 310
Sowell, 29
Spaulding, Miss Laura C. 299
Spear, G.L. 267
Speer 117, 118
Speer, G. L. 4
Speer, G.L. 30, 59, 72, 117, 131, 172
Spence, Robert E.L. 108
Spencer, James A. 151
Sperry, Mr. 198
Spier, 29
Spies, Chas. 182
Spreck, Harvey 181
Spreckles, Claus 53
Springer, 199
Springer, Mr. 186, 208
Stafford, J.N. 264
Stafford, William 324
Staley 135
Stallings 266
Stallings, Congressman 213
Stallings, J. 118
Stallings, J.J. 154
Stallings, Mr. 186, 266
Stambaugh, Dr. 324
Stanfield, J. 124
Stanfield, J.M. 118, 171
Stanfield, J.W. 118, 247
Stanfield, James M. 105
Stanfield, John 311
Stanfield, Mr. 221
Stanfield, Mrs. J.M. 20
Stanford, Senator 96
Stanley, Mrs. M. E.

20
Stanse 15
Stansel 21
Stansel, M.L. 25
Stansel, Mr. 21
Stanton, Lee 96
Staples, Simeon 56
Starr, Bro. 144
Starr, George 56
Steele, 29
Steele, Thomas W. 41
Stein 135
Stein, 135
Stein, E. 18
Stein, Robert 232
Steiner 15, 21
Stelle, John P. 310
Stephens, Alexander 90
Stephens, J. 6
Sterling, J. Morton 38
Stern, Sam 321
Stevens, — 162
Stevens, Bill 47
Stevens, Mr. 317
Stevenson, D. 113
Stevenson, John 167
Stevenson, Mr. and Mrs. 38
Stevenson, Vice-President 149
Stevenson, Vice-president 306, 307
Stevenson, Vice-President-elect 35
Stewart 143, 188, 197, 227, 294, 311
Stewart, Dr. 222, 288
Stewart, J.J.L. 82, 115
Stewart, L.H. 311
Stewart, M.H. 295
Stewart, Mayor 68
Stewart, Miss Ida 229

Stewart, Miss Ollie 275
Stewart, Mr. 208, 215, 216, 225, 226, 235
Stewart, Paymaster-General 114
Stewart, Senator 37, 197, 235, 305, 309
Stewart, W.E. 104, 238, 247, 251, 311
Still Sounooke 257
Stivetts 135
Stockdale, Mr. 198
Stockton, 29
Stoddard, Miss Martha Washington 177
Stokes, F.W. 135
Stokes, J. William 223
Stone, C.W. 198
Stone, Chief Justice 168
Stone, Justice 176
Stoney, Johnstone 223
Story, Brooks 101
Stoughton, George L. 83
Stout 115
Stowell, W.H. 89
Stranz, Lewis 242
Street 168
Street, Alonzo 47
Street, J.C. 27
Strickland, D.J. 233
Strickland, Will 22
Stricklin, J.P. 250
Strock, H.M. 246
Strock, H.W. 237
Strock, John A. 60
Strock, S.J. 104, 184
Strock, Will 43
Stroup, Mrs. Ella 72
Strupson, Jerry 53
Stuart, Henry C. 203

Stutts, J.J. 182
Styles, Ira F. 134
Sugar, Mrs. R.F. 55
Sullivan, 36
Sullivan, Jim 149
Sullivan, John L. 22
Sultan of Johore 177
Sum, Shew Shu 143
Sumner, Henry 10
Surl, Mrs. 56
Surle, W.N. 56
Sutton, W.H. 191, 215
Swann, A.J. 211
Swartz, George W. 113
Swearingen, Dr. 28
Swedenborg, Emmanuel 262
Sweeney, Peter 269
Sweeney, Wm. 300
Sweet, H.B. 114
Swift, Charles A. 157
Swift, Harry P. 18
Swindle, A.C. 214
Swinford, J.R. 213
Swinney, Catherine 233

T

Talbert 190
Talbot, Mr. 208
Talbot, W.B. 26
Taliaferro, E.T. 157
Taliaferro, Henry Pope 295
TALMAGE, DR. 43
Talmage, T. DeWitt 287
Tarrant, Miss Bessie 299
Tarver, Miss Jennie 84
Taubeneck, Chairman 291
Taubeneck, H.E. 91, 130, 154
Taylor, 29

Taylor, A.P. 191
Taylor, Annie 140
Taylor, C.H. 108
Taylor, Dick 44, 50
Taylor, Judge 22
Taylor, T.E. 117, 146
Taylor, W.H. 311
Taylor, William H. 154
Taylor, Wm. J. 158
Teal, Mr. and Mrs. 162
Teall, Early 296
Teel, Henry 297
Teller 227
Teller, Mr. 208, 216, 225, 234, 235
Teller, Senator 226
Terrell, Ben 12, 73, 83
Terront, M. 245
Terry, Tobe 85
Terry, Z. 182
Teton, George 142
Thacker, J.M. 61
Thacker, Miss Julie 213
Thames, Mrs. L.M. 266
Thedford, M.A. 289
Therrel, Zack 181
Thomas 145, 151
Thomas, 32
Thomas, A.L. 123
Thomas, Anderson 72
Thomas, Ben 321
Thomas, Brother 131
Thomas, Deputy Sheriff 149
Thomas, J. Wesley 140
Thomas, J. Westly 169
Thomas, J.L. 123
Thomas, J.W. 92
Thomas, Major 204

352

Thomas, Mrs. 111
Thomas, Norma 311
Thomas, Stewart 72
Thomason, J.F. 299
Thompson, Albert 54
Thompson, Georgia 275
Thompson, Isaac 5
Thompson, Miss Georgia 56, 145, 214
Thompson, Miss Mary Eliza 54
Thompson, Mr. 235
Thompson, Mrs. 235
Thompson, Sheldon 201
Thompson, T.N. 301
Thompson, W.I.R. 186
Thompson, William G. 248
Thornton, (?).A. 105
Thornton, (?).Clair 207
Throne, Conductor 69
Thweatt, J.M. 27
Tib, Tippoo 63
Ticknor, F.B. 163, 169
Tidwell, George 71
Tidwell, Miss Mary 145
Tilden, Miss 125
Tillman, Ben 35
Tillman, Governor 48
Tillman, R.B. 47
Tilton, Mrs. Drusilla E. 80
Timberlake, Edward J.,Jr. 108
Tindall, J.H. 75

Todd, Dr. 206
Todd., E. E. 4
Tom 210
Tompkins, R.A. 241
Toomer, 269
Toomer, Mr. 269
Towles, Charles 266
Townley, John 157
Townsend, 29
Townsend, G. C. 15
Townsend, J.B. 182
Townsend, Mr. 2
Townsend, Mrs. Scott 8
Townsend, William 69
Tracey, Secretary 121
Tracy, Harry 246, 265
Trancort, M. 282
Treadway, 135
Trebien, F. G. 18
Troupe, Mrs. Angeline 113
Tryon, Admiral 143
Tsui, Miss 165
Tuabeneck, H.E. 130
Tucker, G.W. 297
Tullis, John W.,Sr. 27
Tumlin 15, 21
Turner, 29
Turner, George 204
Turner, J.E. 57
Turner, J.H. 130
Turner, Jessie 181
Turner, L.B. 27
Turney, Governor 1
Turnipseed, S.C. 113
Turpie, Mr. 216
Turpin 151, 193, 227
Turpin, 186
Tutwiler, Carl 183
Tutwiller, Deputy Collector 314
Twain, Mark 242, 282
Twist, Geo. W. 82
Twitchell, 211
Tyler, 302
Tyler, ex-president 121
Tyler, Miss Letitia C. 121
Tylor, J.S. 213
Tyron, Governor 143

U

Underwood, Jerry 22
Upchurch, William 101

V

Vail, Leslie 200
Vaillant 302
Vallins, T.N. 283
Van Alen, James J. 313
Van, C.H. 281
Van Houten, Mrs. Anna D. 241
Van Zant, W.E. 32
Vance 227
Vance, Mr. 197, 208
Vance, P.A. 228
Vance, Senator 245
Vanderbert, F.J. 87
Vanderbilt 203
Vanderbilt, Cornelius 10
Vanderbilt, George W. 114
Vanderbilt, Mr. 141
VanDerveer, J.P. 62
Vandiver, Joseph P. 2
Vanngelback, R.A. 89
Varden, Joseph 14
Varden, Miss Sarah E. 124
Varden, R.I. 32
Vauderveer 311
Vauduce, Charles A. 94
Veas(?), Ben 246
Veasey, Ben 292
Verne, Jules 136
Vest 227
Vest, Mr. 181, 188, 189, 197, 305, 312
Vicker, Hatcher 140
Vickers, H.J. 149
Vidocq 279
Vilas 188
Vin-(?), Walter 206
Vincent, Doctor 135
Vincent, N.N. 246
Vincent, saac H. 109
Vines, James 184
Vines, Miss Venecia 184
Vines, V.H. 184
Vines, Venitia 311
Vines, Victor 311
Vinson, E.F. 318
Vinson, J.L. 251
Vinson, J.R. 45, 115, 246
Vinson, Jno. R. 99
Vinson, John 131
Vinson, K.W. 318
Vinson, L.R. 70
Vinson, Manda 80
Vinson, Newton 84
Vinson, Sallie 80
Vlick, Van 114
Volz, Alexander 11
Von Koenitz, Otto 245
Voorhee, Mr. 197
Voorhees 263, 317
Voorhees, Mr. 188, 197, 208, 235
Voorhees, Senator 203, 234, 249, 312
Vorhees, Senator 203
Vose, Horace 298

Vowles, James S. 115

W

Wade, Bill 257
Wade, Wm. 21
Wadsworth, Mr. 55
Wagner, James 184
Wagner, William 162
Wagoner, S.L. 32
Waid, Ernest 302
Waite, Governor 302, 323
Wal(?), Miss Annie 93
Walcott 188, 227
Waldrop, J.R.J. 191
Waldrop, S.E. 60
Waldrup 205
Waldrup, J.L.,Jr. 275
Waldrup, John S. 274
Waldrup, S.E. 246
Waldrup, S.N. 275
Walker 15, 21
Walker, Charles 277, 283, 292
Walker, J.C. 59
Walker, John 139
Walker, John W. 149
Walker, Lee 150, 159, 167, 176
Walker, Lucean J. 159
Walker, Marshall 69
Walker, Meriwether 108
Walker, Miss Annie 130
Walker, R.G. 72
Walker, Robert 261
Walker, William 289
Wallace, David 186, 195
Wallace, J. M. 15
Wallace, Joseph 126
Walldrop, I.L. 97
Walldrop, Mrs. Samanthra 98
Waller, Mr. 26
Walles, Wm. 73
Walles, Wm. E. 73
Walling, R.H. 295
Walter, George 203
Walters, President 90
Walthall 227
Walthall, Mr. 216
Walworth, John 178
Wannatan, Chief 141
Ward 81, 136
Ward, 29
Ward, (?).O. 187
Ward, Amos 3
Ward, Cam 314
Ward, E.L.C. 295
Ward, J.G. 36
Ward, James 23
Ward, Miss Alice 110, 304
Ward, Mrs. A.C. 304
Ward, Representative G. W. 2
Ware, Albert 162
Ware, Eugene 181
Ware, Henry 65
Ware, J.B. 182
Ware, William 38
Warner, A.J. 130, 204
Warner, Charles Dudley 82
Warner, Gen. 236
Warner, Mr. 189
Warner, Smiley & Co. 3
Warren, Andrew 274
Warren, Ben 145, 161
Warren, J.R. 236
Warren, Judson 115
Washburn, Geo F. 130
Washington, George 15
Washington, Mrs. Frank 309
Waters, A.S. 95
Waters, President 95
Watkins, F. 299
Watson, Charles 207
Watson, Congressman 67
Watson, J.A. 261
Watson, James 221
Watson, John 266
Watson, T.W. 249
Watson, Thomas 63
Watson, Thomas E. 265
Watson, Tom 42, 67, 91, 139, 241, 246
Watson, W.J. 231
Watterson, 38
Watts, (?) 81
Watts, Callie 311
Watts, D.B. 261
Watts, Dr. 323
Watts, Leroy 311
Watts, Miss Belle 207, 215
Watts, Miss Callie 81
Watts, Miss Leah 93
Weadock, Mr. 189
Weathers, Thomas 296
Weaver, Gen. 47, 143
Weaver, General 203
Weaver, H.P. 161, 237
Weaver, J.B. 212
Weaver, Miss Alice 145
Weaver, Miss Ella 161
Weaver, Miss Ida 144
Weaver, Miss Minnie 222
Weaver, Misses 161
Weaver, W.A. 115, 161, 246
Webb, Brother 242
Webb, J.E. 25
Webb, Miss Prissy 93
Webb, P.E.J.A. 236
Webster family 258
Webster, Miss Mattie 109
Weeks, E.O. Otto 225
Weeks, W.E. 57
Weems, James 133
Weihl, F.F. 27
Weiss, Dr. 324
Welborn, Charles E. 182
Welch, Aaron 293
Welch, Daisie 116
Welch, Ernest 144
Welch, Sallie 116
Welch, Vesta 144
Weldon, J.W. 104, 215
Weldon, Lula 104, 215
Weldon, Sidney 288
Well 289
Wellden, T.W. 59
Wells, (?).B. 105
Wells, A.C. 31, 37, 50, 55, 61, 118, 125, 133, 153, 154, 162, 163, 196, 206, 222, 238, 284, 288, 294
Wells, B.H. 115, 153, 160, 194, 246, 260
Wells, Ben 31, 62, 195
Wells, David A. 220

Wells, Henry 277, 284
Wells, J.B. 194, 246, 261
Wells, J.W.E. 184
Wells, John 131
Wells, K. 214, 288
Wells, Lee 65
Wells, Minnie 205
Wells, Miss Minnie 124
Wells, Mr. 14
Wells, Rev. - 130
Wells, W.A. 154
Wells, W.H. 60, 214
Wells, Will 261
Wells, Wm. Lyman 320
Welsh, Aaron 84
Wesley, John 255
Wessington 86
West, 29
West, B.G. 74, 287
Wetmore, C.W. 212
Weymath, Daniel 266
Wharton, William F. 38
Whatley, M.W. 182
Whatley, Martin W. 101
Wheaton, Frank 25
Wheaton, Gen. 212
Wheeler 193, 266
Wheeler, 193
Wheeler, Birdie 101
Wheeler, Chairman 186
Wheeler, Congressman 101
Wheeler, Gen. 25, 186
Wheeler, Mr. 306, 312
Wheeler, Representative 109
Whistler, John 201
Whistler, William 201
White 145, 229, 259, 311
White, 29
White, A.L. 183
White, Alexander 313
White, Arnold 249
White, Brother 123
White, C.F. 26
White, E.H. 105
White, Editor 236
White, Frank S. 314
White, J.E. 179, 229
White, Jim 187, 293
White, Joe 145
White, Minion 125
White, Miss Nellie 105, 319
White, Mr. 235, 318
White, T. H. 3, 4, 13
White, T.H. 2, 61, 71, 79, 115, 133, 143, 196, 206, 222, 243, 246, 251, 260
White, W.R. 26, 93
White, W.S. 75
Whitehead 78
Whitehead, Bro. 274
Whitehead, J.M. 79, 182
Whitehead, James W. 258
Whiteheat, J.M. 182
Whitman & Son 75
Whitten, 29
Whittle 299
Whittle, Dr. 168
Whittle, W.A. 287
Whorton 15, 21
Wickstone, C.W. 175
Wigam, H.H.M. 136
Wiggin, E.D. 57
Wiggins, Wesley D. 297
Wigginton, A.R. 21
Wil(?), John 86
WILCOX, C.M. 74
Wilder, Jeff 75
Wilder, T.J. 75
Wiler, John F. 175
Wiley 21
Wiley, George 199
Wiley Littlejohn, Jr. 246
Wiley, Mr. 21
Wilhott, O.L. 252
Wilkerson, Mrs. Jeannie 37
Wilkes, George 57
Wilkins, Doc 293
Wilkins, Doc, 267
Wilkins, Dock 84
Wilkins, G.W. 61
Wilkins, Henry 251
Wilkins, John 98, 144
Wilkins, R.N. 61, 80
Williams, 29
Williams, A.B. 73
Williams, B. Dudley 139
Williams, Benjamin D. 113
Williams, C.F. 184
Williams, Chancellor 192
Williams, Charles 297
Williams, Ely 153
Williams, J.T. 207
Williams, Jacob 113
Williams, Jane 320
Williams, Jeff 139
Williams, John C. 121
Williams, Joseph 86
Williams, Manuel 121
Williams, Melt 118
Williams, Melton 293
Williams, Melvin 111
Williams, Miss Emma 185
Williams, Moses 165
Williams, R.J. 104
Williams, Robert 113, 261
Williams, T.H. 184
Williams, William H. 192
Williamson 15, 21
Williamson, 29
Williamson, J.W. 32
Williamson, Mrs. Rebecca 175
Willingham, Charles M. 220
Willingham, Robert J. 175
Willis, Albert S. 227
Willis, Carter 229
Willis, Ed 30
Willis, Frank 32
Willis, Minister 313
Willis, Mr. 312
Willis, Mrs. Sarah 121
Willis, Wm. 125
Willy, S.J. 114
Wilson 81, 288, 289
Wilson, 234
Wilson, (?)ate 81
Wilson, Albert 277
Wilson, Andrew 261
Wilson, Doctor 163
Wilson, Floyd 284
Wilson, H.A. 169, 230
Wilson, H.J. 32
Wilson, J. H. 15
Wilson, J.E. 93
Wilson, J.J. 32
Wilson, John 293
Wilson, Miss Elmira 319
Wilson, N.W. 131, 172
Wilson, P.D. 311

355

Wilson, Pate 304
Wilson, T.D.L. 101
Wilson, W.M. 289, 311
Wing, Mrs. Louise Scott 150
Winn, Thomas E. 53
Wolcott, Mr. 208, 215
Wood 79
Wood, Colonel 22
Wood, G.W. 302
Wood, Judge 105
Wood, M.A. 260
Wood, M.L. 53
Wood, Mrs. William R. 201
Wood, Sadie 211
Wood, Sidney B. 301
Wood, W. 160
Wood, W.A. 43, 71, 99, 132, 170, 171, 186, 195, 260
Wood, W.J. 75
Wood, W.M. 170, 182, 195
Wood, Wm. M. 153
Woodruff, Miss Julia 157
Woods, Billie 50
Woods, Mrs. A.F. 1
Woodson, Judge 89
Woody, Jake 19
Wooley, Miss Sallie 251
Woolfold, President 42
Woolley, Miner 110
Woolley, Minor 171
Woolley, Miss Fannie 131, 172
Woolley, Miss Sallie 247
Woolly, Miss Fannie 104
Woolsey, King S. 254
Woolsey, William J. 94
Worns, E.C. 55, 100, 105
Wright, A. Himmel 273
Wright, George 219
Wright, John 233, 304
Wright, Mattie 311
Wright, O.H.P. 260
Wright, W. 304
Wright, W.H. 171, 311
Wright, Wm. 320
Wylie, F.J. 152, 162
Wylie, Jasper 36, 110
Wylie, Joe 162, 247
Wylie, Mrs. 162
Wyly, John 104
Wyman, Robert 301
Wyman, Surgeon General 234
Wyman, Surgeon-General 89, 177, 203
Wynne, Congressman 67

Y

Yarbrough, John 216
Yates, Samuel 14
Yielding, Geo. M. 295
York, Ly Wing 313
Yother, John A. 299
Young, Brigham 36, 247
Young, E.B. 27
Young, H.C. 261
Young, H.J. 73
Young, James 182
Young, Miss Lula 20
Young, Mr. 223
Young, Pierce 37
Young, Sam 116
Young, Willis 293
Youngblood, 29

Z

Zinville, Peter 5

www.ingramcontent.com/pod-product-compliance
Lightning Source LLC
Chambersburg PA
CBHW052339230426
43664CB00041B/2224